ORGANIZATIONAL PSYCHOLOGY

ORGANIZATIONAL PSYCHOLOGY

Critical concepts in psychology

Edited by Jo Silvester

**Volume II
Selecting and Developing Employees**

Routledge
Taylor & Francis Group

LONDON AND NEW YORK

First published 2008
by Routledge
2 Park Square, Milton Park, Abingdon, Oxon, OX14 4RN, UK

Simultaneously published in the USA and Canada
by Routledge
270 Madison Avenue, New York, NY 10016

*Routledge is an imprint of the Taylor & Francis Group,
an informa business*

Editorial material and selection © 2008 Jo Silvester;
individual owners retain copyright in their own material

Typeset in Times New Roman by Keyword Group Ltd.
Printed and bound in Great Britain by
TJI Digital, Padstow, Cornwall

All rights reserved. No part of this book may be reprinted or reproduced or utilised in any form or by any electronic, mechanical, or other means, now known or hereafter invented, including photocopying and recording, or in any information storage or retrieval system, without permission in writing from the publishers.

British Library Cataloguing in Publication Data
A catalogue record for this book is available
from the British Library

Library of Congress Cataloging in Publication Data
A catalog record for this book has been requested

ISBN 10: 0-415-40008-2 (Set)
ISBN 10: 0-415-40010-4 (Volume II)

ISBN 13: 978-0-415-40008-4 (Set)
ISBN 13: 978-0-415-40010-7 (Volume II)

Publisher's Note

References within each chapter are as they appear in the original
complete work

CONTENTS

Acknowledgements ix

Introduction 1

PART 3
How organizations attract, select and recruit employees 5

18 The validity and utility of selection methods in personnel psychology: practical and theoretical implications of 85 years of research findings 7
FRANK L. SCHMIDT AND JOHN E. HUNTER

19 The Big Five personality dimensions and job performance: a meta-analysis 35
MURRAY R. BARRICK AND MICHAEL K. MOUNT

20 Five reasons why the "Big Five" article has been frequently cited 59
MICHAEL K. MOUNT AND MURRAY R. BARRICK

21 The motivation to work: what we know 68
EDWIN A. LOCKE

22 Individual differences in work motivation: further explorations of a trait framework 104
RUTH KANFER AND PHILLIP L. ACKERMAN

23 General mental ability in the world of work: occupational attainment and job performance 117
FRANK L. SCHMIDT AND JOHN HUNTER

CONTENTS

24 **Why do assessment centers work? The puzzle of assessment center validity**   **142**
RICHARD KLIMOSKI AND MARY BRICKNER

25 **The perceived fairness of selection systems: an organizational justice perspective**   **159**
STEPHEN W. GILLILAND

26 **Applicants' perceptions of selection procedures and decisions: a critical review and agenda for the future**   **200**
ANN MARIE RYAN AND ROBERT E. PLOYHART

PART 4
Assessing and developing people at work   247

27 **Performance evaluation in work settings**   **249**
R. D. ARVEY AND K. R. MURPHY

28 **Perspectives on models of job performance**   **277**
CHOCKALINGAM VISWESVARAN AND DENIZ S. ONES

29 **Organizational competencies: a valid approach for the future?**   **295**
PAUL SPARROW

30 **Think manager—think male: a global phenomenon?**   **311**
VIRGINIA E. SCHEIN, RUEDIGER MUELLER, TERRI LITUCHY, AND JIANG LIU

31 **The science of training: a decade of progress**   **322**
EDUARDO SALAS AND JANIS A. CANNON-BOWERS

32 **Kirkpatrick's levels of training criteria: thirty years later**   **352**
GEORGE M. ALLIGER AND ELIZABETH A. JANAK

33 **Transfer of training: a review and directions for future research**   **363**
TIMOTHY T. BALDWIN AND J. KEVIN FORD

34 **Application of cognitive, skill-based, and affective theories of learning outcomes to new methods of training evaluation**   405
KURT KRAIGER, J. KEVIN FORD AND EDUARDO SALAS

35 **Building a learning organization**   444
DAVID A. GARVIN

ACKNOWLEDGEMENTS

The publishers would like to thank the following for permission to reprint their material:

The American Psychological Association for permission to reprint Frank L. Schmidt and John E. Hunter, 'The validity and utility of selection methods in personnel psychology: practical and theoretical implications of 85 years of research findings', *Psychological Bulletin*, 124(2), 1998, pp. 262–274. Copyright © 1998 by the American Psychological Association.

Blackwell Publishing for permission to reprint Murray R. Barrick and Michael K. Mount, 'The Big Five personality dimensions and job performance: a meta-analysis', *Personnel Psychology*, 44, 1991, pp. 1–26.

Blackwell Publishing for permission to reprint Michael K. Mount and Murray R. Barrick, 'Five reasons why the "Big Five" article has been frequently cited', *Personnel Psychology*, 51, 1998, pp. 849–857.

Reprinted from *Advances in Motivation and Achievement*, 10, Edwin A. Locke, 'The motivation to work: what we know', pp. 375–412. Copyright © 1997, with permission from Elsevier.

Blackwell Publishing for permission to reprint Ruth Kanfer and Phillip L. Ackerman, 'Individual differences in work motivation: further explorations of a trait framework', *Applied Psychology: An International Review*, 49(3), 2000, pp. 470–482.

The American Psychological Association for permission to reprint Frank L. Schmidt and John Hunter, 'General mental ability in the world of work: occupational attainment and job performance', *Journal of Personality and Social Psychology*, 86(1), 2004, pp. 162–173. Copyright © 2004 by the American Psychological Association.

Blackwell Publishing for permission to reprint Richard Klimoski and Mary Brickner, 'Why do assessment centers work? The puzzle of assessment center validity', *Personnel Psychology*, 40, 1987, pp. 243–260.

ACKNOWLEDGEMENTS

The Academy of Management (NY) in the format of Other Book via Copyright Clearance Center for permission to reprint Stephen W. Gilliland, 'The perceived fairness of selection systems: an organizational justice perspective', *Academy of Management Review*, 18(4), 1993, pp. 694–734. Copyright © 1993 by Academy of Management (NY).

Sage Publications Inc. for permission to reprint Ann Marie Ryan and Robert E. Ployhart, 'Applicants' perceptions of selection procedures and decisions: a critical review and agenda for the future', *Journal of Management*, 26(3), 2000, pp. 565–606. Copyright © 2000 by Sage Publications Inc.

The Annual Review of Psychology for permission to reprint Richard D. Arvey and Kevin R. Murphy, 'Performance evaluation in work settings', *Annual Review of Psychology*, volume 49, pp. 141–168. Copyright © 1998 by Annual Reviews. www.annualreviews.org.

Blackwell Publishing for permission to reprint Chockalingam Viswesvaran and Deniz S. Ones, 'Perspectives on models of job performance', *International Journal of Selection and Assessment,* 8(4), 2000, pp. 216–226.

Blackwell Publishing for permission to reprint Paul Sparrow, 'Organizational competencies: a valid approach for the future?', *International Journal of Selection and Assessment*, 3(3), 1995, pp. 168–177.

John Wiley & Sons Ltd. for permission to reprint Virginia E. Schein, Ruediger Mueller, Terry Lituchy and Jiang Liu, 'Think manager—think male: a global phenomenon?', *Journal of Organizational Behaviour*, 17, pp. 33–41. Copyright © 1996 John Wiley & Sons Ltd.

The Annual Review of Psychology for permission to reprint Eduardo Salas and Janis A. Cannon-Bowers, 'The science of training: a decade of progress', *Annual Review of Psychology*, volume 52, pp. 471–499. Copyright © 2001 by Annual Reviews. www.annualreviews.org.

Blackwell Publishing for permission to reprint George M. Alliger and Elizabeth A. Janak, 'Kirkpatrick's levels of training criteria: thirty years later', *Personnel Psychology*, 42, 1989, pp. 331–342.

Blackwell Publishing for permission to reprint Timothy T. Baldwin and J. Kevin Ford, 'Transfer of training: a review and directions for future research', *Personnel Psychology*, 41, 1988, pp. 63–105.

The American Psychological Association for permission to reprint Kurt Kraiger, J. Kevin Ford and Eduardo Salas, 'Application of cognitive, skill-based, and affective theories of learning outcomes to new methods of training evaluation', *Journal of Applied Psychology*, 78, 1993, pp. 311–328. Copyright © 1993 by the American Psychological Association.

ACKNOWLEDGEMENTS

Harvard Business School for permission to reprint David A. Garvin, 'Building a learning organization', *Harvard Business Review*, 71, July–August 1993, pp. 78–91.

Disclaimer

The publishers have made every effort to contact authors/copyright holders of works reprinted in *Organizational Psychology: Critical Concepts in Psychology*. This has not been possible in every case, however, and we would welcome correspondence from those individuals/companies whom we have been unable to trace.

INTRODUCTION

One of the most important claims made by organizational psychologists is that they provide organizations with the necessary tools and know-how for ensuring that employees work more effectively, healthily and productively. Underlying this claim is the belief that scientific methods can be used to identify universal psychological principles that guide behaviour and ultimately work performance. The development of theory based on these psychological constructs can then be used to design robust and fair systems for attracting and recruiting the best individuals for the job; development programmes that enable employees to learn important skills and apply them in the workplace, and; performance management systems that reliably motivate and reward staff for their performance. It is therefore not surprising that employee selection and development have become core areas within organizational psychology.

Selection and development are also two of the oldest areas of interest. Based on the idea of person–job fit, some of the earliest activities in this area were concerned with selecting and developing military personnel in the Second World War. Faced with the need to allocate large numbers of conscripts to suitable roles quickly and efficiently, the US and UK governments approached psychologists for support. Many of the methods used at that time would not look too dissimilar to methods used today (e.g. interviews, job analysis, assessment centres), but as a consequence of the tremendous amount of research conducted subsequently on the reliability and validity of different methods we now know far more about why methods work and how they can be used to improve return on investment. The scientific approach to evaluating systems and generating evidence to support people strategies at work has contributed substantially to the popularity of organizational psychology among organizational clients. It is also worth celebrating the role that has been played by organizational psychologists in challenging inequalities in the workplace through the provision of empirical evidence and methods needed to minimise subjectivity and bias in evaluation and assessment.

This second volume in the Critical Concepts series concentrates on the contribution of organizational psychology to improving employee performance at work. As such, it takes an employee-centric approach focusing on efforts to build the capacity of individuals, rather than organizational performance per se. The first section focuses on how organizations attract, select and recruit employees, and includes articles discussing the impact of individual differences (e.g. cognitive ability, personality, knowledge, skills and motivational traits) on work performance. The second section concentrates on employees once in the organization and considers strategies for enhancing job performance: articles in this section relate to defining and measuring work performance and training and development.

The first contribution in this volume is a seminal paper by Schmidt and Hunter (1998) who essentially 'sum up' the validity and utility of different methods of employee selection report by conducting a meta-analysis of 85 years of research studies. They found that work sample tests had the highest validity, but that validity was superior when selection techniques were combined with tests of general mental ability (GMA). The next two papers, by Barrick and Mount (1991) and Mount and Barrick (1998), describe the relationship between the Big Five personality dimensions (otherwise known as the five-factor model: FFM) and work performance. Personality measures have become a mainstay of personnel selection and Barrick and Mount's (1991) meta-analysis provided important empirical evidence for their use. Whilst the authors found relationships between all personality dimensions and different occupations, the strongest relationships were with conscientiousness for all job performance criteria. A second, later paper by Mount and Barrick discusses subsequent studies and identifies five reasons why the 'Big Five' article has been frequently cited.

The next two papers focus on motivation to work. Unlike personality, where researchers have successfully developed psychometric measures capable of quantifying relatively stable individual differences, motivation remains a more elusive concept. In his paper Locke (1997) examines several theories of motivation and proposes a model based on goal-setting theory and self-efficacy. Kanfer and Ackerman (2000) take a trait approach in their effort to identify stable individual differences in work motivation. They present evidence of construct validity for a motivational trait taxonomy. Schmidt and Hunter's (2004) second paper is another classic study, which provides summarizing evidence for the relationship between general mental ability (GMA) and work performance. They present evidence that GMA predicts occupational level and occupational performance better than job experience, other measures of ability, traits or dispositions, and present a theory of job performance theory that focuses on GMA.

The final three papers in the first section consider why selection systems work and the impact they can have on applicants. Although Klimoski and Brickner's (1987) paper is now more than twenty years old, it is still an important reminder that factors other than our efforts to identify individuals with relevant knowledge skills and abilities can influence the success of selection systems. The authors point out that selection outcomes influence managers' expectations as well as the individual's role-related self-efficacy. Klimoski and Brickner's work emphasizes the need to ask *why* selection methods work rather than rely simply on outcome measures such as criterion-related validity. Finally, Gilliland (1993) discusses the importance of taking account of applicants' views of how fair selection systems are and Ryan and Ployhart (2000) develop Gilliland's model of organizational and distributive justice by identifying areas important for future research.

The second part of Volume II concentrates on employees once they have entered the workplace and looks at organizational strategies for enhancing individual performance. The first paper, by Arvey and Murphy (1998), provides an important review of theory and research into performance evaluation that stretches from more traditional research areas such as bias in supervisor ratings, to recent developments such as multi-source feedback. The next two papers provide different perspectives on work by organizational psychologists to define and describe work roles. Viswesvaran and Ones (2000) review several models of job performance and look at how dimensions of job performance have been developed. They suggest that positive correlations between different facets of job performance may indicate a general factor. In contrast, Sparrow (1995) discusses the use of competencies in defining different aspects of roles and argues for researchers to take a more strategic approach.

Although validity and reliability are common themes in selection and assessment contexts, research described by Schein and her colleagues (1996) reminds us of the persistent threat of stereotyping to the fairness and utility of selection procedures. Following on from her seminal 'think manager, think male' work in the 1970s, Schein finds that the stereotype of linking men rather than women with management roles persists as a global phenomenon. Despite increasing numbers of women in manager roles, there is still a need to make assessors aware of unconscious bias when making evaluative decisions.

Finally, the remaining five papers each discuss an aspect of employee training and development. Salas and Cannon-Bowers (2001) provide an extensive review of training research conducted during the 1990s, identifying key themes and future needs. Alliger and Janak's (1989) paper describes one of very few studies to have collected evidence of the impact of training programmes at individual through to organizational levels of performance. Findings from their investigation of Kirkpatrick's popular framework of training evaluation challenge assumptions about the hierarchical relations between each of the four levels of training criteria. Baldwin and Ford's (1988) paper focuses on the transfer of learning literature. They suggest that inorder to better understand factors that lead trainees to apply their learning back in the workplace, research should address the effects of training design, work environment and trainee characteristics. Kraiger, Ford and Salas (1993) present a refined evaluation model based on learning outcomes derived from cognitive, skill-based and affective components of learning. Finally, last but not least, Garvin's (1993) paper moves beyond the level of individual psychology by considering what constitutes a learning organization, how one might be developed, and how we might measure whether it is successful.

Part 3

HOW ORGANIZATIONS ATTRACT, SELECT AND RECRUIT EMPLOYEES

18

THE VALIDITY AND UTILITY OF SELECTION METHODS IN PERSONNEL PSYCHOLOGY

Practical and theoretical implications of 85 years of research findings

Frank L. Schmidt and John E. Hunter

Source: *Psychological Bulletin* 124(2) (1998): 262–274.

Abstract

This article summarizes the practical and theoretical implications of 85 years of research in personnel selection. On the basis of meta-analytic findings, this article presents the validity of 19 selection procedures for predicting job performance and training performance and the validity of paired combinations of general mental ability (GMA) and the 18 other selection procedures. Overall, the 3 combinations with the highest multivariate validity and utility for job performance were GMA plus a work sample test (mean validity of .63), GMA plus an integrity test (mean validity of .65), and GMA plus a structured interview (mean validity of .63). A further advantage of the latter 2 combinations is that they can be used for both entry level selection and selection of experienced employees. The practical utility implications of these summary findings are substantial. The implications of these research findings for the development of theories of job performance are discussed.

From the point of view of practical value, the most important property of a personnel assessment method is predictive validity: the ability to predict future job performance, job-related learning (such as amount of learning in training and development programs), and other criteria. The predictive validity coefficient is directly proportional to the practical economic value (utility) of the assessment method (Brogden, 1949; Schmidt, Hunter, McKenzie, & Muldrow, 1979). Use of hiring methods with increased predictive validity leads to substantial increases in employee performance as measured in percentage increases in output, increased monetary value of output, and increased learning of job-related skills (Hunter, Schmidt, & Judiesch, 1990).

Today, the validity of different personnel measures can be determined with the aid of 85 years of research. The most well-known conclusion from this research is that for hiring employees without previous experience in the job the most valid predictor of future performance and learning is general mental ability ([GMA], i.e., intelligence or general cognitive ability; Hunter & Hunter, 1984; Ree & Earles, 1992). GMA can be measured using commercially available tests. However, many other measures can also contribute to the overall validity of the selection process. These include, for example, measures of conscientiousness and personal integrity, structured employment interviews, and (for experienced workers) job knowledge and work sample tests.

On the basis of meta-analytic findings, this article examines and summarizes what 85 years of research in personnel psychology has revealed about the validity of measures of 19 different selection methods that can be used in making decisions about hiring, training, and developmental assignments. In this sense, this article is an expansion and updating of Hunter and Hunter (1984). In addition, this article examines how well certain combinations of these methods work. These 19 procedures do not all work equally well; the research evidence indicates that some work very well and some work very poorly. Measures of GMA work very well, for example, and graphology does not work at all. The cumulative findings show that the research knowledge now available makes it possible for employers today to substantially increase the productivity, output, and learning ability of their workforces by using procedures that work well and by avoiding those that do not. Finally, we look at the implications of these research findings for the development of theories of job performance.

Determinants of practical value (utility) of selection methods

The validity of a hiring method is a direct determinant of its practical value, but not the only determinant. Another direct determinant is the variability of job performance. At one extreme, if variability were zero, then all applicants would have exactly the same level of later job performance if hired. In this case, the practical value or utility of all selection procedures would be zero. In such a hypothetical case, it does not matter who is hired, because all workers are the same. At the other extreme, if performance variability is very large, it then becomes important to hire the best performing applicants and the practical utility of valid selection methods is very large. As it happens, this "extreme" case appears to be the reality for most jobs. Research over the last 15 years has shown that the variability of performance and output among (incumbent) workers is very large and that it would be even larger if all job applicants were hired or if job applicants were selected randomly from among those that apply (cf. Hunter et al., 1990; Schmidt & Hunter, 1983; Schmidt et al., 1979). This latter variability is called the applicant pool variability, and in hiring this is the variability that operates to determine practical value. This is because one is selecting new employees from the applicant pool, not from among those already on the job in question.

The variability of employee job performance can be measured in a number of ways, but two scales have typically been used: dollar value of output and output as a percentage of mean output. The standard deviation across individuals of the dollar value of output (called SD_y) has been found to be at minimum 40% of the mean salary of the job (Schmidt & Hunter, 1983; Schmidt et al., 1979; Schmidt Mack, & Hunter, 1984). The 40% figure is a lower bound value; actual values are typically considerably higher. Thus, if the average salary for a job is $40,000, then SD_y is at least $16,000. If performance has a normal distribution, then workers at the 84th percentile produce $16,000 more per year than average workers (i.e., those at the 50th percentile). And the difference between workers at the 16th percentile ("below average" workers) and those at the 84th percentile ("superior" workers) is twice that: $32,000 per year. Such differences are large enough to be important to the economic health of an organization.

Employee output can also be measured as a percentage of mean output; that is, each employee's output is divided by the output of workers at the 50th percentile and then multiplied by 100. Research shows that the standard deviation of output as a percentage of average output (called SD_p) varies by job level. For unskilled and semi-skilled jobs, the average SD_p figure is 19%. For skilled work, it is 32%, and for managerial and professional jobs, it is 48% (Hunter et al., 1990). These figures are averages based on all available studies that measured or counted the amount of output for different employees. If a superior worker is defined as one whose performance (output) is at the 84th percentile (that is, 1 SD above the mean), then a superior worker in a lower level job produces 19% more output than an average worker, a superior skilled worker produces 32% more output than the average skilled worker, and a superior manager or professional produces output 48% above the average for those jobs. These differences are large and they indicate that the payoff from using valid hiring methods to predict later job performance is quite large.

Another determinant of the practical value of selection methods is the selection ratio—the proportion of applicants who are hired. At one extreme, if an organization must hire all who apply for the job, no hiring procedure has any practical value. At the other extreme, if the organization has the luxury of hiring only the top scoring 1%, the practical value of gains from selection per person hired will be extremely large. But few organizations can afford to reject 99% of all job applicants. Actual selection ratios are typically in the .30 to .70 range, a range that still produces substantial practical utility.

The actual formula for computing practical gains per person hired per year on the job is a three way product (Brogden, 1949; Schmidt et al., 1979):

$$\Delta \bar{U}/\text{hire}/\text{year} = \Delta r_{xy} SD_y \bar{Z}_x \quad \text{(when performance is measured in dollar value)} \quad (1)$$

$$\Delta \bar{U}/\text{hire}/\text{year} = \Delta r_{xy} SD_p \bar{Z}_x \quad \text{(when performance is measured in percentage of average output).} \quad (2)$$

In these equations, Δr_{xy} is the difference between the validity of the new (more valid) selection method and the old selection method. If the old selection method has no validity (that is, selection is random), then Δr_{xy} is the same as the validity of the new procedure; that is, $\Delta r_{xy} = r_{xy}$. Hence, relative to random selection, practical value (utility) is directly proportional to validity. If the old procedure has some validity, then the utility gain is directly proportional to Δr_{xy}. $\bar{Z}_x$ is the average score on the employment procedure of those hired (in z-score form), as compared to the general applicant pool. The smaller the selection ratio, the higher this value will be. The first equation expresses selection utility in dollars. For example, a typical final figure for a medium complexity job might be $18,000, meaning that increasing the validity of the hiring methods leads to an average increase in output per hire of $18,000 per year. To get the full value, one must of course multiply by the number of workers hired. If 100 are hired, then the increase would be (100) ($18,000) = $1,800,000. Finally, one must consider the number of years these workers remain on the job, because the $18,000 per worker is realized each year that worker remains on the job. Of all these factors that affect the practical value, only validity is a characteristic of the personnel measure itself.

The second equation expresses the practical value in percentage of increase in output. For example, a typical figure is 9%, meaning that workers hired with the improved selection method will have on average 9% higher output. A 9% increase in labor productivity would typically be very important economically for the firm, and might make the difference between success and bankruptcy.

What we have presented here is not, of course, a comprehensive discussion of selection utility. Readers who would like more detail are referred to the research articles cited above and to Boudreau (1983a, 1983b, 1984), Cascio and Silbey (1979), Cronshaw and Alexander (1985), Hunter, Schmidt, and Coggin (1988), Hunter and Schmidt (1982a, 1982b), Schmidt and Hunter (1983), Schmidt, Hunter, Outerbridge, and Trattner (1986), Schmidt, Hunter, and Pearlman (1982), and Schmidt et al. (1984). Our purpose here is to make three important points: (a) the economic value of gains from improved hiring methods are typically quite large, (b) these gains are directly proportional to the size of the increase in validity when moving from the old to the new selection methods, and (c) no other characteristic of a personnel measure is as important as predictive validity. If one looks at the two equations above, one sees that practical value per person hired is a three way product. One of the three elements in that three way product is predictive validity. The other two—SD_y or SD_p and $\bar{Z}_x$—are equally important, but they are characteristics of the job or the situation, not of the personnel measure.

Validity of personnel assessment methods: 85 years of research findings

Research studies assessing the ability of personnel assessment methods to predict future job performance and future learning (e.g., in training programs) have been conducted since the first decade of the 20th century. However, as early as the 1920s it became apparent that different studies conducted on the same assessment procedure did not appear to agree in their results. Validity estimates for the same method and same job were quite different for different studies. During the 1930s and 1940s the belief developed that this state of affairs resulted from subtle differences between jobs that were difficult or impossible for job analysts and job analysis methodology to detect. That is, researchers concluded that the validity of a given procedure really was different in different settings for what appeared to be basically the same job, and that the conflicting findings in validity studies were just reflecting this fact of reality. This belief, called the theory of situational specificity, remained dominant in personnel psychology until the late 1970s when it was discovered that most of the differences across studies were due to statistical and measurement artifacts and not to real differences in the jobs (Schmidt & Hunter, 1977; Schmidt, Hunter, Pearlman, & Shane, 1979). The largest of these artifacts was simple sampling error variation, caused by the use of small samples in the studies. (The number of employees per study was usually in the 40–70 range.) This realization led to the development of quantitative techniques collectively called meta-analysis that could combine validity estimates across studies and correct for the effects of these statistical and measurement artifacts (Hunter & Schmidt, 1990; Hunter, Schmidt, & Jackson, 1982). Studies based on meta-analysis provided more accurate estimates of the average operational validity and showed that the level of real variability of validities was usually quite small and might in fact be zero (Schmidt, 1992; Schmidt et al., 1993). In fact, the findings indicated that the variability of validity was not only small or zero across settings for the same type of job, but was also small across different kinds of jobs (Hunter, 1980; Schmidt, Hunter, & Pearlman, 1980). These findings made it possible to select the most valid personnel measures for any job. They also made it possible to compare the validity of different personnel measures for jobs in general, as we do in this article.

Table 1 summarizes research findings for the prediction of performance on the job. The first column of numbers in Table 1 shows the estimated mean validity of 19 selection methods for predicting performance on the job, as revealed by meta-analyses conducted over the last 20 years. Performance on the job was typically measured using supervisory ratings of job performance, but production records, sales records, and other measures were also used. The sources and other information about these validity figures are given in the notes to Table 1.

Table 1 Predictive validity for overall job performance of general mental ability (GMA) scores combined with a second predictor using (standardized) multiple regression

Personnel measures	Validity (r)	Multiple R	Gain in validity from adding supplement	% increase in validity	Standardized regression weights GMA	Standardized regression weights Supplement
GMA tests[a]	.51					
Work sample tests[b]	.54	.63	.12	24%	.36	.41
Integrity tests[c]	.41	.65	.14	27%	.51	.41
Conscientiousness tests[d]	.31	.60	.09	18%	.51	.31
Employment interviews (structured)[e]	.51	.63	.12	24%	.39	.39
Employment interviews (unstructured)[f]	.38	.55	.04	8%	.43	.22
Job knowledge tests[g]	.48	.58	.07	14%	.36	.31
Job tryout procedure[h]	.44	.58	.07	14%	.40	.20
Peer ratings[i]	.49	.58	.07	14%	.35	.31
T & E behavioral consistency method[j]	.45	.58	.07	14%	.39	.31
Reference checks[k]	.26	.57	.06	12%	.51	.26
Job experience (years)[l]	.18	.54	.03	6%	.51	.18
Biographical data measures[m]	.35	.52	.01	2%	.45	.13
Assessment centers[n]	.37	.53	.02	4%	.43	.15
T & E point method[o]	.11	.52	.01	2%	.39	.29
Years of education[p]	.10	.52	.01	2%	.51	.10
Interests[q]	.10	.52	.01	2%	.51	.10
Graphology[r]	.02	.51	.00	0%	.51	.02
Age[s]	−.01	.51	.00	0%	.51	−.01

Note: T & E = training and experience. The percentage of increase in validity is also the percentage of increase in utility (practical value). All of the validities presented are based on the most current meta-analytic results for the various predictors. See Schmidt, Ones, and Hunter (1992) for an overview. All of the validities in this table are for the criterion of overall job performance. Unless otherwise noted, all validity estimates are corrected for the downward bias due to measurement error in the measure of job performance and range restriction on the predictor in incumbent samples relative to applicant populations. The correlations between GMA and other predictors are corrected for range restriction but not for measurement error in either measure (thus they are smaller than fully corrected mean values in the literature). These correlations represent observed score correlations between selection methods in applicant populations. [a]From Hunter (1980). The value used for the validity of GMA is the average validity of GMA for medium complexity jobs (covering more than 60% of all jobs in the United States). Validities are higher for more complex jobs and lower for less complex jobs, as described in the text. [b]From Hunter and Hunter (1984, Table 10). The correction for range restriction was not possible in these data. The correlation between work sample scores and ability scores is .38 (Schmidt, Hunter, & Outerbridge, 1986). [c,d]From Ones, Viswesvaran, and Schmidt (1993, Table 8). The figure of .41 is from predictive validity studies conducted on job applicants.

The validity of .31 for conscientiousness measures is from Mount and Barrick (1995, Table 2). The correlation between integrity and ability is zero, as is the correlation between conscientiousness and ability (Ones, 1993; Ones *et al.*, 1993). [e,f]From McDaniel, Whetzel, Schmidt, and Maner (1994, Table 4). Values used are those from studies in which the job performance ratings were for research purposes only (not administrative ratings) The correlations between interview scores and ability scores are from Huffcutt, Roth, and McDaniel (1996, Table 3). The correlation for structured interviews is .30 and for unstructured interviews, .38. [g]From Hunter and Hunter (1984, Table 11). The correction for range restriction was not possible in these data. The correlation between job knowledge scores and GMA scores is .48 (Schmidt, Hunter, & Outerbridge, 1986). [h]From Hunter and Hunter (1984, Table 9). No correction for range restriction (if any) could be made. (Range restriction is unlikely with this selection method.) The correlation between job tryout ratings and ability scores is estimated at .38 (Schmidt, Hunter, & Outerbridge, 1986); that is, it was taken to be the same as that between job sample tests and ability. Use of the mean correlation between supervisory performance ratings and ability scores yields a similar value (.35, uncorrected for measurement error). [i]From Hunter and Hunter (1984, Table 10). No correction for range restriction (if any) could be made. The average fully corrected correlation between ability and peer ratings of job performance is approximately .55. If peer ratings are based on an average rating from 10 peers, the familiar Spearman–Brown formula indicates that the interrater reliability of peer ratings is approximately .91 (Viswesvaran, Ones, & Schmidt, 1996). Assuming a reliability of .90 for the ability measure, the correlation between ability scores and peer ratings is $.55\sqrt{.91}(.90) = .50$. [j]From McDaniel, Schmidt, and Hunter (1988a). These calculations are based on an estimate of the correlation between T & E behavioral consistency and ability of .40. This estimate reflects the fact that the achievements measured by this procedure depend on not only personality and other noncognitive characteristics, but also on mental ability. [k]From Hunter and Hunter (1984, Table 9). No correction for range restriction (if any) was possible. In the absence of any data, the correlation between reference checks and ability was taken as .00. Assuming a larger correlation would lead to lower estimated incremental validity. [l]From Hunter (1980), McDaniel, Schmidt, and Hunter (1988b), and Hunter and Hunter (1984). In the only relevant meta-analysis, Schmidt, Hunter, and Outerbridge (1986, Table 5) found the correlation between job experience and ability to be .00. This value was used here. [m]The correlation between biodata scores and ability scores is .50 (Schmidt, 1988). Both the validity of .35 used here and the intercorrelation of .50 are based on the Supervisory Profile Record Biodata Scale (Rothstein, Schmidt, Erwin, Owens, and Sparks, 1990). (The validity for the Managerial Profile Record Biodata Scale in predicting managerial promotion and advancement is higher [.52; Carlson, Scullen, Schmidt, Rothstein, & Erwin, 1998]. However, rate of promotion is a measure different from overall performance on one's current job and managers are less representative of the general working population than are first line supervisors). [n]From Gaugler, Rosenthal, Thornton, and Bensor (1987, Table 8). The correlation between assessment center ratings and ability is estimated at .50 (Collins, 1998). It should be noted that most assessment centers use ability tests as part of the evaluation process; Gaugler *et al.* (1987) found that 74% of the 136 assessment centers they examined used a written test of intelligence (see their Table 4). [o]From McDaniel, Schmidt, and Hunter (1988a, Table 3) The calculations here are based on a zero correlation between the T & E point method and ability; the assumption of a positive correlation would at most lower the estimate of incremental validity from .01 to .00. [p]From Hunter and Hunter (1984, Table 9). For purposes of these calculations, we assumed a zero correlation between years of education and ability. The reader should remember that this is the correlation within the applicant pool of individuals who apply to get a particular job. In the general population, the correlation between education and ability is about .55. Even within applicant pools there is probably at least a small positive correlation; thus, our figure of .01 probably overestimates the incremental validity of year of education over general mental ability. Assuming even a small positive value for the correlation between education and ability would drive the validity increment of .01 toward .00. [q]From Hunter and Hunter (1984, Table 9). The general finding is that interests and ability are uncorrelated (Holland, 1986), and that was assumed to be the case here. [r]From Neter and Ben-Shakhar (1989), Ben-Shakhar (1989), Ben-Shakhar, Bar-Hillel, Bilu, Ben-Abba, and Flug (1986), and Bar-Hillel and Ben-Shakhar (1986). Graphology scores were assumed to be uncorrelated with mental ability. [s]From Hunter and Hunter (1984, Table 9). Age was assumed to be unrelated to ability within applicant pools.

Many of the selection methods in Table 1 also predict job-related learning; that is, the acquisition of job knowledge with experience on the job, and the amount learned in training and development programs. However, the overall amount of research on the prediction of learning is less. For many of the procedures in Table 1, there is little research evidence on their ability to predict future job-related learning. Table 2 summarizes available research findings for the prediction of performance in training programs. The first column in Table 2 shows the mean validity of 10 selection methods as revealed by available meta-analyses. In the vast majority of the studies included in these meta-analyses, performance in training was assessed using objective measures of amount learned on the job; trainer ratings of amount learned were used in about 5% of the studies.

Unless otherwise noted in Tables 1 and 2, all validity estimates in Tables 1 and 2 are corrected for the downward bias due to measurement error in the measures of job performance and to range restriction on the selection method in incumbent samples relative to applicant populations. Observed validity estimates so corrected estimate operational validities of selection methods when used to hire from applicant pools. Operational validities are also referred to as true validities.

In the pantheon of 19 personnel measures in Table 1, GMA (also called general cognitive ability and general intelligence) occupies a special place, for several reasons. First, of all procedures that can be used for all jobs, whether entry level or advanced, it has the highest validity and lowest application cost. Work sample measures are slightly more valid but are much more costly and can be used only with applicants who already know the job or have been trained for the occupation or job. Structured employment interviews are more costly and, in some forms, contain job knowledge components and therefore are not suitable for inexperienced, entry level applicants. The assessment center and job tryout are both much more expensive and have less validity. Second, the research evidence for the validity of GMA measures for predicting job performance is stronger than that for any other method (Hunter, 1986; Hunter & Schmidt, 1996; Ree & Earles, 1992; Schmidt & Hunter, 1981). Literally thousands of studies have been conducted over the last nine decades. By contrast, only 89 validity studies of the structured interview have been conducted (McDaniel, Whetzel, Schmidt, & Mauer, 1994). Third, GMA has been shown to be the best available predictor of job-related learning. It is the best predictor of acquisition of job knowledge on the job (Schmidt & Hunter, 1992; Schmidt, Hunter, & Outerbridge, 1986) and of performance in job training programs (Hunter, 1986; Hunter & Hunter, 1984; Ree & Earles, 1992). Fourth, the theoretical foundation for GMA is stronger than for any other personnel measure. Theories of intelligence have been developed and tested by psychologists for over 90 years (Brody, 1992; Carroll, 1993; Jensen, 1998). As a result of this massive related research literature, the meaning of the construct of intelligence is much clearer than, for example, the meaning of what is measured by interviews or assessment centers (Brody, 1992; Hunter, 1986; Jensen, 1998).

The value of .51 in Table 1 for the validity of GMA is from a very large meta-analytic study conducted for the U.S. Department of Labor (Hunter, 1980;

Table 2 Predictive validity for overall performance in job training programs of general mental ability (GMA) scores combined with a second predictor using (standardized) multiple regression

Personnel measures	Validity (r)	Multiple R	Gain in validity from adding supplement	% increase in validity	Standardized regression weights GMA	Standardized regression weights Supplement
GMA Tests[a]	.56					
Integrity tests[b]	.38	.67	.11	20%	.56	.38
Conscientiousness tests[c]	.30	.65	.09	16%	.56	.30
Employment interviews (structured and unstructured)[d]	.35	.59	.03	5%	.59	.19
Peer ratings[e]	.36	.57	.01	1.4%	.51	.11
Reference checks[f]	.23	.61	.05	9%	.56	.23
Job experience (years)[g]	.01	.56	.00	0%	.56	.01
Biographical data measures[h]	.30	.56	.00	0%	.55	.03
Years of education[i]	.20	.60	.04	7%	.56	.20
Interests[j]	.18	.59	.03	5%	.56	.18

Note: The percentage of increase in validity is also the percentage of increase in utility (practical value). All of the validities presented are based on the most current meta-analytic results reported for the various predictors. All of the validities in this table are for the criterion of overall performance in job training programs. Unless otherwise noted, all validity estimates are corrected for the downward bias due to measurement error in the measure of job performance and range restriction on the predictor in incumbent samples relative to applicant populations. All correlations between GMA and other predictors are corrected for range restriction but not for measurement error. These correlations represent observed score correlations between selection methods in applicant populations.
[a]The validity of GMA is from Hunter and Hunter (1984, Table 2). It can also be found in Hunter (1980). [b,c]The validity of .38 for integrity tests is from Schmidt, Ones, and Viswesvaran (1994). Integrity tests and conscientiousness tests have been found to correlate zero with GMA (Ones, 1993; Ones, Viswesvaran & Schmidt, 1993). The validity of .30 for conscientiousness measures is from the meta-analysis presented by Mount and Barrick (1995, Table 2). [d]The validity of interviews is from McDaniel, Whetzel, Schmidt, and Mauer (1994, Table 5). McDaniel et al. reported values of .34 and .36 for structured and unstructured interviews, respectively. However, this small difference of .02 appears to be a result of second order sampling error (Hunter & Schmidt, 1990, Ch. 9). We therefore used the average value of .35 as the validity estimate for structured and unstructured interviews. The correlation between interviews and ability scores (.32) is the overall figure from Huffcutt, Roth, and McDaniel (1996, Table 3) across all levels of interview structure. [e]The validity for peer ratings is from Hunter and Hunter (1984, Table 8). No correction for range restriction (if any) was possible in the data. [f]The validity of reference checks is from Hunter and Hunter 1984, Table 8). No correction for reference checks and ability was taken as .00. Assumption of a larger correlation will reduce the estimate of incremental validity. No correction for range restriction was possible. [g]The validity of job experience is from Hunter and Hunter (1984, Table 6). These calculations are based on an estimate of the correlation between job experience and ability of zero. (See note 1 to Table 1). [h]The validity of biographical data measures is from Hunter and Hunter (1984, Table 8). This validity estimate is not adjusted for range restriction (if any). The correlation between biographical data measures and ability is estimated at .50 (Schmidt, 1988). [i]The validity of education is from Hunter and Hunter (1984, Table 6). The correlation between education and ability within applicant pools was taken as zero. (See note p to Table 1). [j]The validity of interests is from Hunter and Hunter (1984, Table 8). The correlation between interests and ability was taken as zero (Holland, 1986).

Hunter & Hunter, 1984). The database for this unique meta-analysis included over 32,000 employees in 515 widely diverse civilian jobs. This meta-analysis examined both performance on the job and performance in job training programs. This meta-analysis found that the validity of GMA for predicting job performance was .58 for professional-managerial jobs, .56 for high level complex technical jobs, .51 for medium complexity jobs, .40 for semi-skilled jobs, and .23 for completely unskilled jobs. The validity for the middle complexity level of jobs (.51)—which includes 62% of all the jobs in the U.S. economy—is the value entered in Table 1. This category includes skilled blue collar jobs and mid-level white collar jobs, such as upper level clerical and lower level administrative jobs. Hence, the conclusions in this article apply mainly to the middle 62% of jobs in the U.S. economy in terms of complexity. The validity of .51 is representative of findings for GMA measures in other meta-analyses (e.g., Pearlman *et al.*, 1980) and it is a value that produces high practical utility.

As noted above, GMA is also an excellent predictor of job-related learning. It has been found to have high and essentially equal predictive validity for performance (amount learned) in job training programs for jobs at all job levels studied. In the U.S. Department of Labor research, the average predictive validity performance in job training programs was .56 (Hunter & Hunter, 1984, Table 2); this is the figure entered in Table 2. Thus, when an employer uses GMA to select employees who will have a high level of performance on the job, that employer is also selecting those who will learn the most from job training programs and will acquire job knowledge faster from experience on the job. (As can be seen from Table 2, this is also true of integrity tests, conscientiousness tests, and employment interviews.)

Because of its special status, GMA can be considered the primary personnel measure for hiring decisions, and one can consider the remaining 18 personnel measures as supplements to GMA measures. That is, in the case of each of the other measures, one can ask the following question: When used in a properly weighted combination with a GMA measure, how much will each of these measures increase predictive validity for job performance over the .51 that can be obtained by using only GMA? This "incremental validity" translates into incremental utility, that is, into increases in practical value. Because validity is directly proportional to utility, the percentage of increase in validity produced by the adding the second measure is also the percentage of increase in practical value (utility). The increase in validity (and utility) depends not only on the validity of the measure added to GMA, but also on the correlation between the two measures. The smaller this correlations is, the larger is the increase in overall validity. The figures for incremental validity in Table 1 are affected by these correlations. The correlations between mental ability measures and the other measures were estimated from the research literature (often from meta-analyses); the sources of these estimates are given in the notes to Tables 1 and 2. To appropriately represent the observed score correlations between predictors in applicant populations, we corrected all correlations between GMA and other predictors for range restriction but not for measurement error in the measure of either predictor.

Consider work sample tests. Work sample tests are hands-on simulation of part or all of the job that must be performed by applicants. For example, as part of a work sample test, an applicant might be required to repair a series of defective electric motors. Work sample tests are often used to hire skilled workers, such as welders, machinists, and carpenters. When combined in a standardized regression equation with GMA, the work sample receives a weight of .41 and GMA receives a weight of .36. (The standardized regression weights are given in the last two columns of Tables 1 and 2.) The validity of this weighted sum of the two measures (the multiple R) is .63, which represents an increment of .12 over the validity of GMA alone. This is a 24% increase in validity over that of GMA alone—and also a 24% increase in the practical value (utility) of the selection procedure. As we saw earlier, this can be expressed as a 24% increase in the gain in dollar value of output. Alternatively, it can be expressed as a 24% increase in the percentage of increase in output produced by using GMA alone. In either case, it is a substantial improvement.

Work sample tests can be used only with applicants who already know the job. Such workers do not need to be trained, and so the ability of work sample tests to predict training performance has not been studied. Hence, there is no entry for work sample tests in Table 2.

Integrity tests are used in industry to hire employees with reduced probability of counterproductive job behaviors, such as drinking or drugs on the job, fighting on the job, stealing from the employer, sabotaging equipment, and other undesirable behaviors. They do predict these behaviors, but they also predict evaluations of overall job performance (Ones, Viswesvaran, & Schmidt, 1993). Even though their validity is lower, integrity tests produce a larger increment in validity (.14) and a larger percentage of increase in validity (and utility) than do work samples. This is because integrity tests correlate zero with GMA (vs. .38 for work samples). In terms of basic personality traits, integrity tests have been found to measure mostly conscientiousness, but also some components of agreeableness and emotional stability (Ones, 1993). The figures for conscientiousness measures per se are given in Table 1. The validity of conscientiousness measures (Mount & Barrick, 1995) is lower than that for integrity tests (.31 vs. .41), its increment to validity is smaller (.09), and its percentage of increase in validity is smaller (18%). However, these values for conscientiousness are still large enough to be practically useful.

A meta-analysis based on 8 studies and 2,364 individuals estimated the mean validity of integrity tests for predicting performance in training programs at .38 (Schmidt, Ones, & Viswesvaran, 1994). As can be seen in Table 2, the incremental validity for integrity tests for predicting training performance is .11, which yields a 20% increase in validity and utility over that produced by GMA alone. In the prediction of training performance, integrity tests appear to produce higher incremental validity than any other measure studied to date. However, the increment in validity produced by measures of conscientiousness (.09, for a 16% increase) is only slightly smaller. The validity estimate for conscientiousness is based on

21 studies and 4,106 individuals (Mount & Barrick, 1995), a somewhat larger database.

Employment interviews can be either structured or unstructured (Huffcutt, Roth, & McDaniel, 1996; McDaniel *et al.*, 1994). Unstructured interviews have no fixed format or set of questions to be answered. In fact, the same interviewer often asks different applicants different questions. Nor is there a fixed procedure for scoring responses; in fact, responses to individual questions are usually not scored, and only an overall evaluation (or rating) is given to each applicant, based on summary impressions and judgments. Structured interviews are exactly the opposite on all counts. In addition, the questions to be asked are usually determined by a careful analysis of the job in question. As a result, structured interviews are more costly to construct and use, but are also more valid. As shown in Table 1, the average validity of the structured interview is .51, versus .38 for the unstructured interview (and undoubtedly lower for carelessly conducted unstructured interviews). An equally weighted combination of the structured interview and a GMA measure yields a validity of .63. As is the case for work sample tests, the increment in validity is .12 and the percentage of increase is 24%. These figures are considerably smaller for the unstructured interview (see Table 1). Clearly, the combination of a structured interview and a GMA test is an attractive hiring procedure. It achieves 63% of the maximum possible practical value (utility), and does so at reasonable cost.

As shown in Table 2, both structured and unstructured interviews predict performance in job training programs with a validity of about .35 (McDaniel *et al.*, 1994; see their Table 5). The incremental validity for the prediction of training performance is .03, a 5% increase.

The next procedure in Table 1 is job knowledge tests. Like work sample measures, job knowledge tests cannot be used to evaluate and hire inexperienced workers. An applicant cannot be expected to have mastered the job knowledge required to perform a particular job unless he or she has previously performed that job or has received schooling, education, or training for that job. But applicants for jobs such as carpenter, welder, accountant, and chemist can be administered job knowledge tests. Job knowledge tests are often constructed by the hiring organization on the basis of an analysis of the tasks that make up the job. Constructing job knowledge tests in this manner is generally somewhat more time consuming and expensive than constructing typical structured interviews. However, such tests can also be purchased commercially; for example, tests are available that measure the job knowledge required of machinists (knowledge of metal cutting tools and procedures). Other examples are tests of knowledge of basic organic chemistry and tests of the knowledge required of roofers. In an extensive meta-analysis, Dye, Reck and McDaniel (1993) found that commercially purchased job knowledge tests ("off the shelf" tests) had slightly lower validity than job knowledge tests tailored to the job in question. The validity figure of .48 in Table 1 for job knowledge tests is for tests tailored to the job in question.

As shown in Table 1, job knowledge tests increase the validity by .07 over that of GMA measures alone, yielding a 14% increase in validity and utility. Thus job knowledge tests can have substantial practical value to the organization using them.

For the same reasons indicated earlier for job sample tests, job knowledge tests typically have not been used to predict performance in training programs. Hence, little validity information is available for this criterion, and there is no entry in Table 2 for job knowledge tests.

The next three personnel measures in Table 1 increase validity and utility by the same amount as job knowledge tests (i.e., 14%). However, two of these methods are considerably less practical to use in many situations. Consider the job tryout procedure. Unlike job knowledge tests, the job tryout procedure can be used with entry level employees with no previous experience on the job in question. With this procedure, applicants are hired with minimal screening and their performance on the job is observed and evaluated for a certain period of time (typically 6–8 months). Those who do not meet a previously established standard of satisfactory performance by the end of this probationary period are then terminated. If used in this manner, this procedure can have substantial validity (and incremental validity), as shown in Table 1. However, it is very expensive to implement, and low job performance by minimally screened probationary workers can lead to serious economic losses. In addition, it has been our experience that supervisors are reluctant to terminate marginal performers. Doing so is an unpleasant experience for them, and to avoid this experience many supervisors gradually reduce the standards of minimally acceptable performance, thus destroying the effectiveness of the procedure. Another consideration is that some of the benefits of this method will be captured in the normal course of events even if the job tryout procedure is not used, because clearly inadequate performers will be terminated after a period of time anyway.

Peer ratings are evaluations of performance or potential made by one's co-workers; they typically are averaged across peer raters to increase the reliability (and hence validity) of the ratings. Like the job tryout procedure, peer ratings have some limitations. First, they cannot be used for evaluating and hiring applicants from outside the organization; they can be used only for internal job assignment, promotion, or training assignment. They have been used extensively for these internal personnel decisions in the military (particularly the U.S. and Israeli militaries) and some private firms, such as insurance companies. One concern associated with peer ratings is that they will be influenced by friendship, or social popularity, or both. Another is that pairs or clusters of peers might secretly agree in advance to give each other high peer ratings. However, the research that has been done does not support these fears; for example, partialling friendship measures out of the peer ratings does not appear to affect the validity of the ratings (cf. Hollander, 1956; Waters & Waters, 1970).

The behavioral consistency method of evaluating previous training and experience (McDaniel, Schmidt, & Hunter, 1988a; Schmidt, Caplan, *et al.*, 1979) is based on the well-established psychological principle that the best predictor of future performance is past performance. In developing this method, the first step is to determine what achievement and accomplishment dimensions best separate top job performers from low performers. This is done on the basis of information obtained from experienced supervisors of the job in question, using a special set of procedures (Schmidt, Caplan, *et al.*, 1979). Applicants are then asked to describe (in writing or sometimes orally) their past achievements that best illustrate their ability to perform these functions at a high level (e.g., organizing people and getting work done through people). These achievements are then scored with the aid of scales that are anchored at various points by specific scaled achievements that serve as illustrative examples or anchors.

Use of the behavioral consistency method is not limited to applicants with previous experience on the job in question. Previous experience on jobs that are similar to the current job in only very general ways typically provides adequate opportunity for demonstration of achievements. In fact, the relevant achievements can sometimes be demonstrated through community, school, and other nonjob activities. However, some young people just leaving secondary school may not have had adequate opportunity to demonstrate their capacity for the relevant achievements and accomplishments; the procedure might work less well in such groups.

In terms of time and cost, the behavioral consistency procedure is nearly as time consuming and costly to construct as locally constructed job knowledge tests. Considerable work is required to construct the procedure and the scoring system; applying the scoring procedure to applicant responses is also more time consuming than scoring of most job knowledge tests and other tests with clear right and wrong answers. However, especially for higher level jobs, the behavioral consistency method may be well worth the cost and effort.

No information is available on the validity of the job tryout or the behavioral consistency procedures for predicting performance in training programs. However, as indicated in Table 2, peer ratings have been found to predict performance in training programs with a mean validity of .36 (see Hunter & Hunter, 1984, Table 8).

For the next procedure, reference checks, the information presented in Table 1 may not at present be fully accurate. The validity studies on which the validity of .26 in Table 1 is based were conducted prior to the development of the current legal climate in the United States. During the 1970s and 1980s, employers providing negative information about past job performance or behavior on the job to prospective new employers were sometimes subjected to lawsuits by the former employees in question. Today, in the United States at least, many previous employers will provide only information on the dates of employment and the job titles the former employee held. That is, past employers today typically refuse to release information on quality or quantity of job performance, disciplinary record of the past employee, or whether the former employee quit voluntarily or was dismissed. This is especially likely to be the case if the information is requested in writing; occasionally, such information will be revealed by telephone or in face to face conversation but one cannot be certain that this will occur.

However, in recent years the legal climate in the United States has been changing. Over the last decade, 19 of the 50 states have enacted laws that provide immunity from legal liability for employers providing job references in good faith to other employers, and such laws are under consideration in 9 other states (Baker, 1996). Hence, reference checks, formerly a heavily relied on procedure in hiring, may again come to provide an increment to the validity of a GMA measure for predicting job performance. In Table 1, the increment is 12%, only two percentage points less than the increments for the five preceding methods.

Older research indicates that reference checks predict performance in training with a mean validity of .23 (Hunter & Hunter, 1984, Table 8), yielding a 9% increment in validity over GMA tests, as shown in Table 2. But, again, these findings may no longer hold; however, changes in the legal climate may make these validity estimates accurate again.

Job experience as indexed in Tables 1 and 2 refers to the number of years of previous experience on the same or similar job; it conveys no information on past performance on the job. In the data used to derive the validity estimates in these tables, job experience varied widely: from less than 6 months to more than 30 years. Under these circumstances, the validity of job experience for predicting future job performance is only .18 and the increment in validity (and utility) over that from GMA alone is only .03 (a 6% increase). However, Schmidt, Hunter, and Outerbridge (1986) found that when experience on the job does not exceed 5 years, the correlation between amount of job experience and job performance is considerably larger: .33 when job performance is measured by supervisory ratings and .47 when job performance is measured using a work sample test. These researchers found that the relation is nonlinear: Up to about 5 years of job experience, job performance increases linearly with increasing experience on the job. After that, the curve becomes increasingly horizontal, and further increases in job experience produce little increase in job performance. Apparently, during the first 5 years on these (mid-level, medium complexity) jobs, employees were continually acquiring additional job knowledge and skills that improved their job performance. But by the end of 5 years this process was nearly complete, and further increases in job experience led to little increase in job knowledge and skills (Schmidt & Hunter, 1992). These findings suggest that even under ideal circumstances, job experience at the start of a job will predict job performance only for the first 5 years on the job. By contrast, GMA continues to predict job performance indefinitely (Hunter & Schmidt, 1996; Schmidt, Hunter, Outerbridge, & Goff, 1988; Schmidt, Hunter, Outerbridge, & Trattner, 1986).

As shown in Table 2, the amount of job experience does not predict performance in training programs teaching new skills. Hunter and Hunter (1984, Table 6) reported a mean validity of .01. However, one can note from this finding that job experience does not retard the acquisition of new job skills in training programs as might have been predicted from theories of proactive inhibition.

Biographical data measures contain questions about past life experiences, such as early life experiences in one's family, in high school, and in hobbies and other pursuits. For example, there may be questions on offices held in student organizations, on sports one participated in, and on disciplinary practices of one's parents. Each question has been chosen for inclusion in the measure because in the initial developmental sample it correlated with a criterion of job performance, performance in training, or some other criterion. That is, biographical data measures are empirically developed. However, they are usually not completely actuarial, because some hypotheses are invoked in choosing the beginning set of items. However, choice of the final questions to retain for the scale is mostly actuarial. Today antidiscrimination laws prevent certain questions from being used, such as sex, marital status, and age, and such items are not included. Biographical data measures have been used to predict performance on a wide variety of jobs, ranging in level from blue collar unskilled jobs to scientific and managerial jobs. These measures are also used to predict job tenure (turnover) and absenteeism, but we do not consider these usages in this article.

Table 1 shows that biographical data measures have substantial zero-order validity (.35) for predicting job performance but produce an increment in validity over GMA of only .01 on average (a 2% increase). The reason that the increment in validity is so small is that biographical data correlates substantially with GMA (.50; Schmidt, 1988). This suggests that in addition to whatever other traits they measure, biographical data measures are also in part indirect reflections of mental ability.

As shown in Table 2, biographical data measures predict performance in training programs with a mean validity of .30 (Hunter & Hunter, 1984, Table 8). However, because of their relatively high correlation with GMA, they produce no increment in validity for performance in training.

Biographical data measures are technically difficult and time consuming to construct (although they are easy to use once constructed). Considerable statistical sophistication is required to develop them. However, some commercial firms offer validated biographical data measures for particular jobs (e.g., first line supervisors, managers, clerical workers, and law enforcement personnel). These firms maintain control of the proprietary scoring keys and the scoring of applicant responses.

Individuals who are administered assessment centers spend one to several days at a central location where they are observed participating in such exercises as leaderless group discussions and business games. Various ability and personality tests are usually administered, and in-depth structured interviews are also part of most assessment centers. The average assessment center includes seven exercises or assessments and lasts 2 days (Gaugler, Rosenthal, Thornton, & Benson, 1987). Assessment centers are used for jobs ranging from first line supervisors to high level management positions.

Assessment centers are like biographical data measures: They have substantial validity but only moderate incremental validity over GMA (.01, a 2% increase). The reason is also the same: They correlate moderately highly with GMA—in part because they typically include a measure of GMA (Gaugler *et al.*, 1987). Despite the fact of relatively low incremental validity, many organizations use assessment centers for managerial jobs because they believe assessment centers provide them with a wide range of insights about candidates and their developmental possibilities.

Assessment centers have generally not been used to predict performance in job training programs; hence, their validity for this purpose is unknown. However, assessment center scores do predict rate of promotion and advancement in management. Gaugler *et al.* (1987, Table 8) reported a mean validity of .36 for this criterion (the same value as for the prediction of job performance). Measurements of career advancement include number of promotions, increases in salary over given time spans, absolute level of salary attained, and management rank attained. Rapid advancement in organizations requires rapid learning of job related knowledge. Hence, assessment center scores do appear to predict the acquisition of job related knowledge on the job.

The point method of evaluating previous training and experience (T&E) is used mostly in government hiring—at all levels, federal, state, and local. A major reason for its widespread use is that point method procedures are relatively inexpensive to construct and use. The point method appears under a wide variety of different names (McDaniel *et al.*, 1988a), but all such procedures have several important characteristics in common. All point method procedures are credentialistic; typically an applicant receives a fixed number of points for (a) each year or month of experience on the same or similar job, (b) each year of relevant schooling (or each course taken), and (c) each relevant training program completed, and so on. There is usually no attempt to evaluate past achievements, accomplishments, or job performance; in effect, the procedure assumes that achievement and performance are determined solely by the exposures that are measured. As shown in Table 1, the T&E point method has low validity and produces only a 2% increase in validity over that available from GMA alone. The T&E point method has not been used to predict performance in training programs.

Sheer amount of education has even lower validity for predicting job performance than the T&E point method (.10). However, its increment to validity, rounded to two decimal places, is the same .01 as obtained with the T&E point method. It is important to note that this finding does not imply that education is irrelevant to occupational success; education is clearly an important determinant of the level of job the individual can obtain. What this finding shows is that among those who apply to get a particular job years of education does not predict future performance on that job very well. For example, for a typical semi-skilled blue collar job, years of education among applicants might range from 9 to 12. The validity of .10 then means that the average job performance of those with 12 years of education will be only slightly higher (on average) than that for those with 9 or 10 years.

As can be seen in Table 2, amount of education predicts learning in job training programs better than it predicts performance on the job. Hunter and

Hunter (1984, Table 6) found a mean validity of .20 for performance in training programs. This is not a high level of validity, but it is twice as large as the validity for predicting job performance.

Many believe that interests are an important determinant of one's level of job performance. People whose interests match the content of their jobs (e.g., people with mechanical interests who have mechanical jobs) are believed to have higher job performance than with nonmatching interests. The validity of .10 for interests shows that this is true only to a very limited extent. To many people, this seems counterintuitive. Why do interests predict job performance so poorly? Research indicates that interests do substantially influence which jobs people prefer and which jobs they attempt to enter. However, once individuals are in a job, the quality and level of their job performance is determined mostly by their mental ability and by certain personality traits such as conscientiousness, not by their interests. So despite popular belief, measurement of work interests is not a good means of predicting who will show the best future job performance (Holland, 1986).

Interests predict learning in job training programs somewhat better than they predict job performance. As shown in Table 2, Hunter and Hunter (1984, Table 8) found a mean validity of .18 for predicting performance in job training programs.

Graphology is the analysis of handwriting. Graphologists claim that people express their personalities through their handwriting and that one's handwriting therefore reveals personality traits and tendencies that graphologists can use to predict future job performance. Graphology is used infrequently in the United States and Canada but is widely used in hiring in France (Steiner, 1997; Steiner & Gilliland, 1996) and in Israel. Levy (1979) reported that 85% of French firms routinely use graphology in hiring of personnel. Ben-Shakhar, Bar-Hillel, Bilu, Ben-Abba, and Flug (1986) stated that in Israel graphology is used more widely than any other single personality measure.

Several studies have examined the ability of graphologists and nongraphologists to predict job performance from handwriting samples (Jansen, 1973; Rafaeli & Klimoski, 1983; see also Ben-Shakhar, 1989; Ben-Shakhar, Bar-Hillel, Bilu et al., 1986; Ben-Shakhar, Bar-Hillel, & Flug, 1986). The key findings in this area are as follows. When the assessees who provide handwriting samples are allowed to write on any subject they choose, both graphologists and untrained nongraphologists can infer some (limited) information about their personalities and job performance from the handwriting samples. But untrained nongraphologists do just as well as graphologists; both show validities in the .18–.20 range. When the assessees are required to copy the same material from a book to create their handwriting sample, there is no evidence that graphologists or nongraphologists can infer any valid information about personality traits or job performance from the handwriting samples (Neter & Ben-Shakhar, 1989). What this indicates is that, contrary to graphology theory, whatever limited information about personality or job performance there is in the handwriting samples comes from the content and not the characteristics of the handwriting. For example, writers differ in style of writing, expressions of emotions, verbal fluency, grammatical skills, and so on. Whatever information about personality and ability these differences contain, the training of graphologists does not allow them to extract it better than can people untrained in graphology. In handwriting per se, independent of content, there appears to be no information about personality or job performance (Neter & Ben-Shakhar, 1989).

To many people, this is another counterintuitive finding, like the finding that interests are a poor predictor of job performance. To these people, it seems obvious that the wide and dramatic variations in handwriting that everyone observes must reveal personality differences among individuals. Actually, most of the variation in handwriting is due to differences among individuals in fine motor coordination of the finger muscles. And these differences in finger muscles and their coordination are probably due mostly to random genetic variations among individuals. The genetic variations that cause these finger coordination differences do not appear to be linked to personality; and in fact there is no apparent reason to believe they should be.

The validity of graphology for predicting performance in training programs has not been studied. However, the findings with respect to performance on the job make it highly unlikely that graphology has validity for training performance.

Table 1 shows that age of job applicants shows no validity for predicting job performance. Age is rarely used as a basis for hiring, and in fact in the United States, use of age for individuals over age 40 would be a violation of the federal law against age discrimination. We include age here for only two reasons. First, some individuals believe age is related to job performance. We show here that for typical jobs this is not the case. Second, age serves to anchor the bottom end of the validity dimension: Age is about as totally unrelated to job performance as any measure can be. No meta-analyses relating age to performance in job training programs were found. Although it is possible that future research will find that age is negatively related to performance in job training programs (as is widely believed), we note again that job experience, which is positively correlated with age, is not correlated with performance in training programs (see Table 2).

Finally, we address an issue raised by a reviewer. As discussed in more detail in the next section, some of the personnel measures we have examined (e.g., GMA and conscientiousness measures) are measures of single psychological constructs, whereas others (e.g., biodata and assessment centers) are methods rather than constructs. It is conceivable that a method such as the assessment center, for example, could measure different constructs or combinations of constructs in different applications in different firms. The reviewer therefore questioned whether it was meaningful to compare the incremental validities of different methods (e.g., comparing the incremental validities produced by the structured interview and the assessment center). There are two responses to this. First, this article is concerned with personnel measures as used in the real world of employment. Hence, from that point of view, such comparisons of incremental validities would be meaningful, even if they represented only crude average differences in incremental validities.

However, the situation is not that grim. The empirical evidence indicates that such methods as interviews, assessment centers, and biodata measures do not vary much from application to application in the constructs they measure. This can be seen from the fact that meta-analysis results show that the standard deviations of validity across studies (applications), after the appropriate corrections for sampling error and other statistical and measurement artifacts, are quite small (cf. Gaugler *et al.*, 1987; McDaniel *et al.*, 1994; Schmidt & Rothstein, 1994). In fact, these standard deviations are often even smaller than those for construct-based measures such as GMA and conscientiousness (Schmidt & Rothstein, 1994).

Hence, the situation appears to be this: We do not know exactly what combination of constructs is measured by methods such as the assessment center, the interview, and biodata (see the next section), but whatever those combinations are, they do not appear to vary much from one application (study) to another Hence, comparisons of their relative incremental validities over GMA is in fact meaningful. These incremental validities can be expected to be stable across different applications of the methods in different organizations and settings.

Toward a theory of the determinants of job performance

The previous section summarized what is known from cumulative empirical research about the validity of various personnel measures for predicting future job performance and job-related learning of job applicants. These findings are based on thousands of research studies performed over eight decades and involving millions of employees. They are a tribute to the power of empirical research, integrated using meta-analysis methods, to produce precise estimates of relationships of interest and practical value. However, the goals of personnel psychology include more than a delineation of relationships that are practically useful in selecting employees. In recent years, the focus in personnel psychology has turned to the development of theories of the causes of job performance (Schmidt & Hunter, 1992). The objective is the understanding of the psychological processes underlying and determining job performance. This change of emphasis is possible because application of meta-analysis to research findings has provided the kind of precise and generalizable estimates of the validity of different measured constructs for predicting job performance that are summarized in this article. It has also provided more precise estimates than previously available of the correlations among these predictors.

However, the theories of job performance that have been developed and tested do not include a role for all of the personnel measures discussed above. That is because the actual constructs measured by some of these procedures are unknown, and it seems certain that some of these procedures measure combinations of constructs (Hunter & Hunter, 1984; Schmidt & Rothstein, 1994). For example, employment interviews probably measure a combination of previous experience, mental ability, and a number of personality traits, such as conscientiousness; in addition, they may measure specific job-related skills and behavior patterns. The average correlation between interview scores and scores on GMA tests is .32 (Huffcutt *et al.*, 1996). This indicates that, to some extent, interview scores reflect mental ability. Little empirical evidence is available as to what other traits they measure (Huffcutt *et al.*, 1996). What has been said here of employment interviews also applies to peer ratings, the behavioral consistency method, reference checks, biographical data measures, assessment centers, and the point method of evaluating past training and experience. Procedures such as these can be used as practical selection tools but, because their construct composition is unknown, they are less useful in constructing theories of the determinants of job performance. The measures that have been used in theories of job performance have been GMA, job knowledge, job experience, and personality traits. This is because it is fairly clear what constructs each of these procedures measures.

What has this research revealed about the determinants of job performance? A detailed review of this research can be found in Schmidt and Hunter (1992); here we summarize only the most important findings. One major finding concerns the reason why GMA is such a good predictor of job performance. The major direct causal impact of mental ability has been found to be on the acquisition of job knowledge. That is, the major reason more intelligent people have higher job performance is that they acquire job knowledge more rapidly and acquire more of it; and it is this knowledge of how to perform the job that causes their job performance to be higher (Hunter, 1986). Thus, mental ability has its most important effect on job performance indirectly, through job knowledge. There is also a direct effect of mental ability on job performance independent of job knowledge, but it is smaller. For nonsupervisory jobs, this direct effect is only about 20% as large as the indirect effect; for supervisory jobs, it is about 50% as large (Borman, White, Pulakos, & Oppler, 1991; Schmidt, Hunter, & Outerbridge, 1986).

It has also been found that job experience operates in this same manner. Job experience is essentially a measure of practice on the job and hence a measure of opportunity to learn. The major direct causal effect of job experience is on job knowledge, just as is the case for mental ability. Up to about 5 years on the job, increasing job experience leads to increasing job knowledge (Schmidt, Hunter, & Outerbridge, 1986), which, in turn, leads to improved job performance. So the major effect of job experience on job performance is indirect, operating through job knowledge. Again, there is also a direct effect of job experience on job performance, but it is smaller than the indirect effect through job knowledge (about 30% as large).

The major personality trait that has been studied in causal models of job performance is conscientiousness. This research has found that, controlling for mental ability, employees who are higher in conscientiousness develop higher levels of job knowledge, probably because highly conscientious individuals exert greater efforts and spend more time "on task." This job knowledge, in turn, causes higher levels of job performance. From a theoretical point of view, this research suggests that the central determining variables in job performance may be GMA, job experience (i.e., opportunity to learn), and the personality trait of conscientiousness. This is consistent with our conclusion that a combination of a GMA test and an integrity test (which measures mostly conscientiousness) has the highest high validity (.65) for predicting job performance. Another combination with high validity (.63) is GMA plus a structured interview, which may in part measure conscientiousness and related personality traits (such as agreeableness and emotional stability, which are also measured in part by integrity tests).

Limitations of this study

This article examined the multivariate validity of only certain predictor combinations: combinations of two predictors with one of the two being GMA. Organizations sometimes use more than two selection methods, and it would be informative to examine the incremental validity from adding a third predictor. For some purposes, it would also be of interest to examine predictor combinations that do not include GMA. However, the absence of the needed estimates of predictor intercorrelations in the literature makes this impossible at the present time. In the future, as data accumulates, such analyses may become feasible.

In fact, even within the context of the present study, some of the estimated predictor intercorrelations could not be made as precise as would be ideal, at least in comparison to those estimates that are based on the results of major meta-analyses. For example, the job tryout procedure is similar to an extended job sample test. In the absence of data estimating the job tryout–ability test score correlation, this correlation was estimated as being the same as the job sample–ability test correlation. It is to be hoped that future research will provide more precise estimates of this and other correlations between GMA and other personnel measures.

Questions related to gender or minority subgroups are beyond the scope of this study. These issues include questions of differential validity by subgroups, predictive fairness for subgroups, and subgroup differences in mean score on selection procedures. An extensive existing literature addresses these questions (cf. Hunter & Schmidt, 1996; Ones *et al.*, 1993; Schmidt, 1988; Schmidt & Hunter, 1981; Schmidt, Ones, & Hunter, 1992; Wigdor & Garner, 1982). However, the general findings of this research literature are obviously relevant here.

For differential validity, the general finding has been that validities (the focus of this study) do not differ appreciably for different subgroups. For predictive fairness, the usual finding has been a lack of predictive bias for minorities and women. That is, given similar scores on selection procedures, later job performance is similar regardless of group membership. On some selection procedures (in particular, cognitive measures), subgroup differences on means are typically observed. On other selection procedures (in particular, personality and integrity measures), subgroup differences are rare or nonexistent. For many selection methods (e.g., reference checks and evaluations of education and experience), there is little data (Hunter & Hunter, 1984).

For many purposes, the most relevant finding is the finding of lack of predictive bias. That is, even when subgroups differ in mean score, selection procedure scores appear to have the same implications for later performance for individuals in all subgroups (Wigdor & Garner, 1982). That is, the predictive interpretation of scores is the same in different subgroups.

Summary and implications

Employers must make hiring decisions; they have no choice about that. But they can choose which methods to use in making those decisions. The research evidence summarized in this article shows that different methods and combinations of methods have very different validities for predicting future job performance. Some, such as interests and amount of education, have very low validity. Others, such as graphology, have essentially no validity; they are equivalent to hiring randomly. Still others, such as GMA tests and work sample measures, have high validity. Of the combinations of predictors examined, two stand out as being both practical to use for most hiring and as having high composite validity: the combination of a GMA test and an integrity test (composite validity of .65); and the combination of a GMA test and a structured interview (composite validity of .63). Both of these combinations can be used with applicants with no previous experience on the job (entry level applicants), as well as with experienced applicants. Both combinations predict performance in job training programs quite well (.67 and .59, respectively), as well as performance on the job. And both combinations are less expensive to use than many other combinations. Hence, both are excellent choices. However, in particular cases there might be reasons why an employer might choose to use one of the other combinations with high, but slightly lower, validity. Some examples are combinations that include conscientiousness tests, work sample tests, job knowledge tests, and the behavioral consistency method.

In recent years, researchers have used cumulative research findings on the validity of predictors of job performance to create and test theories of job performance. These theories are now shedding light on the psychological processes that underlie observed predictive validity and are advancing basic understanding of human competence in the workplace.

The validity of the personnel measure (or combination of measures) used in hiring is directly proportional to the practical value of the method—whether measured in dollar value of increased output or percentage of increase in output. In economic terms, the gains from increasing the validity of hiring methods can amount over time to literally millions of dollars. However, this can be viewed from the opposite point of view: By using selection methods with low validity, an organization can lose millions of dollars in reduced production.

In fact, many employers, both in the United States and throughout the world, are currently using suboptimal selection methods. For example, many organizations in France, Israel, and other countries hire new employees based on handwriting analyses by graphologists. And many organizations in the United States rely solely on unstructured interviews, when they could use more valid methods. In a competitive world, these organizations are unnecessarily creating a competitive disadvantage for themselves (Schmidt, 1993). By adopting more valid hiring procedures, they could turn this competitive disadvantage into a competitive advantage.

Acknowledgments

An earlier version of this article was presented to Korean Human Resource Managers in Seoul, South Korea, June 11, 1996. The presentation was sponsored by Tong Yang Company. We would like to thank President Wang-Ha Cho of Tong Yang for his support and efforts in this connection. We would also like to thank Deniz Ones and Kuh Yoon for their assistance in preparing Tables 1 and 2 and Gershon Ben-Shakhar for his comments on research on graphology.

References

Baker, T. G. (1996). Practice network. *The Industrial-Organizational Psychologist, 34,* 44–53.

Bar-Hillel, M., & Ben-Shakhar, G. (1986). The a priori case against graphology: Methodological and conceptual issues. In B. Nevo (Ed.), *Scientific aspects of graphology* (pp. 263–279). Springfield, IL: Charles C Thomas.

Ben-Shakhar, G. (1989). Nonconventional methods in personnel selection. In P. Herriot (Ed.), *Handbook of assessment in organizations: Methods and practice for recruitment and appraisal* (pp. 469–485). Chichester, England: Wiley.

Ben-Shakhar, G., Bar-Hillel, M., Bilu, Y., Ben-Abba, E., & Flug, A. (1986). Can graphology predict occupational success? Two empirical studies and some methodological ruminations. *Journal of Applied Psychology, 71,* 645–653.

Ben-Shakhar, G., Bar-Hillel, M., & Flug, A. (1986). A validation study of graphological evaluations in personnel selection. In B. Nevo (Ed.), *Scientific aspects of graphology* (pp. 175–191). Springfield, IL: Charles C Thomas.

Borman, W. C., White, L. A., Pulakos, E. D., & Oppler, S. H. (1991). Models evaluating the effects of ratee ability, knowledge, proficiency, temperament, awards, and problem behavior on supervisory ratings. *Journal of Applied Psychology, 76,* 863–872.

Boudreau, J. W. (1983a). Economic considerations in estimating the utility of human resource productivity improvement programs. *Personnel Psychology, 36,* 551–576.

Boudreau, J. W. (1983b). Effects of employee flows or utility analysis of human resources productivity improvement programs. *Journal of Applied Psychology, 68,* 396–407.

Boudreau, J. W. (1984). Decision theory contributions to human resource management research and practice. *Industrial Relations, 23,* 198–217.

Brody, N. (1992). *Intelligence.* New York: Academic Press.

Brogden, H. E. (1949). When testing pays off. *Personnel Psychology, 2,* 171–183.

Carlson, K. D., Scullen, S. E., Schmidt, F. L., Rothstein, H. R., & Erwin, F. W. (1998). *Generalizable biographical data: Is multi-organizational development and keying necessary?* Manuscript in preparation.

Carroll, J. B. (1993). *Human cognitive abilities: A survey of factor analytic studies.* New York: Cambridge University Press.

Cascio, W. F., & Silbey, V. (1979). Utility of the assessment center as a selection device. *Journal of Applied Psychology, 64,* 107–118.

Collins, J. (1998). *Prediction of overall assessment center evaluations from ability, personality, and motivation measures: A meta-analysis.* Unpublished manuscript, Texas A & M University, College Station, TX.

Cronshaw, S. F., & Alexander, R. A. (1985). One answer to the demand for accountability: Selection utility as an investment decision. *Organizational Behavior and Human Performance, 35,* 102–118.

Dye, D. A., Reck, M., & McDaniel, M. A. (1993). The validity of job knowledge measures. *International Journal of Selection and Assessment, 1,* 153–157.

Gaugler, B. B., Rosenthal, D. B., Thornton, G. C., & Benson, C. (1987). Meta-analysis of assessment center validity. *Journal of Applied Psychology, 72,* 493–511.

Holland, J. (1986). New directions for interest testing. In B. S. Plake & J. C. Witt (Eds.), *The future of testing* (pp. 245–267). Hillsdale, NJ: Erlbaum.

Hollander, E. P. (1956). The friendship factor in peer nominations. *Personnel Psychology, 9,* 435–447.

Huffcutt, A. I., Roth, P. L., & McDaniel, M. A. (1996). A meta-analytic investigation of cognitive ability in employment interview evaluations: Moderating characteristics and implications for incremental validity. *Journal of Applied Psychology, 81,* 459–473.

Hunter, J. E. (1980). *Validity generalization for 12,000 jobs: An application of synthetic validity and validity generalization to the General Aptitude Test Battery (GATB).* Washington, DC: U.S. Department of Labor, Employment Service.

Hunter, J. E. (1986). Cognitive ability, cognitive aptitudes, job knowledge, and job performance. *Journal of Vocational Behavior, 29,* 340–362.

Hunter, J. E., & Hunter, R. F. (1984). Validity and utility of alternative predictors of job performance. *Psychological Bulletin, 96,* 72–98.

Hunter, J. E., & Schmidt, F. L. (1982a). Fitting people to jobs: Implications of personnel selection for national productivity. In E. A. Fleishman & M. D. Dunnette (Eds.), *Human performance and productivity. Volume I: Human capability assessment* (pp. 233–284). Hillsdale, NJ: Erlbaum.

Hunter, J. E., & Schmidt, F. L. (1982b). Quantifying the effects of psychological interventions on employee job performances and work force productivity. *American Psychologist, 38,* 473–478.

Hunter, J. E., & Schmidt, F. L. (1990). *Methods of meta-analysis: Correcting error and bias in research findings.* Beverly Hills, CA: Sage.

Hunter, J. E., & Schmidt, F. L. (1996). Intelligence and job performance: Economic and social implications. *Psychology, Public Policy, and Law, 2,* 447–472.

Hunter, J. E., Schmidt, F. L., & Coggin, T. D. (1988). Problems and pitfalls in using capital budgeting and financial accounting techniques in assessing the utility of personnel programs. *Journal of Applied Psychology, 73,* 522–528.

Hunter, J. E., Schmidt, F. L., & Jackson, G.B. (1982). *Meta-analysis: Cumulating research findings across studies.* Beverly Hills, CA: Sage.

Hunter, J. E., Schmidt, F. L., & Judiesch, M. K. (1990). Individual differences in output variability as a function of job complexity. *Journal of Applied Psychology, 75,* 28–42.

Jansen, A. (1973). *Validation of graphological judgments: An experimental study.* The Hague, The Netherlands: Monton.

Jensen, A. R. (1998). *The g factor: The science of mental ability.* West-port, CT: Praeger.

Levy, L. (1979). Handwriting and hiring. *Dun's Review, 113,* 72–79.

McDaniel, M. A., Schmidt, F. L., & Hunter, J. E. (1988a). A meta-analysis of the validity of methods for rating training and experience in personnel selection. *Personnel Psychology, 41,* 283–314.

McDaniel, M. A., Schmidt, F. L., & Hunter, J. E. (1988b). Job experience correlates of job performance. *Journal of Applied Psychology, 73,* 327–330.

McDaniel, M. A., Whetzel, D.L., Schmidt, F. L., & Mauer, S. D. (1994). The validity of employment interviews: A comprehensive review and meta-analysis. *Journal of Applied Psychology, 79,* 599–616.

Mount, M. K., &. Barrick, M. R. (1995). The Big Five personality dimensions: Implications for research and practice in human resources management. In G. R. Ferris (Ed.), *Research in personnel and human resources management* (Vol. 13, pp. 153–200). JAI Press.

Neter, E., & Ben-Shakhar, G. (1989). The predictive validity of graphological inferences: A meta-analytic approach. *Personality and Individual Differences, 10,* 737–745.

Ones, D. S. (1993). *The construct validity of integrity tests.* Unpublished doctoral dissertation, University of Iowa, Iowa City.

Ones, D. S., Viswesvaran, C., & Schmidt, F. L. (1993). Comprehensive meta-analysis of integrity test validities: Findings and implications for personnel selection and theories of job performance. *Journal of Applied Psychology Monograph, 78,* 679–703.

Pearlman, K., Schmidt, F. L., & Hunter, J. E. (1980). Validity generalization results for tests used to predict job proficiency and training criteria in clerical occupations. *Journal of Applied Psychology, 65,* 373–407.

Rafaeli, A., & Klimoski, R. J. (1983). Predicting sales success through handwriting analysis: An evaluation of the effects of training and handwriting sample context. *Journal of Applied Psychology, 68,* 212–217.

Ree, M. J., & Earles, J. A. (1992). Intelligence is the best predictor of job performance. *Current Directions in Psychological Science, 1,* 86–89.

Rothstein, H. R., Schmidt, F. L., Erwin, F. W., Owens, W. A., & Sparks, C. P. (1990). Biographical data in employment selection: Can validities be made generalizable? *Journal of Applied Psychology, 75,* 175–184.

Schmidt, F. L. (1988). The problem of group differences in ability scores is employment selection. *Journal of Vocational Behavior, 33,* 272–292.

Schmidt, F. L. (1992). What do data really mean? Research findings, meta analysis, and cumulative knowledge in psychology. *American Psychologist, 47,* 1173–1181.

Schmidt, F. L. (1993). Personnel psychology at the cutting edge. In N. Schmitt & W. Barman (Eds.), *Personnel selection* (pp. 497–515). San Francisco: Jossey Bass.

Schmidt, F. L., Caplan, J. R., Bemis, S. E., Decuir, R., Dinn, L., & Antone, L. (1979). *Development and evaluation of behavioral consistency method of unassembled examining* (Tech. Rep. No. 79–21). U.S. Civil Service Commission, Personnel Research and Development Center.

Schmidt, F. L., & Hunter, J. E. (1977). Development of a general solution to the problem of validity generalization. *Journal of Applied Psychology, 62,* 529–540.

Schmidt, F. L., & Hunter, J. E. (1981). Employment testing: Old theories and new research findings. *American Psychologist, 36,* 1128–1137.

Schmidt, F. L., & Hunter, J. E. (1983). Individual differences in productivity : An empirical test of estimates derived from studies of selection procedure utility. *Journal of Applied Psychology, 68,* 407–415.

Schmidt, F. L., & Hunter, J. E. (1992). Development of causal models of processes determining job performance. *Current Directions in Psychological Science, 1,* 89–92.

Schmidt, F. L., Hunter, J. E., McKenzie, R. C., & Muldrow, T. W. (1979). The impact of valid selection procedures on work-force productivity. *Journal of Applied Psychology, 64,* 609–626.

Schmidt, F. L., Hunter, J. E., & Outerbridge, A. N. (1986). The impact of job experience and ability on job knowledge, work sample performance, and supervisory ratings of job performance. *Journal of Applied Psychology, 71,* 432–439.

Schmidt, F. L., Hunter, J. E., Outerbridge, A. N., & Goff, S. (1988). The joint relation of experience and ability with job performance: A test of three hypotheses. *Journal of Applied Psychology, 73,* 46–57.

Schmidt, F. L., Hunter, J. E., Outerbridge, A. M., & Trattner, M. H. (1986). The economic impact of job selection methods on the size, productivity, and payroll costs of the federal work-force: An empirical demonstration. *Personnel Psychology, 39,* 1–29.

Schmidt, F. L., Hunter, J. E., & Pearlman, K. (1980). Task difference and validity of aptitude tests in selection: A red herring. *Journal of Applied Psychology, 66,* 166–185.

Schmidt, F. L., Hunter, J. E., & Pearlman, K. (1982). Assessing the economic impact of personnel programs on workforce productivity. *Personnel Psychology, 35,* 333–347.

Schmidt, F. L., Hunter, J. E., Pearlman, K., & Shane, G. S. (1979). Further tests of the Schmidt-Hunter Bayesian Validity Generalization Model. *Personnel Psychology, 32,* 257–281.

Schmidt, F. L., Law, K., Hunter, J. E., Rothstein, H. R., Pearlman, K., & McDaniel, M. (1993). Refinements in validity generalization methods: Implications for the situational specificity hypothesis. *Journal of Applied Psychology, 78,* 3–13.

Schmidt, F. L., Mack, M. J., & Hunter, J. E. (1984). Selection utility in the occupation of U.S. Park Ranger for three modes of test use. *Journal of Applied Psychology, 69,* 490–497.

Schmidt, F. L., Ones, D. S., & Hunter, J. E. (1992). Personnel selection. *Annual Review of Psychology, 43,* 627–670.

Schmidt, F. L., Ones, D. S., & Viswesvaran, C. (1994, June 30–July 3). *The personality characteristic of integrity predicts job training success.* Presented at the 6th Annual Convention of the American Psychological Society, Washington, DC.

Schmidt, F. L., & Rothstein, H. R. (1994). Application of validity generalization methods of meta-analysis to biographical data scores in employment selection. In G. S. Stokes, M. D. Mumford, & W. A. Owens (Eds.), *The biodata handbook: Theory, research, and applications* (pp. 237–260). Palo Alto, CA: Consulting Psychologists Press.

Steiner, D.D. (1997). International forum. *The Industrial-Organizational Psychologist, 34,* 51–53.

Steiner, D. D., & Gilliland, S. W. (1996). Fairness reactions to personnel selection techniques in France and the United States. *Journal of Applied Psychology, 81,* 134–141.

Viswesvaran, C., Ones, D. S., & Schmidt, F. L. (1996). Comparative analysis of the reliability of job performance ratings. *Journal of Applied Psychology, 81,* 557–560.

Waters, L. K., & Waters, C. W. (1970). Peer nominations as predictors of short-term role performance. *Journal of Applied Psychology, 54,* 42–44.

Wigdor, A. K., & Garner, W. R. (Eds.). (1982). *Ability testing: Uses, consequences, and controversies* (Report of the National Research Council Committee on Ability Testing). Washington, DC: National Academy of Sciences Press.

19

THE BIG FIVE PERSONALITY DIMENSIONS AND JOB PERFORMANCE

A meta-analysis

Murray R. Barrick and Michael K. Mount

Source: *Personnel Psychology* 44 (1991): 1–26.

Abstract

This study investigated the relation of the "Big Five" personality dimensions (Extraversion, Emotional Stability, Agreeableness, Conscientiousness, and Openness to Experience) to three job performance criteria (job proficiency, training proficiency, and personnel data) for five occupational groups (professionals, police, managers, sales, and skilled/semi-skilled). Results indicated that one dimension of personality, Conscientiousness, showed consistent relations with all job performance criteria for all occupational groups. For the remaining personality dimensions, the estimated true score correlations varied by occupational group and criterion type. Extraversion was a valid predictor for two occupations involving social interaction, managers and sales (across criterion types). Also, both Openness to Experience and Extraversion were valid predictors of the training proficiency criterion (across occupations). Other personality dimensions were also found to be valid predictors for some occupations and some criterion types, but the magnitude of the estimated true score correlations was small ($\rho < .10$). Overall, the results illustrate the benefits of using the 5-factor model of personality to accumulate and communicate empirical findings. The findings have numerous implications for research and practice in personnel psychology, especially in the subfields of personnel selection, training and development, and performance appraisal.

Introduction

Over the past 25 years, a number of researchers have investigated the validity of personality measures for personnel selection purposes. The overall conclusion from these studies is that the validity of personality as a predictor of job performance is quite low (e.g., Ghiselli, 1973; Guion & Gottier, 1965; Locke & Hulin, 1962; Reilly & Chao, 1982; Schmitt, Gooding, Noe, & Kirsch, 1984). However, at the time these studies were conducted, no well-accepted taxonomy existed for classifying personality traits. Consequently, it was not possible to determine whether there were consistent, meaningful relationships between particular personality constructs and performance criteria in different occupations.

In the past 10 years, the views of many personality psychologists have converged regarding the structure and concepts of personality. Generally, researchers agree that there are five robust factors of personality (described below) which can serve as a meaningful taxonomy for classifying personality attributes (Digman, 1990). Our purpose in the present study is to examine the relationship of these five personality constructs to job performance measures for different occupations, rather than to focus on the overall validity of personality as previous researchers have done.

Emergence of the 5-factor model

Systematic efforts to organize the taxonomy of personality began shortly after McDougall (1932) wrote that, "Personality may to advantage be broadly analyzed into five distinguishable but separate factors, namely intellect, character, temperament, disposition, and temper ..." (p. 15). About 10 years later, Cattell (1943, 1946, 1947, 1948) developed a relatively complex taxonomy of individual differences that consisted of 16 primary factors and 8 second-order factors. However, repeated attempts by researchers to replicate his work were unsuccessful (Fiske, 1949; Tupes, 1957; Tupes & Christal, 1961) and, in each case, researchers found that the 5-factor model accounted for the data quite well. For example, Tupes and Christal (1961) reanalyzed the correlations reported by Cattell and Fiske and found that there was good support for five factors: Surgency, Emotional Stability, Agreeableness, Dependability, and Culture. As it would turn out later, these factors (and those of McDougall 35 years before) were remarkably similar to those generally accepted by researchers today. However, as Digman (1990) points out, the work of Tupes and Christal had only a minor impact because their study was published in an obscure Air Force technical report. The 5-factor model obtained by Fiske (1949) and Tupes and Christal (1961) was corroborated in four subsequent studies (Borgatta, 1964; Hakel, 1974; Norman, 1963; Smith, 1967). Borgatta's findings are noteworthy because he obtained five stable factors across five methods of data gathering. Norman's work is especially significant because his labels (Extraversion, Emotional Stability, Agreeableness, Conscientiousness, and Culture) are used commonly in the literature and have been referred to, subsequently, as "Norman's Big Five" or simply as the "Big Five."

During the past decade, an impressive body of literature has accumulated which provides compelling evidence for the robustness of the 5-factor model: across different theoretical frameworks (Goldberg, 1981); using different instruments (e.g., Conley, 1985; Costa & McCrae, 1988; Lorr & Youniss, 1973; McCrae, 1989; McCrae & Costa, 1985, 1987, 1989); in different cultures (e.g., Bond, Nakazato, & Shiraishi, 1975; Noller, Law, & Comrey, 1987); using ratings obtained from different sources (e.g., Digman & Inouye, 1986; Digman & Takemoto-Chock, 1981; Fiske, 1949; McCrae & Costa, 1987; Norman, 1963; Norman & Goldberg, 1966; Watson, 1989); and with a variety of samples (see Digman, 1990, for a more detailed discussion). An important consideration for the field of personnel psychology is that these dimensions are also relatively independent of measures of cognitive ability (McCrae & Costa, 1987).

It should be pointed out that some researchers have reservations about the 5-factor model, particularly the imprecise specification of these dimensions (Briggs, 1989; John, 1989; Livneh & Livneh, 1989; Waller & Ben-Porath, 1987). Some researchers suggest that more than five dimensions are needed to encompass the domain of personality. For example, Hogan (1986) advocates six dimensions (Sociability, Ambition, Adjustment, Likability, Prudence, and Intellectance). The principle difference seems to be the splitting of the Extraversion dimension into Sociability and Ambition.

Interpretations of the "Big Five"

While there is general agreement among researchers concerning the number of factors, there is some disagreement about their precise meaning, particularly Norman's Conscientiousness and Culture factors. Of course, some variation from study to study is to be expected with factors as broad and inclusive as the 5-factor model. As shown below, however, there is a great deal of commonality in the traits that define each factor, even though the name attached to the factor differs.

It is widely agreed that the first dimension is Eysenck's Extraversion/Intraversion. Most frequently this dimension has been called Extraversion or Surgency (Botwin & Buss, 1989; Digman & Takemoto-Chock, 1981; Hakel, 1974; Hogan, 1983, Howarth, 1976; John, 1989; Krug & Johns, 1986; McCrae & Costa, 1985; Noller et al., 1987; Norman, 1963; Smith, 1967). Traits frequently associated with it include being sociable, gregarious, assertive, talkative, and active. As mentioned above, Hogan (1986) interprets this dimension as consisting of two components, Ambition (initiative, surgency, ambition, and impetuous) and Sociability (sociable, exhibitionist, and expressive).

There is also general agreement about the second dimension. This factor has been most frequently called Emotional Stability, Stability, Emotionality, or Neuroticism (Borgatta, 1964; Conley, 1985; Hakel, 1974; John, 1989; Lorr & Manning, 1978; McCrae & Costa, 1985; Noller et al., 1987; Norman, 1963; Smith, 1967). Common traits associated with this factor include being anxious, depressed, angry, embarrassed, emotional, worried, and insecure. These two dimensions (Extraversion and Emotional Stability) represent the "Big Two" described by Eysenck over 40 years ago.

The third dimension has generally been interpreted as Agreeableness or Likability (Borgatta, 1964; Conley, 1985; Goldberg, 1981; Hakel, 1974; Hogan, 1983; John, 1989; McCrae & Costa, 1985; Noller et al., 1987; Norman, 1963; Smith, 1967; Tupes & Christal, 1961). Others have labeled it Friendliness (Guilford & Zimmerman, 1949), Social Conformity (Fiske, 1949), Compliance versus Hostile Non-Compliance (Digman & Takemoto-Chock, 1981), or Love (Peabody & Goldberg, 1989). Traits associated with this dimension include being courteous, flexible, trusting, good-natured, cooperative, forgiving, soft-hearted, and tolerant.

The fourth dimension has most frequently been called Conscientiousness or Conscience (Botwin & Buss, 1989; Hakel, 1974; John, 1989; McCrae & Costa, 1985; Noller et al., 1987; Norman, 1963), although it has also been called Conformity or Dependability (Fiske, 1949; Hogan, 1983). Because of its relationship to a variety of educational achievement measures and its association with volition, it has also been called Will to Achieve or Will (Digman, 1989; Smith, 1967; Wiggins, Blackburn, & Hackman, 1969), and Work (Peabody & Goldberg, 1989). As the disparity in labels suggests, there is some disagreement regarding the essence of this dimension. Some writers (Botwin & Buss, 1989; Fiske, 1949; Hogan, 1983; John, 1989; Noller et al., 1987) have suggested that Conscientiousness reflects dependability; that is, being careful, thorough, responsible, organized, and planful. Others have suggested that in addition to these traits, it incorporates volitional variables, such as hardworking, achievement-oriented, and persevering. Based on the evidence cited by Digman (1990), the preponderance of evidence supports the definition of conscientiousness as including these volitional aspects (Bernstein, Garbin, & McClellan, 1983; Borgatta, 1964; Conley, 1985; Costa & McCrae, 1988; Digman & Inouye, 1986; Digman & Takemoto-Chock, 1981; Howarth, 1976; Krug & Johns, 1986; Lei & Skinner, 1982; Lorr & Manning, 1978; McCrae & Costa, 1985, 1987, 1989; Norman, 1963; Peabody & Goldberg, 1989; Smith, 1967).

The last dimension has been the most difficult to identify. It has been interpreted most frequently as Intellect or Intellectence (Borgatta, 1964; Digman & Takemoto-Chock, 1981; Hogan, 1983; John, 1989; Peabody and Goldberg, 1989). It has also been called Openness to Experience (McCrae & Costa, 1985) or Culture (Hakel, 1974; Norman, 1963). Digman (1990) points out that it is most likely all of these. Traits commonly associated with this dimension include being imaginative, cultured, curious, original, broad-minded, intelligent, and artistically sensitive.

The emergence of the 5-factor model has important implications for the field of personnel psychology. It illustrates that personality consists of five relatively independent dimensions which provide a meaningful taxonomy for studying individual differences. In any field of science, the availability of such an orderly classification scheme is essential for the communication and accumulation of empirical findings. For purposes of this study, we adopted names and definitions similar to those used by Digman (1990): Extraversion, Emotional Stability, Agreeableness, Conscientiousness, and Openness to Experience.

Expected relations between personality dimensions and job performance

In the present study, we investigate the validity of the five dimensions of personality for five occupational groups (professionals, police, managers, sales, and skilled/semi-skilled) and for three types of job performance criteria (job proficiency, training proficiency, and personnel data) using meta-analytic methods. We also investigate the validity of the five personality dimensions for objective versus subjective criteria.

We hypothesize that two of the dimensions of personality, Conscientiousness and Emotional Stability, will be valid predictors of all job performance criteria for all jobs. Conscientiousness is expected to be related to job performance because it assesses personal characteristics such as persistent, planful, careful, responsible, and hardworking, which are important attributes for accomplishing work tasks in all jobs. There is some evidence that in educational settings there are consistent correlations between scores on this dimension and educational achievement (Digman & Takemoto-Chock, 1981; Smith, 1967). Thus, we expect that the validity of this dimension will generalize across all occupational groups and criterion categories. We also expect that the validity of Emotional Stability will generalize across occupations and criterion types. Viewing this dimension from its negative pole, we expect that employees exhibiting neurotic characteristics, such as worry, nervousness, temperamentalness, high-strungness, and self-pity, will tend to be less successful than more emotionally stable individuals in all occupations studied because these traits tend to inhibit rather than facilitate the accomplishment of work tasks.

We expect that other personality dimensions may be related to job performance, but only for some occupations or some criteria. For example, in those occupations that involve frequent interaction or cooperation with others, we expect that two personality dimensions, Extraversion and Agreeableness, will be valid predictors. These two dimensions should be predictive of performance criteria for occupations such as management and sales, but would not be expected to be valid predictors for occupations such as production worker or engineer.

In a similar vein, we expect that Openness to Experience will be a valid predictor of one of the performance criteria, training proficiency. This dimension is expected to be related to training proficiency because it assesses personal characteristics such as curious, broadminded, cultured, and intelligent, which are attributes associated with positive attitudes toward learning experiences. We believe that such individuals are more likely to be motivated to learn upon entry into the training program and, consequently, are more likely to benefit from the training.

Finally, we investigated a research question of general interest to personnel psychologists for which we are not testing a specific hypothesis. The question is whether the validity coefficients for the five personality dimensions differ for two types of criteria, objective and subjective. A recent meta-analysis by Nathan and Alexander (1988) indicates that, in general, there is no difference between the magnitude of the validities for cognitive ability tests obtained for objective and subjective criteria for clerical jobs. In another study, Schmitt et al. (1984) investigated the validity of personality measures (across dimensions and occupations) for different types of criteria, but no definitive conclusions were apparent from the data. The average validity for the subjective criterion (performance ratings) was .206. Validities for three of four objective criteria were lower (.121 for turnover, .152 for achievement/grades, and .126 for status change), whereas the validity was higher for wages (.268). Thus, conclusions regarding whether the validities for personality measures are higher for objective, compared to subjective, criteria depend to a large extent on which objective measures are used. Because our study examines personality using a 5-factor model, we are able to assess whether dimensions have differential relationships to various objective and subjective criteria.

In summary, the following hypotheses will be tested in this study. Of the five dimensions of personality, Conscientiousness and Emotional Stability are expected to be valid predictors of job performance for all jobs and all criteria because Conscientiousness measures those personal characteristics that are important for accomplishing work tasks in all jobs, while Emotional Stability (when viewed from the negative pole) measures those characteristics that may hinder successful performance.

In contrast, Extraversion and Agreeableness are expected to correlate with job performance for two occupations, sales and management, because interpersonal dispositions are likely to be important determinants of success in those occupations. Finally, Openness to Experience is expected to correlate with one of the criterion types, training proficiency, because Openness to Experience appears to assess individuals' readiness to participate in learning experiences. In addition, we investigated the validity of various objective and subjective criteria for the five personality dimensions.

Method

Literature review

A literature search was conducted to identify published and unpublished criterion-related validity studies of personality for selection purposes between 1952 and 1988. Three strategies were used to search the relevant literature. First, a computer search was done of PsycINFO (1967–1988) and Dissertation Abstracts (1952–1988) in order to find all references to personality in occupational selection. Second, a manual search was conducted that consisted of checking the sources cited in the reference section of literature reviews, articles, and books on this topic, as well as personality inventory manuals, *Buros Tests in Print* (volumes 4–9,

1953–1985), and journals that may have included such articles (including the *Journal of Applied Psychology, Personnel Psychology, Academy of Management Journal, Organizational Behavior and Human Decision Processes/Organizational Behavior and Human Performance, Journal of Management, Journal of Vocational Behavior, Journal of Personality and Social Psychology, Journal of Personality,* and *Journal of Consulting and Clinical Psychology*). Finally, personality test publishers and over 60 practitioners known to utilize personality inventories in selection contexts were contacted by letter, requesting their assistance in sending or locating additional published or unpublished validation studies.

Overall, these searches yielded 231 criterion-related validity studies, 117 of which were acceptable for inclusion in this analysis. The remaining 114 studies were excluded for several reasons: 44 reported results for interest and value inventories only and were excluded because they did not focus on the validity of personality measures; 24 used composite scores or, conversely, extracted specific items from different scales and instruments; 19 reported only significant validity coefficients; 15 used military or laboratory "subjects"; and 12 either were not selection studies or provided insufficient information.

A total of 162 samples were obtained from the 117 studies. Sample sizes ranged from 13 to 1,401 ($M = 148.11$; $SD = 185.79$), yielding a total sample of 23,994. Thirty-nine samples were reported in the 1950s, 52 in the 1960s, 33 in the 1970s, and 38 in the 1980s. Fifty samples (31%) were collected from unpublished sources, most of which were unpublished dissertations.

The studies were categorized into five major occupational groupings and three criterion types. The occupational groups were *professionals* (5% of the samples), which consisted of engineers, architects, attorneys, accountants, teachers, doctors, and ministers; *police* (13% of the samples); *managers* (41% of the samples), which ranged from foremen to top executives; *sales* (17% of the samples); and *skilled/semi-skilled* (24% of the samples), which consisted of jobs such as clerical, nurses aides, farmers, flight attendants, medical assistants, orderlies, airline baggage handlers, assemblers, telephone operators, grocery clerks, truck drivers, and production workers.

The three criterion types were *job proficiency* (included in 68% of the samples), *training proficiency* (12% of the samples), and *personnel data* (33% of the samples). It should be noted that in 21 samples, data were available from two of the three criterion categories, which explains why the total percent of sample for the three criterion types exceeds 100%. Similarly, the total sample size on which these analyses are based will be larger than those for analyses by occupation. Job proficiency measures primarily included performance ratings (approximately 85% of the measures) as well as productivity data; training proficiency measures consisted mostly of training performance ratings (approximately 90% of the measures) in addition to productivity data, such as work sample data and time to complete training results; and personnel data included data from employee files, such as salary level, turnover, status change, and tenure.

SELECTING AND DEVELOPING EMPLOYEES

Key variables of interest in this study were the validity coefficients, sample sizes, range restriction data for those samples, reliability estimates for the predictors and criteria, the personality scales (and the inventories used), and the types of occupations. A subsample of approximately 25% of the studies was selected to assess interrater agreement on the coding of the key variables of interest. Agreement was 95% for these variables and disagreement between coders was resolved by referring back to the original study.

Scales from all the inventories were classified into the five dimensions defined earlier (i.e., Extraversion, Emotional Stability, Agreeableness, Conscientiousness, and Openness to Experience) or a sixth Miscellaneous dimension. The personality scales were categorized into these dimensions by six trained raters. Five of these raters had received Ph.D.s in psychology (three were practicing consulting psychologists with responsibilities for individual assessment; the other two were professors of psychology and human resources management, respectively, and both had taught personnel selection courses) and the other taught similar courses while completing his Ph.D. in human resources management and was very familiar with the literature on personality. A short training session was provided to the raters to familiarize them with the rating task and examples were provided. The description of the five factors provided to the raters corresponded to those presented by Digman (1990) and as described above. Raters were provided a list of the personality scales and their definitions for each inventory and were instructed to assign each to the dimension to which it best fit. A sixth category, Miscellaneous, was used in those cases where the scale could not be assigned clearly into one of the five categories. If at least five of the six raters agreed on a dimension, the scale was coded in that dimension. If four of the six raters agreed and the two authors' ratings (completed independently of the raters) agreed with the raters, the scale was coded into that dimension. If three or fewer raters agreed, the scale was coded into the Miscellaneous dimension. At least five of six raters agreed in 68% of the cases, four of six raters agreed in 23% of the cases, and three or fewer raters agreed on 9% of the cases. Of the 191 scales, 39 were categorized as representing Emotional Stability; 32 as Extraversion; 31 as Openness to Experience; 29 as Agreeableness; 32 as Conscientiousness; 28 as Miscellaneous. (A list of the inventories, their respective scales, and dimensional category assigned are available from the first author.) It should be noted that an alternative method for assigning the scales would be to use empirical data, such as factor analyses of inventories or correlations among scales from different inventories. However, we were unable to locate sufficient factor analytic studies or correlational data to allow us to use these approaches because in both cases data was available for only about half of the variables.

To arrive at an overall validity coefficient for each scale from an inventory, the following decision rules were applied in situations where more than one validity coefficient was reported from a sample: (a) If an overall criterion was provided, that coefficient was used and (b) when multiple criteria were provided, they were assigned to the appropriate criterion category (job proficiency, training proficiency, or personnel data). If there were multiple measures from a criterion category, the coefficients were averaged. However, because our analyses focused on personality *dimensions* rather than individual personality *scales* (from various inventories), the following decision rules were applied to establish the validity coefficient for each personality dimension from a sample: (a) If a personality dimension had only one scale categorized into that dimension for that sample, the overall validity coefficient from that scale (calculated as previously explained) was used and (b) if multiple scales were available for a dimension, the coefficients from each of these scales from that sample were averaged and the resulting average validity coefficient was used in all analyses.

A number of analyses were conducted. The first was an analysis of the validities for the five personality dimensions for each occupational group (across criterion types). The second was an analysis of personality dimensions for the three criterion types (across occupations). The final analysis investigated the validity of the dimensions for objective versus subjective criteria (across occupations and criterion types).

The meta-analytic procedure adopted in this study used the formulas available in Hunter and Schmidt (1990)[1] and corrected the mean and variance of validity coefficients across studies for artifactual variance due to sampling error, range restriction, and attenuation due to measurement error. However, because the vast majority of studies did not report information on range restriction and measurement error, particularly predictor reliabilities, it was necessary to use artifact distributions to estimate artifactually induced variance on the validity coefficients (Hunter & Schmidt, 1990).

Because reliability coefficients for predictors were only rarely presented in the validity studies, the distributions were based upon information obtained from the inventories' manuals. The mean of the predictor reliability distribution was .76 ($SD = .08$). Similarly, because information for the criterion reliabilities was available in less than one-third of the studies, we developed an artifact distribution for criterion reliabilities based on data provided by Hunter, Schmidt, and Judiesch (1990) for productivity data (with a mean of .92, $SD = .05$) and Rothstein (1990) for performance ratings (with a mean of .52, $SD = .05$). It should be noted, however, that 30 studies included criteria which were categorized as personnel data. For these criteria (e.g., turnover, tenure, accidents, wages, etc.), reliability estimates were unknown because no estimates have been provided in the literature. Therefore, the artifact distributions for criterion reliabilities did not include reliability estimates for these criteria. Thus, for the objective versus subjective analysis, the productivity and performance rating artifact distributions were used in each analysis, respectively, for each personality dimension. For all other analyses, the two criterion distributions were combined (with a mean value of .56, $SD = .10$). Finally, the artifact distribution for range restriction data was based upon those studies that reported both restricted and unrestricted standard deviation data (i.e., from accepted and rejected applicants). The effects on the mean validities due to range restriction were relatively small because the mean range restriction was .94 ($SD = .05$).

As previously stated, the Schmidt-Hunter non-interactive validity generalization procedure (Hunter & Schmidt, 1990) was applied to the data for assumed (predictors and criteria) and sample-based artifact distributions (range restriction). (These distributions are available from the first author.) However, because the purpose of our study is to enhance theoretical understanding of the five personality constructs, we present fully corrected correlations that correct for unreliability in the predictor as well as the criterion.

Finally, there has been some confusion regarding the use and interpretation of confidence and credibility values in meta-analysis (Whitener, 1990). The confidence interval is centered around the sample-size weighted mean effects sizes ($\bar{r}$, before being corrected for measurement error or range restriction) and is used to assess the influence of sampling error on the uncorrected estimate. In contrast, the credibility value is centered around the estimated true score correlations (generated from the corrected standard deviation) and is used to assess the influence of moderators. Our purpose in the present study is to understand the true score correlations between the personality dimensions and job performance criteria for different occupations and to assess the presence of moderators. Therefore, the focus in this study is on ρ and the corresponding credibility values.

Results

Analysis by occupational group

The number of correlations upon which the meta-analysis is based is shown in Table 1 for the five personality dimensions, five occupational types, and three criterion types. It can be seen that the frequencies differ substantially from cell to cell. For example, the number of correlations for the job proficiency criterion is generally larger for all personality dimensions and occupations than for the other criterion types. It can also be seen that the number of correlations for the management occupation is greater than for the other occupations. The table also shows that for some cells there are two or fewer correlations for professionals and sales for the training proficiency criterion, and for professionals and police for the personnel data criterion. Consequently, we were unable to analyze the data using the 3-way categorization (personality dimension by occupational type by criterion type).

Table 2 presents the results of the meta-analysis for the five personality dimensions across the occupational groups (professionals, police, managers, sales, and skilled/semi-skilled labor). The first six columns of the table contain, respectively, the total sample size, the number of correlation coefficients on which each distribution was based, the uncorrected (i.e., observed) mean validity, the estimated true correlation (ρ), the estimated true residual standard deviation (SD_ρ),

Table 1 Call frequencies of correlations for personality dimensions, occupational groups, and criterion types

Occupational group	Personality dimensions				
	Extraversion	Emotional stability	Agreeableness	Conscientiousness	Openness to experience
Job proficiency					
Professionals	4	5	7	6	4
Police	10	12	8	12	8
Managers	29	26	25	25	19
Sales	16	14	11	17	8
Skilled/Semi-skilled	16	15	17	16	10
Training proficiency					
Professionals	0	0	0	0	0
Police	6	6	6	5	5
Managers	9	10	9	10	7
Sales	1	1	1	1	1
Skilled/Semi-skilled	3	4	4	3	1
Personnel data					
Professionals	0	0	0	0	0
Police	0	0	0	2	0
Managers	21	19	13	17	11
Sales	5	4	4	3	3
Skilled/Semi-skilled	4	7	5	6	5

and the lower bound of the 90% credibility value for each distribution, based on its true correlation and SD_ρ estimates. The true SD_ρ is the square root of the variance that was not attributed to the four artifacts (i.e., sampling error and between-study differences in test unreliability, criterion unreliability, and degree of range restriction), after correcting for those artifacts. The last column in Table 2 reports the percentage of observed variance that was accounted for by the four artifacts.

As shown in Table 2, the correlations for the occupational categories differed across the five personality dimensions. Consistent with our hypothesis, the Conscientiousness dimension was a valid predictor for all occupational groupings. It can be seen that the estimated true score correlations are noticeably larger for Conscientiousness compared to the other personality dimensions and are remarkably consistent across the five occupational groups (ρ ranges from .20 to .23).

Very little support was found for the hypothesis regarding Emotional Stability. Compared to the Conscientiousness dimension, the correlations for Emotional Stability are lower (ρ ranges from $-.13$ to $.12$). In fact, for professionals the relationship was in the opposite direction predicted ($\rho = -.13$).

It was also hypothesized that Extraversion and Agreeableness would be valid predictors for the two occupations involving interpersonal skills, managers and

Table 2 Meta-analysis results for personality dimension-occupation combinations (all criterion types included)

Occupational group	Total N	Number of r's	Obs r̄	ρ̂	SD$_\rho$	90% C.V.	% Variance accounted
Extraversion							
Professionals	476	4	−.05	−.09	.05	−.03	92
Police	1,496	16	.05	.09	.00	.09	127
Managers	11,335	59	.11	.18	.13	.01	48
Sales	2,316	22	.09	.15	.16	−.05	54
Skilled/Semi-Skilled	3,888	23	.01	.01	.08	−.10	72
Mean (across occupations)			.08	.13	.11	−.01	69[a]
Emotional stability							
Professionals	518	5	−.07	−.13	.04	−.07	92
Police	1,697	18	.06	.10	.00	.10	138
Managers	10,324	55	.05	.08	.09	−.04	65
Sales	2,486	19	.04	.07	.19	−.18	38
Skilled/Semi-Skilled	3,694	26	.05	.12	.10	−.06	50
Mean (across occupations)			.05	.08	.10	−.05	63[a]
Agreeableness							
Professionals	557	7	.01	.02	0	.02	158
Police	1,437	14	.06	.10	0	.10	121
Managers	8,597	47	.05	.10	.03	.06	94
Sales	2,344	16	.00	.00	.24	−.31	25
Skilled/Semi-Skilled	4,585	28	.04	.06	.17	−.16	37
Mean (across occupations)			.04	.07	.09	−.05	54[a]
Conscientiousness							
Professionals	767	6	.11	.20	.00	.20	106
Police	2,045	19	.13	.22	.20	−.03	40
Managers	10,058	52	.13	.22	.10	.09	64
Sales	2,263	21	.09	.23	.00	.23	150
Skilled/Semi-Skilled	4,588	25	.12	.21	.09	.09	67
Mean (across occupations)			.13	.22	.09	.10	70[a]
Openness to experience							
Professionals	476	4	−.05	−.08	.04	−.03	94
Police	1,364	13	.00	.00	.00	.00	181
Managers	7,611	37	.05	.08	.16	−.12	37
Sales	1,566	12	−.01	−.02	.16	.18	46
Skilled/Semi-Skilled	3,219	16	.01	.01	.12	−.15	49
Mean (across occupations)			.03	.04	.13	.13	59[a]

[a] An unbiased estimate of mean percentage of variance accounted for across meta-analyses, calculated by taking the reciprocal of the average of reciprocals of individual predicted to observed variance ratios (Hunter & Schmidt, 1990).

sales representatives. This hypothesis was supported for Extraversion for both occupations ($\rho = .18$ and .15, respectively). However, very little support was obtained for Agreeableness, as $\rho = .10$ for managers and .00 for sales. With respect to the other dimensions, the remaining true score correlations reported in the table were quite low (i.e., $\rho = .10$ or less).

Analysis by criteria type

Table 3 shows the correlation coefficients for the five personality dimensions for the three criterion types. Consistent with our hypothesis, Conscientiousness is a valid predictor for each of the three criterion types. As was the case with the occupational analysis in Table 2, the results for Conscientiousness are quite consistent across the criterion types (ρ ranges from .20 to .23). As reported, the correlations are generally higher than for the other personality dimensions. Also consistent with our hypothesis, Openness to Experience predicted the training proficiency criterion relatively well ($\rho = .25$). Interestingly, Extraversion was also a significant predictor of training proficiency ($\rho = .26$). Most of the remaining correlations for the three criterion types are relatively small (i.e., $\rho = .10$ or less).

Table 3 Meta-analysis results for personality dimension and criteria (pooled across occupational groups)

Criterion type	Total N	Number of r's	Obs r̄	$\hat{\rho}$	SD_ρ	90% C.V.	% Variance accounted
Extraversion							
Job proficiency	12,396	89	.06	.10	.10	−.03	69
Training proficiency	3,101	17	.15	.26	.14	.08	49
Personnel data	6,477	33	.06	.11	.18	−.12	33
Mean (across criteria)			.08	.13	.13	−.01	47[a]
Emotional stability							
Job proficiency	11,635	87	.04	.07	.11	−.07	64
Training proficiency	3,283	19	.04	.07	0	.07	120
Personnel data	5,644	29	.05	.09	.16	−.11	38
Mean (across criteria)			.05	.08	.10	−.05	60[a]
Agreeableness							
Job proficiency	11,526	80	.04	.06	.14	−.12	49
Training proficiency	3,685	19	.06	.10	0	.10	134
Personnel data	4,474	26	.08	.14	.11	.00	59
Mean (across criteria)			.04	.07	.10	−.05	68[a]
Conscientiousness							
Job proficiency	12,893	92	.13	.23	.10	.10	70
Training proficiency	3,585	17	.13	.23	.15	.04	41
Personnel data	6,175	32	.11	.20	.10	.07	71
Mean (across criteria)			.13	.22	.10	.08	57[a]
Openness to experience							
Job proficiency	9,454	55	−.02	−.03	.04	.00	93
Training proficiency	2,700	14	.14	.25	.16	.05	40
Personnel data	3,785	22	.01	.01	.15	−.18	44
Mean (across criteria)			.03	.04	.09	−.02	51[a]

[a] An unbiased estimate of mean percentage of variance accounted for across meta-analyses, calculated by taking the reciprocal of the average of reciprocals of individual predicted to observed variance ratios (Hunter & Schmidt, 1990).

Analysis by objective and subjective criteria

Table 4 shows the validity of the five personality dimensions for criteria categorized as objective and subjective. It should be noted that this analysis is different from that reported in Table 3 because two of the three criterion types contain some objective and subjective measures. First, it can be seen that the subjective criteria are used about twice as frequently as objective criteria. Second, the estimated true score correlations are generally higher for subjective, compared to objective, criteria. In fact, only one objective criterion, status change, has true score correlations equal to or larger than the subjective ratings for four of the personality dimensions. For the fifth personality dimension, Conscientiousness, the estimated true correlations for the subjective criteria are higher ($\rho = .23$) than for all objective criteria (ρ ranges from .12 to .17).

We conducted additional analyses of the correlation coefficients by personality dimensions, criterion types, and occupational subgroups. Data from these analyses are not reported here (though available upon request) because for many of the subgroup categories there were too few validity studies. Overall, however, the results for those subcategories where data were available do not alter the conclusions reported above.

A key outcome in any meta-analysis of selection studies is the amount of variation in the validities that is attributed to different situations. For a majority of the analyses reported in Tables 2, 3, and 4, the percentage of variance accounted for by the four statistical artifacts (i.e., sampling error and between-study differences in test unreliability, criterion unreliability, and degree of range restriction) failed to exceed the 75% rule (Hunter & Schmidt, 1990). This suggests that differences in correlations may exist across subpopulations.

Discussion

This study differs from previous studies by using an accepted taxonomy to study the relation of personality to job performance criteria. The results illustrate the benefits of using this classification scheme to communicate and accumulate empirical findings. Using this taxonomy, we were able to show that there are differential relations between the personality dimensions and occupations and performance criteria.

Before discussing the substantive findings, a comment is in order regarding the relatively small observed and true score correlations obtained in this study. We would like to re-emphasize that our purpose was not to determine the overall validity of personality; in fact, we question whether such an analysis is meaningful. Rather, the purpose was to increase our understanding of the way the Big Five personality dimensions relate to selected occupational groups and criterion types.

It is likely that the purpose and methodology used in the present study, both of which differ from other reviews, may have contributed to the lower correlations. For example, in the present study, only those samples that reported zero-order

Table 4 Meta-analysis results for personality dimensions and objective and subjective criteria (pooled across occupational groups)

Criterion type	Total N	Number of r's	Obs r̄	ρ̂	SD$_\rho$	90% C.V.	% Variance accounted
Extraversion							
Productivity data	1,774	12	.07	.10	.03	.06	95
Turnover/Tenure	1,437	13	−.03	−.03	.12	.12	52
Status change	4,374	15	.10	.14	.16	−.06	31
Salary	666	4	.04	.06	.08	−.04	68
Objective mean (across criteria)			.07	.10	.11	−.04	52[a]
Subjective ratings	12,943	93	.08	.14	.14	−.05	52
Emotional stability							
Productivity data	1,436	11	−.03	−.04	.14	−.14	45
Turnover/Tenure	1,495	13	.01	.02	.17	−.20	37
Status change	3,483	12	.08	.11	.11	−.03	38
Salary	666	4	−.01	−.01	0	−.01	181
Objective mean (across criteria)			.04	.05	.12	−.10	49[a]
Subjective ratings	12,739	95	.05	.09	.07	.00	83
Agreeableness							
Productivity data	2,082	15	−.03	−.05	.23	.24	28
Turnover/Tenure	1,838	15	.06	.09	0	.09	129
Status change	2,515	9	.09	.13	.13	−.04	30
Salary	121	2	−.01	−.02	0	−.02	143
Objective mean (across criteria)			.04	.05	.14	−.13	48[a]
Subjective ratings	12,467	83	.05	.09	.08	−.01	76
Conscientiousness							
Productivity data	1,639	14	.10	.17	0	.17	176
Turnover/Tenure	2,759	19	.09	.12	.08	.02	47
Status change	2,698	8	.11	.15	.04	.10	88
Salary	718	5	.13	.17	.02	.14	97
Objective mean (across criteria)			.10	.14	.03	.10	82[a]
Subjective ratings	14,059	94	.15	.26	.12	.11	60
Openness to experience							
Productivity data	1,060	9	.00	.01	0	.01	161
Turnover/Tenure	1,628	12	−.08	−.11	.06	−.03	80
Status change	1,766	5	.09	.12	0	.12	119
Salary	121	2	.04	.05	0	.05	120
Objective mean (across criteria)			.01	.02	.09	−.10	113[a]
Subjective ratings	10,639	62	.02	.04	.16	−.16	42

[a] An unbiased estimate of mean percentage of variance accounted for across meta-analyses, calculated by taking the reciprocal of the average of reciprocals of individual predicted to observed variance ratios (Hunter & Schmidt, 1990).

correlations for all scales from an inventory were included in the analysis. Studies were excluded if they reported composite validities or reported only those scales with significant correlations. Thus, the results for each of the five dimensions are based on the average of the correlations between personality scales and job performance criteria. Further, for those studies reporting multiple measures for each dimension, an average correlation was used in the meta-analysis, rather than a composite score correlation (which adjusts the average correlation by the sum of the covariances among the measures incorporated in the average estimate). Use of the composite score correlation *always* results in a mean validity estimate larger in size than that resulting from the average correlation (Hunter & Schmidt, 1990). However, because intercorrelations among personality scales or dimensions were generally not reported (even inventory manuals report only a few intercorrelations), it was not possible to use the composite score correlation in this analysis. A better estimate of the validity of a personality dimension would be provided by combining all scales measuring a single dimension into a predictor composite. Doing this would provide a better measure of the predictive validity of the construct in question. Therefore, in interpreting the results of this study, the reader should focus on understanding which dimensions are the best predictors for specific occupations and criterion types rather than on the magnitude of the validities because they are underestimates.

The most significant finding in the study relates to the Conscientiousness dimension. It was found to be a consistently valid predictor for all occupational groups studied and for all criterion types. Thus, this aspect of personality appears to tap traits which are important to the accomplishment of work tasks in all jobs. That is, those individuals who exhibit traits associated with a strong sense of purpose, obligation, and persistence generally perform better than those who do not. Similar findings have been reported in educational settings where correlations between scores on this dimension and educational achievement (Digman & Takemoto-Chock, 1981; Smith, 1967) and vocational achievement (Takemoto, 1979) have consistently been reported in the range of .50 to .60.

Further evidence that this dimension is a valid predictor of job performance is found in two studies conducted as part of the U.S. Army Selection and Classification Study (Project A) (Hough, Hanser, & Eaton, 1988; McHenry, Hough, Toquam, Hanson, & Ashworth, 1990). Two of the personality constructs, Achievement Orientation and Dependability, were found to be valid predictors of job performance measures in both studies. Although the relationship of the personality constructs investigated by the researchers to the 5-factor taxonomy was not specified, it appears that these two constructs (Achievement/Achievement Orientation and Dependability) are aspects of the Conscientiousness dimension as defined earlier. Achievement taps traits such as planful, organized, persistent, and hardworking, whereas Dependability assesses traits such as careful, thorough, and responsible.

An important area of future research suggested by these results is to further delineate the boundaries of the Conscientiousness dimension. There is some disagreement among researchers about the precise meaning of this construct. Some define it in terms of responsibility or dependability (e.g., Hogan, 1986), whereas others view it as also including volitional aspects, such as hardworking, persistent, and achievement-oriented (e.g., Conley, 1985; Costa & McCrae, 1988; Digman & Inouye, 1986; Digman & Takemoto-Chock, 1981; Krug & Johns, 1986; McCrae & Costa, 1985, 1987, 1989). It is not likely that there will ever be complete agreement among researchers regarding the content of this or any of the other dimensions. However, results of recent studies by researchers in the field of personality psychology, in which scales from personality inventories are factor analyzed and assessed via the 5-factor model, may yield valuable insight into the content of the Conscientiousness dimension (and the four others as well) (McCrae, 1989).

Another area of research suggested by these results is to investigate whether measures of Conscientiousness should be incorporated into theories which attempt to account for work performance. For example, Hunter (1983) has shown that cognitive ability has an indirect effect on supervisory ratings of performance through its effects on the acquisition of job knowledge, which in turn impacts work sample performance. In view of the relatively low correlation between Conscientiousness and cognitive ability (McCrae, 1989), it seems plausible that this aspect of personality may account for unique variance in the acquisition of job knowledge and (therefore) in job performance. Of course, an important issue is whether the effects of Conscientiousness on job performance are direct or indirect, or both, and whether the resulting model would generalize to different occupations. We believe that this is a fertile area for future research.

Consistent with our hypotheses, Extraversion was a valid predictor (across the criterion types) for two occupations, managers and sales. For both types of jobs, interaction with others is a significant portion of the job. Thus traits such as sociable, gregarious, talkative, assertive, and active would lead to effective performance in these jobs, whereas these traits would be less important in jobs such as skilled/semi-skilled (e.g., secretaries, orderlies, assemblers, accountants, production workers) and professionals (e.g., engineers, architects). In both of these cases, however, the estimated true score correlations are less than .20.

The results with respect to Openness to Experience suggest some fruitful areas for future research. This personality construct was found to be a valid predictor of one of the criterion categories, training proficiency, but not for the other two, job proficiency or personnel data. One possible explanation of these findings is that individuals who score high on this dimension (e.g., intelligent, curious, broad-minded, and cultured) are more likely to have positive attitudes toward learning experiences in general. Several researchers have shown that a key component in the success of training programs is the attitude of the individual when s/he enters the training program. As Goldstein (1986) states, "... it is also clear that individuals who are motivated upon entry into the training program have an advantage from the very beginning" (p. 70). Research by Ryman and Biersner (1975) supports this, as they found that scores on a scale designed to measure attitudes of trainees prior to the training (e.g., "If I have trouble during training I will try harder"; "I will get more from this training than most people") predicted eventual graduation from a Navy School for Divers. Similarly, Sanders and Vanouzas (1983) have shown that the attitudes and expectations of the trainees influence whether or not learning is likely to occur. That is, trainees who accepted personal responsibility for the learning process and were willing to participate in discussions, engage in self assessment, and so forth, were more likely to benefit from the training. Thus, measures of Openness to Experience may identify which individuals are "training ready"— those who are most willing to engage in learning experiences—and, consequently, may be useful in identifying those who are most likely to benefit from training programs. As a final comment, it should also be recognized that this dimension has the highest correlation (uncorrected, $r = .20$ to $.30$) of any of the personality dimensions with measures of cognitive ability (McCrae & Costa, 1987). Therefore, it is possible that Openness to Experience is actually measuring ability to learn as well as motivation to learn.

Similarly, Extraversion was found to predict the training proficiency criterion relatively well. Although the relationship with Extraversion was not hypothesized, in retrospect the findings are not surprising, especially in light of the types of training programs that were used in these studies. Most required a high energy level among participants and were highly interactive, such as assessment centers, police academy training, on-the-job training for sales and flight attendants, and so forth. Because Extraversion assesses traits associated with general activity level (talkative, active, assertive) and sociability, these relationships would be expected. As Burris (1976) indicates, based on his review of the literature, research and experience suggest overwhelmingly that learning is more effective when the learner is active rather than passive. However, it seems logical that these relations would not exist in training programs that do not involve social interaction (e.g., lectures, computer assisted instruction, videotapes). The results for Openness to Experience and Extraversion suggest that the relation of personality measures to training proficiency is an important area for future research.

Most of the correlations for Emotional Stability were relatively low. These findings may be due to a type of range restriction, based on a "selecting-out" process, which was not accounted for in the present study. At the extreme, those individuals who are highly neurotic are unable to function effectively on their own and, as a result, are not likely to be in the labor force. More generally, individuals may have "self-selected out" based on their own interests or perceptions of their emotional stability. Another explanation is that there may not be a linear relation between Emotional Stability and job performance beyond the "critically unstable" range. That is, as long as an individual possesses "enough" Emotional Stability, the predictive value of any differences are minimized.

Finally, it was interesting to observe that the coefficient for professionals for this dimension was in a negative direction, suggesting that individuals who are worrying, nervous, emotional, and high-strung are better performers in these jobs. It is difficult to explain these results, although it is possible that the causal direction may be such that in some professional jobs pressures related to high performance cause the individuals to display neurotic traits. Given that these results are based on only five samples, however, they should be interpreted cautiously.

The results for Agreeableness suggest that it is not an important predictor of job performance, even in those jobs containing a large social component (e.g., sales or management). Such results are in contrast with the other socially based personality dimension, Extraversion. Thus, it appears that being courteous, trusting, straight forward, and soft-hearted has a smaller impact on job performance than being talkative, active, and assertive.

An issue of general interest to many personnel psychologists is whether objective measures of job performance result in different validity results than subjective criteria, particularly because objective and subjective measures often cannot be treated as substitutes for one another (Heneman, 1986). In general, for the five personality dimensions, the true score correlations for subjective criteria were larger than for objective criteria. However, for one objective measure, status change, the correlations were equal to or larger than subjective measures for four of the five personality dimensions.

However, for one dimension, Conscientiousness, the correlations for all objective criteria were smaller than for the subjective ratings. This result is particularly intriguing because this dimension was found to be the most predictive personality dimension in this study. A possible explanation for the lower correlations is that the objective criteria are contaminated or deficient, or both. An alternative explanation is that the subjective measures may be susceptible to bias resulting from the individual's personality. For example, Hogan (in press) suggests that one meaning of personality refers to a person's social reputation; that is to the manner in which he or she is perceived by friends, co-workers, and supervisors. Viewed in this way, personality concerns the amount of esteem, regard, and status accorded by his or her social groups. Thus, according to Hogan, reputations summarize what individuals say about a person's past behaviors and may be used to forecast future performance or, at least, what others are likely to say about a person's future behavior. The higher correlations for the subjective criteria in the present study suggest that one's reputation may influence judgments of performance.

The results of the present study have implications for both research and practice in personnel selection. From a practitioner's standpoint, the results suggest that if the purpose is to predict job performance based on an individual's personality, then those measures associated with Conscientiousness are most likely to be valid predictors for all jobs. In fact, it is difficult to conceive of a job in which the traits associated with the Conscientiousness dimension would not contribute to job success. Interestingly, this dimension, which measures traits such as planful, organized, hardworking, persistent, and achievement oriented, has been labeled Work by Peabody and Goldberg (1989) in recognition that these personality traits are closely related to the performance of work tasks.

Of course this does not preclude the possibility that some measures from other personality dimensions may predict job performance. For example, Hogan and

Hogan (1989) developed and validated a personality instrument called Employee Reliability, which was composed of relevant measures from the five personality dimensions studied in this analysis. A large component of this instrument was associated with dependability and carefulness, traits which are representative of the Conscientiousness dimension in the present study. Thus, their finding that the Employee Reliability instrument was a valid predictor of job performance criteria (in addition to counterproductive work behaviors) is consistent with the results of the present study. Taken together, these results further strengthen the conclusion that the most predictive measures of personality are those that emphasize traits associated with the Conscientiousness dimension. (For another example, the reader is directed to the Work Orientation Scale developed by Gough (1985), based on items from multiple scales of the CPI).

In retrospect, it is not surprising that the overall validity of personality measures has been found to be relatively low. As one example, the MMPI is often seen as the prototypical personality inventory. However, a fact that cannot be overlooked is that the MMPI was not designed to predict job performance in normal populations. Thus, findings that the MMPI is a relatively poor predictor of job performance would be expected, based on the results of this study, because most scales on the MMPI measure Emotional Stability and none measure Conscientiousness directly (based on the classifications made by the raters in this study and based on factor analyses of the MMPI by Johnson, Null, Butcher, & Johnson, 1984). Thus, the results of the present study are also useful in explaining why some personality inventories are likely to be better predictors of job performance than others.

Of interest to those in the training and development field are the findings that two of the personality dimensions, Openness to Experience and Extraversion, are related to performance in training programs. Very little research has investigated the relation of individual measures of personality to measures of training readiness and training success. Perhaps future research and practice in the training and development field will be stimulated by the availability of a classification scheme for organizing individual differences in personality.

In summary, in order for any field of science to advance, it is necessary to have an accepted classification scheme for accumulating and categorizing empirical findings. We believe that the robustness of the 5-factor model provides a meaningful framework for formulating and testing hypotheses relating individual differences in personality to a wide range of criteria in personnel psychology, especially in the subfields of personnel selection, performance appraisal, and training and development.

Acknowledgments

Both authors contributed equally to this study. We would like to thank Frank Schmidt, Ralph Alexander, Paul Costa, Mike Judiesch, Wendy Dunn, and Jacob Sines for thoughtful comments about the article and some of the data analyses. We gratefully acknowledge the assistance of Mike Judiesch, Wendy Dunn,

Eric Neumann, Val Arnold, and Duane Thompson in categorizing the personality scales.

Note

1 All analyses were conducted using a microcomputer program developed by Frank Schmidt and reported in Hunter and Schmidt, 1990.

References

Bernstein IH, Garbin CP, McClellan PG. (1983). A confirmatory factoring of the California Psychological Inventory. *Educational and Psychological Measurement, 43*, 687–691.

Bond MH, Nakazato HS, Shiraishi D. (1975). Universality and distinctiveness in dimensions of Japanese person perception. *Journal of Cross-Cultural Psychology, 6*, 346–355.

Borgatta EF. (1964). The structure of personality characteristics. *Behavioral Science, 12*, 8–17.

Botwin MD, Buss DM. (1989). Structure of act-report data: Is the five-factor model of personality recaptured? *Journal of Personality & Social Psychology, 56*, 988–1001.

Briggs SR. (1989). The optimal level of measurement for personality constructs. In Buss DM, Cantor N (Eds.), *Personality Psychology: Recent trends and emerging directions.* New York: Springer-Verlag.

Burris RW. (1976). Human Learning. In Dunnette MD. (*Ed.*), *Handbook of Industrial and Organizational Psychology*. Chicago, Rand McNally.

Cattell RB. (1943). The description of personality: basic traits resolved into clusters. *Journal of Abnormal Social Psychology, 38*, 476–506.

Cattell RB. (1946). *The description and measurement of personality*. Yonkers, NY: World Book.

Cattell RB. (1947). Confirmation and clarification of primary personality factors. *Psychometrika, 12*, 197–220.

Cattell RB. (1948). The primary personality factors in women compared with those in men. *British Journal of Psychology, 1*, 114–130.

Conley JJ. (1985). Longitudinal stability of personality traits: A multitrait-multimethod-multioccasion analysis. *Journal of Personality & Social Psychology, 49*, 1266–1282.

Costa PT Jr., McCrae RR. (1988). From catalog to classification: Murray's needs and the five factor model. *Journal of Personality & Social Psychology, 55*, 258–265.

Digman JM. (1989). Five robust trait dimensions: Development, stability, and utility. *Journal of Personality, 57*, 195–214.

Digman JM. (1990). Personality structure: Emergence of the five-factor model. *Annual Review of Psychology, 41*, 417–440.

Digman JM, Inouye J. (1986). Further specification of the five robust factors of personality. *Journal of Personality & Social Psychology, 50*, 116–123.

Digman JM, Takemoto-Chock NK. (1981). Factors in the natural language of personality: Re-Analysis, comparison, and interpretation of six major studies. *Multivariate Behavioral Research, 16*, 149–170.

Fiske DW. (1949). Consistency of the factorial structures of personality ratings from different sources. *Journal of Abnormal Social Psychology, 44*, 329–344.

Ghiselli EE. (1973). The validity of aptitude tests in personnel selection. *Personnel Psychology, 26*, 461–477.

Goldberg LR. (1981). Language and individual differences: The search for universals in personality lexicons. In Wheeler L. (Ed.), *Review of Personality and Social Psychology* (Vol. 2, pp. 141–166). Beverly Hills, CA: Sage Publications.

Goldstein IL. (1986). *Training in Organizations: Needs Assessment, Development, and Evaluation.* Monterey, CA: Brooks/Cole.

Gough HG. (1985). A work orientation scale for the California Psychological Inventory. *Journal of Applied Psychology, 70*, 505–513.

Guilford JP, Zimmerman WS. (1949). *The Guilford-Zimmerman Temperament Survey.* Beverly Hills, CA: Sheridan Supply.

Guion RM, Gottler RF. (1965). Validity of personality measures in personnel selection. *Personnel Psychology, 18*, 135–164.

Hakel MD. (1974). Normative personality factors recovered from ratings of personality descriptors: The beholder's eye. *Personnel Psychology, 27*, 409–421.

Heneman RL. (1986). The relationship between supervisory ratings and results-oriented measures of performance: A meta-analysis, *Personnel Psychology, 39*, 811–826.

Hogan R. (1983). A socioanalytic theory of personality. In Page MM. (Ed.), *Personality—current theory & research: Nebraska symposium on motivation.* Lincoln, NE: University of Nebraska Press.

Hogan R. (1986). *Manual for the Hogan Personality Inventory.* Minneapolis: National Computer Systems.

Hogan R. (In press). Personality and personality measurement. In Dunnette MD. (Ed.), *Handbook of Industrial and Organizational Psychology.* Palo Alto, CA: Consulting Psychologists Press.

Hogan J, Hogan R. (1989). How to measure reliability. *Journal of Applied Psychology, 74*, 273–279.

Hough LM, Hanser LM, Eaton NK. (1988). *Literature review: Utility of temperament, biodata, and interest assessment for predicting job performance.* Alexandria, VA: U.S. Army, Research Institute for the Behavioral and Social Sciences (ARI research note 88–02).

Howarth E. (1976). Were Cattell's 'personality sphere' factors correctly identified in the first instance? *British Journal of Psychology, 67*, 213–230.

Hunter JE. (1983). A causal analysis of cognitive ability, job knowledge, job performance, and supervisory ratings. In Landy F, Zedeck S, Cleveland J (Eds.), *Performance Measurement and Theory* (pp. 257–266). Hillsdale, NJ: Lawrence Earlbaum.

Hunter JE, Schmidt FL. (1990). *Methods of meta-analysis: correcting error and bias in research findings.* Newbury Park, CA: Sage Publications.

Hunter JE, Schmidt FL, Judiesch MK. (1990). Individual differences in output as a function of job complexity. *Journal of Applied Psychology, 75*, 28–42.

John OP. (1989). Towards a taxonomy of personality descriptors. In Buss DM, Cantor N (Eds.), *Personality psychology: Recent trends and emerging directions.* New York: Springer-Verlag.

Johnson JH, Null C, Butcher JN, Johnson KN. (1984). Replicated item level factor analysis of the full MMPI. *Journal of Personality and Social Psychology, 47*, 105–114.

Krug SE, Johns EF. (1986). A large scale cross-validation of second-order personality structure defined by the 16PF. *Psychological Reports, 59*, 683–693.

Lei H, Skinner HA. (1982). What difference does language make? Structural analysis of the personality research form. *Multivariate Behavioral Research, 17*, 33–46.

Livneh H, Livneh C. (1989). The five-factor model of personality: Is evidence for its crossmedia premature? *Personality and Individual Differences, 10*, 75–80.

Locke EA, Hulin CL. (1962). A review and evaluation of the validity studies of activity vector analysis, *Personnel Psychology, 15*, 25–42.

Lorr M, Manning TT. (1978). Higher-order personality factors of the ISI. *Multivariate Behavioral Research, 13*, 3–7.

Lorr M, Youniss RP. (1973). An inventory of interpersonal style. *Journal of Personality Assessment, 37*, 165–173.

McCrae RR. (1989). Why I advocate the five-factor model: Joint factor analyses of the NEO-PI with other instruments. In Buss DM, Cantor N (Eds.), *Personality psychology: Recent trends and emerging directions*. New York: Springer-Verlag.

McCrae RR, Costa PT Jr. (1985). Updating Norman's "adequate taxonomy": Intelligence and personality dimensions in natural language and in questionnaires. *Journal of Personality & Social Psychology, 49*, 710–721.

McCrae RR, Costa PT Jr. (1987). Validation of the five-factor model of personality across instruments and observers. *Journal of Personality & Social Psychology, 52*, 81–90.

McCrae RR, Costa PT Jr. (1989). The structure of interpersonal traits: Wiggin's circumplex and the five-factor model. *Journal of Personality & Social Psychology, 56*, 586–595.

McDougall W. (1932). Of the words character and personality. *Character Personality, 1*, 3–16.

McHenry JJ, Hough LM, Toquam JL, Hanson MA, Ashworth S. (1990). Project A validity results: The relationship between predictor and criterion domains. *Personnel Psychology, 43*, 335–367.

Nathan BR, Alexander RA. (1988). A comparison of criteria for test validation: A meta-analytic investigation, *Personnel Psychology, 41*, 517–535.

Noller P, Law H, Comrey AL. (1987). Cattell, Comrey, and Eysenck personality factors compared: More evidence for the five robust factors? *Journal of Personality and Social Psychology, 53*, 775–782.

Norman WT. (1963). Toward an adequate taxonomy of personality attributes: Replicated factor structure in peer nomination personality ratings. *Journal of Abnormal & Social Psychology, 66*, 574–583.

Norman WT, Goldberg LR. (1966). Raters, ratees, and randomness in personality structure. *Journal of Personality & Social Psychology, 4*, 681–691.

Peabody D, Goldberg LR. (1989). Some determinants of factor structures from personality-trait descriptors. *Journal of Personality & Social Psychology, 57*, 552–567.

Reilly RR, Chao GT. (1982). Validity and fairness of some alternative employee selection procedures, *Personnel Psychology, 35*, 1–62.

Ryman DH, Biersner RJ. (1975). Attitudes predictive of training success. *Personnel Psychology, 28*, 181–188.

Sanders P, Vanouzas JN. (1983). Socialization to learning. *Training and Development Journal, 37*, 14–21.

Schmitt N, Gooding RZ, Noe RA, Kirsch M. (1984). Meta-analyses of validity studies published between 1964 and 1982 and the investigation of study characteristics. *Personnel Psychology, 37*, 407–422.

Smith GM. (1967). Usefulness of peer ratings of personality in educational research. *Educational and Psychological Measurement, 27*, 967–984.

Takemoto NK. (1979). *The prediction of occupational choice from childhood and adolescent antecedents*. Unpublished masters thesis, University of Hawaii, Honolulu, HI.

Tupes EC. (1957). *Personality traits related to effectiveness of junior and senior Air Force officers* (USAF Personnel Training Research, No. 57–125). Lackland Airforce Base, TX: Aeronautical Systems Division, Personnel Laboratory.

Tupes EC, Christal RE. (1961, May), *Recurrent personality factors based on trait ratings* (ASD-TR-61-97), Lackland Air Force Base, TX: Aeronautical Systems Division, Personnel Laboratory.

Waller NG, Ben-Porath YS. (1987). Is it time for clinical psychology to embrace the five-factor model of personality? *American Psychologist, 42*, 887–889.

Watson D. (1989). Strangers' ratings of the five robust personality factors: Evidence of a surprising convergence with self-report. *Journal of Personality & Social Psychology, 57*, 120–128.

Whitener EM. (1990). Confusion of confidence intervals and credibility intervals in Meta-Analysis. *Journal of Applied Psychology, 75*, 315–321.

Wiggins N, Blackburn M, Hackman JR. (1969). The prediction of first-year success in psychology: Peer ratings. *Journal of Educational Research, 63*, 81–85.

20

FIVE REASONS WHY THE "BIG FIVE" ARTICLE HAS BEEN FREQUENTLY CITED

Michael K. Mount and Murray R. Barrick

Source: *Personnel Psychology* 51 (1998): 849–857.

Abstract

This study investigated the relation of the "Big Five" personality dimensions (Extraversion, Emotional Stability, Agreeableness, Conscientiousness, and Openness to Experience) to three job performance criteria (job proficiency, training proficiency, and personnel data) for five occupational groups (professionals, police, managers, sales, and skill/semi-skilled). Results indicated that one dimension of personality, Conscientiousness, showed consistent relations with all job performance criteria for all occupational groups. For the remaining personality dimensions, the estimated true score correlations varied by occupational group and criterion type. Extraversion was a valid predictor for two occupations involving social interaction, managers and sales (across criterion types). Also, both Openness to Experience and Extraversion were valid predictors of the training proficiency criterion (across occupations). Other personality dimensions were also found to be valid predictors for some occupations and some criterion types, but the magnitude of the estimated true score correlations was small ($\rho < .10$). Overall, the results illustrate the benefits of using the 5-factor model of personality to accumulate and communicate empirical findings. The findings have numerous implications for research and practice in personnel psychology, especially in the subfields of personnel selection, training and development, and performance appraisal.

The most frequently cited article of the 1990s

The Big Five personality dimensions and job performance: a meta-analysis

The idea for our study grew out of our belief that people do, in fact, have long term, dispositional traits that influence their behavior in work settings. Although this idea is relatively well accepted now, at the time we conducted our 1991 study most conclusions in the literature about the usefulness of personality measures in personnel selection were quite pessimistic (e.g., Guion & Gottier, 1965; Mischel, 1968; Weiss & Adler, 1984). Nonetheless, we believed that there were meaningful relationships between individuals' personalities and performance outcomes at work that, for whatever reason, had not been discovered in previous research. We felt that the time was right to conduct a large-scale review of the personality-job performance literature. The critical issue facing us was how our study would contribute in ways that other studies had not.

We reviewed the literature with an eye toward understanding why the conclusions reached by previous researchers were so pessimistic. Based on our interpretation of the literature, we arrived at two major observations. First, literally thousands of personality traits had been investigated and/or potentially could be investigated. The sheer number of such traits made a review of research findings in this area unwieldy. To complicate matters, in a limited number of cases traits with the same names had different meanings, and in other cases traits with different names had the same meaning. The second observation was that most prior reviews of personality and performance were narrative reviews, which limited the nature of the inferences that could be drawn.

Based on the first concern, we recognized that it would be necessary to reduce the thousands of traits to a much smaller number of factors, and to do so in a way that was defensible and accepted by the field. How to do this became the number one priority, as we did not think the study would be worth undertaking unless this could be done in a conceptually meaningful way. As a starting point, we consulted with Jacob Sines of the Psychology Department at the University of Iowa. We are indebted to him for pointing us in the direction of the Big Five. We read the literature pertaining to the structure of personality and were especially influenced by Digman's (1990) chapter in the *Annual Review of Psychology*. Among other things, it showed that while there was not unanimous agreement among researchers, the views of a number of personality psychologists were converging (more or less) on five basic factors of personality. Particularly impressive was the evidence showing that these five factors had been obtained in different cultures, with different languages, using different instruments and with different theoretical frameworks. The solid scientific foundation of this taxonomy provided a defensible organizing framework that enabled us to proceed with our study. In our opinion, this was the missing link in studies seeking to understand personality–performance relationships.

Based on the second concern, we recognized that meta-analysis would be an appropriate data analytic tool for cumulating the personality–performance relationships across studies, and would provide numerous advantages over a narrative approach. Frank Schmidt and Jack Hunter had used validity generalization methods to demonstrate the validity of General Mental Ability (GMA) across jobs and organizations. Many of the same problems that had plagued the research pertaining to GMA also applied to research pertaining to personality: sampling error due to small samples, measurement error in criteria and predictors, range restriction, and dichotomization of continuous measures—all of which distorted the research findings. We envisioned that by using meta-analytic methods we might be able to demonstrate validity generalization for one or more of the Big Five dimensions. If we could find even one personality factor whose validity generalized across jobs and occupations, it would have important practical and theoretical implications.

We felt that the use of the Big Five framework coupled with meta-analytic methods provided a solid foundation for investigating the questions of interest. Privately, however, we worried that the I-O field might not embrace the 5-factor model, particularly given that it was new to many in the field, and that it was not universally accepted by all personality researchers. Nonetheless, we proceeded with the idea that we would be able to ask and, hopefully, answer meaningful questions in a different way than those researchers before us.

We reanalyzed all available published and unpublished research from 1952 to 1988 by categorizing scales from personality inventories into the 5-factor model categories (i.e., Extraversion, Emotional Stability, Agreeableness, Conscientiousness, and Openness to Experience) or into a sixth, miscellaneous category. We examined the predictive validity of these scales for three performance criteria (i.e., job proficiency, training proficiency, and personnel data) in five different occupational groups (i.e., professionals, police, managers, sales, and skilled/semi-skilled).

The major finding was that one of the Big Five dimensions, Conscientiousness, correlated positively with job performance in all five occupational groups. Individuals who are dependable, persistent, goal directed and organized tend to be higher performers on virtually any job; viewed negatively, those who are careless, irresponsible, low achievement striving and impulsive tend to be lower performers on virtually any job. In addition, we found that extraversion was a valid predictor for two occupations (across criterion types), managers and sales, where interactions with others are a significant portion of the job. Thus, traits such as being sociable, talkative, assertive, and energetic contribute to performance in such jobs.

We also found that Extraversion and Openness to Experience were valid predictors of training proficiency across occupations. Being active, sociable, and open to new experiences may lead individuals to be more involved in training and, consequently, learn more. As an aside, we have been somewhat surprised that this finding has not had more of an impact. Most of the citations of our article pertain to personality in selection contexts. There remains a relative void in the literature regarding the relationship between personality dimensions and training outcomes.

On one hand, we were excited and heartened by the findings regarding Conscientiousness and believed they could play a key role in developing comprehensive theories of job performance. Our research in subsequent years has investigated the processes by which Conscientiousness affects job performance. On the other hand, we were somewhat disappointed and a little dismayed at the relatively low magnitude of the correlations for Conscientiousness ($\rho = .21$ to $.23$) and the other four dimensions. However, we reasoned that the raw correlations used in the meta-analyses were based on single scales from personality inventories, which are imperfect measures of the Big Five constructs. For example, when composite measures of Conscientiousness are used the true validity is .31 (Mount & Barrick, 1995). We also found that Conscientiousness is more strongly related to those criteria that are substantially determined by motivational effort or "will do" factors ($\rho = .42$) rather than by ability or "can do" factors ($\rho = .25$). This underscores the importance of the conscientiousness construct as a measure of trait-oriented motivation. The magnitude of these validities was more encouraging, though still well below those for GMA.

The finding that Extraversion predicted successful performance in jobs involving interactions with others was also intriguing, and we believed it could also have important practical and theoretical implications. A recent meta-analysis builds on these findings (Mount, Barrick & Stewart, 1998) by examining the relationship of personality to performance in jobs involving considerable interpersonal interaction, either with customers or with other employees. Findings indicate that Emotional Stability, Agreeableness, and Conscientiousness are also positively related to on-the-job success in these jobs. Furthermore, these relations appear to be stronger for jobs requiring teamwork interactions among employees than for jobs requiring interpersonal interactions with customers. Consequently, in such jobs, viewed from the negative pole, those who are anxious, insecure, emotional, and tense (low emotional stability), argumentative, inflexible, uncooperative, and uncaring (low agreeableness), and impulsive, irresponsible, careless, and lazy (low conscientiousness) tend to be less effective in interactions with others at work. These findings demonstrate that Big Five personality characteristics other than Conscientiousness are meaningfully related to criteria, but their predictive efficiency is more situationally specific than Conscientiousness.

At the time we conducted our study, two other meta-analyses of personality–performance relationships were being conducted (Hough, Eaton, Dunnette, Kamp & McCloy, 1990; Tett, Jackson & Rothstein, 1991). Subsequently, another meta-analysis of studies in the European community was conducted (Salgado, 1997). Some of the validities reported for Big Five constructs in these studies differed from those reported in our study, and in some cases the differences were quite large. For example, true score validities for the same construct differed by .30 or more. For agreeableness, Tett et al. reported a validity of .33, whereas Hough et al. and Salgado reported a validity of −.01 (for job proficiency and ratings of performance, respectively). And, for openness to experience Tett et al. reported a validity of .27, whereas we reported a validity of −.03 (for job proficiency). Further, we found that conscientiousness was a valid predictor of job performance in all jobs studied and for all criterion types, but Tett et al. found that it had lower validity than three other personality constructs: Agreeableness, Openness to Experience, and Emotional Stability. Moreover, the highest validity in the Tett et al. study was for Agreeableness. Goldberg (1993) pointed out that this inconsistency in the findings between two large-scale quantitative reviews of a similar body of knowledge was "befuddling."

Two articles that appeared in *Personnel Psychology* in 1994 (Ones, Mount, Barrick & Hunter, 1994; Tett, Jackson, Rothstein & Reddon, 1994) sought to explain these discrepant results. At least some of the differences can be explained by the fact that the studies had different purposes and made different assumptions in the meta-analytic procedures. In retrospect, however, we believe the debate was only moderately successful in resolving the discrepancies between the two studies. We, like most people we talked to informally who had read the original articles and the ensuing critiques, felt that although some important issues had been clarified, those pertaining to the Big Five results had not. Perhaps the most important outcome of the debate was that it stimulated additional research and illustrated that there are complex methodological and theoretical issues that must be considered when conducting research in this area. Clearly, the field of personnel psychology has made great strides in the past decade in understanding the role of personality measures in personnel selection. Nonetheless, much needs to be done before we understand the intricate relationships that exist between particular personality constructs and job performance measures. One useful study would be to examine existing meta-analytic studies that have used the Big Five framework with the objective of identifying and resolving the apparent discrepancies in results. It is possible that if methodological differences and statistical artifacts are corrected in similar ways across the meta-analyses, there may actually be more consistencies in the findings than appears at present.

The foregoing has highlighted why we conducted the study, some of the issues we addressed in conducting the study, and the major findings. The issue John Hollenbeck asked us to address was why we think this article has been cited so frequently. As of July 1, 1998, the article had been cited slightly more than 200 times (Social Science Citation Index). We don't know for certain what factors led to our article being widely cited; nonetheless, we have several ideas and we discuss them below. We also thought it would be interesting and worthwhile to pose this question to other researchers. We asked a non-random sample of prominent researchers in the field for their views on this question. Their responses revealed several common themes that agreed quite closely with our views. In the paragraphs that follow, we offer five (what else) possible reasons why our study has been frequently cited.

First, our paper addressed one of the most fundamental topics in the field of industrial-organizational psychology. Understanding individual differences and their implications for behavior at work is one of the central tenets of our field, and personality characteristics are central to understanding individual differences. Thus, our topic is important to the field and has widespread appeal as a result.

Second, the study was one of the first to introduce the Big Five personality framework to the industrial-organizational psychology field. It is a simple and parsimonious way to classify the thousands of personality traits that exist in the English language. This taxonomy was well known in the field of personality psychology, though not universally accepted at the time the article was written; however it was less well known and understood in the field of industrial-organizational psychology. Thus the taxonomy itself had informational value to the field quite aside from the findings of the study. It is quite possible that if someone had written a review article about the Big Five (without the meta-analytic analysis) and had discussed the numerous implications of the taxonomy for the I-O field, the article would have been widely cited. Clearly, it would have been difficult for us to conduct our study and for it to have the impact it has had without the Big Five taxonomy. It was instrumental in organizing the multitude of traits and was equally important as a vehicle for parsimoniously communicating the results.

Third, the timing of the study was a factor. Several people mentioned that it was the right article at the right time. (Sometimes you just get lucky.) Around the time we conducted our study, we think die field of industrial-organizational psychology was receptive to a paradigmatic shift in thinking about the utility of non-cognitive predictors such as personality measures. Meta-analytic evidence accumulated during the 1980s showed that cognitive ability tests were valid predictors of performance in most, if not all, jobs in the U.S. economy (Hunter & Hunter, 1984; Schmidt, Hunter & Pearlman 1981; Schmitt, Gooding, Noe & Kirsch, 1984). Following this finding there was considerable interest in the field in identifying additional predictors to add incremental validity to cognitive ability in predicting job performance while simultaneously reducing adverse impact.

In the 1970s and 1980s there was relatively little research being published that directly examined the validity of personality measures for predicting performance. Some have referred to this period humorously as the time when we had no personalities. There had been a few presentations at SIOP and some limited research published in journals in the 1980s that investigated personality and its relationship to job performance. Yet not enough consistent information had accumulated to alter the prior pessimistic conclusions. As mentioned earlier, unbeknownst to us at the time we embarked on our study, Leatta Hough and her colleagues (e.g., Hough et al. 1990) had also concluded that the best way to study the predictive validity of personality was to use a construct-oriented approach to examine the relationship between specific personality traits and performance measures. We would like to acknowledge their contributions in moving the field forward. In a similar fashion Bob and Joyce Hogan were conducting research in the 1980s showing relationships between personality and job performance pertaining to customer service, integrity, and other criteria, at a time when most people *knew* that such research was a waste of time (e.g., Hogan & Hogan, 1989; Hogan, Hogan & Busch, 1984). The work of these researchers paved the way for our research by creating a climate receptive to future research on personality. They shared our conviction that we do, in fact, have personalities and what's more they do matter.

Fourth, related to the point above, our study used meta-analysis, which was rapidly becoming a well accepted data analytic technique at the time we conducted our study. The goal of our study was to identify broadly defined personality characteristics whose validity would generalize across different criteria and different occupational groupings. Using meta-analysis allowed us to quantitatively summarize the results of a large number of studies while correcting for statistical artifacts that could account for the seemingly contradictory findings in prior research. We suspect that large-scale meta-analytic reviews such as ours are more likely to be widely cited than single, empirical studies or narrative reviews. It will be interesting to see if the most frequently cited articles in *Personnel Psychology* 50 years from now are meta-analyses.

Fifth, the results of the study enhanced understanding and contributed to the theoretical development of causal models explaining job performance. This was especially the case with the findings for Conscientiousness, the only dimension of the Big Five whose validity was found to generalize across occupations and criterion types. We believe Conscientiousness to be the important trait-oriented motivation variable that has long eluded I-O psychologists. This meant that there are now two dispositional predictors in our field whose validity generalizes: general mental ability and conscientiousness. Thus, no matter what job you are selecting for, if you want employees who will turn out to be good performers, you should hire those who work smarter and work harder. An equally important development was in demonstrating that measures of other Big Five dimensions also predicted success in certain jobs or with specific criteria, and again, these relationships could be hypothesized a priori.

We were also asked what advice we have for researchers who desire to conduct research that is likely to have an impact on the field. We don't profess to have all the answers to this question. (If we did, all of our articles would be as frequently cited as this one.) So we would be the first to admit that writing a highly cited article is a low probability event that involves hard work, creativity, good timing and luck. Nonetheless, here are some ideas based on our experiences in this project.

First, ask questions that are of interest to you, personally, and that you think will be of interest to the field. In our case we had a strong belief that there were meaningful, consistent relationships between certain aspects of personality and job performance, and that they were stronger than the results portrayed in the literature. Second, be committed to your theory. Any study that challenges traditional thinking in the field will encounter difficult obstacles. Possessing strong beliefs about a theory enables one to persist in the face of such obstacles. Third, read the research literature very broadly. Research in the personality psychology area was invaluable to us in conducting our study. Similarly, we believe that reading the social psychology literature would be helpful to many researchers in I-O psychology. Fourth, if possible, look at the research question in a different way. This is related to the third point above. Reading different, but related, literatures can help bring a fresh perspective to a question. This was particularly true in our case, where there were conflicting findings in the literature, and where the research in our field appeared to have stagnated. Fifth, have the good fortune to obtain results that are relatively straightforward and understandable. Research findings do not have to be complex to be important. Our finding that the validity of conscientiousness generalized across occupational groups was simple to understand, easy to remember and had implications for the field. Finally, never underestimate the importance of dispositional traits. Always be persistent, dependable, organized, efficient, careful, thorough, hard working and achievement striving when conducting your research.

Acknowledgments

We acknowledge the helpful comments of Wally Borman, Mike Campion, Bob Hogan, Tim Judge, Tom Lee, Deniz Ones, Joe Rosse, Craig Russell, Paul Sackett, and Greg Stewart for their helpful comments.

References

Digman JM. (1990). Personality structure: Emergence of the five-factor model. *Annual Review of Psychology*, *41*, 417–440.

Goldberg LR. (1993). The structure of phenotypic personality traits. *American Psychologist*, *48*, 26–34.

Guion RM, Gottier RF. (1965). Validity of personality measures in personnel selection. *Personnel Psychology*, *18*, 135–164.

Hogan J, Hogan R. (1989). How to measure employee reliability. *Journal of Applied Psychology*, *74*, 273–279.

Hogan J, Hogan R, Busch CM. (1984). How to measure service orientation. *Journal of Applied Psychology*, *69*, 167–173.

Hough LM, Eaton NK, Dunnette MD, Kamp JD, McCloy RA. (1990). Criterion-related validities of personality constructs and the effect of response distortion on those validities (Monograph). *Journal of Applied Psychology*, *75*, 581–595.

Hunter JE, Hunter RF. (1984). Validity and utility of alternate predictors of job performance. *Psychological Bulletin*, *96*, 72–98.

Mischel W. (1968). *Personality and assessment*. New York: Wiley.

Mount MK, Barrick MR. (1995). The Big Five personality dimensions: Implications for research and practice in human resource management. *Research in Personnel and Human Resources Management*, *13*, 153–200.

Mount MK, Barrick MR, Stewart GL. (1998). Personality predictors of performance in jobs involving interaction with others. *Human Performance*, *11*, 145–166.

Ones DS, Mount MK, Barrick MR, Hunter JE. (1994). Personality and job performance: A critique of Tett, Jackson, and Rothstein (1991) meta-analysis. *Personnel Psychology*, *47*, 147–156.

Salgado JF. (1997). The five-factor model of personality and job performance on the European community. *Journal of Applied Psychology, 82*, 30–43.

Schmidt FL, Hunter JE, Pearlman K. (1981). Task differences and validity of aptitude tests in selection: A red herring. *Journal of Applied Psychology, 66*, 166–185.

Schmitt N, Gooding RZ, Noe RA, Kirsch M. (1984). Meta-analysis of validity studies published between 1964 and 1982 and the investigation of study characteristics. *Personnel Psychology, 37*, 407–422.

Tett RP, Jackson DN, Rothstein M. (1991). Personality meaures as predictors of job performance: A meta-analytic review, *Personnel Psychology, 44*, 703–742.

Tett RP, Jackson DN, Rothstein M, Reddon JR. (1994). Meta-analysis of personality-job performance relationship: A reply to Ones, Mount, Barrick, and Hunter (1994). *Personnel Psychology, 47*, 157–172.

Weiss HM, Adler S. (1984). Personality and organizational behavior. In Staw BM, Cummings LL (Eds.), *Research in organizational behavior*, (*Vol. 6*), (pp. 1–50). Greenwich, CT: JAI Press.

21

THE MOTIVATION TO WORK

What we know

Edwin A. Locke

Source: *Advances in Motivation and Achievement* 10 (1997): 375–412.

This chapter integrates several decades of empirical research on work motivation and selected elements of eight work motivation theories to formulate a model of work motivation. The core of the model is based on goal-setting theory which approaches motivation from the viewpoint of the individual's conscious performance goals. Essential to the model is social-cognitive theory, especially the concept of self-efficacy which has many motivational effects. The theory encompasses not only work performance but personality, values, emotions (especially job satisfaction) and responses to emotions. In addition to goal theory and social-cognitive theory, the model includes aspects of: personality theory, valence-instrumentality-expectancy (VIE) theory, attribution theory, equity theory, procedural justice theory, and job characteristics theory.

When I was in graduate school (early 1960s) two approaches to the study of human motivation were dominant. The behaviorist approach (e.g., Skinner, 1953) asserted that you could understand human action without regard to the fact that man is conscious—on the grounds that consciousness is not a legitimate scientific concept. I was shocked by how deeply behaviorism had taken hold of the field—and by how thoroughly frightened people were to oppose it, especially considering that you could refute the entire enterprise with 30 seconds of introspection. Later I realized that there were deep-seated (and very wrong) philosophical premises underlying behaviorism which had to be exposed and refuted (e.g., materialism, environmental determinism, the Humean approach to causality and the rejection of introspection as a scientific method [see Locke, 1969, 1971, 1972, 1977, 1980, 1995, 1996]). Ultimately behaviorism failed because it did not and could not, considering the false premises underlying it, work (see, e.g., Bandura, 1986).

The second approach accepted the fact that man was a being possessing consciousness but focused on subconscious rather than conscious motivation. This approach is best exemplified by McClelland (1953). Freudianism—which is no more scientific than behaviorism (Locke, 1980)—aside, there is no doubt that people can be motivated by subconscious motives, that is, motives or premises which they actually possess but which they cannot readily report or access through introspection (e.g., see Bargh & Barndollar, 1996). However, the subconscious approach faced daunting scientific challenges, of which the key one was measurement. McClelland (1953, 1961) used the fantasy, or TAT (thematic apperception test), approach which proved difficult due to such factors as: the multiple possible meanings of fantasy stories, the unreliability of scores across TAT pictures and across time, and the difficulty of specifying the domain to which a particular fantasy dimension applied. Though this approach had some success (e.g., McClelland, 1961; Spangler, 1992), it also came under criticism, especially because the findings tended to be unreliable.

The common premise of the behaviorist and subconscious motive approaches was that the study of conscious motivation was not of great, if any, scientific value. A professor of mine in graduate school, T.A. Ryan disagreed. He was equally skeptical of both of the then-predominant approaches to motivation. Ryan advocated trying to see how much human action we could explain if we focused on conscious motivation. Specifically, he suggested that situationally specific intentions, that is, what the person was trying to do or accomplish on a particular task or in a given situation, was worth studying, and he decided to write a book on the topic which also reviewed the relevant experimental literature (Ryan, 1970). I read early drafts of his 1970 book chapters, took them to heart, tried out his ideas and they worked. I am still following this approach more than 30 years later.

There was a second element involved in my decision to study the conscious side of motivation. I realized, based on Rand (1964), that goal-directedness was a cardinal attribute of the actions of all living organisms (Binswanger, 1990; Locke, 1969). At the vegetative level (the level characteristic of plants and the internal organs of higher organisms), goal-directed action is non-conscious and automatic (e.g., the root growth of a plant, the heartbeat of a man). But at the sensory-perceptual level (animals), molar action is directed by consciousness—in the case of animals by a limited number of desires and aversions which involve concrete, immediate goals (e.g., get the bone). At the conceptual level (man), molar actions are guided by conscious purposes (though purposes can also be sub-conscious); goals can be volitionally chosen and vary widely in content, scope and time perspective. Furthermore, in man, these purposes or goals can be identified through introspection. Thus I was convinced that the study of conscious purposes in man was both biologically sound and practically feasible.

Since my approach is based on a situational and task-specific approach, a word is in order about the issue of general (e.g., trait, motive) vs. specific (e.g., intention, goal) measures and approaches—a topic which has a long history of debate within psychology (e.g., see Bandura, 1986). The critical point to be made here is that every action that a person takes is specific, that is, it involves a concrete action in a concrete context. There is no such thing as "action in general." Therefore, regardless of what view one has of the meaning or usefulness of general values, traits, motives, or over-arching, long-range purposes, these can only operate within and with respect to specific situations. Thus a plausible experimental strategy is to identify the conscious mental contents and processes that most directly regulate such action. This approach produces what T.A. Ryan (1958) called a first-level explanation of action. First-level explanations are clearly not the whole story, but they are a good place to start. Second-level explanations would explain the first-level factors, and, as we shall see, we have made a start at this also.

Motivation and goals

Goal content

A goal is the object or aim of an action. The content of a consciously held goal (purpose) is the end the person wants to achieve. In Aristotle's terminology the causal form is both teleological and efficient; the idea of the goal is the efficient cause of a desired future state. Intention theories in social psychology (e.g., Ajzen, 1991) have focused on the relationship between goal content and discrete actions, for example, the relation between the intent to buy coffee and actually buying it. In contrast, psychology research has focused primarily on the effect of specific attributes of goal content.

Goal attributes

As a budding Industrial-Organizational psychologist my early interest, and that of my colleague, Gary Latham, was in explaining, ability aside, why some people perform better on work tasks than others. Thus our early research—which has continued to this day—focused on the different types of performance goals people try for when working on a task. The most complete statement of goal theory can be found in Locke and Latham (1990). Based on earlier work of C.A. Mace (1935), we have looked at two attributes of performance goals: difficulty and specificity.

Goal difficulty

The attribute of *goal difficulty* (not to be confused with task difficulty; Campbell & Ilgen, 1976) was the more intriguing of the two attributes, because there were competing theoretical predictions as to how difficulty affected performance. Atkinson's (1958) theory, predicted a curvilinear relationship between probability of success, with performance being highest (especially if need for achievement were high) at intermediate (.50) probability levels—implying a moderate goal level. In contrast, valence-instrumentality-expectancy, or VIE theory (Vroom, 1964), predicted a positive relationship between effort-performance expectancy and performance, holding V and I constant. At first, our results seemed paradoxical in that they contradicted both theories. We found that the *lower* the average expectancy of success in reaching one's goal—which meant the higher the actual goal level—the better the performance (Locke, 1968). The relation of goal difficulty to performance is shown in Figure 1. Note that performance drops if knowledge or ability are inadequate or if commitment is low. If normative group data are used to set goals, difficult goals are typically set at the 90th percentile, moderate goals at the 50th percentile and easy goals at the 10th percentile. Goals can also be individualized and can be based on percent improvement rather than absolute attainments (see Wright, 1990).

The paradox was eventually resolved (Locke, Motowidlo, & Bobko, 1986). Goal difficulty is positively related and expectancy negatively related to performance *across* goal levels; for example, trying to produce 25 widgets an hour leads to higher average productivity than trying to produce 15, which in turn is better than trying to produce five. However, *within* any given goal level, where the performance referent for measuring expectancy is held constant, the higher the expectancy, the higher the performance (Van Eerde & Thierry, 1996).

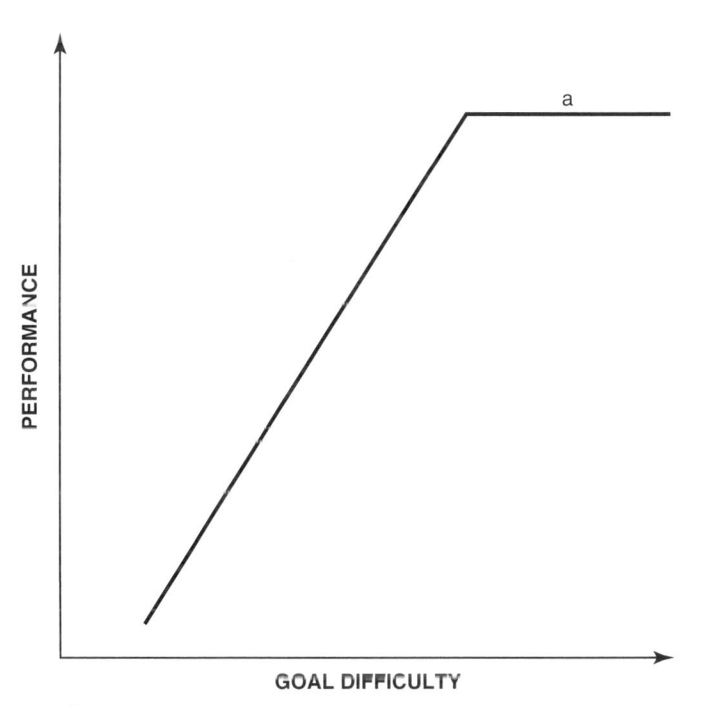

Note: [a]This section indicates lack of sufficient knowledge or ability, or low commitment.

Figure 1 The goal difficulty function.

Goals and self-efficacy

Here goal theory can be integrated with social-cognitive theory (Bandura, 1986, 1997). Especially pertinent is the concept of self-efficacy, which refers to the confidence that one can attain a certain performance level or result. Self-efficacy is related in meaning to the concept of expectancy in VIE theory but is broader in scope. Expectancy refers to effort-performance expectancy, whereas self-efficacy refers to one's confidence in attaining a given performance achievement using not just effort but one's total capacity to orchestrate subskills, overcome setbacks, maintain cognitive self-control, solve problems, and so forth. Self-efficacy should not be confused with locus of control which is a trait rather than a state measure and focuses more on control over the outcomes of performance than performance itself (Bandura, 1997). The relationship between goal difficulty, self-efficacy and performance is shown in Figure 2. If goals are assigned they affect self-set goals and may also affect self-efficacy in that they express confidence in the subordinate. The goals a person sets or accepts have a direct effect on performance, and self-efficacy has both a direct and an indirect effect, the latter through its effect on goal choice (Earley & Lituchy, 1991).

A benefit of using self-efficacy rather than expectancy measures in goal-setting research is that self-efficacy is measured in terms of confidence in reaching each performance level across a range of performance levels, as opposed to any one performance level; thus the referent is always held constant (Locke *et al.*, 1986).

As an aside, it should be noted that because there is usually high covariation (resulting from the causal relation) between self-efficacy and goals which are self-set, regression models which enter both variables together may show one of the two not to have a significant performance effect. If one is entered before the other, the first one entered will take the lion's share of the variance. Locke (in press) suggests that the two could be combined and entered as a single variable. Alternatively, self-efficacy could be entered simply as a cause of goals.

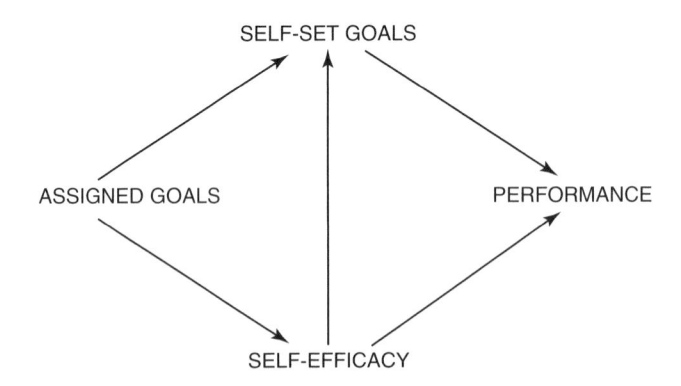

Figure 2 The relationship between goals, self-efficacy, and performance.

Goal specificity

Goal specificity refers to the clarity of the goal or the degree to which the goal refers to an explicit versus a vague performance outcome. The typical vague goal used in our studies (from Mace, 1935) is "do your best," a motivational instruction that people, including managers, routinely give to themselves and to others. We have found that people do not do their best when they are trying to do their best. The reason is that this goal is so vague that it is compatible with a wide variety of performance attainments. Although people trying to do their best typically outperform people trying for an easy goal, they routinely do less well than people who are trying for goals which are both specific and difficult (Locke & Latham, 1990). Specificity is usually best attained by stating goals in quantitative terms. If specific, challenging long-term goals are set, people benefit from setting specific, proximal goals as a means to the end goals (Bandura & Simon, 1977).

Goal specificity by itself does not necessarily lead to high performance. If goals are specific and easy, performance will be low. However, goals which are specific do reduce the variance in performance as compared to goals which are vague, as the performance attainments are more clear cut (Locke, Chah, Harrison, & Lustgarten, 1989), assuming that performance is controllable. When specific goals are very difficult, variation is increased because some people are better able to attain high levels of performance than others.

Individual, group and organizational goals

Goal setting has been studied most often at the individual level and is supported by the results of several hundred studies, conducted in both laboratory and field settings, using 88 different tasks and more than 40,000 subjects in eight countries, employing time spans from minutes to years, involving many different measures of performance, including creativity (Shalley, 1991), and many forms of goals, for example, assigned, self-set, and participative. (See Locke & Latham, 1990, for a summary and meta-analyses.)

Goal-setting effects do not just apply at the individual level, however. Studies of group goal setting find that specific and difficult goals are superior to other types of goals, as for individuals (O'Leary-Kelly, Martocchio, & Frink, 1994). Group goals are most suitable on interdependent tasks (Mitchell & Silver, 1990). However, there are potentially complicating factors that can emerge at the group level (Locke, Durham, Poon, & Weldon, in press). These include cooperation versus conflict, communication and interpersonal influence, all of which can help or hurt effectiveness, and the need to get all members committed. Individual goals may need to be set for each individual's contribution to the group to prevent loafing. In developing task strategies, it may be difficult for group members to decide who, if anyone has the relevant knowledge, especially since the most influential or dominant member is not necessarily the most able.

Goal setting is also effective at the organizational level. Organizational goal setting used to be called Management by Objectives (MBO), although the term is rarely used today, despite the fact that virtually all organizations set goals of some type. Rodgers and Hunter (1991) reviewed 70 MBO studies and found that outcomes improved in 68 of them, although the MBO studies in question were typically conducted at the department or unit level rather than at the level of the entire organization. Rodgers and Hunter also found that a critical factor in the success of MBO programs was commitment by top management. Commitment in this case meant personal participation in the MBO program as opposed to delegating it to lower-level managers. As we shall see below, commitment to goals is also critical at the individual level.

Mediators of goal and self-efficacy effects

It is widely accepted that there are three attributes of motivated action: direction, intensity (effort), and duration (persistence). Goals affect all three; thus, these are mediators of the effect of goals. Goal effects are also mediated by the task strategies people use. Self-efficacy affects effort, persistence, and task strategies.

Goals *direct attention and action* toward performance outcomes relevant to the goal and, as a result, away from other outcomes (Locke & Bryan, 1969). For example, people trying for high quantity are likely to neglect quality (Bavelas & Lee, 1978) and vice versa. People who are highly committed to attaining difficult, individual goals are less likely to help other people with their work since this might distract them from attaining their own goals (Wright, George, Farnsworth, & McMahan, 1993). People can successfully pursue more than one goal providing they can prioritize them as to importance; performance is best for the goal with the highest priority (Edmister & Locke, 1987). Prioritizing can be easier when one goal is hard and the other easy (Gilliland & Landis, 1992). When there are two or more goals in the absence of clear priorities, goal conflict may result. When people are pulled in two directions at once, performance on both goals suffers in comparison to people trying for just one goal or the other (Locke, Smith, Erez, Chah, & Shaffer, 1994). Goal differences can also be a source of conflict between individuals (White & Neale, 1994). When the task requires coordination and cooperation among individuals, the most effective way to motivate high group performance is a combination of group goals and goals for each individual's contribution to the group (Crown & Rosse, 1995).

Goals *arouse effort* (intensity) in approximate proportion to the difficulty of the goal; effort is typically revealed in terms of rate of work (Bryan & Locke, 1967). However, effort may also be revealed by direct measurements of physical exertion (Bandura & Cervone, 1983), physiological arousal (Sales, 1970; Gellatly & Meyer, 1992) and subjective effort indices (Brickner & Bukatko, 1987, study 1), although this last is not always a reliable measure. Self-efficacy also enhances effort, especially when the individual is faced with obstacles (Bandura, 1986).

Persistence (duration) is enhanced by goal difficulty (LaPorte &Nath, 1976), assuming people are free to decide how much time they wish to spend on the task, and there is commitment to the goal. In bargaining situations, people with difficult goals hold out longer to get the deal they want than those with easy goals (Neale & Bazerman, 1985). It should be noted that when time is not limited, there may be a partial trade-off between rate of work and duration of work. Self-efficacy enhances persistence as it does effort.

Goals cannot always be attained by attention, effort, and tenacity (Wood & Locke, 1990). The benefits of motivation pre-suppose some knowledge of what to do, that is, what *task strategies* to use to perform the task. For example, trying hard at chess does not help very much unless you know how to move the pieces and how to coordinate your moves to defend your king and at the same time attack your opponent's pieces. Frequently, suitable task strategies are not known and must be discovered through problem-solving. The more complex the task, the more important task strategies become. Of special interest to goal theory is the relationship between goal type, task strategies, and performance. Here is what we know so far:

(a) When the task is non-routine, specific, difficult goals stimulate planning in general (Smith, Locke, & Barry, 1990), and the search for specific, goal-relevant strategies (Audia, Kristof-Brown, Brown, & Locke, 1996).

(b) If effective task strategies are already known, based on previous experience or on recent training, then specific, difficult goals increase the likelihood that such strategies will be used and thus performance is enhanced (Latham & Baldes, 1975; Earley & Perry, 1987). This is not just an issue of automatic activation, though this may occur if people are "primed" through training or instruction, but also of a deliberate choice to use the strategies that work best.

(c) When people have to discover appropriate or effective task strategies on their own, those who are able to discover effective strategies and have specific, difficult goals perform best. This interaction (which is actually a moderator effect) supplements or supercedes the main effects of goals and strategies (Chesney & Locke, 1991; Durham, Knight, & Locke, 1997).

(d) There is often a time lag in the effect of goals on performance (Audia *et al.*, 1996; DeShon & Alexander, 1996; Smith *et al.*, 1990) which is a result of subjects having to discover suitable strategies. This is most likely to occur on complex tasks or tasks where there are multiple paths to the goal.

(e) When subjects are given a new, complex task without training and are pressured with difficult goals and limited time, they often but not always (Cervone, Jiwani, & Wood, 1991) fail to develop effective strategies due to "tunnel" vision and unsystematic planning. They perform, therefore, no better than or even worse than subjects with "do your best" goals (DeShon & Alexander, 1996; Earley, Connolly, & Ekegren, 1989). Cervone and associates (1991) discovered that subjects with hard goals who were dissatisfied with their progress actually worked harder and yet used poorer analytic strategies than subjects who were satisfied. DeShon and Alexander (1996) found that increasing the time allowed for strategy discovery resulted in subjects with specific, hard goals discovering better strategies and outperforming subjects with "do best" goals. In addition to allowing more time for planning, subjects given hard goals on complex tasks may benefit from initially being given learning goals rather than performance goals (Winters & Latham, 1996).

(f) People with high self-efficacy are more likely than those with low self-efficacy to discover effective task strategies (Wood & Bandura, 1989; Latham, Winters, & Locke, 1994). Selecting effective strategies, in turn, enhances self-efficacy.

Moderators

Moderators refer to interactions between goals and other factors. Moderators are equivalent in meaning to boundary conditions. It was noted above that in addition to mediating goal effects, goals and task strategies may interact such that the combination of high goals and effective strategies lead to higher performance than other combinations. Here we discuss additional moderators.

Feedback

The concept of feedback has a long and somewhat contentious history in psychology (Kluger & DeNisi, 1996). We must begin by making a distinction between instructive feedback, which tells people what they are doing wrong and/or how to improve, and knowledge of progress (i.e., knowledge of score or results). Usually the first type is directly, though not inevitably, beneficial in that it provides task knowledge. Goals themselves may stimulate knowledge-seeking, if relevant information is accessible.

Knowledge of results or progress is a *moderator* of the effect of goals on subsequent performance. Is most effective and usually only effective if individuals have knowledge of their progress in relation to the goal (Erez, 1977; Locke & Latham, 1990). For example, those who are progressing at a slower rate than required to meet the goal need to know this in order to be able to adjust their effort level or change their strategies. Those who are exceeding their goal but want to just meet it need to know that they can continue as they were or even slow down. In the absence of such information, people have to rely on subjective judgments of the adequacy of their progress, and these are often inaccurate.

On the other side of the goal-feedback coin, goals *mediate* the effect of knowledge of results on subsequent performance. Feedback that leads to the setting of high goals is most likely to improve performance (Locke, Cartledge, & Koeppel, 1968). Self-efficacy also plays a critical role here. Those who receive negative information about their progress are most likely to improve subsequently if they set high goals and have high self-efficacy (Bandura & Cervone, 1986; Locke & Latham, 1990).

Commitment

It is virtually axiomatic that if people are not *really* trying for a goal, then the goal will not lead to improved performance. Thus the ultimate proof of commitment is action, although for practical reasons it is often useful to try to measure commitment with an attitude measure before action takes place. Performance corresponds more closely to goals when commitment is high than when it is low. Commitment to high goals means trying not to fall short of them, whereas commitment to low goals means not exceeding them—although commitment to low goals can also be interpreted as performing *at least* up to that level. Commitment is harder to get and therefore especially critical when goals are difficult (Erez & Zidon, 1984; Hollenbeck & Klein, 1987). Commitment depends on the conviction that the goal is: (a) important and (b) possible to reach or approach (Hollenbeck, Williams, & Klein, 1989). There are numerous ways to convince people that a goal is *important*. These include leadership, for example, the use of legitimate authority, providing a rationale for the goal, role modeling, recognition, inspiration through vision (Kirkpatrick & Locke, 1996); peer pressure; norms and role models (Earley & Kanfer, 1985; Earley & Erez, 1991); group cohesion (Klein & Mulvey, 1995); making commitments in public (Hollenbeck *et al.*, 1989); and tying the goal to important personal values.

If money is valued, incentives can be used to gain commitment (e.g., Wright, 1989). However, there are some very complex issues involved here—over and above the amount of the incentive (Locke & Latham, 1990). If incentives are given for attaining easy goals, performance will be routinely low; and if incentives are given only for fully attaining goals which are too difficult to actually reach, self-set goal difficulty, self-efficacy and performance may actually drop over time rather than increase (Lee, Locke, & Phan, in press). This result is shown in Figure 3. In the bonus condition, in which subjects are paid only if they fully attain their goals, performance drops when goals are too hard to reach. People do not like to be offered incentives which they cannot get. Thus to motivate high performance, the incentives must somehow be detached from full goal success. For example, pay could be based on a multi-tier or piece-rate system so that the more you do the more you get, regardless of whether you reach the most difficult goal level or not (Locke & Latham, 1990). Another potential problem with incentive plans is that people learn on the job so that a difficult goal may soon become easy and thereby undermine the desire for further improvement.

Deci and Ryan (1985) have argued that money incentives undermine task interest; however, subsequent research has found their theory wanting in a number of respects (Bandura, 1986, 1997; Locke & Latham, 1990). First, Deci and Ryan use as their preferred measure of interest the free time spent on the task *after* the incentives have been withdrawn; in business settings, however, the purpose of incentives is to motivate people to work hard *while* the incentives are in effect. Second, studies have shown that the effect of incentives using the Deci experimental paradigm depends on whether there is high initial interest in the task. If initial

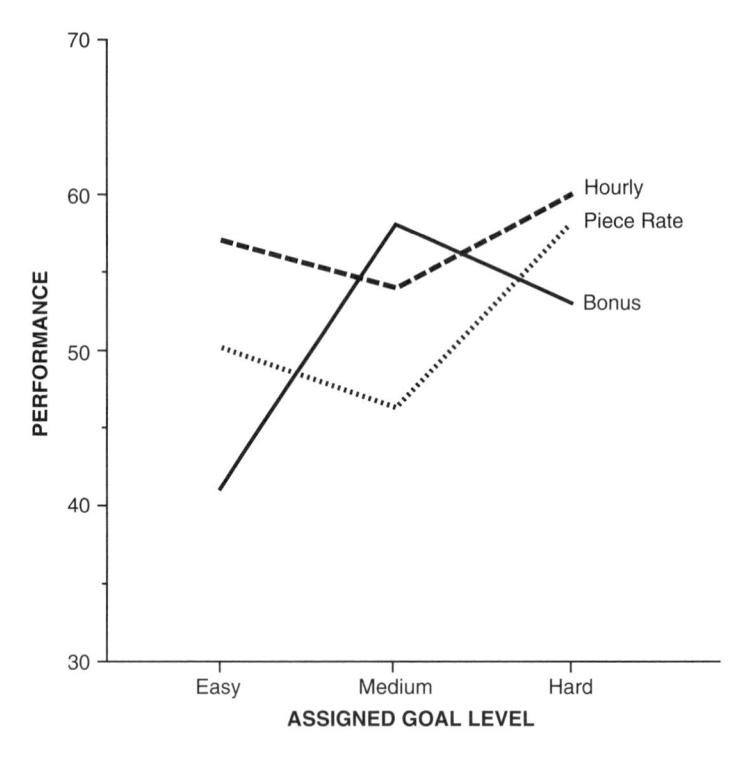

Figure 3 The effect of goals and type of incentive on performance (based on Lee, Locke, & Phan, in press; second of two trials).

interest is high, incentives do not lower interest (Bandura, 1986). Third, the effect of incentives depends on whether or not they are framed as payments for excellent performance, that is, competence (see below). Such forms of payment can raise self-efficacy and subsequently enhance interest. Fourth, an explanation for Deci and Ryan's original findings remains elusive. They theorized that incentive schemes lower interest because, or to the extent that, they undermine the needs for autonomy and competence; but mediator studies have not been done to verify this explanation using free time spent on the task as the criterion. On the other hand, Bandura (1986, 1997) has shown that self-efficacy, which is closely related to the idea of competence but not part of Deci's model, is a critical element in the development of task interest.

The most recent meta-analysis of the "Deci effect" (Eisenberger & Cameron, 1996), reveals that using free time spent on the task as the dependent variable, rewards only undermined motivation, that is, reduced time spent on the task, when the rewards were: tangible, expected (i.e., announced in advance), and independent of performance (i.e., pay for taking part rather than for attainment). All other combinations had either no detrimental effect (e.g., pay for attainment) or a beneficial effect (verbal recognition or praise) on subsequent interest. Using attitudes (e.g., expressed task interest) as the dependent variable revealed no detrimental effect of rewards and beneficial effects for verbal rewards and for tangible rewards based on normative attainments. These results indicate that rewards are not inherently de-motivating even after they have been taken away.

To convince people that challenging goals are *possible to reach or at least approach*, it is necessary to induce high self-efficacy. Bandura (1986, 1997) identifies four methods that can be used to do this: increase enactive mastery through training, guided instruction and practice; show effective role models who are similar to the focal persons (or use self-modeling); persuade the focal persons that they are capable by giving plausible reasons why they can excel; or show people how to interpret their physiological tension in a favorable way, for example, "I have lots of energy." Leader confidence in new subordinates can have significant effect on follower performance (Eden, 1990). In addition, people can be taught various meta-cognitive or thought control skills such as how to interpret their past performance difficulties in a positive way such as that knowledge and skill are not fixed but acquirable.

There is no simple relationship between effort or ability attributions as such and subsequent performance. What is critical is whether the attributions made raise or lower self-efficacy (Bandura, 1997). Mone and Baker (1992) and Thomas and Mathieu (1994) found that self-efficacy increases when past success is attributed to stable causes but does not increase if it is attributed to unstable causes. Conversely, self-efficacy decreases when failure is attributed to stable causes but not when it is attributed to unstable causes, the latter presumably being controllable. Positive mood inductions also can raise efficacy (Baron, 1990). Finally, people can be taught to think through detailed plans for implementing their goals (e.g., Gollwitzer, Heckhausen, & Ratajczak, 1990), a procedure which presumably increases their confidence in being able to attain them.

Goal setting theory ties in nicely with VIE theory in the realm of commitment in that people are most likely to commit themselves to goals which they think they can attain (in agreement with social-cognitive theory) and which are perceived as leading to the attainment of valued outcomes (Hollenbeck & Klein, 1990), which implies that the goals are important.

I must add here that the determinants of goal commitment are fundamentally the same as the determinants of goal choice. People choose high goals when they believe that high performance is important and that they can achieve or approach it (Locke & Latham, 1990).

Subordinate participation in goal setting

Few issues in the history of psychology have been as controversial as that regarding the value of employee participation in decision making (Locke & Schweiger, 1979; Locke, Alavi, & Wagner, 1997). The reason is that some have regarded participation as a moral imperative which must be used regardless of the consequences, whereas others view it as a scientific question. The scientific assumption is that participation enhances motivation, especially commitment, by giving subordinates a sense of "ownership" in the decisions which affect them. Objective analyses, including meta-analyses of the participation literature, however, reveal that it is not a very robust phenomenon in terms of its effects on performance and attitudes (Locke et al., 1997), especially when r-r designs, that is, those studies which correlate self-reports of participation with self-reports of performance or satisfaction and thus which may inflate the correlations, are eliminated from the analyses (Wagner & Gooding, 1987). In the goal setting domain, the results are no more consistent. Participation in has very marginal effects on goal commitment and performance as compared to simply telling people what goal to pursue (assigned; Locke et al., 1997; Locke & Latham, 1990). The exception is that if goals are assigned in a very curt fashion with no explanation of the rationale for the goals, commitment and performance do drop (Latham, Erez, & Locke, 1988). Basically, assigned, participative (joint) and self (i.e., delegated) goal-setting are all effective as compared to not setting specific goals (Locke & Latham, 1990), although most employees may be less likely to set extreme "stretch" goals for themselves than are charismatic leaders who may inspire their followers to perform beyond expectations (Bass, 1985).

We have found that the real value of subordinate participation in decision making is not motivational (i.e., commitment-enhancing) but cognitive (i.e., knowledge enhancing). That is, by seeking subordinate input, supervisors or managers can gain knowledge that they would not otherwise have and thus be able to make higher quality decisions than they would be able to make alone. There is increasing evidence that subordinate knowledge and insight can be valuable for the purpose of developing better task strategies (Durham, Knight, & Locke, 1997; Latham, Winters, & Locke, 1994), assuming that subordinates have or can discover relevant knowledge which the supervisor lacks (Scully, Kirkpatrick, & Locke, 1995). Locke and associates (1997) have recently reconceptualized participation as a knowledge-exchange device.

Ability

Ability, of course, has a direct effect on performance, although this may be partly or wholly mediated by self-efficacy (Bandura, 1986, 1996). There is some, although not conclusive, evidence that ability and goals may interact to boost performance (Locke & Latham, 1990). In other words, high goals may enhance the benefits of high ability or high ability may enhance the effects of high goals.

Task complexity

Wood, Mento, and Locke (1987) found that goal effects were larger on simple tasks than on complex tasks. The reasons, as implied earlier, are that (a) on complex tasks and even some simple but multi-path tasks (e.g., Audia et al., 1996), the issue of effective strategies is usually more critical than on simple tasks since there are many more possible paths to the goal—some of which work much better than others; (b) goals do not always lead people to choose the best strategies, especially, as noted earlier, on new, complex tasks for which there is no training and high pressure to perform.

Self-regulation

Although in work settings and many, though not all, laboratory studies, goals are assigned or set participatively with a supervisor or manager, there is substantial evidence that with or even without training, goals are or can be used by individuals to manage themselves. Frayne and Latham (1987) and Latham and Frayne (1989) used self-management training to help employees reduce their own absenteeism. Self goal-setting was one of several components in the training program. Other components included self-feedback, self-commitment, and problem-solving. Gist, Bavetta, and Stevens (1990) and Gist, Stevens, and Bavetta (1991) successfully trained people to gain and retain salary negotiation skills. Again self goal-setting was one of the components. In the real world, of course, people set goals for themselves all the time, including long-term goals. For example, in the AT&T 25-year managerial progress study (Howard & Bray, 1988) personal ambition predicted how many levels the managers would be promoted. The key component of the ambition measure was a one-item question asking the managers how many levels ahead they wanted to get (A. Howard, personal communication). Incidentally, TAT measures in this study, after new data were added and scoring errors in the original analysis corrected, were only minimally related to managerial progress.

Goals as mediators of personality, values, and incentives

In 1968, based on Mace (1935), I suggested that goals could mediate the effects of incentives on performance. In 1991, I suggested that goals might also mediate the effects of needs and values, including personality, on performance. In that paper (Locke, 1991), I further indicated that self-efficacy (based on Bandura, 1986) should be an added mediator. I called the combination of goals and self-efficacy the "motivation hub"—a hub being where the action is. I argued that goals, assuming there was goal commitment, and self-efficacy were the most immediate, situationally and task-specific, conscious, motivational determinants of action and the mechanisms through which other incentives operated. These two variables represent what you are trying to do and whether you think you can do it. This model did not deal with subconscious motivation which could, of course, affect action independently of these conscious determinants. The model assumed that ability, knowledge, and skill were important but were not included since it was only a motivational model. The social psychology intention models, incidentally, use intentions and self-efficacy, or their equivalent, as immediate predictors (Ajzen, 1991).

It is only in recent years that the beginnings of a real body of research relevant to the mediation issue began to emerge (see Locke, in press, for a summary). Previously, we had found that the effect of feedback or knowledge of results were mediated by goals (Locke & Latham, 1990). Also there was some evidence that to the extent that participation in decision making did affect the motivation to perform, it did so through its effects on goal commitment (Erez, Earley, & Hulin, 1985) and/or self-efficacy (Latham, Erez, & Locke, 1988). More recently we found that job enrichment, that is, increased responsibility, was mediated through goals (Kirkpatrick, 1992), and that charismatic leadership, specifically, leader vision, was mediated through its effects on followers' performance goals and self-efficacy (Kirkpatrick & Locke, 1996). Other studies have found that the effects of assigned goals are mediated through self-set goals and self-efficacy (Locke, in press).

Money incentives

It is well established that both individual and group incentives systems, when properly designed, motivate higher productivity (Kopelman, 1986). However, Lee, Locke, and Phan (in press) found that the effects of various types of money incentives, for example, piece-rate versus bonus, were fully mediated by self-set goals and self-efficacy—that is, the incentives motivated performance through their effects on the goals subject set in response to them and their degree of confidence. Mediation effects of incentives have also been found by others (e.g., Wright, 1989).

Personality

The largest number of mediation studies to date have been done with respect to personality. Although personality traits are not strongly related to work performance, meta-analyses indicate that there are consistent effects of some "big 5" dimensions on work performance, especially conscientiousness (Barrick & Mount, 1991). Thus far, eight different studies have found that self-set goals and self-efficacy partially or fully mediated the effects of personality traits on performance (Locke, in press). For example, Lerner and Locke (1995) found that the effect of sports competitiveness on sit-up performance was completely mediated by these two variables. Similarly, Gellatly (1996) found that the effects of conscientiousness on the performance of an arithmetic task was fully mediated by expectancy (actually a self-efficacy measure) and personal (actually self-set) goals. This result is shown in Figure 4. These two laboratory studies were complemented by a field study of sales representatives by Barrick, Mount, and Strauss (1993). Goals and goal commitment partially mediated the effects of conscientiousness and sales; self-efficacy was not measured.

Note that I have not mentioned need theories, such as Maslow's need hierarchy theory, in this discussion. Although people are born with needs (Locke, McClear,

CONSCIENTIOUSNESS AND PERFORMANCE

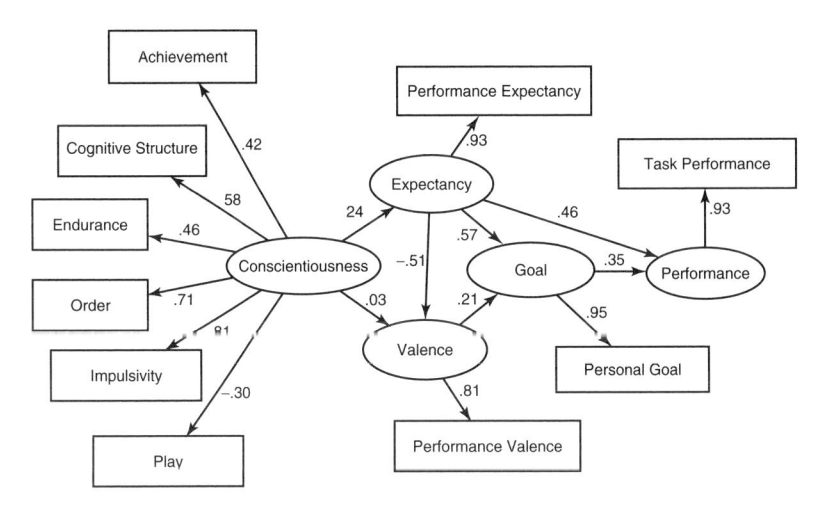

Figure 4 Mediation of the relationship of personality to performance by goals and self-efficacy (from Gellattly, 1996; copyright by American Psychological Association).

& Knight, 1996), there is no evidence that they are born with any built-in need hierarchy or that one could use Maslow's theory to make any predictions regarding job performance (Locke, 1976, 1991). Although needs do motivate action, there are many steps between the existence of needs or the experience of need deprivation and action, including: discovering what your needs are, discovering how to satisfy them, allocating priorities among them, finding the time and resources to satisfy them (or anticipate them) and taking specific actions in specific situations in order to fulfill them. Very little can be predicted from simply knowing that a person has a need or even that a need has been frustrated, because there are many possible reactions to need deprivation and many alternative paths to the satisfaction or attempted satisfaction of most needs. Certainly one can predict that all surviving civilizations will find a way to produce and store food, but this is a long way from predicting what a given individual will do to get nourishment on a given day in a given circumstance.

Affect

Brain disorders and hormonal imbalances aside, *emotions* are the form in which we experience automatic, subconscious appraisals of objects, actions, events, ideas or actions according to the standard of our explicit or implicit values (Locke, 1976; Locke & Latham, 1990). The *appraisal theory* of emotions was first presented in philosophy by Rand (1964, though conceptualized earlier) and in psychology by

Arnold (1960) and later by Lazarus (Lazarus & Folkman, 1984). Only Rand (1964) explicitly identified the fact that the appraisal process involves values or more specifically, value judgments. Emotions, of course, also involve stored conceptual and perceptual knowledge, for example, before you can fear a bear you have to perceive that it exists and has the potential to harm you. Every emotion is the result of a particular type of value appraisal, for example, guilt: you have violated a moral value; anxiety: there is a future threat to your well being; anger: someone took an action they should not have taken; love: some object or person is an important value, and so forth. The emotion of satisfaction is the result of the appraisal: I got or have what I wanted. All emotions are a form of implicit psychological measurement, namely, this object, event or person to some degree furthers or threatens my values, including the value I place on myself. For the application of appraisal theory to job satisfaction see Locke (1976).

Goals and affect

Goals are the specific form of values. For example, if I value ambition, I may set a goal to get promoted to the next position. If I value improvement in my knowledge or being a good student, I may set a goal to get a 3.8 GPA. Achieving specific goals is the means to attaining values. The same is true, incidentally, in the realm of moral values and virtues. How does one attain the virtue of honesty? By resolving to be honest in each and every situation one encounters—although there are exceptions, such as when one is confronted by a criminal (Locke & Woiceshyn, 1995).

Thus performance goals are at the same time ends to aim for and standards by which to judge one's performance (Bandura, 1986; Locke & Latham, 1990). These are not two separate estimates or motivational elements but two sides of the same coin. To commit to and try for a goal *means* to consider the attainment of that goal to be desirable and the failure to attain it undesirable; therefore, reaching the goal leads to satisfaction and not reaching it produces dissatisfaction (Lewin, 1958).

Given this, it is obvious that there must be a strong relationship between frequency of success in attaining goals and satisfaction with performance—which there is (Locke & Latham, 1990). However, a number of interesting theoretical puzzles arise here. For example, high goals lead to *less* performance satisfaction than easy goals. This may seem paradoxical but Figure 5 reveals the explanation. Easy goals set the satisfaction "bar" at a low level; thus, attaining the goal is satisfying and attaining a performance level higher than the goal is even more satisfying. Hard goals set the "bar" much higher. For people with high goals, reaching the easy goal level produces dissatisfaction, and reaching the hard goal level turns dissatisfaction into satisfaction, but not as much satisfaction as for the easy goal people who, if they perform at this level, have greatly exceeded their goals. (For empirical data, see Mento, Locke, & Klein, 1992.)

One might ask in view of this, why hard goals are more motivating than easy goals if they provide less performance satisfaction. The answer is implicit in the

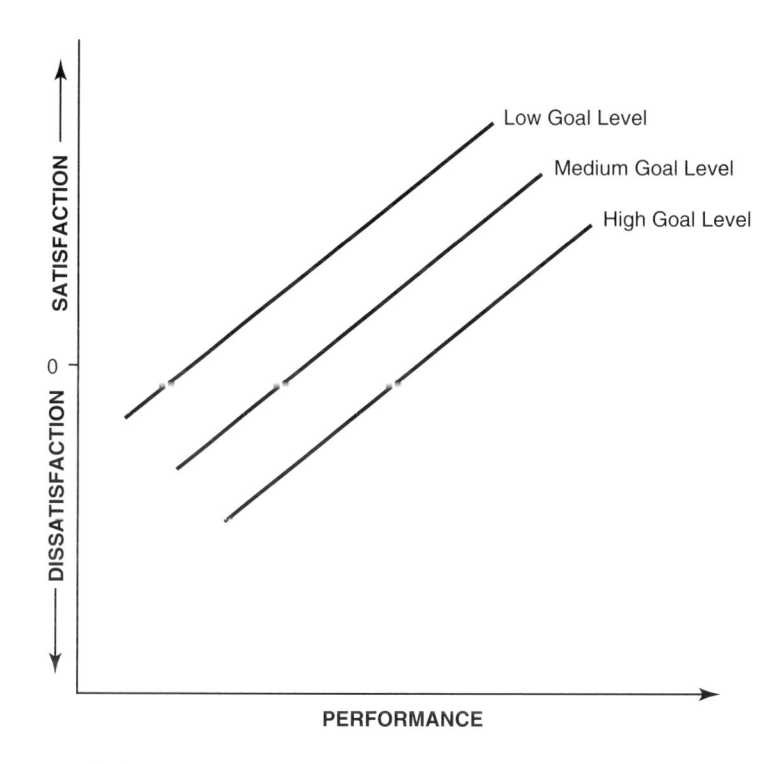

Figure 5 Relationship of goal level (difficulty) and performance to satisfaction.

question; it is *because* people with high goals demand more of themselves in order to feel satisfied that they need to strive harder than people with easy goals.

The obvious question arises here as to why everyone doesn't set easy goals and feel good with minimal effort. There are two answers to this: (a) in life, the greatest rewards, for example, best salaries, most challenging jobs, go to those who achieve the most; thus in VIE theory terms, high goals are more instrumental than low goals (Mento *et al.*, 1992), and (b) people choose goals based, in part, on their self-concept or ideal self, the kind of person they want to be. Thus they would say: settling for less just isn't me. That's not how I see myself or my life. The two answers, of course, are not unrelated. The self-concept can involve specific outcomes which one plans to achieve.

Satisfaction is not only a matter of the number of successes in relation to the goal and the level of the goal (Locke & Latham, 1990). Satisfaction can also be affected by more than one goal or standard, for example, the goal for this trial, and also progress in relation to an end goal; changes in standards over time; the trajectory of performance (is it improving or not?); the importance of the goal or how is it tied into deeper values such as achievement and life success and important needs such as self-esteem; the degree of deviation above or below the standard; and causal attributions, for example, was success or failure caused by me or someone else? Thomas and Mathieu (1994), for example, found that satisfaction with success was experienced only if the success was attributed to the self.

Other job values

Satisfaction with the job is not solely a function of perceived degree of success in meeting performance goals. Several other work motivation theories identify job values other than task success. Hackman and Oldham's (1980) *job characteristics theory* asserts that work attributes such as: variety, feedback, personal importance of the work, autonomy and responsibility, and identity (a whole piece of work) foster job satisfaction. The integrating theme across these attributes can be called job scope or job challenge. There is strong evidence supporting the relationship of the above dimensions to job satisfaction (Locke & Henne, 1986; Stone, 1986). The relationship tends to be stronger for those who place greater value on growth (Oldham, 1996).

Another theory relevant to job satisfaction is *equity theory*. Equity pertains to the value of fairness or justice, especially in administering rewards. Adams' (1965) theory of equity focuses on the effect of *distributive justice*, specifically the ratio of the focal person's outputs, for example, wages, to inputs, for example, performance, as compared to the ratios of comparison others. People feel dissatisfied when they believe that rewards have been distributed unjustly.

In recent years, another justice theory has gained popularity. This theory focuses on *procedural justice* (Greenberg, 1987, 1993)—the degree to which people think the process by which decisions were made and the way in which organizational members interact with them is fair. Perceptions of procedural fairness are based upon such criteria as: non-bias, accuracy, consistency, trust, and feedback (Leventhal, 1980; Tyler, 1989; Tyler & Lind, 1992). There is strong evidence that perceptions of procedural justice influence job satisfaction (McFarlin & Sweeney, 1992).

A recent meta-analysis by Brockner and Wiesenfeld (1996) revealed that distributive and procedural justice have an interactive effect on satisfaction. This is shown in Figure 6. The key result is that people are most dissatisfied when both distributive and procedural justice are low. If distributive justice is high, people are not affected by procedural issues and, if procedural justice is high, people are not upset by distributive problems. The interesting point here is that high procedural justice can compensate for low distributive justice but not vice versa. This brings up, of course, a puzzling question: how can a fair process lead to an unfair outcome? This question is obviously worth further study. One answer may be: through honest error.

Although virtually everyone claims to value fairness and justice, different people and cultures may have different conceptions of what fairness consists of and this

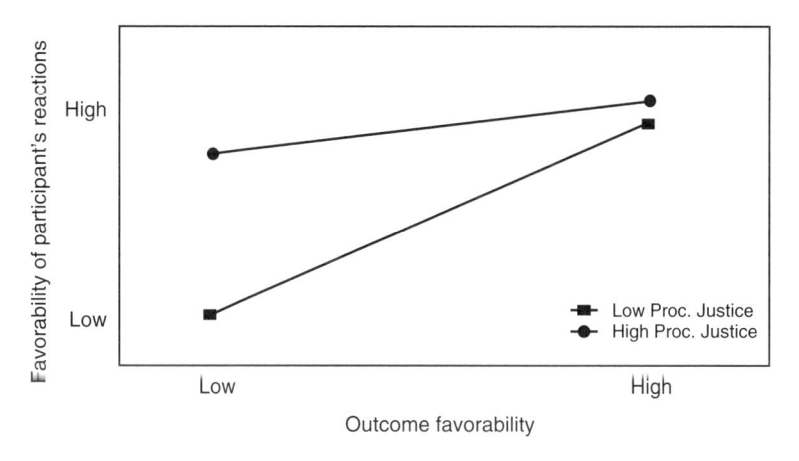

Figure 6 Relationship of outcome favorability and procedural justice to participant reactions (from Brockner & Wiesenfeld, 1996; copyright by American Psychological Association).

is a source of organizational conflict—not to mention political conflict. Union-management conflict is just one example.

There are other factors affecting satisfaction which do not fall clearly under the mantle of any particular theory; although *VIE theory* (Vroom, 1964), since it does not specify any particular value content but contends that satisfaction occurs when people see their actions and choices as instrumental in attaining their values, can accommodate any content. VIE theory can be viewed as a type of consciously calculated, as opposed to automatic, subconscious, appraisal: if you get what you want, you are happy. There are, of course, limits to this principle; people who seek irrational values, for example, dope addiction, do not attain happiness (Locke, 1976). Theories of person-job "fit" are compatible with VIE theory and Locke's (1976) theory in asserting that jobs which match the employee's values are most likely to bring satisfaction (Kristof, 1996). Job attributes such as: competent and honest leadership, considerate supervision, job security, fringe benefits, congenial and competent coworkers, pleasant surroundings, good equipment, convenient location and safety are commonly held values, which when attained, contribute to job satisfaction.

Affect and dispositions

Job satisfaction is not solely a function of the perceived job in relation to one's job values. There are deeper causal factors involved, specifically *personal dispositions* or traits. We discussed these above as predictors of performance; here we are concerned with their relation to job and life satisfaction. The traits of positive and negative affectivity have been the most frequently discussed dispositional traits, especially the latter (Watson & Clark, 1984). Negative affectivity has been treated as equivalent to neuroticism. Positive affectivity is less clearly understood, but has sometimes been viewed as extroversion and at other times as positive mood on a mood scale such as the positive and negative affectivity scale (PANAS) (Watson, Clark, & Tellegen, 1988).

Recently, Judge, Locke, and Durham (1997) conceptualized positive affectivity as involving such traits as: self-esteem, generalized (not task-specific) efficacy, locus of control and optimism. In the most extensive study to date of dispositions in relation to job attitudes, Judge, Locke, and Durham (1997) measured these and other dispositions (e.g., neuroticism, trust in others, benevolent versus malevolent world view) using both self-reports and reports of significant others. They found that a bi-polar factor focused around the theme of self-esteem, generalized (not task-specific) efficacy and internal locus of control versus neuroticism and had strong direct and indirect effects on job satisfaction in two cultures. The indirect effect was through the relation of dispositions to the perception of job attributes. Those with high self-esteem were more likely to see the job as possessing Hackman and Oldham's (1980) core work attributes (e.g., variety, autonomy) than those with low self-esteem. Trust in others' and one's world view had no effect on job or life satisfaction over and above that attributable to self-esteem. It is worth considering, in this context, whether one's view of others and the world is shaped fundamentally by one's view of oneself. Do people who like themselves and have confidence in their ability to function in the world thereby assume, at least in a free country, that the world is a benevolent place where values are achievable and that other people are a source of pleasure rather than a threat? Do people who believe they are unworthy and inefficacious thereby conclude that the world is a dangerous place and that other people will hurt them? These are fascinating questions worthy of future study.

Moods

Moods are enduring emotional states. Clearly, they can be an aspect of dispositions (Williams, 1990). For example, neuroticism entails enduring negative emotions as one of its defining components. Unless one gets counseling or medication, such moods can last indefinitely or recur in frequent cycles. Moods, however, can also result from such enduring life circumstances as health, finances, family, work. An enduring work situation would involve job conditions which one likes; namely, a competent, honest and inspiring boss, challenging work, or dislikes; for example, an unpleasant, inconsiderate boss whom one cannot avoid, work that has no personal meaning or interest. These types of moods would change either when the job situation changed or the person developed a different way of appraising it, namely, my boss is a jerk so I'll just try to ignore him. Shorter-term moods can result from single events which produce conflict that is not resolved, for example, an argument with one's spouse that ends in an impasse or harsh words.

Other attitudes

There is a consistent, strong relationship between job satisfaction and *organizational commitment*, which involves the desire to remain with and accept the goals of the organization (Locke & Latham, 1990). There is some debate over the issue of which causes which, but I believe that the main causal sequence is: satisfaction → commitment, the argument being that you commit yourself to an organization because you are getting what you want from it and presumably expect to do so in the future.

Job involvement

Job involvement is defined as psychological identification with one's work and is correlated highly with both job satisfaction and organizational commitment. However, unlike commitment which is related to subsequent action such as turnover, involvement shows little relationship to actions on the job (Brown, 1996), although one study has shown it to be related to effort (Brown & Leigh, 1996). Thus involvement may best be viewed, in terms of its effects, primarily as a psychological expression or correlate of satisfaction. Locke (1976) argued that involvement was the result of viewing one's job as important, which can be tied to the values and personality people bring to the job (Brown, 1996), but that does not preclude its being affected by job experiences.

Stress and affect

Stress is a particular type of value appraisal, focused around the emotion of anxiety. Thus stress results from the experience of threat (Lazarus & Folkman, 1984; Locke & Taylor, 1990). Threat is experienced when an important value is at stake and one has low self-efficacy, that is, when one lacks confidence in one's ability to control the external situation and/or one's negative thoughts about it (Bandura, 1986, 1997). The most common causes of stress on the job seem to be: time pressure and lack of job security (Sandman, 1992). Although stress is axiomatically unpleasant, stress scales typically load on a different factor than job satisfaction scales (Sandman, 1992), indicating that people can distinguish between not getting what they want and being threatened with conditions they cannot control.

The consequences of affect

The next question we must address is: given that people experience a certain emotion on the job, then what? Industrial-organizational psychologists have tried desperately to show that job satisfaction was beneficial because it lead to high productivity, but in study after study, this hypothesis has been shown to be false (e.g., Podsakoff & Williams, 1986). This does not mean that emotions have no relationship to action, but rather that the satisfaction-productivity hypothesis is too simple.

Emotions, by their nature, contain an implicit action tendency (Arnold, 1960). The tendency is to approach, protect or keep objects appraised as beneficial and to avoid objects appraised as harmful. But this is only a tendency or felt urge. People have the power to override their impulses and avoid things they like, for example, cigarettes, and to approach things they fear, for example, combat, statistics classes, when they are rationally convinced that such a course of action is to their ultimate benefit. Man is not pre-programmed, like the lower animals, to blindly follow his impulses. He has the power to think (Binswanger, 1991) and to decide whether or not to act in response to an emotion and, if he decides to act, he has the power to decide what action to take (Locke & Kristof, 1996). Furthermore, there are many subtle variants on approach and avoidance which reflect the human capacity for creative thought.

There are six major classes of response to job satisfaction and/or dissatisfaction (Fisher & Locke, 1992). Responses to dissatisfaction, of course, are the more interesting and relevant because the usual response to satisfaction is to keep things as they were, although success or satiation can lead to the search for new challenges.

1. *Approach or avoidance of the job.* In line with the inherent action tendencies involved, people stay on jobs they like and leave jobs they dislike. The most reliable effect of job dissatisfaction on action is turnover (Horn, Caranikas-Walker, Prussia, & Griffeth, 1992). However, turnover is not automatic. If the individual makes a decision to act on his dissatisfaction based on all factors he considers relevant, for example, financial condition, job alternatives, he forms an intent to quit which is the more direct precursor of actually quitting (Horn *et al.*, 1992). An intention, a determination to act in a certain way, is of course, the equivalent of a goal. Self-efficacy affects such determinations (Ajzen, 1991) as well as having a direct effect on actions such as job search (Bandura, 1997). Organizational commitment is often a better predictor of turnover than satisfaction, being logically closer in meaning to the intention to quit. Temporary avoidance is possible through absenteeism, though this choice may be constrained by organizational controls. Transfers may be requested if the problem is with the particular job rather than the company.

2. *Approach or avoidance of the work.* The work is only one, albeit the most central, aspect of a job. People may attempt to avoid doing the actual work by coming late, taking long breaks or doing things other than the work, for example, talking, reading, chatting on phone. They may become passive and fail to show initiative. Farrell (1983) calls this neglect. On the other side of the coin, people may come early, work through lunch and take work home. Obviously, satisfaction is not the whole story here. Peoples' work habits also depend on their values, personality and ambition as well as their enjoyment of the work. People who dislike their work do not always avoid it; for example, they may see the work as a stepping stone to promotion to a better job at a later date; they may view it as a point of honor to do

a conscientious job; or they may work hard because they need the money and do not want to be fired.

3. *Constructive helping or attempts to change the situation.* Satisfied employees are more likely to engage in organizational "citizenship" behaviors which better the organization such as helping co-workers, paying attention to customers, and passing along information (Organ, 1988). When employees are unhappy, and especially when they perceive themselves to be the victims of distributive or procedural injustice, there is a desire to remedy the situation. There are many possible ways to do this. The simplest is to complain to the boss and attempt to convince the boss to correct the problem. This failing, the employees can appeal to higher levels of the organization. This is made easier if the organization has effective, formal "voice" mechanisms, for example, appeal or grievance procedures. When such procedures are in place, organizational turnover is lower (Spencer, 1986). Employees may also solve problems by changing themselves, for example, getting more education or training to increase their chances of promotion.

If attempts to improve the situation fail, the employee may move to other, more extreme, categories of actions. One possibility is to become more aggressive. An example would be taking legal action (e.g., a lawsuit), an increasingly popular remedy in the United States. Lawsuits often have a joint purpose: to remedy the wrong or get compensation for it and to punish the wrong doer.

4. *Aggressive or vengeful actions.* If an employee decides that redress is impossible, an alternative is simply to get even. Depending on the employees' preferences and moral scruples, retaliatory action may involve: theft, vandalism, sabotage, lying, leaking unsavory information to the press, giving away or selling company secrets to competitors, or undermining morale (starting rumors, badmouthing managers).

5. *Defiance.* Whereas vengeful actions are motivated by the desire to harm the organization, defiant actions, such as disobeying orders, flouting rules and regulations, skipping meetings, failing to follow instructions, talking back and the like are more likely to be motivated by the desire to assert oneself, not be pushed around, or to get even on a more quid pro quo basis: if you're not nice to me, then I won't help you out.

6. *Psychological adjustment.* Sometimes no overt action is taken in response to job dissatisfaction. The employee may not know what to do or have the nerve to do it or may not think action is appropriate. Adjustment may involve changing one's aspirations or values to match organizational realities, for example, lowering one's promotion or pay goals. It may also involve suppression of feelings and even psychological dissociation from the job, thereby making it unimportant. In more extreme cases, it could mean alcohol and drug abuse to mask painful emotions. Those who can afford it may seek psychological counseling.

It must be stressed that all the actions noted above may be taken for reasons other than job dissatisfaction. An employee may quit not because he dislikes the present job but because another job is more in line with his long-term goals. Another may steal because he wants unearned benefits, or he may defy his boss for reasons of poor mental health, for example, repressed anger at his father.

It remains, however, to explain, in those cases where dissatisfaction does lead to action, how employees choose among the various alternatives? This issue has not been studied very much to date, so what follows is somewhat speculative. It can be safely assumed that many factors come into play. Moral values are one factor. Some people will steal with little or no provocation and others will not, even under extreme provocation. Another factor is personality. Extroverts may be more likely to engage in organizational citizenship behavior than introverts. People with high self-esteem may feel more deserving of satisfaction than those with low self-esteem and therefore be more prone to take action to attain it. At the task-specific level, people with high self-efficacy for a certain type of action, for example, protesting to the boss, will be more likely to take that action than those with low self-efficacy. Organizations which have a reputation for just dealings and well-publicized appeal mechanisms are likely to encourage more constructive protest than those with a reputation for cavalier or unjust treatment.

The integrated model

Figure 7 presents an integrated model which ties together the essential findings and theories described above. It must be stressed that *the model in this figure is not speculative but is, with one exception, entirely empirical.* The key concepts are in solid rectangles and the key causal connections are noted with arrows accompanied by numbers. The key relevant theories are in the dotted rectangles; the main spheres of application of each theory are shown with dotted arrows. Each causal arrow is described briefly below.

1. Needs to values. This is the least empirically researched of the causal connections. Although motivation must start with needs, that is, the objective requirements of the organism's survival and well-being, how work values grow out of needs has not been studied. Although Maslow was partly correct in claiming that people value what they need, there are numerous exceptions to this claim. These exceptions, of course, are one of the reasons why we need both a science of mental health and a code of ethics.
2. Values and personality to satisfaction. This pertains to the relation of self-esteem and neuroticism to job perceptions and job satisfaction.
3. Values and personality to goals and self-efficacy. Values and personality affect goals and self-efficacy and their effects on performance are mediated by goals and efficacy.
4. Incentives to goals and self-efficacy. Like personality, incentives affect goals and self-efficacy which in turn mediate the effects of incentives.

5. Self-efficacy to goals. Efficacy affects goal choice and especially goal difficulty.
6. and 7. Self-efficacy and goals to mechanisms. Goals and efficacy affect performance through their effects on direction, effort, persistence, and task strategies or tactics.
8. Goals, that is, goal mechanisms, to performance. Goals, especially goal difficulty, affect performance and performance, depending on the organization's policies, affects rewards.
9. Goal moderators. Goal effects are enhanced by feedback, commitment, ability, and (low) task complexity.
10. Performance to efficacy. Performance, including the attributions one makes for performance, affects self-efficacy.
11. Performance to satisfaction. Success and rewards produce satisfaction.
12. Work characteristics to satisfaction. Mental challenge and related job attributes enhance satisfaction.
13. Organizational policies to satisfaction. The perceived fairness of the organization's policies, procedural justice, and the perceived fairness of the results of these policies, distributive justice, affect satisfaction.
14. Satisfaction to involvement. Job satisfaction enhances job involvement.
15. Satisfaction to organizational commitment. Satisfaction enhances organizational commitment.
16. and 16a. Satisfaction and commitment to action. Satisfaction and commitment, along with other factors, affect action, especially approach and avoidance of the job or work. Several limitations of this model should be noted:

- To limit cognitive-perceptual overload some causal arrows are omitted. For example, self-efficacy affects commitment and presumably choices among action alternatives in the face of dissatisfaction. Personality and values can also affect action taken in response to job dissatisfaction. Perceived injustice undoubtedly affects goal commitment.
- The various theories, aside from goal theory, are not fully elaborated. For example, there are many complexities involved in procedural justice and a number of competing sub-theories.
- Recursive effects are not shown, except in the case of self-efficacy to performance. In the real world, almost any output can become an input over time.
- The model is static, not dynamic. Mone (1994) has done dynamic analyses of the goal-efficacy-performance relationship and found the basic static model to hold.

- Ability, knowledge and skill are critical to performance but, with one exception, are not shown in the motivation model. Self-efficacy, of course, reflects how people assess their skills and abilities.
- The model focuses on conscious motivation and omits the subconscious, except insofar as it is acknowledged as being involved in emotions.
- The model does not include theories with dubious or highly limited support (e.g., Maslow, Deci).

Despite these limitations, it is clear we have sufficient empirical data to make possible the beginnings of a model of work motivation—a model that explains both performance and affect and that includes a variety of theoretical perspectives. Nevertheless, there is much more to be done, especially with respect to: the role of needs, the effect of the subconscious on action, and the integration of the various theories with each other.

Although I regard needs, defined as requirements of health and well being, as a critical concept both in biology and psychology, we know very little about how needs give rise to specific action choices. The issue is complex because there are different types of needs, for example, physical and psychological, and because many possible steps can occur between the experience of need frustration and response. These include need identification, appraisal of the meaning of the need, specification of action alternatives, assessment of alternatives, choice of action, including the choice not to act, suppression, defense mechanisms, and so forth. Knowledge, values, goals, and the subconscious all come into play. Furthermore, all action is not a response to need frustration; much human action is anticipatory in nature. No existing theory comes close to dealing with all of these complexities.

With respect to the subconscious, I cannot agree with Freud that we are dominated by fictional, unconscious entities like the id. (By subconscious, I mean "in consciousness but not now in focal awareness, though capable of entering awareness." This is closer in meaning to Freud's concept of the preconscious than to his concept of the unconscious which to him meant "not capable of entering awareness.") There is no evidence that man possesses any unconscious instincts (inborn, goal-directed desires). If men were the instinct-driven brutes that Freud claimed, the human race would have become extinct long ago. It was the part of the personality that Freud most neglected, the ego, that is, man's rational faculty, that made possible man's climb from the swamps to the stars. Nevertheless, it is obvious that people are not always fully conscious of what they are doing and why—that is a major reason why they have problems with their own psychology and with their own lives. Introspection is, after all, a volitional act (Binswanger, 1991) and many people do not bother to do it, and those who do, do not always do it well. The problem, as noted earlier, has always been, and still is, how to measure subconscious premises and motives accurately.

As to theoretical integration, one might argue that reality is complex and that we will need more and more specific theories to deal with different aspects of

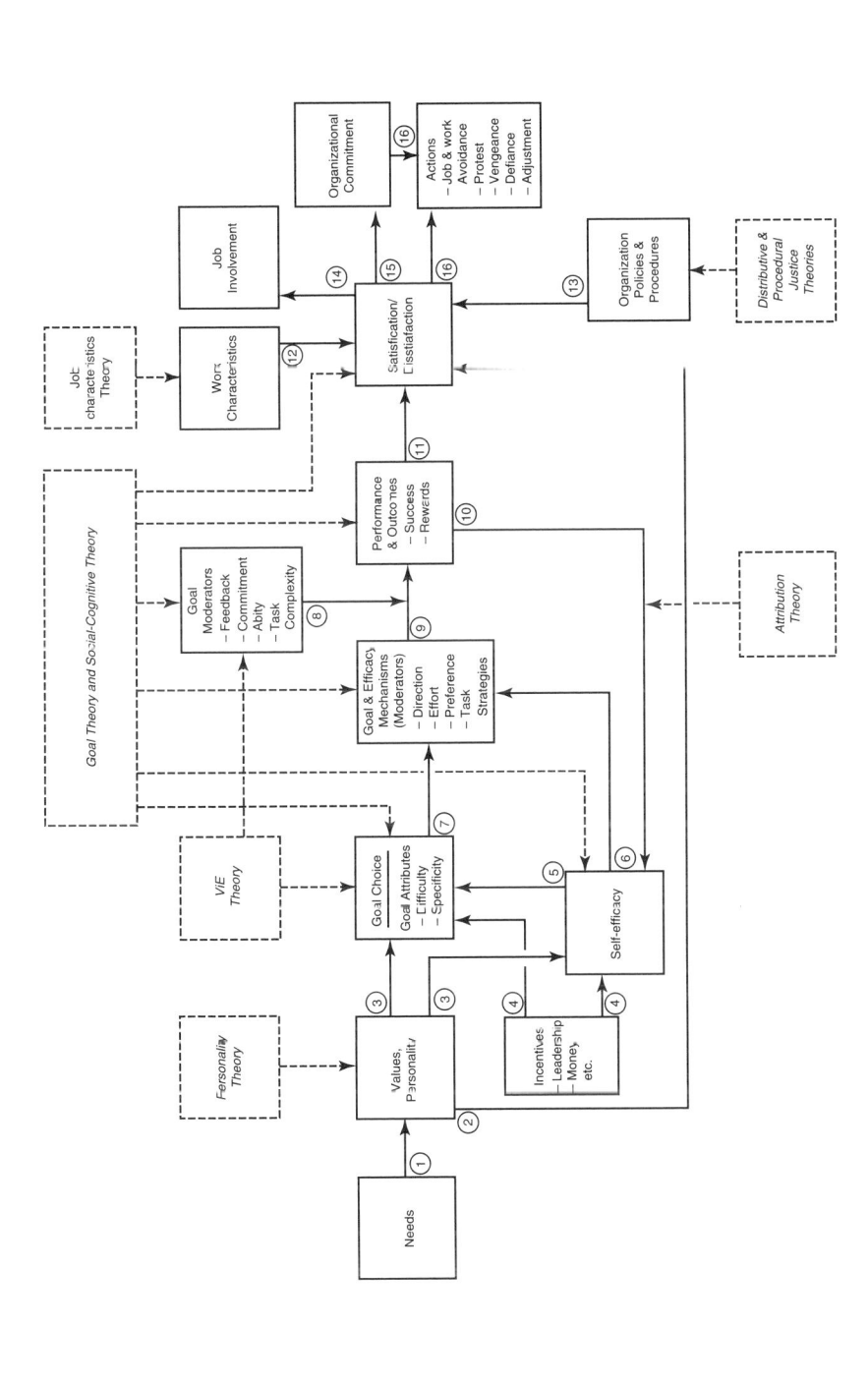

Figure 7 The integrated model of work motivation.

the motivation process. Thus some may argue that rather than seeking theoretical integration we should seek more theoretical proliferation. If you look, for example, at biology, every new discovery seems to entail new mechanisms and increased complexity. Theoretical proliferation, *if* the theories are valid, reflects the discovery of new knowledge. Actually we need *both* proliferation and integration. When the time comes to predict the specific actions people will take at work and the specific reactions they will have in response to various conditions of work, we will need to have some method of putting all the pieces together.

All these problems and others will provide enormous challenges for researchers in the realm of work motivation for decades to come.

Acknowledgment

Preparation of this manuscript was facilitated by contract #MDA903-93-K-0016 from the Army Research Institute. The views, opinions, and/or findings contained in this paper are those of the authors and should not be construed as an official Department of the Army position, policy, or decision.

References

Adams, J.S. (1965). Inequity in social exchange. In L. Berkowitz (Ed.), *Advances in experimental social psychology* (Vol. 2). New York: Academic Press.

Ajzen, I. (1991). The theory of planned behavior. *Organizational Behavior and Human Decision Processes, 50*, 179–211.

Arnold, M.B. (1960). *Emotion and personality: Psychological aspects* (Vol. 1). New York: Columbia University Press.

Atkinson, J.W. (1958). Towards experimental analysis of human motivation in terms of motives, expectancies, and incentives. In J.W. Atkinson (Ed.), *Motives in fantasy, action and society*. Princeton, NJ: Van Nostrand.

Audia, G., Kristof-Brown, A., Brown, K.G., & Locke, E.A. (1996). The relationship of goals and micro-level work processes to performance on a multi-path, manual task. *Journal of Applied Psychology, 81*, 483–497.

Bandura, A. (1986). *Social foundations of thought and action: A social-cognitive view*. Englewood Cliffs, NJ: Prentice Hall.

Bandura, A. (1997). *Self-efficacy: The exercise of control*. New York: W.H. Freeman.

Bandura, A., & Cervone, D. (1986). Differential engagement of self-reactive influences in cognitive motivation. *Organizational Behavior and Human Decision Processes, 38*, 92–113.

Bandura, A., & Simon, K.M., (1977). The role of proximal intentions in self-regulation of refractory behavior. *Cognitive Therapy and Research, 1*, 177–193.

Bargh, J.A., & Barndollar, K. (1996). Automaticity in action: The unconscious as repository of chronic goals and motives. In P.M. Gollwitzer & J.A. Bargh (Eds.), *The psychology of action*. New York: The Guilford Press.

Baron, R.A. (1990). Environmentally induced affect: Its impact on self-efficacy, task performance, negotiation, and conflict. *Journal of Applied Social Psychology, 20*, 368–384.

Barrick, M.R., & Mount, M.K. (1991). The big five personality dimensions and job performance: A meta-analysis. *Personnel Psychology, 44*, 1–26.

Barrick, M.R., Mount, M.K., & Strauss, J.P. (1993). Conscientiousness and performance of sales representatives: Test of the mediating effects of goal setting. *Journal of Applied Psychology, 78*, 715–722.

Bass, B.M. (1985). *Leadership and performance beyond expectations*. New York: The Free Press.

Bavelas, J., & Lee, E.S. (1978). Effect of goal level on performance: A trade-off of quantity and quality. *Canadian Journal of Psychology, 32*, 219–240.

Binswanger, H. (1990). *The biological basis of teleological concepts*. Los Angeles: Ayn Rand Institute Press.

Binswanger, H. (1991). Volition as cognitive self-regulation. *Organizational Behavior and Human Decision Processes, 50*, 154–178.

Brickner, M.A., & Bukatko, P.A. (1987). *Locked into performance: As a moderator of the social loafing effect*. University of Akron, unpublished manuscript.

Brockner, J., & Wiesenfeld, B.M. (1996). An integrative framework for explaining reactions to decisions: Interactive effects of outcomes and procedures. *Psychological Bulletin, 120*, 189–208.

Brown, S.P. (1996). A meta-analysis and review of organizational research on job involvement. *Psychological Bulletin, 120*, 235–255.

Brown, S.P., & Leigh, T.W. (1996). A new look at psychological climate and its relationship to job involvement, effort, and performance. *Journal of Applied Psychology, 81*, 358–368.

Bryan, J.F., & Locke, E.A. (1967). Parkinson's law as a goal-setting phenomenon. *Organizational Behavior and Human Performance, 2*, 258–275.

Campbell, D.J., & Ilgen, D.R. (1976). Additive effects of task difficulty and on subsequent task performance. *Journal of Applied Psychology, 61*, 319–324.

Cervone, D., Jiwani, N., & Wood, R. (1991). Goal setting and the differential influence of self-regulatory processes on complex decision-making performance. *Journal of Personality and Social Psychology, 61*, 257–266.

Chesney, A.A., & Locke, E.A. (1991). An examination of the relationship among goal difficulty, business strategies, and performance on a complex management simulation task. *Academy of Management Journal, 34*, 400–424.

Crown, D.F., & Rosse, J.G. (1995). Yours, mine, and ours: Facilitating group productivity through the integration of individual and group goals. *Organizational Behavior and Human Decision Processes, 61*, 138–150.

Deci, E.L., & Ryan, R.M. (1985). *Intrinsic motivation and self-determination in human behavior*. New York: Plenum Press.

DeShon, R.P., & Alexander, R.A. (1996). Goal setting effects on implicit and explicit learning of complex tasks. *Organizational Behavior and Human Decision Processes. 65*, 18–36.

Durham, C., Knight, D., & Locke, E.A. (1997). *Effects of leader role, team-set goal difficulty, team-efficacy, and team tactics on team effectiveness*. Unpublished manuscript, University of Maryland.

Earley, P.C., Connolly, T., & Ekegren, G. (1989). Goals, strategy development and task performance: Some limits on the efficacy of goal setting. *Journal of Applied Psychology, 74*, 24–33.

Earley, P.C., & Erez, M. (1991). Time-dependency effects of goals and norms: The role of cognitive processing on motivational models. *Journal of Applied Psychology, 76*, 717–724.

Earley, P.C., & Kanfer, R. (1985). The influence of component participation and role models on goal acceptance, goal satisfaction and performance. *Organizational Behavior and Human Decision Processes, 36*, 378–90.

Earley, P.C., & Lituchy, T.R. (1991). Delineating goal and efficacy effects: A test of three models. *Journal of Applied Psychology, 76*, 81–98.

Earley, P.C., & Perry, B.C. (1987). Work plan availability and performance: An assessment of task strategy priming on subsequent task completion. *Organizational Behavior and Human Decision Processes, 39*, 279–302.

Eden, D. (1990). *Pygmalion in management.* Lexington, MA: Lexington Books.

Edmister, R.O., & Locke, E.A. (1987). The effects of differential goal weights on the performance of a complex financial task. *Personnel Psychology, 40*, 505–517.

Eisenberger, R., & Cameron, J. (1996). Detrimental effects of reward: Reality or myth? *American Psychologist, 51*, 1153–1166.

Erez, M. (1977). Feedback: A necessary condition for the goal setting-performance relationship. *Journal of Applied Psychology, 62*, 624–627.

Erez, M., Earley, P.C., & Hulin, C.L. (1985). The impact of participation on goal acceptance and performance: A two-step model. *Academy of Management Journal, 28*, 50–66.

Erez, M., & Zidon, I. (1984). Effect of goal acceptance on the relationship of goal difficulty to performance. *Journal of Applied Psychology, 69*, 69–78.

Farrell, D. (1983). Exit, voice, loyalty, and neglect as responses to job dissatisfaction: A multidimensional scaling analysis. *Academy of Management Journal, 26*, 596–607.

Fisher, C.D., & Locke, E.A. (1992). The new look in job satisfaction research and theory. In C.J. Cranny, P.C. Smith, & E.R. Stone (Eds.), *Job satisfaction.* New York: Lexington-Macmillan.

Frayne, C.A., & Latham, G.P. (1987). Application of social learning theory to employee self-management of attendance. *Journal of Applied Psychology, 72*, 387–392.

Gellatly, I.R. (1996). Conscientiousness and task performance: Test of a cognitive process model. *Journal of Applied Psychology, 81*, 474–482.

Gellatly, I.R., & Meyer, J.P. (1992). The effects of goal difficulty on physiological arousal, cognition, and task performance. *Journal of Applied Psychology, 77*, 694–704.

Gilliland, S.W., & Landis, R.S. (1992). Quality and quantity goals in a complex decision task: Strategies and outcomes. *Journal of Applied Psychology, 77*, 672–681.

Gist, M.E., Bavetta, A.G., & Stevens, C.K. (1990). Transfer training method: Its influence on skill generalization, skill repetition, and performance level. *Personnel Psychology, 43*, 501–523.

Gist, M.E., Stevens, C.K., & Bavetta, A.G. (1991). Effects of self-efficacy and post-training intervention on the acquisition and maintenance of complex interpersonal skills. *Personnel Psychology, 44*, 837–861.

Gollwitzer, P.M., Heckhausen, H., & Ratajczak, H. (1990). From weighing to willing: Approaching a change decision through pre- or post-decisional mentation. *Organizational Behavior & Human Decision Processes, 45*, 41–65.

Greenberg, J. (1987). Reactions to procedural injustice in payment distribution: Do the means justify the ends? *Journal of Applied Psychology, 72*, 55–61.

Greenberg, J. (1993). The social side of fairness: Interpersonal and informational classes of organizational justice. In R. Cropanzano (Ed.), *Justice in the workplace:*

Approaching fairness in human resource management. Hillsdale, NJ: Lawrence Erlbaum Associates.

Hackman, J.R., & Oldham, G.R. (1980). *Work redesign.* Reading, MA: Addison-Wesley.

Hollenbeck, J.R., & Klein, H.J. (1987). Goal commitment and the goal-setting process: Problems, prospects and proposals for future research. *Journal of Applied Psychology, 72,* 212–220.

Hollenbeck, J.R., Williams, C.R., & Klein, H.J. (1989). An empirical examination of the antecedents of commitment to difficult goals. *Journal of Applied Psychology, 74,* 18–23.

Hom, P.W., Caranikas-Walker, F., Prussia, G.E., & Griffeth, R.W. (1992). A meta-analytical structural equations analysis of a model of employee turnover. *Journal of Applied Psychology, 77,* 890–909.

Howard, A., & Bray, D.W. (1988). *Managerial lives in transition.* New York: Guilford Press.

Judge, T., et al. *Dispositions and job and life satisfaction: Dispositional effects on job and life satisfaction in two cultures.* Unpublished manuscript, University of Iowa.

Judge, T., Locke, E., & Durham, C. (1997). The dispositional causes of job satisfaction: A core evaluations approach. In B. Staw & L. Cummings (Eds.) *Research in organizational behavior* (Vol. 19). Greenwich, CT: JAI Press.

Kirkpatrick, S.A. (1992). *The effects of psychological variables on the job characteristics–work outcomes relationship.* Presented at the 1992 Eastern Academy of Management Meeting, Baltimore, Maryland.

Kirkpatrick, S.A., & Locke, E.A. (1996). Direct and indirect effects of three core charismatic leadership components on performance and attitudes. *Journal of Applied Psychology, 81,* 36–51.

Klein, H.J., & Mulvey, P.W. (1995). Two investigations of the relationships among group goals, goal commitment, cohesion, and performance. *Organizational Behavior and Human Decision Professes, 61,* 44–53.

Kluger, A.N., & DeNisi, A. (1996). The effects of feedback interventions on performance: A historical review, a meta-analysis, and a preliminary feedback intervention theory. *Psychological Bulletin, 119,* 254–284.

Kopelman, R.E. (1986). *Managing productivity in organizations: A practical, people-oriented perspective.* New York: McGraw-Hill.

Kristof, A.L. (1996). Person-organization fit: An integrative review of its conceptualizations, measurement, and implications. *Personnel Psychology, 49,* 1–49.

LaPorte, R.E., & Nath, R. (1976). Role of performance goals in prose learning. *Journal of Educational Psychology, 68,* 260–264.

Latham, G.P., & Baldes, J.J. (1975). The "practical significance" of Locke's theory of goal-setting. *Journal of Applied Psychology, 60,* 122–124.

Latham, G.P., Erez, M., & Locke, E.A. (1988). Resolving scientific disputes by the joint design of crucial experiments by the antagonists: Application to the Erez-Latham dispute regarding participation in goal setting. *Journal of Applied Psychology* (Monograph), *73,* 753–772.

Latham, G.P., & Frayne, C.A. (1989). Self-management training for increasing job attendance: A follow-up and a replication. *Journal of Applied Psychology, 74,* 411–416.

Latham, G.P., Winters, D.C., & Locke, E.A. (1994). Cognitive and motivational effects of participation: A mediator study. *Journal of Organizational Behavior, 15,* 49–63.

Lazarus, R.S., & Folkman, S. (1984). *Stress, appraisal, and coping.* New York: Springer.
Lee, T.W., Locke, E.A., & Phan, S.H. (in press). Explaining the assigned goal-incentive interaction: the role of self-efficacy and personal goals. *Journal of Management.*
Lerner, B.S., & Locke, E.A. (1995). The effects of goal setting, self-efficacy, competition and personal traits on the performance of an endurance task. *Journal of Sport & Exercise Psychology, 17,* 138–152.
Leventhal, G.S. (1980). What should be done with equity theory? In K.J. Gergen, M.S. Greenberg, & R.H. Willis (Eds.), *Social exchange: Advances in theory and research.* New York: Plenum.
Lewin, K. (1958). Psychology of success and failure. In C.L. Stacey & M.F. Demartino (Eds.), *Understanding human motivation.* Cleveland: Howard Allen.
Locke, E.A. (1968). Toward a theory of task motivation and incentives. *Organizational Behavior and Human Performance, 3,* 157–189.
Locke, E.A. (1969). Purpose without consciousness: A contradiction. *Psychological Reports, 25,* 991–1009.
Locke, E.A. (1971). Is "Behavior Therapy" behavioristic? (An analysis of Wolpe's psychotherapeutic methods.) *Psychological Bulletin, 76,* 318–327.
Locke, E.A. (1972). Critical analysis of the concept of causality in behavioristic psychology. *Psychological Reports, 31,* 175–197.
Locke, E.A. (1976). The nature and causes of job satisfaction. In M.D. Dunnette (Ed.), *Handbook of industrial and organizational psychology.* Chicago: Rand McNally.
Locke, E.A. (1977). The myths of behavior mod in organizations. *Academy of Management Review, 2,* 543–553.
Locke, E.A. (1980). Behaviorism and psychoanalysis: Two sides of the same coin. *Objectivist Forum, 1*(1), 10–15.
Locke, E.A. (1991). The motivation sequence, the motivation hub and the motivation core. *Organizational Behavior and Human Decision Processes, 50,* 288–299.
Locke, E.A. (1995). Beyond behaviorism and materialism, or isn't it time we took consciousness seriously? *Journal of Behavior Therapy and Experimental Psychiatry, 26,* 265–273.
Locke, E.A. (1996). Science, philosophy and man's mind. *Journal of Behavior Therapy and Experimental Psychiatry, 27,* 363–368.
Locke, E. (in press). Self-set goals and self-efficacy as mediators and causal links. To appear in M. Erez, H. Thierry, & U. Kleinbeck (Eds.), *Work motivations: a multi-level approach. The individual, the group, the organization and the culture.* Hillsdale, NJ: Erlbaum.
Locke, E.A., Alavi, M., & Wagner, J. (1997). Participation in decision-making: An information exchange perspective. In G. Ferris (Ed.), *Research in personnel and human resources management* (Vol. 15). Greenwich, CT: JAI Press.
Locke, E.A., & Bryan, J.F. (1969). The directing function of goals in task performance. *Organizational Behavior and Human Performance, 4,* 35–42.
Locke, E.A., Cartledge, N., & Koeppel, J. (1968). Motivational effects of knowledge of results: A goal-setting phenomenon? *Psychological Bulletin, 70,* 474–485.
Locke, E.A., Chah, D.O., Harrison, S., & Lustgarten, N. (1989). Separating the effects of goal specificity from goal level. *Organizational Behavior and Human Decision Processes, 43,* 270–287.
Locke, E.A., Durham, C., Poon, J., & Weldon, E. (in press). Goal setting, planning and performance on work tasks for individuals and groups. To appear in S. Freidman &

E. Scholnick (Eds.), *Why, how and when do we plan? The developmental psychology of planning*. Hillsdale, NJ: Erlbaum.

Locke, E.A., & Henne, D. (1986). Work motivation theories. In C. Cooper & I. Robertson (Eds.), *International review of industrial and organizational psychology*. Chichester, England: Wiley Ltd.

Locke, E.A., & Kristof, A.L. (1996). Volitional choices in the goal-achievement process. In P. Gollwitzer & J. Bargh (Eds.), *The psychology of action: Linking cognition and motivation to behavior*. New York: Guilford Press.

Locke, E.A., & Latham, G.P. (1990). *A theory of goal setting and task performance*. Englewood Cliffs, NJ: Prentice Hall.

Locke, E.A., McClear, K., & Knight, D. (1996). Self-esteem and work. In C. Cooper & I. Robertson (Eds.), *International review of industrial & organizational psychology*. Chichester, England: Wiley Ltd.

Locke, E.A., Motowidlo, S.J., & Bobko, P. (1986). Using self-efficacy theory to resolve the conflict between goal-setting theory and expectancy theory in organirational behavior and industrial/organizational psychology. *Journal of Social and Clinical Psychology, 4*, 328–338.

Locke, E.A., & Schweiger, D.M. (1979). Participation in decision-making. One more look. In B.M. Staw (Ed.), *Research in organizational behavior* (Vol. 1). Greenwich, CT: JAI Press.

Locke, E.A., Smith, K.G., Erez, M., Chah, D-O.K., & Schaffer, A. (1994). The effects of intra-individual goal conflict on performance. *Journal of Management, 20*, 67–91.

Locke, E.A., & Taylor, M.S. (1990). Stress, coping and the meaning of work. In A. Brief & W. Nord (Eds.), *The meaning of work in America*. Lexington, MA: Lexington Books.

Locke, E.A., & Woiceshyn, J. (1995). Why businessmen should be honest: The argument from rational egoism. *Journal of Organizational Behavior, 16*, 405–414.

Mace, C.A. (1935). *Incentives: Some experimental studies*. Industrial Health Research Board (Great Britain). Report No. 72.

Maslow, A.H. (1954). *Motivation and personality*. New York: Harper.

McClelland, D.C. (1961). *The achieving society*. Princeton, NJ: Van Nostrand.

McClelland, D.C., Atkinson, J.W., Clark, R.A., & Lowell, E.L. (1953). *The achievement motive*. New York: Appleton-Century-Crofts.

McFarlin, D.B., & Sweeney, P.D. (1992). Distributive and procedural justice as predictors of satisfaction with personal and organizational outcomes. *Academy of Management Review, 35*, 626–637.

Mento, A.J., Locke, E.A., & Klein, H. (1992). Relationship of goal level to valence and instrumentality. *Journal of Applied Psychology, 77*, 395–405.

Mitchell, T., & Silver, W. (1990). Individual and group goals when workers are interdependent: Effects on task strategies and performance. *Journal of Applied Psychology, 75*, 185–193.

Mone, M.A. (1994). Comparative validity of two measures of self-efficacy in predicting academic goals and performance. *Educational and Psychological Measurement, 54*, 516–529.

Mone, M.A., & Baker, D.D. (1992). A social-cognitive, attributional model of personal goals: An empirical evaluation. *Motivation and Emotion, 16*, 297–321.

Neal, M.A., & Bazerman, M.H. (1985). The effect of externally set goals on reaching integrative agreements in competitive markets. *Journal of Occupational Behavior, 6*, 19–32.

Oldham, G.R. (1996). Job Design. In C. Cooper &. I. Robertson (Eds.), *International review of industrial and organizational psychology*. Chichester, England: Wiley Ltd.

O'Leary-Kelly, A.M., Martocchio, J.J., & Frink, D.D. (1994). A review of the influence of group goals on group performance. *Academy of Management Journal, 37*, 1285–1301.

Organ, D.W. (1987). *Organizational citizenship behavior: The good soldier syndrome*. Lexington, MA: Lexington.

Podsakoff, P.M., & Williams, L.J. (1986). The relationship between job performance and job satisfaction. In E.A. Locke (Ed.), *Generalizing from laboratory to field settings*. Lexington, MA: Lexington Books.

Rand, A. (1964). The objectivist ethics. In A. Rand (Ed.), *The virtue of selfishness*. New York: New American Library.

Rodgers, R., & Hunter, J.E. (1991). Impact of management by objectives on organizational productivity. *Journal of Applied Psychology Monograph, 76*, 322–336.

Ryan, T.A. (1958). Drives, tasks, and the initiation of behavior. *American Journal of Psychology, 71*, 74–93.

Ryan, T.A. (1970). *Intentional behavior*. New York: Ronald Press.

Sales, S.M. (1970). Some effects on role overload and role underload. *Organizational Behavior and Human Performance, 5*, 592–608.

Sandman, B.A. (1992). The measurement of job stress: Development of the job stress index. In C.J. Cranny, P.C. Smith, & E.F. Stone (Eds.), *Job satisfaction*. New York: Lexington-Macmillan.

Scully, J., Kirkpatrick, S., & Locke, E.A. (1995). Locus of knowledge as a determinant of the effects of participation on performance, affect and perceptions. *Organizational Behavior & Human Decision Processes, 61*, 276–288.

Shalley, C.E. (1991). Effects of productivity goals, creativity goals, and personal discretion on individual creativity. *Journal of Applied Psychology, 76*, 179–185.

Skinner, B.F. (1953). *Science and human behavior*. New York: Macmillan.

Smith, K.G., Locke, E.A., & Barry, D. (1990). Goal setting, planning and organizational performance: An experimental simulation. *Organizational Behavior and Human Decision Processes, 46*, 118–134.

Spangler, W.D. (1992). The validity of questionnaire and TAT measures of need for achievement: Three meta-analyses. *Psychological Bulletin, 112*, 140–154.

Spencer, D.G. (1986). Employee voice and employee retention. *Academy of Management Journal, 29*, 488–502.

Stone, E.F. (1986). Job scope-job satisfaction and job scope-job performance relationships. In E.A. Locke (Ed.), *Generalizing from laboratory to field settings*. Lexington, MA: Lexington Books.

Thomas, K.M., & Mathieu, J.E. (1994). Role of causal attributions in dynamic self-regulation and goal processes. *Journal of Applied Psychology, 79*, 812–818.

Tyler, T.R. (1989). The psychology of procedural justice: A test of the group-value model. *Journal of Personality and Social Psychology, 57*, 830–838.

Tyler, T.R., & Lind, E.A. (1992). A relational model of authority in groups. In M. Zanna (Ed.), *Advances in experimental social psychology* (Vol. 25). New York: Academic Press.

Van Eerde, W., & Thierry, H. (1996). Vroom's expectancy models and work-related criteria: A meta-analysis. *Journal of Applied Psychology, 81*, 575–586.

Vroom, V. (1964). *Work and motivation*. New York: Wiley.

Wagner, J.A., & Gooding, R.Z. (1987). Shared influence and organizational behavior: A meta-analysis of situational variables expected to moderate participation-outcome relationships. *Academy of Management Journal*, *30*, 524–541.

Watson, D., & Clark, L.A. (1984). Negative affectivity: The disposition to experience aversive emotional states. *Psychological Bulletin*, *96*, 465–490.

Watson, D., Clark, L.A., & Tellegen, A. (1988). Development and validation of brief measures of positive and negative affect: The PANAS scales. *Journal of Personality and Social Psychology*, *54*, 1063–1070.

White, S.B., & Neale, M.A. (1994). The role of negotiator aspirations and settlement expectancies in bargaining outcomes. *Organizational Behavior and Human Decision Processes*, *57*, 303–317.

Williams, D.G. (1990). Effects of psychoticism, extraversion, and neuroticism in current mood: A statistical review of six studies. *Personality and Individual Differences*, *11*, 615–630.

Winters, D., & Latham, G. (1996). The effect of learning versus outcome goals on a simple versus a complex task. *Group and Organization Management*, *21*, 236–250.

Wood, R., & Bandura, A. (1989). Social-cognitive theory of organizational management. *Academy of Management Review*, *14*, 361–384.

Wood, R.E., & Locke, E.A. (1990). Goal setting and strategy effects on complex tasks. In B. Staw & L. Cummings (Eds.), *Research in organizational behavior* (Vol. 12). Greenwich, CT: JAI Press.

Wood, R.E., Mento, A.J., & Locke, E.A. (1987). Task complexity as a moderator of goal effects: A meta-analysis. *Journal of Applied Psychology*, *72*, 416–425.

Wright, P.M. (1989). Test of the mediating role of goals in the incentive-performance relationship. *Journal of Applied Psychology*, *74*, 699–705.

Wright, P.M. (1990). Operationalization of goal difficulty as a moderator of the goal difficulty-performance relationship. *Journal of Applied Psychology*, *75*, 227–234.

Wright, P.M., George, J.M., Farnsworth, S.R., & McMahan, G.C. (1993). Productivity and extra-role behavior: The effects of goals and incentives on spontaneous helping. *Journal of Applied Psychology*, *78*, 374–381.

22
INDIVIDUAL DIFFERENCES IN WORK MOTIVATION
Further explorations of a trait framework

Ruth Kanfer and Phillip L. Ackerman

Source: *Applied Psychology: An International Review* 49(3) (2000): 470–482.

Abstract

Empirical evidence on the conceptual and construct validity of the motivational trait taxonomy proposed by Kanfer and Heggestad is presented. Two hundred and twenty eight adults completed a shortened form of the Motivational Trait Questionnaire (MTQ), along with a battery of personality and ability measures. Relationships of the MTQ with personality measures show evidence of convergent and discriminant validity for trait constructs of Personal Mastery, Competitive Excellence, and Motivation Related to Anxiety. In addition, MTQ scale scores were generally unrelated to composite measures of fluid and crystallised intelligence. Examination of age differences showed a pattern of developmental decline in the achievement trait complex, but not the anxiety complex.

Introduction

A crucial problem in contemporary work motivation theory and research pertains to how best to conceptualise and assess individual differences in motivational tendencies. Although most researchers agree on the existence of individual differences in motivational preferences or traits, the development of an adequate taxonomic structure of such traits has lagged far behind work in the ability traits domain. However, work motivation researchers have focused on a variety of constructs, ranging from broad constructs, such as need for achievement, to narrow trait-state constructs, such as mastery orientation. Similarly, measures of target constructs also vary widely and range from scales taken from multitrait inventories to situation-specific, customised scales. Not surprisingly, the slow progress in this area and the lack of coherence in research efforts aimed at elucidating these person influences on motivational processes has made it extremely difficult to aggregate results across studies.

Nonetheless, the maturation of work motivation theories over the past decade has prompted organisational researchers to focus greater attention on the identification of nonability person factors that may play a role in work motivation (Austin & Klein, 1996). Advances in personality psychology, along with increasing organisational needs to identify and develop worker motivational traits, provide further impetus for overcoming the taxonomic problem. Such developments have spurred the creation of an articulated nomological network of person constructs as they relate to the adoption of organisationally valued goals and the development of motivational skills for accomplishing work goals. In this paper we present the results of an empirical study aimed at further evaluating the validity of a theory-based measure of work motivation traits. First, though, we address the current "received" view of personality—called the Five-Factor Model (FFM)—in the context of motivational traits.

The Five-Factor Model (FFM) of personality vs. motivational traits

Advocates of the FFM of personality have argued that trait motivation variance is largely captured by individual differences in conscientiousness (e.g. Barrick & Mount, 1991; Schmidt & Hunter, 1992). However, a growing number of researchers have shown that important motivational trait elements can be linked to other factors, such as extroversion and neuroticism (e.g. Kanfer, Dugdale, & McDonald, 1994; Kuhl & Fuhrmann, 1999; Zuckerman, Joireman, Kraft, & Kuhlman, 1999).

The FFM provides an unsatisfactory taxonomy of motivational traits for both conceptual and empirical reasons. Conceptually, the FFM provides a structure of personality that encompasses far more than individual differences in motivational tendencies. Although the FFM may arguably provide the most parsimonious representation of the structure of personality as a whole, empirical research (see e.g. Barrick, Mount, & Stauss, 1993; Hough & Schneider, 1996) suggests that it is not an optimal structure for the evaluation of individual differences in motivational tendencies. Moreover, there is an additional question of the "consistency" or "specificity" of personality traits across domains of function (see e.g. Murtha, Kanfer, & Ackerman, 1996). In this paper, we adopt a midrange perspective that permits examination of motivational traits and tendencies in achievement settings, with respect to broader cross-situational measures of personality.

Approach/avoidance conceptions vs. motivational traits

A number of social-personality researchers have recently suggested that individual differences in achievement motivation may be best conceptualised in terms of individual differences in goals (Cassidy & Lynn, 1989; Elliott & Dweck, 1988;

Elliott & Church, 1997). Although researchers differ in terms of the type of goals they study (e.g. classroom goals vs. life goals), most researchers in this area distinguish between appetitive (approach) and aversive (avoidance) motivational orientations. Results of studies of children in the classroom, adult work adjustment and job performance indicate a relationship between goal orientation (approach vs. avoidance), subsequent self-regulatory activities, and performance. VandeWalle (1997), for example, extended the approach/avoidance goal formulation to develop a self-report measure that assessed three aspects of adult work goal orientation (i.e. learning, performance prove, and performance avoid). Using the measure, VandeWalle, Brown, Cron, and Slocum (1999) found a positive relationship between (approach) learning goal orientation, effective self-regulatory activities, and performance. In contrast, individual differences in the measures of "performance prove" and "performance avoid" (avoidance) goal orientations were only weakly and inconsistently related to goal-striving measures and criterion performance.

The approach/avoidance goal taxonomy takes advantage of advances in achievement motivation and more recent motivation process research. Whereas the FFM conceptualisation embeds motivational traits in a comprehensive structure of personality, the goal orientation formulation embeds motivational traits in a narrow structure of goal striving that emphasises how approach and avoidance tendencies affect action in the context of goal-directed behaviour. Further, this line of research is fully consistent with classic approaches in terms of the presumed latent-trait structure of motivation. However, the measures developed in the goal-based framework suffer from many of the same problems as measures used in classic approaches, including for example, concerns about the dimensionality of traits and the appropriate level of goal assessment.

The motivational traits formulation

In 1997, Kanfer and Heggestad (1997) reviewed the work and achievement motivation literatures and self-report measures of motivational traits. Based upon this review, they proposed a developmental theory that distinguishes between distal influences on action, in the form of relatively stable motivational traits, and proximal influences on performance associated with individual differences in self-regulatory, or motivational, skills. Two specific shortcomings identified by Kanfer and Heggestad (1997) pertained to the lack of attention to individual differences in strength of competitive excellence motives and to individual differences in aversively oriented motivational traits (such as worry and emotionality with respect to performance situations). Although a full description of the formulation lies beyond the scope of this paper, Kanfer and Heggestad (1997) argued that the success of a comprehensive account of work motivation would require that greater attention be paid to the motivational trait structure. In particular, they showed that: (a) there has been a substantial narrowing of focus for assessment of motivational traits over the past 30 years, and (b) that much of the motivational trait construct space was underrepresented in most current multitrait personality inventories.

The Motivational Traits Questionnaire (MTQ)

In a series of empirical investigations, Heggestad and Kanfer (e.g. Heggestad, 1997; Heggestad & Kanfer, 1999) developed a multiple trait motivational inventory designed explicitly to address those portions of the construct space frequently neglected in extant measures. The Motivational Trait Questionnaire (MTQ) long form contains 183 items that compose nine separate scales. These nine scales, in turn, load substantially on three underlying factors identified as: Personal Mastery, Competitive Excellence, and Motivation-Related Anxiety (for details on the development and validation of these scales, see Heggestad and Kanfer, 1999).

A short form of the MTQ was also developed to provide assessment of the three major motivational trait factors identified in the original investigations. The MTQ short form has 48 items taken from the original long form measure, and these comprise six of the original nine scales, as follows: Desire to Learn, Mastery, Other Referenced Goals, Competitiveness, Worry, and Emotionality. Descriptions of the scales and sample items are provided below, including Cronbach's α internal consistency reliability estimates.

Personal mastery

Desire to learn

This scale is composed of items that focus on a need to achieve in the context of learning new skills or acquiring knowledge. (8 items; $\alpha = 0.81$; Example item: "I prefer activities that provide me the opportunity to learn something new.")

Mastery

Items comprising this scale focus on personal goal setting and other aspects of the achievement context that represent an orientation toward continued task improvement or mastery—even when it is not required. (8 items; $\alpha = 0.83$; Example: "I set high standards for myself and work toward achieving them.")

Both of the Personal Mastery scales are considered to assess approach-oriented motivational traits.

Competitive excellence

Other referenced goals

Items on this scale involve comparisons to other performers (e.g. coworkers and peers) for the purpose of establishing a social reference context for the individual's performance. (7 items; α = 0.85; Example: "Whether or not I feel good about my performance depends on how it compares to the performance of others.")

Competitiveness

This scale involves comparisons of personal performance with others—with the main focus on competition and performing better than coworkers or peers. (6 items; $\alpha = 0.89$; Example: "I would rather cooperate than compete." [reverse-scored])

While Competitiveness is clearly represented as an approach-oriented trait, Other Referenced Goals involves both approach- and avoidance-related tendencies.

Motivation related to anxiety

Worry

This scale is composed of items that focus on worry and other aspects of evaluation apprehension in performance contexts. (10 items; $\alpha = 0.88$; Example: "Before beginning an important project, I think of the consequences of failing.")

Emotionality

This scale focuses on emotions associated with performance in evaluation contexts. (9 items; $\alpha = 0.79$; Example: "I am able to remain calm and relaxed before I take a test." [reverse-scored])

Both the Worry and Emotionality scales represent avoidance-related tendencies.

MTQ—personality and intelligence relations

Initial investigations of the motivational trait structure involved administration of developmental versions of the MTQ long form and a battery of personality measures to three samples of college students. These investigations yielded results showing strong evidence of convergent and discriminant validity for the hypothesised trait clusters of Personal Mastery, Competitive Excellence, and Anxiety (Heggestad & Kanfer, 1999).

To provide additional construct validity information and extend these findings using the MTQ short form, we embedded the 48-item measure in a study of adult knowledge, intelligence, and personality. The study (reported in Ackerman, 2000), consisted of a sample of 228 adults recruited from flyers and newspaper advertisements at a large public university—78 men and 150 women (M age = 34.2 years, SD age = 10.6 years, age range of 21–62 years). The main inclusion criterion was completion of at least a baccalaureate level of education. Roughly half of the sample was between the ages of 21 and 30 ($N = 111$) and the other half was between the ages of 31 and 62 ($N = 116$). For the sake of convenience, the younger group was designated "young adult" and the older group was designated "middle-aged group". In addition to the administration of the short form of the MTQ, we also administered four personality scales from Tellegen's (1982) Multi-dimensional Personality Questionnaire (MPQ; Social Potency, Social Closeness, Absorption, and Traditionalism). An extensive three-hour ability battery provided assessments of: (1) fluid intelligence (Raven Progressive Matrices, Spatial Analogy, Number Series, Diagramming Relations, Number Span, Problem Solving, and Necessary Facts); and (2) crystallised intelligence (Nelson–Denny Reading Speed and Comprehension, Multidimensional Aptitude Battery Comprehension, Multi-dimensional Aptitude Battery Synonyms, Word Beginnings, Vocabulary, and the Wechsler Adult Intelligence Scale—Revised Information scale). For additional details about these measures, see Ackerman (2000).

Table 1 shows the means, standard deviations, and intercorrelations among the MTQ scales, the MPQ scales, intelligence, age, and gender. Several aspects of these data are noteworthy with respect to issues of construct validity and conceptual clarity. These are discussed below in terms of: (a) the relations among MTQ scales, (b) the relations between MTQ scales and the personality-oriented MPQ scales, and (c) the relations among MTQ scales and intelligence, age, and gender.

MTQ scale intercorrelations

As hypothesised, substantial correlations were found between pairs of MTQ scales that purport to measure similar constructs (i.e. Desire to Learn and Mastery, $r = 0.64$; Other Reference Goals and Competitiveness, $r = 0.64$; Worry and Emotionality, $r = 0.76$). These correlations are highly supportive of convergent validity of the scales. Discriminant validation was also demonstrated with the six MTQ scales, as shown by the small correlations between scales that were hypothesised to represent differentiated constructs (e.g. Desire to Learn and Other Referenced Goals, $r = 0.07$).

A particularly interesting pattern of results pertains to the relationships obtained among Competitive Excellence and Motivation Related to Anxiety measures. As conceptualised, the two measures comprising the Motivation Related to Anxiety factor were designed to tap the "aversive" (e.g. fear of failure) aspects of motivation. In contrast, the two measures comprising the Competitive Excellence factor were designed to capture the "appetitive" aspects of motivation described by Murray in terms of "to rival and surpass others" (Murray, 1938, p. 164). However, as shown in Table 1, although the two measures of each higher-order factor are substantially correlated, the two measures of Competitive Excellence are *differentially related* to the Motivation Related to Anxiety measures. Specifically, the Other Referenced Goals scale shows a pattern of positive correlations with the Worry and Emotionality scales ($rs = 0.34$ and 0.25, respectively), whereas the Competitiveness scale is unrelated to the Worry and Emotionality scales ($rs = -0.06$ and 0.08, respectively). One way of reconciling these seemingly inconsistent results is to recognise that individuals may compare their own performance to that of

Table 1 Means, SDs, and intercorrelations

	Mean	SD	1	2	3	4	5	6	7	8	9	10	11	12	13
1. Desire to Learn	37.99	4.98													
2. Mastery	35.90	5.85	.639**												
3. Other Referenced Goals	26.43	5.98	.068	.212**											
4. Competitiveness	19.30	6.03	.069	.251**	.642**										
5. Worry	38.34	8.63	−.105	−.038	.340**	−.061									
6. Emotionality	28.52	6.93	−.050	.040	.248**	−.085	.756**								
7. Social Potency	10.54	6.29	.195**	.306**	.320**	.445**	−.187**	−.114							
8. Social Closeness	14.01	5.35	.011	.181**	−.010	.026	−.182**	−.071	.256**						
9. Absorption	18.74	6.93	.263**	.255**	.029	−.046	.057	.108	.210**	−.032					
10. Traditionalism	14.46	5.83	.003	.250**	.101	.029	.040	−.014	.023	.157*	−.076				
11. Fluid Intelligence (Gf)	.00	1.00	.012	−.034	.150*	.033	.130	.012	.106	−.075	.001	−.124			
12. Crystallised Intelligence (Gc)	.00	1.00	.163*	−.080	.079	−.050	.100	−.005	−.138*	−.188**	.046	−.215**	.589**		
13. Age	34.22	10.58	−.006	−.171**	−.180**	−.188**	−.063	−.080	−.071	−.127	−.053	−.081	−.388**	.143*	
14. Gender (1 = Male, 2 = Female)	1.66	.48	.147*	.291**	.008	−.098	.113	.195**	−.029	.177**	.187**	.087	−.107	−.060	−.041

*$P < 0.05$; **$P < 0.01$.

others for two very different reasons: (a) to evaluate whether they are performing better than others (e.g. competition), or (b) to evaluate whether others are doing better than they are (e.g. fear of failure). With this conceptualisation in mind, the pattern of correlations makes sense. That is, both appetitive and aversive aspects of motivation are captured in an individual's tendency to reference other actors' performance. Whether these two different aspects of the comparison process can be resolved with more refined measures is an open question that awaits further research.

Motivational trait (MTQ) and personality trait (MPQ) relations

Further evidence on the validity of the MTQ scales is provided by considering MTQ–MPQ scale correlations. In contrast to the FFM model, which provides only a broad assessment of the construct of extroversion, the MPQ has the advantage of separating two aspects of extroversion, namely: Social Potency and Social Closeness. As shown in Table 1, the appetitive motivational traits (i.e. Desire to Learn, Mastery, Competitiveness, and Other Referenced Goals) are positively and significantly correlated with Social Potency, but only the MTQ Mastery scale is significantly correlated with Social Closeness. With respect to the aversive motivational trait scales, Emotionality is not significantly related to either aspect of extroversion, whereas Worry is significantly and negatively related to both Social Potency and Social Closeness. Taken together, these results are consistent with previous suggestions that both appetitive and aversive motivational traits relate to extroversion.

Table 1 also shows significant positive correlations between the MPQ Absorption scale and the MTQ Personal Mastery scales—but not the Competitive Excellence Scales. Again, this pattern of results makes good theoretical sense, in that individuals are unlikely to be absorbed in a task at the same time that they are comparing their performance to that of others. Finally, it should be noted that Mastery was significantly and positively correlated with Traditionalism. Consistent with the positive correlation of this MTQ scale with Social Closeness, it appears that this scale may reflect aspects of a traditional work ethic construct, such as the desire for doing a job well and getting along well with others.

Motivational traits and intelligence

Overall, MTQ measures were generally unrelated to measures of crystallised and fluid intelligence. (Two significant correlations obtained between MTQ scales and measures of intelligence were generally modest in magnitude [$r = 0.15$ and 0.16].) These results, obtained using an extensive battery of ability tests, are consistent with prior results showing little overlap between individual differences in motivational traits and ability traits—at least among samples of educated adults (see e.g. Kanfer, Dugdale, & McDonald, 1994; Kuhl & Fuhrmann, 1999). Using multiple correlation techniques, the MTQ scales were found to have only 5% shared variance with fluid intelligence ($r^2 = 0.05$, $P = 0.06$), and 12% of shared variance with crystallised intelligence ($r^2 = 0.12$, $P < 0.01$). Such results indicate that even though communalities among motivational traits and intellectual abilities are rather modest, the locus of most of the communality is in the domain of experiential and educationally-based abilities (see Horn, 1968 for a more extensive discussion of fluid and crystallised intelligence constructs).

Motivational traits, age, and gender

As indicated in Table 1, significant negative correlations were obtained between age and the appetitive motivational traits (e.g. Mastery, Competitiveness). These findings are consistent with prior results showing that middle-aged and older adults are less likely to have the same achievement-oriented motive strength as younger adults (Heckhausen, 1997).

Results obtained for gender differences indicate that women reported significantly higher levels of Mastery and Emotionality than men do. As Kanfer and Heggestad (1997) suggested, individuals with simultaneously high trait levels of appetitive and aversive motivational tendencies may experience increased conflict and problems in the workplace. For these individuals, the positive effects of adopting challenging goals may be substantially offset by intensified anxiety during goal striving. The results obtained in this study indicate that women are more likely to demonstrate this trait pattern than men are. Further research to investigate the generalisability of these findings in the larger population and across cultures appears warranted.

An ANOVA summary

Because the sample was split into two approximately equal groups of participants under the age of 30 and over the age of 30 ($N = 111$ and 116, respectively), it was possible to provide a contrast between these groups on the MTQ scales within an ANOVA framework. Even with recognition that these are cross-sectional data, and may thus be influenced by cohort differences, post hoc analyses of the age and gender data suggest that there may be interesting developmental patterns for several of the MTQ scales.

Table 2 shows the results of 2 (age) × 2 (gender) ANOVAs for each of the six MTQ scales. As expected, the main effects mirror the correlational findings; namely significant gender differences (all with women having higher scores) for Desire to Learn, Mastery, and Emotionality, with the largest gender differences found for Mastery (Cohen's $d = 0.61$). Also, significant age differences (under 30/over 30) were found for all but one of the appetitive trait scales (i.e. Mastery, Other Referenced Goals, and Competitiveness). Not surprisingly, younger adults showed higher average levels than middle-aged adults on each scale, with the largest age differences found for Competitiveness (Cohen's $d = 0.53$). In contrast, no significant age differences were obtained for the aversive trait scales.

Table 2 Age (under 30 vs. over 30) by gender ANOVAs on the MTQ scales—
F ratios and effect sizes (Cohen's d)

MTQ scale	F Ratio (Cohen's d)					
	Gender		Age		Gender × Age	
1. Desire to Learn	4.64*	(.31)	.16	(.08)	.16	(.03)
2. Mastery	20.28**	(.61)	6.23*	(.36)	.13	(.04)
3. Other Referenced Goals	.01	(.02)	7.03**	(.41)	1.18	(.13)
4. Competitiveness	2.07	(.21)	11.85**	(.53)	4.12*	(.23)
5. Worry	2.65	(.24)	.55	(.14)	.19	(.07)
6. Emotionality	8.97**	(.41)	.08	(.08)	.64	(.11)

*$P < 0.05$; **$P < 0.01$
All comparisons: $df = 1$ (numerator), $df = 221$ (denominator)

Finally, a significant Gender × Age interaction was found for Competitiveness. Specifically, middle-aged women showed the lowest level of Competitiveness compared to the other three groups. Together, these results suggest that women report higher trait levels for situations that provide opportunities for mastery, but report lower competition-seeking, especially as they transition from young adults to middle age. What may be perhaps problematic is that there is no concomitant decline in Worry or Emotionality scores for these middle-aged women—again suggesting a source of apparently conflicting motivational traits.

Summary and future directions

The findings reported here add to the corpus of evidence supporting the motivational trait taxonomy proposed by Kanfer and Heggestad (1997). Consistent with classic conceptions of achievement motivation, but in contrast to most contemporary trends in motivational trait measurement, the results indicate a clear differentiation between appetitive/approach traits related to Personal Mastery and Competitive Excellence. The MTQ scales pertaining to Personal Mastery appear to tap those aspects of achievement most commonly evaluated in extant personality and achievement-oriented individual differences measures. In contrast, the two Competitive Excellence MTQ scales appear to capture less well-understood aspects of approach and avoidance traits. In particular, the observed differential relationship of the two Competition Seeking scales with the Motivation Related to Anxiety trait scales is fully consistent with the notion that extrinsic motivational orientations may occur in concert with high levels of approach or avoidance-oriented traits (e.g. Harackiewicz, Sansone, & Manderlink, 1985). Further research to investigate the validity of these scales and their influence in work motivation processes clearly appears warranted.

A long-standing issue in the trait domain pertains to the extent to which motivational traits may be clearly distinguished from intellectual traits. The results of this study add to the growing body of evidence demonstrating the independence of individual differences in motivation and individual differences in intellectual abilities—as indexed by measures that aim primarily at assessing g. In this study, however, individual differences in intellectual abilities were evaluated with respect to fluid (Gf) and crystallised intelligence (Gc) (for a description of these constructs, see Horn, 1968). Given that the Gc measure of intelligence represents a central index of the results of lifelong learning, and that our measure of Gc (a composite of seven separate tests) was broad and extensive, the weak association between this composite and Personal Mastery scales of the MTQ is surprising. That is, although Gf and motivational traits may be unrelated, it seems reasonable to expect a slightly higher association between individuals' cumulative level of knowledge (Gc) and their trait tendencies toward learning and mastery. Additional research, to determine whether the specificity of an individual's "desire to learn" affects this relation, appears warranted. From a pragmatic perspective, the extent to which specificity may influence this relation has potential implications for personnel selection and training, particularly among middle-aged workers.

The pattern of results obtained for MTQ scores as a function of gender and age suggests that work motivation researchers should pay greater attention to how demographic variables exert their influence on motivational processes and work outcomes. For example, our findings show a relative decline in trait strength related to mastery and learning among "middle-aged" (above 30) individuals. As such, it may be that motivational interventions designed to compensate for, rather than attempt to rekindle, lower levels of intrinsic motivation may be more effective among middle-aged workers.

From an assessment perspective, the MTQ short form demonstrates a number of desirable properties with respect to internal consistency scale reliabilities and construct validity. Together with previous results obtained with the MTQ long form, these findings suggest that the MTQ serves as a promising tool for use in theory and research investigating the influence of individual differences in motivational traits as they affect goal choice and striving in work place/achievement settings.

Acknowledgments

This research was supported in part by a grant to the first author from the National Science Foundation (NSF/SBR9223357) and a grant to both authors from the National Institute of Aging (AG16648).

References

Ackerman, P.L. (2000). Domain-specific knowledge as the "dark matter" of adult intelligence: Gf/Gc, personality and interest correlates. *Journal of Gerontology: Psychological Sciences, 55* (2), P69–P84.

Austin, J.T., & Klein, H.J. (1996). Work motivation and goal striving. In K.R. Murphy (Ed.), *Individual Differences and Behavior in Organizations* (pp. 209–257). San Francisco: Jossey-Bass.

Barrick, M.R., & Mount, M.K. (1991). The Big Five personality dimensions and job performance: A meta-analysis. *Personnel Psychology*, *44*, 1–26.

Barrick, M.R., Mount, M.K., & Strauss, J.P. (1993). Conscientiousness and performance of sales representatives: Test of the mediating effects of goal setting. *Journal of Applied Psychology*, *78*, 715–722.

Cassidy, T., & Lynn, R. (1989). A multi-factorial approach to achievement motivation: The development of a comprehensive measure. *Journal of Occupational Psychology*, *62*, 301–312.

Elliott, A.J., & Church, M.A. (1997). A hierarchical model of approach and avoidance achievement motivation. *Journal of Personality and Social Psychology*, *72*, 218–232.

Elliott, E.S., & Dweck, C.S. (1988). Goals: An approach to motivation and achievement. *Journal of Personality and Social Psychology*, *54*, 5–12.

Harackiewicz, J.M., Sansone, C., & Manderlink, G. (1985). Competence, achievement orientation and intrinsic motivation: A process analysis. *Journal of Personality and Social Psychology*, *48*, 493–508.

Heckhausen, J. (1997). Developmental regulation across adulthood: Primary and secondary control of age-related challenges. *Developmental Psychology*, *33*, 176–187.

Heggestad, E.D. (1997). Motivation from a personality perspective: The development of a measure of motivational traits. Unpublished doctoral dissertation, University of Minnesota, Minneapolis.

Heggestad, E.D., & Kanfer, R. (April, 1999). Individual differences in trait motivation. Development of the Motivational Trait Questionnaire. Poster presented at the Annual Meetings of the Society of Industrial and Organizational Psychology, Atlanta, Georgia.

Horn, J.L. (1968). Organization of abilities and the development of intelligence. *Psychological Review*, *75*, 242–259.

Hough, L.M., & Schneider, R.J. (1996). Personality traits, taxonomies, and applications in organizations. In K.R. Murphy (Ed.), *Individual Differences and Behavior in Organizations* (pp. 31–88). San Francisco: Jossey-Bass.

Kanfer, R., Dugdale, B., & McDonald, B. (1994). Empirical findings on the Action Control Scale in the context of complex skill acquisition. In J. Kuhl & J. Beckmann (Eds.), *Volition and Personality: Action- and State-Oriented Modes of Control* (pp. 61–77). Göttingen, Germany: Hogrefe & Huber.

Kanfer, R., & Heggestad, E.D. (1997). Motivational traits and skills: A person-centered approach to work motivation. In L.L. Cummings & B.M. Staw (Eds.), *Research in Organizational Behavior* (Vol. 19, pp. 1–56). Greenwich, CT: JAI Press, Inc.

Kuhl, J., & Fuhrmann, A. (1999). Decomposing self-regulation and self-control. The Volitional Components Inventory. In J. Heckhausen & C.S. Dweck (Eds.), *Motivation and Self-Regulation Across the Life Span* (pp. 15–49). Cambridge: Cambridge University Press.

Murray, H.A. (1938). *Explorations in Personality*. New York: Oxford University Press.

Murtha, T.C., Kanfer, R., & Ackerman, P.L. (1996). Towards an interactionist taxonomy of personality and situations: An integrative situational-dispositional representation of personality traits. *Journal of Personality and Social Psychology*, *71*, 193–207.

Schmidt, F.L., & Hunter, J.E. (1992). Development of a causal model of processes determining job performance. *Current Directions in Psychological Science*, *1*, 89–92.

Tellegen, A. (1982). *Brief Manual for the Multidimensional Personality Questionnaire (MPQ)*. Minneapolis, MN: Author.

VandeWalle, D. (1997). Development and validation of a work domain goal orientation instrument. *Educational and Psychological Measurement, 57,* 995–1015.

VandeWalle, D., Brown, S.P., Cron, W.L., & Slocum J.W. (1999). The influence of goal orientation and self-regulation tactics on sales performance: A longitudinal field test. *Journal of Applied Psychology, 84,* 249–259.

Zuckerman, M., Joireman, J., Kraft, M., & Kuhlman, D.M. (1999). Where do motivational and emotional traits fit within three factor models of personality? *Personality and Individual Differences, 26,* 487–504.

23

GENERAL MENTAL ABILITY IN THE WORLD OF WORK

Occupational attainment and job performance

Frank L. Schmidt and John Hunter

Source: *Journal of Personality and Social Psychology* 86(1) (2004): 162–173.

Abstract

The psychological construct of general mental ability (GMA), introduced by C. Spearman (1904) nearly 100 years ago, has enjoyed a resurgence of interest and attention in recent decades. This article presents the research evidence that GMA predicts both occupational level attained and performance within one's chosen occupation and does so better than any other ability, trait, or disposition and better than job experience. The sizes of these relationships with GMA are also larger than most found in psychological research. Evidence is presented that weighted combinations of specific aptitudes tailored to individual jobs do not predict job performance better than GMA alone, disconfirming specific aptitude theory. A theory of job performance is described that explicates the central role of GMA in the world of work. These findings support Spearman's proposition that GMA is of critical importance in human affairs.

During the 1960s when we were graduate students, we frequently heard predictions from experimental psychologists and experimental social psychologists that in 20 or so years differential psychology would be a dead field, because experimental research would explain all individual differences as effects of past or present (environmental) treatment conditions. Obviously, this has not happened. In fact, in recent years there has been a strong resurgence of interest in the psychology of individual differences (Lubinski, 2000). This resurgence embraces general intelligence (general mental ability, GMA), specific aptitudes and abilities, personality traits, interests, values, and other traits showing important differences between individuals and groups.

This resurgence has been particularly strong in connection with GMA, a construct first postulated and defined nearly 100 years ago by Spearman (1904). A number of developments and findings have contributed to renewed interest in GMA. The accumulated evidence has become very strong that GMA is correlated with a wide variety of life outcomes, ranging from risky health-related behaviors, to criminal offenses, to the ability to use a bus or subway system (Gottfredson, 1997; Lubinski & Humphreys, 1997). In addition, the more highly a given GMA measure loads on the general factor in mental ability (the *g* factor), the larger are these correlations. The relative standing of individuals on GMA has been found to be stable over periods of more than 65 years (Deary, Whalley, Lemmon, Crawford, & Starr, 2000). Findings in behavior genetics, including studies of identical twins reared apart and together (e.g., Bouchard, Lykken, McGue, Segal, & Tellegen, 1990), have shown beyond doubt that GMA has a strong genetic basis (e.g., Bouchard, 1998; McGue & Bouchard, 1998). Heritability has been shown to increase with age and to reach levels of .80 or higher in elderly persons. (The square root of .80 is .89, indicating a correlation of nearly .90 between genes and GMA in elderly persons.) Molecular genetic research has identified specific genes that affect particular traits (e.g., Hamer & Copeland, 1998), and this research effort and its findings have changed the intellectual zeitgeist and affected many basic assumptions. Other factors include Carroll's (1993) book on the factor structure of human abilities, Jensen's two major books on GMA (Jensen, 1980, 1998), and Herrnstein and Murray's (1994) *Bell Curve*, the only social science book ever to appear on *The New York Times* bestseller list. Another development has been the demonstration that GMA predicts both later occupational level and performance within one's chosen occupation—and predicts both outcomes more strongly than any other trait. These latter two developments are the subject of this article. Because of the vastness of this literature and space limitations, our review of necessity cannot be exhaustive. However, we address the major conclusions in this literature and we cite a representative sample of the relevant research.

The remainder of this article is organized as follows. First, we present the evidence indicating that GMA predicts occupational level attained. We then review the research evidence showing that GMA predicts performance within jobs and occupations—both performance in learning the job (training performance) and performance on the job—for both civilian and military occupations. Third, we examine other traits and variables that affect training and job performance—personality traits, specific aptitudes, and job experience—and show that these factors, although important, exert weaker effects on both occupational level and job performance than does GMA. Last, we describe a theory of job performance that explains these findings.

GMA and attainment of occupational level

Cross-sectional studies

Both cross-sectional and longitudinal studies have related GMA to occupational level. We first examine cross-sectional studies. People's rankings or ratings of the occupational level or prestige of different occupations are very reliable; correlations between mean ratings across studies are in the .95 to .98 range, regardless of the social class, occupation, age, or country of the raters (Dawis, 1994; Jensen, 1980, pp. 339–347). These occupational level ratings correlate between .90 and .95 with average GMA scores of people in the occupations (Jensen, 1998, p. 293). Individual level correlations are of course not this large. In the U.S. Employment Service's large database on the General Aptitude Test Battery (GATB, Hunter, 1980), the individual level correlation between the GMA measure derived from that battery and occupational level is .65 (.72 corrected for measurement error; Jensen, 1998). Much military data exist from both world wars (when samples of draftees were very representative of the U.S. male population) showing an increase in mean GMA scores as occupational level (as determined by ratings of the sort discussed here) increases (Harrell & Harrell, 1945; Stewart, 1947; Yerkes, 1921). Table 1, showing findings for 18,782 White enlisted men in the Army Air Force Command (Harrell & Harrell, 1945), presents typical findings. The GMA measure used was the Army General Classification Test (Schmidt, Hunter, & Pearlman, 1981). Mean GMA scores clearly increase with occupational level. It is also apparent that standard deviations and score ranges decrease with increasing occupational level, indicating that although lower level occupations can and do contain very high-scoring individuals, individuals with low GMA scores apparently find it hard to enter higher level occupations. It is apparent that the upper end of the GMA range is quite similar across all occupations, whereas the lower end increases with increasing occupational level, suggesting minimum GMA requirements for higher level occupations.

Longitudinal studies

Longitudinal studies are important because they show that GMA measured earlier in life predicts later occupational attainment. Wilk, Desmarais, and Sackett (1995), using the 3,887 young adults in the National Longitudinal Survey—Youth Cohort (NLSY; Center for Human Resource Research, 1989) for whom the required data were available, showed that over the 5-year period from 1982 to 1987, GMA measured in 1980 predicted movement in the job hierarchy. Those with higher GMA scores in 1980 moved up the hierarchy, whereas those with lower GMA scores moved down in the hierarchy. In a larger follow-up study that was based on somewhat different methodology, Wilk and Sackett (1996) examined two large government databases: the National Longitudinal Study of the Class of 1972 (NLS-72) and the National Longitudinal Survey of Labor Market

Table 1 Mean GCT standard scores, standard deviations, and range of scores of 18,782 AAF White enlisted men by civilian occupation (from Harrell & Harrell, 1945, pp. 231–232)

Occupation	N	M	Mdn	SD	Range
Accountant	172	128.1	128.1	11.7	94–157
Lawyer	94	127.6	126.8	10.9	96–157
Engineer	39	126.6	125.8	11.7	100–151
Public-relations man	42	126.0	125.5	11.4	100–149
Auditor	62	125.9	125.5	11.2	98–151
Chemist	21	124.8	124.5	13.8	102–153
Reporter	45	124.5	125.7	11.7	100–157
Chief clerk	165	124.2	124.5	11.7	88–153
Teacher	256	122.8	123.7	12.8	76–155
Draftsman	153	122.0	121.7	12.8	74–155
Stenographer	147	121.0	121.4	12.5	66–151
Pharmacist	58	120.5	124.0	15.2	76–149
Tabulating-machine operator	140	120.1	119.8	13.3	80–151
Bookkeeper	272	120.0	119.7	13.1	70–157
Manager, sales	42	119.0	120.7	11.5	90–137
Purchasing agent	98	118.7	119.2	12.9	82–153
Manager, production	34	118.1	117.0	16.0	82–153
Photographer	95	117.6	119.8	13.9	66–147
Clerk, general	496	117.5	117.9	13.0	68–155
Clerk-typist	468	116.8	117.3	12.0	80–147
Manager, miscellaneous	235	116.0	117.5	14.8	60–151
Installer-repairman, tel. & tel.	96	115.8	116.8	13.1	76–149
Cashier	111	115.8	116.8	11.9	80–145
Instrument repairman	47	115.5	115.8	11.9	82–141
Radio repairman	267	115.3	116.5	14.5	56–151
Printer, job pressman, lithographic pressman	132	115.1	116.7	14.3	60–149
Salesman	494	115.1	116.2	15.7	60–153
Artist	48	114.9	115.4	11.2	82–139
Manager, retail store	420	114.0	116.2	15.7	52–151
Laboratory assistant	128	113.4	114.0	14.6	76–147
Tool-maker	60	112.5	111.6	12.5	76–143
Inspector	358	112.3	113.1	15.7	54–147
Stock clerk	490	111.8	113.0	16.3	54–151
Receiving and shipping clerk	436	111.3	113.4	16.4	58–155
Musician	157	110.9	112.8	15.9	56–147
Machinist	456	110.1	110.8	16.1	38–153
Foreman	298	109.8	111.4	16.7	60–151
Watchmaker	56	109.8	113.0	14.7	68–147
Airplane mechanic	235	109.3	110.5	14.9	66–147
Sales clerk	492	109.2	110.4	16.3	42–149
Electrician	289	109.0	110.6	15.2	64–149
Lathe operator	172	108.5	109.4	15.5	64–147
Receiving & shipping checker	281	107.6	108.9	15.8	52–151
Sheet metal worker	498	107.5	108.1	15.3	62–153

(*Continued*)

Table 1 (Cont'd)

Occupation	N	M	Mdn	SD	Range
Lineman, power and tel. & tel.	77	107.1	108.8	15.5	70–133
Assembler	498	106.3	106.6	14.6	48–145
Mechanic	421	106.3	108.3	16.0	60–155
Machine-operator	486	104.8	105.7	17.1	42–151
Auto serviceman	539	104.2	105.9	16.7	30–141
Riveter	239	104.1	105.3	15.1	50–141
Cabinetmaker	48	103.5	104.7	15.9	66–127
Upholsterer	59	103.3	105.8	14.5	68–131
Butcher	259	102.9	104.8	17.1	42–147
Plumber	128	102.7	104.8	16.0	56–139
Bartender	98	102.2	105.0	16.6	56–137
Carpenter, construction	451	102.1	104.1	19.5	42–147
Pipe-fitter	72	101.9	105.2	18.0	56–139
Welder	493	101.8	103.7	16.1	48–147
Auto mechanic	466	101.3	101.8	17.0	48–151
Molder	79	101.1	105.5	20.2	48–137
Chauffer	194	100.8	103.0	18.4	46–143
Tractor driver	354	99.5	101.6	19.1	42–147
Painter, general	440	98.3	100.1	18.7	38–147
Crane-hoist operator	99	97.9	99.1	16.6	58–147
Cook and baker	436	97.2	99.5	20.8	20–147
Weaver	56	97.0	97.3	17.7	50–135
Truck driver	817	96.2	97.8	19.7	16–149
Laborer	856	95.8	97.7	20.1	26–145
Barber	103	95.3	98.1	20.5	42–141
Lumberjack	59	94.7	96.5	19.8	46–137
Farmer	700	92.7	93.4	21.8	24–147
Farmhand	817	91.4	94.0	20.7	24–141
Miner	156	90.6	92.0	20.1	42–139
Teamster	77	87.7	89.0	19.6	46–145

Note. GCT = General Classification Test; AAF = Army Air Force; tel. & tel. = telephone and telegraph.

Experience—Youth Cohort (NLSY). In both databases, Wilk and Sackett found that job mobility was predicted by the congruence between individuals' GMA scores (measured several years earlier) and the objectively measured complexity of their jobs. If their GMA exceeded the complexity level of their job, they were likely to move into a higher complexity job. And if the complexity level of their job exceeded their GMA level, they were likely to move down into a less complex job. The job complexity measure used is highly correlated with the measures of occupational level discussed above.

In another study drawn from this same large database, Murray (1998) found that GMA predicted later income even with unusually thorough control for socioeconomic status (SES) and other background variables. This control took advantage of the large variability of GMA within families and was achieved by use of a sample of male full biological siblings, hence controlling for home background and many other variables (e.g., schools, neighborhoods). Murray found that the siblings with higher GMA scores received more education, entered more prestigious occupations, had higher income, and were employed more regularly. When the siblings were in their late 20s (in 1993), a person with average GMA was earning on average almost $18,000 less per year than his brighter sibling who had an IQ of 120 or higher and was earning more than $9,000 more than his duller sibling who had an IQ of less than 80. This pattern of findings held up even in a subsample of persons who were all from "advantaged" homes (his "utopian" sample). This addresses the objection that it may not be GMA per se that causes differences in occupational level and income but other variables such as quality of schools, availability of opportunities, and so on, that are not well captured by standard measures of SES and, hence, are not fully controlled for when standard measures of SES are statistically partialed out.

Judge, Higgins, Thoresen, and Barrick (1999) related GMA measures taken at around 12 years of age to occupational outcomes in the age range of 41 to 50 years. They found that childhood GMA scores predicted adult occupational level with a correlation of .51 and predicted adult income with a correlation of .53. Ball (1938) found that GMA measured in childhood correlated .47 with occupational level 14 years later and .71 with occupational level 19 years later. Other such studies include Brown and Reynolds (1975), Dreher and Bretz (1991), Gottfredson and Crouse (1986), Howard and Bray (1990), Siegel and Ghiselli (1971), and Thorndike and Hagen (1959).

It is clear that GMA is related to occupational level (and income) longitudinally as well as cross-sectionally. Furthermore, the relationship is relatively strong. Correlations of .50 or higher are rare in psychology and the social sciences and are considered large (Cohen & Cohen, 1988). As discussed in the section *Personality and Job Performance*, certain personality traits are also predictive of occupational level, but the magnitude of the relationships is considerably smaller, with the possible exception of one personality trait (conscientiousness).

GMA predicts one's ultimate attained job level, but it does not predict which occupation at that level one will enter. That role falls to interests. There is considerable evidence that interests predict the particular occupation (or at least the occupational family) that a person will choose (Holland, 1985, 1996; Savickas & Spokane, 1999). However, interests are poor predictors of performance once one has entered an occupation (Schmidt & Hunter, 1998).

GMA and performance within occupations and jobs

In the world of work, and particularly in the hiring of employees, measures of GMA have been used since the end of World War I (Yerkes, 1921). The tests used are typically paper-and-pencil tests containing questions and problems related to verbal material, quantitative material, spatial material, and sometimes mechanical material. Although there are a variety of such instruments, probably the most representative of these—and certainly the most widely used today—is the Wonderlic Personnel Test (Hunter, 1989; Wonderlic, 1992). This test is given with a time limit of 10 min and consists of 50 free-response items, with verbal, quantitative and spatial material about equally represented. The Wonderlic test has numerous psychometrically parallel forms available, and it is supplied with extensive norm data. On the basis of instruments of this sort, thousands of validity studies have accumulated since the early part of the 20th century.

It has long been believed among both psychologists and lay-people that GMA is important for academic performance but has little to do with real-world performances after schooling is over. In particular, it was held that GMA had little relation to performance on the job (e.g., Jencks, 1972). Within industrial–organizational psychology, a related but not identical belief was dominant between 1910 and about 1980: the so-called theory of situational specificity. This theory held that GMA did predict job performance but only sporadically; that is, it held that the validity of GMA (and other measures) for predicting job performance was highly situational: It might predict for one job in one employment setting but fail to do so for what was apparently the same job in another organization. This theory was supported by the finding that observed validity coefficients for similar tests and jobs varied substantially across different validity studies and the finding that some (about half) of these validity coefficients were statistically significant and the rest were not. The explanation offered for this puzzling variability was that jobs that appeared to be the same actually differed in important but subtle ways in what was required to perform them. Because of this, validity had to be estimated anew in each separate setting. Over the last 25 years, application of meta-analysis methods (Hunter & Schmidt, 1990) to validity databases has disconfirmed this theory and has shown that the variability in validity findings is mostly due to statistical and measurement artifacts such as sampling error variance, measurement error in job performance measures, restriction in range on GMA scores, and other artifacts. These artifacts have two effects beyond the creation of variability in observed validities: They reduce statistical power to around .50 and they bias validity estimates downward (except for sampling error, which does not exert a downward bias). After correction for the effects of these methodological artifacts, it was found that there was little or no variation in validity findings (cf. Schmidt et al., 1993) and that GMA measures were predictive of job performance (in varying degrees) for all jobs. (Similar findings of minimal actual variability under conditions of large apparent variability have also been reported in other research areas; cf. Schmidt, 1992.) Hundreds of such meta-analyses (called validity generalization studies) have now been conducted (Schmidt & Hunter, 1998) and have included a wide variety of measures used to predict job performance: aptitudes, personality traits, and other measures, in addition to GMA measures.

Results for GMA are typified by the findings of the large study conducted by Hunter (1980; Hunter & Hunter, 1984) for the U.S. Employment Service using the database on the General Aptitude Test Battery (GATB). On the basis of 425 validity studies ($N = 32,124$) conducted on civilian jobs spanning the occupational spectrum, Hunter and Hunter (1984) and Hunter (1980) reported the results shown in Table 2. Hunter assigned each job to one of five job families based on *complexity* (i.e., the information processing requirements of the job, measured using U.S. Department of Labor job analysis data for each job). This is the largest database available using a measure of performance on the job (measured using supervisory ratings of job performance). As can be seen, validity for predicting performance on the job ranges from .58 for the highest complexity jobs (professional, scientific, and upper management jobs) to .23 at the lowest complexity level (feeding/off-bearing jobs). Job Family 2 (2.5% of all jobs in the economy) consists of complex technical jobs such as computer-systems trouble shooting or complex manufacturing set-up jobs. Job Family 3, with almost 63% of all jobs in the economy, includes skilled workers, technicians, mid-level administrators, paraprofessionals, and similar jobs. Job Family 4 is semiskilled work. Clearly, GMA predicts performance on higher level jobs better that it does for lower level jobs. However, there is substantial validity for all job levels. In particular, GMA predicts performance even for the simplest 2.4% of jobs (Job Family 5).

Other findings are reported in Table 3. On the basis of 194 studies ($N = 17,539$) of performance in clerical jobs, Pearlman, Schmidt, and Hunter (1980) reported a mean GMA validity for job performance of .52. For law enforcement jobs, Hirsh, Northrup, and Schmidt (1986) reported a mean validity for job performance of .38. In a large scale, multiyear military study on enlisted Army personnel (called "Project A"), McHenry, Hough, Toquam, Hanson, and Ashworth (1990)

Table 2 Validity of the general mental ability (GMA) measure in the general aptitude test battery

Complexity level of job[a]	% of workforce	Performance measures On the job	In training
1	14.7	.58	.59
2	2.5	.56	.65
3	62.7	.51	.57
4	17.7	.40	.54
5	2.4	.23	NR

Note. For the lowest complexity job category, no training performance studies were reported. Performance on the job was measured using supervisory ratings of overall job performance. Training performance was typically assessed using tests measuring amount learned in training. There were 425 studies of job performance ($N = 32,124$) and 90 studies of performance in training programs ($N = 6,496$). Correlations are corrected for measurement error in the dependent variable and for range restriction but not for measurement error in the GMA measure; hence, these are estimates of operational validities, not construct-level correlations. Construct-level correlations are approximately 8.5% larger. All values reported are mean values; after correction for artifacts, variability around these mean values was limited, and almost all values in each distribution were positive and substantial. NR = not reported. Adapted from Hunter (1980) and from "Validity and Utility of Alternate Predictors of Job Performance," by J. E. Hunter and R. F. Hunter, 1984, *Psychological Bulletin, 96*. Table 2, p. 82. Copyright 1984 by the American Psychological Association.
[a] 1 = highest; 5 = lowest.

Table 3 The relation between general mental ability (GMA) and performance in job training and on the job: representative findings from meta-analyses

Study	Occupation	Performance measures	
		On the job	In training
Hunter and Hunter (1984)	Medium complexity[a]	.51	.57
Pearlman et al. (1980)	Clerical	.52	.71
Hirsh et al. (1986)	Law enforcement	.38	.76
McHenry et al. (1990)	Military—enlisted	.63[b]	NR
McHenry et al. (1990)	Military—enlisted	.65[c]	NR
Hunter (1986)	Military—enlisted	NR	.63
Ree et al. (1994)	Military—enlisted	.45	NR
Ree and Earles (1991)	Military—enlisted	NR	.60
Schmidt et al. (1979)	First-line supervisors	.64	NR
Schmidt et al. (1979)	Administrative clerks	.67	NR
Schmidt et al. (1980)	Computer programmers	.73	NR
Callender and Osburn (1981)	Refinery workers	.31	.50

Note. McHenry et al. (1990) and Ree et al. (1994) used job sample measures of job performance. Other studies measured job performance using supervisory ratings of overall job performance. Training performance was typically measured using tests of amount learned in the training program. Correlations are corrected for measurement error in the dependent variable and for range restriction but not for measurement error in the GMA measures; hence, these are estimates of the operational validities, not construct-level correlations. Construct-level correlations are 8% to 12% larger. All values reported are mean values; after correction for artifacts, variability around these mean values was limited and almost all values in each distribution were positive and substantial. NR = not reported, (i.e., the relationship was not examined in the study).
[a]Results for medium-complexity jobs (63% of jobs). Results for other job complexity levels are given in Table 2. [b]Criterion was "core technical proficiency." [c]Criterion was "general soldiering proficiency."

reported that GMA predicted "Core Technical Proficiency" with a validity of .63 and "General Soldiering Performance" with a validity of .65. Both job performance measures were based on hands-on work-sample measures. (Validities were not as high for ratings of "Effort and Leadership" [.31], "Personal Discipline" [.16], and "Physical Fitness and Military Bearing [.20], which are secondary criterion measures with fewer cognitive demands.) Using similar job sample measures of job performance, Ree, Earles, and Teachout (1994) reported a mean value of .45 across seven Air Force jobs.

Validities for the prediction of performance in training programs are even larger. As can be seen in Table 2, in the GATB training database (90 studies; $N = 6,496$) used by Hunter and Hunter (1984), GMA predicted performance in job training programs for all job families for which data existed with a correlation above .50. The database for training performance is larger for military jobs. Hunter (1986) meta-analyzed military databases totaling over 82,000 trainees and reported an average validity of .63 for GMA. On the basis of 77,958 Air Force trainees, Ree and Earles (1991) reported a very similar value of .60. On the basis of 65 studies with an N of 32,157, Pearlman et al. (1980) reported a mean validity of .71 for

GMA in predicting training performance of clerical workers, whereas Hirsh et al. (1986) found a mean value of .76 for predicting performance in police and other training academies for law enforcement trainees. These findings and others are shown in Table 3. Additional data of this sort are presented in Schmidt (2002).

A rough summary can be obtained by averaging the findings shown in Table 3. Across the meta-analyses reported there, the unweighted average validity of GMA is .55 for predicting performance on the job and .63 for predicting performance in job training programs.

Other traits and variables that affect job performance

Variables beyond GMA that have been hypothesized to affect job and training performance include specific aptitudes (e.g., verbal ability, quantitative ability, etc.), job experience, and personality traits.

Specific aptitudes and specific aptitude theory

Cognitive abilities that are narrower than GMA are called specific aptitudes, or often just aptitudes. Examples include verbal aptitude, spatial aptitude, and numerical aptitude. Differential or specific aptitude theory hypothesizes that performance on different jobs requires different cognitive aptitudes and, therefore, regression equations computed for each job and incorporating measures of several specific aptitudes will optimize the prediction of performance on the job and in training. In the last 10 years, research has strongly disconfirmed this theory. Differentially weighting specific aptitude tests produces little or no increase in validity over the use of a measure of GMA. An explanation for this finding has been discovered. It has been found that specific aptitude tests measure GMA; in addition to GMA, each measures something specific to that aptitude (e.g., specifically numerical aptitude, over and above GMA). The GMA component appears to be responsible for the prediction of job and training performance, whereas the factors specific to the aptitudes appear to contribute little or nothing to prediction. The research showing this is presented and reviewed in Hunter (1986); Jensen (1986); Thorndike (1986); Olea and Ree (1994); Ree and Earles (1992); Ree et al. (1994); Schmidt, Ones, and Hunter (1992); and Sackett and Wilk (1994), among other sources.

A particularly dramatic refutation of specific aptitude theory comes from the large sample military research conducted by Hunter (1983b) for the Department of Defense on the performance of military personnel in job training programs. Four large samples were analyzed separately: 21,032 Air Force personnel, 20,256 Marines, and two Army samples of 16,618 and 79,926, respectively. In all samples, test data were obtained some months prior to measurement of performance in job training programs. In all samples, causal analysis modeling (with corrections for measurement error and range restriction) was used to pit specific aptitude theory against GMA in the prediction of performance. In the case of all four samples, models with causal arrows from specific aptitudes to training performance failed to fit the data. However, in all the samples, a hierarchical model showing a single causal path from GMA to performance—and no paths from specific aptitudes to performance—fit the data quite well. Figure 1 shows the findings for the Marines sample. The causal model that fit the data shows GMA as the cause of the specific aptitudes of quantitative, verbal, and technical (i.e., these specific aptitudes were indicators—or measures—of GMA). Specific subtests of the Armed Services Vocational Aptitude Battery (ASVAB, Forms 6/7) were, in turn, caused by these three specific aptitudes (i.e., they were indicators of these aptitudes). For example, the Math Knowledge and Arithmetic Reasoning subtests were indicators of quantitative aptitude. There is no causal arrow from any of the aptitudes or subtests to training performance. Training performance is determined only by GMA, with the standardized path coefficient from GMA to performance being very large (.62). The findings for the other three samples were essentially identical (Hunter, 1983b).

It is well known that analysis of causal models with correlational data cannot prove a theory. However, such analyses—especially when samples are very large, as here—can disconfirm theories. Theories that do not fit the data are disconfirmed. In these studies, specific aptitude theory is strongly disconfirmed.

Job experience, GMA, and job performance

Learning, and hence job experience, plays a major role in the determination of job performance. Experience provides the medium for learning, and thus, people with more experience have had more opportunity to learn and to achieve a higher level of job performance (Schmidt, Hunter, & Outerbridge, 1986).

However, individual differences in learning are also important. If one worker learns faster than another, the same amount of experience will produce a higher

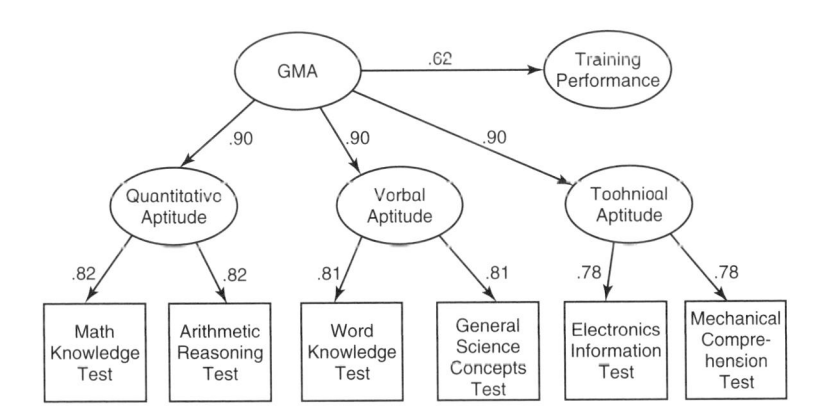

Figure 1 The standardized path model for the U.S. Marine data ($N = 20,256$) from Hunter (1983b) showing relationships among general mental ability (GMA), specific aptitudes, and subtests of the Armed Services Vocational Aptitude Battery (Forms 6/7). Adapted from Hunter (1983b).

level of performance in the fast learner than in the slow learner. It is GMA that turns experience into increased job knowledge and hence higher performance.

Ability differences over time

One might hypothesize that the validity of GMA declines over time as workers obtain more job experience. However, research does not support this hypothesis. Schmidt, Hunter, Outerbridge, and Goff (1988) analyzed data for four military occupations in which workers had been assessed for job knowledge, objectively measured actual performance, and performance ratings. Their data allowed mean comparisons between high and low GMA groups (upper and lower halves of the distribution) for each year of experience out to 5 years. For job knowledge, Schmidt et al. (1988) found large and constant differences between the two ability groups at all levels of experience over the 5-year period. For objectively measured job performance, the same finding was observed. For performance ratings, Schmidt et al. found definite though smaller differences between the two ability groups at all levels of experience up to 5 years. Again, the size of the difference was the same after 5 years as after 1 year of experience.

McDaniel (1985) analyzed United States Employment Services (USES) data for groups whose level of job experience extended beyond 5 years. Controlling for differences in variability of GMA across groups, McDaniel correlated GMA with performance ratings for each level of experience to 12 years and up. The results are summarized in Table 4. As the level of experience increases, the predictive validity does not decrease. Validity goes from .36 for 0–6 years, up to .44 for 6–12 years, up to .59 for more than 12 years (although the last value is based on a very small sample). If anything, McDaniel's data suggest an increase in the validity of GMA for predicting performance ratings as level of worker experience increases.

These findings indicate that the predictive validity of GMA is at least stable over time and does not decrease. The work of Ackerman (1986, 1987, 1988, 1990, 1992)

Table 4 The correlation between general mental ability (GMA) and job performance ratings for job incumbents with various levels of job experience

Years of experience	Total sample size	GMA with performance correlation
0–3	4,424	.35
3–6	3,297	.37
6–9	570	.44
9–12	84	.44
12+	22	.59

Note. From *The Evaluation of a Causal Model of Job Performance: The Interrelationships of General Mental Ability, Job Experience, and Job Performance* (p. 76), by M. A. McDaniel, 1985, unpublished doctoral dissertation, George Washington University. Adapted with permission of the author.

has been the basis for predictions of declining GMA validities over time. Ackerman distinguished between consistent tasks and inconsistent tasks. Consistent tasks are simple enough (or noncognitive enough) that their performance can be automated; hence, after a time, such tasks draw minimally on cognitive resources and performance on such tasks comes over time to show a low correlation with GMA (e.g., riding a bicycle). Inconsistent tasks are just the opposite: They are complex enough that no matter how long they are performed, they continue to draw on cognitive resources (and to require controlled information processing), and they therefore continue to show a large correlation with GMA over time. Using a variety of tasks in laboratory research, Ackerman (1987) has provided evidence to support his theory of controlled and automated information processing. On the basis of Ackerman's theory and research, Murphy (1989) advanced a theory that predicts declining validity over time for GMA in predicting job performance. (Ackerman himself has not made such a prediction.) Murphy's theory posits *maintenance stages*, during which job tasks are well learned and can be performed with minimal mental effort (automatic information processing), resulting in low or zero GMA validities. The empirical evidence summarized above disconfirms this theory and suggests that when the measure in question is overall job performance, the task remains complex enough that it cannot be automated; it continues to require controlled information processing and hence continues to correlate with GMA (Schmidt et al., 1992). There may be a temptation in this area to generalize inappropriately from narrow and automatable tasks to broader, more complex, and less automatable real-world job performance composites.

Predictive validity of job experience

Hunter and Hunter (1984) found the mean predictive validity of job experience to be .18 across 373 studies (corrected for measurement error in the job performance ratings). Controlling for differences in variability of experience across categories of experience, McDaniel, Schmidt, and Hunter (1988) examined the validity of job experience at different mean levels of experience using the USES individual worker database. The results are summarized in Table 5. Some training advocates hypothesize that experience differences become increasingly important as workers become more and more experienced. The pattern of findings in Table 5 is opposite to the prediction from this hypothesis. Differences in experience are very important among newly hired employees: The correlation between experience and performance ratings is .49 for those who have been on the job 0–3 years. (Schmidt et al., 1986, likewise found substantial correlations between job experience and performance when all workers were on the low end of the experience continuum [less than 5 years]. The mean value for supervisory ratings was .33, and for work sample measures of performance it was .47.) This correlation then drops gradually to a low of .15 for those who have been on the job 12 years or more. This is explained by other data presented in McDaniel (1985) showing the nonlinear relationship between experience and performance. The relation between

Table 5 The correlation between amount of job experience and performance ratings for job incumbents with various levels of job experience

Years of experience	Total sample size	Experience with performance correlation
0–3	4,490	.49
3–6	5,088	.32
6–9	3,588	.25
9–12	1,274	.19
12+	1,618	.15

Note. Differences in variability of experience across categories of experience were controlled for. From "Job Experience Correlates of Job Performance," by M. A. McDaniel, F. L. Schmidt, and J. E. Hunter, *Journal of Applied Psychology*, 73, p. 329. Copyright 1988 by the American Psychological Association.

experience and job performance shows the same shape as other learning curves: It is nonlinear and monotonic (Schmidt & Hunter, 1992: Schmidt et al., 1988).

Ability versus experience as predictors

Tables 4 and 5 show that as workers gain job experience, the correlation between experience and performance decreases whereas the correlation between GMA and performance remains constant or increases. GMA not only matters during the early stages of job learning but throughout the worker's tenure. This pattern may be even more pronounced today because of the rapidly changing product life cycles that require workers to learn new methods of production at ever shorter intervals.

Personality and job performance

In our experience, laypeople consider personality a more important determinant of job performance than GMA. It is easy to think of individuals who experienced difficulty at work because of personality conflicts with supervisors or because of failure to be organized and achievement oriented at work. Many people may also believe that personality is more important than GMA in determining ultimate occupational level. However, research supports the conclusion that personality is less important than GMA in both areas.

In recent years, most personality research has been organized around the Big Five model of personality (Goldberg, 1990). Considerable evidence has accumulated suggesting that most personality measures intended for individuals without psychopathology can be subsumed under the umbrella of the five-factor model. The five traits included in this model are Extroversion, Agreeableness, Neuroticism, Openness to Experience, and Conscientiousness. These same five personality factors have been found in analyses of trait adjectives in a variety of different languages, factor-analytic studies of existing personality inventories, and decisions regarding the dimensionality of existing measures made by expert judges

(McCrae & John, 1992). The five-factor structure has been found in a wide variety of cultures (McCrae & Costa, 1997; Pulver, Allik, Pulkkinen, & Hamalainen, 1995; Salgado, 1997; Yoon, Schmidt, & Ilies, 2002) and remains stable over time (Costa & McCrae, 1988, 1991). Although the five-factor model of personality has its critics (e.g., see Block, 1995; Butcher & Rouse, 1996), it is widely accepted today.

As indicated earlier, Judge et al. (1999) found that three of the Big Five personality traits measured in childhood predicted adult occupational level and income. For Conscientiousness, these longitudinal correlations were .49 and .41, respectively; these values are only slightly smaller than the corresponding correlations in this study for GMA (discussed in the *Longitudinal Studies* section, above) of .51 and .53, respectively. For Openness to Experience (which correlates positively with GMA), the correlations were .32 and .26. Finally, Neuroticism produced longitudinal correlations of −.26 and −.34, for occupational level and income, respectively.

Because of the unique nature of Judge et al.'s (1999) study, we conducted additional analyses of the data from this study. Because occupational level and income were highly correlated ($r = .83$) and loaded on the same factor, we combined them into one equally weighted measure of career success. After correcting for the biasing effects of measurement error, we found that the three Big Five personality traits predicted this index of career success with a (shrunken) multiple correlation of .56. It is interesting to examine the standardized regression weights (betas). For Neuroticism, $\beta = -.05$ ($SE = .096$); for Openness, $\beta = .16$ ($SE = .10$); and for Conscientiousness, $\beta = .44$ ($SE = .123$). Hence, in the regression equation, Conscientiousness is by far the most important personality variable, and Neuroticism appears to have little impact after controlling for the other two personality traits.

However, it is also important to control for the effects of GMA. When GMA is added to the regression equation, the (shrunken) multiple correlation rises to .63. Again, it is instructive to examine the beta weights: Neuroticism, $\beta = -.05$ ($SE = .096$); Openness, $\beta = -.03$ ($SE = .113$); Conscientiousness, $\beta = .27$ ($SE = .128$); and GMA, $\beta = .43$ ($SE = .117$). From these figures, it appears that the burden of prediction is borne almost entirely by GMA and Conscientiousness, with GMA being 59% more important than Conscientiousness (i.e., $.43/.27 = 1.59$). In fact, when only GMA and Conscientiousness are included in the regression equation, the (shrunken) multiple correlation remains the same, at .63. The standardized regression weights are then .29 for Conscientiousness ($SE = .102$) and .41 for GMA ($SE = .096$). These analyses suggest that Conscientiousness may be the only personality trait that contributes to career success.

As far as we were able to determine, there are no other data sets comparable with Judge et al.'s (1999) data; that is, data sets that relate both personality and ability measures to career success and are longitudinal in nature. In fact, even cross-sectional data sets that relate personality and GMA to career success are rare. This is unfortunate; it would be highly desirable to compare findings across different such longitudinal data sets.

In the prediction of performance on the job, only one of the Big Five traits—Conscientiousness—has been found in meta-analytic studies to function like GMA in that it consistently predicts job performance in all job families studied (Barrick & Mount, 1991; Mount & Barrick, 1995). The level of validity is higher when Conscientiousness is assessed using ratings by others rather than self-report personality inventories (Mount, Barrick, & Strauss, 1994). Conscientiousness also predicts performance in job training programs (Mount & Barrick, 1995; Schmidt & Hunter, 1998). In one primary study, Barrick and Mount (1993) found that the validity of Conscientiousness was higher for managers in high-autonomy jobs than for those in low-autonomy jobs. Barrick, Mount, and Strauss (1993) proposed that Conscientiousness affects motivational states and stimulates goal setting and goal commitment. They found in their primary study, which was designed to test this causal model, that Conscientiousness had both direct and indirect effects (through goal setting and commitment) on performance. They concluded that Conscientiousness functions as a motivational contributor to job performance. The traits Extroversion and Agreeableness are sporadically valid: They predict performance on certain kinds of jobs under certain conditions but are not job related for most jobs (Barrick & Mount, 1993; Barrick, Mount, & Judge, 2001; Barrick, Stewart, Neubert, & Mount, 1998). For example, Barrick et al. (1998) found that in work teams in which members must cooperate closely, Agreeableness, Extraversion, and Emotional Stability, in addition to Conscientiousness, were related to supervisor ratings of team performance.

The best meta-analytic estimate for the validity of Conscientiousness, measured with a reliable scale, for predicting job performance is .31 (Mount & Barrick, 1995). Hence, the validity of GMA is 60% to 80% larger (depending on the GMA validity estimate used) than that of Conscientiousness. However, Conscientiousness measures contribute to validity over and above the validity of GMA, because the two are uncorrelated (Schmidt & Hunter, 1998). As noted above, Hunter and Hunter (1984) estimated the validity of GMA for medium complexity jobs (63% of all jobs) to be .51, The multiple correlation produced by use of measures of both GMA and Conscientiousness in a regression equation for such jobs is .60, an 18% increase in validity over that of GMA alone (Schmidt & Hunter, 1998). The best meta-analytic estimate of the validity of Conscientiousness for predicting performance in job training is .30 (Mount & Barrick, 1995). The multiple correlation produced by simultaneous use of GMA and Conscientiousness measures is .65 (vs. .56 for GMA alone; Schmidt & Hunter, 1998).

Integrity tests can also be considered personality measures because they have been found to measure Conscientiousness primarily, with some representation of Agreeableness and Neuroticism (reverse scored; Ones, 1993). Integrity tests have been shown to have validity for all jobs studied (Ones, Viswesvaran, & Schmidt, 1993) and to have validity that is somewhat higher than that of Conscientiousness measures (.41 for job performance and .38 for training performance). However, these validities are still considerably smaller than those for GMA. For predicting job performance, integrity tests produce a 27% increase in validity over that of GMA alone (to a multiple R of .65). For training performance, the increment is 20% (to a multiple R of .67; Schmidt & Hunter, 1998).

These findings, which are based on hundreds of studies subjected to meta-analysis, indicate that although personality (as conceptualized in the Big Five model) is indeed important in job and training performance, it is less important than GMA. Contrary to what may be the common intuition, ability is more important than personality in the workplace (Ree & Carretta, 1998; Schmidt & Hunter, 1998).

A reviewer enquired as to whether job performance is unidimensional. Performance on any job can be broken down analytically and rationally into its various component dimensions. Campbell and his associates (e.g., Campbell, McCloy, Oppler, & Sager, 1992) have identified dimensions of job performance that are general across different jobs. As they acknowledged, performance on these dimensions is likely to be positively correlated. However, even if this was not the case, one could still create and use a composite index of job performance that represents overall job performance (Schmidt & Kaplan, 1971), as was done in the validity studies reviewed in this article. In addition, there is empirical evidence that there is a general factor in job performance. Viswesvaran, Schmidt, and Ones (2002) developed a statistical method for removing from job performance ratings the halo error that inflates the correlations among rated dimensions of job performance. They found that even after this bias was removed, there was still a large general factor in job performance. The fact that GMA and Conscientiousness affect performance on all job performance dimensions is almost certainly part of the explanation for this general factor.

Why is GMA so important for job performance?

It can be difficult for people to accept facts and findings they do not like if they see no reason why the findings should or could be true. When Alfred Weggner advanced the theory of plate tectonics early in the 20th century, geologists could think of no means by which continents or continental plates could move around. Not knowing of any plausible mechanism or explanation for the movement of continents, they found Weggner's theory implausible and rejected it. Many people have had the same reaction to the empirical findings showing the GMA is highly predictive of job performance. The finding does not seem plausible to them because they cannot think of a reason why such a strong relationship should exist. In fact, their intuition may tell them that personality and other noncognitive traits are more important than GMA (Hunter & Schmidt, 1996). However, as in the case of plate tectonics theory, there is an explanation. Causal analyses of the determinants of job performance show that the major effect of GMA is on the acquisition of job knowledge: People who are higher in GMA acquire more job knowledge and acquire it faster. The amount of job-related knowledge required on even less complex jobs is much greater than is generally realized. Higher levels of job knowledge lead to higher levels of job performance. Viewed negatively, not knowing what one should be doing—or even not knowing all that one should about what one should be doing—is detrimental to job performance. In addition, knowing what one should be doing and how to do it depends strongly on GMA.

The research showing that the major mediating link between GMA and job performance is job knowledge is described in Borman, Hanson, Oppler, and Pulakos (1993); Borman, White, Pulakos, and Oppler (1991); Hunter (1983a); Hunter and Schmidt (1996); Schmidt (2002); Schmidt and Hunter (1992); and Schmidt et al. (1986). We illustrate this research using the findings that Hunter and Schmidt (1996) reported separately for military and civilian jobs. Figure 2 shows the basic path analysis results. (The differences between military and civilian jobs are quantitative rather than qualitative and are not discussed here.) As can be seen, in both data sets, the major effect of GMA is on the acquisition of job knowledge, and job

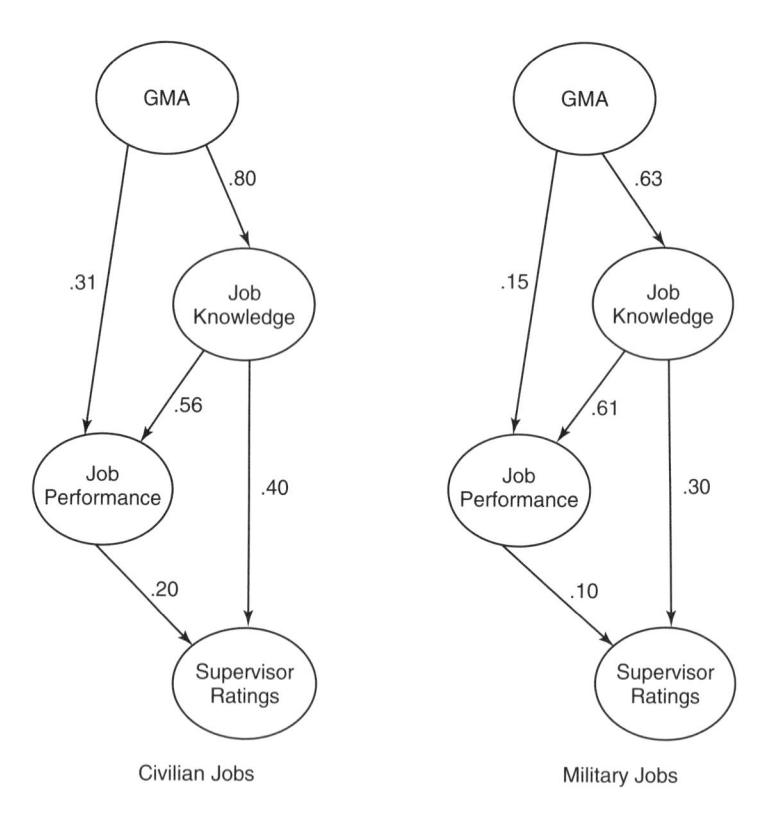

Figure 2 A path analysis of relations among general mental ability (GMA), job knowledge, job performance, and supervisor ratings. Reprinted from "Intelligence and Job Performance: Economic and Social Implications," by J. E. Hunter and F. L. Schmidt, 1996, *Psychology, Public Policy, and Law*, 2, Figure 1, p. 464. Copyright 1996 by the American Psychological Association.

knowledge in turn is the major determinant of job performance (measured using hands-on job sample tests). GMA does have a direct effect on job performance independent of job knowledge in both data sets, but this effect is smaller than its indirect effect through job knowledge (direct effect of .31 for civilian jobs vs. an indirect effect of .80 × .56 = .45; direct effect of .15 for military jobs vs. an indirect effect of .63 × .61 = .38). These results also show that supervisory ratings of job performance are determined in both data sets by both job knowledge and job sample performance. Hunter and Schmidt (1996) and Schmidt and Hunter (1992) presented an extended theory that predicts and explains findings such as these.

For practical purposes of prediction in personnel selection, it does not matter why GMA predicts job performance. However, scientific understanding requires theoretical explanation. Theoretical explanation is also required to gain acceptance of findings from those who question the plausibility of a central role for GMA in the determination of job performance. It is easier to accept an empirical finding when there is a theoretical explanation for that finding.

Summary

It has been nearly 100 years since Spearman (1904) defined the construct of GMA and proposed its central role in human cognition and learning. During the middle part of the 20th century, interest in the construct of GMA declined in some areas of psychology, but in the last 20 to 25 years there has been a resurgence of interest in GMA and its role in various life areas. This article has focused on the world of occupations and work and has presented the research evidence, most of it being recent, showing that GMA predicts both the occupational level attained by individuals and their performance within their chosen occupation. GMA correlates above .50 with later occupational level, performance in job training programs, and performance on the job. Relationships this large are rare in psychological research and are considered "large" (Cohen & Cohen, 1988). Other traits, particularly personality traits, also affect occupational level attained and job performance, but these relationships are generally not as strong as those for GMA. Evidence was summarized indicating that weighted combinations of specific aptitudes (e.g., verbal, spatial, or quantitative aptitude) tailored to individual jobs do not predict job performance better than GMA measures alone, thus disconfirming specific aptitude theory. It has been proposed that job experience is a better predictor of job performance than GMA, but the research findings presented in this article support the opposite conclusion. Job experience (i.e., amount of opportunity to learn the job) does relate to job performance, but this relationship is weaker than the relation with GMA and it declines over time, unlike the GMA job performance relationship.

Empirical facts about relationships are important but are scientifically unsatisfactory without theoretical explanation. This article describes a theory that accounts for the central role of GMA in job training programs and in job performance and cites the research evidence supporting this theory.

Nearly 100 years ago, Spearman (1904) proposed that the construct of GMA is central to human affairs. The research presented in this article supports his proposal in the world of work, an area of life critical to individuals, organizations, and the economy as a whole.

References

Ackerman, P. L. (1986). individual differences in information processing: An investigation of intellectual abilities and task performance during practice. *Intelligence, 10,* 101–139.

Ackerman, P. L. (1987). Individual differences in skill learning: An integration of psychometric and information processing perspectives. *Psychological Bulletin, 102,* 3–27.

Ackerman, P. L. (1988). Determinants of individual differences during skill acquisition: Cognitive abilities and information processing. *Journal of Experimental Psychology: General, 117,* 288–318.

Ackerman, P. L. (1990). A correlational analysis of skill specificity: Learning, abilities, and individual differences. *Journal of Experimental Psychology: Learning, Memory, and Cognition, 16,* 883–901.

Ackerman, P. L. (1992). Predicting individual differences in complex skill acquisition: Dynamics of ability determinants. *Journal of Applied Psychology, 77,* 598–614.

Ball, R. S. (1938). The predictability of occupational level from intelligence. *Journal of Consulting Psychology, 2,* 184–186.

Barrick, M. R., & Mount, M. K. (1991). The Big Five personality dimensions and job performance: A meta-analysis. *Personnel Psychology, 41,* 1–26.

Barrick, M. R., & Mount, M. K. (1993). Autonomy as a moderator of the relationships between the big five personality dimensions and job performance. *Journal of Applied Psychology, 78,* 111–118.

Barrick, M. R., Mount, M. K., & Judge, T. A. (2001). The FFM personality dimensions and job performance: Meta-analysis of meta-analyses. *International Journal of Selection and Assessment, 9,* 9–30.

Barrick, M. R., Mount, M. K., & Strauss, J. P. (1993). Conscientiousness and performance of sales representatives: Test of the mediation effects of goal setting. *Journal of Applied Psychology, 78,* 715–722.

Barrick, M. R., Stewart, G. L., Neubert, M. J., & Mount, M. K. (1998). Relating member ability and personality to work-team processes and team effectiveness. *Journal of Applied Psychology, 83,* 377–391.

Block, J. (1995). A contrarian view of the five factor approach to personality. *Psychological Bulletin, 117,* 226–229.

Borman, W. C., Hanson, M. A., Oppler, S. H., & Pulakos, E. D. (1993). The role of early supervisor experience in supervisor performance. *Journal of Applied Psychology, 78,* 443–449.

Borman, W. C., White, E. D., Pulakos, E. D., & Oppler, S. H. (1991). Models evaluating the effects of ratee ability, knowledge, proficiency, temperament, awards, and problem behavior on supervisor ratings. *Journal of Applied Psychology, 76,* 863–872.

Bouchard, Jr., T. J. (1998). Genetic and environmental influences on adult intelligence and special mental abilities. *Human Biology, 70*, 257–279.

Bouchard, Jr., T. J., Lykken, D. T., McGue, M., Segal, N. L., & Tellegen, A. (1990, October 12). Sources of human differences: The Minnesota study of twins reared apart. *Science, 250*, 223–228.

Brown, W. W., & Reynolds, M. O. (1975). A model of IQ, occupation, and earnings. *American Economic Review, 65*, 1002–1007.

Butcher, J. N., & Rouse, S. V. (1996). Personality: Individual differences and clinical assessment. *Annual Review of Psychology, 47*, 87–111.

Callender, J. C., & Osburn, H. G. (1981). Testing the constancy of validity with computer generated sampling distributions of the multiplicative model variance estimate: Results for the petroleum industry validation research. *Journal of Applied Psychology, 66*, 274–281.

Campbell, J. P., McCloy, R. A., Oppler, S. H., & Sager, C. E. (1992). A theory of performance, In N. Schmitt & W. Borman (Eds.), *New developments in selection and placement* (pp. 49–56). San Francisco: Jossey-Bass.

Carroll, J. B. (1993). *Human cognitive abilities*. Cambridge, England: Cambridge University Press.

Center for Human Resource Research, (1989). *The future of NLS research*. Columbus, OH: Center for Human Resource Research, The Ohio State University.

Cohen, J., & Cohen, P. (1988). *Applied multiple regression/correlation analysis for the behavioral sciences* (2nd ed.). Hillsdale, NJ: Erlbaum.

Costa, P. T., Jr., & McCrae, R. R. (1988). Personality in adulthood: A six-year longitudinal study of self-reports and spouse ratings on the NEO Personality Inventory. *Journal of Personality and Social Psychology, 54*, 853–863.

Costa, P. T., Jr., & McCrae, R. R. (1991). Four ways five factors are basic. *Personality and Individual Differences, 13*, 653–665.

Dawis, R. V. (1994). Occupations. In R. T. Sternberg (Ed.), *Encyclopedia of human intelligence, Vol. 2* (pp. 781–785). New York: Macmillan.

Deary, I. J., Whalley, L. J., Lemmon, H., Crawford, J. R., & Starr, J. M. (2000). The stability of individual differences in mental ability from childhood to old age: Follow-up of the 1932 Scottish mental survey. *Intelligence, 28*, 49–55.

Dreher, G. F., & Bretz, R. D. (1991). Cognitive ability and career attainment: The moderating effects of early career success. *Journal of Applied Psychology, 76*, 392–397.

Goldberg, L. R. (1990). An alternative "description of personality": The Big Five factor structure. *Journal of Personality and Social Psychology, 59*, 1216–1229.

Gottfredson, L. S. (1997). Why *g* matters: The complexity of everyday life. *Intelligence, 24*, 79–132.

Gottfredson, L. S., & Crouse, J. (1986). Validity versus utility of mental tests. Examples of the SAT. *Journal of Vocational Behavior, 29*, 363–378.

Hamer, D., & Copeland, P. (1998). *Living with our genes: Why they matter more than you think*. New York: Doubleday.

Harrell, T. W., & Harrell, M. S. (1945). Army general classification test scores for civilian occupations. *Educational and Psychological Measurement, 5*, 229–239.

Herrnstein, R. J., & Murray, C. (1994). *The bell curve*. New York: The Free Press.

Hirsh, H. R., Northrup, L., & Schmidt, F. L. (1986). Validity generalization results for law enforcement occupations. *Personnel Psychology, 39*, 399–420.

Holland, J. L. (1985). *Making vocational choices: A theory of vocational personalities and work environments*. Odessa, FL: Psychological Assessment Resources.

Holland, J. L. (1996). Exploring careers with a typology. *American Psychologist, 51*, 397–406.

Howard, A., & Bray, D. W. (1990). Predictions of managerial success over time: Lessons from the Management Progress Study. In K. E. Clark & M. B. Clark (Eds.), *Measures of leadership* (pp. 113–130). West Orange, NJ: Leadership Library of America.

Hunter, J. E. (1980). *Test validation for 12,000 jobs: An application of synthetic validity and validity generalization to the General Aptitude Test Battery (GATB)*. Washington, DC: U.S. Department of Labor.

Hunter, J. E. (1983a). A causal analysis of cognitive ability, job knowledge, job performance, and supervisor ratings. In F. Landy, S. Zedeck, & J. Cleveland (Eds.), *Performance measurement and theory* (pp. 257–266). Hillsdale, NJ: Erlbaum.

Hunter, J. E. (1983b). *The prediction of job performance in the military using ability composites: The dominance of general cognitive ability over specific aptitudes*. Report for Research Applications in partial fulfillment of Department of Defense Contract F41689-83-C-0025.

Hunter, J. E. (1986). Cognitive ability, cognitive aptitudes, job knowledge, and job performance. *Journal of Vocational Behavior, 29*, 340–362.

Hunter, J. E. (1989). *The Wonderlic Personnel Test as a predictor of training success and job performance*. Libertyville, IL: Wonderlic.

Hunter, J. E., & Hunter, R. F. (1984). Validity and utility of alternate predictors of job performance. *Psychological Bulletin, 96*, 72–98.

Hunter, J. E., & Schmidt, F. L. (1990). *Methods of meta-analysis: Correcting error and bias in research findings*. Newbury Park, CA: Sage.

Hunter, J. E., & Schmidt, F. L. (1996). Intelligence and job performance: Economic and social implications. *Psychology, Public Policy, and Law, 2*, 447–472.

Jencks, C. (1972). *Inequality: A reassessment of the effect of family and schooling in America*. New York: Harper & Row.

Jensen, A. R. (1980). *Bias in mental testing*. New York: Free Press.

Jensen, A. R. (1986). g: Artifact or reality? *Journal of Vocational Behavior, 29*, 301–331.

Jensen, A. R. (1998). *The g factor: The science of mental ability*. Westport, CT: Praeger.

Judge, T. A., Higgins, C. A., Thoresen, C. J., & Barrick, M. R. (1999). The Big Five personality traits, general mental ability, and career success across the life span. *Personnel Psychology, 52*, 621–652.

Lubinski, D. (2000). Scientific and social significance of assessing individual differences: "Sinking shafts at a few critical points." *Annual Review of Psychology, 51*, 405–444.

Lubinski, D., & Humphreys, L. G. (1997). Incorporating general intelligence into epidemiology and the social sciences. *Intelligence, 24*, 159–201.

McCrae, R. R., & Costa, Jr., P. T. (1997). Personality trait structure as a human universal. *American Psychologist, 52*, 509–516.

McCrae, R. R., & John, O. P. (1992). An introduction to the five-factor model and its applications. *Journal of Personality, 60*, 175–215.

McDaniel, M. A. (1985). *The evaluation of a causal model of job performance: The interrelationships of general mental ability, job experience, and job performance*. Unpublished doctoral dissertation, George Washington University.

McDaniel, M. A., Schmidt, F. L., & Hunter, J. E. (1988). Job experience correlates of job performance. *Journal of Applied Psychology, 73*, 327–330.

McGue, M., & Bouchard, Jr., T. J. (1998). Genetic and environmental influences on human behavioral differences. *Annual Review of Neuroscience, 21*, 1–14.

McHenry, J. J., Hough, L. M., Toquam, J. L., Hanson, M. A., & Ashworth, S. (1990). Project A validity results: The relationship between predictor and criterion domains. *Personnel Psychology, 43*, 335–354.

Mount, M. K., & Barrick, M. R. (1995). The big five personality dimensions: Implications for research and practice in human resources management. In G. Ferris (Ed.), *Research in personnel and human resources management* (Vol. 13, pp. 153–200). Greenwich, CT: JAI Press.

Mount, M. K., Barrick, M. R., & Strauss, J. P. (1994). Validity of observer ratings of The Big Five personality dimensions. *Journal of Applied Psychology, 79*, 272–280.

Murphy, K. R. (1989). Is the relationship between cognitive ability and job performance stable over time? *Human Performance, 2*, 183–200.

Murray, C. (1998). *Income and inequality*. Washington, DC: AEI Press.

Olea, M. M., & Ree, M. J. (1994). Predicting pilot and navigator criteria: Not much more than g. *Journal of Applied Psychology, 79*, 845–851.

Ones, D. S. (1993). *The construct validity of integrity tests*. Unpublished doctoral dissertation, University of Iowa.

Ones, D. S., Viswesvaran, C., & Schmidt. F. L. (1993). Comprehensive meta-analysis of integrity test validities: Findings and implications for personnel selection and theories of job performance. *Journal of Applied Psychology, 78*, 679–703.

Pearlman, K., Schmidt, F. L., & Hunter, J. E. (1980). Validity generalization results for tests used to predict job proficiency and training criteria in clerical occupations. *Journal of Applied Psychology, 65*, 373–407.

Pulver, A., Allik, J., Pulkkinen, L., & Hamalainen, M. (1995). A Big Five personality inventory in two non-Indo-European languages. *European Journal of Personality, 9*, 109–124.

Ree, M. J., & Carretta, T. R. (1998). General cognitive ability and occupational performance. In C. Cooper & I. Robertson (Eds.), *International review of industrial organizational psychology, 1998* (pp. 159–184). New York: Wiley.

Ree, M. J., & Earles, J. A. (1991). Predicting training success: Not much more than g. *Personnel Psychology, 44*, 321–332.

Ree, M. J., & Earles, J. A. (1992). Intelligence is the best predictor of job performance. *Current Directions in Psychological Science, 1*, 86–89.

Ree, M. J., Earles, J. A., & Teachout, M. (1994). Predicting job performance: Not much for than g. *Journal of Applied Psychology, 79*, 518–524.

Sackett, P. R., & Wilk, S. L. (1994). Within-group norming and other forms of score adjustment in pre-employment testing. *American Psychologist, 49*, 929–954.

Salgado, J. F. (1997). The five factor model of personality and job performance in the European Community (EC). *Journal of Applied Psychology, 82*, 30–43.

Savickas, M. L., & Spokane, A. R. (1999). *Vocational interests: Their meaning, measurement, and use in counseling*, Palo Alto, CA: Davies-Black.

Schmidt, F. L. (1992). What do data really mean? Research findings, meta-analysis, and cumulative knowledge in psychology. *American Psychologist, 47*, 1173–1181.

Schmidt, F. L. (2002). The role of general cognitive ability and job performance: Why there can be no debate. *Human Performance, 15*, 187–210.

Schmidt, F. L., Gast-Rosenberg, I. F., & Hunter, J. E. (1980). Validity generalization results for computer programmers. *Journal of Applied Psychology, 65*, 643–661.

Schmidt, F. L., & Hunter, J. E. (1992). Causal modeling of processes determining job performance. *Current Directions in Psychological Science, 1*, 89–92.

Schmidt, F. L., & Hunter, J. E. (1998). The validity and utility of selection methods in personnel psychology: Practical and theoretical implications of 85 years of research findings. *Psychological Bulletin, 124*, 262–274.

Schmidt, F. L., Hunter, J. E., & Outerbridge, A. N. (1986). The impact of job experience and ability on job knowledge, work sample performance and supervisory ratings of job performance. *Journal of Applied Psychology, 71*, 432–439.

Schmidt, F. L., Hunter, J. E., Outerbridge, A. N., & Goff, S. (1988). The joint relation of experience and ability with job performance: A test of three hypotheses. *Journal of Applied Psychology, 73*, 46–57.

Schmidt, F. L., Hunter, J. E., Pearlman, K., & Shane, G. S. (1979). Further tests of the Schmidt–Hunter Bayesian validity generalization model. *Personnel Psychology, 32*, 257–281.

Schmidt, F. L., Hunter, J. E., & Pearlman, K. (1981). Task differences and validity of aptitude tests in selection: A red herring. *Journal of Applied Psychology, 66*, 166–185.

Schmidt, F. L., & Kaplan, L. B. (1971). Composite vs. multiple criteria: A review and resolution of the controversy. *Personnel Psychology, 24*, 419–434.

Schmidt, F. L., Law, K., Hunter, J. E., Rothstein, H. R., Pearlman, K., & McDaniel, M. (1993). Refinements in validity generalization methods: Implications for the situational specificity hypothesis. *Journal of Applied Psychology, 78*, 3–13.

Schmidt, F. L., Ones, D. S., & Hunter, J. E. (1992). Personnel selection. *Annual Review of Psychology, 43*, 627–670.

Siegel, J. P., & Ghiselli, E. E. (1971). Managerial talent, pay, and age. *Journal of Vocational Behavior, 1*, 129–135.

Spearman, C. (1904). "General intelligence," objectively determined and measured. *American Journal of Psychology, 15*, 201–293.

Stewart, N. (1947). AGCT scores of Army personnel grouped by occupation. *Occupations, 26*, 5–41.

Thorndike, R. L. (1986). The role of general ability in prediction. *Journal of Vocational Behavior, 29*, 332–339.

Thorndike, R. L., & Hagen, E. (1959). *Ten thousand careers*. New York: Wiley.

Viswesvaran, C., Schmidt, F. L., & Ones, D. S. (2002). *Is there a general factor in job performance ratings independent of halo error?* Manuscript submitted for publication. Florida International University.

Wilk, S. L., Desmarais, L. B., & Sackett, P. R. (1995). Gravitation to jobs commensurate with ability: Longitudinal and cross-sectional tests. *Journal of Applied Psychology, 80*, 79–85.

Wilk, S. L., & Sackett, P. R. (1996). Longitudinal analysis of ability-job complexity fit and job change. *Personnel Psychology, 49*, 937–967.

Wonderlic, E. F. (1992). *Wonderlic Personnel Test user's manual*. Libertyville, IL: Wonderlic.

Yerkes, R. M. (Ed.). (1921). *Psychological examining in the U.S. Army: Memoirs of the National Academy of Sciences* (Vol. 15). Washington, DC: U.S. Government Printing Office.

Yoon, K., Schmidt, F. L., & Ilies, R. (2002). Cross-cultural construct validity of the five-factor model of personality among Korean employees. *Journal of Cross-Cultural Psychology, 33*, 217–235.

24

WHY DO ASSESSMENT CENTERS WORK?

The puzzle of assessment center validity

Richard Klimoski and Mary Brickner

Source: *Personnel Psychology* 40 (1987): 243–260.

Abstract

The finding that assessment centers are successful in making valid predictions of managerial success is well established in the literature. Unfortunately, it is not clearly understood *why* assessment centers work. For example, construct validity of assessment center dimensions is rarely obtained. In this paper we affirm the evidence for predictive validity of assessment centers and conclude that assessment centers can work for a variety of purposes and in numerous contexts. But we also assert that we do not know why they work. The bulk of the paper goes on to raise possible explanations for the predictive validity observed in assessment centers and raises implications for practice and guidance of future research.

Assessment centers appear to be the modern enigma in human resource practices. The use of assessment center procedures for assessments of managerial potential is prevalent in corporations, large and small. Although assessment centers are generally considered valid predictors of managerial success, the nature of those predictions and the underlying dynamics of assessment center practices remain a puzzle. A number of questions surrounding assessment centers have been raised. In this paper we will try to piece the assessment center picture together by considering questions that surround assessment center practices.

Do assessment centers work?

A number of articles on assessment center validity have appeared in the literature. Meta-analyses of assessment center research results have been reported by Schmitt, Gooding, Noe, & Kirsch (1984), Hunter & Hunter (1984), and by Gaugler,

Rosenthal, Thornton & Bentson (1985). Early summaries of research (Cohen, 1980; Klimoski & Strickland, 1977) reported moderate to high validity coefficients for assessment center predictions. More recently, Schmitt, Gooding, *et al.* (1984) compared validity studies for different types of performance predictors. Their reported mean predictive validity for assessment centers was .407. Meta-analyses by Hunter & Hunter (1984) and Gaugler and her colleagues reported validities in the range of 37–43.

Given the predictive validities consistently reported in reviews, we would have to conclude that indeed assessment centers do work. Assessment centers are useful tools for predicting the future success of potential managers.

For whom do assessment centers work?

Available studies demonstrate the usefulness of assessment centers for predicting managerial success regardless of educational level (Huck, 1973), prior assessment center experience (Struth, Frank, & Amato, 1980), race (Huck & Bray, 1976; Moses, 1973), or gender (Moses, 1973; Moses & Boehm, 1975). These studies supported the usefulness of assessment centers in predicting managerial success fairly regardless of membership in subgroups.

Where do assessment centers work?

Assessment centers have been used in a wide variety of organizational settings. This selection tool has been effectively utilized in manufacturing companies (Turnage & Muchinsky, 1982), government (Struth *et al.*, 1980), military services (Borman, 1982; Tziner & Duran, 1982), utility companies (Schmitt, 1977), oil companies (Norton, 1977), educational institutions (Schmitt, Noe, Merritt, & Fitzgerald, 1984) and by the FBI (Neidig, Martin, & Yates, 1979).

For what purposes do assessment centers work?

Assessment centers have proven to be useful for a variety of purposes beyond promotion and selection (Cascio & Silbey, 1979). They are useful in training and development (Lorenzo, 1984), for career planning (Gaugler, Rosenthal, Thornton, & Bentson, 1985), and in improving important managerial skills in assessors (Lorenzo, 1984). However in the few comparative studies they have been most predictive of advancement criteria (Klimoski & Strickland, 1981; Turnage & Muchinsky, 1984).[1]

Why do assessment centers work?

The studies reviewed above establish that the assessment center is a useful tool for predicting managerial success, across organizations and types of employees and for a number of purposes. Given the extensive literature, however, we believe it appropriate (even long overdue) to ask "Why?".

As straightforward as this question must seem, it appears to us that no firm answer is yet available. Quite the contrary, given the nature of assessment center research and the evidence generated in the last ten years, there appear to be several plausible explanations.

The traditional explanation

Assessment centers have been designed to predict managerial success by providing raters with an opportunity to infer personal qualities and traits that have been determined, through careful job analysis, to be relevant to success (Byham, 1980). That is, assessment centers are standardized devices to allow assessments of traits, which are then used for predicting future success on the job. The traditional argument is that assessment centers work because they do a good job of measuring and integrating information regarding an individual's traits or qualities (Byham, 1980). But do they?

The evidence for the construct validity of the dimensions used in assessment centers is not encouraging. The bulk of the reported literature shows little support for the view that assessment center procedures do in fact produce scores that serve as valid representations of separate constructs or that those constructs are used in evaluation decisions in the manner proposed by assessment center designers.

Sackett and Hakel (1979) examined how individuals used assessment center information in forming overall ratings. They found that assessors used only a small number of dimensions although they had been instructed to use all of them in making their judgments. Three dimensions (leadership, organizing and planning, and decision making) accurately predicted overall ratings. Considered pessimistically, their results imply the existence of only general and diffuse measurements of behaviors. Alternatively, it may be that the dimensionality of effectiveness is not that complex. In either case, this raises real questions about both the need and the potential for centers to discriminate among a large number of dimensions.

Turnage and Muchinsky (1982) reported that assessment center trait ratings gave little help beyond what could be obtained from a global rating. The average correlation between dimension ratings and the overall rating was .91. They reported a lack of discriminant validity and high levels of convergent validity across traits. This was considered an indication that assessors were making global evaluations rather than differentiating among traits.

Sackett and Dreher (1982) studied the interrelationships among dimensions between and within assessment center exercises in three different organizations. In all three organizations they found within-exercise ratings correlated more highly with each other than did dimensional ratings across exercises. In two of the organizations there was no convergence among the various measures of a dimension (the average correlation was zero). Method variance predominated over the shared variance of measures of a single trait. In the third organization, all ratings were highly correlated with all other ratings. This indicates a lack of discriminant validity for the dimensions considered. They concluded that there was little evidence that assessment center ratings accurately reflect the complex traits that they purport to measure (p. 401).

Russell (1985, 1986) sought to further our understanding of the decision-making processes of assessors in assessment centers. His findings were consistent with previous research (Sackett & Hakel, 1979): assessors did not use specific dimensions in making their judgments. In his study, assessors' perceptions of center participants were strongly affected by an underlying factor (either interpersonal skills or problem-solving skills). In his later study, halo across the six dimensions assessed in two exercises was great. Russell suggests that "the best guesses of assessment center architects and job analysts should not be expected necessarily to exhibit rigorous evidence of construct validity" (Russell, 1985, p. 743). He too emphasizes that the bases for the predictive validity of assessment centers are not understood.

The available research consistently demonstrates a lack of evidence for the construct validity of assessment center dimension ratings. Moreover, it convinces us that assessment centers are *not* working as designed. If they have predictive validity, it is not because they are effectively measuring and using traits (Zedeck & Cascio, 1984). We must look elsewhere for the answer.

Some alternative explanations

A variety of alternative explanations for why assessment centers appear to work can be gleaned from the literature. The following are presented as possibilities. In many cases they appear as suggestions made by various writers. Few have been carefully evaluated.

Actual criteria contamination explanation

The apparent predictive validity of assessment centers could arise out of the unintended but real possibility that promotions in organizations (or other criterion decisions) are partially based on assessment center judgments. Thus, individuals who get favorable ratings are considered for promotion over those who do not. A future analysis of the relationship between center assessments and promotions would then appear to show a correspondence between assessment center ratings and success criteria.

In the early literature (e.g., Kraut & Scott, 1972), this dynamic was popularly referred to as the "crown prince (princess)" system of promotions. In true predictive studies (e.g., Bray & Grant, 1966), of course, this type of criterion contamination is not possible (unless the assessment center ratings are allowed to be "leaked out"). However, in many studies (e.g., Klimoski & Strickland, 1981) data are gathered from operational centers. That is, assessment center evaluations are obtained and used for purposes of administrative action (e.g., selecting individuals for promotions). Under these circumstances criterion contamination is quite possible.

As of 1974, Howard listed ten studies reporting validity data in which center ratings had been used for promotions. Not surprisingly, all of these showed significant relationships. She argued, however, that while such contamination could indeed artificially inflate the apparent validity of center predictions, it was not a major problem because center ratings would be used less frequently as a basis for advancement in later years. Kraut and Scott (1972) were similarly reassuring. They maintained that a favorable rating was not sufficient to be promoted, with the "possible exception of the top 5% who receive the very highest rating" (p. 128). If some companies use center ratings for promotions, however, it is only for the initial move. Beyond this, other dynamics operate to determine who gets ahead (Stumpf & London, 1981). Silzer (1985) reported that 73% of those providing on-the-job ratings had never seen assessment reports; 9% had seen them three to nine years before providing criterion information. Finally, Gaugler et al. (1985) found little support for the actual contamination hypotheses. In their metaanalysis, study design did not moderate assessment center validity. Specifically, reports from operational centers did not show higher validities than those where center ratings (as potential predictors) were thought not to be used. Nevertheless, in the face of so little research to test this notion specifically, it cannot be ruled out as a potential explanation for apparent center validity.

"Subtle" criterion contamination

Klimoski and Strickland (1977) proposed the notion that assessment center validity might be affected by a form of criterion contamination that operates in an indirect or subtle fashion. Their reasoning was based on the fact that a great deal of evidence for the validity of assessment centers was based on predictions of promotions or promotion-linked criteria (e.g., salary growth). They proposed that, instead of looking for behavioral evidence of specific traits or personal qualities, assessment center staff in fact observe and evaluate candidates on the basis of their knowledge of those factors needed to get ahead in the company. Instead of systematically evaluating each person on the dimensions created for the center, they attempt to perform a policy-capturing function and to mimic what future decision makers might do in making a promotion decision. This may or may not be based on performance. Thus, judgments made by center staff would tend to correlate with judgments made by managers in the field.

Once again there is little definitive research on this potential explanation; most evidence is circumstantial. For example, if this dynamic were operating, assessment center validities would be higher for promotion criteria than for other success indicators (e.g., performance in grade). As mentioned, this does appear to be the case. Similarly, the explanation implies that assessment center staff characteristics would affect the magnitude of the validities obtained. That is, staff who come from or who have intimate knowledge of the corporate setting into which center participants will go after being assessed should be better able to predict (or anticipate) the promotion criteria and processes. They should produce judgments with higher validities than outsiders or consultants. Silzer (1985) did find higher validities for staff who had greater familiarity with norms in one versus another company. In fact, he agrees with Holt (1970) that such knowledge is an indispensable feature of a good clinical prediction paradigm. In contrast, Gaugler *et al.* (1985) reported in their meta-analysis that validities were higher when assessors were psychologists rather than managers. Presumably the former would have less familiarity with organizational decision making about promotions than the latter. Still other studies have reported equivocal results (e.g., Borman, Eaton, Bryan, & Rosse, 1983).

One other line of evidence relevant to the argument that subtle criterion contamination may be operating has been raised by Dunnette & Borman (1979). They observed that assessments of overall performance or potential in assessment centers tend to correlate more highly with organizational success criteria than do ratings of specific dimensions. Moreover, the average validity coefficients for dimension ratings are much lower than those obtained for overall ratings (e.g., Tumage & Muchinsky, 1984). They reason that overall assessment ratings are thus likely to be influenced by factors that are presumably linked to success in the company but not reflected in the dimensions (e.g., proper background, appearance, etc.). In our opinion, the subtle criterion contamination hypothesis of Klimoski and Strickland cannot be ruled out as a significant contributor to assessment center validity.

Self-fulfilling prophecy explanation

Another possible explanation for the apparent validity of assessment centers relates to a self-fulfilling prophecy dynamic operating for assessees. It could be argued that being selected to participate in an assessment center may reinforce the feelings of self-efficacy for competent managerial candidates. Bandura (1982) notes that judgments of self-efficacy affect how much effort a person will direct toward a goal and how long he or she will persist in striving to attain a goal. He suggests that if a person has a strong sense of self-efficacy, that person will exert more effort and be more persistent in meeting a challenge. Moreover, competent managerial candidates, after experiencing success on assessment center tasks, may also have increased feelings of self-efficacy. This state results in the candidate directing more effort toward the development of skills and abilities that are important to managerial success. In this way, the selection of competent people for participation in the assessment center becomes a self-fulfilling prophecy. Even if individuals are put through centers as a matter of course (as a result of seniority or a court ruling), receiving favorable feedback on performance in the center would reinforce an "effective-manager" self-image. This, in turn, would result in greater effort and persistence in developing the managerial skills and abilities important to managerial success. Such increased effort in the development of managerial skills should result (given the assessed capacity), in greater managerial capability.

Finally, higher levels of managerial skill would increase the probability of selection or promotion to a managerial position. In a sense, the assessee can make the staff prediction come true.

Both Russell (1986) and Gaugler *et al.* (1985) refer to these notions and the potential role of self-efficacy. Moreover, we know that expectations for high performance on the part of others can be communicated and do have an impact (Rosenthal & Jacobson, 1968). For example, in a field experiment in a training context, Eden found that staff members who believed in the high potential of their trainees (regardless of their actual capabilities) had classes with disproportionate numbers of high performers. More to the point, this high performance continued even when the original trainers had been transferred for administrative reasons (Eden & Ravid, 1982; Eden & Shari, 1982). Thus, instructor expectancies appeared to have been perceived, reinforced, and internalized as part of the trainees' self-images, with positive outcomes as a result (see also Crawford, Thomas, & Fink, 1980). While little data to test this notion in an assessment center context are available, we do know that center participation alone can change or reinforce self-perceptions (Schmitt *et al.*, 1986).

Performance consistency explanation

Judgments in assessment centers are supposed to be based on trait inferences made from observations of behavior elicited by the center exercises and tasks.

It is possible, however, that a different process might be operating. That is, staff may be evaluating the past and present performance of individuals and basing overall assessments on these, thus bypassing the judgment of traits entirely. High performers in the centers are thus predicted to be high performers in future managerial roles.

This explanation is based on certain features of the typical assessment center. One is that a great deal of achievement-relevant background information in the form of autobiographical information is available to staff before they make assessment evaluations. This information is gathered at a number of points in the center process, most notably in the extensive, in-depth interviews that are usually conducted. The vast literature on the value of biodata for predicting job success (Campbell, Dunnette, Lawler & Weick, 1970; Childs & Klimoski, 1986; Owens, 1976) makes it clear that the validity of staff predictions could be enhanced by relying on such information. Past history of successes would thus be expected to relate to future success.

As straightforward as this explanation is, it is also true that there seems to be little evidence available to evaluate it. Studies have attempted to examine components of the assessment center for their contributions to the center's prediction of success (e.g., Hinrichs & Haanpera, 1976; Wollowick & McNamara, 1969), but the biodata component has rarely been explicitly considered. Borman (1982) found little evidence of the predictive validity of a structured interview in an assessment center created for evaluating Army recruiters. But it is not clear how much biodata was actually obtained in the interviews conducted for the study.

On the other hand, Hinrichs (1969) noted that data from existing personnel records were highly predictive of overall ratings obtained from a two-day assessment center program. He suggested that a careful evaluation of personnel records and employment history could provide much of the same information (or at least the predictive power) as a lengthy and expensive assessment program (p. 431). Turnage & Muchinsky (1984) did use assessment center data in which there was a biodata component, but the results (with the exception of age) were not that supportive of the past history explanation of center ratings.

Alternatively, the predictive validity of assessment centers may rest on a second feature, the fact that center exercises serve as job samples. To the extent that the exercises (as job samples) reflect behavior and performance that is relevant and representative of future managerial job requirements, evaluations should be related to and predict managerial success. Such evaluations, however, would serve as indications of current levels of performance (a sample) rather than assessments of managerial potential (a sign; Wernimont & Campbell, 1968). To phrase it differently, present performance (in center exercises) predicts future performance (as managers).

The designs of most assessment centers are based on the results of job analyses (Byham, 1980). Most specialists would agree that this is a necessary step in the development of any center. Nevertheless, there is some controversy as to just how job analysis information is to be used. Traditionally, it has provided the bases for the identification of managerial job requirements–the traits or qualities to be assessed. In fact, it serves to produce what is usually referred to as the construct validity for assessment centers (Sackett & Dreher, 1984). But job analysis can also be the source of information for creating the actual simulations used. That is, it can be the basis for establishing a center's content validity. For example, Neidig and Neidig (1984) contend that an accurate sampling of relevant work situations in a center is critical for establishing the job relatedness of the assessment center. In this way job analysis can ensure that good performance on the exercises will relate to good on-the-job performance because the candidate is presumed to have the requisite knowledge, abilities, and traits if he/she does well. But it should be stressed that the measurement of performance levels on samples (as predictors) need not even involve the notion of underlying constructs (see, e.g., Campion, 1972).

We will not attempt to restate, much less resolve, the arguments about whether assessment centers should have construct validity or content validity (or both). The interested reader is referred to Brush and Schoenfeldt (1977), Byham (1980), Dreher and Sackett (1981), Neidig and Neidig (1984), Norton (1977, 1981), and Sackett and Dreher (1982, 1984). The point is that most centers *do* involve the use of apparently content (face?) valid exercises or simulations (i.e., job samples). Assessment centers may work (be valid) because levels of performance on these exercises, not inference with regard to particular traits, form the bases for predicting managerial job success.

A managerial intelligence explanation

A final hypotheses with regard to the reasons for assessment center validity bears some relationship to the subtle criterion contamination notion. It is sufficiently distinct, however, to merit special mention. To put it simply, assessment centers may predict managerial success because the ratings obtained reflect the level of intellectual functioning of candidates.

There seems to be no doubt that intelligence is important for managerial effectiveness. Most analyses of managerial job requirements refer to the importance of verbal skills (manifested in oral and written communications), analytic or reasoning skills, the regular use of short- and long-term reasoning, including well-developed plans or routines (for example, scripts) for the combining of information. Effective managerial functioning is also thought to involve what has been called the application of "tacit knowledge" (Wagner & Sternberg, 1985). Research suggests that tacit knowledge appears to be acquired and developed by intellectually more capable individuals. In short, intelligence can be defined by that old phrase, "what one needs when you don't know what to do". Given the nature of managerial work, intelligence must be viewed as a major determinant of managerial success (Lord, DeVader, & Alliger, 1986; Yukl, 1981).

Actually, the empirical relationship between intelligence and managerial performance has long been established (Ghiselli, 1966, 1971, 1973; McCormick & Tiffin, 1974; Miner, 1957). Ghiselli (1966) reported intelligence tests as the best predictors of future performance for foremen, managers, administrators, and executives. Moderate correlations (.25–.30) between intelligence and performance are frequently obtained. In his (1971) study of managerial talent he was also able to report moderate correlations (.28–.45) between intelligence and performance for managers and personnel officers. Lower correlations (.01–.07), however, were found in studies of line managers in packing plants. Similarly, in 1973, Ghiselli determined that intelligence tests were useful for predicting trainability, job proficiency, and performance among foremen, administrators, and executives (correlation ranging from .28–.36). These data provide evidence for the consistent relationship observed between intelligence and effective managerial performance. Miner also (1957) reviewed a number of studies of intelligence and success in military contexts.

The importance of intelligence has also been recognized explicitly by the assessment center literature. To begin with, it is frequently part of the measurement plan of assessment centers. Thornton and Byham (1982) refer to a number of centers that incorporated intelligence measures. Bray and Grant (1966) used three intelligence tests in their famous Management Progress Study.

Scores from these tests all correlated significantly with staff predictions of success for managers. Moses (1973) found that SCAT scores were significantly correlated with intelligence in a longitudinal study of assessment center evaluations and managerial performance. Huck (1973) reported moderate correlations (.40) between SCAT test scores and overall assessment ratings. And Carleton (1970) found moderate correlations between intelligence test scores and a composite criterion of behavioral ratings in assessment centers. This was also true of a recent study by Wolfson (1985) at IBM. Schmitt (1977) reported high correlations between intelligence test scores (SCAT) and overall dimension ratings.

Finally, the observed predictive validity of assessment centers may be attributable, in part, to assessment centers as measures of intelligence. For example, Tziner and Dolan (1982) compared assessment center results with some traditional forms of evaluation (i.e., tests of verbal intelligence, supervisory evaluation, evaluations for selection interviews). They found that verbal intelligence scores were highly predictive of future performance. In fact, these scores were better than individual exercises and overall assessment ratings for predicting future performance. Intelligence scores accounted for the largest portion of variance. Moreover, Klimoski and Strickland (1981) found that paper and pencil measures of intelligence predicted future managerial performance ratings better than did assessment centers.

All this is not to argue that measures of intelligence are superior to assessment centers as predictors or that assessment ratings are to be characterized as perfect surrogates for intelligence tests. In fact, the evidence is too equivocal to do this. The interested reader can contrast the findings of Schmitt, Gooding, et al. (1984), Turnage and Muchinsky (1984), Russell (1985), and Gaugler et al. (1985).

What does seem clear, however, is that both center behavior and assessor judgments are influenced in part by the level of general intellectual functioning of assessees. Further, the on-the-job performance of these same individuals is likely to be similarly affected. If assessment centers predict job success, their apparent validity may be due, in part, to this underlying nomological network. At this point, however, we just don't know the extent of this happening.

In this section we have discussed several possible explanations for the predictive validity that is so characteristic of assessment center predictions. These explanations (or hypotheses) include criterion contamination, policy capturing, self-fulfilling prophecies for assessees, construct and context capturing capacity, and assessment centers as measures of intelligence. These explanations are not mutually exclusive and are probably not equally complete or plausible. However, they do provide implications for both practice and future research.

Implications for practice

The various explanations for the mechanisms by which assessment centers appear to obtain their validity would seem to make a difference for practices in this area. That is to say, the beliefs of and assumptions made by managers would guide choices among different assessment center formats and the likelihood of their use.

Managers frequently have a real need to assess or inventory the personal traits or qualities of individuals. For example, they may wish to provide accurate and specific developmental feedback to employees. Thus, they might well turn to assessment centers as the technique of choice. The available research evidence suggests it would be a mistake to do this. They might be better advised to consider alternative devices (e.g., standardized paper-and-pencil instruments, clinical inferences by trained professionals).

If, however, managers believe that the assessment center has the potential to be construct valid, certain steps are warranted. They might start by limiting the number of dimensions or qualities to be assessed. The latter could be selected to reflect higher order constructs or broader attributes than is usually the case (e.g., interpersonal skill vs. behavior flexibility), thus acknowledging both the ecological relationship among human traits and the limits of human (assessor) capacities to discriminate. For example, Barr and Hitt (1986) reported that experienced managers used substantially fewer factors yet produced decisions with more explanatory power than did naive subjects.

Furthermore, staff might be given longer periods of training than seem to be the case with centers set up more recently. Similarly, individuals might be given extended "tours of duty" as staff assessors. In this regard, it is interesting to note that in the classical (or AT&T) model, assessor assignments could last as long as a year. In such cases, the expertise developed and the resultant capacities to discriminate among traits would seem to be much greater than would occur among individuals serving as staff at a center set up for a single group of candidates. In any event, during training and throughout the life of the center, staff judgments should be calibrated against other construct valid indicators.

Finally, several suggestions (even programs) can be found in the literature for how one might improve the validity of trait judgments, depending on whether the problem is believed to derive from human information-processing errors occurring during the encoding of behavioral information (McElroy & Downey, 1982; Nathan & Alexander, 1985) or when it is retrieved at the time assessment ratings are made (Alba & Hasher, 1983; Johnson & Raye, 1981).

In contrast, the manager may not be that concerned about constructs but may still be interested in valid prediction; our review implies several alternatives. If an assessment center format is to be retained (and for procedural justice reasons we can see why this might be the case), a content-based model might be followed. Assessment center exercises would be designed as work-sample tests. As is frequently the case anyway, the major tasks to be performed in the managerial role would be simulated in the center. In contrast with present practices, however, the way candidate performance is assessed and scored would be different. Instead of obtaining staff ratings on behavioral dimensions, points would be allocated for appropriate actions taken by candidates. Staff would no longer be required to provide inferences about a candidate on some underlying construct but would only have to record whether or not something actually occurred (see Campion, 1972, and Schmitt & Ostroff, 1986, for an example of how such work samples might be scored).

The dynamics of some of the other "explanations" could actually be utilized to meet the needs of the organization—or attempts might be made to mitigate them. For example, high levels of (practical) intelligence might be recognized as relevant and appropriate in managerial candidates. Standardized measures could then be used as the preferred assessment tool (Sternberg, 1979). Similarly, high performers in the center might be encouraged to take pride in this accomplishment and to do things to strengthen this self-image. On the other hand, if subtle criterion contamination is felt to be a problem, it may be wise to use individuals as assessors who have limited knowledge of the organization. In fact, candidates might be sent to "generic" centers conducted by specialized consulting firms or sponsored by industry groups.

Implications for research

While the above advice might be given to practitioners, it must frequently be based on inferences from the available research literature. The fact is, most evidence for the alternative dynamics of center validity is circumstantial. Thus, almost any of the suggestions provided should be considered tentative and the starting point for research.

In terms of priorities, however, given the real need of organizations to assess potential (apart from competencies), it would seem most important to establish if, or under what conditions, assessment centers can be made to produce valid measures of constructs. Given what we now know about human judgment and social cognition, there is some reason to be optimistic about finding a solution. Recent theories in these areas should be applied to the assessment center process (see Zedeck, 1986, for an excellent treatment of this).

Specifically, numerous and potentially relevant variables could be experimentally manipulated to determine their impact on discriminant and convergent validities of staff ratings. For example, Silverman, Dalessio, Woods, and Johnson (1986) predicted on the basis of current models of cognitive processing that there would be differences in the dimensionality and construct validity of assessments made by staff who were instructed to form dimension ratings right after each center exercise (a common practice) and by those who would have to postpone making such judgments until all the exercises had been completed. This was indeed found to be true. Unfortunately, the authors did not go on to see to what extent criterion-related validities were similarly affected. Turnage and Muchinsky (1982) also stressed the potential impact of limiting the number of dimensions to be assessed on construct validity.

Similarly, Zajonc's (1960) concept of cognitive tuning implies that individuals have a tendency to simplify social information and to reduce or minimize attention to discrepant information. This is especially true when we expect to have to pass on impressions to other people. If this is occurring in assessment centers, perhaps centers should be redesigned so that certain staff would provide the behavioral information but others would actually make the dimension rating. To take this one step further, one might speculate on the consequences for better construct validity if separate staff were used to make the overall assessment ratings or predictions of likely success with trait ratings as input from others.

Research on the impact of staff specialization (with regard to dimensions) or exercise specialization (e.g., where exercises are designed to produce behavior relevant to a single dimension) might reveal advantages of these approaches (see Cohen & Sands, 1978, for a parallel example). Finally, alternative methods of reaching overall assessment ratings might be examined. Instead of having staff follow a majority or consensus-decision rule, dialectical or devil's advocacy models could be incorporated. There is some evidence that the latter would produce better quality (more construct valid) evaluations (Schweiger, Sandberg, & Ragan, 1986; Zedeck, 1986). Other suggestions for research on the potential impact on group processes on overall assessment ratings can be found in the work of Klimoski, Friedman, and Weldon (1980).

But studies may reveal that it is just not possible to establish assessment centers as valid measures of constructs (at least in the number and variety of interest to managers). If this were to be the case, there would still appear to be any number of programs of research that could be built around some of the alternative explanations for the assessment center's apparent predictive validity as presented in this paper. The point is, to establish the correctness of one or more of these would lead to sound recommendations for practice. This in turn, would increase our confidence that we actually know what we are doing in the use of whatever selection/promotion devices we end up with. It should also reduce the nagging feeling (as reported by one reviewer of this paper) that when assessment centers actually work, one has just been through some sort of a "voodoo rite."

Conclusion

For all we do know about assessment centers, we don't know enough. We know that these procedures are useful for predicting managerial success. Nevertheless, the predictive validity of assessment centers remains a puzzle. We agree with Russell (1985) when he states, "although assessors are apparently not doing what assessment center architects thought they were doing, the reasons behind assessment center predictive validity remain unknown" (p. 743).

In this paper we have attempted to define some of the pieces used in putting the assessment center picture together. By identifying some of the possible explanations for the predictive validity of assessment centers, we believe we provide a framework for a better understanding of the assessment center method.

Note

1 The above findings should not be used to conclude that assessment centers are performing better than alternatives in predicting these different criteria. The limited number of comparative studies which contrast alternative predictions suggest that they are not (cf. Borman, 1982; Hinrichs, 1978; Hunter & Hunter, 1984; Klimoski & Strickland, 1981).

References

Alba JW, Hasher L. (1983). Is memory schematic? *Psychological Bulletin, 92,* 203–231.

Bandura A. (1982). Self-efficacy mechanism in human agency. *American Psychologist, 37,* 122–147.

Barr SH, Hitt MA. (1986). A comparison of selection decision models in manager versus student samples. *Personnel Psychology, 39,* 599–618.

Borman WC. (1982). Validity of behavioral assessment for predicting military recruiter performance. *Journal of Applied Psychology, 67,* 3–9.

Borman WC, Eaton NK, Bryan JD, Rosse RL. (1983). Validity of Army recruiter behavioral assessment: Does the assessor make a difference. *Journal of Applied Psychology, 68,* 415–419.

Bray DW, Grant DL. (1966). The assessment center in the measurement of potential for business management. *Psychological Monographs, 80* (17 whole No. 625).

Brush DH, Schoenfeldt LF. (1980, May–June). Identifying managerial potential: An alternative to assessment centers. *Personnel,* pp. 68–76.

Byham WC. (1980, February). Starting an assessment center the correct way. *Personnel Administrator,* pp. 27–32.

Campion JE. (1972). Work sampling for personnel selection. *Journal of Applied Psychology, 56,* 40–44.

Campbell JP, Dunnette MD, Lawler EE III, Weick KB Jr. (1970). *Managerial behavior, performance, and effectiveness.* New York: McGraw Hill.

Carlton FO. (1970). *Relationships between follow-up evaluations and information developed in a management assessment center.* Paper presented at the annual meeting of the American Psychological Association, Miami Beach, FL.

Cascio WF, Silbey V. (1979). Utility of the assessment center as a selection device. *Journal of Applied Psychology, 64,* 107–118.

Childs A, Klimoski RJ. (1986). Successfully predicting career success: An application of biographical inventory. *Journal of Applied Psychology, 71,* 3–8.

Cohen SL. (1980, February). The bottom line on assessment center technology. *Personnel Administrator,* pp. 50–56.

Cohen SL, Sands L. (1978). The effects of order of exercise presentation on assessment center performance: one standardization concern, *Personnel Psychology, 31,* 35–46.

Crawford KS, Thomas BD, Fink JJ. (1980). Pygmalion at sea: Improving the work effectiveness of low performers. *Journal of Applied Behavioral Science, 16,* 482–505.

Dunnette MD, Borman WC. (1979). Personnel selection and classification systems. *Annual Review of Psychology, 30,* 477–525.

Dreher GF, Sackett PR. (1981). Some problems with applying content validity evidence to assessment center procedures. *Academy of Management Review, 6,* 551–560.

Eden D, Ravid G. (1982). Pygmalion versus self-expectancy: Effects of instructor and self-expectancy on trainee performance. *Organizational Behavior and Human Performance, 30,* 352–364.

Eden D, Shani A. (1982). Pygmalion goes to boot camp: Expentancy, leadership and trainee performance. *Journal of Applied Psychology, 67,* 194–199.

Gaugler BB, Rosenthal DB, Thornton GC III, Bentson C. (1985). *Meta-analyses of assessment center validity.* Paper presented at the annual meeting of the American Psychological Association, Los Angeles.

Ghiselli EE. (1966). *The validity of occupational aptitude tests.* New York: Wiley & Sons.

Ghiselli EE. (1971). *Explorations in managerial talent.* New York: Springer Publishing Co.

Ghiselli EE. (1973). The validity of aptitude tests in personnel selection. *Personnel Psychology, 26,* 461–477.

Hinrichs JR. (1969). Comparison of "real life" assessments of management potential with situational exercises, paper-and-pencil ability tests, and personality inventories. *Journal of Applied Psychology, 53,* 425–432.

Hinrichs JR. (1978) An eight-year follow-up of a management assessment center. *Journal of Applied Psychology, 63,* 596–601.

Hinrichs Jr, Haanpera S. (1976). Reliability of measurement in situational exercises: An assessment of the assessment center method. *Personnel Psychology, 29,* 32–40.

Holt RR. (1970). Yet another look at clinical and statistical prediction: Or is clinical psychology worthwhile. *American Psychologist, 25,* 337–349.

Howard A. (1974). An assessment of assessment centers. *Academy of Management Journal, 17,* 115–134.

Huck JR. (1973). Assessment centers: A review of the external and internal validities. *Personnel Psychology, 26,* 191–212.

Huck JR, Bray DW. (1976). Management assessment center evaluations and subsequent job performance of white and black females. *Personnel Psychology, 29,* 13–30.

Hunter JE, Hunter RF. (1984). Validity and utility of alternative predictors of job performance. *Psychological Bulletin, 96,* 72–98.

Johnson MK, Raye CL. (1981). Reality monitoring. *Psychology Review, 88,* 67–85.

Klimoski RJ, Friedman BA, Weldon E. (1980). Leader influence in the assessment of performance. *Personnel Psychology, 33,* 389–401.

Klimoski RJ & Strickland WJ. (1977). Assessment centers—valid or merely prescient. *Personnel Psychology, 30,* 353–361.

Klimoski RJ, Strickland WJ. (1981). *A comparative view of assessment centers: A case analysis,* Unpublished manuscript.

Kraut AI, Scott GJ. (1972). Validity of an operational management assessment program. *Journal of Applied Psychology, 56,* 124–129.

Lord RG, DeVader CL, Alliger GM. (1986). A meta-analysis of the relation between personality traits and leadership perceptions: An application of validity generalization procedures. *Journal of Applied Psychology, 71,* 402–410.

Lorenzo RV. (1984). Effects of assessorship on managers' proficiency in acquiring, evaluating, and communicating information about people. *Personnel Psychology, 37,* 617–634.

McCormick EJ, Tiffin J. (1974). *Industrial psychology.* Englewood Cliffs: Prentice Hall Inc.

McElroy JC, Downey HK. (1982). Observation in organization research: Panacea to the performance-attribution effect? *Academy of Management Journal, 25,* 822–835.

Miner JB. (1957). *Intelligence in the United States.* New York: Springer Publishing Co.

Moses JL. (1973). The development of an assessment center for the early identification of supervisory potential. *Personnel Psychology, 26,* 569–580.

Moses JL, Boehm VR. (1975). Relationship of assessment center performance to management progress of women. *Journal of Applied Psychology, 60,* 527–529.

Nathan BR, Alexander RA. (1985). The role of inferential accuracy in performance rating. *Academy of Management Review, 10,* 109–115.

Neidig RD, Martin JC, Yates RE. (1979). The contribution of exercise skill ratings to final assessment center evaluations. *Journal of Assessment Center Technology, 2,* 21–23.

Neidig RD, Neidig PJ. (1984). Multiple assessment center exercises and job relatedness. *Journal of Applied Psychology, 69,* 182–186.

Norton SD. (1977). The empirical and content validity of assessment centers vs. traditional methods for predicting managerial success. *Academy of Management Review, 2,* 442–452.

Norton SD. (1981). The assessment center process and content validity: A reply to Dreher and Sackett. *Academy of Management Review, 6,* 561–566.

Owens WA. (1976). Background data. In Dunnette MD (Ed.) *Handbook of industrial and organizational psychology* (pp. 609–644). Chicago: Rand McNally.

Rosenthal R, Jacobson L. (1968). *Pygmalian in the classroom.* New York: Holt.

Russell CJ. (1985). Individual decision processes in an assessment center. *Journal of Applied Psychology, 70,* 737–746.

Russell CJ. (1986). *An examination of person characteristic vs. role congruency explanations for post exercise assessment center ratings.* Unpublished Manuscript.

Sackett PR, Dreher GF. (1982). Constructs and assessment center dimensions: Some troubling empirical findings. *Journal of Applied Psychology, 67,* 401–410.

Sackett PR, Dreher GF. (1984). Situation specificity of behavior and assessment center validation strategies: A rejoinder to Neidig and Neidig. *Journal of Applied Psychology, 69,* 187–190.

Sackett PR, Hakel MD. (1979). Temporal stability and individual differences in using assessment information to form overall ratings. *Organizational Behavior and Human Performance, 23,* 120–137.

Schmitt N. (1977). Interrater agreement in dimensionality and combination of assessment center judgments. *Journal of Applied Psychology, 63,* 171–176.

Schmitt N, Ford JK, Stultz DM. (1986). Changes in self-perceived ability as a function of performance in an assessment center. *Journal of Occupational Psychology, 59,* 327–335.

Schmitt N, Gooding RZ, Noe RA, Kirsch M. (1984). Meta-analysis of validity studies published between 1964 and 1982 and the investigation of study characteristics. *Personnel Psychology, 37,* 407–422.

Schmitt N, Noe RA, Meritt R, Fitzgerald MP. (1984). Validity of assessment center ratings for the prediction of performance ratings and school climate of school administrators. *Journal of Applied Psychology, 69,* 20–213.

Schmitt N, Ostroff S. (1986). Operationalizing the "behavioral consistency" approach: Selection test development based on a content-oriented strategy. *Personnel Psychology, 39,* 91–108.

Schweiger D, Sandberg WR, Ragan JW. (1986). Group approaches for improving strategic decision making: A comparative analysis of dialectical inquiry, devil's advocacy, and consensus. *Academy of Management Journal, 29,* 51–71.

Silverman WH, Dalessio A, Woods SB, Johnson RL. (1986). Influence of assessment center methods on assessor ratings. *Personnel Psychology, 39,* 565–579.

Silzer RE. (1985). Assessment center validity across two organizations. In symposium, *Assessment center validity: Recent data and current status.* Presented at annual meeting of the American Psychological Association. Los Angeles, CA.

Sternberg RJ. (1979). The nature of mental abilities. *American Psychologist, 34,* 214–230.

Struth MR, Frank FD, Amato A. (1980). Effects of assessor training on subsequent performance as an assessee. *Journal of Assessment Center Technology, 3,* 17–22.

Stumpf SA, London M. (1981). Management promotions: Individual and organizational factors influencing the decision process. *Academy of Management Review, 6,* 539–549.

Thornton GC III, Byham WC. (1982). *Assessment centers and managerial performance.* New York: Academic Press.

Turnage JJ, Muchinsky PM. (1982). Transituational variability in human performance with assessment centers. *Organizational Behavior and Human Performance, 30,* 174–200.

Turnage JJ, Muchinsky PM. (1984). A comparison of the predictive validity of assessment center evaluations versus traditional measures in forecasting supervisory job performance: Interpretive implications of criterion distortion for the assessment center. *Journal of Applied Psychology, 69,* 595–602.

Tziner A, Dolan S. (1982). Validity of an assessment center for identifying future female officers in the military. *Journal of Applied Psychology, 67,* 728–736.

Wagner RK, Sternberg RJ. (1985). Practical intelligence in real world pursuits: The role of tacit knowledge. *Journal of Personality and Social Psychology, 49,* 436–458.

Wemimont PR, Campbell JP. (1968). Signs, samples and criteria. *Journal of Applied Psychology, 52,* 372–376.

Wolfson A. (1985). Assessment centers ten years later. In symposium, *Assessment center validity: Recent data and current status.* Presented at the annual meeting of the American Psychological Association, Los Angeles, CA.

Wollowick HB, McNamara WJ. (1969). Relation of components of an assessment center to management success. *Journal of Applied Psychology, 53,* 348–352.

Yukl GA. (1981). *Leadership in organizations.* Englewood Cliffs: Prentice Hall, Inc.

Zajonc RB. (1960). The process of cognitive timing in communications. *Journal of Abnormal and Social Psychology, 61,* 159–167.

Zedeck S. (1986). A process analysis of the assessment center method. In Staw B, Cummings LL (Eds.), *Research in Organizational Behavior,* 8, 259–296.

Zedeck S, Cascio WF. (1984). Psychological issues in personnel decisions. *Annual Review of Psychology, 35,* 461–518.

25

THE PERCEIVED FAIRNESS OF SELECTION SYSTEMS

An organizational justice perspective

Stephen W. Gilliland

Source: *Academy of Management Review* 18(4) (1993): 694–734.

Abstract

A justice model of applicants' reactions to employment-selection systems is proposed as a basis for organizing previous findings and guiding future research. Organizational justice literature is briefly reviewed, and key findings are used to provide a framework for the proposed model and to support hypotheses. The procedural justice of selection systems is examined in terms of 10 procedural rules, wherein the satisfaction and violation of these rules provide the basis for fairness reactions. Distributive justice of hiring decisions is examined with respect to equity, equality, and needs. The model also includes the interaction of procedural and distributive justice and the relationship of fairness reactions to individual and organizational outcomes.

Dominant concerns in the personnel selection literature are issues of the psychometric soundness of tests (e.g., reliability), the validity of inferences made with tests (Schmitt, Gooding, Noe, & Kirsch, 1984), the utility of selection procedures (Hunter & Hunter, 1984), and the fairness with which selection procedures have an impact on protected subgroups (Schmitt, 1989). Although all of these topics have been studied from a psychometric perspective, rarely has attention been directed to the social side of the selection process (Herriot, 1989b). In particular, the study of fairness has been focused on concerns about test bias, differential prediction, and the relative impact of subgroup differences on expected organizational productivity and subgroup hiring rates (Hartigan & Wigdor, 1989; Schmitt, 1989). One important yet often overlooked aspect of test fairness is the reaction of applicants to testing and selection decisions (Schmitt & Gilliland, 1992).

It can be argued that just as the establishment of psychometrically fair selection procedures is important from business, ethical, and legal perspectives, applicants' perceptions of test fairness are also important from these perspectives. From a business perspective, reactions to selection procedures may influence the ability of the organization to attract and hire highly qualified applicants, which, in turn, can influence the overall utility of selection procedures (Boudreau & Rynes, 1985; Murphy, 1986). From an ethical perspective, organizations should be concerned with the effects of selection procedures on the psychological well-being of applicants. For example, the perceived fairness of selection testing may influence the efficacy and self-esteem of rejected applicants (Robertson & Smith, 1989). Finally, from a legal perspective, the perceived fairness of the selection procedure may influence applicants' decisions to pursue discrimination cases. Additionally, the 1991 amendments to the Civil Rights Bill allow for jury trials in discrimination cases, creating the possibility that issues of face validity and perceptions of fairness may become a more salient issue with statistically naive jurors.

In addition to these practical outcomes associated with the perceived fairness of selection systems, research in this domain can be of theoretical importance. Although few attempts have been made to empirically assess reactions to selection procedures, even less attention has been given to developing a theoretical model of these perceptual processes. Preliminary models of reactions to selection systems have been proposed (e.g., Arvey & Sackett, 1993; Schuler, 1993), but all of these lack a solid theoretical framework. A natural theoretical orientation that can be used to organize this area of research is that of organizational justice theories (e.g., Greenberg, 1990b).

This article extends theories from the organizational justice literature to the selection domain with the goal of advancing both organization justice theory and the understanding of selection fairness. In this article a comprehensive model that describes procedural and distributive factors influencing applicants' reactions to selection systems is developed. The model also links fairness perceptions to a variety of attitudinal and behavioral outcomes. To provide a basis for this model, the major tenets of organizational justice theory are briefly reviewed, highlighting issues of importance for the extension of justice literature to selection processes. During the discussion of the model, selection research that has examined reactions to selection procedures is reviewed in an effort to establish what has been investigated and where further research is needed.

Organizational justice theory

Traditional discussions of organizational justice have emphasized the role of *distributive justice*, or the fairness of organizational outcome distributions (Bierhoff, Cohen, & Greenberg, 1986). Adams' (1965) equity theory was a dominant motivation theory in the 1960s and early 1970s, and research on equity theory constitutes the bulk of investigation into distributive justice (Greenberg, 1987b). Researchers also have examined perceptions of *procedural justice*, or the fairness of procedures that are used to divide valued organizational outcomes (Folger & Greenberg, 1985; Lind & Tyler, 1988). Current developments in organizational justice are aimed at examining fairness involved with the implementation of procedures (*interactional justice*; Bies & Moag, 1986) and the integration of procedural and distributive justice perspectives (Folger, 1987). Perhaps because of this diversity, a number of researchers have attempted to integrate and organize research and theory (e.g., Cohen, 1987; Greenberg, 1987b, 1990b; Lind & Tyler, 1988). Therefore, only a brief overview of organizational justice is given here, highlighting issues of importance in developing a model of the fairness of selection systems.

Distributive justice

Authors of distributive justice theories propose that individuals will evaluate distributions of outcomes with respect to some distributive rule, the most common of which is equity (Cohen, 1987). Equity assessment involves a comparison of one's inputs and obtained outcomes relative to a referent comparison other. Evaluations of inequitable distributions are thought to produce negative emotions, which, in turn, motivate individuals to change their behavior or distort the cognitions associated with perceptions of unfairness (Adams, 1965). Attitudes are also affected by perceived inequity, and dissatisfaction becomes greater as the inequity increases. Inequity is hypothesized to exist under conditions of both underpayment and overpayment, and although the underpayment prediction is more commonly supported (Campbell & Pritchard, 1976), Greenberg (1982) concluded that support exists for both predictions.

Deutsch (1975) extended equity theory by incorporating the possibility that other distributional rules of relative contribution may influence perceptions of distributive fairness. In addition to equity, Deutsch suggested rules of equality (all individuals should be rewarded equally regardless of inputs) and needs (rewards should be based on relative needs). Although organizational justice researchers have tended to examine distributive justice only from the equity perspective, researchers in social psychology have supported the existence of equality and needs rules (Cohen, 1987). Specifically, this research suggests that even though the dominant distribution rule is equity, equality and needs rules may become more salient when individuals are exposed to violations of rules (Bierhoff et al., 1986).

Procedural justice

Procedural justice theorists are concerned with the perceived fairness of procedures used in making decisions (Folger & Greenberg, 1985). Two major perspectives or models have initiated much of the current research and interest in procedural justice. Thibaut and Walker (1975) approached procedural justice from a legal perspective and emphasized the role of process control or "voice" of the individual in fairness perceptions. Their basic finding is that procedures are perceived to be more fair when affected individuals have an opportunity to either influence the decision process or offer input. In contrast to the process-control model of procedural justice, Leventhal (1980) approached the issue by identifying the structural components that are thought to exist in individuals' cognitive conceptualizations of a reward-allocation decision process. Procedural justice was suggested to be a function of the extent to which a number of procedural rules are satisfied or violated. Specifically, procedural rules suggested that decisions should be made consistently, without personal biases, with as much accurate information as possible, with interests of affected individuals represented in a way that is compatible with their ethical values, and with an outcome that could be modified. Other justice researchers have found similar rules in the domains of managerial fairness (Sheppard & Lewicki, 1987) and performance appraisal (Greenberg, 1986a) and have added rules such as the importance of two-way communication. Leventhal (1980) also suggested that different procedural rules are not necessarily weighted equally because different rules may be emphasized at different times; however, he gave no indication of the types of factors that may influence these weightings.

A more recent perspective of procedural justice was suggested by Bies and Moag (1986), who illustrated concerns about the fairness of decision makers' behavior during the enactment of procedures, a perspective which they labeled *interactional justice*. Interactional justice refers to both what is said to individuals during the decision process and how it is said (Tyler & Bies, 1990). One aspect of interactional justice (i.e., providing an explanation for a decision) has received recent attention; researchers have demonstrated that justification for an adverse decision can lessen negative consequences associated with that decision (Bies & Shapiro, 1988; Greenberg, 1990a). A second component of interaction justice is the interpersonal treatment an individual receives during the decision process. It reflects issues of respect and rudeness and the propriety of questions asked and statements made (Bies & Moag, 1986). Thus, procedural justice can be summarized as being composed of three components: (a) formal characteristics of procedures, (b) explanation of procedures and decision making, and (c) interpersonal treatment (Greenberg, 1990b).

Integrating procedural and distributive justice

Thibaut and Walker (1975) suggested that procedural justice and distributive justice are independent dimensions. Some researchers have supported that procedural and distributive justice perceptions are statistically independent (Alexander & Ruderman, 1987; Greenberg, 1986a). Others have indicated that perceptions of procedural and distributive justice are highly correlated (Folger & Konovsky, 1989; Fryxell & Gordon, 1989). A second question about the relationship between procedural and distributive justice is the relative importance of each in relation to individual reactions and organizational outcomes. Theorists have clearly demonstrated that in many situations perceptions of procedural justice account for more variance in a variety of dependent measures than do perceptions of distributive justice (Alexander & Ruderman, 1987; Dipboye & de Pontbriand, 1981; Folger & Konovsky, 1989; Konovsky & Cropanzano, 1991).

The statistical interaction between procedural and distributive justice also has been examined. Greenberg (1987a) found that perceived fairness of the outcome was related to the interaction between outcome favorableness (which has tended to be related to distributive fairness) and procedural justice such that just procedures led to perceptions of fair outcomes, even when the outcome was not favorable. Similar findings were obtained by Leung and Li (1990) when they evaluated individuals' reactions to a new subway-fare scheme. In this case, increased process control was found to be related to more favorable reactions with negative outcomes, but it was less related to favorable reactions with positive outcomes.

Summary

This brief overview of justice literature highlights the following points that are likely to be important in the extension of organizational justice literature to the selection process:

1. Organizational justice theories clearly distinguish dimensions of procedural and distributive justice and demonstrate the importance of each.
2. Although equity appears to be the primary distribution rule underlying distributive justice perceptions, situational factors may increase the salience of the alternate distribution rules of equality and needs.
3. Procedural justice theories also suggest a number of rules that influence perceptions of procedural justice, the most commonly studied of which is process control. Additional procedural rules include consistency, bias suppression, representativeness, and two-way communication, all of which are discussed in greater detail in the following sections.
4. Interactional justice is an important component of procedural fairness. The most commonly studied factor has been the effect of offering justification for a procedure or outcome on perceptions of fairness.
5. Some evidence has suggested a statistical interaction between procedural and distributive justice on some perceptual outcomes so that procedural justice may override some of the disappointment associated with unfair distributions.

A model of applicants' reactions to selection systems

Reactions to selection procedures have been studied from both the interests of recruiting, whereby perceptions and reactions are related to job-choice intentions (Liden & Parsons, 1986; Schmitt & Coyle, 1976), and the interests of demonstrating how certain selection procedures are more favorable, for example, work-sample tests (Schmidt, Greenthal, Hunter, Berner, & Seaton, 1977) or assessment centers (Dodd, 1977). As a result, research is largely fragmented, and authors have made little effort to share methodology or results. Further, the recruiting literature does not consider the favorableness of different types of selection procedures, and the literature regarding the favorableness of selection procedures does not consider the implications for recruiting. Though Schmitt and Gilliland (1992) provided an initial review of this literature, clearly an integration is needed.

Previous attempts to model social issues involved in the selection process can be found (Arvey & Sackett, 1993; Herriot, 1989a; Schuler, 1993), but these models tend to be only catalogs of possible determinants of fairness perceptions. For example, Schuler (1993) suggested that the following four factors influence the perceived acceptability of selection situations: (a) the presence of job-relevant information that can aid job-acceptance decisions, (b) participation or representation in the development of the selection process, (c) understanding of the evaluation process and the task relevance of the selection procedures, and (d) content and form of feedback. Similarly, Arvey and Sackett (1993) proposed that perceived fairness can be influenced by the content of the selection system (e.g., job relatedness; thoroughness of KSA of knowledge, skills, and abilities coverage; invasiveness of questions; ease of faking answers), an understanding of the system-development process, the administration of the selection process (e.g., consistency, confidentiality, opportunity for reconsideration, and prior information), and the organizational context (e.g., the selection ratio). Regarding these models, little attention has been paid to the psychological process underlying these perceptions, and no indication has been given regarding how the various determinants combine to form perceptions of fairness.

Robertson and his colleagues (Iles & Robertson, 1989; Robertson & Smith, 1989) began to address these issues by discussing the psychological impact of personnel selection methods on individual candidates. Their model hypothesized that features of the selection method and the nature (e.g., accept versus reject) and specificity of decision feedback would influence applicants' cognitive and affective reactions toward the process. In turn, applicants' cognitive and affective reactions should influence outcomes such as work commitment, performance, turnover, psychological well-being, and personal agency. As with the other models, Robertson and Smith (1989) presented their model as an initial conceptualization or a preliminary model, and they acknowledged that research is needed to more completely understand the underlying factors and processes.

Although the model presented by Robertson and his colleagues provides an initial examination of the psychological process and personnel selection, it is still missing a solid link to psychological theory. Additionally, in this model a review of the existing literature on reactions to the selection process was sparse and isolated. In an effort to improve upon these previous models, I propose a model of applicants' reactions to selection processes that includes both psychological theory from organizational justice and prior research on reactions to selection procedures. This model provides a framework for organizing current research, and it provides many research propositions that suggest directions for future research. In addition, some organizational justice issues that have not been previously addressed are developed.

The model

According to the model presented in Figure 1, situational and personal conditions influence the extent to which procedural and distributive rules are perceived as satisfied or violated. That is, conditions such as test type, human resource policy, and behavior of human resource personnel influence applicants' perceptions of the procedural justice of the selection system. Procedural justice is conceptualized in terms of procedural rules. Perceptions of the extent to which each of these rules is satisfied or violated are combined to form an overall evaluation of the fairness of the selection system. Applicants' prior experiences with selection and hiring processes also may influence the salience of the procedural rules and the evaluation of the fairness of the selection system. In terms of distributive justice, performance expectations are hypothesized to influence perceptions of equity in either the test outcome or the hiring-decision outcome. Although equity is predicted to be the primary distributive rule, in situations with increased salience of discrimination or applicants' special needs, the equality and needs distributive rules also should contribute to evaluations of test outcome and the fairness of the hiring decision. In addition to these main effects, procedural rules are predicted to moderate the distributive justice to the fairness of the outcome relationship, and distributive rules are predicted to moderate the procedural justice to the fairness of the process relationship.

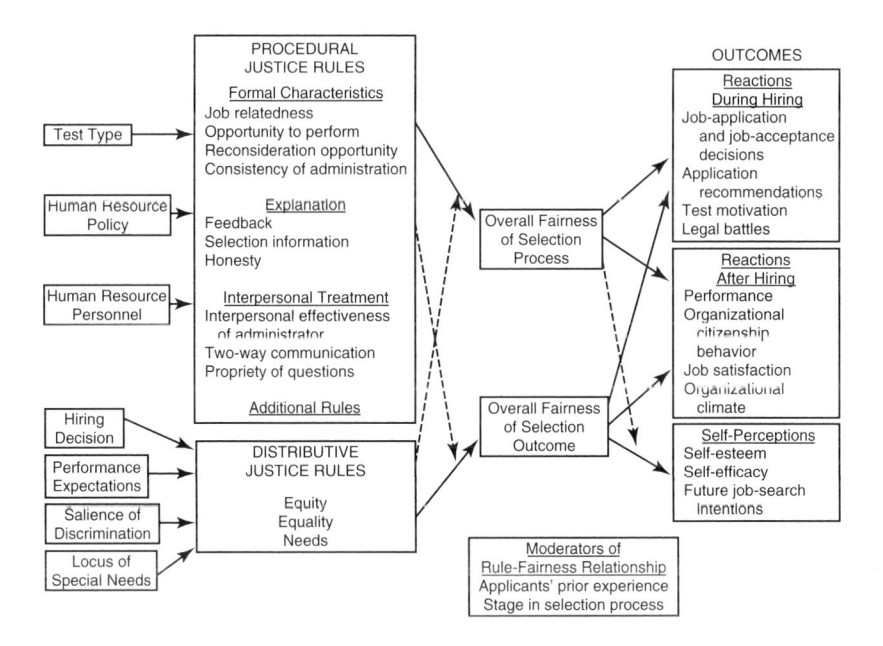

Figure 1 Model of applicants' reactions to employment selection systems.

A final part of the model deals with the relationship between fairness perceptions and individual and organizational outcomes. These outcomes include some variables common to both accepted and rejected candidates (job-application decisions, test motivation, self-esteem, self-efficacy, and endorsement of the company's products), some variables specific to the accepted candidates (job-acceptance decisions, job satisfaction, performance, organizational citizenship behavior, and organizational climate), and a variable specific to rejected applicants (future job-search intentions). These relationships, as well as all of the other relationships outlined in this brief overview, are discussed in the following sections and are related to findings in the organizational justice and reactions to selection procedures literatures. First, the procedural justice rules presented by Leventhal (1980) are discussed as they relate to the selection context and existing research. Then, propositions regarding the determinants and outcomes of perceived violation or satisfaction of these rules are presented.

Procedural justice rules

According to the perspective of procedural justice initiated by Leventhal (1980), overall evaluations of procedural justice are thought to be composed of the satisfaction or violation of 10 procedural rules. All of these rules are adapted from procedural rules discussed in organizational justice research on allocation decisions (Leventhal, 1980), managerial fairness (Sheppard & Lewicki, 1987), performance appraisal (Greenberg, 1986a), communication fairness in recruiting (Bies & Moag, 1986), and interactional justice norms (Tyler & Bies, 1990). Additionally, all of the rules have been mentioned in some of the previous models of applicants' reactions to selection procedures (Arvey & Sackett, 1993; Iles & Robertson, 1989; Schuler, 1993). The procedural rules and their relationships to prior theory are summarized in Table 1. Procedural justice can be summarized in terms of three components: formal characteristics, explanation, and interpersonal treatment (Greenberg, 1990b). Consistent with this trichotomy of procedural antecedents, the 10 procedural rules are grouped into three categories, including formal characteristics of the selection system, explanations offered during the selection process, and interpersonal treatment. Formal characteristics of the selection system include job relatedness, opportunity to perform, opportunity for reconsideration, and consistency of administration. Explanation or information offered to applicants in the form of feedback, selection information, and honesty in treatment composes the next category. The final three rules, interpersonal effectiveness of the administrator, two-way communication, and propriety of questions, all relate to the interpersonal treatment of applicants. Figure 1 and Table 1 also allow for the possibility of other procedural rules that may influence fairness perceptions but that are not directly linked to organizational justice literature and have not been examined in the applicant reactions literature. Two such possible procedures relate to concerns about the ease of faking answers and the invasiveness of questions. The following discussion elaborates on each of these procedural rules.

Table 1 Relationships among procedural rules and other justice and reactions models

Procedural rule	Organizational justice theory[a]	Applicant reactions model[b]
Formal Characteristics		
Job relatedness	Accuracy rule (L), Representativeness (S&L)	Job relatedness (A&S), (I&R), Transparency (S)
Opportunity to perform	Voice (T&W), Soliciting input (G), Resource (S&L)	Thoroughness of knowledge, skills, and abilities coverage (A&S)
Reconsideration opportunity	Ability to modify rule (L), Ability to correct (S&L), Ability to challenge (G)	Opportunity for reconsideration (A&S), Review scores (A&S)
Consistency	Consistency rule or standard (L), (S&L), (G), (T&B)	Consistency across candidates (A&S)
Explanation		
Feedback	Timely feedback (T&B), Timeliness (S&L)	Feedback form (S), Type/degree of feedback (I&R)
Selection information	Information (S&L), Communication (S&L), Explanation (T&B)	Information (S), (A&S), System-development process (A&S)
Honesty	Truthfulness (B&M)	Feedback honesty (S)
Interpersonal Treatment		
Interpersonal effectiveness	Respect (B&M)	Sympathetic treatment (I&R)
Two-way communication	Two-way communication (G), Consider views (T&B)	Participation (S)
Propriety of questions	Propriety of questions (B&M), Personal bias (L), Bias suppression (S&L), (T&B)	Illegal variables (A&S)
Other possible rules:		
Ease of faking answers	?	(A&S)
Invasiveness of questions	?	(A&S) (I&R)

[a]Notation for justice theories: L—Leventhal (1980), S&L—Sheppard and Lewicki (1987), G—Greenberg (1986a), B&M—Bies and Moag (1986), T&B—Tyler & Bies (1990), T&W—Thibaut & Walker (1975).

[b]Notation for applicant reactions models: A&S—Arvey and Sackett (1993), S—Schuler (1993), I&R—Iles & Robertson (1989).

Job relatedness

Perhaps the greatest procedural influence on fairness perceptions is the job relatedness of the selection device. *Job relatedness* refers to the extent to which a test either appears to measure content relevant to the job situation or appears to be valid. The appearance of validity can be captured in both the content validity sense (i.e., test content related to job content) and the criterion-related validity sense (i.e., performance on the test is likely related to performance on the job)

(Smither & Pearlman, 1991). Job relatedness should be distinguished from *face validity*, which refers to "what the test appears to measure" or "whether the test looks valid" (Anastasi, 1988:136). A test can appear face valid (appear to measure what it actually measures) without appearing job related, and a test can appear job related (in the criterion-related sense) without appearing face valid.

In the organizational justice literature, Leventhal (1980) defined the *accuracy rule* as decisions being based on as much good information as possible, and he suggested that procedural fairness is violated when performance is evaluated on the basis of inappropriate information. Similarly, Sheppard and Lewicki (1987) found evidence for a resource rule, which suggests that decisions should be based on accurate resources and expertise. Prior models of applicants' reactions to testing include job relatedness (Arvey & Sackett, 1993), job relevance (Iles & Robertson, 1989), and task relevance (Schuler, 1993).

Many researchers have examined the job relatedness of tests and the effects of this relatedness on perceptions of fairness. Positive reactions in terms of perceived face validity, perceived accuracy, and perceived fairness have been documented at assessment centers (Dodd, 1977) and with work-sample tests (Schmidt et al., 1977), which are both highly job related. Schmitt, Gilliland, Landis, and Devine (1993) found that both perceived job relevance and overall perceived fairness were higher with a content-valid, computerized work-sample test than with simple typing and dictation tests. In this case, job relevance was highly correlated with perceived fairness. Smither, Reilly, Millsap, Pearlman, and Stoffey (1993) assessed perceived job relatedness for different types of selection tests and found that interviews, assessment-center tasks, and cognitive ability tests that included concrete items were perceived to be more job related than personality tests, biodata forms, and cognitive ability tests that included abstract items. In a second study, Smither and his colleagues (1993) found that perceived predictive validity and perceived face validity correlated with both procedural and distributive justice perceptions. Similarly, Kluger and Rothstein (1991) assessed both the perceived relevance and the perceived fairness of cognitive ability tests and biographical data inventories, and they demonstrated a significant correlation between relevance and perceived fairness. Gilliland (1993) manipulated job relatedness in a hiring situation and found direct influences on perceptions of procedural and distributive fairness. Finally, research from the drug-testing literature is somewhat related; drug testing is seen as more acceptable if the job includes characteristics such as perceived danger (Murphy, Thornton, & Prue, 1991). Regarding drug testing, the procedural rule may be more aptly described as job relevance rather than job relatedness.

Opportunity to perform

Research in the organizational justice literature on voice suggests that procedures are perceived to be more fair if recipients of the decision outcome have the opportunity to express themselves prior to the decision (Thibaut & Walker, 1975). Greenberg (1986a) identified solicitation of input as one factor that influences the perceived fairness of performance appraisals, and Dipboye and de Pontbriand (1981) found that the opportunity to offer information during a performance appraisal was related to perceived fairness. Sheppard and Lewicki (1987) proposed a rule related to collecting input in the domain of managerial fairness. In the selection domain, voice can be interpreted as having adequate opportunity to demonstrate one's knowledge, skills, and abilities in the testing situation (Arvey & Sackett, 1993) or the possibility of exerting control in a selection situation (Schuler, 1993). Kluger and Rothstein (1991) found that individuals perceived greater control over their test performance with biodata inventories than they did with cognitive ability tests. Bies and Shapiro (1988) presented individuals with recruiting interview scenarios in which the interviewee either did or did not have the opportunity to demonstrate competencies and ask questions of the interviewer. Perceptions of procedural fairness were higher when the interviewee had the opportunity to offer input.

It can be hypothesized that interviews provide the most direct opportunity for applicants to perform or have a voice in the process because interviews provide the opportunity to express oneself directly to the interviewer rather than indirectly through test questions. The satisfaction of the opportunity to perform procedural rules may help explain why so few lawsuits are filed on the basis of selection interviews (Campion & Arvey, 1989).

Reconsideration opportunity

An often-cited factor that contributes to perceptions of procedural justice is the opportunity to challenge or modify the decision-making evaluation process (i.e., to receive a second chance) (Greenberg, 1986a; Leventhal, 1980; Sheppard & Lewicki, 1987). The opportunity for reconsideration and the opportunity to review scores and scoring were both issues proposed by Arvey and Sackett (1993) as important in determining perceived fairness of selection systems. The only testing domain in which reconsideration opportunity has been examined with regard to applicant reactions is drug testing. Drug testing was given high ratings of justifiability (a construct presumably related to fairness) when test results were checked with a second testing method (Murphy, Thornton, & Reynolds, 1990). Further research should consider the impact that reconsideration opportunities have on applicant reactions.

Consistency of administration

Consistency or standardization is a procedural factor discussed in much of the procedural justice literature (Greenberg, 1986a; Leventhal, 1980; Sheppard & Lewicki, 1987; Tyler & Bies, 1990). *Consistency* refers to ensuring that decision procedures are consistent across people and over time. Arvey and Sackett (1993) suggested that consistency across people refers to consistency in the content of the selection system, in scoring, and in the interpretation of scores. When considering consistency across people, Leventhal (1980) pointed out that this rule is similar to the distributive rule of equality, which suggests that all people should have an equal chance of obtaining the decision outcome.

Concerns for standardization or consistency of test administration have been demonstrated with drug-testing programs, which received greater acceptance or perceived effectiveness when they involved all individuals or only those with a history of drug use and not a random selection of individuals (Gomez-Mejia & Balkin, 1987; Murphy et al., 1990). It seems reasonable to expect that concerns for consistency may be influenced by the type of test and may be more salient for some types (e.g., interviews) than for others (e.g., paper-and-pencil tests). This procedural rule suggests a prediction that structured interviews should be perceived as more consistent in administration, and, therefore, they are considered more fair than unstructured interviews. Although individuals may not always be aware of the treatment given to others and, therefore, are unable to evaluate consistency, a clear example of a violation of consistency across people is the situation in which applicants receive jobs because of who they know, not what they know.

Given that consistency evaluations rely on comparisons with other people or previous experiences, two factors that may influence the salience of the consistency rule are the previous experiences of the applicant and the time at which perceived fairness is assessed. Applicants who have experienced both structured and unstructured interviews may be more likely to associate interview structure with consistency of administration. With regard to time or stage of the selection process, applicants may be more aware of consistency after a selection decision has been made and applicants have learned the basis for the decision from organizational sources or from conversations with other applicants.

Feedback

The provision of timely and informative feedback is cited as an important factor in perceptions of interactional justice (Tyler & Bies, 1990). Timeliness is also a rule of managerial fairness suggested by Shep-pard and Lewicki (1987). In previous models of applicant reactions, researchers have discussed feedback form (Schuler, 1993) and the type or degree of feedback (Iles & Robertson, 1989).

Empirical evidence from the testing literature indicates that reactions to testing were more favorable among people who had received feedback on their test performance than among those who had not (Lounsbury, Bobrow, & Jensen, 1989). This study used a 17-item measure to assess reactions that included perceptions of fairness and procedural dimensions such as opportunity to perform and propriety of questions and global reactions toward employment testing. Researchers have also specifically addressed the issues of timeliness and informativeness. Schmidt, Urry, and Gugel (1978) cited the speed with which feedback was provided, both in terms of test performance and qualification for a job, as an advantage of computer-adaptive testing over paper-and-pencil tests. With respect to the selection process in general, Arvey, Gordon, Massengill, and Mussio (1975) found that as the time lag between initial application for a job and initiation of the selection process increased, the percentage of applicants withdrawing from the selection process also increased. Rynes, Bretz, and Gerhart (1991) interviewed job seekers and found that one of the reasons individuals lost interest in companies or turned down offers for site visits was delays in the recruiting process. Many individuals attributed delays to personal rejection and this resulted in lower self-confidence and qualifications. Although these studies did not assess perceived fairness, they do indicate that a procedural aspect of the selection situation can influence outcomes of organizational concern.

In terms of the informativeness of feedback, Dodd (1977) indicated that feedback that is developmental and provides information on how to remedy deficiencies is valued regardless of the selection or promotion decision. The timeliness and informativeness of feedback may represent an important procedural factor because it is one factor that organizations could easily improve without the additional costs associated with selection-system development.

Selection information

One of the most commonly examined variables in the interactional justice literature is the provision of justification for a decision (Greenberg, 1990a; Leventhal, 1980). For example, Bies and Shapiro (1988) found that perceptions of the procedural fairness of scenario-based recruiting situations were greater when justification was offered for a negative decision than when no justification was offered. Procedural rules that are related to selection information include information and communication (Sheppard & Lewicki, 1987) and explanation for the decision (Tyler & Bies, 1990). In terms of explanation or justification for a selection procedure, perceptions of fairness are likely to be influenced by information on the validity of the selection process, information on scoring and the way in which scores are used in decision making, and justification for a particular selection decision. Lounsbury and colleagues (1989) found that attitudes toward testing were more favorable when people were told how the test related to future job performance. It is possible that validity evidence would be particularly useful for tests with low face validity, such as cognitive ability tests (Huffcutt, 1990). With the current interest in cognitive ability testing, the provision of validity evidence may be one relatively cost-free method for improving the acceptance of such testing.

Arvey and Sackett (1993) suggested that validity evidence may be perceived differently by the public than by selection specialists. Specifically, whereas selection specialists are concerned with improved overall prediction, the public may be more concerned with the extent to which the selection system makes mistakes. This may be particularly true of integrity testing and drug testing, where negative outcomes suggest that rejected applicants may engage in some form of deviant behavior.

Another type of selection information that may influence perceptions of fairness is a priori information on the selection process. Arvey and Sackett (1993) hypothesized that the reduction in uncertainty that such information would provide, particularly with unfamiliar selection processes, would reduce applicants' beliefs that they performed poorly because they did not know what to expect. Stone and Kotch (1989) found more negative attitudes (defined in terms of perceived fairness and invasion of privacy) toward drug-testing programs that provided no advance notice of testing than those that did.

Honesty

Bies and Moag (1986) highlighted the importance of honesty and truthfulness when communicating with recruitees. In particular, instances of either candidness or deception would likely be particularly salient. Schuler (1993) discussed the importance of openness and honesty as components of feedback content. Although honesty may be inherent with other forms of explanation (e.g., selection information or feedback), research suggests that it is a distinct and important component of applicants' reactions. For example, research on interviews has demonstrated that interviewer correctness, sincerity, and believability are strong predictors of affect toward reactions to the interview, impressions of the organization, and intentions to accept a job offer (Liden & Parsons, 1986; Schmitt & Coyle, 1976).

Interpersonal effectiveness of administrator

The interpersonal effectiveness of the test administrator refers to the degree to which applicants are treated with warmth and respect. Bies and Moag (1986) analyzed by content recruitees' descriptions of fair and unfair treatment and found that one dimension of fairness was related to respect or, alternately, rudeness. Similarly, Iles and Robertson (1989) discussed the possible impact that sympathetic treatment may have on applicants during the selection process.

Research on reactions to interviews demonstrated that the warmth and thoughtfulness of an interviewer was the strongest predictor of impressions of the company and expectations regarding job offers and acceptance of those offers (Schmitt & Coyle, 1976). Similarly, Liden and Parsons (1986) found that the strongest predictor of general affect of an interview was the extent to which the interviewer was personable. Rynes (1991) summarized the research on recruiters' personality and behavior traits and indicated the factor that explained the most variance in various dependent variables was the affect of the recruiter (e.g., warmth and empathy). It is important to note that interviewer and recruiter research cited with regard to both honesty and interpersonal effectiveness did not directly assess the impact of honesty and interpersonal effectiveness of reactions to fairness. Although dependent variables included impressions of recruiter, affect toward reactions to the interview, and probability of accepting a job offer, the direct impact on reactions to fairness has not been assessed.

Although interpersonal effectiveness is clearly an important factor in applicants' reactions to interviews, it may also be an important factor in other aspects of the selection process. For example, a test administrator who simply administers a paper-and-pencil, work-sample, or drug test may be able to affect the comfort and stress level of applicants and influence applicants' reactions to the testing process in general. Rynes (1993) provided an example of an applicant who felt like a criminal during drug testing because she was escorted by a uniformed guard to a doorless toilet stall.

Two-way communication

Two-way communication refers to the opportunity for applicants to offer input or to have their views considered in the selection process (Tyler & Bies, 1990), but it differs from the opportunity to perform in that it relates primarily to interpersonal interaction. The research by Martin and Nagao (1989) demonstrated the difference between two-way communication and opportunity to perform. Simulated applicants for a high-status job expressed more anger and resentment toward computerized and paper-and-pencil interviewing than toward traditional face-to-face interviewing. Though all interviewing formats presumably provided adequate opportunity to perform, the nontraditional interview formats did not allow for the two-way communication that applicants appear to expect from interviews. Similarly, Schuler (1993) cited research that demonstrated more favorable impressions and reactions to nondirective interviews than to directive interviews. Although not a selection situation, research has found that the opportunity for appraisees to express their feelings was one of the strongest predictors of perceived accuracy and fairness of performance appraisals (Landy, Barnes, & Murphy, 1978).

Two-way communication also can refer to the opportunity to ask questions regarding the job, the organization, or even the selection process. The selection system must provide applicants with adequate opportunity to gain information that is relevant to making acceptance decisions. If such opportunities are not found, applicants' satisfaction with the selection process will likely be lessened. Clearly, procedural justice research on performance evaluation demonstrates the importance of two-way communication (Greenberg, 1986a). Because applicants are not likely to expect two-way communication during all aspects of the selection process, it would be useful to determine for which selection procedures two-way communication is a salient issue.

Propriety of questions

Bies and Moag (1986) found that one of the dimensions that influenced recruitees' perceptions of fairness was the propriety of questions asked during recruitment. Question propriety included both improper questioning and prejudicial statements. Similarly, the suppression of personal bias was discussed by Leventhal (1980), Sheppard and Lewicki (1987), and Tyler and Bies (1990) as a rule of procedural justice. Stone and Stone (1990) discussed the impact that question propriety has on perceived invasion of privacy, which may be related to perceived fairness. Although Arvey and Sackett (1993) discussed the possible impact that illegal variables have on perceived fairness of a selection system, and it is easy to speculate on the significant impact this treatment has on fairness perceptions and later decision making, researchers have not yet examined this issue. Perhaps a reason for the lack of research in this area is the illegality of asking such questions during the selection process (Arvey & Sackett, 1993). Many companies are not likely to admit that such behavior occurs, and for some it may not even be recognized (Rynes, 1993). A reasonable first step for research on this procedural factor would be to define and document the existence and prevalence of the problem because these issues are probably known with less certainty than the impact that such questions have on applicants.

Other possible procedural rules

The 10 procedural rules have ties to both organizational justice theory and applicant reactions models and research (see Table 1). Although these rules capture most of the variance in perceptions of procedural fairness, two other factors have been discussed in some of the models of applicant reactions. Neither of these factors has direct ties to organizational justice theory and neither has been examined with regard to perceived fairness, so they are not included in the list of procedural rules. The first factor, ease of faking answers, refers to the extent to which applicants *believe* information can be distorted in a socially desirable manner during the selection process. Arvey and Sackett (1993) indicated that ease of faking answers may influence fairness reactions, and they discussed a scenario in which applicants may be torn between wanting to be honest and wanting to tell the interviewer what they think the interviewer wants to hear. Such uncertainty in terms of how to respond may violate a reasonableness procedural rule (Sheppard & Lewicki, 1987), or it may in some other way influence perceived fairness. This would seem to be a particular concern with overt integrity tests where applicants may believe they know what the "correct" response should be. Kluger and Rothstein (1991) found biodata inventories to be perceived as easier to fake than cognitive ability tests, training tests, and work-sample tests. Somewhat surprising was their finding that the correlation between perceptions of ease of faking answers and test fairness was almost zero. A possible explanation of this lack of relationship can be found in a discussion by Stone and Stone (1990) of test transparency and invasion of privacy. They argued that if applicants know what is being assessed through a selection procedure, they can actively control the amount and nature of information they share. In this way, a transparent test (one that seems easy to fake) may actually increase perceived fairness.

The second possible additional rule is invasiveness of questions or invasion of privacy. Both Arvey and Sackett (1993) and Iles and Robertson (1989) suggested that the invasiveness or intrusiveness of a selection procedure may influence applicants' reactions to that procedure. Stone and Stone (1990) provided an excellent review of the types of factors that influence individuals' perceptions of invasion of privacy. Among other influences, they discussed the impact of selection test type on the invasion of privacy and indicated that both the test type and the way it is implemented can have an impact on perceived invasion of privacy. For example, research indicates that reactions to drug-testing programs are influenced by the existence of safeguards to ensure privacy and confidentiality (Gomez-Mejia & Balkin, 1987; Murphy et al., 1990). The importance of invasion of privacy can be seen in a recent California Supreme Court case (*Soroka v. Dayton Hudson*), which was filed on the grounds that certain test questions constituted an invasion of privacy (Brown, 1992). Further research is needed to link both faking of answers and invasiveness of questions to perceived fairness and procedural justice.

Summary of procedural rules

The 10 procedural rules (as well as two additional rules) all represent factors that may contribute to overall perceptions of the fairness of the selection process. As indicated in Figure 1, the type of selection test, human resource policy, and human resource personnel are expected to influence the extent to which each of the 10 procedural rules is satisfied or violated. More specifically:

> *Proposition 1:* The type of selection test is expected to influence perceptions of job relatedness, opportunity to perform, consistency of administration, feedback, and two-way communication.

Direct support for this proposition is limited, but the previously mentioned research of Smither and colleagues (1993) demonstrated the link between the type of selection test and perceived job relatedness, and Kluger and Rothstein (1991) demonstrated a relationship between test type and opportunity to perform (perceived control). Indirect support for the influence of test type on the other procedural rules was cited in the previous literature review pertaining to opportunity to perform (Bies & Shapiro, 1988), feedback (Schmidt et al., 1978), and two-way communication (Martin & Nagao, 1991).

The type of human resource policy will also influence the satisfaction or violation of a number of procedural rules.

> *Proposition 2:* Fairness reactions based on the procedural rules of reconsideration opportunity, consistency of administration, feedback, and selection information will be influenced by the extent to which the human resource policy accommodates these concerns.

As discussed, research indicates that drug-testing programs have greater acceptance when retesting opportunities are provided, when the programs are uniformly administered (Murphy et al., 1990), and when advance notice is provided (Stone & Kotch, 1989). Lounsbury and colleagues (1989) demonstrated the impact that telling applicants how tests relate to future job performance had on these applicants' attitudes toward testing.

Finally, much research on selection and recruiting interviews has indicated the importance of the behavior of human resource personnel on reactions to the selection process. Perceptions of recruiter behavior (related to honesty and interpersonal treatment) have been related to a variety of affective and intentional outcomes (see Rynes, 1991). Bies and Moag (1986) also demonstrated the influence that recruiters have on reaction of fairness and dimensions of honesty, respect, and question propriety.

> *Proposition 3:* Behavior of human resource personnel will influence examinees' satisfaction and perceived violation of procedural rules related to honesty, interpersonal effectiveness, two-way communication, and propriety of questions.

Combination of procedural rules

Leventhal (1980) suggested that procedural rules combine to form overall evaluations of fairness based on a weighted average. That is, in certain situations, some procedural rules may be more salient than others, but across situations all 10 of the procedural rules should contribute to the overall perceived fairness of the selection process.

> *Proposition 4:* The 10 procedural rules should explain most of the variance in overall perceived fairness of the selection system. Though not all of the procedural rules will be salient in all selection situations, each procedural rule will be important in certain selection situations.

Although Leventhal (1980) suggested that different situations may influence the relative weights of different procedural rules, he offered few suggestions regarding specific features of situations that may influence these weights. Indeed, one area in which organizational justice theory can be advanced is through the current discussion of factors that influence weights of procedural rules. It is possible to make some predictions about the types of factors that influence the salience of procedural rules, although theoretical bases for these predictions are weak and they must be examined through subsequent research. The following factors are predicted to influence the salience of procedural rules: (a) types of selection procedures encountered, (b) the extent to which a procedural rule is violated, (c) previous experiences of the applicant, and (d) the time at which fairness reactions are collected.

The types of selection procedures encountered will likely have an impact on the relative weighting of procedural rules. For example, given the predominance of research examining interviewer effects in selection and recruiting interviews (Rynes, 1991), interpersonal treatment rules (i.e., interpersonal effectiveness, two-way communication, and propriety of questions) will likely be most salient when interviews are experienced as part of the selection process. Opportunity to perform was also suggested to be an important procedural rule regarding interviews. Similarly, job relatedness has been a research concern with paper-and-pencil tests (Smither & Pearlman, 1991), and it has been cited as an advantage of work-sample tests and assessment centers (Dodd, 1977; Schmidt et al., 1977); therefore, the job-relatedness procedural rule will likely be the dominant component in perceptions of the fairness of these procedures. The following proposition summarizes these possible relationships:

Proposition 5: The types of selection procedures experienced will have an impact on the relative weighting of the 10 procedural rules in overall evaluations of procedural fairness.

Although the research and theory behind this proposition are somewhat weak, initial support is offered from one study (Gilliland, 1992). Newly hired individuals related incidents of fair and unfair treatment during the selection processes of their latest job search, and these incidents were sorted into procedural categories that were roughly correspondent to the 10 procedural rules. Distribution of incidents in the procedural categories differed for different selection procedures, suggesting that concerns of job relatedness were most salient with paper-and-pencil tests and work-sample tests, whereas ease of faking answers was the dominant concern with honesty and personality tests.

A second factor that may influence the relative weighting of procedural rules in forming fairness perceptions is the extent to which a rule is violated. Research on impression formation and individual decision making indicates that negative information is often more salient and, therefore, weighs more heavily when an individual forms an evaluation, compared to either neutral or positive information (e.g., Fiske & Taylor, 1984; Wright, 1974). Similar findings have been consistently observed in evaluations related to selection interviews (Schmitt, 1976) and performance appraisals (Steiner & Rain, 1989). Extended to the domain of procedural justice, this research suggests that rule violation is likely to be more salient than rule satisfaction. From a decision strategy perspective, noncompensatory strategies such as the conjunctive rule (i.e., satisficing—Simon, 1955) or elimination by aspects (Tversky, 1972) are based on the idea that decision makers reject an alternative if it does not meet a minimal criterion for each attribute that describes that criterion (Svenson, 1979). These strategies are labeled noncompensatory because high levels of some attributes cannot compensate for substandard levels of other attributes. When forming evaluations of procedural fairness, job applicants may use a similar evaluation strategy such that they perceive a selection system as unfair if any one of the procedural rules is violated.

Proposition 6: Instances of rule violation will be more salient and therefore weigh more heavily in overall evaluations of procedural fairness than instances of rule satisfaction.

A third factor that is predicted to influence the weighting of procedural rules is an applicant's prior experience with selection procedures. Again, if the process of weighing procedural rules to form an overall fairness perception is considered as an evaluation or decision-making process, then research in social cognition on impression formation and judgment is relevant and useful for forming predictions. Considerable evidence in impression formation suggests that people have scripts or schemata that guide information attention and evaluation, and information tends to be weighted more heavily if it is consistent with these scripts or schemata (Fiske & Taylor, 1984). Although this finding may seem at odds with Proposition 6, it is important to realize the distinction between rule violation and schema inconsistency. A particular selection procedure, such as a personality test, may *violate* the job relatedness rule for an applicant, but this violation may also be *consistent* with an applicant's schema for that selection procedure.

In terms of fairness reactions, prior experiences with different types of selection procedures may lead to the development of selection scripts or schemata that are characterized by salient procedural rules. For example, a person who has experienced primarily interviews in previous selection experiences will likely believe that the interpersonal procedural rules are more salient than formal characteristics of the selection process. Additionally, as suggested previously, a person who has experienced both structured and unstructured interviews may have the consistency of administration rules salient during future interview situations. Finally, a person who has had a negative experience with a particular selection test, such as a personality inventory, may find that the procedural rules associated with that test (e.g., job relatedness) are more salient in his or her judgment of procedural fairness.

Proposition 7: Prior experiences with different types of selection procedures and with selection procedures that clearly violated one or more of the procedural rules will increase the salience of the procedural rules associated with those experiences.

A final factor that may influence the weighting of procedural rules is the time at which perceived fairness is assessed. Early in the selection process, the selection information procedural rule may be particularly salient because individuals want to know what is going on. After the selection process, feedback should be a more salient procedural justice rule as individuals wait to receive feedback or have recently received feedback. Therefore, if perceived fairness is assessed immediately following the selection process, the feedback procedural rule should be weighted more heavily than other procedural rules. Finally, the discussion of the consistency of administration rule included the possibility that consistency may be more salient after a selection decision has been made.

Proposition 8: The time at which perceived fairness is assessed during the selection process will influence the salience of different procedural justice rules and, therefore, the weighting of these rules in overall perceptions of procedural fairness.

Although researchers have not assessed the impact of stage of selection process on fairness reactions, they have examined recruitment activities and applicants' reactions toward a company. Taylor and Bergmann (1987) found that recruitment activities only influenced perceived company attractiveness and probability of offer acceptance early in the recruitment process. Later, job attributes provided the primary influence on these perceptions.

Conclusions

The model outlined in Figure 1 suggests that test type, human resources policy, and human resources personnel are expected to influence the extent to which each of the 10 procedural rules is violated. In addition, some of the rules may be more salient in specific situations. The types of selection procedures encountered, the extent to which a procedural rule is violated, the previous selection experiences of the applicant, and the time at which fairness reactions are collected are all expected to influence the salience of procedural rules. A final factor that may influence the salience of procedural rules is the outcome of the hiring decision. This possibility is discussed in a following section of this article when the interaction between procedural and distributive justice is considered.

Distributive justice rules

In the most general form, distributive justice theories are concerned with the extent to which recipients receive outcomes in an amount that is consistent with a given distribution rule. In the selection situation, this translates into a determination of whether or not applicants receive the hiring decisions they feel they deserve. Although applicants clearly define the recipients in selection situations, researchers have assessed distributive justice in a more general fashion, reflecting the distributive justice of a selection program rather than an individual's experience in the program. For example, Konovsky and Cropanzano (1991) conceptualized outcome fairness in terms of whether people generally get what they deserve as a result of drug testing, which is almost an instrumentality assessment. This is clearly distinct from traditional theories of distributive justice that are concerned with the outcomes an individual receives personally.

The most salient outcome in the selection situation is the hiring decision, although it may also be possible to consider the distributive justice of a selection test score. Greenberg (1986b) discussed a similar distinction between the distributive justice of a performance evaluation versus the distributive justice of outcomes that result from the evaluation (e.g., salary increase or promotion). Specification of the outcome as a hiring decision also may oversimplify the nature of this decision, in that the position for which an applicant is accepted, the conditions or benefits that accompany the acceptance decision, or the nature of rejection (rejected outright versus being the first alternate) all add dimensions to the hiring decision and suggest that selection outcome is more likely a continuum than a dichotomy.

A final aspect of the distributive justice of selection systems is the determination of what one deserves, which can be made on the basis of one or more distributive rules. Three distributional rules have been identified in the distributive justice literature: equity, equality, and special needs. Although equity is clearly the dominant rule that guides perceptions of distributive fairness, under some circumstances the other procedural rules may become more salient (Bierhoff et al., 1986; Deutsch, 1975). Each of these distribution rules is considered with respect to the selection situation.

Equity

The equity distribution rule suggests that people should receive rewards that are consistent with the inputs they contribute to a distribution situation, relative to a referent comparison. Inputs in a selection situation can be conceptualized as self-perceptions of ability or qualifications for the job. At first glance, equity may not appear applicable to the selection situation because of the lack of opportunity to compare one's inputs to the inputs of other job applicants. However, Goodman (1974) suggested that the use of an "other" as the referent comparison is only one of three possible referents. Structural aspects of the *system*, such as contracts, and *self* -referents compose the other two categories of referents, and it is this latter category that should be most applicable to selection-system equity. With self-referents, people compare their current input/outcome ratio with a past input/outcome ratio or an ideal input/ outcome that is held for the situation. Pritchard (1969:206) suggested that it is from the self-referent or internal standard that "feelings of inequity arise *first* and *foremost*."

The use of a self-referent in forming equity perceptions translates into an evaluation of met expectations. Based on one's past qualifications, one's past success at attaining a job, and one's current qualifications, an expectation is formed regarding the likelihood that the job will be attained.[1] This *performance expectation* may be conceptually similar to the self-efficacy construct because both refer to the perceived likelihood of success. Because an individual may have a variety of past experiences to draw upon for the self-referent, characteristics of the current situation, such as competition for the job, will likely be used to select a past referent that is most representative of the current referent. The assessment of equity is made by comparing the outcome of the hiring decision with one's performance expectations. People will perceive a hiring decision as inequitable and, therefore, unfair if they think they have a good chance of getting a job and they are turned down. More important, rejection may be perceived as more fair or less inequitable if the individual really did not expect to receive a job offer but applied "just in case he or she got lucky."

The results of perceptions of inequity have been discussed in terms of affect, cognition, and behavior. Inequity results in negative emotions, which, in turn, result in cognitive and behavioral attempts to restore equity (Adams, 1965). Negative emotions can result both from perceptions of underpayment inequity (i.e., not getting a job offer when it was expected) and overpayment inequity (i.e., getting a job offer when it was not expected). The negative emotions associated with underpayment are anger toward the company and dissatisfaction with the hiring decision, whereas overpayment is thought to result in feelings of guilt and dissatisfaction (Adams, 1965). Cognitive and behavioral attempts to restore underpayment inequity may take the form of devaluing the job (e.g., "It was not really a very good position anyway"), devaluing the organization, revaluating one's self-perceived abilities and qualifications (and possibly lowering one's self-efficacy toward job attainment), and warning others away from similar jobs with the organization. Responses to overpayment inequity and guilt may include increasing one's self-perceived abilities, qualifications, and possibly self-efficacy toward job performance (e.g., "I must be a stronger applicant than I thought"); increasing initial work performance on the job (as a direct response to inequity and as a result of increased self-efficacy); and increasing extra job behaviors such as organizational citizenship behavior. The bases for and responses to inequity are summarized in the following propositions:

Proposition 9: Applicants' expectations of receiving a job offer (performance expectations) will result from their self-perceived ability or qualifications and their prior experience in similar selection situations.

Proposition 10: Perceptions of equity will emerge from the matching of applicants' expectations with the outcome of the hiring decision such that (a) If applicants expect to get the job and then receive a job offer, they perceive the selection decision as equitable and fair; (b) If applicants expect to get the job and then do not receive a job offer, they perceive the selection decision as inequitable (underpayment) and unfair; (c) If applicants do not expect to get the job and then receive a job offer, they perceive the selection decision as inequitable (overpayment) and unfair; (d) If applicants do not expect to get the job and then do not receive a job offer, they perceive the selection decision as equitable and fair.

Proposition 11: Perceptions of underpayment inequity that result from not receiving a job when it was expected will result first in anger and then in organizational devaluing and self-devaluing.

Proposition 12: Perceptions of overpayment inequity that result from receiving a job offer when it was not expected will result first in guilt, but they will also result in higher self-efficacy and positive outcomes after the person is hired.

Researchers of selection fairness have not considered many of these issues involving equity; however, research on equity theory and compensation is related and can be offered as support for some of the above propositions. Early researchers of equity theory manipulated underpayment by offering fewer rewards than expected (e.g., Lawler & O'Gara, 1967), but often they manipulated overpayment by telling people they were not qualified for the job (e.g., Adams & Rosenbaum, 1962; Friedman & Goodman, 1967; Lawler, Koplin, Young, & Fadem, 1968). This overpayment manipulation of inequity may be more relevant to the issue of hiring equity than it was to compensation equity. Consistent with Proposition 10c and Proposition 12, when individuals were led to believe they were not qualified for the job but were given the job anyway, they responded with higher work quality and increased self-perceived qualifications. Work quantity often decreased in these studies, but as noted by Pritchard (1969), this decrease may have had more to do with deflation of self-esteem than with inequity.

It should be noted that overpayment effects of inequity have not been as consistently demonstrated as underpayment effects, and in many cases overpayment effects are short lived (Campbell & Pritchard, 1976; Kanfer, 1990). In addition. Proposition 10 does not preclude the possibility that the hiring decision will also have a main effect on fairness reactions. Applicants who do not expect to get the job and then receive an offer will likely see the decision as more fair than those who expect to get a job and do not receive an offer.

Equality

Equality suggests that all individuals should have an equal chance of receiving the outcome, regardless of differentiating characteristics such as knowledge or ability. In the selection situation, the satisfaction of equality would suggest random hiring rather than hiring based on ability or experience. However, the equality rule may be more important in terms of its violation rather than its satisfaction, and it may be more salient for job-irrelevant differentiating characteristics (e.g., sex or ethnic background) than for relevant characteristics (e.g., qualifications). Thus, if a person is hired on the basis of ability, equality is not violated, but if sex or ethnic background appears to bias the hiring decision, equality is clearly violated.

Proposition 13: Violations of equality based on job-irrelevant differentiating characteristics will contribute to perceptions of selection outcome unfairness, but violations of equality based on job-relevant differentiating characteristics will not influence fairness perceptions.

Although researchers have not directly assessed this proposition, one need only look toward our social and legal reactions to adverse impact to see support for this proposition. *Adverse impact*, defined in terms of the proportion of minority candidates hired relative to the number of nonminority candidates hired, must be defended by an employer on the grounds of validity in the selection process. Thus, violations of equality on the basis of job-relevant characteristics can be legally defensible, whereas violations of equality on the basis of job-irrelevant characteristics are not legally defensible. The attention given to equality and fairness in employee selection (Hartigan & Wigdor, 1989) also indicates the importance of the equality distributive rule.

Much research on distributive justice has found that equity is the dominant distributive rule (Bierhoff et al., 1986); however, in some situations concerns for equality become more salient and also influence distributive justice reactions. For example, people have been shown to be more sensitive to discrimination, a violation in equality, after seeing a clear-cut example of discrimination (Crosby, Burris, Censor, & MacKethan, 1986). In a selection situation, prior exposure to discrimination or membership in a group against which discriminatory practices are directed (e.g., women and minorities) may influence the salience of the equality distribution rule. Thus, a man losing a job because of discrimination against males would be less likely to perceive the hiring decision as unfair than a female losing a job for the same reason.

> *Proposition 14:* Equality will have a greater impact on overall outcome fairness for those individuals who have had prior exposure to discrimination and those who are members of frequently discriminated upon groups than for individuals for whom discrimination is less salient.

Even though research on the salience of the equality distributive rule is sparse (Cohen, 1987), research examining equality in reactions to selection decisions is nonexistent. Researchers could add to this proposition by examining the salience of equality or violations of equality for males and females or for minority and nonminority subgroups.

Needs

The needs distribution rule suggests that rewards should be distributed on the basis of individual needs. Special needs in the employment situation may be referred to as preferential treatment for a subgroup of disadvantaged employees, such as that provided by affirmative action programs (Hartigan & Wigdor, 1989). Special needs also may become more salient when reasonable accommodation is given to individuals with disabilities or handicaps (Arvey & Sackett, 1993). In both cases, the special consideration that the needy individual receives is most likely to be perceived as fair, if the special needs rule is salient.

Proposition 15: The extent to which the needs distributive rule is more salient than the other distributive rules will positively influence the perceived outcome fairness of a hiring decision that was influenced by affirmative action consideration or hiring involving disabled or handicapped people.

It may be possible for the selection process to be adapted to meet the special needs of disadvantaged subgroups or disabled individuals and, at the same time, to maintain the distributive justice of such a selection system, as long as the special needs rule is salient. Just as research related to equality has demonstrated that people are more sensitive to equality after seeing or experiencing discrimination (Crosby et al., 1986), research has demonstrated that reward allocation decisions are influenced by the needs distributive rule to a greater extent when individual needs are made salient to the allocator (Schwinger, 1986). This finding is strongest when the needs are externally and unintentionally caused rather than internally or intentionally caused. Although these results were produced with allocation decisions, similar findings may hold for perceptions of outcome fairness. If the basis for the special needs consideration during the hiring decision is made salient to job applicants, the needs rule may become more dominant in fairness evaluations, and the decision will be seen as more fair (less unfair) by both positively and negatively affected applicants.

Proposition 16: Special needs considerations will have a greater impact on overall outcome fairness reactions when the basis for the special needs consideration is made clear and attributable to external causes.

Proposition 16 is likely somewhat simplistic because equity and equality injustice may always overshadow attempts to establish justice on a needs basis. The following section addresses this problem and some possible solutions.

Conclusion

Three distributive rules, equity, equality, and special needs, are directly applicable to perceived fairness in the selection situation. One problem that arises is that one distributive rule is not always salient for all applicants, and given the nature of these rules, satisfaction of one distributive rule will always lead to violation of the other distributive rules. For example, an affirmative action program may satisfy the special needs rule but violate the equity and equality rules, thereby influencing the attitudes and behaviors of those employees receiving preferential treatment and those observing preferential treatment (Kleiman & Faley, 1988). Heilman, Simon, and Repper (1987) highlighted this problem in their research on sex-based preferential selection. In a laboratory, females assigned leadership roles on the basis of sex had lower self-perceptions of their leadership ability, performance, and desire to remain a leader than those assigned on the basis of merit.

Similarly, Jacobson and Koch (1977) found that female supervisors were viewed more negatively by subordinates if their position had been attained through preferential treatment. These results suggest that violations of equity and equality during the selection and promotion processes can have a negative impact on attitudes that is not compensated by the satisfaction of the special needs rule.

One solution to the problem of a treatment satisfying one rule but violating another rule is to try to increase the salience of the distributive rule that is being satisfied and thereby decrease the impact that the violated rule has on overall perceptions of distributive justice. This procedure may be destined to fail if Proposition 6 for procedural justice is extended to the distributive justice situation. Based on social cognition and decision-making research, Proposition 6 suggested that instances of rule violation will always be more salient than instances of rule satisfaction. Thus, an affirmative action program will violate equality and equity, and these violations will be more salient than the satisfaction of special needs. A second recommendation, from procedural justice research, would be to highlight just aspects of the selection or promotion procedure as a means of reducing overall perceptions of injustice (for a similar argument see Nacoste, 1990).

Combining procedural and distributive justice

In both the discussions of procedural justice rules and distributive justice rules, it was suggested that evaluations of the satisfaction or violation of different rules are combined to form overall perceptions of the fairness of the system and the outcome. In addition to the direct influences of procedural justice rules on system fairness and distributive justice rules on outcome fairness, Figure 1 suggests that distributive rules moderate the procedural relationship and that procedural rules moderate the distributive relationship.

More specifically, it is predicted that procedural rules will have the greatest impact on system fairness in situations in which distributive rules have been violated. Thus, if job applicants receive job offers that they think they deserve, they will not be as concerned about the fairness of the selection process as if they did not receive a job offer. Similarly, the relationship between distributive justice and outcome fairness will be greatest when procedural rules are violated. That is, applicants will tend to be most dissatisfied with hiring decisions if the procedures used to select them violate their sense of procedural justice.

> *Proposition 17:* Distributive justice will moderate the relationship between procedural rules and overall fairness of the selection process such that the relationship will be strongest when distributive justice has been violated.
>
> *Proposition 18:* Procedural justice will moderate the relationship between distributive rules and overall fairness of the selection outcome

such that the relationship will be strongest when procedural justice has been violated.

Some support for these propositions can be found in the organizational justice literature. In support of Proposition 18, Greenberg (1987a) found that fairness varied as a function of outcome in the procedurally unfair condition but not in the procedurally fair condition. Proposition 17 is supported by the research of Leung and Li (1990) who found process-control (procedural justice) effects on distributive and procedural fairness only with a negative outcome and not with a positive outcome. Similarly, much of the research on procedural justice effects has utilized conditions of distributive injustice (Folger & Greenberg, 1985).

In the selection procedures reaction literature, researchers have only recently examined the impact of different types of selection procedures on both accepted and rejected candidates, and the results are not consistent with organizational justice findings (Kluger & Rothstein, 1991). In a simulated selection situation, these researchers failed to find significant interactions between a hiring decision and selection procedures on a number of attitudinal measures. In contrast, Gilliland (1993) found an interaction between the job relatedness of the selection procedure (procedural justice) and the hiring decision (distributive justice) on perceptions of outcome fairness but not perceptions of process fairness. This finding is consistent with Greenberg (1987a).

The need to further examine reactions of both accepted and rejected candidates is paramount. From a company's perspective, the most important individuals are those who are hired, and if procedural factors have a relatively minor influence on accepted applicants, then the impact of this line of research from a corporate perspective would be substantially reduced. Of course, from a scientific or practical but individually oriented perspective, the impact of selection procedures on rejected applicants is of equal importance to its impact on accepted applicants.

Organizational outcomes

The central features of the proposed model of applicants' reactions to selection systems are fairness perceptions. However, the importance of studying these perceptions is emphasized by documenting the relationship between fairness perceptions and important individual and organizational outcomes. These outcomes include applicants' behavior during selection and hiring processes (e.g., job-application and job-acceptance decisions, self-perceptions such as self-esteem and self-efficacy, and behavior after a person is hired such as work performance and organizational citizenship behavior) (see Figure 1).

When considering the relationships of fairness perceptions to outcomes, it is important to note that the selection process for one job is not isolated from other concurrent selection experiences. The process and outcome fairness of the selection system for an alternate job may influence the fairness to outcome relationship for the current job. For example, the absence of alternate job offers would likely weaken the relationship between selection fairness and job-acceptance decisions. Similarly, previous job rejections may influence the relationship between outcome fairness and self-concept. Although these influences of alternate selections procedures on fairness-outcome relationships is acknowledged, for the sake of simplicity the following discussion only considers the influences of one selection system on these outcomes.

An important feature of previous research relating justice perceptions to organizational outcomes is that some variables have been more strongly related to procedural justice and some variables have been more strongly related to distributive justice. In fact, one of the consistent findings in the organizational justice literature is that procedural justice perceptions tend to account for more variance in attitudes and reactions than do distributive justice perceptions (e.g., Folger & Konovsky, 1989; Konovsky & Cropanzano, 1991; Lind & Tyler, 1988).

> *Proposition 19:* Procedural justice and the fairness of the selection process will be more strongly related to both individual outcomes, such as acceptance decisions and application recommendations, and organizational outcomes, such as work performance and job satisfaction, than will distributive justice or the fairness of the selection outcome.

Proposition 19 is certainly counterintuitive in the selection situation where intuition would suggest that the fairness associated with whether or not one received the job has more of an impact than the fairness of the process by which one was evaluated. It is possible that the relative impact of distributive justice compared to procedural justice is dependent on the valence of the outcome being allocated. The outcome of receiving versus not receiving a job offer may be considerably more valent than typical outcomes associated with justice studies.

Attitudes and behavior during selection and hiring

The perceived fairness of the selection process and outcome can influence job-application and job-acceptance decisions, application recommendations, test motivation, and possibly legal battles. If job seekers know in advance what type of selection process is being used and the selection process is perceived to be unfair, they may be dissuaded from applying for the job. This effect was found in an examination of attitudes toward integrity testing where 10 percent of college students indicated they would refuse an integrity test in an actual employment situation (Ryan & Sackett, 1987). Similarly, Crant and Bateman (1990) found that the presence of a drug-testing program reduced individuals' intentions to apply for a job. Another way in which the perceived fairness of the selection system may have an impact on job-application decisions is through recommendations by applicants who have experienced the selection process. Companies can gain reputations for how they treat applicants during the selection process (Rynes, 1993), and these reputations may influence the ability of organizations to recruit high-quality applicants (Rynes & Barber, 1990). Smither and colleagues (1993) demonstrated relationships between both procedural and distributive justice perceptions and recommendation intentions.

> *Proposition 20:* Decisions to apply for a job and recommendations to others to apply for a job will be influenced by procedural and distributive fairness. That is, individuals will be less likely to apply for a job if they perceive the hiring process as unfair, and they will be less likely to recommend a job to others if they perceived their hiring experience (both process and outcome) to be unfair.

The fairness of the selection system also may influence applicants' decisions to remain in the selection process or to accept job offers. For example, Arvey and colleagues (1975) found that as the time lag between initial application for a job and initiation of the selection process increased (thereby violating the feedback rule), so did the percentage of applicants withdrawing from selection. Reactions to interview procedures also have been shown to influence individuals' intentions to accept job offers (e.g., Linden & Parsons, 1986; Schmitt & Coyle, 1976). Although most research has examined job acceptance in terms of acceptance intentions, it is important to also examine actual job-acceptance decisions because the two may not be as closely related as one would expect (Rynes, 1992).

> *Proposition 21:* Applicants will be less likely to accept a job offer if they perceive the selection process as unfair than if they perceive it as fair, although this relationship may be weaker for individuals who perceive high as opposed to low distributive fairness.

Perceived fairness may influence job-acceptance decisions directly (e.g., because of resentment) or indirectly in terms of a realistic organization preview (Wanous, 1980). Poor treatment may be taken as an indication of how a company treats its employees or the stake that a company places in human resources.

In addition to application and acceptance decision making, perceived fairness may influence the motivation of applicants during the selection process. Individuals' a priori impressions of test fairness may influence their motivation in the testing process. Similarly, system and outcome fairness of one selection process may influence motivation on a subsequent selection process. If a test violates perceptions of procedural justice, motivation to complete the test may be low.

> *Proposition 22:* The motivation for taking a test may be lower among individuals with a priori beliefs that this selection procedure is unfair rather than fair.

Though research has not directly addressed this possibility, researchers have demonstrated that motivation toward taking a test differs for paper-and-pencil versus computer-adaptive testing (Arvey, Strickland, Drau-den, & Martin, 1990). Given some evidence for the impact of test-taking motivation on criterion-related validity (Schmit & Ryan, 1992), concern for the impact of fairness on test motivation is even more important.

A final issue related to applicants' behavior is the relationship between perceived fairness and decisions to file discrimination charges. Although researchers have not directly examined this relationship, Cascio and Phillips (1979) demonstrated lower incidence of applicants' complaints regarding testing following the introduction of job-related performance testing. Additionally, there is some indication that perceptions of the fairness of the selection system influence decisions by lawyers to pursue plaintiffs' discrimination cases (Seymour, 1988).

Proposition 23: Applicants' complaints and decisions to file discrimination charges are likely related to both procedural and distributive fairness of the selection system.

Self-perceptions

Self-esteem, self-efficacy toward a job and toward the job-search process, and self-perceived ability may be influenced by the selection system and the fairness of the outcome. In terms of self-esteem, research regarding interviews indicates that social comparisons in the interview process can have an impact on an applicant's self-esteem (Morse & Gergen, 1970). Additionally, considerable research in social psychology has examined the impact that feedback on success and failure has on self-esteem (e.g., Jones, Rhodewalt, Berglas, & Skelton, 1981; McFarland & Ross, 1982). Although feedback regarding failure has been shown to have a detrimental effect on self-esteem, attributions surrounding such feedback are an important moderator of this effect. McFarland and Ross (1982) gave individuals feedback on either success or failure under conditions where performance could be attributed to either the task or one's ability. When performance was attributed to the task, feedback had no effect on resultant self-esteem. However, when the attribution was to ability, feedback regarding success increased self-esteem and feedback regarding failure decreased self-esteem.

Consistent with predictions from attribution theory (Weiner, 1985), if the perceived fairness of the selection system can be questioned, external attributions are more likely and the outcome of a selection decision will not have a great impact on applicants' self-esteem. Alternately, if the test is perceived to be fair, internal attributions are more likely, and the selection outcome will likely affect applicants' self-esteem. The implication of this reasoning is that if an organization strives to attain a procedurally fair selection system, it may be raising the self-esteem of the selected individuals but lowering the self-esteem of rejected individuals. From a psychological standpoint, rejected applicants would be better off being rejected through a procedurally unfair selection system than through a procedurally fair system. Clearly this point is at odds with the advantages of procedurally fair selection systems hypothesized for the other organizational outcomes.

Proposition 24: An interaction between procedural and distributive fairness will be observed on self-esteem such that distributive fairness will not influence the self-esteem of applicants evaluated through a procedurally unfair selection system, but it will have an impact on those selected through a procedurally fair selection system. Among this latter group of applicants, the distributive fairness of the selection process will increase the self-esteem of accepted individuals and will decrease the self-esteem of rejected individuals.

Similar reasoning can be used to generate hypotheses with regard to self-efficacy and self-perceived ability. Job seekers likely have efficacy beliefs about gaining any job, attaining a given job, performing well on a particular selection procedure, and performing the job once it is attained.

Proposition 25: Procedural and distributive justice will interact in their impact on self-efficacy toward the job, the job-search process, and self-perceived ability such that the distributive justice impact on self-perceptions will be greatest when procedural justice is satisfied rather than violated (see Propositions 11, 12, and 24).

Support for this proposition can be found in a study by Gilliland (1993). In a hiring situation, self-efficacy toward job performance was increased for applicants who were selected through a job-related selection procedure, and it was decreased for applicants who were rejected through this same procedure. Self-efficacy was not influenced by the hiring decision when the selection procedure was low in job relatedness. Additionally, Schmitt, Ford, and Stults (1986) found that self-perceived ability changed as a result of participation in an assessment center.

Self-efficacy is related to motivation and subsequent performance (Gist & Mitchell, 1992), so the perceived fairness of selection may have an impact on motivation, self-perceptions, and performance both during the selection process and after the person is hired. Further, self-esteem and self-efficacy may influence the motivation of rejected applicants to continue their job search. Ellis and Taylor (1983) found that self-esteem predicted the sources that individuals used to find jobs, individuals' satisfaction with the job-search process, number of offers received, job-offer acceptance, and length of intended tenure. Similarly, Kluger and Rothstein (1991) found that hiring decision and, to some extent, test type influenced individuals' positive and negative coping mechanisms with regard to the job search. Although they did not assess self-concept, Schmitt and Coyle (1976) found that interviewers' characteristics and the information conveyed during an interview were related to applicants' intentions to pursue further job opportunities.

Outcomes after hiring

It is likely that experiences during the selection process also have an impact on attitudes and behavior of hired individuals on the job, and they may even shape an organization's climate. Obviously, these outcomes are only relevant for individuals who have been offered and have accepted jobs. At least three lines of research offer support for this prediction. First, organizational justice research demonstrates the relationship among justice perceptions, job attitudes, and job behaviors (e.g., Alexander & Ruderman, 1987; Folger & Konovsky, 1989; Moorman, 1991). For example, Moorman (1991) found that justice perceptions associated with supervisors' treatment of subordinates were related to supervisors' evaluations of subordinates' organizational citizenship behaviors (OCB), which include altruism, courtesy, and conscientiousness. Extending this finding to the selection domain would lead to the prediction that perceptions of procedural fairness, particularly fairness associated with explanation and interpersonal treatment, would predict future OCB. If one receives courteous, honest, informative treatment during the selection process, one may be more likely to exhibit these behaviors in the workplace. More directly relevant to organizational justice of selection, Konovsky and Cropanzano (1991) found that perceptions of procedural justice and an explanation for a drug-testing program were related to work performance, job satisfaction, and organizational commitment. Although this study assessed incumbents' perceptions of procedural justice, a similar effect would be expected between applicants' reactions to a selection process and later job performance.

Second, research examining realistic job previews has demonstrated that providing applicants with realistic information about the nature of the job will lead to small but significant increases in performance, organizational commitment, job satisfaction, and tenure (Premack & Wanous, 1985). Finally, individuals' initial impressions are formed early in the information-acquisition process, and these initial impressions are often resistant to change (Nisbett & Ross, 1980). The selection process can serve as the first information an individual receives regarding an organization's treatment of employees. If this person is hired, it seems reasonable to expect that the initial impressions developed during the selection process would have a substantial impact on later impressions of the organization and the job. This perspective is consistent with the Attraction-Selection-Attrition model proposed to describe the etiology of organizational behavior, in general, and organizational climate more specifically (Schneider, 1987). The fairness of the selection process may influence both attraction to and attrition from an organization.

> *Proposition 26:* Evaluations of selection process and outcome fairness will have an impact on the work behavior of a person who is hired, which is exhibited through work performance, organizational citizenship behaviors, his or her attitudes such as job satisfaction and organizational commitment, and the organizational climate.

Initial research indicates some support for the impact of selection-process justice on job satisfaction and work performance (Gilliland, 1993), although the results of this study were more complicated than Proposition 26 suggests. Clearly more research is needed before these links can be considered as anything beyond research propositions.

It is important to note that the current model does not represent an attempt to capture all of the variance in attitudes and behavior after a person is hired, nor is it offered as an alternate explanation of the etiology of these constructs. Rather, the goal of the current discussion is to highlight the influence that individuals' reactions to the fairness of the selection process may have on their outcomes after they are hired.

Conclusions

The model of applicants' reactions to selection systems demonstrates the importance of considering these reactions as a property of the selection process. This perspective is consistent with Herriot's (1989b) assertion that selection research should consider more carefully the social processes surrounding selection. Organizational justice theory provides both the framework for examining procedural and distributive components of selection reactions and a basis for generating research propositions. Although fragmented, prior research on reactions to selection procedures supported the importance of a number of the proposed components and relationships in the model.

During the presentation of the model, a number of venues for future research were developed. The following is a brief summary of some of the most important research issues.

1. One of the foremost research needs is to examine the validity and importance of the 10 procedural rules that are proposed to underlie applicants' reactions to the fairness of a selection system. Researchers should determine whether these 10 rules capture the entire domain of procedural concerns, whether some of the rules are not important to job applicants, and whether the rules could be reduced to a more succinct group.
2. Another issue related to the 10 procedural rules is the salience of these factors under different selection situations. Some of the rules may be more important in certain selection situations (e.g., two-way communication in selection interviews). Do other factors, such as rule violation, prior experiences, and stage in the selection process, influence the salience of certain procedural rules?
3. In terms of distributive justice, researchers should examine the relationship of applicants' performance expectations to their perceptions of equity and distributive justice. What are the relative influences of the hiring decision and performance expectations on distributive justice?
4. Do equality and needs distributive justice rules have an influence on applicants' perceptions of distributive fairness, and can the salience of these rules

be manipulated by presenting instances of discrimination or by highlighting individual needs?
5. The relative influence of procedural and distributive factors on applicants' perceptions of fairness should be examined, as should the interaction between these factors. Does procedural justice moderate the relationship between distributive features and distributive fairness, and does distributive justice moderate the relationship between procedural features and procedural fairness?
6. Finally, research is needed that links applicants' perceptions of procedural and distributive fairness to preemployment and postemployment outcomes. Demonstrating the links to important organizational outcomes will help establish the importance of the study of applicants' perceptions of the fairness of selection systems.

Acknowledgments

Parts of this article were based upon the author's dissertation, and thanks are given to the committee members: Neal Schmitt, Dan Ilgen, Steve Kozlowski, and Mike Lindell. The author would also like to thank Jose Cortina, Cynthia Gilliland, and Craig Russell for their helpful comments on various drafts of this article.

Note

In terms of formally expressed outcome to input ratios (e.g., Adams, 1965), equity can be defined in the following manner:

$$\frac{O_c}{I_c} = \frac{O_p}{I_p}$$

Where: O_c = current outcomes (receiving job offer)
I_c = current inputs (perceived qualifications)
O_p = past outcomes (received/not received job offer)
I_p = past inputs (perceived qualifications)

To evaluate the current outcome, the person examines his or her current inputs in the context of his or her past outcomes and inputs. That is:

$$O_c = I_c(O_p/I_p) = (I_c/I_p)O_p$$

The combination of current inputs and past inputs and outcomes can be conceptualized as performance expectations, or the extent to which a person thinks he or she will get the job.

References

Adams, J. S. 1965. Inequity in social exchange. In L. Berkowitz (Ed.), *Advances in experimental social psychology,* vol. 2: 267–299. New York: Academic Press.

Adams, J. S., & Rosenbaum, W. E. 1962. The relationship of worker productivity to cognitive dissonance about wage inequities. *Journal of Applied Psychology,* 46: 161–164.

Alexander, S., & Ruderman, M. 1987. The role of procedural and distributive justice in organizational behavior. *Social Justice Research,* 1: 177–198.

Anastasi, A. 1988. *Psychological testing* (6th ed.). New York: Macmillan.

Arvey, R. D., Gordon, M. E., Massengill, D. P., & Mussio, S. J. 1975. Differential dropout rates of minority and majority job candidates due to "time-lags" between selection procedures. *Personnel Psychology,* 28: 175–180.

Arvey, R. D., & Sackett, P. R. 1993. Fairness in selection: Current developments and perspectives. In N. Schmitt & W. Borman (Eds.), *Personnel selection*: 171–202. San Francisco: Jossey-Bass.

Arvey, R. D., Strickland, W., Drauden, G., & Martin, C. 1990. Motivational components of test taking. *Personnel Psychology,* 43: 695–716.

Bierhoff, H. W., Cohen, R. L., & Greenberg, J. 1986. *Justice in social relations.* New York: Plenum.

Bies, R. J., & Moag, J. S. 1986. Interactional justice: Communication criteria of fairness. *Research on Negotiation in Organizations,* 1: 43–55.

Bies, R. J., & Shapiro, D. L. 1988. Voice and justification: Their influence on procedural fairness judgments. *Academy of Management Journal,* 31: 676–685.

Boudreau, J. W., & Rynes, S. L. 1985. The role of recruitment in staff utility analysis. *Journal of Applied Psychology,* 70: 354–366.

Brown, D. C. 1992. Soroka v. Dayton Hudson. *Industrial-Organizational Psychologist,* 30(1): 28.

Campbell, J. P., & Pritchard, R. D. 1976. Motivation theory in industrial and organizational psychology. In M. Dunnette (Ed.), *Handbook of industrial and organizational psychology:* 63–130. Chicago: Rand McNally.

Campion, J. E., & Arvey, R. D. 1989. Unfair discrimination in the employment interview. In R. W. Eder & G. R. Ferris (Eds.), *The employment interview: Theory, research, and practice:* 61–72. Newbury Park, CA: Sage.

Cascio, W. F., & Phillips, N. F. 1979. Performance testing: A rose among thorns? *Personnel Psychology,* 32: 751–766.

Cohen, R. L. 1987. Distributive justice: Theory and research. *Social Justice Research,* 1: 19–40.

Crant, J. M., & Bateman, T. S. 1990. An experimental test of the impact of drug-testing programs on potential job applicants' attitudes and intentions. *Journal of Applied Psychology,* 75: 127–131.

Crosby, F., Burris, L., Censor, C., & MacKethan, E. R. 1986. Two rotten apples spoil the justice barrel. In H. W. Bierhoff, R. L. Cohen, & J. Greenberg (Eds.), *Justice in social relations:* 267–281. New York: Plenum.

Deutsch, M. 1975. Equity, equality, and need: What determines which value will be used as the basis of distributive justice? *Journal of Social Issues,* 31(3): 137–149.

Dipboye, R. L., & de Pontbriand, P. 1981. Correlates of employee reactions to performance appraisals and appraisal systems. *Journal of Applied Psychology,* 66: 248–251.

Dodd, W. E. 1977. Attitudes toward assessment center programs. In J. L. Moses & W. C. Byham (Eds.), *Applying the assessment center method:* 161–183. New York: Pergamon Press.

Ellis, R. A., & Taylor, M. S. 1983. Role of self-esteem within the job search process. *Journal of Applied Psychology,* 68: 632–640.

Fiske, S. T., & Taylor, S. E. 1984. *Social cognition.* New York: Random House.

Folger, R. 1987. Distributive and procedural justice in the workplace. *Social Justice Research,* 1: 143–159.

Folger, R., & Greenberg, J. 1985. Procedural justice: An interpretive analysis of personnel systems. *Research in Personnel and Human Resources Management,* 3: 141–183.

Folger, R., & Konovsky, M. A. 1989. Effects of procedural and distributive justice on reactions to pay raise decisions. *Academy of Management Journal,* 32: 115–130.

Friedman, A., & Goodman, P. S. 1967. Wage inequity, self-qualifications, and productivity. *Organizational Behavior and Human Performance,* 3: 340–352.

Fryxell, G. E., & Gordon, M. E. 1989. Workplace justice and job satisfaction as predictors of satisfaction with union and management. *Academy of Management Journal,* 32: 851–866.

Gilliland, S. W. 1992. *Fairness from the applicant's perspective: Reactions to employee selection procedures.* Unpublished manuscript.

Gilliland, S. W. 1993. *Procedural and distributive justice: Reactions to a selection system.* Paper presented at the 8th annual conference of the Society for Industrial and Organizational Psychology, San Francisco.

Gist, M. E., & Mitchell, T. R. 1992. Self-efficacy: A theoretical analysis of its determinants and malleability. *Academy of Management Review,* 17: 183–211.

Gomez-Mejia. L. R., & Balkin, D. B. 1987. Dimensions and characteristics of personnel manager perceptions of effective drug-testing programs. *Personnel Psychology,* 40: 745–763.

Goodman, P. S. 1974. An examination of referents used in the evaluation of pay. *Organizational Behavior and Human Performance,* 12: 170–195.

Greenberg, J. 1982. Approaching equity and avoiding inequity in groups and organizations. In J. Greenberg & R. L. Cohen (Eds.), *Equity and justice in social behavior:* 389–435. New York: Academic Press.

Greenberg, J. 1986a. Determinants of perceived fairness of performance evaluations. *Journal of Applied Psychology,* 71: 340–342.

Greenberg, J. 1986b. The distributive justice of organizational performance evaluations. In H. W. Bierhoff, R. L. Cohen, & J. Greenberg (Eds.), *Justice in social relations:* 337–351. New York: Plenum.

Greenberg, J. 1987a. Reactions to procedural injustice in payment distributions: Do the means justify the ends? *Journal of Applied Psychology,* 72: 55–61.

Greenberg, J. 1987b. A taxonomy of organizational justice theories. *Academy of Management Review,* 12: 9–22.

Greenberg, J. 1990a. Employee theft as a reaction to underpayment inequity: The hidden cost of pay cuts. *Journal of Applied Psychology,* 75: 561–568.

Greenberg, J. 1990b. Organizational justice: Yesterday, today, and tomorrow. *Journal of Management,* 16: 399–432.

Greenberg, J., & Tyler, T. R. 1987. Why procedural justice in organizations. *Social Justice Research,* 1: 127–142.

Hartigan, J. A., & Wigdor, A. K. 1989. *Fairness in employment testing: Validity generalisation, minority issues, and the general aptitude test battery.* Washington, DC: National Academy Press.

Heilman, M. E., Simon, M. C., & Repper, D. P. 1987. Intentionally favored, unintentionally harmed? Impact of sex-based preferential selection of self-perceptions and self-evaluations. *Journal of Applied Psychology,* 72: 62–68.

Herriot, P. 1989a. Interactions with clients in personnel selection. In P. Herriot (Ed.), *Assessment and selection in organizations:* 219–226. Chichester, England: Wiley.

Herriot, P. 1989b. Selection as a social process. In M. Smith & I. Robertson (Eds.), *Advances in selection and assessment:* 171–187. Chichester, England: Wiley.

Huffcutt, A. 1990. Intelligence is not a panacea in personnel selection. *The Industrial-Organizational Psychologist,* 27(3): 66–67.

Hunter, J. E., & Hunter, R. F. 1984. Validity and utility of alternative predictors of job performance. *Psychological Bulletin,* 96: 72–38.

Iles, P. A., & Robert, I. T. 1989. The impact of personnel selection procedures on candidates. In P. Herriot (Ed.), *Assessment and selection in organizations:* 257–271. Chichester, England: Wiley.

Jacobson, M. B., & Koch, W. 1977. Women as leaders: Performance evaluation as a function of method of leader selection. *Organizational Behavior and Human Performance,* 20: 149–157.

Jones, E. E., Rhodewalt, F., Berglas, S., & Skelton, J. A. 1981. Effects of strategic self-presentation on subsequent self-esteem. *Journal of Personality and Social Psychology,* 41: 407–421.

Kanfer, R. 1990. Motivation theory and industrial/organizational psychology. In M. D. Dunnette & L. M. Hough (Eds.), *Handbook of industrial and organizational psychology,* vol. 1: 75–170. Palo Alto, CA: Consulting Psychologists Press.

Kleiman, L. S., & Faley, R. H. 1988. Voluntary affirmative action and preferential treatment: Legal and research implications. *Personnel Psychology,* 41: 481–496.

Kluger, A. N., & Rothstein, H. R. 1991. The influence of selection test type on applicant reactions to employment testing. In R. R. Reilly (Chair), *Perceived validity of selection procedures: Implications for organizations.* Symposium conducted at the 6th annual conference of the Society for Industrial and Organizational Psychology, St. Louis.

Konovsky, M. A., & Cropanzano, R. 1991. The perceived fairness of employee drug testing as a predictor of employee attitudes and job performance. *Journal of Applied Psychology,* 76: 698–707.

Landy, F. J., Barnes, J. L., & Murphy, K. R. 1978. Correlates of perceived fairness and accuracy of performance evaluation. *Journal of Applied Psychology,* 63: 751–754.

Lawler, E. E., III, Koplin, C. A., Young, T. F., & Fadem, J. A. 1988. Inequity reduction over time in an induced overpayment situation. *Organizational Behavior and Human Performance,* 3: 253–268.

Lawler, E. E., III, & O'Gara, P. W. 1967. Effects of inequity produced by underpayment on work output, work quality, and attitudes toward the work. *Journal of Applied Psychology,* 51: 403–410.

Leung, K., & Li, W. 1990. Psychological mechanisms of process-control effects. *Journal of Applied Psychology,* 75: 613–620.

Leventhal, G. S. 1980. What should be done with equity theory? New approaches to the study of fairness in social relationship. In K. J. Gergen, M. S. Greenberg, & R. H. Willis (Eds.), *Social exchange: Advances in theory and research*: 27–55. New York: Plenum.

Liden, R. C., & Parsons, C. K. 1986. A field study of job applicant interview perceptions, alternative opportunities, and demographic characteristics. *Personnel Psychology,* 39: 109–122.

Lind, E. A., & Tyler, T. 1988. *The social psychology of procedural justice.* New York: Plenum.

Lounsbury, J. W., Bobrow, W., & Jensen, J. B. 1989. Attitudes toward employment testing: Scale development, correlates, and "known-group" validation. *Professional Psychology: Research and Practice,* 20: 340–349.

Martin, C. L., & Nagao, D. H. 1989. Some effects of computerized interviewing on job applicant responses. *Journal of Applied Psychology,* 74: 72–80.

McFarland, C., & Ross, M. 1982. Impact of causal attributions on affective reactions to success and failure. *Journal of Personality and Social Psychology,* 43: 937–946.

Moorman, R. H. 1991. The relationship between organiational justice and organizational citizenship behaviors: Do fairness perceptions influence employee citizenship? *Journal of Applied Psychology,* 76: 845–855.

Morse, S., & Gergen, K. J. 1970. Social comparison, self-consistency, and the concept of self. *Journal of Personality and Social Psychology,* 16: 148–156.

Murphy, K. R. 1986. When your top choice turns you down: Effects of rejected offers on utility of selection tests. *Psychological Bulletin,* 99: 133–138.

Murphy, K. R., Thornton, G. C., III, & Prue, K. 1991. Influence of job characteristics on the acceptability of employee drug testing. *Journal of Applied Psychology,* 76: 447–453.

Murphy, K. R., Thornton, G. C., III, & Reynolds, D. H. 1990. College students' attitudes toward employee drug testing programs. *Personnel Psychology,* 43: 615–631.

Nacoste, R. B. 1990. Sources of stigma: Analyzing the psychology of affirmative action. *Law & Policy,* 12: 175–195.

Nisbett, R., & Ross, L. 1980. *Human inference: Strategies and shortcomings of social judgment.* Englewood Cliffs, NJ: Prentice-Hall.

Premack, S. L., & Wanous, J. P. 1985. A meta-analysis of realistic job review experiments. *Journal of Applied Psychology.* 70: 706–719.

Pritchard, R. D. 1969. Equity theory: A review and critique. *Organizational Behavior and Human Performance,* 4: 176–211.

Robertson, I. T., & Smith, M. 1989. Personnel selection methods. In M. Smith & I. Robertson (Eds.), *Advances in selection and assessment:* 89–112. Chichester, England: Wiley.

Ryan, A. M., & Sackett, P. R. 1987. Pre-employment honesty testing: Fakability, reactions of test takers, and company image. *Journal of Business and Psychology,* 1: 248–256.

Rynes, S. L. 1991. Recruitment, job choice, and post-hire consequences: A call for new research directions. In M. D. Dunnette (Ed.), *Handbook of industrial and organizational psychology:* 399–444. Palo Alto, CA: Consulting Psychologists Press.

Rynes, S. L. 1993. Who's selecting whom? Effects of selection practices on applicant attitudes and behaviors. In N. Schmitt & W. Borman (Eds.), *Personnel selection in organizations:* 240–274. San Francisco: Jossey-Bass.

Rynes, S. L., & Barber, A. E. 1990. Applicant attraction strategies: An organizational perspective. *Academy of Management Review,* 15: 286–310.

Rynes, S. L., Bretz, R. D., Jr., & Gerhart, B. 1991. The importance of recruitment in job choice: A different way of Looking. *Personnel Psychology,* 44: 487–521.

Schmidt, F. L., Greenthal, A. L., Hunter, J. E., Berner, J. G., & Seaton, F. W. 1977. Job sample v. paper-and-pencil trades technical tests: Adverse impact and examinee attitudes. *Personnel Psychology,* 30: 187–197.

Schmidt, F. L., Urry, V. M., & Gugel, J. F. 1978. Computer assisted tailored testing: Examinee reactions and evaluations. *Educational and Psychological Measurement,* 38: 265–273.

Schmit, M. J., & Ryan, A. M. 1992. Test-taking disposition: A missing link? *Journal of Applied Psychology,* 77: 629–637.

Schmitt, N. 1976. Social and situational determinants of interview decisions: Implications for the employment interview. *Personnel Psychology,* 29: 79–101.

Schmitt. N. 1989. Fairness in employee selection. In M. Smith & I. Robertson (Eds.), *Advances in selection and assessment:* 131–153. Chichester, England: Wiley.

Schmitt, N., & Coyle, B. W. 1976. Applicant decisions in the employment interview. *Journal of Applied Psychology,* 61: 184–192.

Schmitt, N., Ford, J. K., & Stults, D. M. 1986. Changes in self-perceived ability as a function of performance in an assessment centre. *Journal of Occupational Psychology,* 59: 327–335.

Schmitt, N., & Gilliland, S. W. 1992. Beyond differential prediction: Fairness in selection. In D. M. Saunders (Ed.), *New approaches to employee management: fairness in employee selection,* vol. 1: 21–46. Greenwich, CT: JAI Press.

Schmitt. N., Gilliland, S. W., Landis, R. S., & Devine, D. 1993. Computer-based testing applied to selection of secretarial applicants. *Personnel Psychology,* 46: 149–165.

Schmitt, N., Gooding, R. Z., Noe, R. A., & Kirsch, M. 1984. Metaanalyses of validity studies published between 1964 and 1982 and the investigation of study characteristics. *Personnel Psychology,* 37: 407–422.

Schneider, B. 1987. The people make the place. *Personnel Psychology,* 40: 437–453.

Schuler, H. 1993. Social validity of selection situations: A concept and some empirical results. In H. Schuler, J. L. Farr, & M. Smith (Eds.), *Personnel selection and assessment; Individual and organizational perspectives:* 11–26. Hillsdale, NJ: Erlbaum.

Schwinger, T. 1986. The need principle of distributive justice. In H. W. Bierhoff, R. L. Cohen, & J. Greenberg (Eds.), *Justice in social relations:* 211–225. New York: Plenum.

Seymour, R. T. 1988. Why plaintiffs' counsel challenge tests, and how they can successfully challenge the theory of "validity generalization." *Journal of Vocational Behavior,* 33: 331–364.

Sheppard, B. H., & Lewicki, R. J. 1987. Toward general principles of managerial fairness. *Social Justice Research,* 1: 161–176.

Simon, H. A. 1955. A behavioral model of rational choice. *Quarterly Journal of Economics,* 69: 99–118.

Smither, J. W., & Pearlman, K. 1991. Perceptions of the job-relatedness of selection procedures among college recruits and recruiting/employment managers. In R. R. Reilly (Chair), *Perceived validity of selection procedures: Implications for organizations.* Symposium conducted at the 6th annual conference of the Society for Industrial and Organizational Psychology, St. Louis.

Smither, J. W., Reilly, R. R., Millsap, R. E., Pearlman, K., & Stoffey, R. W. 1993. Applicant reactions to selection procedures. *Personnel Psychology,* 46: 49–76.

Steiner, D. D., & Rain, J. S. 1989. Immediate and delayed primacy and recency effects in performance evaluation. *Journal of Applied Psychology,* 74: 136–142.

Stone, D. L., & Kotch, D. A. 1989. Individuals' attitudes toward organizational drug testing policies and practices. *Journal of Applied Psychology,* 74: 518–521.

Stone, E. F., & Stone, D. L. 1990. Privacy in organizations: Theoretical issues, research findings, and protection mechanisms. *Research in Personnel and Human Resource Management,* 8: 349–411.

Svenson, O. 1979. Process descriptions of decision making. *Organizational Behavior and Human Performance,* 23: 86–112.

Taylor, M. S., & Bergmann, T. J. 1987. Organizational recruitment activities and applicants' reactions at different stages of the recruitment process. *Personnel Psychology,* 40: 261–285.

Thibaut, J., & Walker, L. 1975. *Procedural justice: A psychological analysis.* Hillsdale, NJ: Erlbaum.

Tversky, A. 1972. Elimination by aspects: A theory of choice. *Psychological Review,* 79: 281–299.

Tyler, T. R., & Bies, R. J. 1990. Beyond formal procedures: The interpersonal context of procedural justice. In J. S. Carroll (Ed.), *Applied social psychology and organizational settings*; 77–98. Hillsdale, NJ: Erlbaum.

Wanous, J. P. 1980. *Organizational entry: Recruitment, selection, and socialization of newcomers.* Reading, MA: Addison-Wesley.

Weiner, B. 1985. An attribution theory of achievement motivation and emotion. *Psychological Review,* 92: 548–573.

Wright, P. 1974. The harassed decision maker: Time pressure, distractions, and the use of evidence. *Journal of Applied Psychology,* 59: 555–561.

26

APPLICANTS' PERCEPTIONS OF SELECTION PROCEDURES AND DECISIONS

A critical review and agenda for the future

Ann Marie Ryan and Robert E. Ployhart

Source: *Journal of Management* 26(3) (2000): 565–606.

Abstract

This review critically examines the literature from 1985 to 1999 on applicant perceptions of selection procedures. We organize our review around several key questions: What perceptions have been studied? What are determinants of perceptions? What are the consequences or outcomes associated with perceptions applicants hold? What theoretical frameworks are most useful in examining these perceptions? For each of these questions, we provide suggestions for key research directions. We conclude with a discussion of the practical implications of this line of research for those who design and administer selection processes.

Over the past decade, there has been a surge of interest in studying how job applicants view the employee selection process. This research interest has been sparked by a number of forces. First, the greater competition for employees due to low unemployment rates (Nassar, 1999) has led organizational decision makers to think about how various components of selection processes might influence the attractiveness of the organization. Second, leading recruiting researchers, such as Rynes (1991, 1993), have called for better research on applicant perspectives. Third, researchers in the area of organizational justice have suggested and begun to explore the applicability of social justice theory concepts to applicant perceptions of selection methods (e.g., Gilliland, 1993). Fourth, the increasing diversity of the workforce (Cox, 1993; Jackson & Associates, 1992) has led employers to be concerned that certain procedures might make an organization less attractive to qualified minority group members. In addition to examining racial differences in perceptions of selection processes, researchers interested in lessening the adverse impact of selection procedures have been interested in whether attitudes about tests might account for some of the performance differences observed between minority and majority group members on certain selection methods.

The basic premise of research on applicant perceptions of selection processes and procedures has been that these perceptions affect how the applicant views the organization (i.e., the process sends a signal; Rynes, 1993), his or her decision to join the organization, and subsequent behaviors (e.g., future product/service purchases, recommendations to others). Thus, understanding when and why applicants have more or less favorable impressions of a selection process might increase the ability to influence those perceptions and related applicant attitudes and behavior.

In this paper, we provide a review of the research on applicant perceptions of selection processes. We use the terms perceptions and selection processes broadly so as to provide a comprehensive review. That is, we discuss literature related to any attitudes, affect, or cognitions an individual might have about the hiring process, with several exceptions. First, there is a great deal of research on the effects of affirmative action and specifically on preferential selection (e.g., Heilman & Herlihy, 1984: Heilman Lucas, & Kaplow, 1990; Heilman, Simon, & Repper 1987). This research is relevant because it examines applicant perceptions of a particular characteristic of a selection process. However, as this is reviewed comprehensively elsewhere (Kravitz et al., 1997; Turner & Pratkanis, 1994), we do not review this area but simply note its relevance to the study of applicant perceptions of selection procedures. Second, elsewhere in this issue, a review is provided of the research on recruiter effects on applicant perceptions (Breaugh, 2000). Thus, we do not discuss how recruiter characteristics and recruitment materials affect applicant perceptions, although we do discuss perceptions of interviews as a selection procedure in contrast to other selection methods. Third, there is research on attitudes toward drug testing of current employees; we exclude this from our review and focus only on drug testing in selection contexts.

We have organized the review in the following manner. First, we provide a brief overview to orient the reader. We then present a tabular summary of the published empirical work in this area. There have also been numerous unpublished conference papers related to this topic and we discuss these in the text where relevant. We limit this review to the last 15 years for the sake of parsimony, but also because most work has occurred since that time. We discuss the table's contents and theoretical work in the area in terms of the following questions:

- What applicant perceptions have been studied? What should be studied?
- What are the determinants of applicant perceptions?
- What are the consequences of holding more positive or negative perceptions (i.e., to what outcomes have they been linked)? What moderates these relations?
- What theoretical frameworks have been presented? How well have they been applied? What other theoretical viewpoints need consideration?

In each section, we include what we see as key research needs on the topic of applicant perceptions. We end with suggestions for new research directions and some practical implications.

Overview of the research area

Researchers have mentioned applicant perceptions of selection procedures as an avenue of inquiry for quite some time (e.g., Mosier, 1947). In the late 1980s and early 1990s, a number of book chapters and theoretical pieces appeared that suggested there was not enough attention being paid by researchers to the fact that selection involves two parties: the organization selects employees but applicants also select—where they will apply and where they will work (e.g., Herriot, 1989; Rynes, 1991, 1993; Schuler, 1993). Although the recruiting research literature was certainly addressing what drives applicant decisions, it was not focused on the selection process as an element in those decisions. In particular, Rynes (1993) pointed out some key research needs in studying applicant perceptions that spurred other research.

Schmitt and Gilliland (1992) and Gilliland (1993) developed a model of how and why situational factors in the selection process influence perceptions of the fairness of the process and how these perceptions influence applicant attitudes and behaviors. Gilliland proposed that situational characteristics (e.g., test type, organization human resource policy, the behavior of human resource personnel) influence applicant perceptions of the procedural justice of the selection system. He noted that perceptions of the extent to which specific procedural rules (e.g., job relatedness, consistency of administration. priority of questions) are satisfied or violated are combined to form an overall evaluation of the fairness of the selection process. He also noted that an applicant's prior experiences with a selection process would influence this evaluation. Gilliland proposed that perceptions of distributive fairness (i.e., the fairness of either the test outcome or the hiring decision) are influenced by the distributive justice rules of equity, equality, and need, which in turn are influenced by such things as performance expectations and the salience of discrimination. Consistent with the justice literature, his model proposes an interaction of procedural and distributive rules in forming fairness perceptions of the process and of the outcome. Gilliland indicated that fairness perceptions should relate to outcomes such as job application decisions, test motivation, self-esteem, self-efficacy, endorsement of the company's products, job acceptance decisions, job satisfaction, and performance, among others. We refer the reader to his article for a comprehensive discussion of this model. Gilliland's conceptualization has served as the basis for a large number of the studies in the applicant perceptions literature.

Two other influential pieces that did not derive from Gilliland's conceptualization but can be seen as focusing on "justice-related" perceptions are Arvey and Sackett (1993) and Smither, Reilly, Millsap, Pearlman and Stoffey (1993). Arvey and Sackett (1993) proposed a slightly different set of factors as influencing perceptions of fairness, some of which remain unexamined to date. Smither et al. (1993) looked specifically at job-relatedness, which is one of the justice rules in Gilliland's model, and developed a two-factor measure of it—face validity and perceived predictive validity—that has been widely used in subsequent research.

A second stream of applicant perceptions research comes from attempts to understand what drives performance on cognitive ability tests. Although research on this topic has led in many directions (e.g., understanding the nature of intelligence, examining effects of methods of testing and question variants), some has been directed specifically at how the perceptions of the test taker affect test performance. Although this was not the primary force behind its development, Arvey, Strickland, Drauden, and Martin's measure of test attitudes for use in selection contexts (Arvey, Strickland, Drauden, & Martin, 1990) serves as a seminal piece in the applicant perceptions literature that follows this research trend. The factor accounting for the most variance in their measure was test-taker motivation, and they noted that motivational differences might account for some portion of racial differences in cognitive ability test scores. Subsequent researchers have used Arvey et al.'s measure to further examine this question (e.g., studies by Chan and colleagues).

Thus, there have been two major thrusts to the applicant perceptions literature: a focus on fairness and other characteristics of the selection methods as potential influences on applicant attraction to an organization (referencing Gilliland, 1993; Smither et al., 1993), and a focus on test-taker attitudes as an influence on how applicants perform in the selection process (referencing Arvey et al., 1990). Note that the former focuses on perceptions of procedures and decisions, while the latter focuses more on perceptions of one's own cognitions and behaviors while experiencing those procedures and decisions. We feel both streams of research are important for understanding what an applicant might think, feel, and do based on having participated in a selection process.

Table 1 provides a summary of published empirical studies on applicant perceptions conducted since 1985. We chose to point out particular features of studies that relate to some key concerns in this research area. The second column—types of perceptions—addresses the question of what phenomena are being studied. The next three columns—procedures studied, timing of measurement and type of sample—all focus on the generalizability of this area of research. We then chose to highlight "determinants" and "outcomes" of perceptions because the critical research questions are: 1) What leads to perceptions? and 2) Do these perceptions lead to any attitudes or behaviors of importance? Note that characterizing variables as "determinants" was somewhat finessed, as some authors clearly labeled non-manipulated variables as simply correlates, others manipulated such variables to indicate they were determinants, and in other cases causality was assumed. We mention variables studied that we feel deserve further consideration as *potential* determinants of reactions. Also, we note that some authors were interested in the perceptions or reactions of applicants as the dependent variable of interest, whereas others were interested in how these perceptions influenced

Table 1 Summary of research

Study	Perceptions	Selection procedure	Timing of measurement	Type of participant	Determinants examined	Outcomes examined	Key findings
Arvey, Strickland, Drauden, & Martin (1990)	Motivation, lack of concentration, belief in tests, comparative anxiety, test case, external attribution, general need achievement, future effects, preparation	Mechanical and math tests (1) Comparison, math and work sample test (2) Test, not described (3)	Post-test (1&2) Pre-test and post-test (3)	Applications & incumbents for highway maintenance worker (1) Applicants for county financial worker (2) Applicants for financial planner (3)	Gender, age & race	Test performance; job performance	• Applicants reported more positive attitudes than incumbents • Attitudes are related to test performance • Racial differences in test scores may be due to test attitudes • Limited findings on whether motivation moderates test validity
Bauer, Maertz, Dolen, & Campion (1998)	Procedural justice: information, chance to perform, treatment at test site, consistency of test administration, job-relatedness	Cognitive aptitude and knowledge test	Pre-test; post-test; post feedback	Entry-level job applicants in accounting	Pass/fail status on test; perceptions at earlier points in process	Organizational attractiveness, intentions toward the organization, general attitude toward test fairness, test taking self-efficacy	• Procedural justice perceptions had some incremental value beyond outcome favorability in determining general attitudes, test fairness, and test-taking self-efficacy but not organizational attractiveness or intentions toward the organization
Burke, Normand, & Raju (1987)	General acceptance of computer-administered testing; ease of testing	12 computer-administered tests (10 clerical ability, personality and verbal ability)	Post-test	Clerical employees	Education level, computer-related experience, work processing experience	Test performance	• Word-processing experience and verbal ability have small effects on attitudes toward computerized testing

Chan (1997)	Perceived predictive validity	Personality and cognitive ability	Post-test	Students	Race, test performance	Test performance	• Blacks had lower predictive validity perceptions for cognitive tests, but no race differences were found for personality test perceptions • Perceptions of the cognitive ability test related to test performance
Chan & Schmitt (1997)	Face validity	Situational judgment test	Post-test	Students	Race, Test method (video or paper-and-pencil)	Test performance	• Higher face validity ratings were given to the video than paper-and-pencil • Black-white difference in perceptions was greater for paper-and-pencil than video • Face validity perceptions accounted for a portion of the race × method interaction on performance
Chan, Schmitt, DeShon, Clause, & Delbridge (1997)	Face validity, test-taking motivation	Cognitive ability test battery	Post one form of test, pre parallel form	Students	Race	Test performance	• Test-taking motivation affects test performance after controlling for effects of race and prior test performance • Face validity affects performance indirectly through motivation • Racial differences in face validity perceptions may be explained by racial differences in cognitive ability performance

(Continued)

Table 1 cont'd

Study	Perceptions	Selection procedure	Timing of measurement	Type of participant	Determinants examined	Outcomes examined	Key findings
Chan, Schmitt, Jennings, Clause, & Delbridge (1998)	Job-relatedness, test fairness	Reading comprehension test, video-based procedures test	Post-test	State trooper applicants	Perceived performance, actual performance	—	• Applicant perceptions of fairness and job relevance are influenced by perceived performance
Chan, Schmitt, Sacco, & Deshon (1998)	Belief in tests, face validity, predictive validity, fairness	Cognitive ability battery, personality test	Pre-test and post-test	Students	Race	Test performance	• Pre-test and post-test perceptions of cognitive ability tests have different determinants; pre-test are function of general beliefs in tests and post-test are partly a function of test performance. These relations are not found for personality tests.
Crant & Bateman (1990)	—	Drug testing scenarios	—	Students	Explanation of need for testing, subjective drug testing	Attitude toward company, intention to apply	• Presence of drug testing and giving an explanation affected attitudes toward company and intentions to apply • Subjects had less positive attitudes toward a company that did testing if subjective norms indicated less approval
Cunningham (1989)	Outguessing, test minimization	Integrity test	Post-test	Applicants various positions	—	Hire recommendation	• Those not recommended were more likely to believe they could outguess the test and played down test importance

Gilliland (1994)	Procedural fairness; distributive fairness	Work sample, cognitive ability, overt integrity	Post-feedback	Student; paid job	Hiring status; explanation provided; hiring expectations; job-relatedness	Performance on job; recommendation intentions; self-efficacy	• Expectations for being hired were positively related to fairness for selected applicants and negatively related for rejected applicants • Job-relatedness affects distributive justice most for those rejected • Rejected applicants were more likely to recommend project when given explanation; explanation did not relate to fairness and had a negative effect on performance quality • Fair procedures result in higher self-efficacy for those hired and lower self-efficacy for those rejected
Gilliland (1995)	Fair and unfair treatment	Generated critical incidents	—	Recent college grads; factory worker applicants	—	—	• More unfair than fair incidents were recalled for justice rules of fakability, dishonesty, and question propriety • Some rules were more salient in their violation while others were more salient in their satisfaction • Fairness among accepted applicants arises from different procedural rules than unfairness among rejected applicants

(Continued)

Table 1 cont'd

Study	Perceptions	Selection procedure	Timing of measurement	Type of participant	Determinants examined	Outcomes examined	Key findings
Kluger & Rothstein (1993)	Fairness, difficulty, fakability, usefulness of feedback, improvability of performance (1) Control, involvement, intrusion, relevance, cognitive interference (2)	Computerized biodata, computerized cognitive ability, computerized trainability test, computerized work sample	Post-failure feedback (1) Pre-feedback and post-feedback (2)	Students	Self-assessed test performance	Mood, coping, anticipated job performance, intentions to take test again, organization perceptions, attributions for failure, attributed locus of failure	• Biodata was viewed most favorably; conclude this is due to less cognitive effort (i.e., seen as less difficult) • Perceptions varied by test type
Kohn & Dipboye (1998)	Interview fairness, perceptions of the interviewer	Transcripts of structured and unstructured interviews (1); interview scenarios (2)	—	Students	Demographics, Big 5 personality characteristics, self-esteem	Perceptions of the organizations	• Those reading unstructured interviews viewed the organization and interviewer more favorably and saw the interview as more fair. • Standarization has more negative effects when there is more applicant voice

Latham & Finnegan (1993)	Perceptions of interview format	Descriptions of patterned, situational, and unstructured interviews	—	Managers, applicants, attorneys	—	• Managers and attorneys viewed the situational interview as most practical. • Student applicants preferred the unstructured interview
Lounsbury, Bobrow, & Jensen (1989)	General attitude toward employment testing	Test in general	N/a (1) Post-test or post-feedback (2)	Random sample telephone directory (1) Sewing mechanic or marker maker applicants (2)	Sex, age, race, occupation, education level experience with testing	• No demographic differences in study 1; in study 2, more favorable attitudes for Hispanics and younger • Having received information on how the test is related to the job and feedback on performance were related to more favorable attitudes • Those hired and those who had not yet heard a decision had more positive attitudes than those rejected
Macan, Avecon, Paese, & Smith (1994)	Face validity, fairness, control, overall satisfaction with process	Cognitive ability, assessment center	Post-test	Applicants	Self-assessed performance job liking, organizational attractiveness, sex, race, employment status	Acceptance intention, purchase intention, test performance	• Perceptions are related to job acceptance intentions but job and organization impressions are key predictors • Test scores were unrelated to perceptions • Buying intentions were only weakly related to perceptions

(Continued)

Table 1 cont'd

Study	Perceptions	Selection procedure	Timing of measurement	Type of participant	Determinants examined	Outcomes examined	Key findings
Martin & Nagao (1989)	Affective reaction to interview	Computerized interview, paper-and-pencil interview form, face-to-face interview in warm or cold manner	Post-interview	Students	Job status	Socially desirable responding	• Those interviewed for a high-status job by computer or paper-and-pencil expressed greater resentment than those interviewed face-to-face
Murphy, Thornton, & Prue (1991)	Acceptability of procedure	Drug testing	—	Students; mail survey of adults	PAQ and DOT rating	—	• PAQ factors accounted for variance in ratings of acceptability of drug testing across jobs
Murphy, Thornton, & Reynolds (1990)	Acceptability of procedure	Various drug testing procedures	N/A	Students	Background characteristics, job type, testing circumstances	—	• Drug testing viewed as more appropriate for jobs with responsibility for safety of others or dangerous activities • Considerable variability in attitudes; attitudes only weakly related to qualifications
Ployhart & Ryan (1997)	Process fairness, outcome fairness	GRE, GPA, research and work experiences, research interests, letters of recommendation, personal statement	Pre-application, post-offer	Graduate school applicants	Admission status, attributions for decision	Recommendation, application, acceptance, and reapplication intentions; self-efficacy, self-esteem, self-assessed performance	• Procedures perceived as fair produced more favorable intentions and self-assessed performance, and this increased as outcome fairness increased

Ployhart & Ryan (1998)	Process fairness, outcome fairness	Cognitive ability test	Pre-test, post-test, post-feedback	Students	Consistency of administration, hiring status	Performance expectations, job acceptance intentions, future experiment intentions, reapplication intentions, recommendation intentions, withdrawal	• Self-efficacy was lowest for those who were selected and perceived unfair procedures • Applicants engaged in self-serving attributions only with fair procedures • Positive inconsistency does not result in different perceptions of fairness than consistency • Most unfavorable reactions occurred with an unfair process and positive outcome • Prior intentions and outcome key influences in reactions
Ployhart, Ryan, & Bennett (1999)	Process fairness, explanation adequacy	Scenarios: Cognitive ability and job knowledge test (1); GRE, GPA, research interests, personal statement, research experience, work experience, letter of recommendation (2)	—	Students (1); Recent graduate program applicants (2)	Explanation for selection decision—information and sensitivity features; hiring status	Self-perceptions, organizational perceptions	• Perceptions of process fairness are enhanced by providing personal or procedural information • Self-perceptions of rejected are damaged by personal information and enhanced by diversity justification; opposite is true for accepted

(Continued)

Table 1 cont'd

Study	Perceptions	Selection procedure	Timing of measurement	Type of participant	Determinants examined	Outcomes examined	Key findings
Robertson, Iles, Gratton, & Sharpley (1991)	Beliefs about adequacy of selection procedures, perceived career impact	Biodata, situational interview, assessment center	Post-feedback, at various points in program	Assessees within a management development program	Pass/fail status	Withdrawal cognitions, organizational commitment, psychological health	• Different types of procedural information in an explanation for a decision produce different effects on fairness, self-perceptions and organizational outcomes • Candidates perceived negative decisions as having negative impact on their careers • Psychological health was unrelated to decisions • Beliefs about adequacy were higher for assessment center than situational interview • Those who passed saw procedures as more adequate and exhibited higher organizational commitment
Rosse, Miller, & Stecher (1994)	Privacy protection and appropriateness	Interview *or* personality test and interview *or* personality and ability tests and interview	Post-test	Applicants for seasonal jobs	—	—	• Reactions were generally positive but were more negative if personality inventory was required • Considerable variance in reactions was found

Ryan & Chan (1999a)	Procedural fairness, information, interpersonal treatment, consistency of administration, face validity, predictive validity, motivation, anxiety, belief in tests, outcome satisfaction, outcome fairness	Multiple choice knowledge exam	Post-test and post feedback	Psychology licensure candidates	Test score, pass/fail status, background information, cognitive interference, self-assessed performance	—	• Test score is positively related to perceptions, but many high scorers had negative perceptions of job relatedness
Ryan & Greguras (1998)	Response format preference, test fairness	—	—	Applicants at employment services	Race	—	• No preference for a particular format • Minorities indicated less positive perceptions of multiple-choice tests
Ryan, Greguras, & Ployhart (1996)	Job-relatedness, fairness, consistency, improvement beliefs, practice effects, typical v. maximal performance, timing of tests, order,	Descriptions of various physical ability tests (PATs)	—	Firefighters	Experience, current fitness level, department fitness climate, self-efficacy	—	• Self-efficacy and experience related to job-relatedness perceptions • Maximal performance tests are seen as less job related than typical performance tests • Test order is seen as affecting performance

(Continued)

Table 1 cont'd

Study	Perceptions	Selection procedure	Timing of measurement	Type of participant	Determinants examined	Outcomes examined	Key findings
	rest periods between tests, scoring options, training programs						• Fairness perception related to job-relatedness and consistency perceptions
Ryan, Ployhart, Greguras, & Schmit (1998)	Motivation (2), anxiety (2)	Ability exam	Pre-test (1) Post-test (2)	Firefighter applicants	Test-taking self-efficacy (1), personality measures, test preparation program attendance	Test performance	• Motivation, anxiety, test self-efficacy related to test performance • Greater anxiety associated with lower stress tolerance, lower school success, and being African–American • African–Americans reported lower motivation • Program attendance unrelated to attitudes
Ryan, Sacco, McFarland, & Kriska (2000)	Predictive validity, fairness, selection information, Interpersonal treatment, perceptions of interview, perceptions of cognitive ability	Cognitive ability/biodata test; writing sample; panel interview	Questionnaire at time of application; interview with those withdraw-ing	Police officer applicants	Perceptions of organization, job commitment, job expectations, employment status, need to relocate, social influence	Test performance, withdrawal from selection process	• Perceptions were generally unrelated to withdrawing from the selection process • Perceptions were most positive for those subsequently selected by the organization and least positive for those who failed the paper-and-pencil test • African–Americans had more negative perceptions

Ryan & Sackett (1987)	Perceptions of integrity tests	Over- integrity test	Post-test	Students	Test performance, age	Organization image	• Few of those interviewed mentioned the process as a reason for withdrawing • Test was seen as an appropriate management tool • No evidence of negative impressions of organizations using integrity tests
Rynes & Connerley (1993)	General reaction, beliefs about employer's ability to accurately interpret, beliefs about whether employer needs information, beliefs about performance	Scenarios: Generic interview, cognitive ability, psychological assessment, reference checks, simulation-based interview, handwriting sample, written simulation, drug test, overt integrity test, business-related test, personality inventory	Post-scenario	Students	Job search self-efficacy, background variables	—	• Reacted more positively to simulation-based interviews, written simulation and business-related test • Most important attitude differentiater was belief in system accuracy • Attitude did not vary by background characteristics

(Continued)

Table 1 cont'd

Study	Perceptions	Selection procedure	Timing of measurement	Type of participant	Determinants examined	Outcomes examined	Key findings
Saks, Leck, & Saunders (1995)	—	Application blank	Post-procedure	Students	Inclusion of discriminatory questions	Organization attractiveness, likelihood of success, motivation to pursue job, job acceptance intention, treatment of employees, organization recommendation	• Those who completed an application blank with discriminatory questions reacted less favorably
Schmit & Ryan (1992)	Test-taking attitude survey	Cognitive ability and personality test	Post-test; post second testing and negative feedback	Students	Negative outcome	GPA	• Criterion-related validity was moderated by test-taking attitudes such that ability test validity was lower and personality test validity was higher for those with less positive test-taking attitudes • Negative feedback and retesting was associated with decreased motivation
Schmit & Ryan (1997)	Motivation, anxiety, belief in tests	Ability examination	Pre-test	Police officer applicants	Race	Test performance, withdrawal form the selection process	• Highly motivated and more anxious individuals were less likely to withdraw from the selection process

Singer (1990)	Self-generated statements, 21 fairness determinants	Selection in general scenario	N/A	Undergraduates and professionals	—

- Caucasians had higher motivation, less anxiety, and believed more in the efficacy of tests
- Identified the followings as key determinants of fairness: consistency in following rules, two-way communication, ethicality, bias avoidance, information soliciting (voice)

Smither, Reilly, Millsap, Pearlman, & Stoffey (1993)	Predictive validity, face validity, perceived knowledge of results, likelihood of improvement, affect, procedural justice, distributive justice	Descriptions of cognitive ability battery (took 5 of 8 described) personality test, in-basket, leaderless group discussion, biodata, unstructured interview, structured interview (had been through both kinds of interviews; 1)	Post 5 tests for entry managers (1); post-test and post-feedback (2)	Newly hired entry-level managers, recruiting managers (1); Civil Service applicants (2)	GPA, test performance, provision of construct definition, face validity of sample items (1) organizational attractiveness (2)	Recommendation intentions

- Manipulating the face validity of items did not enhance perceptions of validity
- Perceived validity did not necessarily correspond with actual validity
- Reactions are positively related to organizational attractiveness and to recommendation intentions
- High-ability applicants are not less likely to see procedures as job related

(Continued)

Table 1 cont'd

Study	Perceptions	Selection procedure	Timing of measurement	Type of participant	Determinants examined	Outcomes examined	Key findings
Steiner & Gilliland (1996)	Process favorability, scientific evidence, face validity opportunity to perform, employer's right, widely used, interpersonal warmth, respectful of privacy	Descriptions of 10 procedures: interviews, resumes, work sample, biodata, written ability tests, personal references, personality tests, honesty tests, personal contacts, graphology	—	Students	Country (France or U.S.)	—	• Those from both countries gave similar evaluations of method favorability • Face validity was strongest correlate of process favorability in both countries • Procedural dimensions less predictive of fairness reactions among French than American students
Thorsteinson & Ryan (1997)	Procedural fairness, distributive fairness	Cognitive ability, personality test, biodata inventory	Post-test and post-feedback	Students	Selection ratio, hiring status, perceived chance of success	GPA—college and high school	• Selection ratio had little effect on perceptions of fairness • Perceptions of the fairness of the cognitive ability test moderated its validity
Truxillo & Bauer (1999)	Outcome fairness, process fairness, perceptions of banding	Multiple-choice and writing sample tests, video test, physical ability test (1) multiple-choice test (2)	Post some tests, pre other hurdles (1); post-test (2); post-test (3)	Police entry level applicants (1,2) Promotion (3)	Race, gender organizational attractiveness, test experience, education	—	• Reactions to banding were a function of race and banding's association with affirmative action (i.e., those who thought it was in their self-interest viewed it more positively) • Positive reactions to banding were associated with belief that banding aids score interpretation and the procedure is understandable

(1), (2) and (3) refer to multiple studies within one publication.

other outcomes. We label perception of the job and organization as outcomes, although many researchers refer to these as "applicant reactions." In the table, we also note one or two key findings from each study, recognizing that this provides only a limited picture of the research. We urge the interested reader to refer to the primary work and to consider the table in light of its purpose: to provide a very broad summary. We now turn to discussing some specific questions that are addressed via the table.

What applicant perceptions have been studied? What should be studied?

The most commonly studied perceptions of applicants are perceptions of the validity or job-relatedness of the selection process, perceptions of the fairness of various aspects of the process and of the outcome of the process, and test-taking motivation. Not surprisingly, these derive directly from the seminal articles we mentioned earlier: Smither et al. (1993), Gilliland (1993), and Arvey et al. (1990). An examination of column 2 of Table 1 provides some examples of other perceptions studied. Rather than discussing each study, we offer the following general suggestions.

Improve perception measurement

One major concern with the research to date on applicant perceptions is the imprecision with which the constructs assessed are defined and the variability with which they are operationalized. This concern makes summarizing research difficult, as one cannot be certain if differences in findings are due to inadequate measurement or the assessment of truly different constructs. Insufficient work has been done on the reliability and validity of measures of applicant perceptions. We state this as researchers who are guilty ourselves of "using the scale most commonly used," rather than working toward improvement. For example, the factor structure of the Test Attitude Survey (Arvey et al., 1990) may not be what the developers proposed (Schmit & Ryan, 1992). Another example would be the clarity and consistency of the referents in measures. Some items/scales are clearly related to a specific procedure or aspect of the selection process (Thorsteinson & Ryan, 1997), while other items/scales relate to the entire process (Gilliland, 1994; Ployhart, Ryan, & Bennett 1999). Some items/scales refer to one's own outcome (Gilliland, 1994), while others refer to the fairness of outcomes in general (Truxillo & Bauer, 1999). Across studies, process or procedural fairness has been assessed with different measures (e.g., Gilliland, 1994; Macan, Avedon, Paese, & Smith, 1994; Truxillo & Bauer, 1999). Although there has been some work on scale development (e.g., Gilliland & Honig, 1994), more is needed. However, first construct definitions must be clarified. For example, interpersonal treatment sometimes refers to the personal or impersonal nature of the process whereas other times it refers to the behavior of administrators.

Clarify how test-taking attitudes relate to fairness perceptions by conducting studies that integrate the two streams of research

A better integration of the research on test attitudes and on fairness is needed to advance understanding. Although the work of Chan and colleagues (Chan, Schmitt, Sacco, & DeShon, 1998) does some linking, this research has focused on only one or two concepts from each line of research. Thus, we do not really know if those who are more anxious view procedures as more unfair, if those who are highly motivated have different perceptions of the fairness of a rejection decision than those with low motivation, or if general beliefs about testing are a greater determinant of perceptions of the fairness of a procedure than characteristics of the procedure and selection situation itself. Note that many test-taking attitude measures are perceptions of oneself in the selection situation (i.e., are you motivated, anxious) whereas justice related perceptions are typically about the procedure or process (i.e., is this test a fair method of hiring). One would expect these two types of perceptions to relate. Indeed, Chan et al. (1997) demonstrated that the effects of face validity (a procedural justice perception) on test performance are fully mediated by motivation. However, Ryan and Chan (1999a) did not find attitudes of licensure candidates (e.g., motivation, anxiety) to add to the prediction of post-feedback process fairness above and beyond pre-feedback process fairness and justice rules.

In general, applicant perceptions research lacks a nominological net—we do not have theoretical or empirical work that provides a broad enough picture of how these various types of perceptions might be expected to relate. (This does not imply there is no theory; as we noted earlier, the expected relations between justice related perceptions have been explicated by Gilliland, 1993.)

Consider measuring other perceptions

Although understanding how an applicant's motivation or perceptions of fairness influences his or her attitudes and behavior is important, researchers may be ignoring other perceptions with important outcomes. For example, Cunningham (1989) measured "outguessing." For many noncognitive measures, issues like perceived fakability may affect applicant behavior. Perceived ease or difficulty of a selection process has been suggested as having effects (e.g., Kluger & Rothstein, 1993) but is not routinely incorporated in this line of research. Another suggestion is "procedural pain" (Ball, Trevino, & Sims, 1993) or the extent to which a negative state such as embarrassment, humiliation, or stress is caused by a procedure, with the privacy of the process and outcome being important determinants of procedural pain. In selection settings where an applicant is relatively anonymous to other applicants, this may not be much of an issue; however, it may be much more important in promotion contexts or very public selection processes (e.g., civil service jobs, university administrators). Other perceptions that may have relevance are the order of testing, whether procedures are timed, the methods of scoring, and other administrative issues (Ryan, Greguras, & Ployhart, 1996).

Ryan and Greguras (1998) noted that one limitation of a focus on fairness perceptions is that it ignores the fact that preference is a different concept from fairness. That is, there is research in the educational arena to show that individuals often prefer methods such as multiple choice testing while indicating they are less valid and less fair than other methods (e.g., essay, recall) (Bridgeman, 1992; Nield & Wintre, 1986; Zeidner, 1987). To fully understand how an applicant reacts to a selection process, we need to consider perceptions other than just fairness as possible influences on behavior.

What are the determinants of applicant perceptions?

Of particular interest is what researchers have seen as the causes and correlates of various applicant perceptions. One difficulty in summarizing this portion of Table 1 is that while some studies treat certain variables as correlates or potential antecedents of perceptions of selection processes (e.g., organizational attractiveness, self-efficacy; Macan et al., 1994; Ryan, Ployhart, Greguras, & Schmit, 1998; Truxillo & Bauer, 1999), others see these same variables as potential outcomes of perceptions (e.g., Bauer, Maertz, Dolen, & Campion, 1998; Ployhart, Ryan, & Bennett, 1999). Such inferences may be appropriate when you have measurement at multiple points in time (as in Bauer et al., 1998); however, the current state of the literature indicates a lack of a clear consensus on what causes or is caused by perceptions. Also, only about half of the studies listed in Table 1 examined determinant-perception links—many researchers have not focused on what determines perceptions.

What are the key determinants of applicant perceptions? Table 1 indicates that perceptions of procedures (e.g., fairness, job-relatedness) appear to be influenced by type of procedure (both the construct assessed (i.e., cognitive ability, personality) and the method of assessment (video, paper and pencil), self-assessed performance, type of job, information provided about the procedure, and, in some cases for some procedures, race of the applicant. A number of studies have suggested that perceptions of the fulfillment of justice rules (e.g., consistency of administration) determine perceptions of the fairness of the process, in keeping with Gilliland's model. We are reluctant to consider these as strongly supported relations in the selection context, despite their solid theoretical grounding in social justice theory, simply because few studies have actually manipulated these justice rules to see if they influence (rather than just correlate with) perceptions of the fairness of selection procedures (exceptions would be Ployhart & Ryan, 1998, which manipulated consistency of administration, and Smither et al., 1993, which manipulated face validity).

We noted earlier that there are two streams of research, and the preceding paragraph speak only to what determines perceptions of selection procedures. Prior performance history and race (for cognitive ability tests) appear to influence test-taking attitudes. Less research has focused on determinants of test-taking attitudes, most likely because extensive literature on topics like cognitive interference with test performance (Sarason, Pierce, & Sarason, 1996) and recent work on stereotype threat (Steele & Aronson, 1995) is seen as addressing determinants.

We also note that many of these determinants may also be moderators of the link between other determinants and perceptions or between perceptions and behavior (e.g., perceptions relate to applicant behavior for unattractive but not for highly attractive organizations). For example, Gilliland (1994) found that hiring expectations influenced the relation between hiring status and fairness perceptions. Because of the lack of clarity in empirical work on the exact role of these variables and inattention to the timing of measurement, we currently have little beyond some interesting correlational findings for many variables.

Based on the findings of studies summarized in the table, we offer the following observations:

1: Whether applicants are accepted or rejected clearly influences perceptions; studies that examine perceptions absent feedback on the selection decision cannot be interpreted similarly to those measuring perceptions post-decision.

The most researched "cause" of perceptions is the outcome of the process itself. That is, whether or not one receives a favorable outcome (hired or not) is seen as a major influence. It is clear that the outcome received by an applicant can influence perceptions (e.g., Arvey et al., 1990; Bauer et al., 1998: Chan, 1997; Chan et al., 1998b; Cunningham, 1989; Ployhart & Ryan, 1997, 1998; Robertson, Iles, Gratton, & Sharpley, 1991; Ryan & Chan, 1999a; Ryan et al., 1998; Ryan, Sacco, McFarland, & Kriska, 2000), and this is consistent with basic research on justice issues (e.g., Greenberg, 1987). Yet many studies have examined reactions post-test, absent feedback. Simply studying how test scores relate to perceptions assessed pre feedback is not sufficient, as in many cases individuals do not self-assess performance well. Indeed, test scores have not always been found to relate to perceptions (e.g., Macan et al., 1994; Whitney, Diaz, Minneghino, & Powers, 1998).

Studies of post-test perceptions may be helpful—these perceptions may relate to behaviors exhibited by applicants during later stages of the process prior to the organization's decision (e.g., withdrawal behavior). However, these behaviors may not be the focal ones of interest. As Greenberg (1986) noted in discussing performance appraisal research, "researchers and theorists should not allow distributive factors to get lost in the shadow of the recent attention paid to procedural determinants of fairness." (p. 342). It seems that this has occurred to some extent in the applicant perceptions literature.

2: All procedures of the same "type" (e.g., personality tests) are not the same, nor are procedures of different types viewed consistently.

Initial research comparing perceptions of different types of procedures (e.g., Kluger & Rothstein, 1993; Kravitz, Stinson, & Chavez, 1994; Rynes & Connerley, 1993) has indicated that mean differences exist between perceptions of different types of tests (e.g., the job-relatedness of biodata and cognitive ability), but there is considerable variability in perceptions. As Ryan and Greguras (1998) noted, the face validity and fairness of specific procedures are not universally shared perceptions. Researchers have also found that although applicants may have general perceptions of a category of procedures (e.g., interviews), they also make distinctions within category. For example, Ryan, Greguras, and Ployhart (1996) noted considerable variability in reactions to different types of physical ability tests for the same job that assess the same abilities. Chan and Schmitt (1997) found differences in face validity perceptions for video and paper-and-pencil versions of the same situational judgment test. Whitney et al. (1998) found differences in some perceptions of overt versus personality based integrity tests.

In studying perceptions of different procedures, there is a need to clarify what procedure characteristics give rise to perceptions (Brutus & Ryan, 1998). For example, how does the method of assessing a construct affect perceptions (Chan & Schmitt, 1997; Ryan & Greguras, 1998; Shotland & Alliger, 1999)? Does the transparency of an assessed construct affect perceptions? Does the ease with which one can self-assess performance affect perceptions (Fredriksen & Collins, 1989)? Does the ability (or perceived ability) to prepare for a procedure affect perceptions (Ryan & Chan, 1999b)? Do physical features (e.g., how "slick" materials look, test length, room in which an interview is conducted) affect perceptions? Does the level of structure in an interview affect perceptions (e.g., Gilliland & Steiner, 1999)? Educational researchers interested in examinee perceptions (e.g., Nevo, 1992, 1995) have examined such features as the convenience of the answer sheet and the test's physical attractiveness. All of these distinctions remain to be researched in the selection context. We caution against a piecemeal approach to a study of procedure characteristics, and we advocate the development of models of antecedents that clarify expected relations. At the conclusion of the paper, we propose a heuristic model to aid in that effort.

3: Perceptions of procedures and decisions should not be studied devoid of context. In field research, context should be well described. In lab research, context should be controlled for or manipulated. We note several context variables that research indicates must be considered

3a : The type of job for which applicants are applying, and job and organization attractiveness, appear to be influences on perceptions. The type of job has been shown to influence how a particular procedure is viewed (e.g., Kravitz et al., 1994), although this is under-researched. One would expect that judgments of job-relatedness would be influenced by the job. For example, research has shown that the acceptability of drug testing as a selection tool is influenced by job characteristics (Murphy, Thornton, & Prue, 1991; Murphy, Thornton, & Reynolds, 1990). In developing models of antecedents of perceptions, we need to specify what specific job characteristics are expected to influence perceptions. For example, does the degree of social interaction required in a job affect perceptions regarding the use of personality tests? "Does the technology level of the job influence perceptions of computerized testing?

Although there has been little research on attractiveness as an antecedent or correlate of reactions, it seems that one might see a more attractive organization as having better selection processes. For example, McCulloch and Turban (1997) found that those who had concerns about a life insurance sales job viewed integrity tests more negatively than those without such concerns. It may be that cognitive dissonance leads one to alter procedure perceptions to be in line with job desirability perceptions (i.e., this is a high paying job so their procedures are "thorough" rather than "invasive"). Similarly, an acceptable reason for not pursuing a job would be "their process turned me off," rather than acknowledging a lack of qualifications Alternatively, individuals may actually view the content of selection procedures for jobs they desire more positively. Attractive organizations may be ones that have the most attractive methods of hiring.

3b: Information provided to applicants regarding a procedure (e.g., constructs assessed, reasons for use) and/or decisions (e.g., explanations for rejection) can make a difference in perceptions; such information should be detailed in study descriptions. Ployhart et al. (1999) found that providing information on why an individual was accepted or rejected (e.g., due to what particular procedure in the process) influenced perceptions of process fairness. This is consistent with the literature on social accounts (Bies, 1987; Bies & Shapiro, 1988, Greenberg, 1990, 1994). However, Gilliland (1994) did not find providing an explanation to relate to fairness perceptions. In field studies, we typically are not provided with much information on how applicants were informed of the decision. Research is needed on what applicants are told and how this is perceived.

In addition to how decisions are explained, researchers should attend to what information is provided about the procedure itself. For example, are applicants told what construct is to be assessed? Have applicants been given a reason why a test is used? Horvath, Ryan, and Stierwalt (in press) found that explanations for why a procedure was used affected fairness perceptions. Crant and Bateman (1990) found that giving an explanation for why drug testing was used affected attitudes toward a company and intentions to apply. Without knowing what applicants are told about a procedure, it is difficult to assess what is driving perceptions. For example, simply being told that a measure is job related may enhance job-relatedness perceptions.

3c: Procedures may be viewed differently depending upon what else is part of the process. Rosse, Miller, and Stecher (1994) demonstrated that perceptions of a personality test were influenced by what other selection procedures were used in the hiring process. Ryan et al. (1996) found opinions on the order of test administration to relate to fairness perceptions. They also suggested that applicants might prefer compensatory selection processes, where they participate in all selection procedures, to multiple hurdle processes, where individuals are excluded at each step. Unless organizations are using a procedure in isolation, studying it in isolation does not make sense. If a procedure is hardly ever used as an initial screening hurdle, treating it as such in a research study is inappropriate. It is important that we consider how inclusion/exclusion of procedures, order of procedures, and the compensatory/noncompensatory nature of the process might influence applicant perceptions.

3d: Organizational context may influence perceptions. Arvey and Sackett (1993) noted that context will influence applicant reactions, yet this has not been systematically examined in the literature. For example, they suggest that organizational history, selection ratio, and organizational resources may influence fairness perceptions. However, Thorsteinson and Ryan (1997) did not find selection ratio to relate to fairness perceptions. Researchers using civil service samples (e.g., Ryan et al., 1998; Ryan et al., 2000; Schmit & Ryan, 1997; Truxillo & Bauer, 1999) note that the public nature of testing, presence of strong affirmative action efforts, and histories of discrimination appear to influence perceptions of selection processes. Given that studies of applicant perceptions have not been multiorganizational, it may take an accumulation of research in different contexts before any conclusions regarding organizational context influence can be made. However, ignoring the role of these variables in discussions of perceptions is misleading.

3e: Reactions to promotion processes and decisions may be very different from those for organizational entry positions. Research has indicated that identification with the organization may play a key role in how one interprets the fairness of a process (Brockner, Tyler, & Cooper-Schneider, 1992; Huo, Smith, Tyler, & Lind, 1996; Tyler & Degoey, 1995). Reactions to promotional procedures deal with individuals who are members of the organization. Thus, we might expect different mechanisms underlying attitude formation. Truxillo and Bauer (1999) found racial differences in perceptions of banding in a promotion sample, but not among entry-level applicants. They suggest that individuals within the organization may be in possession of different information regarding procedures and procedure use.

A few studies have examined perceptions of incumbents in comparison to those of applicants and have found differences, with applicants typically exhibiting more positive perceptions (e.g., Arvey et al., 1990; Brutus & Ryan, 1998). One concern this highlights is that regardless of anonymity assurances, applicant reports of perceptions may be influenced by socially desirable responding. Alternatively, because applicants often possess little information about the job (Barber, 1998), their judgments of job-relatedness and fairness may differ from those of incumbents who have intimate knowledge of the job. Interestingly, Smither et al. (1993) found more experienced managers to have more positive perceptions than new hires of the job-relatedness of only 2 of 14 selection procedures. Finally, applicants may, indeed, simple feel more positively. For example, studies assessing the test-taking motivation of applicants (Schmit & Ryan, 1997; Ryan et al., 1998, 2000) typically find a high mean and restricted range. This raises concerns about how studies of test-taking motivation with nonapplicant samples (e.g., Chan et al., 1997) might generalize to highly motivated applicant samples.

4: Individual differences as potential antecedents of perceptions remain largely unexplored.

Arvey et al. (1990) noted the need to assess whether test taker attitudes are more determined by individual differences or situational characteristics. They note that if the former is true, organizational interventions to affect attitudes may not have large effects. Yet, few studies have looked at individual difference correlates. Indeed, few studies have looked at subjects across multiple types of procedures. Fewer still have looked at subjects longitudinally, either across one selection process or across different job search cycles. We need such research to determine how malleable applicant perceptions are.

Applicants are likely to be drawing on their own past experiences and personal characteristics in making evaluations. Research has shown previous experience with a procedure to influence perceptions (Kravitz et al., 1994; Ryan et al., 1996). Brutus and Ryan (1998) found perceptions of the job-relatedness of various selection procedures to be related to individual differences in preferences and personality that would lead to good performance on those instruments. For example, those who preferred to work alone or had conflictual relations with others did not see an interpersonal skills test as job-related. Researchers have suggested that those with high negative affectivity might have lower perceptions of process and outcome fairness (Ball et al., 1993). However, Greguras and Ryan (1997) did not find perceptions of tests to be related to negative affectivity. We would also suggest openness to experience might affect perceptions of more novel procedures and processes. Three decades ago (Fiske, 1967), it was noted that personality might be a source of variance in reactions to tests: it is time to better explore that possibility in organizational contexts. At the very least, the role of one's evaluative history (i.e., how well one has done on similar procedures in the past) should be assessed.

5: Racial differences in perceptions are sometimes found; appropriate descriptions of context are needed to develop a greater understanding of when they will occur.

The work of Chan and colleagues (Chan et al., 1997, 1998a, 1998b) clearly indicates that racial differences in perceptions of cognitive ability tests may explain and/or be explained by race differences in test performance. However, race differences have not been found in perceptions of personality tests (Chan, 1997) and have been found to be less for certain methods of testing (Chan & Schmidt, 1997). Thus, test type and test format appear to interact with race in the formation of perceptions. Ryan and Greguras (1998) noted that although there is an implicit assumption that minority applicants view performance assessments more favorably than multiple-choice testing, there has not been much research on this point that avoids a confound of test content and format. Because the research on test characteristics that influence perceptions is limited as we noted above, we feel that interactions of test characteristics and race would be a fruitful area of investigation.

Further, whether racial differences in perceptions are present in real-world settings is likely highly influenced by context. In several studies (Ryan, Ployhart, Greguras, & Schmit, 1997; Schmit & Ryan, 1997), African-Americans had more favorable views than whites of the fairness of an ability test in contexts where there were strong affirmative action programs and minorities in visible leadership positions within the organization. In a law enforcement organization with poor relations with the minority community, Ryan et al. (2000) found that African-Americans had more negative perceptions of all aspects of the process (written test, oral boards), although effects were quite small. Similarly, Lemons and Danebower (1997), in a study of perceptions of promotion decisions, found that perceptions of distributive justice increased as the number of female role models in the organization increased, and decreased as departmental segregation increased.

We noted in our opening paragraph that concerns about racial differences in perceptions and the potential effects of these on minority recruiting are a driving force behind applicant perceptions research. At the same time, we find a need for considerably more research if we are to understand when and why these differences might occur. We also note that gender differences have not been systematically examined. There is some research that indicates women tend to have more positive perceptions of distributive justice, potentially because they have been socialized to be more accommodative (Boldizar, Perry, & Perry, 1988; Major & Deaux, 1982). Yet, potential gender differences in distributive justice perceptions in selection contexts remain unexplored.

6: Social information has been neglected as an influence on perceptions.

Research suggests that individuals rely on cues from others when making fairness assessments (Ambrose, Harland, & Kulik, 1991; Lind & Tyler, 1988). However, the applicant perceptions literature has not really examined how the opinions of others influence perceptions of an organization's selection process (one exception is Bazerman, Schroth, Shah, Diekmann, & Tenbrunsel, 1994). Such comparisons have been the basis of much equity theory research on outcome fairness. It may be that applicants change perceptions once they have a chance to gather some comparison information from friends and family about whether the procedure they experienced was fair or unfair in the eyes of others.

What are the consequences of perceptions (i.e., to what outcomes have they been linked)? What moderates these relations?

Column 7 of Table 1 indicates the major dependent variables in applicant perceptions research. Perceptions have been linked to test performance in that studies have shown that test-taking attitudes both influence and are influenced by test performance. Thus, in a given situation an applicant's motivation is likely linked to previous outcomes on similar devices and also influences how he or she performs in the current situation (Chan et al., 1997). Perceptions of procedures may influence organizational attractiveness (e.g., Bauer et al., 1998). Research has also shown correlations between perceptions of procedures (e.g., job relatedness, fairness) and intentions to accept a job and recommend an organization.

Researchers have demonstrated that perceptions of a procedure influence self-perceptions after a selection or rejection decision. Ployhart and Ryan (1997) indicated that there are process × outcome interactions, such that a combination of fair procedures and positive outcomes can have positive effects on self-perceptions. However, being hired under unfair procedures can actually have negative effects on self-perceptions. A different effect occurs for rejected applicants. There is some evidence that being rejected by a fair procedure leads to lowered self-perceptions.

In terms of links between perceptions and applicant behavior, Ryan et al. (2000) showed no connection between perceptions of the process and applicant decisions to drop out of the process. No studies have examined the links between perceptions and actual offer acceptance, Gilliland (1994) showed that job-relatedness perceptions influenced subsequent job performance.

Some key themes emerge after examining this research question:

7: Aside from test performance, few studies assess actual behavior. Researchers have not demonstrated that applicant perceptions "matter."

Because most studies do not assess actual behaviors of applicants (such as do they accept offers, do they self-select out), we may be overestimating the influence of applicant perceptions. Granted, many studies do assess intentions, but potential moderators of intention-behavior links are not considered. Also, Macan et al. (1994) pointed out that job and organizational attractiveness had stronger influences on behavior than applicant perceptions of the selection process. Studies that do not measure and consider these correlates of perceptions might inappropriately infer that perceptions of procedures have a larger influence on behavior than they do.

One problem with the behavioral variable most assessed, test performance, is that studies assume a causal order that is seldom demonstrated. That is, do perceptions influence performance or does previous test performance (which would be correlated with current test performance) influence perceptions? Chan et al. (1997) demonstrated that test-taking motivation did affect performance after controlling for prior performance. However, this issue remains unexamined with other types of applicant perceptions (e.g., fairness) and procedures other than cognitive ability tests.

Applicant self-selection out of a hiring process has not been found to be linked to perceptions of the process (Ryan et al., 2000; Ryan & McFarland, 1997a; Ryan et al., 1997; Schmit & Ryan, 1997), despite the suggestion of a relation by many researchers. Schmit and Ryan (1997) suggested that process unfairness may lead to withdrawal behavior for only a small percentage of applicants (i.e., less than 10%); studies examining retrospective reasons for withdrawal gathered via interviews have supported that contention (Ryan & McFarland, 1997a; Ryan et al., 1997; Ryan et al., 2000). Rather than assuming strong perception-behavior relations, we should pursue why some individuals act on negative perceptions but many do not. Also, we need to examine whether these individuals are ones the organization considers desirable applicants.

Given the lack of attention to actual behavior, one may question the value of any of the research we have reviewed. We feel this research does contribute to our understanding of what influences perceptions, how perceptions change over the course of the selection process, and whether justice theory propositions are applicable to the selection context. However, unless greater attention is given to behavioral outcomes, we feel the research will be dismissed as practically irrelevant.

8: Only about 10% of studies include pre-test measures. Some "outcome" variables may also serve as antecedents (e.g., general attitudes toward test fairness, test-taking self-efficacy (Bauer et al., 1998)).

Without assessing attitudinal measures (e.g., organizational attractiveness) and intentions prior to participating in the selection process, one is hard pressed to be able to definitively attribute a causal order. That is, applicant perceptions of the selection procedure may cause intentions and attitudes, or these intentions and attitudes may lead one to hold certain perceptions of the procedure. For example, as we noted earlier, one may view an organization as attractive and this can cause one to see the selection process in a more favorable light. Powell (1991) noted that research on self-fulfilling prophecies in applicants' decisions about jobs is necessary. Rynes (1991) stated that applicant perceptions and behavior are likely to be influenced by different determinants at different points in the process: thus, time of measurement is an important concern. Researchers need to move away from post-test designs to designs that incorporate pre- and post-measures when possible.

9: Self-perceptions appear to be influenced by perceptions of selection procedures (Gilliland, 1994; Ployhart & Ryan, 1997; Ployhart et al., 1999), but may also influence them.

The literature on preferential selection provides some insights regarding effects of selection processes on self-perceptions. Being hired preferentially leads to lowered self-perceptions of competence and lowered task performance (Heilman et al., 1987, 1990; Heilman, Rivero, & Brett, 1991), but such effects seem to occur for women and not for men. The implication is that benefiting from an "unfair procedure" is viewed differently by different groups. Heilman proposes that this is due to initial self-perceptions being more negative for women. The implication for applicant perceptions research in general is that an applicant's initial self-view may affect perceptions and perception-outcome links. Thus, it is important to understand the role of self-perceptions as an antecedent and not just a consequence of applicant perceptions of procedures.

10: There is some suggestion that perceptions may moderate the validity of selection procedures.

Arvey et al. (1990) suggested that test-taking attitudes might affect the validity of a test and there has been some support for this in lab (e.g., Schmit & Ryan, 1992; Thorsteinson & Ryan, 1997) and field studies (Barbera, Ryan, Desmarais, & Dyer, 1995; Ryan & McFarland, 1997b). Individuals who perceive a selection tool as low in predictive validity or unfair may know that they "test poorly" and that the test is not predictive for them. These studies have generally found small effects; however, small changes in validity can be practically meaningful.

11: Research on potential moderators of perception-outcome links has been limited.

Applicant perceptions research typically considers the direct effects of perceptions on various attitudes, intentions, self-perceptions, and behaviors. Given the complexity of real-world selection settings, it is likely that moderators exist. Further, theories such as justice theory and behavior intention models predict a number of such interactions. For example, Ployhart and Maynard (1999) found that complex interactions exist between job-relatedness, the hiring decision, job desirability, and selection ratio for predicting organizational attitudes and job choice. This suggests that the applicant perception–behavior link might be conditional on job desirability or the amount of competition for the job. For example, fairness–behavior relations might he stronger when the job is highly desirable (perhaps because of good pay, a desirable location, or excellent benefits), the applicant already has an acceptable job or lacks desirable alternatives, or the economy is strong. Indeed, Gilliland (1993) proposed the expectation of being hired to be a key moderator in his justice model.

Bazerman et al. (1994) suggested that the availability of alternative offers would affect the role procedural justice information plays in making a decision about offer acceptance. In a study of interviewer characteristics, Liden and Parsons (1986) found alternative opportunities moderated the relation between affective reactions and job acceptance intentions. Bazerman et al. (1994) noted that when people are questioned about their feelings concerning a single procedure they report being far more concerned about fairness than when asked about their choice among several procedures. Much of the research on applicant perceptions focuses on a single situation (i.e., the fairness of this process for this position). We need to examine the role of perceptions in determining behavior of applicants who have multiple options available.

Another potential moderator of the perception–outcome link is social support. Justice research on revenge indicates that social support plays a key role in allowing individuals to vent about an injustice and may lead to ruminating on the injustice to the point of taking action (Bies & Tripp, 1998; Bies, Tripp, & Kramer, 1997). Whether applicants act on negative perceptions may be dependent upon the opinions and urgings of others.

In sum, there has not been a lot of exploration of potential perception–behavior moderators. Exploration of moderators needs to occur within true experimental designs. To adequately develop a framework of potential moderators, we suggest researchers do not "reinvent the wheel" by ignoring the large literature on recruitment and choice, which provides guidance on what influences applicant behavior.

What theoretical frameworks have been presented? How well have they been applied? What other theoretical viewpoints need consideration?

The predominant theoretical framework that has been applied to studying applicant perceptions is a social justice framework. Although Gilliland's model (Gilliland, 1993) is well received by researchers, little empirical work has focused on specifically testing the propositions of the model (for exceptions see Bauer et al., 1998; Gilliland, 1994; Ployhart & Ryan, 1998; Ryan & Chan, 1999b). Many researchers do not measure or manipulate the procedural or distributive justice rules or their antecedents. For example, Gilliland (1993) presented specific propositions about which procedural justice rules should be influenced by test type, which will be influenced by human resource policy, and which will be influenced by the behavior of HR personnel. He also proposed that justice rule perceptions will explain most of the variance in perceptions of process fairness and provided several propositions regarding rule weighting and rule salience. Yet, these propositions remain largely untested. For example, Ryan and Chan (1999b) found only one rule—job-relatedness—had effects on fairness perceptions of a licensure examination, and it was the only one for which respondents had negative perceptions. Thus, in terms of "what leads to fairness perceptions," theory has largely been unapplied in applicant perceptions research.

The other side of Gilliland's model is the connection of fairness perceptions to individual and organizational outcomes. Here, we note a greater research focus (e.g., Ployhart & Ryan, 1997), but shortcomings as well (i.e., studies have not assessed actual behaviors subsequent to participating in the process itself). For example, Gilliland (1993) proposed that perceptions of underpayment inequity that result from not receiving a job when it is expected will result first in anger and, then, in organizational and self devaluing. No one has examined a sequential set of applicant reactions to a hiring decision. In sum, although justice theory is often invoked in this research arena, many of the propositions derived from justice theory remain untested.

Attribution theory has received some attention in the applicant perceptions literature (Arvey et al., 1990; Kluger & Rothstein, 1993; Ployhart & Ryan, 1997). In social psychology, causal attributions are considered to be a critical component of social perception (e.g., Fiske & Taylor, 1991; Weiner, 1986) and form the basis for a variety of expectations, intentions, and behaviors (Weiner, 1985, 1986).

Thus, to what an applicant ascribes the cause of a selection or rejection decision is likely to be a very strong influence on his or her future behavior. Ployhart and Ryan (1997) found that individuals who were selected reported the selection decision to be caused by more internal, stable, and controllable factors (and those who were rejected reported external, unstable, and uncontrollable causes). This is consistent with social psychology's definition of the self-serving bias (e.g., Fiske & Taylor, 1991). Interestingly, the self-serving bias was only found when the procedures were also perceived as fair. The finding of applicants exhibiting a self-serving bias in selection contexts has been found in other studies, although it has typically been operationalized and measured in ways different from those described in the attribution theory literature (e.g., Chan et al., 1999; Ployhart & Ryan, 1998; Ryan & Chan, 1999b). What are perceived as fair are procedures and outcomes that are favorable for the applicant.

Research seems to support the existence of an applicant self-serving bias, but this is just one of a number of biases suggested by attribution theory. For example, the false-consensus effect occurs when individuals judge their own behavior as being typical, and that others would perform the same behaviors in the same circumstances (when in fact they would not) (Fiske & Taylor, 1991). In applicant perceptions research, one might see the false-consensus effect when applicants who refuse to buy products from a company that did not hire them believe this is a common behavior. In addition to various attribution biases, there are also a variety of alternative attribution theories that have not been explored in applicant reactions research. Fiske and Taylor (1991) provide a nice summary of these various approaches.

We suggest the following theoretical considerations in future research.

Better testing of Gilliland's model, and social justice theory propositions in general

We noted above the limited testing of Gilliland's model in that few studies have systematically manipulated justice rules. We also need to be concerned with how justice theory applies to a selection setting. A selection context differs from other arenas of organizational justice that researchers have investigated because of the lack of a relation between the applicant and organization. Tyler and Dawes (1993) stated that in situations without strong social bonds, people will be egoistical. We noted above the self-serving bias finding in the applicant perceptions literature. Further, researchers have not found the types of process by outcome interactions found in other justice research. Brockner and Wiesenfeld (1996) indicated that procedures matter most when outcomes are unfair or undesirable, yet Ployhart and Ryan (1997) indicated that procedures matter most when outcomes are seen as fair. Ployhart and Ryan noted that this is partly a function of the types of intentions one examines and also perhaps a function of the fact that applicants often have alternative offers they can pursue when rejected. Rather than expecting findings similar to those in other organizational justice areas (e.g., performance appraisal, layoffs), basic social justice theory would predict potentially different findings in a selection context because of the nature of the applicant/organization relationship (i.e., one-shot, limited scope). Of course, those who are accepted by an organization and accept the offer do then commence an ongoing relationship. Justice theory might make different predictions about this group than about other applicant groups.

Also, some aspects of basic theory have been neglected in the applicant perceptions area. For example, Adams' equity theory formulation (Adams, 1965) predicts that the reaction to inequity will be proportional to the magnitude of the inequity, and research has supported this (e.g., Greenberg, 1988). In a selection setting, we need to think about what the likely reaction of an applicant would be if he or she were given an inequitable outcome (i.e., what is the magnitude of the inequity for the applicant). For example, perhaps the reaction is stronger if it is a highly desirable job (e.g., high-paying or high-status) than if one feels an unfair rejection occurred for a low level, generic job.

Consider other theoretical formulations and models

Our understanding of the nature and consequences of applicant perceptions would be enhanced by looking outside the justice literature. As we noted in the section on types of perceptions that have been studied, fairness is but one type of perception an applicant might hold. Frameworks other than justice theory may prove valuable in exploring a wider range of applicant perceptions. However, we note that other existing frameworks (e.g., Arvey & Sackett, 1993) do not provide much understanding of the processes' underlying perception formation or perception–outcome links.

Basic research on attitude formation, measurement, and effects is particularly relevant to applicant perceptions research. As noted earlier, the second predominant stream of research focuses on test-taking attitudes and motivation (e.g., Arvey et al., 1990; work of Chan and colleagues). Research on test-taking attitudes has not been well-grounded theoretically (e.g., test-taking motivation is not well tied to leading theories of motivation such as expectancy theory; self-efficacy is not considered in light of research on how self-efficacy perceptions are formed (Gist & Mitchell, 1992)). Indeed, although this research is on test-taking attitudes, little connection is made to basic attitude research and theory.

One interesting concept is attitude strength. Krosnick and Petty (1995) reviewed the attitude strength literature and suggested it has two components: durability (or stability) and impactfulness (how much the attitude influences other processes). Thus, more durable and impactful attitudes have a stronger influence on behaviors than attitudes lacking these qualities. One can borrow the durability and impactfulness conceptualizations to examine fairness perceptions, test-taking attitudes, and a variety of other applicant perceptions. For example, if test-taking motivation is easily changed (i.e., lacks durability), it may not be strongly held and may not have a consistent relation with applicant behavior.

Another example of attitude research that may be relevant is that on behavioral intention models (e.g., Ajzen & Fishbein, 1980; Ajzen & Madden, 1986; Fishbein & Ajzen, 1975). This research suggests intentions are determined by beliefs, attitudes, subjective norms, and perceptions of control (e.g., Ajzen & Fishbein, 1980). Such intention models might also serve to supplement justice models or be more formally integrated with them to better understand how applicant perceptions connect to applicant behavior. As we noted earlier, social information (such as subjective norms) is not examined well in this research. Perceptions of control are also unexplored, yet they have been suggested as key influences on applicant views of the selection process (Schuler, 1993).

Research on cognitive consistency theories (e.g., cognitive dissonance, balance theory) might also be used to understand reactions to selection decisions (see Abelson et al., 1968; Heider, 1958, for classic examples; and Fiske & Taylor, 1991, for a more recent treatment). Cognitive dissonance suggests that, when there are inconsistencies between a person's behavior and attitudes, the discrepancy will create dissonance and thus motivate the person to reduce the discrepancy. The most typical form of discrepancy reduction is to change one's attitudes to be aligned with the behavior (Fiske & Taylor, 1991). For example, if an applicant applies for a desirable job but then learns the organization uses a selection process he or she is unlikely to do well on, the individual may withdraw from the process and change his or her perceptions of the organization to less favorable ones. One very important feature of cognitive consistency theories is the notion of selective perception. Selective perception suggests that individuals will only attend to information that supports their existing attitudes. For example, if an applicant already holds negative attitudes toward a selection process (e.g., feels cognitive ability tests are unfair), he or she may be highly sensitive to minor justice rule violations (e g., see a by-the-book test administrator as poor interpersonal treatment).

New directions

Figure 1 provides a heuristic model of what we see as the key antecedents, outcomes, and perceptions to be studied, as well as a number of suggested moderators. We borrow from Gilliland's justice model (Gilliland, 1993) and Brutus and Ryan's model of determinants of perceived job-relatedness (Brutus & Ryan, 1998). One contribution of this heuristic is the categorizing of types of applicant perceptions into perceptions of the procedure/process (e.g., justice rule violations, fairness, ease), of one's affective and cognitive state during the procedure (e.g., motivation, anxiety), of the procedure's outcome (e.g., distributive fairness), and of selection processes and procedures in general (e.g., belief in tests, views on affirmative action, preferences for evaluation methods). We feel that more systematic research on the various determinants and outcomes in this model would move this area of research forward greatly.

Figure 1 Heuristic model.

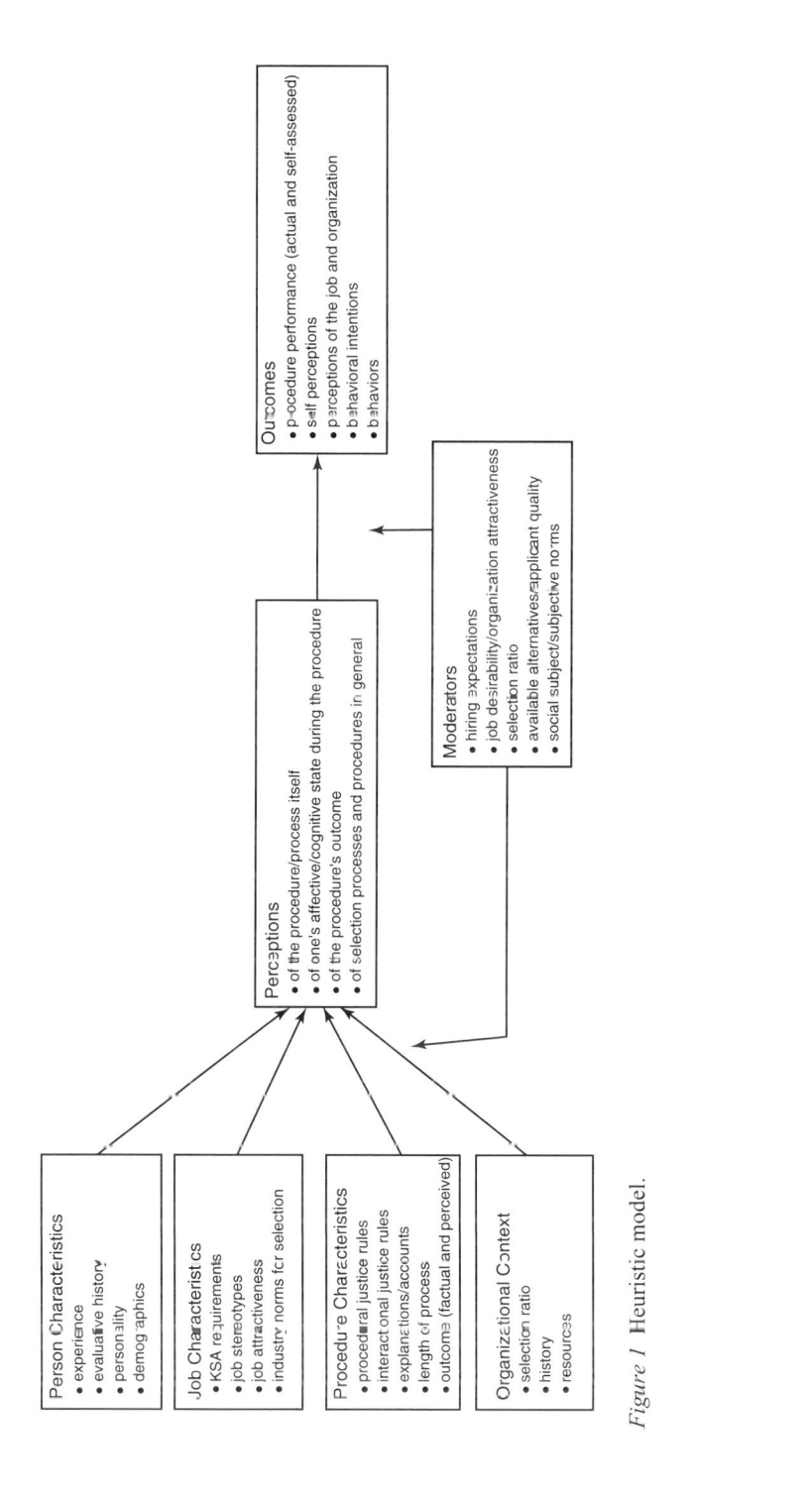

In addition to the specific research ideas mentioned throughout the paper, there are several other issues applicant perceptions researchers need to address. First, we need to consider the stability of various perceptions across the course of a selection process. Researchers have noted changes in perceptions from pre- to post-test (e.g., Chan et al., 1998b) and from post-test to post-outcome (e.g., Ployhart & Ryan, 1998). More distal assessments (e.g., months post-outcome) may differ as well, as individuals "get on with their lives" or experience alternative procedures with other employers as part of their job search. We reiterate the importance of considering time of measurement in evaluating study generalize ability, given what we know to be the natural sequence of events in employee selection.

Second, perhaps there are nonlinear relations between perceptions and behaviors. For example, applicants might not pursue legal action until there is some "breaking point" in terms of what they see as discriminatory behavior. Gilliland, Benson, and Schepers (1998) showed that when one has to make a *decision about taking action* based on considerations of fairness, if more than three justice rule violations have occurred, any non-violations are not considered. When making *judgments* of fairness, justice violations and nonviolations are equally important. In a selection context for a decision about accepting a job offer, it may be that greater weight is given to what is wrong in the process (e.g., the receptionist was rude when she gave me the test) than to what is right. Further, Gilliland (1995) noted that some procedural justice rules are more salient in their violation while others are more salient in their satisfaction, suggesting potentially complex relations with behaviors. Future research directed at understanding how violations and nonviolations combine to influence decisions is needed.

Third, a multiple stakeholder perspective might be helpful. There are others besides applicants who are stakeholders in the selection process, and their perceptions may influence key organizational outcomes. For example, we know little about incumbent managers' perceptions of hiring processes (e.g., Smither et al., 1993). These perceptions might influence important outcomes, such as willingness to use a selection procedure (or to use it as intended) or views and acceptance of new hires. Another group of stakeholders are those in HR with responsibility for administering and evaluating procedures. For example, if a test administrator views a procedure negatively, he or she may adhere less strictly to protocol and be more willing to "assist" applicants on a procedure. Recruiters with negative perceptions of structured interview questions might skip what they see as irrelevant.

Fourth, prominent applicant perceptions researchers such as Chan and Ployhart have repeatedly called for more experimental research (Chan et al., 1998b; Ployhart & Ryan, 1998), even if such research is lab based with student populations. This may seem counter to a need to study actual applicants and actual behaviors. For example, college students are more experienced and comfortable with being tested than those with lower levels of education or who are long removed from the educational system (Ryan & Greguras, 1998). However, these researchers point out some major concerns. First, we cannot assess the effects of a particular justice rule (such as job-relatedness), what leads to a rule being seen us violated, how individual and situational characteristics affect rule salience, etc., unless we conduct research where that rule is systematically manipulated. Such manipulations are less likely to be possible in field settings, where treating one group of applicants differently from another can be seen as unethical or even illegal. Second, we cannot develop a good theoretical understanding of how and why perceptions have effects on personal and organizational outcomes unless we conduct experimental research that enables us to isolate mediators and moderators. Measuring or manipulating these is also less likely in a field setting.

Fifth, Rynes (1993) noted that to identify applicant likes and dislikes, intensive qualitative research should precede surveying. This has not been the case in the applicant perceptions research arena (exceptions include Gilliland, 1995; Ployhart, McFarland, & Ryan, 1998). Rynes noted that doing as she suggested would "avoid the opposing dangers of either prematurely settling on one potentially deficient model, such as justice or expectancy theory, or contribution to underlying process obfuscation via proliferation of seemingly different, but actually similar, constructs" (Rynes, 1993: 252). We feel it is not too late for researchers in this area to heed her warning and backtrack to do intensive qualitative research (e.g., verbal protocol analysis) of applicant perceptions of procedures to formulate a more meaningful framework for this research.

Conclusions

What should an organization do about its selection process based on this literature? We would not advocate that organizations remove valid procedures because of suspected negative reactions. At this stage, we do not have enough evidence that negative perceptions of applicants actually have negative effects (i.e., relate to turning down jobs, badmouthing the organization). Also, given the many potential determinants and moderators of perceptions, generalizations from reported research on a "similar" method may not be prudent. However, the literature on applicant perceptions, as well as the more basic literature on social justice, provides some clear "good ideas" that seem unlikely to harm and likely to help both organizations and individuals.

1. Recognize that test-taking attitudes influence performance in the selection process. Chan and colleague have demonstrated that test-taking motivation can influence performance. Employers may protest that it is not their role to motivate applicants and that they do not want to hire "unmotivated" employees. However, test-taking motivation is not necessarily an indicator of motivation to do a job—it may be influenced by an individual's experiences with a particular type of test. Employers can look at whether their particular selection process demotivates applicants (e.g., is it too lengthy) or unduly raises anxiety e.g., nature of instructions).

2. Provide explanations that give information and are delivered in an interpersonally sensitive manner (Greenberg, 1990, 1994). However, as noted by several researchers (e.g., Bies, 1987; Ployhart et al., 1999), using social accounts to "manage" a situation can lead to distortion of the truth or inappropriate rationalizations. For example, an organization could argue that a procedure with high adverse impact was necessary to maintain a competitive advantage. While this might be true, giving such an explanation does not address the issue of what an organization might do to reduce adverse impact. We note that the research on social accounts has typically focused on cases where there are ongoing relationships between the explanation provider and recipient (Bies, 1987; Bies & Sitkin, 1992). It is unclear how this then applies to a selection context, where the interaction between the applicant and the organization may be a single-time encounter, with no ongoing relationship. We also lack descriptive research on what types of explanations or accounts are currently used in selection contexts or what strategies organizations use in informing applicants of rejection. Our suspicion is that most organizations use a "there were many more qualified applicants than openings" boilerplate statement when explaining a rejection decision.

3. Regularly monitor applicant perceptions. When approached about research, a number of organizational contacts have told us they do not want to ask about things like the fairness of their selection process for fear that it "will plant seeds in applicants minds." The idea of a priming effect is not without scientific merit (Feldman & Lynch, 1988). However, asking incumbents or students for their perceptions does not appear to be a sufficient surrogate for asking actual applicants. Regular monitoring of perceptions can alert an organization to shifts in the quality of selection process administration as well (e.g., pinpointing uninformative interviewers, noting delays in the process).

4. Assess perception–behavior links. Laboratory research can only go so far in assessing the types of behavior of interest (e.g., job offer acceptance). Such links need to be examined in order for researchers to confidently assert that "applicant perceptions matter." In particular, we note that there is not as yet solid evidence that desirable applicants turn down job offers because of their views of the selection process.

5. Recognize that selection involves evaluation. As Fiske (1967) noted, reactions to tests are not just reactions to the procedure itself, but are reactions to being evaluated. Regardless of what changes are made to tools used in decision making, selection is an evaluative process. The real issue is not the total elimination of negative perceptions, but an understanding of whether those who hold negative perceptions are desirable applicants and, if so, how to make certain those perceptions do not affect important behaviors (e.g., accepting job offers). There is much organizations can do to improve applicant perceptions, but such undertakings must not supplant the use of reliable and valid predictors, nor can they erase the fact that, in selection, some people will be unhappy with the negative outcomes they receive.

Applicant perceptions of selection procedures have generated considerable research and applied interest. However, we come to a pessimistic conclusion regarding whether perceptions really matter, as there has been insufficient empirical demonstration of links to behaviors or distal attitudes and self-perceptions. We do feel that this remains an open question and hope that clearer demonstrations of value occur soon. As the area of research matures, a more theoretical and integrated approach is needed. We hope this review can serve as a starting point for that integration.

References

Abelson, R. P., Aronson, E., McGuire, W. J., Newcomb, T. M., Rosenberg. M. J., & Tannebaum, P. H. 1968. *Theories of cognitive consistency: A sourcebook.* Chicago: Rand McNally.

Adams, J. S. 1965. Inequity in social exchange. In L. Berkowitz (Ed.), *Advances in experimental social psychology*, Vol. 2: 267–299. New York: Academic Press.

Ajzen, I., & Fishbein, M. 1980. *Understanding attitudes and predicting social behavior.* Englewood Cliffs, NJ: Prentice-Hall.

Ajzen, I., & Madden, T. J. 1986. Prediction of goal-directed behavior: Attitudes, intentions, and perceived behavioral control. *Journal of Experimental Social Psychology*, 22: 453–474.

Ambrose, M. L., Harland, L. K., & Kulik, C. T. 1991. Influence of social comparisons on perceptions of organizational fairness. *Journal of Applied Psychology*, 76: 239–246.

Arvey, R. D., & Sackett, P. R. 1993. Fairness in selection: Current developments and perspectives. In. N. Schmitt & W. C. Borman (Eds.), *Personnel selection in organizations*: 171–202. San Francisco: Jossey-Bass.

Arvey, R. D., Strickland, W., Drauden, G., & Martin, C. 1990. Motivational components of test-taking. *Personnel Psychology*, 43: 695–716.

Ball, G. A., Trevino, L. K., & Sims, H. P. 1993. Justice and organizational punishment: Attitudinal outcomes of disciplinary events. *Social Justice Research*, 6: 39–66.

Barber, A. E. 1998. *Recruiting employees: Individual and organization perspectives.* Thousand Oaks, CA: Sage.

Barbera, K. M., Ryan, A. M., Desmarais, L. B., & Dyer, P. J. 1995. *Multimedia employment tests: Effects of attitudes and experiences on validity.* Presented at the Tenth Annual Conference of the Society for Industrial and Organizational Psychology, Orlando, FL.

Bauer, T. N., Maertz, C. P., Dolen, M. R., & Campion, M. A. 1998. Longitudinal assessment of applicant reactions to employment testing and test outcome feedback. *Journal of Applied psychology*, 83. 892–903.

Bazerman, M. H., Schroth, H. A., Shah, P. P., Diekmann, K. A., & Tenbrunsel, A. E. 1994. The inconsistent role of comparison others and procedural justice in reactions to hypothetical job descriptions: Implications for job acceptance decisions. *Organizational Behavior and Human Decision Processes*, 60. 326–352.

Bies, R. J. 1987. The predicament of injustice: The management of moral outrage. In L. L. Cummings & B. M. Staw (Eds.), *Research in organizational behavior.* Greenwich: JAI Press.

Bies, R. J., & Shapiro, D. L. 1988. Voice and justification: Their influence an procedural fairness judgments. *Academy of Management Journal*, 31: 676–685.

239

Bies, R. J., & Sitkin, S. B. 1992. Explanation as legitimization: Excuse-making in organizations. In M. L. McLaughlin, M. J. Cody, & S. J. Read (Eds.), *Explaining one's self to others: Reason-giving in a social context*: 183–198. Hillsdale, NJ: Erlbaum.

Bies, R. J., & Tripp, T. M. 1998. Revenge in organizations: The good, the bad, and the ugly. In R. W. Griffin, A. O' Leary-Kelly, & J. M. Collins (Eds.), *Dysfunctional behavior in organizations: Non-violent dysfunctional behavior:* 49–67. Stanford, CT: JAI Press.

Bies, R. J., Tripp, T. M., & Kramer, R. M. 1997. At the breaking point: Cognitive and social dynamics of revenge in organizations. In R. Giacalone & J. Greenberg (Eds.), *Antisocial behavior in organizations*: 18–36. Thousand Oaks, CA: Sage.

Boldizar, J. P., Perry, D. G., & Perry, L. C. 1988. Gender and reward distributions: A test of two hypotheses. *Sex Roles*, 19: 569–579.

Breaugh, J., & Starke, M. 2000. Research on employee recruitment: So many studies, so many remaining questions. *Journal of Management*, 26: 405–434.

Bridgeman, B. 1992. A comparison of quantitative questions in open-ended and multiple choice formats. *Journal of Educational Measurement*, 29: 253–271.

Brocker, J., & Wiesenfeld, B. M. 1996. An integrative framework for explaining reactions to decisions: Interactive effects of outcomes and procedures. *Psychological Bulletin*, 120: 189–208.

Brockner, J., Tyler, T. R., & Cooper-Schneider, R. 1992. The Influence of prior commitment to an institution on reactions to perceived unfairness: The higher they are, the harder they fall. *Administrative Science Quarterly*, 37: 241–261.

Brutus, S., & Ryan, A. M. 1998. *Individual characteristics as determinants of the perceived relatedness of selection procedures.* Presented at 13th Annual SIOP meeting, Dallas, TX.

Burke, M. J., Normand, J., & Raju, N. S. 1987. Examinee attitudes toward computer-administered ability testing. *Computers in Human Behavior*, 3: 95–107.

Chan, D. 1997. Racial subgroup differences in predictive validity perceptions on personality and cognitive ability tests. *Journal of Applied Psychology*, 82: 311–320.

Chan, D., & Schmitt, N. 1997. Video-based versus paper-and-pencil method of assessment in situational judgment tests: Subgroup differences in test performance and face validity perceptions. *Journal of Applied Psychology*, 82: 143–159.

Chan, D., Schmitt, N., DeShon, R. P., Clause, C. S., & Delbridge, K. 1997. Reactions to cognitive ability tests: The relationships between race, test performance, face validity perceptions, and test-taking motivation. *Journal of Applied Psychology*, 82: 300–310.

Chan, D., Schmitt, N., Jennings, D., Clause, C. S., & Delbridge, K. 1998a. Applicant perceptions of test fairness: Integrating justice and self-serving bias perspectives. *International Journal of Selection and Assessment*, 6: 232–239.

Chan, D. Schmitt, N., Sacco, J. M., & DeShon, R. P. 1998b. Understanding pretest and posttest reactions to cognitive ability and personality tests. *Journal of Applied Psychology*, 83: 471–485.

Cox, T. 1993. *Cultural diversity in organizations.* San Francisco: Berrett-Kochler.

Crant, J. M., & Berman, T. S. 1990. An experimental test of the impact of drug-testing programs on potential job applicants' attitudes and intentions. *Journal of Applied Psychology*, 75: 127–131.

Cunningham, M. R. 1989. Test-taking motivations and outcomes on a standardized measure of on-the-job integrity. *Journal of Business and Psychology*, 4: 119–127.

Feldman, J. M., & Lynch, J. G. 1998. Self-generated validity and other effects of measurement on belief, attitude, intention, and behavior. *Journal of Applied Psychology*, 73: 421–435.

Fishbein, M., & Ajzen, I. 1975. *Belief attitude, intentions and behavior: An introduction to theory and research*. Boston, MA: Addison-Wesley.

Fiske, D. W. 1967. The subject reacts to tests. *American Psychologist*, 22: 287–296.

Fiske, S.T., & Taylor, S. E. 1991. *Social cognition*. New York, NY: McGraw Hill.

Fredriksen, J. R., & Collins, A. 1989. A systems approach to educational testing. *Educational Researcher*, 2: 27–32.

Gilliland, S. W. 1993. The Perceived fairness of selection system: An organizational justice perspective. *Academy of Management Review*, 18: 694–734.

Gilliland, S. W. 1994. Effects of procedural and distributive justice on reaction to a selection system. *Journal of Applied Psychology*, 79: 691–701.

Gilliland, S. W. 1995. Fairness from the applicant's perspective: Reactions to employee selection procedures. *International Journal of Selection and Assessment*, 3: 11–19.

Gilliland, S. W., Benson, L., & Schepers, D. H. 1998. A rejection threshold in justice evaluations: Effects on judgment and decision-making. *Organizational Behavior and Human Decision Processes*, 76: 113–131.

Gilliland, S. W., & Honig, H. 1994. *Development of the selection fairness survey*. Paper presented at the 9th Annual Conference of the Society for Industrial and Organizational Psychology, Nashville, TN.

Gilliland, S. W., & Steiner, D. D. 1999. Applicant reactions. In R. W. Eden & M. M. Harris (Eds.), *The employment interview handbook*: 69–82. Thousand Oaks, CA: Sage.

Gist, M. E., & Mitchell, T. R. 1992. Self-efficiency: A theoretical analysis of its determinants and malleability. *Academy of Management Journal*, 17: 183–211.

Greenberg, J. 1986. Determinants of perceived fairness of performance evaluations. *Journal of Applied Psychology*, 71: 340–342.

Greenberg, J. 1987. A taxonomy of organizational justice theories. *Academy of Management Review*, 12: 9–22.

Greenberg, J. 1988. Equity and workplace status: A field experiment. *Journal of Applied Psychology*, 73: 606–613.

Greenberg, J. 1990. Employee theft as a reaction to underpayment inequity: The hidden cost of pay cuts. *Journal of Applied Psychology*, 75: 561–568.

Greenberg, J. 1994. Using socially fair treatment to promote acceptance of a work site smoking ban. *Journal of Applied Psychology*, 79: 288–297.

Greguras, G. J., & Ryen, A. M. 1997. *Test taker reactions, negative affectivity, and test performance*. Presented at the twelfth annual meeting of the Society for Industrial and Organizational Psychology, St. Louis, MO.

Heider, F. 1958. *The psychology of interpersonal relations*. New York: Wiley.

Heilman, M. E., & Herlihy, J. M. 1984. Affirmative action, negative reaction? Some moderating conditions. *Organizational Behavior and Human Performance*, 33: 204–213.

Heilman, M. E., Lucas, J. A., & Kaplow, S. R. 1990. Self derogating consequences of sex-based preferential selection: The moderating role of initial self-confidence. *Organizational Behavior and Human Decision Processes*, 46: 202–216.

Heilman, M. E., Rivero, J. C., & Brell, J. F. 1991. Skirting the competency issue: Effects of sex-based preferential selection on task choices of men and women. *Journal of Applied Psychology*, 76: 99–105.

Heilman, M. E., Simon, M. C., & Repper, D. P. 1987. Intentionally favored, unintentionally harmed?: The impact of sex-based preferential selection on self-perceptions and self-evaluations. *Journal of Applied Psychology*, 72: 62–68.

Herriot, P. 1989. Selection as a social process. In M. Smith and I. T. Robertson (Eds.), *Advances in selection and assessment:* 171–187. London: John Wiley & Sons.

Horvath, M., Ryan, A. M., & Stierwalt, S. (in press). The influence of explanations for selection test use, outcome favorability and self-efficacy on test-taker perceptions. *Organizational Behavior and Human Decision Processes.*

Huo, Y. J., Smith, H. J., Tyler, T. R., & Lind, E. A. 1996. Superordinate identification, subgroup identification, and justice concerns: Is separatism the problem; is assimilation the answer? *Psychological Science*, 7: 1–6.

Jackson, S. E., & Associates. 1992. *Diversity in the workplace: Human resources initiatives.* New York: Guilford Press.

Kluger, A. N., & Rothstein, H. R. 1993. The influence of selection test type on applicant reactions to employment testing. *Journal of Business and Psychology,* 8: 3–25.

Kohn, L. S., & Dipboye, R. L. 1998. The effects of interview structure on recruiting outcomes. *Journal of Applied Social Psychology,* 28: 821–843.

Kravitz, D. A., Harrison, D. A., Turner, M. E., Levine, E. L., Chaves, W., Brannick, M. T., Denning, D. L., Russell, C. J., & Conard, M. A. 1997. *Affirmative Action: A review of psychological and behavioral research.* Bowling Green, OH: The Society for Industrial & Organizational Psychology.

Kravitz, D. A., Stinson, V., & Chavez, T. L. 1994. *Perceived fairness of tests used in making selection and promotion decisions.* Presented at the annual meeting of the Society for Industrial and Organizational Psychology, Nashville, TN.

Krosnick, J. A., & Petty, R. E. 1995. Attitude strength: An overview. In R. E. Petty & J. A. Krosnick (Eds.), *Attitude strength: Antecedents and consequences:* 1–24. Mahwah, NJ: Erlbaum.

Latham, G. P., & Finnegan, B. J. 1993. Perceived practicality of unstructured, patterned, and situational interviews. In H. Schuler, J. L. Farr, & M. Smith (Eds.), *Personnel selection and assessment: Individual and organizational perspectives,* 41–55. Hillsdale, NJ: Erlbaum.

Lemons, M. A., & Danehower, V. C. 1997. *Organizational justice in promotion decision for women: Contextual and cognitive determinants.* Presented at Southern Management Association Meeting.

Liden, R. C., & Parsons, C. K. 1986. A field study of job applicant interview perceptions, alternative opportunities, and demographic characteristics. *Personnel Psychology*, 39: 109–122.

Lind, E. A., & Tyler, T. 1988. *The social psychology of procedural justice.* New York: Plenum.

Lounsbury, J. W., Bobrow, W., & Jensen, J. B. 1989. Attitudes toward employment testing: Scale development, correlates, and "known group" validation. *Professional Psychology: Research and Practice*, 20: 340–349.

Macan, T. H., Avedon, M. J., Paese, M., & Smith, D. E. 1994. The effects of applicants, reactions to cognitive ability tests and an assessment center. *Personnel Psychology*, 47: 715–738.

Major, B., & Deaux, K. 1982. Individual differences in justice behavior. In J. Greenberg & R. L. Cohen (Eds.), *Equity and justice in social behavior.* New York: Academic Press.

Martin, C. L., & Nagao, D. 1989. Some effects of computerized interviewing on job applicant responses. *Journal of Applied Psychology*, 74: 72–80.

McCulloch, M. C., & Turban, D. B. 1997. *Candidate and manager reactions to overt integrity tests*. Presented at the 12th annual conference of the Society for Industrial and Organizational Psychology, St. Louis, MO.

Mosier, C. I. 1947. A critical examination of the concept of face validity. *Educational and Psychological Measurement*, 7: 191–206.

Murphy, K. R., Thornton, G. C., & Prue, K. 1991. Influence of job characteristics on the acceptability of employee drug testing. *Journal of Applied Psychology*, 76: 447–453.

Murphy, K. R., Thornton, G. C., & Reynolds, D. H. 1990. College students' attitudes toward employee drug testing programs. *Personnel Psychology*, 43: 615–631.

Nassar, S. 1999. Jobless rate in the U.S. hits 29-year low. *New York Times*, April 3, C. I.

Nevo, B. 1992. Examinee feedback: Practical guidelines. In M. Zeidner & R. Most (Eds.), *Psychological testing: An inside view:* 377–398. Palo Alto: Consulting Psychologists Press.

Nevo, B. 1995. Examinee feedback questionnaire: Reliability and validity measures. *Educational and Psychological Measurement*, 55: 499–504.

Nield, A. F., & Wintre, M. G. 1986. Multiple choice questions with an option to comment: Student attitudes and use. *Teaching of Psychology*, 13: 196–199.

Ployhart, R. E., & Maynard, D. C. 1999. *Broadening the scope of applicant reactions research: An exploratory investigation of the effects of job characteristics and level of competition*. Paper presented at 14th annual SIOP meeting, Atlanta. GA.

Ployhart, R. E., McFarland, L. A., & Ryan, A. M. 1998. April. *Applicant reactions to selection procedures: Expanding the justice framework*. Presented at 13th annual SIOP meeting, Dallas. TX.

Ployhart, R. E., & Ryan, A. M. 1997. Toward an explanation of applicant reactions: An examination of organizational justice and attribution frameworks. *Organizational Behavior and Human Decision Processes*, 72: 308–335.

Ployhart, R. E., & Ryan, A. M. 1998. Applicants' reaction to the fairness of selection procedures: The effects of positive rule violations and time of measurement. *Journal of Applied Psychology*, 83: 3–16.

Ployhart, R. E., & Ryan, A. M., & Bennett, M. 1999. Explanations for selection decisions: Applicants' reactions to informational and sensitivity features of explanations. *Journal of Applied Psychology*, 84: 87–106.

Powell, G. N. 1991. Applicant reactions to the initial employment interview: Exploring theoretical and methodological issues. *Personnel Psychology*, 44: 67–83.

Robertson, I. T., Iles, P. A., Gratton, L., & Sharpley, D. 1991. The impact of personnel selection and assessment methods on candidates. *Human Relations*, 44: 963–982.

Rosse, J. G., Miller, J. L., & Stecher, M. D. 1994. A field study of job applicants' reactions to personality and cognitive ability testing. *Journal of Applied Psychology*, 79: 987–992.

Ryan, A. M., & Chan, D. 1999a. Perceptions of the EPPP: How do licensure candidates view the process? *Professional Psychology*, 30: 519–530.

Ryan, A. M., & Chan, D. 1999b. *Self-serving biases in perceptions of fairness and the psychology licensing examination*. Paper presented at the 14th annual conference of the Society for Industrial and Organizational Psychology, Atlanta, GA.

Ryan, A. M., & Greguras, G. 1998. Life is not multiple choice: Reactions to the alternatives. In M. D. Hakel (Ed.), *Beyond multiple choice: Alternatives to traditional assessment:* 183–202. Mahwah, NJ: Lawrence Erlbaum.

Ryan, A. M., Greguras, G. J., & Ployhart, R. E. 1996. Perceived job relatedness of physical ability testing for firefighters: Exploring variations in reactions. *Human Performance*, 9: 219–240.

Ryan, A. M., & McFarland, L. A. 1997a. *Influence on applicant withdrawal from selection processes*. Presented at the twelfth annual meeting of the Society for Industrial and Organizational Psychology, St. Louis, MO.

Ryan, A. M., & McFarland, L. A. 1997b. *Perceived job relatedness as a moderator of the validity of cognitive ability and biodata instruments*. Presented at Academy of Management Conference, Boston, MA.

Ryan, A. M., Ployhart, R. E., Greguras, G. J., & Schmit, M. J. 1997. *Predicting applicant withdrawal form applicant attitudes*. Presented at the twelfth annual meeting of the Society for Industrial and Organizational Psychology, St. Louis, MO.

Ryan, A. M., Ployhart, R. E., Greguras, G. J., & Schmit, M. J. 1998. Test preparation programs in selection contexts: Self-selection and program effectiveness. *Personnel Psychology*, 51: 599–622.

Ryan, A. M., Sacco, J. M., McFarland, L. A., & Kriska, S. D. 2000. Applicant self-selection: Correlates of withdrawal from a multiple hurdle process. *Journal of Applied Psychology*, 85: 163–179.

Ryan, A. M., & Sackett, P. R. 1987. Pre-employment honesty testing: Fakability, reactions of test takers, and company image. *Journal of Business and Psychology*, 1(3): 248–256.

Rynes, S. L. 1991. Recruitment, job choice, and post-hire consequences: A call for new research directions. In M. D. Dunnette & L. M. Hough (Eds.), *Handbook of industrial and organizational psychology*, Vol. 2: 399–444. Palo Alto: Consulting Psychologists Press 2nd ed.

Rynes, S. L. 1993. Who's selecting whom? Effects of selection practices on applicant attitudes and behavior. In N. Schmitt & W. C. Borman (Eds.), *Personnel selection in organizations*: 240–274. San Francisco: Jossey-Bass.

Rynes, S. L., & Connerley, M. R. 1993. Applicant reactions to alternative selection procedures. *Journal of Business and Psychology*, 7: 261–277.

Saks, A. M., Leck, J. D., & Saunders, D. M. 1995. Effects of application blanks and employment equity on applicant reactions and job pursuit intentions. *Journal of Organizational Behavior*, 16: 415–430.

Sarason, I. G., Pierce, G. R., & Sarason, B. R. 1996. *Cognitive interference: Theories, methods, and findings*. Mahwah, NJ: Erlbaum.

Schmit, M. J., & Ryan, A. M. 1992. Test-taking dispositions: A missing link? *Journal of Applied Psychology*, 77: 629–637.

Schmit, M. J., & Ryan, A. M. 1997. Applicant withdrawal: The role of test-taking attitudes and racial differences. *Personnel Psychology*, 50: 855–876.

Schmitt, N., & Gilliland, S. W. 1992. Beyond differential prediction: Fairness in selection. In D. M. Saunders (Ed.), *New approaches to employee management: Fairness in employee selection*, Vol. 1: 21–46. Greenwich, CT: JAI Press.

Schuler, H. 1993. Social validity of selection situations: A concept and some empirical results. In H. Schuler, J. L. Farr, & M. Smith (Ed.), *Personnel selection and assessment: Individual and organizational perspectives*: 11–26. Hillsdale, NJ: Erlbaum.

Shotland, A. B., & Alliger, G. M. 1999. *The advantages of employing a face valid, multimedia selection device: Comparison of three measures*. Presented at the 14th Annual Conference of the Society for Industrial and Organizational Psychology, Atlanta, GA.

Singer, M. 1990. Determinants of perceived fairness in selection practices: An organizational justice perspective. *Genetic, Social and General Psychology Monographs*, 116: 477–494.

Smither, J. W., Reilly, R. R., Millsap, R. E., Pearlman, K., & Stoffey, R. W. 1993. Applicant reactions to selection procedures. *Personnel Psychology*, 46: 49–76.

Steele, C. M., & Aronson, J. 1995. Stereotype threat and the intellectual test performance of African Americans. *Journal of Personality and Social Psychology*, 69: 797–811.

Steiner, D., & Gilliland, S. W. 1996. Fairness reactions to personnel selection techniques in France and the United States. *Journal of Applied Psychology*, 81: 134–141.

Thorsteinson, T. J., & Ryan, A. M. 1997. The effect of selection ratio on perceptions of the fairness of a selection test battery. *International Journal of Selection and Assessment*, 5: 159–168.

Turner, M. E., & Pratkanis, A. R. 1994. Affirmative action as help: A review of recipient reactions to preferential selection and affirmative action. *Basic and Applied Social Psychology*, 15: 43–69.

Truxillo, D. M., & Bauer, T. N. 1999. Applicant reactions to test score banding in entry-level and promotional contexts. *Journal of Applied Psychology*, 84: 322–339.

Tyler, T. R., & Dawes, R. 1993. Fairness in groups: Comparing the self-interest and social identity perspectives. In B. Mellers & J. Baron (Eds.), *Psychological perspectives on justice: Theory and applications*: 87–108. Cambridge: Cambridge University Press.

Tyler, T. R., & Degoey, P. 1995. Collective restraint in social dilemmas: Procedural justice and social identification effects on support for authorities. *Journal of Personality and Social Psychology*, 69: 482–497.

Weiner, B. 1985. An attributional theory of achievement motivation and emotion. *Psychological Review*, 92: 548–573.

Weiner, B. 1986. An *attributional theory of motivation and emotion*. New York, NY: Springer-Verlag.

Whimey, D. J., Diaz, J., Minneghino, M. E., & Powers, K. T. 1998. *Test-taker perceptions of overt and personality-based integrity inventories*. Presented at the 13th annual conference for Industrial and Organizational Psychology.

Part 4

ASSESSING AND DEVELOPING PEOPLE AT WORK

27

PERFORMANCE EVALUATION IN WORK SETTINGS

R. D. Arvey and K. R. Murphy

Source: *Annual Review of Psychology* 49 (1998): 141–168.

Abstract

Recent research from 1993 on performance evaluations in work settings is reviewed and integrated with the prior reset and historical bases. Contemporary research reflects several themes: General models of job performance are being developed, the job performance domain is being expanded, research continues to explore the psychometric characteristics of performance ratings, research is developing on potential bias in ratings, rater training is examined, and research continues in terms of efforts to attach utility values to rated performance. We conclude that research is progressing in traditional content areas as well in the exploration of new ground. Researchers are recognizing that job performance is more than just the execution of specific tasks and that it involves a wider array of important organizational activities. There is also an increased optimism regarding the use of supervisory ratings and recognition that such "subjective" appraisal instruments do not automatically translate into rater error or bias.

Introduction

Psychologists have long been attentive to the issue of defining, understanding, and evaluating performance within work contexts. This chapter constitutes the first independent and separate treatment of recent research on this topic in an *Annual Review* format. *Annual Review* chapters on personnel selection by Landy et al (1994) and Borman et al (1997) give some treatment to performance evaluation issues. These reviews primarily focus on the role of job performance measures as criterion variables against which personnel selection methods and systems are validated, and as such, the treatment of personnel evaluation has been embedded within the larger framework of prediction and selection systems.

Our intent in this chapter is to develop and expand on previous treatments as well as to review and integrate more recent research on performance evaluation. We review and discuss recent research associated with job performance and appraisal methods and instrumentation, and we attend to psychological efforts to understand the value of individuals to organizations vis-à-vis their work performance.

We acknowledge at the outset that the value of an individual to a firm may be more than "just" his or her work performance. An individual may be valued by an organization because he or she possesses particular personal characteristics (e.g. valuing diversity; see Chemers et al 1995, Jackson & Ruderman 1995) or skills (see Gerhart & Milkovich 1992, Lawler 1990, Lawler & Jenkins 1992). In addition, the value of an individual is likely to vary substantially depending on the job he or she holds [this is an assumption that is the basis of many job evaluation systems (Lawler 1990)]. Here we take a traditional perspective that the major contributor of an employee's worth to the organization is through work behavior and ultimately performance. In addition, we explicitly deal with individual job performance and do not consider group or team performance or individual performance within teams (for a treatment of team performance, see Guzzo & Dickson 1996). Similarly, we do not deal with economic theories of employee worth that tend to focus on economic or financial definitions and explanations of performance (for an economic treatment of subjectivity in performance appraisals, see, for example, Prendergast & Topel 1996).

The scope of the chapter includes a comprehensive review of major psychological journals from 1993 to present. The decision to focus on recent research is based on a rationale used in previous Annual Review chapters (Borman et al 1997, Landy et al 1994). We reviewed relevant articles cited in *PsychInfo* and sent out a call for additional papers to over 75 professional psychologists. We also examined a variety of seminal articles, books, and reviews that provided context for this review. Many of the issues discussed in recent research can only be understood in the context of papers published before 1993, and our review includes numerous references to research published before this date. Our coverage, however, of research published before 1993 is not designed to be comprehensive.

Historical treatment and context

It is useful to provide brief coverage of some of the historical treatments and models of performance appraisal. Between 1950 and 1980, most research was concerned with improving the instruments used in making performance ratings. Thus, there were hundreds of studies on the advantages and disadvantages of different types of rating scales, of rating vs ranking, and of ways of eliciting ratings that would provide the most objective measures of performance.

In the early 1980s, researchers shifted their focus away from instrumentation issues and toward developing a better understanding of the way raters form impressions and judgments of their subordinates' performance. In particular, Landy & Farr (1980, 1983) directed the attention of researchers toward the links between research on information processing and cognition and the practical questions often faced by performance appraisal researchers. Feldman's (1981) review helped to introduce a number of concepts from social cognition into research on performance appraisal. The next fifteen years saw an explosion in research on information processing in performance appraisal; DeNisi (1997) provides an in-depth review of this research. Many individuals, however, expressed skepticism about the contribution this research made to our understanding of performance appraisal in organizations (DeNisi 1997, Guion & Gibson 1988, Ilgen et al 1993).

There are several noteworthy reviews that are somewhat more restricted in scope than those discussed above. Austin & Villanova (1992) described the history of research on performance criteria, from 1917 to 1992. Folger et al (1992) reviewed research on justice perceptions of fairness in appraisal and suggest a due-process metaphor for understanding many of the questions raised in that literature. Bobko & Colella (1994) reviewed research on the meaning, implications, and determination of performance standards. In a broader context, several papers addressed the impact of ongoing changes in the structure and function of organizations on performance appraisal. Organizations are becoming flatter, more decentralized, and are moving away from individual-based and toward team-based methods of production. Cascio (1995) and Fletcher (1994, 1995) examined the probable impact of these changes on the way performance appraisals will be conducted and used in organizations.

This understanding of the broader context is consistent with several papers that examined in more detail the role of the rating context and the goals pursued by various stakeholders in shaping the behavior of raters, ratees, and other users of performance appraisal. For example, Murphy & Cleveland (1991, 1995) suggest that researchers should consider the rating context before attempting to analyze or evaluate the effectiveness, accuracy, etc, of performance ratings. Cleveland & Murphy (1992) analyzed performance appraisal as goal-oriented behavior and suggested that if the goals pursued by raters were examined more closely, behaviors that are typically treated as rating errors (e.g. giving high ratings to most subordinates) would be seen as adaptive responses to forces in the rating environment.

In a similar vein, Cardy & Dobbins (1994) discussed the relationships between concepts from research on efficient production systems and Total Quality Management (TQM) and performance appraisal. They noted that performance is determined by both the behavior of the individual and the system in which he or she functions. Likewise, Waldman (1994a,b) suggested an integration of TQM principles with performance appraisal/management and noted that an adequate theory of performance should contain both person and system components.

A review of the historical literature concerning personnel evaluation also shows a substantial gap between research and practice in performance appraisal. This was perhaps most obvious during the 1980s, when many of the studies in this area were conducted in the laboratory and focused on the cognitive processes in appraisal and evaluation (Banks & Murphy 1985). However, concerns about the links between appraisal research and practice still remain. Bretz et al (1992) noted that researchers have not typically asked what practitioners and managers regard as the most important questions and that the results of performance appraisal research have had little impact on the practice of appraisal in organizations. There are clearly opportunities for good research-practice linkages (Banks & Murphy 1985). For example, Latham et al (1993) illustrated the interface between practical issues and salient research findings. However, these links are seldom as strong as they could or should be.

One place where a concerted effort has been made to link research and practice is in the Armed Services Joint Performance Measurement project (Wigdor & Green 1991). Substantial efforts on the parts of several branches of the Armed Services were directed at developing the best practical measures of job performance. This project resulted in the development of several "hands-on" performance measures, which typically involved demonstrating proficiency in specific job tasks.

Another area where historically there is an active research-practice interchange is within the legal arena. In court cases involving Title VII charges of bias and discrimination, performance appraisal evaluations often come under attack. Expert witnesses often rely on the published literature to help them reach informed opinions about the adequacy of the appraisal system and instrumentation used by organizations. Reviews by Feild & Holley (1982), Kleiman & Durham (1981), Bernardin & Beatty (1984), and Cascio & Bernardin (1984) analyzed case law to develop principles and themes associated with appraisal systems and formats that appear to influence how courts and juries review the relative fairness of such evaluation systems.

The groundwork for utility analysis was laid decades ago (Brogden 1949, Cronbach & Gleser 1965), and the conceptual models guiding this work have changed little over time. In the area of personnel and human resource management, utility analysis has been used to (a) forecast the effect of some intervention (e.g. a test, a training program) on the performance of employees, and (b) attach a value, often framed in a dollar metric, to that performance. Research on utility estimation over the past several decades has mostly focused on elaborating and applying the basic models developed by Brogden and others.

Definition of job performance

The first broad area of recent performance evaluation research focuses on defining job performance. First, there are several efforts outlining general models of job performance and the determinants of job performance. Drawing from the long-term Selection and Classification project (Project A) sponsored by the military, Campbell et al (1993) proposed the view of job performance as multidimensional in nature and comprised of an eight-factor latent structure. In addition, Campbell et al proposed several broad individual determinants of performance (i.e. Declarative Knowledge, Procedural Knowledge and Skill, and Motivation). Empirical support for this model is presented by McCloy et al (1994), who show significant relationships between the measured and latent variables of performance and specified performance determinants indicating a good fit to their model.

Waldman & Spangler (1989) also developed an integrated model of job performance focusing on characteristics of the individual (e.g. experience, ability), outcomes (e.g. feedback, job security), and the immediate work environment. Campbell et al (1996) reviewed and discussed other models of job performance (e.g. the "classical" general factor model, the critical deficiency model) but again affirmed their belief that performance is best understood as multifactor in nature.

Further specification of the taxonomic structure of job performance is developed in Borman & Brush (1993). Using the results of published and unpublished studies of managerial performance, expert judges sorted performance dimensions into similar content domains. Further psychometric methods were used to develop an 18-factor solution. These 18 factors (e.g. planning and organizing, training, coaching, developing subordinates, technical proficiency) compared well with previous research efforts to derive a taxonomic structure of performance in managerial jobs.

Viswesvaran (1996) suggested that there is a general factor underlying most common performance measures but that there are also important subfactors, including task-specific as well as conscientiousness-oriented factors. One question that surfaces here is whether there might be a "general factor" in performance that corresponds to a "g" factor in cognitive intelligence. Along these lines, Arvey (1986) earlier called attention to a possible general factor (a "p" factor?) resulting from factor analyzing job-analytic information for a number of petrochemical jobs. The implication of this type of research is that performance measures might be differentiated in terms of both performance dimensions and level of abstraction/specificity.

Campbell et al (1996) also drew specific attention to the need to examine more fully the nature of job performance variability across employees. They discussed different methods of estimating variation in job performance (i.e. the coefficient of variation) and the meaning of variance in terms of economic value. Sackett et al (1988) and DuBois et al (1993) also called attention to distributional aspects of performance in their discussion of maximum and typical measures of performance, essentially referring to range difference within ratees.

A second theme is that the job performance domain is expanding. This theme is sounded somewhat broadly by Cascio (1995) and Ilgen & Hollenbeck (1991), who argue that the nature of work is changing and therefore so are the different definitions of what jobs and job performance are all about. There appears to be a general move toward more flexible definitions of work roles and jobs, where jobs are viewed as dynamic and more interchangeable and are defined with less precision. The focus is on the personal competencies required to perform various work roles and jobs rather than a narrow review of specific tasks and duties inherent in fixed jobs and work roles. Hedge & Borman (1995) suggested that different rater types (i.e. peers, self, subordinates) will capture different and valued perspectives in measuring performance, that electronic monitoring devices might be used for measurement purposes, and that attitudes toward appraisal systems will be examined more thoroughly.

Consistent with this theme is that broad distinctions might be made between measures of task proficiency in job performance and what is being called "contextual" performance. Borman & Motowidlo (1993) suggested that task performance relates to the proficiency with which incumbents perform core technical activities that are important for their jobs, whereas contextual performance is defined as extratask proficiency that contributes more to the organizational, social, and psychological environment to help accomplish organizational goals. These contextual factors include such aspects as persisting with enthusiasm and extra effort, volunteering to carry out duties not formally part of one's job, and endorsing and supporting organizational objectives (Borman & Motowidlo 1993). This notion is consistent with the work by Organ (1988), who discusses organizational citizenship behavior; prosocial behavior as discussed by Brief & Motowidlo (1986); and organizational spontaneity (George & Brief 1992). All these labels refer to constructs contributing to organizational goals and reflect the polar opposites of constructs of employee deviance and counterproductivity that detract from organizational goals. Such contextual behaviors serve to facilitate communications, lubricate social communications, and reduce tension and/or disruptive emotional responses, and are viewed as important and contributing to organizational goals.

Recent awareness that it is important for individuals to develop and possess skills that facilitate teamwork that are distinct and are different from specific on-task performance is also consistent with this theme (McIntyre & Salas 1995). Likewise, there is a growing recognition that counterproductive behaviors that detract from organizational goals should also be specified and treated as aspects of performance—perhaps as conditions of employment.

Schmidt (1993) sounded a note of caution regarding the idea of creating a new performance construct called contextual performance, because it appears to be defined as something absent from a job description. He further made the argument that as soon as it becomes part of such a description, it ceases being part of contextual performance. Part of the problem might lie in whether the distinction is only conceptual or whether it has an empirical basis. As such, there are several empirical research efforts to support this distinction. Using supervisory ratings from over 18,000 employees in 42 different entry-level jobs in retail settings, Hunt (1996) developed a taxonomy of "generic" work behavior, or behavior that contributes to performance of jobs independent of technical job roles. These included the following dimensions: Adherence to Confrontational Rules, Industriousness, Thoroughness, Schedule Flexibility, Attendance, Off-Task Behavior, Unruliness, Theft, and Drug Misuse. Motowidlo & Van Scotter (1994) tested the distinction between task and contextual performance using supervisory ratings of over 400 Air Force mechanics. Results showed that both task and contextual performance factors contributed independently to overall performance and showed that personality variables were more highly correlated with contextual performance in accordance with their expectations.

Conway (1996) used a multitrait-multirater database and confirmatory factor analysis to support the validity of task and contextual performance as separate domains. Further, the distinction was more pronounced for nonmanagerial than for managerial jobs. Nonetheless, the two domains show substantial intercorrelations (in the 0.5–0.6 range), indicating that they are certainly not entirely independent from each other. Van Scotter & Motowidlo (1996) added more empirical support to refine the construct of contextual performance by dividing it into two narrower constructs, interpersonal facilitation and job dedication. Results from supervisory ratings of 975 Air Force mechanics indicate that task performance is distinguishable from interpersonal facilitation but not from job dedication. Werner (1994) showed that extrarole behaviors such as citizenship behaviors strongly influenced rater search strategies as well as the eventual ratings given by supervisors evaluating secretarial performance.

One might ask why this kind of distinction has not been developed previously. Part of the answer to this question may be due to the historical attachment of the field of I/O psychology to a pronounced behavioristic/objective orientation which emphasized on-task performance as the only important performance domain. Schmidt et al (1981) called attention to the "behavioral fractionation" of criterion measures and task-oriented job performance measures that were virtually set in concrete in the federal government's Uniform Guidelines on Employee Selection Procedures.

Research suggesting that performance consists of both task-oriented and contextually oriented facets has led to the question of whether the attributes that lead some applicants to excel in specific aspects of performance (e.g. performing individual job tasks) might be different from those that lead some applicants to excel in other aspects of job performance (e.g. working well with others). Several studies suggest that there are differences in the variables that predict task vs contextual performance (Borman et al 1997, Day & Silverman 1989, McCloy et al 1994, McHenry et al 1990, Motowidlo & Van Scotter 1994, Rothstein et al 1994). On the whole, this research suggests that cognitive abilities might be more relevant for predicting task performance, whereas personality variables might be more critical for predicting contextual performance. Arvey et al (1997) hypothesized that constructs associated with individual differences in emotionality might also predict contextual aspects of performance.

Another issue explored in terms of definition of performance is the work by Hofmann et al (1993), who discussed the dynamic nature of performance measures across time. While researchers have previously addressed the issue of whether work performance measures are dynamic, Hofmann et al suggested that emphasis should be placed on decomposing change into the study of intra- and inter-individual differences in observed change.

Measurement of job performance

The second broad area of performance evaluation research focuses on performance appraisal techniques that are used to measure job performance. We have organized this section of the review by thematically grouping relevant research that reflects similar content domains. This grouping was driven by the research and therefore should be considered inductive in nature.

Construct validity/psychometric considerations

Recent research continues to explore the construct validity and other psychometric properties of performance measures. Vance et al (1988) reported a study involving the assessment of construct validity using multitrait-multimethod data obtained for a sample of 256 jet engine mechanics. They used confirmatory factor analysis to support the construct validity of performance ratings provided by self, supervisors, and peers and to relate each to performance data gathered using an objective test of task proficiency. Convergence among the three different rating sources was found as well as significant discriminant validity. Similarly, Conway (1996) reported analyses of multitrait-multimethod designs and estimated the proportion of trait and method variance in ratings.

Viswesvaran et al (1996) reported the results of a meta-analysis of the interrater and intrarater reliabilities of job performance ratings. Their findings indicated that supervisory ratings appear to have higher interrater reliability than peer ratings ($m = .52$ for supervisors, $m = .42$ for peers) and that intrarater estimates of reliability (e.g. coefficient alphas) tend to be higher than interrater estimates. They conclude that the use of intrarater reliability estimates to correct for measurement error will lead to potentially biased research results and recommend the use of interrater reliability estimates. There also appears to be some evidence for differential reliabilities depending on which specific job performance dimension is being used. For example, supervisors rate performance on communication competence and interpersonal competence less reliably, on average, than productivity or quality. This finding suggests that the contextual performance factors mentioned above might be less reliably rated dimensions of performance compared with more task-specific factors.

Finally, Ganzach (1995) challenged the notion that there is a linear relationship between ratings of various dimensional ratings or attributes and an overall performance evaluation and showed that more weight is given to negative attributes than to positive attributes, and that the combination of attributes may be configural in nature. McIntyre & James (1995) showed that rater policies on weighting and combining information about target ratees are target-specific and particularly sensitive to negative information about target ratees.

Alternative measures of performance

A number of recent studies have examined the relative value and interchangeability of different types of performance measures. Bommer et al (1995) assessed the relationships between relatively objective and subjective measures of employee performance. Using meta-analytic techniques to summarize the relationships for over 50 independent samples, the overall corrected mean correlation between the two types of measures was 0.39 (0.32 observed), suggesting that the two measures were significantly and moderately related but not totally substitutable. Subsequent moderator analyses revealed that when objective and subjective measures tapped the same construct, their convergent validity improved substantially and that the measures were reasonably substitutable, a finding that is not surprising. Their discussion is valuable in that they summarize arguments that differences between these two types of measurement may not be as distinctive as once believed (e.g. there is subjectivity in the choice of objective measures and metrics). Likewise, Harris et al (1995) examined the psychometric properties of performance ratings collected for research versus administrative purposes. They found that administrative-based ratings were more lenient, that ratings obtained only for research purposes demonstrated significant correlations with a predictor, and that the two types of ratings were substantially correlated with each other (0.58). Gottfredson (1991) outlined factors to be used to evaluate the equivalence of alternative measures of performance: validity, reliability, susceptibility to compromise (i.e. changes in validity or reliability with extensive use), financial cost, and acceptability to interested parties. This article represents an excellent summary of various psychometric and theoretical issues in assessing the equivalence or nonequivalence of criterion measures.

A discussion of the relative costs of alternative performance measures was provided by Stone et al (1996). As an alternative to a more expensive "handson" performance measure, a low-cost, readily available measure of performance was developed for Air Force specialty jobs using an existing data base that rank-ordered individuals. More research is needed to explore the relative advantages of low-fidelity and low-cost performance measures. Conceivably the relative value of such instruments might be better than more highly specific, high-fidelity instruments if relatively molar decisions are being made about individuals (e.g. promote versus not-promote, high versus low performance). A paper by Yang et al (1996) addressed this concern. They described substituting a low-cost proxy criterion measure for a higher-cost criterion measure to illuminate that such a strategy can pay off when evaluating training programs.

Absenteeism as a criterion measure continues to be the subject of research. Johns (1994) examined the psychometric properties and theoretical perspectives for self-reported absence measures as well as the possibilities of bias in such measures due to common measurement error or distortions due to memory, for example. He provided a number of recommendations for measuring and using self-reports of absence. Likewise, Harrison & Shaffer (1994) examined biases in self-reports of absences and suggested the presence of an underreporting bias when describing oneself and an over-reporting bias when describing perceived norms or others.

Kulick & Ambrose (1993) reported a study comparing performance ratings given for secretarial performance observed under videotaped conditions as well as when typing performance data were delivered in a computerized summary format. Results showed that when evaluating performance, subjects used visual sources of information, but the computerized data were used only when evaluating typing performance. The authors suggested that different processing strategies are used when viewing performance presented via these different modalities. Future research might focus more on potential differential processing and evaluations that could occur as a result of using computer-delivered performance information.

Rating accuracy and rating error

A number of recent studies have examined a number of different variables and processes relating to the accuracy of performance ratings. Several studies have examined the role of affect in performance appraisal. Many studies in this area have focused on the potential biases that may occur when a supervisor likes or dislikes a subordinate (see Cardy & Dobbins 1994 for a review). However, more recent studies of affect and rating have suggested that affective influences on ratings may not represent rating biases. In a well-designed laboratory study, Robbins & DeNisi (1994) showed how affect toward ratees can influence the acquisition and processing of performance information. However, they argued that affect is likely to be a function of how well or poorly a person performs his or her job and is therefore more likely to represent a valid piece of information than an irrelevant source of bias. In a subsequent field study, Varma et al (1996) presented evidence consistent with this argument. Likewise, Ferris et al (1994) proposed a model wherein supervisors' affect toward subordinates was a major influence of rated performance. They tested their model using a sample of 95 staff nurses and 28 nurse supervisors and found a good fit; supervisors' affect toward subordinates correlated 0.74 with performance ratings.

Sanchez & De La Torre (1996) explored the influence of accuracy of memories on the accuracy of ratings of ratee's strengths and weaknesses. Not surprisingly, results show that the accuracy of dimensional ratings are a function of the accuracy of memories. In contrast, their results also show that overall holistic ratings are not related to the accuracy of memories. They suggest that raters overcome memory loss over time by relying on their on-line impressions when forming holistic or overall ratings. Kinicki et al (1995) explored the impact of activating performance prototypes (by giving raters prototypical trait adjectives of effective and ineffective performers) and found that such priming minimally affected ratings of videotaped performance, regardless of whether ratings were made immediately or under a delayed condition. A priming effect was observed when using pencil-and-paper vignettes as opposed to more richly embedded stimuli using videotape methods.

Ryan et al (1995) also investigated the impact of using videotaped performance (in an assessment center context) on rating accuracy and concluded that viewing performance through a videotape modality rather than directly does not affect the accuracy of ratings. Using in-basket and videotape methods to present stimulus information about ratees, Mero & Motowidlo (1995) showed that raters are more accurate in their ratings when they are made to feel accountable by having to justify their evaluations.

In perhaps the only field study investigating the impact of cognitive processes on performance evaluations. DeNisi & Peters (1996) showed that structuring diary-keeping and recall methods helped in terms of recalling information, differentiating among ratees, and generating more positive reactions to the appraisal process. The use of a field study to investigate these issues is very encouraging. However, no direct measurement of the proposed cognitive processes was undertaken in this study.

Some other studies have investigated more traditional rater error topics even though the topic is now thought to be not as important as it was in the past. Murphy et al (1993) reviewed the definitions of rater halo error and noted that the major conceptions about this construct are either wrong or problematic. Their review of the evidence is that halo error is not pervasive, that inflated correlations among rating dimensions are not the norm, and that there are a number of contextual factors that influence when halo might be observed. However, Lance et al (1994) tested the notion that the type of halo that occurs varies as a function of rating context and found that halo is best considered as a unitary phenomenon and should be defined as the influence of a rater's general impression on ratings of specific ratee qualities. Kane (1994) developed a model of the determinants of rater error, hypothesizing that such error has conscious antecedents where raters make decisions to introduce distortion into ratings. The model he developed draws upon subjective expected utility concepts where raters evaluate the relative utility of rating accurately and rating inaccurately, and the probability of being detected for giving inaccurate ratings. No empirical data are presented to substantiate this model, however.

Sumer & Knight (1996) examined the impact of rating previous performance on ratings of subsequent performance from the framework of contrast effects (inappropriate high or low ratings because of prior evaluations). Their findings showed that individuals who reviewed but did not rate the previous performance demonstrated an assimilation effect by rating a second rating in the direction of the previous performance. In addition, individuals who reviewed and actually rated the previous performance engaged in a contrast effect by rating the second performance away from the direction of the previous performance. However, the effect sizes for the main and interaction effects were low. Maurer et al (1993) also investigated contrast effects and showed that the use of checklists and diaries did not reduce potential contrast effects and may even strengthen such effects.

Woehr & Roch (1996) examined the impact of prior evaluations that varied in terms of performance level and ratee gender on subsequent evaluations and on recall of either a male or female of average performance. Results showed that both the performance level and the gender of the target ratee's prior evaluation influenced the subsequent rating. Relatively low performance for the prior target influenced subsequent evaluations differentially for male and female target ratees such that males were given relatively higher evaluations than females. Thus, recent research confirms complex interactions in the rating environment that influence performance ratings.

Schrader & Steiner (1996) reported the results of a study where they investigated the impact of different comparison standards on the ratings of supervisors and on self-ratings. They hypothesized that ratings in which employees are evaluated against clear and specific objective standards will differ from those in which such objective criteria are not specified and the standards are ambiguous. Results supported this proposition. However, ratings made when using internal, relative, or multiple standards of comparison were not terribly different from those made under the more objective conditions both in terms of mean differences and supervisor-self agreement. Thus, a conclusion that employee standards that involve objective and specific standards against which to evaluate individuals are the one "best" method seems premature given the results of this study. A potential problem with this study is that it involves dimensions of performance that lend themselves to precise and objective measurement, a condition that does not generalize to many dimensions of job performance.

Performance ratings as a function of rater source

Several recent investigations have focused on relative differences in performance ratings generated by groups compared with ratings generated by individuals. This topic is important given the contemporary trend toward the use of teams and groups in organizational settings. Using experimental laboratory methods and students as subjects, Jourden & Heath (1996) showed that after completing a task, most individuals ranked their own performance below the median (a negative performance illusion), whereas most group members ranked their group performance above the median (a positive performance illusion), contradicting previous research showing a positive illusion for both individuals and group members. The authors labeled the differences between group and individual perceptions of performance as the "evaluation gap."

Martell & Borg (1993) examined the relative accuracy of having individuals or groups of individuals provide ratings on a behavioral checklist after reviewing a pencil-and-paper vignette depicting the work behavior of a police officer. Ratings were made either immediately or after a five-day delay. Results showed that groups remembered more accurately than individuals under a delayed condition, but no differences were observed when ratings were made immediately. They argued that using groups to provide ratings may be a help but not a panacea for dealing with rating accuracy. Research is just starting to examine the issue of group versus individual rating sources. Before we progress too much further, it might be wise to develop more theoretical specifications of when and why groups may provide more accurate evaluations of performance.

The use of peers as sources of ratings continues to he investigated. Saavedra & Kwun (1993) showed, in a laboratory context, that peer evaluations in self-managed work groups are conditional on self-other comparisons. Individuals who were outstanding contributors tended to be the most discerning evaluators when evaluating their peers. Borman et al (1995) showed that peers and supervisors differed slightly with regard to the different sources of information they use in providing performance ratings of US soldiers.

Self-ratings were examined by Yu & Murphy (1993) across several samples in China. As typically found in Western research, Chinese workers showed leniency effects in their self-ratings, contradicting earlier results demonstrating that Chinese workers would produce modesty bias or self-rate themselves lower than their peers or supervisors.

There is a substantial increase of interest lately in so-called "360-degree" performance measures. Such measures incorporate evaluations from a number of different rater perspectives—supervisor, peer, subordinate, self, and even customers—and are used for feedback and/or personnel decisions. London & Smither (1995) developed a model and propositions regarding the impact of such a multisource system on perceptions of goal accomplishment, reevaluation of self-image, and changes in performance-related outcomes (i.e. goals, development, behavior, and subsequent performance). These authors also articulated a number of potential moderators of the major components of the model.

An excellent starting point in terms of becoming aware of 360-degree instruments and systems is a special issue of *Human Resource Management* (Tornow 1993). Included in this issue is a cluster of articles focusing on understanding the relationship between the self and other ratings (Nilsen & Campbell 1993, Van Velsor et al 1993, Yammarino & Atwater 1993), a cluster focusing on improving the value of others' feedback, and a final cluster dealing with the impact of 360-degree feedback as a management intervention.

Antonioni (1994) presented the results of a field study using 38 managers and their subordinates and showed that subordinates preferred providing appraisal feedback to their managers anonymously. However, managers viewed upward appraisals more positively when such feedback was provided under conditions of accountability or when they were aware of the identity of the subordinates. Under conditions of accountability, subordinates tended to inflate their rating of managers, suggesting that ratee identification may influence such feedback information.

Rating fairness and bias issues

The topic of subgroup differences on performance ratings is an important one. However, the topic has received only modest attention recently, especially given the persistent finding that subgroups receive systematically different scores on a variety of performance measures. Past literature has established that racial differences in performance persistently are found. For example, Ford et al (1986) conducted a meta-analysis across 53 studies, showing that blacks receive slightly lower performance scores than whites on both subjective and objective measures (the corrected point biserial correlations were respectively .209 and .204). Studying a sample of supermarket cashiers, DuBois et al (1993) showed that black-white ratee differences also were significant. The evaluations favored whites on four different performance criteria that reflected two separate performance domains (accuracy and speed) as well as measures of "typical" performance (using computer-monitored operational measures) and "maximum" performance (using work sample tests). These differences were less extreme on the measures of maximum performance.

Kraiger & Ford (1985) conducted a meta-analysis of 74 studies across field and laboratory settings and concluded that an interaction effect existed: White raters rate white ratees higher than black ratees, whereas black raters evaluated black ratees higher than white ratees. Moderator effects were found also for group composition and research setting: Effect sizes increased as the proportion of blacks in the group decreased, and field studies generated larger effect sizes than laboratory studies. Pulakos et al (1989) examined performance ratings for racial differences using a military sample of 8642 enlisted personnel as rating targets. Both between-subjects and within-subjects (where each ratee was evaluated by both a black and white rater and therefore performance is held constant) designs were used. While statistical differences were observed, the amount of variance accounted for by race effects (main and interactions) was quite small across both within- and between-subjects analyses. These authors interpreted their data as being at odds with Kraiger & Ford (1985) but suggested that the military sample was not representative of the larger population.

Sackett & DuBois (1991) represents perhaps the most contemporary investigation of this topic. They challenge the conclusion that raters generally give more favorable ratings to members of their own race. Using a civilian sample of over 36,000 individuals in 174 jobs, and using again a between- and within-subjects design, they showed black employees to be rated lower by both black and white raters, but the difference between black and white ratees was not as great for black ratees as for white ratees. Comparisons were made between the Pulakos et al (1989) military study and the Kraiger & Ford (1985) meta-analysis. Sackett & DuBois found great similarities between their results and those found in the military studies, but both their results and the data from the Pulakos et al (1989) were at odds with the meta-analytic study conducted by Kaiger & Ford (1985). The conclusion that black raters rate black ratees higher than they rate white ratees was not confirmed by either the civilian or the military studies. They suggest that the differences between these two conclusions rest in that the Kraiger & Ford (1985) study involved a limited sample size and that the observed effect was limited to laboratory studies using peer and student samples.

Oppler et al (1992) noted that differences observed between black and white ratees in performance do not necessarily imply bias; such differences could reflect actual and true differences between such samples. One method to tease out whether such differentials reflect bias is to attempt to control for as many job-relevant variables as possible. After controlling for a number of non-rated variables (i.e. Awards and Letters, Disciplinary Actions, Training Achievement), the differences between black and white ratees as rated by supervisors diminished but did not disappear.

Age-performance relationships, a popular topic of past research, has not received much attention within the past few years. Waldman & Avolio (1986) reviewed 40 samples using meta-analytic methods and found that age was significantly positively correlated (mean $r = .27$) with measures of productivity (i.e. unit output over time, number of patents) but negatively correlated with supervisory ratings (mean $r = -.14$). There was some evidence that job type moderated the relationships observed; performance ratings showed more positive relationships with age for professionals compared with nonprofessionals.

A more recent meta-analysis of the age-performance relationship including 96 independent studies was reported by McEvoy & Cascio (1989). Their meta-analysis showed that age and performance generally were unrelated. No evidence was found for moderators of the relationship, either by job type or type of performance measure.

The relationship between gender and performance has received little recent investigation. One exception is the study by Pulakos et al (1989), cited above, which found that males were rated significantly higher than females by peers. However, this difference was not observed for supervisors. All main and interactive effects associated with rater and ratee gender on performance ratings were small, accounting for a minimal amount of rating variance. The study noted earlier by Woehr & Roch (1996) showed that females tend to receive relatively lower ratings compared with males when being rated after the evaluation of a low-performing ratee (either male or female). One hypothesis sometimes put forth to explain why groups might differ is that the antecedents of job performance may not be the same for men and women, or for members of different racial or ethnic groups. Pulakos et al (1996) tested this hypothesis using structural modeling, and their data suggest that the antecedents of performance are similar across gender and racial groups.

The issue of whether rating type or format has anything to do with differential ratings given to racial minorities, women, or older employees is explored in an excellent review by Bernardin et al (1995). They observed that "expert witnesses" working for plaintiffs in discrimination cases often testify that age, race, or gender bias in performance ratings is due to the use of performance-appraisal systems that are too subjective or insufficiently specific. Their review makes it clear that there is no scientific support for the opinion that the format or specificity of appraisal systems has a significant effect on race or gender bias in performance ratings. They note that an "expert" who wishes to link bias or discrimination to specific characteristics of performance appraisal systems will be hard pressed to provide firm scientific support for such testimony.

Traditional treatments of the relative fairness of performance ratings and appraisal systems focus on whether subgroups differ significantly and meaningfully on performance ratings themselves. However, consistent with contemporary treatments of fairness in selection contexts (Arvey & Sackett 1993), researchers are beginning to examine the relative fairness of the appraisal process itself via concepts of due-process and procedural justice. Folger et al (1992) developed three characteristics of a due-process appraisal system. The first is that "adequate notice" be given such that employing organizations publish, distribute, and explain performance evaluation standards and processes. The second is that a "fair hearing" should be provided with a formal review meeting in which an employee is informed of his/her evaluation. A third characteristic is that raters apply performance standards consistently across employees, without distortion by external pressure, corruption, or personal biases ("judgment based on evidence").

Taylor et al (1995) described the results of a study where a performance-appraisal system was designed to ensure that due-process components were embedded in the evaluation processes. Their methodology involved randomly assigning employee–manager pairs to train for and implement the due-process system or to continue using the appraisal system as it was. Results showed that those employees evaluated by managers trained in the due-process system displayed significantly more favorable reactions along a variety of measures (e.g. perceived system fairness, appraisal accuracy, attitudes toward the system). An interesting finding was that the due-process employees received significantly lower evaluations than control employees, suggesting that such an intervention might be helpful in controlling rating inflation.

Other research has focused on the attitudes resulting from the appraisal process. Dickinson (1993) provided a nice review of this research showing that a number of appraisal variables can influence the opinions and attitudes about the fairness, accuracy, and acceptability of appraisal ratings.

Performance evaluation training

Recent research has examined the impact of "frame of reference" (FOR) training on rating outcomes and processes. The primary goal of FOR training is to train raters to share and use common conceptualizations of performance when making evaluations (Woehr 1994). Woehr & Huffcutt (1994) found an average effect size of .83 for studies comparing FOR training with control or no training on the dependent variables of rating accuracy. They concluded that FOR-trained raters typically provide substantially more accurate ratings than do untrained raters. Along these lines, Stamoulis & Hauenstein (1993), investigating FOR training for raters evaluating the performance of job interviewers, found such training to be more effective in terms of some types of rater accuracy than others.

Several recent studies have explored the mechanics of why FOR training improves rater accuracy. Woehr & Feldman (1993) articulated an information-processing model where they suggested that rating are based on both memory and contextual factors. Their study showed that performance accuracy and recall depend on the instructional set given to ratees (i.e. learning versus evaluating) as well as the order in which the evaluation and recall tasks were elicited. In a follow-up study, Woehr (1994) again hypothesized that FOR training will be used by raters as the basis of information processing in the evaluation process and will be demonstrated through improved ratings using different indices of accuracy (i.e. differential elevation, differential accuracy) as dependent variables.

Day & Sulsky (1995) examined the accuracy of ratings after FOR training under various time delays, hypothesizing that different types of accuracy (differential accuracy, distance accuracy) and recall would be better or worse under various time delays based on the notion that raters who receive FOR training will be more capable of correctly categorizing ratees on various performance dimensions even when specific information is forgotten. Some support for the hypotheses was found, but the experiment did not involve direct assessment of any categorization process among raters. They also examined whether the manner in which performance information was presented to subjects (i.e. blocked by person versus some unpredictable mixture of information) might moderate the beneficial impact of FOR training. Support for the moderating hypothesis was not found; instead, both FOR training and the manner in which the performance information was presented exhibited main effects on performance-rating accuracy.

Somewhat noticeable across these FOR studies is that little attempt is made to measure directly the information processing that hypothetically goes on as a result of such training. We also worry that research exploring the impact of training tends to use similar stimulus materials (e.g. standard videotapes of performance) and generally to use students as subjects. Thus, research in this area seems to have limited generalizability across jobs and subjects.

Attaching value to employees: utility assessment

The third broad area of performance-evaluation research focuses on utility analysis. In its most basic form, Brogden's model for estimating utility used linear regression both to forecast future performance and to attach specific values to that performance, using an equation similar to:

$$\text{Predicted value} = (rxy \times Zx \times SD_y) - C,$$

where rxy refers to the validity of the intervention, or the relationship between the intervention and the criterion; Zx refers to the "score" (in z-score form) that an individual receives on the intervention (e.g. test score, whether an individual receives training); SD_y refers to the variability of the criterion (typically in dollar terms); and C refers to the cost, per person, of implementing the intervention. Thus, the results of a utility analysis provide an estimate of the relative benefits over costs of a planned intervention.

A great deal of recent research reflects elaborations on this model. Boudreau (1991) reviewed the increasing complexity and sophistication of utility models that have built on the equation shown above. Adjustments have been proposed to (*a*) take into account a variety of financial parameters (Cascio 1991, 1993); (*b*) include a wider range of costs (e.g. recruiting costs; see Law & Myors 1993, Martin & Raju 1992) and a more realistic assessment of benefits [e.g. relatively lower performance and higher turnover during probationary periods

(De Corte 1994)]; (c) appropriately take into account range restriction (Raju et al 1995); (d) reflect uncertainties in the forecasting process (e.g. rejected job offers, Murphy 1986); and (e) integrate the effects of both recruitment and selection strategies on the quality of the set of individuals who eventually occupy jobs (De Corte 1996). Most discussions of utility analysis have focused on selection testing, but Klaas & McClendon (1996) demonstrated the application of these techniques in evaluating pay policies.

A long-standing barrier to implementing utility analysis has been the difficulty in estimating the dollar value of the variability in job performance (i.e. SD_y). Schmidt et al (1979) proposed a method of obtaining direct estimates by supervisors of the value of employees performing at different levels and showed how this might be used to estimate SD_y. The validity and meaning of such direct estimates of employee value have been examined in detail in numerous studies (for reviews of utility analysis, see Bobko et al 1987, Vance & Colella 1990), and debate still rages concerning the accuracy of SD_y estimates. For example, Judiesch et al (1992) suggested that supervisory estimates of SD_y are downwardly biased, but they also claimed that estimates of the coefficient of variation (i.e. ratio of SD_y to the mean of the performance value distribution) are not seriously biased and may be preferable to direct SD_y estimates. Becker & Huselid (1992) also suggested that traditional procedures underestimate SD_y and illustrated the use of organizational productivity indices in estimating utility.

Recent research on the accuracy of SD_y estimates does not yield clear conclusions about which procedure is best or about which type of estimate is most trustworthy, but it has shed some light on the processes involved in judging the value of employees. Most notably, estimates of the value of employee performance appear to be strongly related to salary levels. Judiesch et al (1992) noted that when supervisors are asked to judge the value of an average employee, these estimates are very close to the average wage for that job. SD_y estimates obtained from supervisory judgments are typically 40–70% as large as mean salaries. One possibility is that judgments of the value of employees are themselves based on salary (Bobko et al 1987). That is, an employee who receives substantial rewards is likely to be judged to be worth more than another who receives lower rewards. However, Roth et al (1994) found factors other than salary (e.g. output levels, initiative) to be the most critical determinants of perceived worth.

Cesare et al (1994) examined a number of factors that may affect these estimates of the value of an employee to an organization and showed what appears to be a very global bias. Estimates of the value of employees to the organization appear to be very closely tied to the supervisor's estimate of his or her own value to the organization (in estimating value of average performer, correlation between self-worth and employee worth is above 0.90). Thus, while job-oriented factors such as skills, personal qualities of subordinates, and job characteristics are rated as being important in evaluating worth, evaluations of one's own worth to the organization may be a critical anchor.

Boudreau et al (1994) suggested that the meaning of utility estimates is often unclear because of a failure to adequately identify and measure the criterion variable Y. In particular, these authors noted that the criteria of interest in utility analyses are usually complex and multivariate but that the analyses themselves are usually simple and univariate. Earlier, we noted that discussions of the construct of job performance have broadened considerably, with a general recognition that both core task proficiency and contextual performance represent critical aspects of job performance. To date, few studies of utility have incorporated this perspective. Most studies instead focus almost exclusively on the correlation between tests, intervention, and the like, and measures of core task performance.

Boudreau et al (1994) suggested that very different conclusions about the utility of various tests and interventions might be reached if a broader conception of the performance domain is adopted. Murphy & Shiarella (1996) presented evidence from a simulation study that supports this suggestion. Their study examined the validity and utility of a selection test battery for predicting a multidimensional criterion, using the two-facet model discussed earlier to characterize the criterion space (i.e. job performance is assumed to represent a composite of task and contextual performance). They showed that both validity and utility could vary considerably, depending on the relative emphasis given to individual- versus group-oriented facets of the criterion domain.

Raju et al (1990) and Becker & Huselid (1992) presented alternative approaches for addressing the criterion problem in utility analysis. Raju et al (1990) suggested that the relationship between performance evaluations and an employee's value to the organization is linear, and they presented a method for directly estimating value without any separate estimate of troublesome parameters such as SD_y, in effect bypassing the criterion problem. This suggestion has received some criticism (Judiesch et al 1993; for a reply, see Raju et al 1993). Becker & Huselid (1992) took another approach, suggesting that utility analyses should be based on organizational-level indices (e.g. overall firm performance) rather than on unreliable estimates of individual-level performance.

Macan & Highhouse (1994) documented the use of utility analysis by human resource specialists, and noted that the dollar metric favored by researchers in this area is not the only useful one; Vance & Colella (1990) made a similar suggestion. However, Latham & Whyte (1994) cautioned that utility analysis may not be useful or credible to managers. In a carefully designed study, they showed that presenting dollar-value utility estimates could *lower* managers' willingness to adopt an intervention.

The sheer volume of research and debate on the estimation of SD_y might suggest that this is a critically important parameter. There are reasons to believe that it is not. First, as noted above, practitioners do not always use a dollar metric for communicating their utility estimates, and when they do, those figures do not seem convincing or credible to managers. Second, as Murphy & Cleveland (1991, 1995) have noted, the scaling of utility estimates rarely has any impact on actual decisions. For example, if an organization is choosing between two different testing programs, it does not matter if utility estimates are phrased in terms of dollars, units of productivity, or completely arbitrary units. The dollar metric is useful if and only if all costs and benefits of each of the options being considered can be accurately scaled in terms of dollars. Rather than focusing so much attention on the estimation of SD_y, we suggest that utility researchers should focus on understanding exactly what Y represents. We expect that future research on utility will feature multivariate rather than univariate models and will take advantage of our growing understanding of the domain of job performance to create more realistic estimates of the impact of tests, interventions, etc, on an organization's effectiveness.

Observations and summary

This review suggests that research on performance evaluation is alive and well in the psychological and management literatures. Our review of recent (and some past) literatures suggests that research is progressing in traditional content areas as well as exploring new ground. Perhaps the most exciting areas of research are the development and elaboration around the notion of contextual aspects of job performance. The notion that job performance is more than just the execution of specific tasks and that it involves a wide variety of organizational activities has important implications for the understanding and measurement of job performance. Such a focus will result in a greater likelihood that performance will be more predictable within job contexts through the use of a larger number of predictor vehicles tapping different constructs. Perhaps a larger trend is the tendency to view performance evaluation in a broader context, in general. One thought here is that ultimately the effects of contextual variables will be observed through their interactions with the rater who ultimately provides an evaluation of performance.

Much progress has been made in terms of delineating broad taxonomies of job performance that cut across most, if not all, jobs. Such a trend will almost surely enhance our understanding of job performance. We note, however, that for practical purposes, organizations will perhaps continue to need more narrow and job-focused measures of performance, often for legal defense purposes as well as to help to provide feedback to employees. It is also true that organizations have very practical needs to limit the costs of measurement and to provide instrumentation that provides for the assessment of performance in terms of broader domains and fluid aspects of performance due to rapidly changing work roles, assignments, etc. The movement toward broader measurement is perhaps consistent with this reality; perhaps there will he more convergence between the research and practitioner domains in the future.

We also find a trend in terms of an increased optimism regarding the use of supervisory ratings and other "subjective" appraisal instruments and formats. There is increased recognition that subjectivity does not automatically translate into rater error or bias and that ratings are most likely valid reflections of true performance and represent a low-cost mechanism for evaluating employees. The notion that performance evaluations and particularly supervisory ratings of performance are biased against racial and gender groups is simply not supported by the empirical data. Such differentials, when exhibited, are typically small and are as likely to be a reflection of true differences as they are to be indications of bias in performance appraisals. This optimism is shared by others as well (e.g. Cardy, as cited in Church 1995).

A similar observation might be made in terms of how contemporary researchers view rater "error;" the trend is not to view such variances and discrepancies as error but true variance that can be traced to a variety of different sources. Thus, such concepts as contrast error, central tendency, halo, etc, which occupied so much research space, are thought to be relatively unimportant, trivial, and due to understandable factors.

We are pleased to see additional progress with regard to utility components of performance estimation, and it is likely that we will see more of this. Efforts to model complex and multidimensional performance patterns that are nonlinear in nature are emerging and will likely receive greater attention in the next few years.

Acknowledgments

We thank the following individuals for their input and help during the various phases in writing this paper: Paul Sackett, Fred Oswald, Melissa Gruys, Sarah Hustis, Maria Rotundo, Jill Ellingson, Tim Tandon, Walter Borman, Frank Landy, George Thornton, Mike Campion, and Jan Cleveland.

Literature cited

Anderson N, Herriot P. eds. 1994. *Assessment and Selection in Organizations: Methods and Practice for Recruitment and Appraisal.* New York: Wiley

Antonioni D. 1994. The effects of feedback accountability on upward appraisal ratings. *Pers. Psychol.* 47:349–56

Arvey RD. 1986. General ability in employment: a discussion. *J. Vocat. Behav.* 29:415–20

Arvey RD, Renz G, Watson T. 1997. Individual differences in emotionality as predictors of job performance. In *Research in Personnel and Human Resources Management*, eds. GR Ferris, KM Rowland, Vol. 15. Greenwich, CT: JAI. In press

Arvey RD, Sackett PR. 1993. Fairness in selection: current developments and perspectives. See Schmitt et al. 1993, pp. 171–202

Austin JT, Villanova P. 1992. The criterion problem: 1917–1992. *J. Appl. Psychol.* 77(6):836–74

Banks CG, Murphy KR. 1985. Toward narrowing the research-practice gap in performance appraisal. *Pers. Psychol.* 38(2):335–45

Becker BE, Huselid MA. 1992. Direct estimates of SD_y and the implications for utility analysis. *J. Appl. Psychol.* 77(3):227–33

Bernardin HJ, Beatty RW. 1984. *Performance Appraisal: Assessing Human Behavior at Work.* Boston: Kent

Bernardin HJ, Hennessey HW Jr, Peyrefitte J. 1995. Age, racial, and gender bias as a function of criterion specificity: a test of expert testimony. *Hum. Resour. Manage. Rev.* 5(1):63–77

Bobko P, Colella A. 1994. Employee reactions to performance standards: a review and research propositions. *Pers. Psychol.* 47(1):1–29

Bobko P, Karren R, Kerkar SP. 1987. Systematic research needs for understanding supervisory-based estimates of SDy in utility analysis. *Organ. Behav. Hum. Decis. Process.* 40(1):69–95

Bommer WH, Johnson JL, Rich GA, Podsakoff PM, MacKenzie SB. 1995. On the interchangeability of objective and subjective measures of employee performance: a meta-analysis. *Pers. Psychol.* 48(3):587–605

Borman WC, Brush DH. 1993. More progress toward a taxonomy of managerial performance requirements. *Hum. Perform.* 6(1):1–21

Borman WC, Hanson M, Hedge J. 1997. Personnel selection. *Annu. Rev. Psychol.* 48: 299–337

Borman WC, Motowidlo SJ. 1993. Expanding the criterion domain to include elements of contextual performance. See Schmitt et al. 1993, pp. 71–98

Borman WC, White LA, Dorsey DW. 1995. Effects of ratee task performance and interpersonal factors on supervisor and peer performance ratings. *J. Appl. Psychol.* 80(1):168–77

Boudreau JW. 1991. Utility analysis for decisions in human resource management. See Dunnette & Hough 1991, pp. 621–745

Boudreau JW, Sturman MC, Judge TA. 1994. Utility analysis: What are the black boxes, and do they affect decisions? See Anderson & Herriot 1994, pp. 77–96

Bretz RD, Milkovich GT, Read W. 1992. The current state of performance appraisal research and practice: concerns, directions, and implications. *J. Manage.* 18(2):321–52

Brief AP, Motowidlo SJ. 1986. Prosocial organizational behaviors. *Acad. Manage. Rev.* 10:710–25

Brogden HE. 1949. When testing pays off. *Pers. Psychol.* 2:171–83

Campbell JP, Gasser MB, Oswald FL. 1996. The substantive nature of job performance variability. In *Individual Differences and Behavior in Organizations*, ed. KR Murphy, pp. 258–99. San Francisco: Jossey-Bass

Campbell JP, McCloy RA, Oppler SH, Sager CE. 1993. A theory of performance. See Schmitt et al 1993, pp. 35–70

Cardy RL, Dobbins GH. 1994. *Performance Appraisal: Alternative Perspectives.* Cincinnati, OH: Southwest

Cascio WF. 1991. *Costing Human Resources: The Financial Impact of Behavior in Organizations.* Boston: Kent. 3rd ed.

Cascio WF. 1993. Assessing the utility of selection decisions: theoretical and practical considerations. See Schmitt et al 1993, pp. 310–40

Cascio WF. 1995. Whither industrial and organizational psychology in a changing world of work? *Am. Psychol.* 50(11):928–39

Cascio WF, Bernardin HJ. 1984. Implications of performance appraisal litigation for personnel decisions. *Pers. Psvchol.* 34(2):211–26

Cesare SJ, Blankenship MH, Giuannetto PW. 1994. A dual focus of SD$_y$ estimations: a test of the linearity assumption and multivariate application. *Hum. Perform.* 7(4):235–55

Chemers MM, Oskamp S, Costanzo MA, eds. 1995. *Diversity in Organizations: New Perspectives for a Changing Workplace.* Thousand Oaks, CA: Sage

Church AH. 1995. Performance appraisal: practical tools or effective measures. *Ind. Organ. Psychol.* 33(2):57–64

Cleveland JN, Murphy KR. 1992. Analyzing performance appraisal as goal-directed behavior. In *Research in Personnel and Human Resources Management*, eds. GR Ferris, KM Rowland, Vol. 10, pp. 121–85. Greenwich, CT: JAI

Conway JM. 1996. Analysis and design of multitrait-multirater performance appraisal studies. *J. Manage.* 22(1):139–62

Cronbach LJ, Gleser GC. 1965. *Psychological Tests and Personnel Decisions.* Urbana: Univ. Ill. Press. 2nd ed.

Day DV, Silverman SB. 1989. Personality and job performance: evidence of incremental validity. *Pers. Psychol.* 42(1):25–36

Day DV, Sulsky LM. 1995. Effects of frame-of-reference training and information configuration on memory organization and rating accuracy. *J. Appl. Psychol.* 80(1):158–67

De Corte W. 1994. Utility analysis for the one-cohort selection-retention decision with a probationary period. *J. Appl. Psychol.* 79(3):402–11

De Corte W. 1996. Recruitment and retention decisions that maximize the utility of a probationary selection to obtain a fixed quota of successful selectees. *Pers. Psychol.* 49(2):399–428

DeNisi AS, 1997. *A Cognitive Approach to Performance Appraisal: A Program of Research.* London: Routledge. In press

DeNisi AS, Peters LH. 1996. Organization of information in memory and the performance appraisal process: Evidence from the field. *J. Appl. Psychol.* 81(6):717–37

Dickinson TL. 1993. Attitudes about performance appraisal. In *Personnel Selection and Assessment: Individual and Organizational Perspectives*, eds. H Schuler, JL Farr, M Smith, pp. 141–62. Hillsdale, NJ: Erlbaum

DuBois CL, Sackett PR, Zedeck S, Fogli L. 1993. Further exploration of typical and maximum performance criteria: definitional issues, prediction, and white-black differences. *J. Appl Psychol.* 78(2):205–11

Dunnette MD, Hough LM, eds. 1991. *Handbook of Industrial and Organizational Psychology*, Vol. 2. Palo Alto, CA: Consult. Psychol. Press. 2nd ed.

Dunnette MD, Hough LM, eds. 1992. *Handbook of Industrial and Organizational Psychology*, Vol. 3. Palo Alto, CA: Consult. Psychol. Press. 2nd ed.

Feild HS, Holley WH. 1982. The relationship of performance appraisal system characteristics to verdicts in selected employment discrimination cases. *Acad. Manage. J.* 25(2):392–406

Feldman JM. 1981. Beyond attribution theory: cognitive processes in performance appraisal. *J. Appl. Psychol.* 66(2):127–48

Ferris GR, Judge TA, Rowland KM, Fitzgibbons DE. 1994. Subordinate influence and the performance evaluation process: test of a model. *Organ. Behav. Hum. Decis. Process.* 58:101–35

Fletcher C. 1994. Performance appraisal in context: organizational changes and their impact on practice. See Anderson & Herriot 1994, pp. 41–55

Fletcher C. 1995. New directions for performance appraisal: some findings and observations. *Int. J. Select. Assess.* 3(3):191–201

Folger R, Konovsky MA, Cropanzano R. 1992. A due process metaphor for performance appraisal. In *Research in Organizational Behavior*, eds. BM Staw, LL Cummings, Vol. 14, pp. 129–77. Greenwich, CT: JAI

Ford JK, Kraiger K, Schechtman SL. 1986. Study of race effects in objective indices and subjective evaluations of performance: a meta-analysis of performance criteria. *Psychol. Bull.* 99(3):330–37

Ganzach Y. 1995. Negativity (and positivity) in performance evaluation: three field studies. *J. Appl. Psychol.* 80(4):491–99

George RA, Brief AP. 1992. Feeling good-doing good: a conceptual analysis of the mood at work-organizational spontaneity relationship. *Psychol. Bull.* 112(2):310–29

Gerbart B, Milkovich GT. 1992. Employee compensation: research and practice. See Dunnette & Hough 1992, pp. 481–569

Gottfredson LS. 1991. The evaluation of alternative measures of job performance. In *Performance Assessment for the Workplace, Tech. Issues*, eds. AK Wigdor, BF Green Jr. Vol. 2, pp. 75–126. Washington, DC: Natl. Acad. Sci.

Guion RM, Gibson WM. 1988. Personnel selection and placement. *Annu. Rev. Psychol.* 37:349–74

Guzzo RA, Dickson MW. 1996. Teams in organizations: recent research on performance and effectiveness. *Annu. Rev. Psychol.* 47:307–38

Harris MM, Smith DE, Champagne D. 1995. A field study of performance appraisal purpose: research versus administrative-based ratings. *Pers. Psychol.* 48(1):151–60

Harrison DA, Shaffer MA. 1994. Comparative examinations of self-reports and perceived absenteeism norms: wading through Lake Wobegon. *J. Appl. Psychol.* 79(2):240–51

Hedge JW, Borman WC. 1995. Changing conceptions and practices in performance appraisal. In *The Changing Nature of Work*, ed. A Howard, pp. 451–81. San Francisco: Jossey-Bass

Hofmann DA, Jacobs R, Baratta JE. 1993. Dynamic criteria and the measurement of change. *J. Appl. Psychol.* 78(2):194–204

Hunt S. 1996. Generic work behavior: an investigation into the dimensions of entry-level, hourly job performance. *Pers. Psychol.* 49(1):51–83

Ilgen DR, Barnes-Farrell JL, McKellin DB. 1993. Performance appraisal process research in the 1980s: What has it contributed to appraisals in use? *Organ. Behav. Hum. Decis. Process.* 54(3):321–68

Ilgen DR, Holienbeck JR. 1991. The structure of work: job design and roles. See Dunnette & Hough 1991, pp. 165–207

Jackson SE, Ruderman MN. 1995. *Diversity in Work Teams: Research Paradigms for a Changing Workplace*. Washington, DC: Am. Psychol. Assoc.

Johns G. 1994. How often were you absent? A review of the use of self-reported absence data. *J. Appl. Psychol.* 79(4):574–91

Jourden FJ, Heath C. 1996. The evaluation gap in performance perceptions: illusory perceptions of groups and individuals. *J. Appl. Psychol.* 81(4):369–79

Judiesch MK, Schmidt FL, Hunter JE. 1993. Has the problem of judgment in utility analysis been solved? *J. Appl. Psychol.* 78(6):903–11

Judiesch MK, Schmidt FL, Mount MK. 1992. Estimates of the dollar value of employee output in utility analyses: an empirical test of two theories. *J. Appl. Psychol.* 77(3):234–50

Kane JS. 1994. A model of volitional rating behavior. *Hum. Resour. Manage. Rev.* 4(3):83–310

Kinicki AJ, Hom PW, Trost MR, Wade KJ. 1995. Effects of category prototypes on performance-rating accuracy. *J. Appl. Psychol.* 80(3):354–70

Klaas BS, McClendon JA. 1996. To lead, lag, or match: estimating the financial impact of pay level policies. *Pers. Psychol.* 49(1):121–41

Kleiman LS, Durham RS. 1981. Performance appraisal, promotion, and the courts: a critical review. *Pers. Psychol.* 34(1):103–21

Kraiger K, Ford JK. 1985. A meta-analysis of ratee race effects in performance ratings. *J. Appl. Psychol.* 70(1):56–65

Kulick CT, Ambrose ML. 1993. Category-based and feature-based processes in performance appraisal: integrating visual and computerized sources of performance data. *J. Appl. Psychol.* 78(5):821–30

Lance CE, LaPointe JA, Stewart AM. 1994. A test of the context dependency of three causal models of halo rater error. *J. Appl. Psychol.* 79(3):332–40

Landy FJ, Farr JL. 1980. Performance rating. *Psychol. Bull.* 87(1):72–107

Landy FJ, Farr JL. 1983. *The Measurement of Work Performance: Methods, Theory, and Applications.* New York: Academic

Landy FJ, Shankster LJ, Kohler SS. 1994. Personnel selection and placement. *Annu. Rev. Psychol.* 45:261–96

Latham GP, Skarlicki D, Irvine D, Siegel JP. 1993. The increasing importance of performance appraisals to employee effectiveness in organizational settings in North America. *Int. Rev. Ind. Organ. Psychol.* 8:87–132

Latham GP, Whyte G. 1994. The futility of utility analysis. *Pers. Psychol.* 47(10):31–46

Law KS, Myors B. 1993. Cutoff scores that maximize the total utility of a selection program: comment on Martin and Raju's (1992) procedure. *J. Appl. Psychol.* 78(5):736–40

Lawler EE III. 1990. *Strategic Pay.* San Francisco: Jossey-Bass

Lawler EE III, Jenkins GD Jr. 1992. Strategic reward systems. See Dunnette & Hough 1992, pp. 1009–55

London M, Smither JW. 1995. Can multi-source feedback change perceptions of goal accomplishment, self-evaluations, and performance-related outcomes? Theory-based applications and directions for research. *Pers. Psychol.* 48(4):803–39

Macan TH, Highhouse S. 1994. Communicating the utility of human resource activities: a survey of I/O and HR professionals. *J. Bus. Psychol.* 8(4)425–36

Martell RF, Borg MR. 1993. A comparison of the behavioral rating accuracy of groups and individuals. *J. Appl. Psychol.* 78(1): 43–50

Martin SL, Raju NS. 1992. Determining cutoff scores that optimize utility: a recognition of recruiting costs. *J. Appl. Psychol.* 77(1):15–23

Maurer TJ, Palmer JK, Ashe DK. 1993. Diaries, checklists, evaluations and contrast effects in measurement of behavior. *J. Appl. Psychol.* 78(2):226–31

McCloy RA, Campbell JP, Cudeck R. 1994. A confirmatory test of a model of performance determinants. *J. Appl. Psychol.* 79(4): 493–505

McEvoy GM, Cascio WF. 1989. Cumulative evidence of the relationship between employee age and job performance. *J. Appl. Psychol.* 74(1):11–17

McHenry JJ, Hough LM, Toquam JL, Hanson MA, Ashworth S. 1990. Project A validity results: the relationship between predictor and criterion domains. *Pers. Psychol.* 43(2):335–55

McIntyre MD, James LR. 1995. The inconsistency with which raters weight and combine information across targets. *Hum. Perform.* 8(2):95–111

McIntyre RM, Salas E. 1995. Measuring and managing for team performance: emerging principles from complex environments. In *Team Effectiveness and Decision Making in Organizations*, eds. R Guzzo, E Salas, pp. 9–45. San Francisco: Jossey-Bass

Mero NP, Motowidlo SJ. 1995. Effects of rater accountability on the accuracy and the favorability of performance ratings. *J. Appl. Psychol.* 80(4):517–24

Motowidlo SJ, Van Scotter JR. 1994. Evidence that task performance should be distinguished from contextual performance. *J. Appl. Psychol.* 79(4):475–80

Murphy KR, 1986. When your top choice turns you down: effect of rejected offers on the utility of selection tests. *Psychol. Bull.* 99(1):133–38

Murphy KR, Cleveland JN. 1991. *Performance Appraisal: An Organizational Perspective.* Needham Heights, MA: Allyn & Bacon

Murphy KR. Cleveland JN. 1995. *Understanding Performance Appraisal: Social. Organizational and Goal-Based Perspectives.* Thousand Oaks, CA: Sage

Murphy KR, Jako RA, Anhalt RL. 1993. Nature and consequences of halo error; a critical analysis. *J. Appl. Psychol.* 78(2):218–25

Murphy K, Shiarella A. 1996. *Estimating the validity and utility of selection test batteries in relation to multi-attribute criteria.* Presented at Annu. Meet. Soc. Ind. Organ. Psychol., 11th, San Diego

Nilsen D, Campbell DP. 1993. Self-observer rating discrepancies: Once an overrater, always an overrater? *Hum. Resour. Manage.* 32(2/3):265–81

Oppler SH, Campbell JP, Pulakos ED, Borman WC. 1992. Three approaches to the investigation of subgroup bias in performance measurement: review, results, and conclusions. *J. Appl. Psychol.* 77(2):201–17

Organ DW. 1988. *Organizational Citizenship Behavior: The Good Soldier Syndrome.* Lexington. MA: Lexington

Prendergast C, Topel RH. 1996. Favoritism in organizations, *J. Polit. Econ.* 104(5):958–78

Pulakos ED, Schmitt N, Chan D. 1996. Models of job performance ratings: an examination of ratee race, ratee gender, and rater level effects. *Hum. Perform.* 9:103–19

Pulakos ED, White LA, Oppler SH, Borman WC. 1989. Examination of race and sex effects on performance ratings. *J. Appl. Psychol.* 74(5):770–80

Raju NS, Burke MJ, Maurer TJ. 1995. A note on direct range restriction corrections in utility analysis. *Pers. Psychol.* 48(1):143–49

Raju NS, Burke MJ, Normand J. 1990. A new approach for utility analysis. *J. Appl. Psychol.* 75(1):3–12

Raju NS, Burke MJ, Normand J, Lezotte DV. 1993. What would be if what is wasn't? Rejoinder to Judiesch, Schmidt, and Hunter (1993). *J. Appl. Psychol.* 78(6):912–16

Robbins TL, DeNisi AS. 1994. A closer look at interpersonal affect as a distinct influence on cognitive processing in performance appraisal *J. Appl. Psychol.* 79(3):341–53

Roth PL, Pritchard RD, Stout JD, Brown SH. 1994. Estimating the impact of variable costs on SD_y in complex situations. *J. Bus. Psychol.* 8(4):437–54

Rothstein MG, Paunonen SV, Rush JC, King GA. 1994. Personality and cognitive ability predictors of performance in graduate business school. *J. Educ. Psvchol.* 86(4): 516–30

Ryan AM, Dawn D, Bauman T, Grisez M, Mattimore K, et al. 1995. Direct, indirect, and controlled observation and rating accuracy. *J. Appl. Psychol.* 80(6):664–70

Saavedra R, Kwun SK. 1993. Peer evaluation in self-managing work groups. *J. Appl. Psychol.* 78(3):450–62

Sackett PR, DuBois CL. 1991. Rater–ratee race effects on performance evaluation: challenging meta-analytic conclusions. *J. Appl. Psychol.* 76(6):873–77

Sackett PR, Zedeck S, Fogli L. 1988. Relations between measures of typical and maximum job performance. *J. Appl. Psychol.* 73(3):482–86

Sanchez JI, De La Torre P. 1996. A second look at the relationship between rating and behavioral accuracy in performance appraisal. *J. Appl. Psychol.* 81(1):3–10

Schmidt FL. 1993. Personnel psychology at the cutting edge. See Schmitt et al. 1993, pp. 497–515

Schmidt FL, Hunter JE, McKenzie RC, Muldrow TW. 1979. Impact of valid selection procedures on work-force productivity. *J. Appl. Psychol.* 64(6):609–26

Schmidt FL, Hunter JE, Pearlman K. 1981. Task differences as moderators of aptitude test validity in selection: a red herring. *J. Appl. Psychol.* 66(5):166–85

Schmitt N, Borman WC, Associates, eds. 1993. *Personnel Selection in Organizations.* San Francisco: Jossey-Bass

Schrader BW, Steiner DD. 1996. Common comparison standards: an approach to improving agreement between self and supervisory performance ratings. *J. Appl. Psychol.* 81(6):813–20

Stamoulis DT, Hauenstein NMA. 1993. Rater training and rating accuracy: training for dimensional accuracy versus training for ratee differentiation. *J. Appl. Psychol.* 78(6):994–1003

Stone BM, Turner KL, Wiggins VL, Looper LT. 1996. Measuring airman job performance using occupational survey data. *Mil. Psychol.* 8(3):143–60

Sumer HC, Knight PA. 1996. Assimilation and contrast effects in performance ratings: effects of rating the previous performance on rating subsequent performance. *J. Appl. Psychol.* 81(4):436–42

Taylor MS, Tracy KB, Renard MK, Harrison JK, Carroll SJ. 1995. Due process in performance appraisal: a quasi-experiment in procedural justice. *Adm. Sci. Q.* 40:495–523

Tornow WW. 1993. Perceptions or reality? Is multi-perspective measurement a means or an end? *Hum. Resour. Manage.* 32:2211–29

Vance RJ, Colella A. 1990. The utility of utility analysis. *Hum. Perform.* 3(2):123–39

Vance RJ, MacCallum RC, Coovert MD, Hedge JW. 1988. Construct validity of multiple job performance measures using confirmatory factor analysis. *J. Appl. Psychol.* 73(1):74–80

Van Scotter JR, Motowidlo SJ. 1996. Interpersonal facilitation and job dedication as separate facets of contextual performance. *J. Appl. Psychol.* 81(5):525–31

Van Velsor E, Taylor S, Leslie JB. 1993. An examination of the relationships among self-perception accuracy, self-awareness, gender, and leader effectiveness. *Hum. Resour. Manage.* 32(2&3):249–63

Varma A, DeNisi AS, Peters LH. 1996. Interpersonal affect and performance appraisal: a field study. *Pers. Psychol.* 49(2):341–60

Viswesvaran C. 1996. *Modeling job performance: Is there a general factor?* Presented at Annu. Meet. Soc. Ind. Organ. Psychol., 11th, San Diego

Viswesvaran C, Ones DS, Schmidt FL. 1996. Comparative analysis of the reliability of job performance ratings. *J. Appl. Psychol.* 81(5):557–74

Waldman DA. 1994a. Contributions of total quality management to the theory of work performance. *Acad. Manage. Rev.* 19:510–36

Waldman DA. 1994b. Designing performance management systems for total quality implementation. *J. Organ. Change* 7(2):31–44

Waldman DA, Avolio BJ. 1986. A meta-analysis of age differences in job performance. *J. Appl. Psychol.* 71(1):33–38

Waldman DA, Spangler WD. 1989. Putting together the pieces: a closer look at the determinants of job performance. *Hum. Perform.* 2(1):29–59

Werner JM. 1994. Dimensions that make a difference: examining the impact of in-role and extrarole behaviors on supervisory ratings. *J. Appl. Psychol.* 79(1):98–107

Wigdor AK, Green BF Jr, eds. 1991. *Performance Assessment for the Workplace*, Vols. 1, 2. Washington, DC: Natl. Acad. Sci.

Woehr DJ. 1994. Understanding frame-of-reference training: the impact of training on the recall of performance information. *J. Appl. Psychol.* 79(4):525–34

Woehr DJ, Feldman J. 1993. Processing objective and question order effects on the causal relation between memory and judgment in performance appraisal: the tip of the iceberg. *J. Appl. Psychol.* 78(2):232–41

Woehr DJ, Huffcutt AI. 1994. Rater training for performance appraisal: a quantitative review. *J. Occup. Organ. Psychol.* 67:189–205

Woehr DJ, Roch SG. 1996. Context effects in performance evaluation: the impact of ratee sex and performance level on performance ratings and behavioral recall. *Organ. Behav. Hum. Decis. Process.* 66(1):31–41

Yammarino FJ, Atwater LE. 1993. Understanding self-perception accuracy: implications for human resource management. *Hum. Resour. Manage.* 32(2&3):231–48

Yang H, Sackett PR, Arvey RD. 1996. Statistical power and cost in training evaluation: some new considerations. *Pers. Psychol.* 49(3):651–68

Yu J, Murphy KR. 1993. Modesty bias in self-ratings of performance: a test of the cultural relativity hypothesis. *Pers. Psychol.* 46(2):357–63

28

PERSPECTIVES ON MODELS OF JOB PERFORMANCE

Chockalingam Viswesvaran and Deniz S. Ones

Source: *International Journal of Selection and Assessment* 8(4) 2000. 216–226.

Abstract

Contemporary models of job performance are reviewed. Links between task performance, contextual performance, organizational citizenship behaviors, counterproductivity and organizational deviance are pointed out. Measurement issues in constructing generic models applicable across jobs are discussed. Implications for human resource management in general, and performance appraisal for selection and assessment in particular, are explored. It is pointed out that the different dimensions or facets of individual job performance hypothesized in the literature are positively correlated. This positive manifold suggests the presence of a general factor which represents a common variance shared across all the dimensions or facets. Although no consensus exists in the extant literature on the meaning and source of this shared variance (i.e., the general factor), rater idiosyncratic halo alone does not explain this general factor. Future research should explain the common individual differences determinants of performance dimensions.

Introduction

Job performance is a central construct in industrial/organizational psychology (Austin and Villanova 1992; Campbell 1990; Murphy and Cleveland 1995; Schmidt and Hunter 1992). Much of personnel selection is predicated on the premise of selecting from a pool of applicants those who are likely to perform better on the job (compared to those not selected). Many training programs are designed to improve job performance. Assessments of individuals are undertaken to identify their strengths and weaknesses in order to design training programs as well as for optimal placement decisions (Guion 1998). Performance appraisal, feedback and even merit pay systems make use of employee performance information. In short, job performance is a construct that is central to much of work psychology. Thus, it is important to know what that construct entails.

Many definitions of job performance have been proposed (e.g., Campbell 1990; Murphy 1989). For our purposes, job performance refers to scalable actions, behavior and outcomes that employees engage in or bring about that are linked with and contribute to organizational goals. Apart from abstract definitions, how do we know what constitutes job performance? To answer this question researchers have applied some combination of one of the following four approaches. First, researchers have reviewed job performance measures used in different contexts and attempted to synthesize what dimensions make up the construct of job performance. This rational method of synthesizing and theory building is likely, however, to be influenced by the focus, interests and perhaps even biases of the individual researchers doing the theorizing.

Second, researchers have relied on job analytic techniques to explain the behavior and associated dimensions for job performance. In this approach, standard techniques of job analysis are used to discover what makes up job performance. For example, Campbell (1990) suggest that the multiple dimensions that constitute job performance manifest themselves in critical incidents analyses, task analyses, and other job analytic analyses. However, although there is much to be said about analyzing jobs and thus discovering behavior incumbents engage in on the job, quite often performance dimensions obtained using job analysis have differed from those obtained using other empirical methods. Factor structures of importance or criticality ratings do not mirror dimensions of actual behavior on the job. Job analysis reveals how the different tasks engaged in by incumbents cluster together whereas job performance focuses on evaluable, scalable behaviors in which individual differences exist.

Third, researchers have developed measures of hypothesized dimensions, collected data on these measures, and factor analyzed the data (e.g., Lance, Teachout, and Donnelly 1992). This is the most direct (and empirical way) of assessing the dimensionality of the performance domain. Unfortunately, this empirical approach is limited by the number and type of measures included in the data collection phase. Recently, Viswesvaran (1993) invoked the lexical hypothesis from personality literature (Goldberg 1995) to address this limitation. The lexical hypothesis states that practically significant individual differences in personality are encoded in the language used, and therefore, a comprehensive description of personality can be obtained by collating all the adjectives found in the dictionary. Viswesvaran, Ones and Schmidt (1996) extended this principle to job performance assessment and argued that a comprehensive specification of the content domain of the job performance construct can be obtained by collating all the measures of job performance that had been used in the extant work psychology literature of the past 80 years.

Finally, researchers (e.g., Welbourne, Johnson, and Erez 1998) have invoked organizational theories to define what the content of the job performance construct should be. Welbourne *et al.* used role theory and identity theory to explain the construct of job performance. Another example of invoking a theory of work organization to explicate the construct of job performance comes in the distinction made between task and contextual performance (Borman and Motowidlo 1993). Distinguishing between task and contextual performance parallels the social and technical systems that are postulated to make up the organization.

In this article, we review some of the models that have been proposed to explicate the construct of job performance. According to Binning and Barrett (1989) models of performance that aim to uncover dimensions can be at different levels of breadth or generality. The developmental context of job performance dimensions can be characterized as either (1) stand-alone, specific, or (2) part of a larger set of dimensions. After reviewing some dimensions that have been developed in a stand-alone manner (e.g., prosocial behavior), we review models that take a more comprehensive view of job performance.

In addition to this dichotomy, one can also classify the models of job performance as those that are developed for specific occupations (e.g., managers, entry-level jobs) as against models of job performance that are applicable across all jobs. That is, the occupational focus of job performance models can either be (1) limited to specific occupations/job families, or (2) applicable across jobs. These two dichotomous classifications (i.e., based on occupational focus and based on developmental context) can be combined to result in four types of models of job performance. Table 1 depicts this framework.

However, in this article, we do not discuss stand-alone, specific dimensions developed for specific jobs. This category contains too numerous dimensions and

Table 1 A framework for reviewing models of job performance

Developmental context of dimensions	Occupational focus	
	Limited to specific occupations/job families	Applicable across jobs
Stand-alone dimensions	Stand-alone, specific dimensions developed to apply to specific occupations	Stand-alone, specific dimensions developed to apply across jobs.
	Too numerous and diverse to be covered in a review	Example models include those proposed by Borman & Motowidlo (1993); Brief & Motowidlo (1986); Organ (1994)
Dimensions developed as part of a set of dimensions	Dimensions developed as a set that are to apply to specific occupations	Dimensions developed as a set that are to apply across jobs
	Example models include those proposed by Borman & Brush (1993); Conway (1999); Hunt (1996)	Example models include those proposed by Campbell (1990); Viswesvaran (1993)

has only limited value for general theories of work behavior. Thus we discuss (1) stand-alone, specific dimensions developed to apply across jobs; (2) dimensions developed as a set that are applicable to specific occupations; and (3) dimensions developed as a set that are applicable across jobs. Following this, we discuss some of the measurement issues involved in the explication of job performance constructs. We close this article with a review of some models of work behavior that postulate job performance antecedents (i.e., how different individual differences variables are linked to different aspects of performance).

Models of job performance

Models of job performance postulating specific, stand alone dimensions developed to apply across jobs can be grouped around primarily three broad dimensions: task performance, organizational citizenship behavior and counterproductive behaviors. We take up each in turn.

Task performance

Early attempts at exploring the job performance construct focused heavily on task requirements. Fleishman (1967) attempted to develop a taxonomy of human performance based on learning theories and training techniques (an earlier, similar attempt was made by Guilford 1954). The objective was to develop homogeneous task clusters applicable across jobs. Although Fleishman's objective was to develop a *comprehensive* taxonomy of job performance dimensions, given the exclusive focus on ability requirements, we classify his model as one postulating specific stand-alone dimensions across jobs. Fleishman (1975) noted four approaches to identify dimensions of job performance (limited to what we now refer to as task performance). The four were: behavior description approach, behavior requirements approach, abilities approach, and task characteristics approach.

In the current work psychology literature, task performance is defined as 'the proficiency with which incumbents perform activities that are formally recognized as part of their jobs; activities that contribute to the organization's technical core either directly by implementing a part of its technological process, or indirectly by providing it with needed materials or services' (Borman and Motowidlo 1993: 73). According to Murphy (1989) task performance entails the accomplishment of duties and tasks that are specified in a job description. However, as Schmidt (1993) points out with changing jobs, job descriptions may not provide solid grounds for defining task performance.

Organizational citizenship behavior

Several researchers over the years have argued that job performance entails more than just task performance (Borman and Motowidlo 1993; Brief and

Motowidlo 1986; Clark and Hollinger 1983; Hogan and Hogan 1989; Organ 1988; Smith, Organ and Near 1983). Although studied for a long time under different names (e.g., cooperation [Roethlisberger and Dickinson 1939]), Smith *et al.* popularized the concept of 'Organizational Citizenship Behavior' (OCB) in the job performance literature. OCB was defined as individual behavior that is discretionary/ extra-role, not directly or explicitly recognized by the formal reward system, and that in the aggregate promotes the effective functioning of the organization (Organ 1988). Distinct sub-dimensions of OCB have been identified as: altruism, courtesy, cheerleading, sportsmanship, civic virtue, and conscientiousness (Organ 1988). Note that in his current conceptualization of OCB, Organ (1997) has dropped the requirement for these behaviors to be extra-role, and not to be directly rewarded. The only requirement is that they are discretionary and contribute to organizational effectiveness.

Over the years several concepts related and overlapping with OCB have been proposed. George and Brief (1992) introduced the concept of 'organizational spontaneity'. George and Brief (1992) defined organizational spontaneity as voluntarily performed extra-role behaviors that contribute to organizational effectiveness. Five dimensions were postulated to comprise organizational spontaneity: helping co-workers, protecting the organization, making constructive suggestions, developing oneself, and spreading goodwill. Organizational spontaneity is distinguished from OCB partly on account of reward systems being designed to recognize organizational spontaneity.

Van Dyne, Cummings and Parks (1995) argued for the use of 'Extra-Role Behavior' (ERB). Based on role theory concepts developed by Katz (1964), ERB has been hypothesized to contribute to organizational effectiveness. Brief and Motowidlo (1986) introduced the related concept of Prosocial Organizational Behavior (POB). POB has been defined as behavior performed with the intention of promoting the welfare of individuals or groups to whom the behavior has been directed. POB can be either role-prescribed or extra-role, and it can be negative towards organizations although positive towards individuals.

Counterproductive behaviors

Behaviors that have negative value for organizational effectiveness have also been proposed as constituting distinct dimensions of job performance. Organizationally deviant behavior has become a topic of research interest. Robinson and Bennett define deviant behavior as 'voluntary behavior that violates significant organizational norms and in so doing threatens the well being of an organization, its members, or both' (1995: 556).

In a multidimensional scaling study, Robinson and Bennett (1995) found that deviant behavior in organizations vary along two continua: (1) organizational/ interpersonal and (2) serious/minor. The resulting typology that crosses these two dimensions produced the following four categories: (1) property deviance (serious deviance directed at the organization); (2) production deviance (minor deviance directed at the organization); (3) personal aggression (serious deviance directed at other individuals); and (4) political deviance (minor deviance directed at other individuals).

Our work on integrity testing (Ones, Viswesvaran and Schmidt 1993) as well as the works of Paul Sackett and colleagues (cf. Sackett and Wanek 1996) have identified the different forms of counterproductive behaviors such as property damage, substance abuse, violence on the job. Withdrawal behaviors have long been studied by work psychologists in terms of lateness or tardiness, absenteeism, and turnover. Work psychologists and social psychologists have explored the antecedents and consequences of social loafing, shirking or the propensity to withhold effort (Kidwell and Bennett 1993).

A striking feature in empirical studies that have explored these specific dimensions developed independently and hypothesized to apply across jobs is the positive correlation found across them (Viswesvaran 1993). Orr, Sackett and Mercer (1989) report that supervisors take into account all these dimensions in their assessments of job performance. Thus, a positive manifold of correlations exist across the various hypothesized dimensions. We will return to this positive manifold and its implications after we discuss (1) specific dimensions developed as a set that are to apply to specific occupations; and (2) specific dimensions developed as a set that are to apply across jobs.

Models of job performance: dimensions developed as a set for specific occupations

Although models of performance have been developed for many occupational groups, due to space constraints, here we focus on three: entry level jobs in the service industry, managers, and military personnel.

Entry level jobs in the service industry

Hunt (1996) developed a model of generic work behavior applicable to entry-level jobs especially in the service industry. Using performance ratings data for over 18,000 employees primarily from the retail sector, Hunt (1996) identified nine dimensions of job performance that do not depend on job-specific knowledge. The nine dimensions were: adherence to confrontational rules, industriousness, thoroughness, schedule flexibility, attendance, off-task behavior, unruliness, theft, and drug misuse. Adherence to confrontational rules reflected an employee's willingness to follow rules that might result in a confrontation between the employee and a customer (e.g., checking for shoplifting). Industriousness captured the constant effort and attention towards work while on the job. Thoroughness was related to the quality of work whereas schedule flexibility reflected the employees' willingness to change their schedule to accommodate demands at work. Attendance captured the employee's presence at work when scheduled to work and punctuality. Off-task behavior involved the use of company time to engage in non-job activities.

Unruliness referred to minor deviant tendencies as well as abrasive and inflammatory attitude towards co-workers, supervisors, and work itself. Finally, theft involved taking money or company property or helping friends steal property whereas drug misuse referred to inappropriate use of drugs and alcohol.

Managers

Specific models of job performance have also been developed for managerial jobs. Brumback and Vincent (1970) factor-analyzed work performance data and identified 26 dimensions of job performance. Kassem and Moursi (1971) examined the models of managerial effectiveness. Komaki, Zlotnick, and Jensen (1986) presented an operant-based taxonomy and index of supervisory behavior. Several commercial instruments have been developed to assess managerial performance. Personnel Decisions Inc. has developed the PROFILOR® which is a 135-item feedback instrument designed specifically for managers. This instrument assesses performance in 24 dimensions identified as relevant for managerial performance. Supervisors provide ratings on the PROFILOR® which are used to provide feedback on different dimensions of performance. The items pertain to specific, job-related skills, rather than managerial style or other abstract concepts that are difficult to translate into on-the-job behaviors. Another taxonomy of managerial behavior was examined by Conway (1999) who meta-analytically accumulated data across studies to develop a three-level hierarchy of managerial performance. In his investigation, Conway relied heavily on an earlier taxonomy of managerial performance presented by Borman and Brush (1993). Borman and Brush (1993) presented 18 dimensions of performance which were derived using 187 behaviors found in the literature. These 18 dimensions can further be grouped into four broad managerial performance dimensions: (1) leadership and supervision; (2) interpersonal relations and communication; (3) technical behaviors and mechanics of management (e.g., administration); and (4) useful behaviors and skills (e.g., handling crises).

Military jobs

Our third example is for military jobs. Both Campbell, McHenry and Wise (1990) and Borman, Motowidlo, Rose and Hansen (1985) developed models of soldier effectiveness based on data collected for Project A. Project A is a multi-year effort undertaken by the US Army to develop a comprehensive model of work effectiveness. As part of that landmark project, Campbell *et al.* (1990) found five performance dimensions across 19 entry-level Amy jobs: (1) core technical proficiency; (2) general soldiering proficiency; (3) effort and leadership; (4) personal discipline; and (5) physical fitness and military bearing. Borman *et al.* (1985) developed a model of job performance for first-tour soldiers that are important for unit effectiveness. Borman *et al.* noted that in addition to task performance, there are three performance dimensions. Organizational commitment and socialization combined to define the 'allegiance' of the individual; socialization and morale combined to define 'teamwork'; and morale and commitment combined to define 'determination'. Each of these three dimensions could be further subdivided. Thus, allegiance involved following orders, following regulations, respect for authority, military bearing, and commitment. Teamwork comprised of cooperation, camaraderie, concern for unit morale, boosting unit morale, and leadership. Determination involved perseverance, endurance, conscientiousness, initiative, and discipline.

Models of job performance: dimensions applicable across occupations

Campbell (1990) describes the general latent structure of job performance in terms of eight distinct dimensions. The eight factors are: job-specific task proficiency, non-job-specific task proficiency, written and oral communication, demonstrating effort, maintaining personal discipline, facilitating peer and team performance, supervision, and management or administration.

Job-specific task proficiency is defined as the degree to which the individual can perform the core substantive or technical tasks that are central to a job and distinguish one job from another. Non-job-specific task proficiency, on the other hand, is used to refer to tasks not specific to a particular job, but is expected of all members of the organization. Demonstrating effort captures the consistency or perseverance and intensity of the individuals to complete the task, whereas maintenance of personal discipline refers to the eschewment of negative behaviors (such as rule infractions) at work. Management or administration differs from supervision in that the former includes performance behaviors directed at managing the organization that are distinct from supervisory or leadership roles. Written and oral communications reflects that component of the job performance that refers to the proficiency of an incumbent to communicate (written or oral) independent of the correctness of the subject matter. The descriptions of these eight dimensions are further elaborated in Campbell (1990) and Campbell, McCloy, Oppler, and Sager (1993). According to Campbell and colleagues, these eight dimensions are sufficient to describe the latent structure of performance at a general level. Campbell *et al.* (1990), however, point out that the salience or importance of these eight dimensions differs across occupational groups. Further, each of the eight factors are proposed to have sub-factors that will also vary in their degree of salience across occupations. Finally, according to Campbell (1990) as well as Campbell *et al.* (1993), the true score correlations between these eight dimensions can be assumed to be small enough to consider them distinct. According to Campbell and colleagues, each dimension is likely to produce rank ordering of employees that is different.

Viswesvaran (1993) proposed a hierarchical latent structure for the construct of job performance. To ensure a comprehensive specification of the content domain of the job performance construct, Viswesvaran (1993) invoked the lexical hypothesis which was first introduced in the personality assessment literature (see also Viswesvaran *et al.* 1996). A central thesis of this lexical approach is that the entire domain of job performance can be captured by culling all job performance measures used in the vast work psychology and human resource management literature. This parallels the lexical hypothesis used in the personality literature which, as first enunciated by Goldberg, holds that a comprehensive description of the personality of an individual can be obtained by examining the adjectives used in the lexicon (e.g., all English language words that could be obtained/culled from a dictionary).

Viswesvaran (1993) listed job performance measures (486 of them) used in published articles over the years. Two raters working independently then derived ten dimensions by grouping conceptually similar measures. The ten dimensions were: overall job performance, job performance or productivity, effort, job knowledge, interpersonal competence, administrative competence, quality, communication competence, leadership, and compliance with rules. Overall job performance captured overall effectiveness, overall work reputation, or was the sum of all individual dimensions rated. Job performance or productivity included ratings of quantity or ratings of volume of work produced. Ratings of effort were statements about the amount of work an individual expends in striving to do a good job. Interpersonal competence was assessments of how well an individual gets along with others whereas administrative competence was a rating measure of the proficiency exhibited by the individual in handling the coordination of the different roles in an organization. Quality was an assessment of how well the job was done and job knowledge was a measure of the expertise demonstrated by the individual. Communication competence reflected how well an individual communicated regardless of the content. Leadership was a measure of the ability to successfully bring out extra performance from others, and compliance with or acceptance of authority assessed the perspective the individual has about rules and regulations. Illustrative examples as well as more elaborate explanations of these dimensions are provided in Viswesvaran *et al.* (1996).

Although the lexical approach is promising, it should be noted that there are two potential concerns here. First, it can be argued that just as the technical nuances of personality may not be reflected in the lexicon, some technical but important aspects of job performance have never been used in the literature—thus, not covered in the ten dimensions identified. Second, it should be noted that generating ten dimensions from a list of all job performance measures used in the extant literature involved the judgmental task of grouping conceptually similar measures, although the intercoder agreement in grouping the conceptually similar measures into the ten dimensions was reported in the 90%s (cf. Viswesvaran 1993).

Of these two concerns, the first is mitigated to the extent that the job performance measures found in the extant literature were identified by industrial-organizational psychologists and other professionals (in consultation with managers in organizations). As such, the list of measures can be construed as a comprehensive specification of the entire domain of the construct of job performance. However, the second concern, the judgmental basis on which the job performance measures were grouped into ten conceptual dimensions, remains a concern, albeit alleviated by high interrater agreement.

Viswesvaran (1993) accumulated results from over 300 studies that reported correlations across the ten dimensions. Both interrater and intrarater correlations, as well as non-ratings-based measures were analyzed. The ten dimensions showed a positive manifold of correlations, suggesting the presence of a general factor across the different dimensions. We return to the substantive meaning of this general factor in the section on measurement issues.

Murphy (1990) describes the construct of job performance as comprising of four dimensions: downtime behaviors, task performance, interpersonal, and destructive behaviors. Task performance focuses on performing role-prescribed activities whereas downtime behaviors refer to lateness, tardiness, absences, or broadly, to the negative pole of time on task (i.e., effort exerted by an individual on the job). Interpersonal behaviors refer to helping others, teamwork ratings, and prosocial behaviors. Finally, destructive behaviors correspond to compliance with rules (or lack of it), violence on the job, theft, and other behaviors counterproductive to the goals of the organization. According to Murphy (1990), each of these dimensions can be related to inputs and outputs in organizational units.

Borman and Motowidlo (1993) describe the construct of job performance as comprising task and contextual performance. Briefly, task performance focuses on performing role-prescribed activities whereas contextual performance accounts for all other helping and productive behaviors (Borman and Motowidlo 1993). Contextual performance encompasses: '(1) persisting with enthusiasm and extra effort as necessary to complete own task activities successfully, (2) volunteering to carry out task activities that are not formally part of own job, (3) helping and cooperating with others, (4) following organizational rules and procedures, (5) endorsing, supporting, and defending organizational objectives.' (ibid.: 82)

Researchers have attempted to develop a theory of individual differences in task and contextual performance (Motowidlo, Borman, and Schmit 1997). Modeling job performance as the aggregated value of episodic, evaluative behaviors, attempts have been made to distinguish the underlying dimensions of the episodes evaluated. Researchers (e.g., Van Scotter and Motowidlo 1996) have argued that individual differences in personality variables are linked more strongly than individual differences in (cognitive) abilities to individual differences in contextual performance. Cognitive ability was hypothesized to be more predictive of task performance than contextual performance. Although persuasive from a theoretical perspective, empirical support for this argument has been mixed. Conscientiousness, a personality variable, has been linked as strongly as cognitive ability to task performance in some studies (cf. Van Scotter and Motowidlo 1996).

Bernardin and Beatty (1984) define performance as the record of outcomes produced on a specified job function or activity during a specified time period. Although a person's job performance depends on some combination of ability, motivation and situational constraints, it can be measured only in terms of some outcomes. This definition contrasts with the stand of Campbell and colleagues that individual job performance should not be defined in terms of outcomes, but rather behaviors. Bernardin and Beatty (1984) then consider the issue of dimensions of job performance. Every job function could be assessed in terms of six dimensions (Kane 1986). The six dimensions are: quality, quantity, timeliness, cost-effectiveness, need for supervision, and interpersonal impact. Some of these dimensions may not be relevant to all job activities. Bernardin and Russell (1998) emphasize the need to understand the interrelationships among the six dimensions of performance. For example, a work activity performed in sufficient quantity and quality but not in time may not be useful to the organization.

Measurement issues

Work psychologists have stressed the need to conduct a thorough job analysis to define the content domain of the construct 'job performance'. This emphasis should not be taken to mean that the construct of job performance is an amorphous construct that changes from job to job. If that were the case, theories of work behavior would simply be impossible to develop. No science of work behavior (for that matter, any science of behavior) is possible if performance in each task is unique. What should be kept in mind is the fact that job performance is an abstract construct. An abstract construct implies two characteristics. First, one cannot point to something physical and concrete and state that 'it' is job performance. One can only point out the manifestations of this construct. Second, there are many manifestations that could indicate job performance. Thus, the specific manifestations may change from job to job, but the dimension of the construct may generalize across jobs. For example, interpersonal competence as a dimension of job performance generalizes across jobs, but the actual manifestation of it may change from job to job with the specific behaviors identified perhaps via a job analysis. This is analogous to domain sampling in measurement where, however comprehensive, no single measure can capture the entire domain of what is being measured.

The assessment of job performance dimensions has primarily relied either on objective counts of specified acts or output maintained in organizational records or on subjective judgments from raters. Although raters have been primarily supervisors (Cascio 1991), recent efforts have used raters from different levels of the organization (e.g., peers, subordinates, etc.). Hunter and Hirsh (1987) argue that organizational records suffer from criterion contamination and deficiency to a greater extent than judgemental assessments. Indeed, judgmental assessments from knowledgeable and motivated raters are likely to have greater criterion relevance. Judgmental assessments of job performance can be either norm-referenced (i.e., rankings) or criterion-referenced (i.e., ratings). Several scale formats have been developed and cumulative research suggests (Landy and Farr 1980) that scale formats do not substantially influence assessments. Scales have been developed that could be used across situations (Welbourne et al. 1998).

Although judgmental assessments have been hypothesized to have adequate criterion relevance, factors such as opportunity to observe (Rothstein 1990) do influence judgmental assessments. Some researchers have argued that job performance is partially a socially constructed phenomenon and that rater disagreements do not constitute error (Murphy and Cleveland 1995). Such an argument assumes that interrater reliability should be construed merely as an index of interrater agreement and that a lack of agreement is a non sequitur. This view is seriously flawed since the basis for any science is interrater (interobserver) or intersource reliability. Reliability refers to consistency of measurement. When ratings are used to measure performance, interrater correlations provide an index of reliability of job performance ratings. While job performance constructs may be a measured using more than just ratings (e.g., organizational records of productivity, discipline problems), without consistency of measurement, the science behind industrial-organizational psychology would disappear. For example, there can be no valid selection. There would no basis for developing training programs, evaluating any human resource intervention, awarding merit pay, etc., because the concept of validation would collapse to a futile exercise if the criterion measures were idiosyncratic to particular raters or specific alternate indices of performance. This in effect would amount to a rejection of the science of organizational and occupational psychology.

Incorporating time into the assessment of job performance has been another measurement issue. Dynamic criteria has been presented to mean one of the following: (1) the mean performance of individuals change over time; (2) the rank order of individuals on performance change over time; and (3) the correlations of performance indicators with external variable change. Barrett, Caldwell, and Alexander (1989) accumulated the existing literature on this issue and found scant evidence for rank order and correlational changes. Researchers (e.g., DuBois, Sackett, Zedeck and Fogli 1993) have distinguished between typical performance that is determined by ability as well as personality characteristics from maximal performance where personality variables such as motivation and drive play only a limited role. It may be important to consider whether different dimensions of job performance have different weights for assessing overall performance over time. Further, although arguments can be made that some of the 'performance dimensions' that have been proposed could be causally related (e.g., job knowledge and effort result in productivity), it should be noted that most models of job performance treat them as performance dimensions. By definition, different dimensions of performance (task, citizenship, etc.) explain variation in overall job performance (Viswesvaran 1993).

In reviewing the various models of job performance, we summarized many dimensions of job performance. Empirical research shows positive correlation across the different dimensions. Viswesvaran (1993) cumulated results across more than 300 studies and found that over 50% of the variance is shared across the different dimensions. There is a general factor in job performance assessments. In our work, we also found that much of this general factor is substantively meaningful and not just a manifestation of halo error. This magnitude of shared variance is similar to that found in factor analyses of cognitive abilities (cf. Jensen 1986). However, stating that there is a general factor in job performance assessments is not the same as saying that the different dimensions are redundant. The specific variance associated with each dimension may be useful in certain circumstances and for certain purposes (e.g., designing training interventions). What is clear is that the structure of job performance can be conceptualized as a hierarchy with the general factor at the apex and various dimensions at the lower levels and each dimension in turn can be divided into further subdimensions. The appropriate level of specificity depends on the purpose of the assessor (Wallace 1965). For example, to construct a theory of work motivation it may be reasonable to focus on the overall general factor of job performance, but to develop a theory of customer orientation we may have to focus not on the general factor of job performance but on interpersonal competence with customers.

Antecedents of job performance dimensions

We close this article with a brief review of models of work behavior that postulate how different individual differences variables are causally linked to different aspects of performance. Hunter (1983) developed and tested a causal model where cognitive ability was a direct causal antecedent to both job knowledge and job performance (also see Schmidt, Hunter and Outerbridge 1986). Job knowledge was an antecedent to job performance. Both job knowledge and job performance contributed to supervisory ratings. These findings suggest that cognitive ability contributes to overall job performance through its effects on learning job knowledge and mastery of required skills. Borman, Hanson, Oppler, Pulakos and White (1993) extend these findings to the role of early experience in supervisory job performance.

McCloy, Campbell and Cudeck (1994) argued for and found empirical evidence for the perspective that all individual differences variables affect the performance dimension by their effects on either procedural knowledge or declarative knowledge or motivation. Barrick, Mount, and Strauss (1993) tested and found support for a model where overall performance was predicted by conscientiousness which exerted its influence through goal setting. Ones and Viswesvaran (1996) argued that conscientiousness has multiple pathways by which it affects overall performance. First, conscientious individuals are likely to spend more time on the task and less time daydreaming (Schmidt and Hunter 1992). This investment of time will result in greater acquisition of job knowledge, which in turn will result in greater productivity and which in turn will result in positive ratings. Further, conscientious individuals are likely to engage in organizational citizenship behaviors which in turn might enhance productivity and ratings. Finally, conscientious individuals are expected to pay more attention to detail and profit more via vicarious learning (Bandura 1977) which would result in higher job knowledge and productivity. Note that supporting the idea of multiple pathways for conscientiousness, Organ and Ryan (1995) found a sizable relationship between organizational citizenship behaviors and conscientiousness.

Borman and Motowidlo (1993) postulated that ability will predict task performance more strongly than individual differences in personality. On the other hand, individual differences in personality were hypothesized to predict contextual performance better than ability. Motowidlo et al. (1997) developed a more nuanced model where contextual performance was modeled as dependent on contextual habits, contextual skills, and contextual knowledge. Although habits and skills were predicated on personality, contextual knowledge was influenced both by personality and cognitive ability. Similarly, task performance is influenced by task habits, task skill and task knowledge. Whereas task skill and task knowledge are influenced solely by cognitive ability, task habits are affected by both cognitive ability and personality variables. Thus, this more nuanced model implies that both ability and personality have a role in explaining task and contextual performance. However, research to date suggests that ability and conscientiousness predict both task and contextual performance.

Most recently, Hunter, Schmidt, Rauschenberger and Jayne (2000) tested a causal model of job performance using correlation matrices reported by Project A researchers. In this research, cognitive ability predicted objectively measured job performance which in turn predicted the overall evaluation by raters. On the other hand, conscientiousness directly predicted not only objectively measured job performance, but also physical condition, and overall evaluation by raters.

The bottom line from the existing research in this area appears to be that each performance dimension is complexly determined (jointly by ability and personality) and that it is impossible to specify a sole cause or antecedent of a particular dimension of job performance. However, we should note that the general factor obtained in our model of job performance implies that there are some common determinants across different job performance dimensions. That is, different performance dimensions are likely to have common individual differences antecedents. Given a large body of research in work psychology, two individual differences variables that would fit the bill are: cognitive ability and conscientiousness (Salgado, Viswesvaran and Ones, in press).

Conclusion

Job performance is perhaps the most central construct in work psychology. Explanation of this construct is important for many functions that we engage in our profession. Explaining the content domain of the construct of job performance is a critical component of our job performance as industrial and organizational psychologists. For many years, industrial-organizational psychologists have concentrated on the predictor side of the equation. This emphasis on predictor space is explainable as attempts by a nascent science to establish its utility (Schmidt and Kaplan 1971). As our profession becomes more mature and secure among the pantheon of scientific disciplines, more attention will be diverted from prediction towards understanding and explanation of phenomena. Under such circumstances, great strides are likely to be made in our understanding of the construct of individual job performance. This article by summarizing the existing models of job performance, sketching some measurement issues, and providing an overview of the determinants of performance, is hopefully one step in that direction.

References

Austin, J.T. and Villanova, P. (1992) The criterion problem: 1917–1992. *Journal of Applied Psychology*, **77**, 836–74.

Bandura, A. (1977) *Social Learning Theory*. Englewood Cliffs, NJ: Prentice-Hall.

Barrett, G.V., Cladwell, M.S., and Alexander, R.A. (1989) The predictive stability of ability requirements for task performance: A critical reanalysis. *Human Performance*, **2**, 167–81.

Barrick, M.R., Mount, M.K. and Strauss, J. (1993) Conscientiousness and performance of sales representatives: Test of the mediating effects of goal setting. *Journal of Applied Psychology*, **78**, 715–22.

Bernardin, H.J. and Beatty, R. (1984) *Performance Appraisal: Assessing Human Behavior at Work*. Boston: Kent-PWS.

Bernardin, H.J. and Russell, J.E.A. (1998) *Human Resource Management: An Experiential Approach* (2nd ed.). Boston: McGraw-Hill.

Binning, J.F. and Barrett, G.V. (1989) Validity of personnel decisions: A conceptual analysis of the inferential and evidential basis. *Journal of Applied Psychology*, **74**, 478–94.

Borman, W.C. and Brush, D.H. (1993) More progress towards a taxonomy of managerial performance requirements. *Human Performance*, **6**, 1–21.

Borman, W.C., Hanson, M.A., Oppler, S.H., Pulakos, E.D. and White, L.A. (1993) Role of early supervisory experience in supervisor performance. *Journal of Applied Psychology*, **78**, 443–9.

Borman, W.C. and Motowidlo, S.J. (1993) Expanding the criterion domain to include elements of contextual performance. In N. Schmitt and W.C. Borman (eds.), *Personnel Selection in Organizations* (pp. 71–98). San Francisco, CA: Jossey Bass.

Borman, W.C., Motowidlo, S.J., Rose, S.R. and Hansen, L.M. (1985) *Development of a Model of Soldier Effectiveness*. Minneapolis, MN: Personnel Decisions Research Institute.

Brief, A.P. and Motowidlo, S.J. (1986) Prosocial organizational behavior. *Academy of Management Review*, **11**, 710–25.

Brumback, G.B. and Vincent, J.W. (1970) Factor analysis of work-performed data for a sample of administrative, professional, and scientific positions. *Personnel Psychology*, **23**, 101–7.

Campbell, J.P. (1990) Modeling the performance prediction problem in industrial and organizational psychology. In M. Dunnette and L. M. Hough (eds.), *Handbook of Industrial and Organizational Psychology* (Vol. 1, 2nd edn., pp. 687–731). Palo Alto, CA: Consulting Psychologists Press.

Campbell, J.P., McCloy, R.A., Oppler, S.H. and Sager, C.E. (1993) A theory of performance. In N. Schmitt and W.C. Borman (eds.), *Personnel Selection in Organizations* (pp. 35–70). San Francisco: Jossey Bass.

Campbell, J.P., McHenry, J.J. and Wise, L.L. (1990) Modeling job performance in a population of jobs. *Personnel Psychology*, **43**, 313–33.

Cascio, W.F. (1991) *Applied Psychology in Personnel Management* (4th edn). Englewood Cliffs, NJ: Prentice-Hall.

Clark, J.P. and Hollinger, R.C. (1983) *Theft by Employees in Work Organizations: Executive Summary*. Washington, DC: National Institute of Justice.

Conway, J.M. (1999) Distinguishing contextual performance from task performance for managerial jobs. *Journal of Applied Psychology*, **84**, 3–13.

DuBois, C.L.Z., Sackett, P.R., Zedeck, S. and Fogli, L. (1993) Further exploration of typical and maximum performance criteria: Definitional issues, prediction, and white-black differences. *Journal of Applied Psychology*, **78**, 205–11.

Fleishman, E.A. (1967) Performance assessment based on an empirically derived task taxonomy. *Human Factors*, **9**, 349–66.

George, J.M. and Brief, A.P. (1992) Feeling good-doing good: A conceptual analysis of the mood at work-organizational spontaneity relationship. *Psychological Bulletin*, **112**, 310–29.

Goldberg, L.R. (1995) What the hell took so long? Donald Fiske and the big-five factor structure. To appear in P.E. Shrout and S.T. Fiske (eds.), *Advances in Personality Research, Methods, and Theory: A Festschrift Honoring Donald W. Fiske*. New York: Erlbaum.

Guilford, J.P. (1954) *Psychometric Methods* (2nd edn.). New York: McGraw-Hill.

Guion, R.M. (1998) *Assessment, Measurement, and Prediction for Personnel Selection*. Mahwah, NJ: Lawrence Erlbaum.

Hogan, J. and Hogan, R. (1989) How to measure employee reliability. *Journal of Applied Psychology*. **74**, 273–9.

Hunt, S.T. (1996) Generic work behavior: An investigation into the dimensions of entry-level, hourly job performance. *Personnel Psychology*, **49**, 51–83.

Hunter, J.E. (1983) *Test Validation for 12,000 Jobs: An Application of Job Classification and Validity Generalization Analysis to the General Aptitude Test Battery* (*GATB*) (Test Research Report No. 45). Washington, DC: United States Employment Service, United States Department of Labor.

Hunter, J.E. and Hirsh, H.R. (1987) Applications of meta-analysis. In C.L. Cooper and I.T. Robertson (eds.), *Review of Industrial Psychology* (Vol 2, pp. 321–57). New York: Wiley.

Hunter, J.E., Schmidt, F.L., Rauschenberger, J.M. and Jayne, M.E.A. (2000) Intelligence, Motivation, and Job Performance. In C.L. Cooper and E.A. Locke (eds.), *Industrial and Organizational Psychology: Linking Theory with Practice*. Oxford: Blackwell.

Jensen, A.R. (1986) g: Artifact or reality? *Journal of Vocational Behavior*, **29**, 301–31.

Kane, J.S. (1986) Performance distribution assessment. In R.A. Berk (Ed.), *Performance Assessment* (pp. 237–73). Baltimore: Johns Hopkins University Press.

Kassem, M.S. and Moursi, M.A. (1971) Managerial effectiveness: A book review essay. *Academy of Management Journal*, **14**, 381–8.

Katz, D. (1964) The motivational basis of organizational behavior. *Behavioral Science*, **9**, 131–46.

Kidwell, R.E. and Bennett, N. (1993) Employee propensity to withhold effort: A conceptual model to intersect three avenues of research. *Academy of Management Review*, **18**, 429–56.

Komaki, J.L., Zlotnick, S. and Jensen, M. (1986) Development of operant-based taxonomy and observational index of supervisory behavior. *Journal of Applied Psychology*, **71**, 260–9.

Lance, C.E., Teachout, M.S. and Donnelly, T.M. (1992) Specification of the criterion construct space: An application of hierarchical confirmatory factor analysis. *Journal of Applied Psychology*, **77**, 437–52.

Landy, F.J. and Farr, J.L. (1980) Performance rating. *Psychological Bulletin*, **87**, 72–107.

McCloy, R.A., Campbell, J.P. and Cudeck, R. (1994) A confirmatory test of a model of performance determinants. *Journal of Applied Psychology*, **79**, 493–505.

Motowidlo, S.J., Borman, W.C. and Schmit, M.J. (1997) A theory of individual differences in task and contextual performance. *Human Performance*, **10**, 71–83.

Murphy, K.R. (1989) Dimensions of job performance. In R. Dillon and J. Pelligrino (eds.), *Testing: Applied and Theoretical Perspectives* (pp. 218–47). New York: Praeger.

Murphy, K.R. (1990) Job performance and productivity. In K.R. Murphy and F. Saal (eds.), *Psychology in Organizations: Integrating Science and Practice* (pp. 157–76). Hillsdale, NJ: Erlbaum.

Murphy, K.R. and Cleveland, J.N. (1995) *Understanding Performance Appraisal: Social, Organizational, and Goal-based Perspectives*. Thousand Oaks, CA: Sage.

Ones, D.S. and Viswesvaran, C. (1996, April) A general theory of conscientiousness at work: Theoretical underpinnings and empirical findings. In J.M. Collins (Chair), *Personality Predictors of Job Performance: Controversial Issues*. Symposium conducted at the eleventh annual meeting of the Society for Industrial and Organizational Psychology, San Diego, CA.

Ones, D.S., Viswesvaran, C. and Schmidt, F.L. (1993) Comprehensive meta-analysis of integrity test validities: Findings and implications for personnel selection and theories of job performance. *Journal of Applied Psychology*, **78**, 679–703.

Organ, D.W. (1988) *Organizational Citizenship Behavior*. Lexington, MA: D.C. Heath.

Organ, D.W. (1997) Organizational citizenship behavior: It's construct clean-up time. *Human Performance*, **10**, 85–97.

Organ, D.W. and Ryan, K. (1995) A meta-analytic review of attitudinal and dispositional predictors of organizational citizenship behavior. *Personnel Psychology*, **48**, 775–800.

Orr, J.M., Sackett, P.R. and Mercer, M. (1989) The role of prescribed and nonprescribed behaviors in estimating the dollar value of performance. *Journal of Applied Psychology*, **74**, 34–40.

Robinson, S.L. and Bennett, R.J. (1995) A typology of deviant workplace behaviors: A multidimensional scaling study. *Academy of Management Journal*, **38**, 555–72.

Roethlisberger, F.J. and Dickinson, W.J. (1939) *Management and the Worker*. Cambridge, MA: Harvard University Press.

Rothstein, H.R. (1990) Interrater reliability of job performance ratings: Growth to asymptote level with increasing opportunity to observe. *Journal of Applied Psychology*, **75**, 322–7.

Sackett, P.R. and Wanek, J.E. (1996) New developments in the use of measures of honesty, integrity, conscientiousness, dependability, trustworthiness and reliability for personnel selection. *Personnel Psychology*, **49**, 787–830.

Salgado, J., Viswesvaran, C., and Ones, D.S. (in press) A look at predictors in work and organizational psychology: individual differences, selection methods and Techniques. In N. Anderson, D.S. Ones, H. Sinangil and C. Viswesvaran (eds.) *Handbook of Work Psychology: Vol. 1*. London: Sage.

Schmidt, F.L. (1993) Personnel psychology at the cutting edge. In N. Schmitt and W.C. Borman (eds.), *Personnel Selection in Organizations* (pp. 497–515). San Francisco: Jossey-Bass.

Schmidt, F.L. and Hunter, J.E. (1992) Causal modeling of processes determining job performance. *Current Directions in Psychological Science*, **1**, 89–92.

Schmidt, F.L., Hunter, J.E. and Outerbridge, A.N. (1986) Impact of job experience and ability on job knowledge, work sample performance, and supervisory ratings of job performance. *Journal of Applied Psychology*, **71**, 432–9.

Schmidt, F.L. and Kaplan, L.B. (1971) Composite versus multiple criteria: A review and resolution of the controversy. *Personnel Psychology*, **24**, 419–34.

Smith, C.A., Organ, D.W. and Near, J.P. (1983) Organizational citizenship behavior: Its nature and antecedents. *Journal of Applied Psychology*, **68**, 655–63.

Van Dyne, L., Cummings, L.L., and Parks, J.M. (1995) Extra-role behaviors: Its pursuit of construct and definitional clarity (a bridge over muddied waters). In L.L. Cummings and B.M. Staw (eds.), *Research in Organizational Behavior* (vol. 17, pp. 215–85) Greenwich, CT: JAI Press.

Van Scotter, J.R. and Motowidlo, S.J. (1996) Interpersonal facilitation and job dedication as separate facets of contextual performance. *Journal of Applied Psychology*, **81**, 525–31.

Viswesvaran, C. (1993) Modeling job performance: Is there a general factor? Unpublished doctoral dissertation, University of Iowa, Iowa City, IA.

Viswesvaran, C., Ones, D.S. and Schmidt, F.L. (1996) Comparative analysis of the reliability of job performance ratings. *Journal of Applied Psychology*, **81**, 557–74.

Wallace, S.R. (1965) Criteria for what? *American Psychologist*, **20**, 411–17.

Welbourne, T.M., Johnson, D.E. and Erez, A. (1998) The role-based performance scale: Validity analysis of a theory-based measure. *Academy of Management Journal*, **41**, 540–55.

29

ORGANIZATIONAL COMPETENCIES

A valid approach for the future?

Paul Sparrow

Source: *International Journal of Selection and Assessment* 3(3) (1995): 168–177.

Abstract

This paper attempts to integrate concepts of organizational competency across a number of levels of analysis. It provides grounded evidence on existing application and practice, and synthesizes research and development in the area of organizationally derived management competencies. Consideration is given to the underlying theoretical assumptions and definitional issues raised by existing practice. The paper highlights the range of human resource strategies or programmes used to integrate activity and implement strategic changes, and examines the shift in thinking about the importance and nature of management competency. Organization-specific approaches are reviewed and the benefits analysed. A critical review of attempts at integration suggests that application of competency-based approaches within organizations has fallen behind advances in strategic human resource management and that there is a need to shift application towards more future-oriented and strategic contexts. Weaknesses associated with existing approaches to management competency are analysed as is the issue of validity. Finally, the implications of considering competencies as an organizational level resource for human resource strategy are discussed.

The language of 'competency' in the singular and 'competences' or 'competencies' in the plural has become one of the big ideas in HRM on a par with management by objectives, total quality management and empowerment (Connock 1992). The approach, initially popular in US and British organizations, is now being transferred into other countries in the Asia/Pacific region (Armstrong 1991; Glass 1990; Macleod and Wyndham 1991; Murdoch 1992), Scandinavia (Hansson 1988) and continental Europe (Hooghiemstra 1990). It becomes important to review this approach in terms of its usefulness, validity and implications for the assessment and selection paradigm. There has been a fierce debate about the term 'competency' with writers asking what psychological constructs do they tap? Are there generic competencies or are they all organization-specific? And are they learnable (developable) or discriminative (selectable)? Answering such questions is made all the more difficult because there are three different perspectives on the nature of management skills, each of which has used the language of competence or competency (Sparrow 1994b; Sparrow and Bognanno 1993). These three separate concepts also essentially represent different levels of analysis. The 'management competence' approach considers effectiveness across occupations and sectors based on samples of key jobs. The 'behavioural competency' approach tends to be applied across the management hierarchy within an organization, summarized in terms of jobs, roles or career streams. The 'core competence' approach adopts an organizational level of analysis. Unfortunately, the terms, methodologies and focus of measurement found in all three perspectives are frequently used quite interchangeably. Not only does this serve to confuse the practitioner or academic, it carries the risk of encouraging organizations to build and integrate HRM systems on a bed of shifting sand. It is essential therefore to draw first some distinctions between these three usages of the term 'competence' or 'competency', by considering:

— what each term describes;
— how they are identified;
— the aspects of organizational life they focus on;
— what they tend to indicate;
— the nature of the performance criteria;
— the typical applications;
— the level of analysis;
— the implicit ownership;
— the assessment onus; and
— the individual motivation to conform to the expressed notion.

Management competencies

The first source of discussion about management competency has come from the management educationalists and national institutions, who responded to a series of influential national reports attacking Britain's poor comparative record of vocational education and training by initiating a review of the essential nature of management. This approach has formed the core of developments in the Management Charter Initiative (MCI) and National Vocational Qualifications (NVQs). It attempts to describe and define specifications of the outcomes, skills, knowledge, attitudes (and handful of personal behaviours) that have to be learned by managers. These descriptions are identified through functional analyses of job roles and responsibilities. The aspect of organizational life that this approach focuses on is the nature of managerial tasks and the associated expectations of workplace performance. The approach therefore indicates areas of competence—or fields of knowledge—which a person has to be able to demonstrate effectively. The performance criterion represents an entry or threshold standard, that is, the common denominator needed for a broad range of management jobs (broken down into a hierarchy of lower, middle and senior management levels). These generic standards are applied to the field of vocational education and training across organizations and occupations. 'Competence' is something owned by national institutions and organizations which can be granted to individuals. The assessment onus is therefore the accreditation of past activities in order to grant professional status and the individual motivation to conform to this picture is the achievement of an externally transferable qualification. The advantages of the approach are that it represents a useful starting point and picture of management competence for small organizations with limited internal resources, a cost-effective way of identifying assessment standards for highly populated external labour markets and resourcing routes, and a way of identifying the training laggards (Fletcher 1992). The disadvantages are that, despite considerable financial and institutional support, a minority of organizations have adopted the approach and the majority of these do not use the information for promotion decisions, do not feel it has influenced the nature of their training, and see it as a bureaucratic, cumbersome process unrelated to the world of work (Personnel Management 1990). The approach does not pick up the organization-specific and in-house nature of management skills and so offers few attractions as a basis for integrating or developing an HRM system.

Behavioural competencies

Perhaps because of such difficulties, a second, more widely adopted model of 'behavioural competency' has been developed from the early work of the McBer Corporation and Harvard Business School (Boyatzis 1982; Spencer and Spencer 1993). This model describes 'competencies' as 'soft skills' that are associated with underlying characteristics of individuals (such as motive, traits, skills, aspects of one's self-image, social roles or bodies of knowledge). They are evidenced through sets of intentional behaviour patterns ('behavioural repertoires') that people 'input' to a broad organizational context, which may be an individual job, a role, a career stream or the organization as a whole given its structure and strategic purpose. Consequently, they are identified through behavioural investigation techniques, which focus on person-centred analyses of effectiveness. They indicate the behaviours that have to be brought to a role by the individual in order to perform to a required level. This performance criterion is based on a range of performance outputs or characteristics of superior (excellent) individual performance that can be produced from a situation if it is managed effectively. The resulting tailored and excellent behaviours are used as a template that can be applied through a variety of tools to reinforce intentional behaviour and therefore integrate all areas of human resource management (Boam and Sparrow 1992; Dale and Iles 1992; Iles 1992; Lawler 1994; Salaman 1992). The competency is held by the individual and is brought to the organization. Consequently, the assessment onus is on the identification of potential in order to ensure the best resourcing decisions. And the motivation of the individual to conform to this picture of effectiveness? It results in internally rewardable achievement and recognition.

This second behavioural approach has found wide application across a range of HRM practices. A review of the literature and conference proceedings (Sparrow 1994b) found a range of benefits reported across the content of HRM in recruitment and selection, career development, performance management and management of change applications. A range of benefits are also associated with the process of identifying, communicating and articulating the behavioural model of effectiveness they reveal (see Table 1). The methodological rigour of these competency profiles is difficult to assess from most reports as is the actual occurrence of the benefits in question. The reports are for the most part based on case study, conveyed in practitioner forums or occasionally through academic articles (see, for example, Cockerill 1989; Craig 1992; Feltham 1992; Glaze 1989; Gratton 1989; Greatex and Philips 1989; Iles 1992; Jackson 1989; Jacobs 1989; Mabey and Iles 1993; Shackleton 1992; Sparrow and Bognanno 1993; Torrington and Blandamer 1992; Woodruffe 1991). However, most of the reported benefits would not need to be supported by independent study since they are based on accepted practice or tenets of occupational psychology. This observation applies to many of the 'process benefits' such as higher ownership of the final profile amongst line managers as a result of involvement in the design process, which tend to be associated with the consulting process required for much organization development work. Other benefits arise from the 'behavioural description' element of the competency approach, such as more accurate and consistent rating from behaviourally anchored scales. However, hidden amongst the practitioner benefits are many as yet untested claims, such as better succession planning, better decisions about organization structure and more appropriate self-selection.

Systematic assessment of the benefits of competency-based approaches is problematic because they tend to be applied in conjunction with a myriad of other organizational changes. Empirical investigation of such claimed benefits has begun (Mabey and Iles 1993; Robertson, Iles, Gratton and Sharpley 1991) but it will be many years before the impact of the competency-based approach on the more strategic aspects of HRM can be assessed. The fear of variable methodology and skill in the process of competency identification and concerns over some as yet unproven benefits have led some authors to criticize the competency approach. Against this, the mass adoption of competency-based approaches by British organizations and the continued development of tools and techniques as sophistication in the area increases, indicates that there is considerable face validity in the approach.

Some behavioural competencies may be measured, some may be developed, some may be modified, whilst others have to be selected. Competency frameworks, such as that developed by Boyatzis (1982), are therefore best treated as

Table 1 The HRM content and process benefits associated with well-designed competency approaches

HRM content benefits

Recruitment and selection
(i) Visible and agreed set of standards to systematic assessment.
(ii) More rigorous job analysis process to defend against equal opportunities legislation.
(iii) Reduces variable practice by individual selectors and assessment on irrelevant person characteristics.
(iv) More sophisticated and flexible targeting of applicants, e.g. women returners, untried labour pools, freedom from previous norms.
(v) Conveying of relevant information to assist self-selection in adverts or assessment centre exercise design.
(vi) Enhancement of application form design to focus on more important aspects of previous experience.
(vii) More informed initial screening and sifting decisions based on targeted questionnaires.
(viii) Informed choices about the types of assessment tools best used in the selection procedure to ensure adequate coverage of competencies.
(ix) Provision of information for situational interviews to assess potential.

Career development
(i) Promotes career restructuring by identifying real 'career bridges' or 'breakpoints' as opposed to the status quo, i.e. results in more cross-functional movement and technical to professional moves.
(ii) Informs decisions about the underlying number of vertical hierarchies in the structure.
(iii) Standards set for progression based on behavioural sets and not on the individual.
(iv) Career decisions made on the basis of future potential, not just on current competency.
(v) Facilitates succession planning.
(vi) Strengths and weaknesses provide a referent for planned development.

Performance management
(i) Provides a guideline for decisions about grading in job evaluation.
(ii) Provides a framework under which objectives for the appraisal system may be developed and set.
(iii) Broadens appraisal systems to consider 'how well it is done' measures as well as the more traditional 'what is achieved' measures.
(iv) Facilitates the development of behaviourally anchored rating scales or language ladders for more accurate performance management assessment.
(v) Concentrates the appraisal interview discussion on performance and effectiveness.
(vi) Provides a language for feedback on sensitive and emotive issues.

HRM process benefits

(i) Involvement of line managers in the identification process and design of assessment tools results in higher ownership of the results.
(ii) Forces a link between the strategic direction and recruitment criteria.
(iii) Identification process creates a shared understanding of the types of people needed in the organization.
(iv) More informed decisions about the most appropriate resourcing decision, i.e. buy, make or design out the competencies.
(v) Provides a language for self-development and self-assessment and a basis for coaching and training.
(vi) Generates useful information to help build successful teams.
(vii) Represents a tool for developing the business culture, forcing clearer articulation of the strategy, or consideration of how new structures or business processes may actually work.

templates against which whole teams should be assessed and resourced, serving as a basis for coaching, training and development. Individuals are unlikely to have strengths against more than three or four competencies. Surface knowledge and skill competencies are the easiest and most costeffective to develop through training and development activities, whilst core motive and trait competencies, at the base of personality, are more difficult to assess and develop, with organizations preferring to select for these characteristics (Spencer and Spencer 1993). The type or level of competencies identified therefore has significant implications for HRM managers. Increasingly, however, the collections of behaviours that evidence a competency combine both surface and base aspects of an individual's make-up.

Validity issues with behavioural competencies

The behavioural competency field will see the development of more complex tools and techniques, a need to tolerate greater ambiguity of performance criteria, and a challenge to many of the selection, assessment and development methods to which it has been applied. There are two problems in particular:

(i) The validity of the performance or 'effectiveness' criteria is being questioned.
(ii) There are a number of methodological problems with even some of the most predictive competency-based selection and assessment tools.

Many competency frameworks are derived through a process of examining the constructs that managers use to differentiate between 'effective' and 'less effective' performance. The paradox is that the need to understand a new competency typically comes at a time when the job holders' knowledge is at its lowest. Identifying such competencies is an educational and values-driven process, rather than the more traditional job analysis process favoured by psychologists. It has therefore become common to build in a learning element to the specification of future-orientated competencies, either by recognizing aspects of learning (such as creativity, mental agility and balanced learning habits) as specific competencies to be assessed, or by recognizing future forecasting as a competency, and incorporating the behaviours and skills associated with reading the future (such as spotting major 'fracture lines' and discontinuities) into corporate profiles. However, there is a thin line between intuitive deduction about future competencies and speculation about 'desirable' organizational characteristics (such as the need to create a learning organization, fewer organizational layers, a reduction of internal boundaries and greater levels of empowerment). Links between such organizational characteristics and individual performance are difficult to prove on conventional grounds.

There is also a problem when more formally defined 'criterion samples' (that is, people who have clearly had success in their jobs) are used. Competencies have to predict something meaningful in the real world and therefore must demonstrate a 'causal intent' that generates action towards the desired outcome. In his pioneering work, Boyatzis (1982) studied 2000 managers holding 41 different jobs in 12 (mainly Anglo-Saxon) organizations, distinguishing between 'threshold' management competencies (which usually means the minimally acceptable level of work) and 'superior' management competencies (defined as the level achieved by one person out of 10). Such 'criterion samples' are typically determined using data from appraisal schemes. Unfortunately, there are a number of circular arguments within this approach to the validity. It assumes that the appraisal schemes used to identify the 'highest' and 'lowest' performers are themselves accurate reflections of truly effective performance. In most instances they are not. Eighty per cent of UK organizations are dissatisfied with their appraisal schemes. Why? Because they tend to focus on measuring the 'what is achieved' side to organizational performance—the outputs necessary to meet targets, standards and objectives. Frequently such individualized measures can be achieved at the expense of fellow departments or the organization as a whole. Contradictions are created in the picture of performance that is managed, in many instances to the detriment of 'horizontal management processes' such as total quality management or customer service measures. Using such flawed measures of performance as a criterion by which to differentiate between effective and ineffective behaviours and resultant competencies is somewhat worrying. Then there is the circularity to consider. In order to overcome the obvious limitations of output-based performance measures, organizations are introducing more sophisticated performance management systems that also take account of 'inputs' or 'how it is achieved' measures (such as the skills, behaviours or values that are considered necessary) and 'external stakeholder' criteria (to reflect the perspectives of external or internal customers, upwards appraisers, and so forth). These are surely better criteria on which to base any differentiation of effective and ineffective performers, but ones that also typically incorporate measures of behavioural competency. We may have to end up using competency-based criteria of performance to determine the validity of competency-based criteria of performance!

Another challenge comes from the call for a more judicious, strategic and targeted approach to competencies seen in the literature on existing assessment centre practice. Despite the emphasis on management competencies, the exact status of the construct is still not clear (Crawley, Pinder and Herriot 1990). Difficulties with the traditional assessment centre approach mainly concern the limited ability of managers to handle complex assessment decisions driven by multiple competencies or dimensions. The validity achieved by assessment centres is surprisingly low given the validity of their component parts (Jones, Herriot, Long and Drakeley 1991; Payne, Anderson and Smith 1992; Tziner, Ronen and Hacohen 1993). Managers seem incapable of assessing accurately cross-situational abilities from most exercises, unduly influenced by the general task performance of the candidate. The design of exercises to assess critical management roles, the creation of exercise-specific behavioural frameworks, scales and checklists (Iles 1992) and reductions in the number of dimensions in order to reflect only higher-order constructs, reduce the memory load and improve their relation to specific outcomes in the organizations (Klimoski and Brickner 1987), have all helped counter this problem to some extent, but serve to add to the cost and complexity of the approach.

Psychologists need to accept that it may be more important to forego their preference for completeness of behavioural description and focus instead on the changing relevance of management competencies and the use of business-sensitive mechanisms to prioritize their assessment. Rather than pursue the traditional search for predictive validity that lies at the heart of many existing selection systems focused around job analysis, the search for the validity of behavioural competencies has to rest on:

— the content validity of the behavioural indicators (that is, their relevance to individual and organizational effectiveness or their motivational power when used as cornerstone of a resourcing policy); and
— the construct validity of the assessment dimensions that may be used to assist resourcing decisions.

Arguments in support of, and confidence in the competency approach, becomes based on an act of faith and a belief in the reliability of the various competency identification and forecasting methodologies (such as behavioural event investigation, repertory grids, critical incidents, structured skills questionnaires, focus groups, subject matter experts, organizational climate surveys, and so forth). Of more concern, however, are some of the deeper problems faced by organizations in ensuring that their competency-based systems continue to fit and develop their future resourcing requirements.

Core organization competencies

This 'act of faith' in the validity of competencies is steeped in a business logic supported by the strategic management writers and theorists (Barney 1991; Fiol 1991; Grant 1991; Hamel and Prahalad 1991; Klein, Edge and Kass 1991; Mahoney and Pandian 1992; Nordhaug and Grønhaug 1994; Reed and DeFillippi 1990). These writers provide the third source of discussion about competency, as they translate the strategic capabilities of organizations into underlying competences in an attempt to provide some 'fixed points' to help deal with high levels of turbulence in the business environment. Many organizations have found that historical cost and quality advantages eroded as new competitors entered the market, innovations in technology spread rapidly throughout the sector, or alternative national 'business systems or logics' proved more effective at creating these advantages (Pettigrew and Whipp 1991). As these advantages lost their potency the importance and exploitation of 'core or organisation-level competences' has been stressed (Hamel and Prahalad 1991).

'Core competences' describe the resources and capabilities of the organization that are linked with business performance. They are identified through market analysis methods and the strategic planning process. Grant (1991) examines what lies beneath core competences (such as the ability to innovate and the development of a learning organization). Organization competences and capabilities represent a meshing together of organization resources (such as the skills of individual people), leadership and more tangible assets such as capital resources, brand reputation and patents held. Klein, Edge and Kass (1991) view 'corporate skills' as strategic combinations of individual (human) competences, hard organizational factors (such as equipment and facilities) and soft organizational factors (such as culture and organization design). Core competences therefore indicate what makes one organization more successful than another, representing fixed sources of competitive advantage. The performance criteria used to assess this are superior records of innovation, learning quality or other long-term business criteria. They are applied to marketing and product strategies and the design of business processes. In terms of ownership, the competence is held by the organization but jointly developed by individuals. The assessment onus is to articulate the unique key success factors and proprietary know-how. The individual motivation to conform to the picture revealed is to ensure that the organization can sustain itself and provide employment and security.

The richer the connection between the capabilities and skills of the organization's human resources, the distinctive areas of high performance and technical know-how of the organization, and the dominant logic or mental models of the top management teams, then the more effective the strategy will be (Reed and DeFillippi 1990; Sparrow 1994a). Strategists view management skills—evidenced by the organization's behaviour and the skills of the total pool of human resources—as being based on the possession of core corporate-level skills, coherence across these skills, and unique know-how in the context of strategic key success factors. Organizations need actively to manage their competency portfolio, analysing emerging and future needs for competence in line with the strategy development process (Morgan 1989; Nordhaug and Grønhaug 1994; Whipp 1991). Klein *et al.* (1991) similarly conclude that as product life-cycles shorten and skill development life-cycles lengthen '... the skillbase must therefore be actively managed as the mainstay of competitive strategy'. Senior managers need to take responsibility for this competency development through promoting productive learning amongst employees and work teams, rather than hoping this strategic attention to competence can be managed by middle managers or HRM staff.

New contexts: new organizational competencies?

We should distinguish between human resources as individuals (who have associated behavioural competences and characteristics) and human resources as the total pool of human capital within the organization (who need to show a behavioural reflection of the strategic competences of the organization). Rather than focus on specific management practices and tools and the way these align individual employee behaviour with strategic goals, HRM strategists need to manage the competency of the total pool of human capital within the organization

(Wright and McMahan 1992). Instead of interpreting the organization's competence base as limited by the existing stock of individuals, organizations need to consider the competencies of individuals and work teams who form part of the total cooperative network or business chain (Nordhaug and Grønhaug 1994). Individual employee behaviour has to be analysed in the context of these organization competencies. Why? Because management skills are increasingly organization-specific. Different organization structures, growth paths and unique career paths have reinforced the development of organization-specific skills, which have in turn become a central source of differential and sustainable competitive advantage (Grant 1991). Whilst the definition of these strategic competences is clearly distinguishable from the concept of behavioural competencies, there is a meeting of the minds between strategists, HRM practitioners and psychologists. The core competences considered in the strategic management literature impact behavioural competencies in two ways:

(i) there must be a behavioural reflection of the specific technical and marketing capabilities they tend to describe; and
(ii) there must be a set of conceptual abilities that are associated with the identification, modification and management of strategic competences.

A challenge to our assumptions about validity?

The selection and assessment of people, indeed the whole range of decisions to be made about resourcing the organization, provide a powerful basis for influencing and organizing human behaviour in line with the organization's strategic direction. Organizations are beginning to appreciate that the process of labelling behavioural indicators into strategically meaningful titles provides a language and forum for capturing cultural change (Iles 1992; Mabey and Iles 1993; Mills and Friesen 1992; Sparrow and Bognanno 1993). Adopting such competency frameworks can produce quite shocking insights into the organization. Sparrow (1994b) provides an example in which, after a downsizing, a major organization found that only 16% of its surviving staff scored above half way on the dimension of leadership. Through the use of the competency approach it was shown that the new 'delayered' organization with its 'empowered' managers simply would not be 'competent' enough. The framework challenged decades of recruitment and selection practice and the historical climate and culture of the old organization.

The changed context for both HRM and behavioural competences in organizations includes: business trends towards flexible work patterns, career and organization structures; new economic arrangement through mergers, acquisitions, strategic alliances, privatization and sub-contracting rationalization, downsizing and delayering of organizations; international labour cost pressures; increasing demands for quality of products and services and business chain management; and the redesign of managerial work resulting from increased availability of information, decision support systems, reduced rules, formalization or internal boundaries, and business process re-engineering. This changed context has resulted in new resourcing equations (Sparrow and Hiltrop 1994).

Faced with such change, many currently accepted assumptions in recruitment, selection and assessment, based on experiences steeped in organization systems, structures and styles that are rapidly disappearing, will need to be re-assessed. On the one hand, research on meta-analysis and validity generalization has challenged the beliefs of psychologists about the importance of many situational variables (a key element of the competencies-based approach) in limiting the validity of historical empirical studies (Schmidt and Hunter 1977). Meta-analysis and validity generalization studies probably represent the most important methodological innovation in psychology within recent decades (Schuler and Guildin 1991). Work on validity generalization suggests that there is substantial transfer in the predictive validity of general cognitive, perceptual and psychomotor abilities for both job proficiency and training success for a wide range of jobs. Moreover, the job components or synthetic validity approach assumes that those jobs with particular activities in common share similar requirements, general skills and abilities and common links to selection predictors, with the validity of most existing psychological tests only altering with large changes in job content (McCormick and Ilgen 1987).

On the other hand, at what point are changes in the managerial task felt to be so great that the rules of the past no longer apply? Ultimately, it is a matter of judgement as to whether psychologists believe that the underlying job components and tasks in managerial jobs have changed sufficiently—or have been made specific to each organization by recent efforts at empowerment, delayering and creation of new organizational forms. Research shows that different task requirements moderate test validities (especially in managerial jobs) such that generalizable cognitive abilities as measured by general mental abilities tend to be relatively less important (Smith and Robertson 1991). Many psychologists now seek new ways of collecting information about management competencies and better methods of matching this to the organization's needs. The strategic HRM literature also points to the need to educate, mobilize and then integrate managers into the strategic change process, as the nature of the relationship between organizations and their managers has evolved. In the past, managerial competency was equated with the possession of specific skills and abilities, but it now rests in '... the development of attitudes, values and "mindsets" that allow managers to confront, understand and deal with a wide range of forces within and outside their organizations' (Morgan 1989). Organizations can no longer continue to drive through the rear-view mirror, analysing what they and other excellent organizations already do.

Pedler, Burgoyne and Boydell (1991) note that the competencies identified by many organizations are orientated to the skills needed to allow the organization to continue doing what it is already doing. If such competencies are used as part of an HRM strategy they only serve to reinforce and fix the current or historical ways of doing things, dragging the cloak of the old business into the new. If a competency framework creates too much homogeneity amongst managers it may reduce the potential for novel ideas and viewpoints to emerge. Indeed, psychologists now focus on the importance of cognitive diversity in top teams in order to facilitate strategic implementation (Bantel and Jackson 1989; Sparrow 1994a).

Therefore, what is required is a more proactive, less prescriptive and more future-orientated approach to competencies, intended to anticipate likely strategic changes and the position of the organization and its members to address these challenges. An example is the life-cycle analysis and portfolio management of competencies, based upon their relevance to the organizational and human resource strategy (Boam and Sparrow 1992; Sparrow 1994b; Sparrow and Bognanno 1993).

Conclusions

Organization-level behavioural competencies have profound implications for HRM. Psychologists have traditionally identified a taxonomy of skills based on the abilities of individuals, profiled specific jobs along this taxonomy, and then made resourcing decisions. Once organizations build HRM strategies around competencies, then the competency, not the individual, becomes the unit of analysis, especially once this competency becomes a behavioural reflection of the strategic capabilities of the organization. Organizations will make more sophisticated resourcing decisions intended to design themselves around these higher-level 'competencies'. Only then will they audit the skills and abilities of their people. Resourcing decisions that may be informed by the identification and knowledge of organizational-level competencies include:

— the selection or deselection of people (or units of their time) on the basis of the relevance of their competency to the task or to the team;
— large-scale development programmes to close competency gaps with competitors;
— designing out of the need for competencies that are time-consuming to develop through technology or work structuring; and
— contracting out of under-developed competencies (through choices and assessments of partners in alliances or joint ventures, or the practice of executive leasing).

It seems likely that the field will develop this way given developments both in HRM strategy and the business environment. The question is, will psychologists be able to inform organizations and guide their efforts, or will organizational practice supersede our ability to contribute? Will organizational competencies be identified by line managers and internal staff—with the associated risk of lax methodology and limited consideration of the assessment task? As assessment psychologists we have to ask ourselves about our own competencies. Perhaps the best guidance is to consider some of the characteristics that have helped personnel managers make the transition to a more strategic HRM role (Sparrow 1994b). There is time to close the gap. For the competency approach to develop in a more strategic direction there is a potentially huge research agenda for industrial psychologists. The most important methodological and research developments should include:

— an audit of existing practice, the levels of integration of HRM systems actually achieved and the perceived benefits and problems;
— examination of international practice, and clarification of the variation in behavioural indicators of competencies from one country to another;
— the building up of a repertoire of future orientated data collection techniques;
— development of methods to weight competencies in terms of their relevance, development time, and the depth of talent pool; and
— identification of methods to determine 'fracture lines' between competencies, that is, when behavioural indicators represent significantly new demands that should be used to structure careers or organizations.

As organizations and HR directors emerge from the current chaos in the business environment—as the downsizings continue and the problems these create come to the fore, as complete business processes are 're-engineered'—then they will be looking for ways to re-integrate the organization and its HRM systems. Helping organizations create broad selection and assessment systems based around organizational-level behavioural competencies may offer an attractive way forward.

References

Armstrong, A. (1991) Management skills and performance audit. *Asia Pacific Human Resource Management,* Summer, 25–39.

Bantel, K. and Jackson, S. (1989) Top management and innovation in banking. Does the composition of top teams make a difference? *Strategic Management Journal,* 10, 107–124.

Barney, J. (1991) Firm resources and sustainable competitive advantage. *Journal of Management,* 17(1), 99–120.

Boam, R. and Sparrow, P.R. (eds) (1992) *Designing and Achieving Competency: A Competency-Based Approach to Managing People and Organisations.* London: McGraw-Hill.

Boyatzis, R. (1982) *The Competent Manager.* New York: John Wiley.

Cockerill, A. (1989) The kind of competence for rapid change. *Personnel Management,* 21(9), 52–56.

Connock, S. (1992) The importance of 'big ideas' to HR managers. *Personnel Management,* 24(6), 24–29.

Craig, S. (1992) Using competencies in career development. In R. Boam and P. Sparrow (eds), *Designing and Achieving Competency: A Competency-Based Approach to Managing People and Organizations.* London: McGraw-Hill.

Crawley, B., Pinder, R. and Herriot, P. (1990) Assessment centre dimensions, personality and aptitudes. *Journal of Occupational Psychology,* 63(3), 211–216.

Dale, M. and Iles, P. (1992) *Assessing Management Skills: A Guide to Competencies and Evaluation Techniques.* London: Kogan Page.

Feltham, R. (1992) Using competencies in recruitment and selection. In R. Boam and P. Sparrow (eds), *Designing and Achieving Competency: A Competency-Based Approach to Managing People and Organisations.* London: McGraw-Hill.

Fiol, C.M. (1991) Managing culture as a competitive resource: an identity-based view of sustainable competitive advantage. *Journal of Management*, 17(1), 191–211.

Fletcher, S. (1992) *Competence-Based Assessment Techniques.* London: Kogan Page.

Glass, P. (1990) Skills required for effective performance by hospital managers. Asia *Pacific Human Resource Management*, February, 24–40.

Glaze, A. (1989) Cadbury's dictionary of competence. *Personnel Management*, 21(7), 44–48.

Grant, R.M. (1991) The resource-based theory of competitive advantage: implications for strategy formulation. *California Management Review*, 33(3), 114–135.

Gratton, L. (1989) Work of the manager. In P. Herriot (ed.), *Assessment and Selection in Organizations.* Chichester: John Wiley.

Greatex, J. and Philips, P. (1989) Oiling the wheels of competence. *Personnel Management*, 21(8), 36–39.

Hamel, G. and Prahalad, C.K. (1991) Corporate imagination and expeditionary marketing. *Harvard Business Review*, 69(4), 81–92.

Hansson, J. (1988) *Creative Human Resource Management: Competence as Strategy.* Stockholm: Prisma.

Hooghiemstra, T. (1990) Management of talent. *European Management Journal*, 8(2), 142–149.

Iles, P. (1992) Centres of excellence? Assessment and development centres, managerial competence, and human resource strategies. *British Journal of Management*, 3(2), 79–90.

Jackson, L. (1989) Turning airport managers into high-fliers. *Personnel Management*, 21(10), 80–85.

Jacobs, R. (1989) Getting the measure of managerial competence. *Personnel Management*, 21(6), 32–37.

Jones, A., Herriot, P., Long, B. and Drakeley, R. (1991) Attempting to improve the validity of well-established assessment centre. *Journal of Occupational Psychology*, 64(1), 1–21.

Klein, J., Edge, G. and Kass, T. (1991) Skill-based competition. *Journal of General Management*, 16(4), 1–15.

Klimoski, R. and Brickner, M. (1987) Why do assessment centres work? The puzzle of assessment centre validity. *Personnel Psychology*, 40(2), 243–260.

Lawler, E. (1994) From job-based to competency based organisations. *Journal of Organisational Behaviour*, 15(1), 3–16.

McCormick, E.J. and Ilgen, D. (1987) *Industrial and Organisational Psychology* (8th edn). London: Routledge.

Mabey, C and Iles, P. (1993) The strategy integration of assessment and development practices: succession planning and new management development. *Human Resource Management Journal*, 3(4), 16–34.

Macleod, G. and Wyndham, J. (1991) Developing the competent manager. *Asia Pacific Human Resource Management*, Winter, 69–78.

Mahoney, J.T. and Pandian, J.R. (1992) The resource-based view within the conversation of strategic management. *Strategic Management Journal*, 13(2), 363–380.

Mills, D.Q. and Friesen, B. (1992) The learning organisation. *European Management Journal*, 10(2), 146–156.

Morgan, G. (1989) *Riding the Waves of Change: Developing Managerial Competencies for a Turbulent World*. Oxford: Jossey-Bass.

Murdoch, V.J. (1992) Assessment centres: through the glass brightly. *Asia Pacific Journal of Human Resources*, Spring, 29–41.

Nordhoug, O. and Grønhoug, K. (1994) Competencies and resources in firms. *International Journal of Human Resource Management*, 5(1), 89–106.

Payne, T., Anderson, N. and Smith, T. (1992) Assessment centres, selection systems and cost effectiveness: an evaluative case study. *Personnel Review*, 21(4), 48–56.

Pedler, M., Burgoyne, J. and Boydell T. (1991) *The Learning Company: A Strategy for Sustainable Development*. London: McGraw-Hill.

Personnel Management (1990) Management Charter Initiative has had little impact so far. *Personnel Management*, 22(1), 14.

Pettigrew, A. and Whipp, R. (1991) *Managing Change for Competitive Success*. Oxford: Blackwell.

Reed, R. and DeFillippi, R.J. (1990) Causing ambiguity, barriers to imitation, and sustainable competitive advantage. *Academy of Management Review*, 15(1), 88–102.

Robertson, I.T., Iles, P.A., Gratton, L. and Sharpley, D. (1991) The impact of personnel selection and assessment methods on candidates. *Human Relations*, 44(9), 963–982.

Salaman, G. (ed.) (1992) *Human Resource Strategies*. London: Sage.

Schmidt, F.L. and Hunter, J.E. (1977) Development of a general solution to the problem of validity generalisation. *Journal of Applied Psychology*, 68, 407–414.

Schuler, H. and Guildin, A. (1991) Methodological issues in personnel selection research. In C.L. Cooper and I.T. Robertson (eds), *International Review of Industrial and Organisational Psychology*, (vol. 6). Chichester: John Wiley.

Shackleton, V. (1992) Using a competency approach in a business change setting. In R. Boam and P. Sparrow (ed.), *Designing and Achieving Competency: A Competency-Based Approach to Managing People and Organizations*. London: McGraw-Hill.

Smith, M. and Robertson, I. (1991) *Advances in Selection and Assessment*. Chichester: John Wiley.

Sparrow, P.R. (1994a) The psychology of strategic management: emerging themes of diversity and cognition. In C.L. Cooper and I.T. Robertson (eds), *International Review of Industrial and Organisational Psychology*, (vol. 9). London: John Wiley.

Sparrow, P.R. (1994b) Organisational competencies: creating a strategic behavioural framework for selection and assessment. In N. Anderson and P. Herriot (eds), *Handbook of Assessment and Appraisal*. London: John Wiley.

Sparrow, P.R. and Bognanno, M. (1993) Competency requirement forecasting: issues for international selection and assessment. *International Journal of Selection and Assessment*, 1, 50–58.

Sparrow, P.R. and Hiltrop, J.M. (1994) *European Human Resource Management in Transition*. London: Prentice-Hall.

Spencer, L.M. and Spencer, S.M. (1993) *Competence at Work: Models for Superior Performance*. London: Wiley.

Torrington, D. and Blandamer, W. (1992) Competency, pay and performance management. In R. Boam and P. Sparrow (eds), *Designing and Achieving Competency: A Competency-Based Approach to Managing People and Organizations*. London: McGraw-Hill.

Tziner, A., Ronen, S. and Hacohen, D. (1993) A four-year validation study of an assessment centre in a financial corporation. *Journal of Organisational Behaviour*, 14(3), 225–237.

Whipp, R. (1991) Human resource management, strategic change and competition: the role of learning. *International Journal of Human Resource Management*, 2(2), 165–191.

Woodruffe, C. (1991) Competent by any other name. *Personnel Management*, 23(9), 30–33.

Wright, P. and McMahan, G. (1992) Theoretical perspectives for strategic human resource management. *Journal of Management*, 18(2), 295–320.

30

THINK MANAGER—THINK MALE

A global phenomenon?

Virginia E. Schein, Ruediger Mueller, Terri Lituchy, and Jiang Liu

Source: *Journal of Organizational Behavior* 17 (1996): 33–41.

Summary

The relationship between sex role stereotypes and characteristics perceived as necessary for management success was examined among 361 male and 228 female management students in Japan and the People's Republic of China. The results revealed that males and females in both countries perceive that successful middle managers possess characteristics, attitudes and temperaments more commonly ascribed to men in general than to women in general. These results were compared with previous studies done in the U.S., Great Britain and Germany, using the same Schein 92-item Descriptive Index, and similar samples and procedures. The comparison supports the view that 'think manager—think male' is a global phenomenon, especially among males. Regardless of country context, there was a strong and similar degree of managerial sex typing among male management students in all five countries. Among females, the managerial sex typing hypothesis was confirmed in every country except the U.S., in which men and women are seen as equally likely to possess requisite management characteristics. Unlike those of their male counterparts, the females' pattern of outcomes varied across countries, possibly a reflection of their respective opportunities for managerial participation. The implications of managerial sex typing as a global phenomenon are discussed.

Introduction

In the early 1970s Schein's empirical investigations of managerial sex role stereotyping revealed that 'think manager—think male' was a strongly held belief among middle managers in the United States. Both male (Schein, 1973) and female (Schein, 1975) managers perceived that the characteristics associated with managerial success were more likely to be held by men than by women. Recent U.S. replications reveal that this view is still held today by male managers (Brenner, Tomkiewicz and Schein, 1989; Heilman, Block, Martell and Simon, 1989) and male management students (Schein, Mueller and Jacobson, 1989). Female managers (Brenner *et al*., 1989) and female management students (Schein *et al*., 1989), however, no longer sex type the managerial position. They perceive women to be as likely as men to possess characteristics required of successful managers.

Despite changes in women's progress in the workforce, males, unlike their female counterparts, continue to perceive the managerial position as requiring masculine characteristics. To the extent this attitude is unchecked by structural limitations, the male decision-maker may still favor the male candidate. As a psychological barrier to the advancement of women in management, the 'think manager—think male' phenomenon can foster bias against women in managerial selection, placement, promotion and training decisions.

The globalization of management brings to the forefront the need to examine this phenomenon in the international arena. Antal and Izraeli (1993), in an overview of women in management worldwide state that, 'probably the single most important hurdle for women in management in all industrialized countries is the persistent stereotype that associates management with being male' (p. 63). In an empirical test of this assertion Schein and Mueller (1992) found that German and British management students of both sexes perceive the managerial position to require characteristics more commonly held by men than by women. The psychological barriers to women in management worldwide appear to be strong. As such, we need to determine to what extent 'think manager—think male' may be a global phenomenon.

Internationalizing the research question suggests studies in several countries, in more than one continent, preferably using the same instrument for comparison purposes (e.g. Haire, Ghiselli and Porter, 1966; Hofstede, 1980). The present research attempts such a global look by expanding the stereotyping research to another continent, Asia, and testing the hypothesis in two countries, the People's Republic of China and Japan, within that continent.

In Japan only 5 per cent of all managers and professionals are women (Sato, 1990). Although Japanese women constitute 40 per cent of the workforce (*The New York Times*, 1992), they hold different types of jobs and earn less money than their male counterparts (Rosenfeld and Kallenberg, 1990). Most working women in large corporations are 'office ladies'—clerical workers who serve tea to businessmen (Toshiko, 1983). Since women are expected to 'retire' when they become married (Hiroshi, 1982) or raise children, they are viewed as part-time workers who receive low pay and none of the benefits that male employees receive (Cook and Hayashi, 1980).

Since the 1949 revolution in the People's Republic of China, official government policies have promoted the equality of the sexes and all Chinese women are expected to take part in production (Stacey, 1984). Although the employment of women in China is relatively high, about 78 per cent of the female labor force work in low tech industries and sections (Yi-hong, 1992). Hildebrandt and Liu (1988) report that 8.9 per cent of Chinese managers are women. Korabik's (1992) interview study of Chinese managers suggests that this may be somewhat higher if all types of industries and enterprises are considered. 'Women hold posts as factory production workers, workshop directors, chief accountants, although they still account for only a small percentage compared to men ... the higher the post, the fewer the women' (p. 204).

The purpose of the research was to examine the relationship between sex role stereotypes and requisite management characteristics in these two Asian countries and compare the results to those found by Schein and Mueller (1992) in Western Europe and Schein *et al.* (1989) in the United States, all using similar samples and procedures. As with the previous studies, it was hypothesized that males and females in both Asian countries would perceive successful middle managers as possessing characteristics, attitudes and temperaments more commonly ascribed to men in general than to women in general.

Method

Sample

The Chinese sample consisted of 123 female and 150 male undergraduate upper class students enrolled in a school of business in a large city in China. The Japanese sample was composed of 105 females and 211 males enrolled in business courses at a university in a large Japanese city. All of the male students and 36 per cent of the female students were in the university's four-year business program. The remainder of the females were enrolled in a two-year college on the same university campus.

Measuring instrument

The 92 item Schein Descriptive Index (Schein, 1973, 1975) was used to define sex role stereotypes and the characteristics of successful managers. Three forms of the Index were used. Each contained the same descriptive terms and instructions, except that the one form asked for a description of women in general (Women), one for a description of men in general (Men), and one for a description of successful middle managers (Managers). Each of the forms were back-translated (Brislin, 1970) into either Chinese or Japanese.

The instructions on the three forms of the Index were as follows:

'On the following pages you will find a series of descriptive terms commonly used to characterize people in general. Some of these terms are positive in connotation, others are negative and some are neither very positive nor very negative.

We would like you to use this list to tell us what you think (women in general, men in general or successful middle managers) are like. In making your judgments, it might be helpful to imagine you are about to meet a person for the first time and the only thing you know in advance is that the person is (an adult female, an adult male, or a successful middle manager). Please rate each word or phrase in terms of how characteristic it is of (women in general, men in general, or successful middle managers)'.

The ratings were made according to a 5-point scale, ranging from 1 (not characteristic) to 5 (characteristic) with a neutral rating of 3 (neither characteristic nor uncharacteristic). The respondents used arabic numbers to make the ratings. Items from the Index include: leadership ability, intuitive, aggressive, emotionally stable, dominant, curious and competent.

Procedure

The procedure was similar in both countries. Course instructors at the institutions were given a packet containing distribution instructions and the Schein Descriptive Index. Care was taken with any specific instruction that might be different from usual country procedures, such as placing of the responses before or after the descriptive terms. Each packet contained an equal number of Women, Men and Manager forms so that the Index could be distributed randomly within each class. The questionnaires were completed during class time and returned to the instructor immediately after completion. Each student received only one form of the Index and was not made aware of the purpose of the study. For the questionnaires eliciting descriptions of Women, Men and Managers, respectively, the number responding to each form, by country and gender, was as follows: Chinese males, 53, 45, 52; Chinese females, 37, 42, 44; Japanese males, 77, 82, 52; and Japanese females, 29, 39, 37.

Analyses

The degree of resemblance between the descriptions of men and managers and between women and managers was determined by computing intraclass correlation coefficients (r') from two randomized-groups analyses of variance (see Hays, 1963, p. 424). The classes (or groups) were the 92 descriptive items. In the first analysis, the scores within each class were the mean item ratings of men and managers, while in the second analysis they were the mean item ratings of women and managers. According to Hays, the larger the value of r', the more similar do the observations in the class tend to be relative to the observations in different classes. Thus, the smaller the within-item variability, relative to the between-item variability, the greater the similarity between the mean item ratings of either men and managers or women and managers.

Results

Chinese sample

As shown in Table 1, for males there was a large and significant resemblance between the ratings of men and managers and a near zero, insignificant resemblance between the ratings of women and managers. For females, there was also a large and significant resemblance between the ratings of men and the ratings of managers. Although there was a small significant resemblance between the ratings of women and the ratings of managers, this coefficient was significantly lower than that of the intraclass coefficient between men and managers ($z = 8.38, p < 0.01$). Thus, for both males and females the hypothesis that managers are perceived to possess characteristics more commonly ascribed to men than to women is confirmed.

Japanese sample

As shown in Table 2, there was a large and significant relationship between the ratings of men and managers and a near zero, non-significant relationship between the ratings of women and managers for the males. Before testing the hypothesis

Table 1 Analyses of variance of mean item ratings and intraclass coefficients

Source	\multicolumn{2}{c}{Chinese sample}	F	r'
	df	Mean square		
Males				
Managers and Men				
Between items	91	1.74	22.33	0.91*
Within items	92	0.08		
Managers and Women				
Between items	91	0.63	0.92	−0.04
Within items	92	0.69		
Females				
Managers and Men				
Between items	91	1.75	20.29	0.91*
Within items	92	0.09		
Managers and Women				
Between items	91	0.94	1.76	0.28*
Within items	92	0.53		

*$p < 0.01$.

Table 2 Analyses of variance of mean item ratings and intraclass coefficients

Source	Japanese sample df	Mean square	F	r′
Males				
Managers and Men				
Between items	92	0.64	3.31	0.54*
Within items	91	0.19		
Managers and Women				
Between items	92	0.43	0.88	−0.07
Within items	91	0.49		
Females				
Managers and Men				
Between items	92	0.89	5.26	0.68*
Within items	91	0.17		
Managers and Women				
Between items	92	0.46	0.92	−0.04
Within items	91	0.50		

*$p < 0.01$.

within the female sample, a check for possible response differences between those in the two-year versus the four-year degree program was made. There were no significant differences between the overall mean ratings of each subgroup on the three questionnaire forms (Women, $t = -0.61, p > 0.05$; Men, $t = 1.83, p > 0.05$; Managers, $t = 0.78, p > 0.05$) and the data were pooled for the analyses. Among the females, there was a large and significant relationship between the ratings of men and managers and a near-zero, non-significant relationship between the ratings of women and managers. As such, the hypothesis is confirmed for both males and females.

Item comparisons

An exploratory examination of the individual items was done to gain further understanding of the outcomes. The 15 items with the highest means for each target, i.e. men, women and managers, were displayed by gender within each country. In the Chinese sample, males and females agreed on 14 items as being very characteristic of managers. Of these 14 items, males and females agreed that analytical ability, self confident, competitive, firm, ambitious, creative and vigorous were characteristic of managers and men. Males also saw leadership ability and self-controlled as characteristic of managers and men, while females included competent and prompt as very descriptive of managers and men. Females viewed understanding as very characteristic of managers and women. Males had no over lapping manager–women descriptive terms. Finally, both males and females viewed skilled in business matters and emotionally stable as very characteristic of managers, but neither gender included them among the items seen as most descriptive of either men or women.

In the Japanese sample, males and females agreed on 12 items as being very characteristic of managers. Of these 12 items, males and females viewed desires responsibility and decisive as very characteristic of managers and men. Females also saw prompt and knows the way of the world as highly characteristic of managers and men. Six items—leadership ability, analytical ability, competent, self-controlled, assertive and well informed—were highly characteristic of managers, but not among the items viewed as most descriptive of men or women by either gender. Finally, two items, curious and sociable, were viewed as very characteristic of managers, men, and women by both males and females.

International managerial sex typing

Table 3 displays the Chinese and Japanese outcomes, along with those found by Schein and Mueller (1992) for male and female British and German management students and by Schein *et al.* (1989) for male and female U.S. management students. The comparison reveals that males in all five countries perceive successful middle managers as possessing the characteristics, attitudes and temperaments more commonly ascribed to men in general than women in general. Within all five country samples there was a high and significant resemblance between ratings of men and managers and a low, often close to zero, resemblance between descriptions of women and managers. The Chinese male sample exhibited the highest degree of male-manager similarity, suggesting the greatest degree of managerial sex typing.

Among the females, the comparison reveals that the managerial sex typing hypothesis is confirmed in every country except the U.S. Females in the U.S. see

Table 3 Intraclass coefficients for five country samples

Source	Country sample				
	China	Japan	Germany*	U.K.*	U.S.†
Males					
Managers and Men	0.91‡	0.54‡	0.74‡	0.67‡	0.70‡
Managers and Women	−0.04	−0.07	−0.04	0.02	0.11
Females					
Managers and Men	0.91‡	0.68‡	0.66‡	0.60‡	0.51‡
Managers and Women	0.28‡	0.04	0.19§	0.31‡	0.43‡

* From Schein and Mueller (1992).
† From Schein *et al.* (1989).
‡ $p < 0.01$; § $p < 0.05$.

males and females as equally likely to possess requisite management characteristics. The major cross country difference shown in Table 3 is the varying degrees to which females in each country perceive women to be similar to managers. As with the U.S. females, the British, Chinese and German females also exhibited varying, but significant degrees of resemblance between descriptions of women and descriptions of managers. Unlike the U.S. sample, however, all of these coefficients were significantly smaller than their respective manager–men coefficients. Only the Japanese female sample exhibited no significant resemblance between ratings of managers and ratings of women.

Discussion

Overall, the results lend strong support to the view that 'think manager—think male' is a global phenomenon, especially among males. The strong degree of managerial sex typing found among Chinese and Japanese male management students is similar to that previously found among British, German and U.S. male management students. Despite the many historical, political and cultural differences that exist among these five countries, the view of women as less likely than men to possess requisite management characteristics is a commonly held belief among male management students worldwide.

The Chinese males show a very strong degree of managerial sex typing. These outcomes are perhaps not unexpected. Chinese women have been considered men's appendage during the many thousands of years of feudal society (Xi-hong, 1992). Gender discrimination is often not considered as such, but rather as a true difference based upon a belief in the males' basic superiority (Korabik, 1992). Even women who do become managers are termed 'iron women', meaning that they are masculine or without innate female characteristics (Xiao-tian, 1992). Despite government policies promoting equality (Stacey, 1984), the Chinese male appears to have strongly-held attitudes more closely akin to those of his feudal patriarchal history than to modern day reforms.

On the other hand, Chinese females hold somewhat less closely to the managerial stereotype. Unlike their male counterparts, females see some resemblance between characteristics held by women and requisite management characteristics. The increased participation of women, perhaps dramatic given the years of patriarchal submission, a long time government commitment to equality, as well as their opportunities for female role models and networking, especially through the All-China Women's Federation, (Korabik, 1994) may account for the slightly more positive view of women as managers among Chinese females.

Japanese females see no similarity between women and managers, sharing closely the view of their male counterparts. This may reflect a culture without any impetus to improve opportunities for women. Indeed, barriers such as long work hours, extensive socializing after work, family pressures for university women graduates to marry a manager rather than be one (Steinhoff and Tanaka, 1988), and an equal employment opportunity law with no teeth and passed reluctantly by Parliament (*The New York Times*, 1992) seem to reinforce the status quo for women in Japan.

The display of items within the Chinese sample highlights the characteristics underlying the strong male–manager resemblance found among both males and females. Within the Japanese sample, the target item comparisons highlight several characteristics descriptive of managers, but less descriptive of either men or women, reflective of the significant, but lower male–manager resemblance than that found within the Chinese samples. While the sex role stereotyping hypothesis is confirmed within the Chinese and Japanese samples, that there may be somewhat different views of managerial characteristics as they relate to masculine and feminine characteristics warrants further research.

The global nature of managerial sex typing among males should be of concern to those interested in promoting gender equality worldwide. The similar pattern of outcomes found among male management students in five different countries suggests that attitudinal barriers to women's advancement may be in place for some time. As they become the managers and decision makers of the future, their stereotypical attitudes are apt to limit women's access to and promotions within management internationally.

Schein and Mueller (1992) recommend continued international efforts for equal employment opportunity legislation and the encouragement of corporate structural mechanisms to circumvent the negative impact of stereotypical attitudes on women's opportunities. In addition, more research examining the development of stereotypical attitudes, mitigating factors and approaches to change is also needed. This research might include experimental studies to determine effective interventions during the educational years. With such research and interventions, coupled with continued legal pressures, there may be hope for changes in gender equality as these students of today become our managers of tomorrow.

The variations in the females' degree of managerial sex typing, both in these results and in the comparisons across the five countries, may reflect their views of opportunities for and actual participation of women in management. For example, in the U.S., with large numbers of women in management and strong efforts for continuing change, females do not sex type the position. Direct investigations of explanations for these variations, including the effects of perceived or actual opportunities for women, as well as efforts for change, would seem warranted.

Finally, as a global phenomenon, research on the relationship between sex role stereotypes and requisite management characteristics can be expanded from a sample and a geographical perspective. Managers, as well as management students, need to be investigated and studies of managerial sex typing conducted in South American (see Adaniya and de Perez-Costa, 1992) and African countries, as well as other countries. Such empirical investigations can fuel further research and applied efforts promoting gender equality in management worldwide.

Acknowledgments

The authors would like to thank Kay Tracy, Jill Lynch, Reiko Tsusuki, Kayo Hattori, Keiko Gakuta and Jennifer Williams for help with this research project.

References

Adaniya, A. and de Perez-Costa, R. (1992). Women in Management: The case of Peru. Paper presented at the Women and Management Global Research Conference, Ottawa, Canada.

Antal, A. B. and Izraeli, D. N. (1993). 'A global comparison of women in management: Women managers in their homelands and as expatriates'. In: Fagenson, E. A. (Ed.) *Women in Management: Trends, Issues, and Challenges in Managerial Diversity*. Sage, Newbury Park, pp. 52–96.

Brenner, O. C., Tomkiewicz, J. and Schein, V. E. (1989). 'The relationship between sex role stereotypes and requisite management characteristics revisited', *Academy of Management Journal*, **32**, 662–669.

Brislin, R. W. (1970). 'Back translation for cross cultural research'. *Journal of Cross-Cultural Psychology*, **1**, 185–216.

Cook, A. H. and Hayashi, H. (1980). *Working Women in Japan: Discrimination, Resistance and Reform*, Industrial and Labor Relations School, Cornell University, Ithaca, NY.

Haire, M., Ghiselli, E. E., and Porter, L. W. (1966). *Managerial Thinking: An International Study*, Wiley, New York.

Hays, W. L. (1963). *Statistics for Psychologists*, Holt, Rinehart & Winston, New York.

Heilman, M. E., Block, C. K., Martell, R. F. and Simon, M. C. (1989). 'Has anything changed? Current characteristics of men, women and managers', *Journal of Applied Psychology*, **74**, 935–942.

Hildebrandt, H. and Liu, J. (1988). 'Chinese women managers: A comparison with their U.S. and Asian counterparts', *Human Resource Management*, **27**, 291–314.

Hiroshi, T. (1982). 'Working women in business corporations: the management viewpoint', *Japan Quarterly*, **29**, 319–323.

Hofstede, G. (1980). *Culture's Consequences: International Differences in Work Related Values*, Sage, Beverly Hills, CA.

Korabik, K. (1992). 'Women hold up half the sky: the status of managerial women in China', *Advances in Chinese Industrial Studies*, **3**, 197–211.

Korabik, K. (1994). 'Managerial women in the People's Republic of China: The long march continues'. In: Adler, N. J. and Izraeli, D. N. (Eds) *Competitive Frontiers: Women Managers in a Global Economy*, Blackwell, Cambridge, MA, pp. 114–126.

Rosenfeld, R. A. and Kallenberg, A. L. (1990). 'A cross cultural comparison of gender gap in income', *American Journal of Sociology*, **96**, 69–106.

Sato, G. (1990). Role of women in the workplace. Presented at the 1990 American Chamber of Commerce in Japan Employment Practices Conference, November 29.

Schein, V. E. (1973). 'The relationship between sex role stereotypes and requisite management characteristics', *Journal of Applied Psychology*, **57**, 95–100.

Schein, V. E. (1975). 'The relationship between sex role stereotypes and requisite management characteristics among female managers', *Journal of Applied Psychology*, **60**, 340–344.

Schein, V. E. and Mueller, R. (1992). 'Sex role stereotyping and requisite management characteristics: A cross cultural look', *Journal of Organizational Behavior*, **13**, 439–447.

Schein, V. E., Mueller, R. and Jacobson, C. (1989). 'The relationship between sex role stereotypes and requisite management characteristics among college students', *Sex Roles*, **20**, 103–110.

Stacey, J. (1984). *Patriarchy and Socialist Revolution*, University of California Press, Berkeley, CA.

Steinhoff, P. G. and Tanaka, K. (1988). 'Women managers in Japan'. In: Adler, N. J. and Izraeli, D. N. (Eds) *Women in Management Worldwide*, M. E. Sharpe, Armonk, NY, pp. 103–121.

The New York Times (1992). 'Women in Japan job market find the door closing again', December 1, pp. 1+.

Toshiko, F. (1983). 'Women in the labor force', *Kodansha Encyclopedia of Japan*, **8**, 261–269.

Xi-hong, J. (1992). 'From indirect-exist to replacement of achievement', *China Woman*, February, p. 14.

Xiao-tian, T. (1992). 'Changing female image', *China Woman*, July 16–18.

Yi-hong, J. (1992). 'The cultural quality of the Chinese female', *China Woman*, July, 26–27.

31

THE SCIENCE OF TRAINING
A decade of progress

Eduardo Salas and Janis A. Cannon-Bowers

Source: *Annual Review of Psychology* 52(2001): 471–499.

Abstract

This chapter reviews the training research literature reported over the past decade. We describe the progress in five areas of research including training theory, training needs analysis, antecedent training conditions, training methods and strategies, and posttraining conditions. Our review suggests that advancements have been made that help us understand better the design and delivery of training in organizations, with respect to theory development as well as the quality and quantity of empirical research. We have new tools for analyzing requisite knowledge and skills, and for evaluating training. We know more about factors that influence training effectiveness and transfer of training. Finally, we challenge researchers to find better ways to translate the results of training research into practice.

Introduction

In the 30 years since the first review of training in the *Annual Review of Psychology*, things have progressed dramatically in terms of both the science and practice of training. On the practice side, socio-cultural, technological, economic, and political pressures have all combined to force modern organizations to take a closer look at their human capital in general, and training in particular (Thayer 1997, Howard 1995). In fact, now more than ever, organizations must rely on workplace learning and continuous improvement in order to remain competitive (London & Moore 1999). In addition, organizations have shifted their views about training from a separate, stand-alone event to a fully integrated, strategic component of the organization. New training-related approaches, including action learning, just-in-time training, mentoring, coaching, organizational learning, and managing skill portfolios are all currently being explored. Finally, modern organizations must cope with training needs associated with the changing demographics of the population—both an older and more diverse workforce can be expected as we move into the new millennium.

It is important to note that improved training comes at a cost. Recent estimates suggest that the investment in training activities in organizations ranges from $55.3 billion to $200 billion annually (Bassi & Van Buren 1999, McKenna 1990), an investment that has not only created a growing interest in training, but also in learning technologies and performance-improvement processes, practices, and services. In fact, there is an increasing concern in organizations that the investment made in training must be justified in terms of improved organizational performance—increased productivity, profit, or safety; reduced error, enhanced market share (e.g. Huselid 1995, Martocchio & Baldwin 1997, Salas et al 2000).

The past 30 years have also witnessed tremendous growth in training research. This trend has been so pronounced that we are led to conclude that there has been nothing less than an explosion in training-related research in the past 10 years. More theories, models, empirical results, reviews, and meta-analyses are available today than ever before. Whether this research is having an effect on training practice—that is, a meaningful impact on how organizations actually train—is a matter of some debate. We return to this issue after documenting the many advances in training research over the past decade.

This is the sixth review of training and development to appear in the *Annual Review of Psychology* (see Campbell 1971, Goldstein 1980, Wexley 1984, Latham 1988, Tannenbaum & Yukl 1992). In this review, we focus on research published from 1992 to January 2000. Similar to Tannenbaum &Yukl's (1992), our review is selective and descriptive. We focus primarily on the research that is concerned with the design, delivery, and evaluation of training in work organizations. Our review is organized as follows. We first discuss the recent theoretical advancements in training over the past decade. Then we address the relevant research on training needs analysis, including organization, job/task, and person analysis. Following this, we address antecedent training conditions (i.e. pretraining variables) that may enhance or disrupt learning. Next we turn our discussion to research on training methods and instructional strategies. In this section we discuss recent developments in simulation-based training, learning approaches, team training, and the influence of technology on training research and practice. Finally we review the research on post-training conditions. This includes a discussion of training evaluation and transfer of training. Wherever appropriate we point out the research needs and gaps. We conclude with a few observations and trends and a word about the future. Consistent with previous reviews, this review does not cover basic issues involved in skill acquisition and learning, organizational development, socialization in organizations, or educational psychology. We also do not synthesize the large literature in practitioner-oriented publications.

Initial observations

Our first observation is that in 30 years of documenting the progress of training research, it is clear that the field, by any measure, has changed dramatically—for the better. Now, as recent reviews have documented, training-related theories abound. As noted earlier, there is also more empirical training-related research going on—in the field as well as in the lab—than ever before. Researchers are adopting a systems view of training and are more concerned with the organizational context. There are new models, constructs (e.g. opportunity to perform), and influences (e.g. technology) in the reported research. The traditional training evaluation paradigm has been expanded, and there are more evaluations being conducted and reported. There are better tools with which to conduct training evaluations, and better (and more practical) experimental designs have emerged. The field can now offer sound, pedagogically based principles and guidelines to practitioners and instructional developers. Furthermore, the impact of training on performance and organizational effectiveness is being felt (Bassi & Van Buren 1999), although clearly more documentation is needed here. Finally, there are more books and textbooks related to training (e.g. Ford et al 1997, Quinones & Ehrestein 1997, Noe 1999, Wexley & Latham 2000, Goldstein 1993; plus over 20 more that have been reviewed in *Personnel Psychology*).The science of training has progressed and matured—it is now truly an exciting and dynamic field. As evidence for this assertion, we summarize some of the latest theoretical advances in the next section.

Theoretical developments

There have been some influential theories developed about training since 1992. In fact, the past decade has offered us myriad new and expanded theoretical frameworks, as well as concepts and constructs. This thinking is deeper, richer, more comprehensive, and more focused. More importantly, the field has been energized by these developments so that empirical work has followed. Some of these frameworks and concepts are broad, general, and integrating. For example, Tannenbaum and colleagues provided an integrative framework for all the variables that influence the design and delivery of training (see Tannenbaum et al 1993, Cannon-Bowers et al 1995). The framework outlines in detail the pretraining and during-training conditions that may influence learning, as well as the factors that may facilitate the transfer of skills after training. Kozlowski & Salas (1997), drawing from organizational theory, discussed the importance of characterizing the factors and processes in which training interventions are implemented and transferred in organizations. Moreover, Kozlowski and colleagues (Kozlowski et al 2000) consider organizational system factors and training design issues that influence the effectiveness of vertical transfer processes. Vertical transfer refers to the upward propagation of individual-level training outcomes that emerge as team- and organizational-level outcomes. This issue has been largely neglected by researchers yet is suggested to be crucial to training effectiveness. Similarly, researchers have begun to understand and outline the barriers and myths that exist in organizations as they implement training (Dipboye 1997, Salas et al 1999). In other work, Kraiger et al (1993) provided new conceptualizations of learning and evaluation theory, approaches, and measurement. These authors expanded Kirkpatrick's (1976) evaluation typology by incorporating recent notions in cognitive psychology.

Other conceptual developments are more focused. For example, Ford et al (1997) invoked "the opportunity to perform" construct as a way to understand the transfer of training process. Colquitt et al (2000) summarized (qualitatively and quantitatively) the literature on training motivation and offered a new, integrative model. Cannon-Bowers & Salas (1997) proposed a framework for how to conceptualize performance measurement in training. Thayer & Teachout (1995) developed a model to understand the climate for transfer in organizations, as well as in-training conditions that enhance transfer. Cannon-Bowers et al (1998) advanced a number of conditions, concepts, and interventions that may enhance practice. Ford and colleagues have looked at individual differences and learner control strategies (e.g. Ford et al 1998). Training researchers have also examined variables such as the pretraining context (e.g. Baldwin & Magjuka 1997, Quinones 1995), conscientiousness and training outcomes (e.g. Colquitt & Simmering 1998, Martocchio & Judge 1997), individual and situational characteristics that influence training motivation (e.g. Facteau et al 1995, Mathieu & Martineau 1997), and participation in developmental activities (e.g. Noe & Wilk 1993, Baldwin & Magjuka 1997), just to name a few.

In sum, these theoretical advancements have provided a much needed forum in which to discuss debate, analyze, and understand better the design and delivery of training in organizations. Moreover, they have provided an organized framework in which systematic research could be couched. Our conclusion is that training research is no longer atheoretical as charged by our predecessors. We believe the field is healthier because of these influences and all the empirical work that has followed.

Training needs analysis

It is well acknowledged that one of the most important steps in training development is conducting a training needs analysis. This first step in training development focuses on the process of deciding who and what should be trained. A training needs analysis is primarily conducted to determine where training is needed, what needs to be taught, and who needs to be trained (Goldstein 1993). This phase has several outcomes. One is the specification of learning objectives, which in turn shape the design and delivery of training, as well as the process of criterion development. Consistent with Tannenbaum & Yukl (1992), we found a limited amount of empirical work on training needs analysis. In this section we discuss two components: organizational analysis and job/task analysis. We briefly address the third phase—person analysis.

Organizational analysis

The purpose of an organizational analysis is to outline the systemwide components of the organization that may affect the delivery of a training program (Goldstein 1993). That is, it focuses on the congruence between training objectives with such factors as organizational goals, available resources, constraints, and support for transfer. Unfortunately, many training programs fail to reach their goals because of organizational constraints and conflicts, which could have been identified and ameliorated before training was implemented. Hence, conducting an organizational analysis is an important first-step training design. The best treatment of this topic can be found in Goldstein (1993).

Only recently have training researchers begun to pay attention to organizational analysis. One study, conducted by Rouiller & Goldstein (1993) in a chain of fast food restaurants, demonstrated that organizational climate (e.g. situational cues, consequences) was a powerful predictor of whether trainees transferred the learned skills. A second study conducted in a chain of supermarkets by Tracey et al (1995) showed that organizational climate and culture were directly related to posttraining behaviors. Clearly, these two studies illustrate how powerful an effect the organizational environment can have on whether newly acquired knowledge, skills, and attitudes (KSAs) are applied on the job (see also the transfer of training section).

As job requirements change, so does the need to help organizations plan their human resources activities. A number of issues have emerged that are related to organizational analysis. For example, authors have expressed the need to understand how the organizational context influences human resources strategies (e.g. Tannenbaum & Dupuree-Bruno 1994) to enhance continuous learning environments (e.g. London & Moore 1999), to manage knowledge effectively (e.g. Tannenbaum 1997), and to determine the best organizational strategy (e.g. who is responsible for training?) for learning and training (e.g. Martocchio & Baldwin 1997). Obviously, organizational analysis is crucial for ensuring the success of a training program. However, more research is needed to develop practical and diagnostic tools to determine the organizational context relative to training.

Job/task analysis

Historically, job/task analysis has been used to identify the information necessary to create the learning objectives (Goldstein 1993). A job/task analysis results in a detailed description of the work functions to be performed on the job, the conditions under which the job is to be performed, and the KSAs needed to perform those tasks.

In the past decade, new research aimed at developing solid methods, approaches, and knowledge elicitation techniques for determining training needs and requirements have emerged. For example, Arvey et al (1992) explored the use of task inventories to forecast skills and abilities necessary for a future job. The results indicated that such forecasting predictions could represent useful information to training analysis. Wilson & Zalewski (1994) tested an expert system program as a way to estimate the amount of 11 abilities required for performing a job. The results indicated that most incumbents preferred the expert system method to the traditional ability rating scales.

Some attention has been given to better understanding the job/task analysis process for training purposes. For example, Ford et al (1993) examined the impact of task experience and individual factors on task ratings of training emphasis. Results indicated that as experience (and self-efficacy) increased over time, it tended to cause trainees to increase their ratings of training emphasis. Also, a few researchers have focused on outlining a task analysis procedure for teams (e.g. Baker et al 1998, Bowers et al 1993, Blickensderfer et al 2000). Much more research is needed, however. Specifically, we need to design and develop a methodology that helps instructional designers and analysts uncover the team-based tasks and their related KSAs.

Cognitive task analysis

Cognitive task analysis refers to a set of procedures for understanding the mental processing and mental requirements for job performance. It has received much attention recently (see Dubois et al 1997/1998, Schraagen et al 2000), fueled primarily by interest in understanding how trainees acquire and develop knowledge, and how they organize rules, concepts, and associations (see Zsambok & Klein 1997). In addition, research aimed at uncovering the nature of expertise and how experts make decisions in complex natural environments has led to the development of tools such as cognitive task analysis (see Salas & Klein 2000, Schraagen et al 2000).

Cognitive task analysis is based on techniques (e.g. verbal protocols) used by cognitive scientists to elicit knowledge from subject matter experts. Products of a cognitive task analysis include information-generating templates for mental model development, cues for fostering complex decision-making skills, cues for developing simulation and scenarios used during training, and information for designing performance measurement and feedback protocols. For example, Neerincx & Griffoen (1996) applied a cognitive task analysis to assess the task load of jobs and to provide indicators for the redesign of jobs. This new application showed its benefits over the "old" task load analysis.

A cognitive task analysis can complement existing (behavioral) forms of training-need analysis. For example, research on meta-cognition suggests that through continued practice or experience, individuals automatize complex behaviors, thus freeing up cognitive resources for monitoring and evaluating behavior

(Rogers et al 1997). By determining trainees' current complex cognitive skills, instructional designers can gain insight into trainees' capacity for proficiency and diagnose performance deficiencies. Thus, training-needs analysis should identify not only the requisite knowledge and skills to perform tasks, but also the cues and cognitions that enable trainees to know when to apply those skills. By incorporating the development of these skills into training, instructional designers can provide trainees with valuable self-help tools. Cognitive task analysis is becoming a useful tool but needs more development. Specifically, a theoretically driven methodology that clearly outlines the steps to take and how to analyze the data is needed.

We found no empirical work regarding the third phase of training-needs analysis—person analysis. However, the emerging literature of 360° feedback may be relevant. This approach identifies individual strengths and weaknesses, but perhaps more importantly, provides suggestions for improvement that often revolve around training and development activities.

In summary, it is interesting to note that whereas most training researchers believe and espouse that training-needs analysis is the most important phase in training, this phase remains largely an art rather than a science. We need more research that would enable us to develop a systematic methodology to determine the training needs of organizations.

Antecedent training conditions

Events that occur before training can be as important as (and in some cases more important than) those that occur during and after training. Research has shown that activities that occur prior to training have an impact on how effective training turns out to be (Tannenbaum et al 1993). These factors fall into three general categories: (*a*) what trainees bring to the training setting, (*b*) variables that engage the trainee to learn and participate in developmental activities, and (*c*) how the training can be prepared so as to maximize the learning experience. Each of these is described in more detail below.

Individual characteristics

Cognitive ability

Research aimed at understanding how characteristics the trainee brings to the training environment influence learning has proliferated in the past decade. For example, Ree et al (1995) developed a causal model showing the role of general cognitive ability and prior job knowledge in subsequent job-knowledge attainment and work-sample performance during training. The resulting model showed that ability influenced the attainment of job knowledge directly, and that general cognitive ability influenced work samples through job knowledge. Similar findings have been obtained by Ree & Earles (1991), Colquitt et al (2000), Randel et al

(1992), Quick et al (1996), Kaemar et al (1997), Warr & Bunce (1995), and many others. Therefore, it is safe to conclude, based on this body of evidence (and others as well, e.g. Hunter 1986), that *g* (general intelligence) is good—it promotes self-efficacy and performance, and it helps a great deal with skill acquisition. Clearly, those who have high cognitive ability (all other things being equal) will likely learn more and succeed in training.

At this point, we probably need to look more closely at low-ability trainees and conduct research on how to optimize learning for them. Also, it might be worthwhile to examine in more depth concepts such as tacit knowledge and practical intelligence (Sternberg 1997) and their relation to on-the-job learning. Finally, it is worth noting that cognitive ability is a viable predictor of training performance (i.e. learning), but not necessarily performance on the job. Many jobs have requirements that go beyond cognitive ability (e.g. psychomotor demands), and/or depend on other factors (e.g. motivation) for success. Therefore, it is important to understand the nature of the job to determine whether cognitive ability will be a valid predictor of training transfer.

Self-efficacy

This construct has been widely studied in this past decade. The findings are consistent: Self-efficacy, whether one has it before or acquires it during training, leads to better learning and performance. Self-efficacy (the belief that one can perform specific tasks and behaviors) is a powerful predictor of performance, as has been shown time and time again (e.g. Cole & Latham 1997, Eden & Aviram 1993, Ford et al 1998, Mathieu et al 1993, Martocchio 1994, Martocchio & Webster 1992, Mathieu et al 1992, Quinones 1995, Mitchell et al 1994, Phillips & Gully 1997, Stevens & Gist 1997, Stajkovic & Luthans 1998). Self-efficacy also mediates a number of personal variables including job satisfaction, organizational commitment, intention to quit the job, the relationship between training and adjustment in newcomers (Saks 1995), and the relationship between conscientiousness and learning (Martocchio & Judge 1997). Self-efficacy has also been shown to have motivational effects (e.g. Quinones 1995), to influence training reactions (Mathieu et al 1992), and to dictate whether trainees will use training technology (Christoph et al 1998).

In sum, it is well established that self-efficacy enhances learning outcomes and performance. A research need that still remains is to expand what we know about self-efficacy at the team level. Whereas a few studies have investigated collective efficacy in training (e.g. Guzzo et al 1993, Smith-Jentsch et al 2000), considerably more work is needed to better understand the mechanisms of collective efficacy in learning as a means to raise team performance. In addition, it might be useful to consider the use of self-efficacy as a deliberate training intervention (i.e. developing training targeted at raising self-efficacy), as well as a desirable outcome of training (i.e. as an indicator of training success).

Goal orientation

Goal orientation has received considerable attention in recent years (e.g. Brett & VandeWalle 1999, Ford et al 1998, Phillips & Gully 1997). This construct is broadly conceptualized as the mental framework used by individuals to interpret and behave in learning- or achievement-oriented activities. Two classes of goal orientation have been identified (Dweck 1986, Dweck & Leggett 1988): (*a*) mastery (or learning) goal orientation, whereby individuals seek to develop competence by acquiring new skills and mastering novel situations, and (*b*) performance goal orientation, whereby individuals pursue assurances of their own competence by seeking good performance evaluations and avoiding negative ones. There is a debate in the literature as to whether goal orientation is a disposition, a state, or both (e.g. Stevens & Gist 1997), whether it is a multidimensional construct (e.g. Elliot & Church 1997, VandeValle 1997), or whether these two goal strategies are mutually exclusive (Buttom et al 1996). Although continued research will bring more conceptual clarity, recent studies have shown, in general, that goal orientation influences learning outcomes and performance. For example, Fisher & Ford (1998) found that a mastery orientation was a strong predictor of a knowledge-based learning outcome. Ford et al (1998) showed that mastery orientation was positively related to the meta-cognitive activity of the trainee. Phillips & Gully (1997) demonstrated that mastery goal orientation was positively related to self-efficacy. All these results are promising. More research is needed to determine how goal orientation is developed. Specifically, it must be determined whether goal orientation is a relatively stable trait, or if it can be modified prior to training. Should the latter be true, then efforts to move trainees toward a mastery orientation should be developed.

Training motivation

Training motivation can be conceptualized as the direction, effort, intensity, and persistence that trainees apply to learning-oriented activities before, during, and after training (Kanfer 1991, Tannenbaum & Yukl 1992). Recently, several studies have found (and confirmed) that trainees' motivation to learn and attend training has an effect on their skill acquisition, retention, and willingness to apply the newly acquired KSAs on the job (e.g. Martocchio & Webster 1992, Mathieu et al 1992, Quinones 1995, Tannenbaum & Yukl 1992). Whereas the literature is, in general, clear about the influence of training motivation on learning outcomes, it has lacked some conceptual precision and specificity, and has been somewhat piecemeal. An exception is a recent effort by Colquitt et al (2000) that has shed light on the underlying processes and variables involved in understanding training motivation throughout the training process. Their integrative narrative and meta-analytic review suggest that training motivation is multifaceted and influenced by a set of individual (e.g. cognitive ability, self-efficacy, anxiety, age, conscientiousness) and situational (e.g. climate) characteristics. This effort provides the beginnings of an integrative theory of training motivation—a much needed synthesis and organization.

A number of important implications for research and practice can be drawn from Colquitt et al's review. For example, they point out the need to assess trainee's personality during training-needs analysis, a much neglected or ignored assessment during person analysis. In fact, Colquitt et al also called for the need to expand the kind of personality variables we have examined in recent years to include emotions, adaptability, trait goal orientation, and other Big Five variables. Another important implication is the link they found between age and motivation to learn—older workers showed lower motivation, learning, and post-training efficacy. However, it may be prudent to consider this conclusion carefully because a host of other issues must be considered when discussing the training needs of older workers (including the design of training itself). Clearly, in an era of technology-driven instruction and an aging workforce, a challenge for instructional developers will be to design learning environments where older trainees can be trained (and retrained) with ease.

In the future, we also need to continue gaining a deeper understanding of training motivation because it is crucial for learning and has direct implications for the design and delivery of training. Future work should consider those factors that influence training motivation for job development activities and for situations in which workers acquire new skills through informal learning mechanisms. Longitudinal studies are also needed.

Training induction and pretraining environment

Considerable research has gone into understanding which factors help trainees to optimize the benefits of training. These are usually interventions employed before training to ensure that the trainee gets the most out of the learning experience.

Prepractice conditions

It is well documented that practice is a necessary condition for skill acquisition. However, all practice is not equal. In fact, the precise nature of practice and its relationship to learning outcomes has been largely ignored or misunderstood. Recent thinking and research is beginning to suggest that practice may be a complex process, not simply task repetition (e.g. Ehrenstein et al 1997, Shute & Gawlick 1995, Schmidt & Bjork 1992); we address this issue further in Specific Learning Approaches. For example, Cannon-Bowers et al (1998) provided a framework for delineating the conditions that might enhance the utility and efficacy of practice in training. They drew from the literature a number of interventions (e.g. meta-cognitive strategies, advanced organizers, and preparatory information) that can be applied before actual practice as a way to prepare the trainee for training. Empirical verification of these interventions needs to be conducted.

The pretraining environment and climate

Can pretraining contextual factors also affect learning outcomes? Recent research suggests that the manner in which the organization frames the training and the nature of trainees' previous experiences in training do influence learning outcomes. For example, Quinones (1995) demonstrated that the manner in which training was framed (i.e. as advanced or remedial) influenced training motivation and learning (see also Quinones 1997). Martocchio (1992), who labeled the training assignment as an "opportunity," showed similar findings. Smith-Jentsch et al (1996a) demonstrated that trainees' previous experiences with training (e.g. prior negative events) affected learning and retention. Baldwin & Magjuka (1997) explored the notion of training as an organizational episode and laid out a framework of other pretraining contextual factors (e.g. voluntary versus mandatory attendance) that may influence motivation to learn. These studies suggest that experience with training (both task-based and event-based) is important to subsequent training outcomes. This is certainly a neglected area, and one in which much more work is needed. Specifically, we need to know how these experiences shape self-efficacy, expectations about the training, motivation to learn and apply skills on the job, and learning.

Training methods and instructional strategies

Instructional strategies are defined as a set of tools (e.g. task analysis), methods (e.g. simulation), and content (i.e. required competencies) that, when combined, create an instructional approach (Salas & Cannon-Bowers 1997). Most effective strategies are created around four basic principles: (*a*) They present relevant information or concepts to be learned; (*b*) they demonstrate the KSAs to be learned; (*c*) they create opportunities for trainees to practice the skills; and (*d*) they provide feedback to trainees during and after practice. Because there is no single method to deliver training, researchers continue to address how to best present targeted information to trainees. Specifically, researchers are seeking cost-effective, content-valid, easy-to-use, engaging, and technology-based methods (e.g. Baker et al 1993, Bretz & Thompsett 1992, Steele-Johnson & Hyde 1997). In the next section, we review research related to instructional strategies in several major categories. First, we review specific learning approaches and learning technologies and distance training. Next, we cover simulation-based training and games, followed by a review of recent work in team training.

Specific learning approaches

Traditionally, training researchers have investigated how to optimize learning and retention by manipulating feedback, practice intervals, reinforcement schedules, and other conditions within the learning process itself. In this regard, Fisk, Kurlik, and colleagues (Kirlik et al 1998) improved performance in a complex decision-making task by training consistently mapped components of the task to automaticity (i.e. so that they could be performed with little or no active cognitive control). Along these same lines, Driskell et al (1992) conducted a meta-analysis of the effects of overlearning on retention. The results of their analysis showed that overlearning produces a significant effect on retention which, in turn, is moderated by the degree of overlearning, length of retention period, and type of task.

Attention has also been focused on developing collaborative training protocols. This is distinguished from team training (see below) by the fact that team training applies to training competencies that are required for performance of a team task. Collaborative learning, on the other hand, refers to situations where trainees are trained in groups, but not necessarily to perform a team task. The idea is that there are features of group interaction that benefit the learning process (e.g. the opportunity for vicarious learning or interaction with peers). For example, Arthur et al (1997) provided strong support and justification for the ongoing use of innovative dyadic protocols (i.e. training two trainees at once) for the training of pilots and navigators in both military and nonmilitary settings. However, Arthur et al (1996) showed that the comparative effectiveness of dyadic versus individual protocols for computer-based training is moderated by trainees' level of interaction anxiety, with only low interaction anxiety trainees benefiting from dyadic protocols (see also Arthur et al 1997). Collaborative protocols have also been shown to reduce required instructor time and resources by half (Shebilske et al 1992), and to provide observational learning opportunities that compensate for hands-on practice efficiently and effectively, as predicted by social learning theory (Shebilske et al 1998).

Researchers have also studied the conditions of practice as they relate to learning. For example, Goettl et al (1996) compared an alternating task module protocol, which alternated sessions on video game–like tasks and algebra word problems, with a massed protocol, which blocked sessions on the tasks. The findings showed that alternating task modules provided an advantage in learning and retention in both the video games and algebra word problems.

Along these lines, Bjork and colleagues (Schmidt & Bjork 1992, Ghodsian et al 1997) have provided an interesting reconsideration of findings regarding practice schedules. These authors argued that introducing difficulties for the learner during practice will enhance transfer (but not necessarily immediate posttraining performance). By reconceptualizing interpretation of data from several studies, Schmidt & Bjork (1992) provided a compelling case for a new approach to arranging practice. This approach includes introducing variation in the way tasks are ordered for practice, in the nature and scheduling of feedback, and in the versions of the task to be practiced, and also by providing less frequent feedback. In all cases, the authors argue that even though acquisition (i.e. immediate) performance may be decreased, retention and generalization are enhanced owing to additional—and most likely deeper—information processing requirements during practice. Shute & Gawlick (1995) supported this conclusion in an investigation of computer-based training for flight engineering knowledge and skill.

In other work, Driskell and colleagues (Driskell & Johnston 1998, Johnston & Cannon-Bowers 1996; JE Driskell, E Salas, JH Johnston, submitted) have investigated the use of stress-exposure training (SET) as a means to prepare trainees to work in high stress environments. SET, which is based on clinical research into stress inoculation, has several phases. In the first phase, trainees are provided with preparatory information that includes a description of which stressors are likely to be encountered in the environment and what the likely impact of those stressors on the trainee will be. The second phase—skill acquisition—focuses on behavioral- and cognitive-skills training designed to help trainees cope with the stress. In the final phase, application and practice of learned skills is conducted under conditions that gradually approximate the stress environment. Results of investigations of this protocol have indicated that SET is successful in reducing trainees' subjective perception of stress, while improving performance. Moreover, the effects of SET generalized to novel stressors and tasks.

Learning technologies and distance training

There is no doubt that technology is shaping how training is delivered in organizations. While still relying heavily on classroom training, organizations have begun to explore technologies such as video conferencing, electronic performance support systems, video discs, and on-line Internet/Intranet courses. Indeed, Web-based training may make "going-to" training obsolete. It is being applied in education, industry, and the military at an alarming rate (these days, one can get a PhD through the Web). What is probably more alarming is that this implementation is happening without much reliance on the science of training. Many issues about how to design distance learning systems remain open. Theoretically-based research is needed to uncover principles and guidelines that can aid instructional designers in building sound distance training. A few have begun to scratch the surface (e g. Schreiber & Berge 1998) of this topic, but a science of distance learning and training needs to evolve. Specifically, it must be determined what level of interaction is needed between trainees and instructors. Moreover, the nature of such interaction must be specified. For example, do instructors need to see trainees in order to conduct effective instruction? Do trainees need to see instructors or is it better for them to view other material? What is the best mechanism for addressing trainee questions (e.g. through chat rooms or e-mail)? Should learners have control over the pace and nature of instruction [some evidence from studies of computer-based training support the use of learner control (see Shute et al 1998), but the extent of its benefits for distance learning is not known]? These and other questions must be addressed as a basis to develop sound distance-training systems.

Advances in technology are also enabling the development of intelligent tutoring systems that have the potential to reduce or eliminate the need for human instructors for certain types of learning tasks. Early indications are that intelligent software can be programmed to successfully monitor, assess, diagnose, and remediate performance in tasks such as computer programming and solving algebra problems (e.g. see Anderson et al 1995). As this technology becomes more widely available (and less costly to develop), it may provide organizations with a viable alternative to traditional computer-based or classroom training.

Simulation-based training and games

Simulation continues to be a popular method for delivery training. Simulators are widely used in business, education, and the military (Jacobs & Dempsey 1993). In fact, the military and the commercial aviation industry are probably the biggest investors in simulation-based training. These simulations range in cost, fidelity, and functionality. Many simulation systems (including simulators and virtual environments) have the ability to mimic detailed terrain, equipment failures, motion, vibration, and visual cues about a situation. Others are less sophisticated and have less physical fidelity, but represent well the KSAs to be trained (e.g. Jentsch & Bowers 1998). A recent trend is to use more of these low-fidelity devices to train complex skills. There is also more evidence that skills transfer after training that uses these simulations (e.g. MT Brannick, C Prince, E Salas, unpublished manuscript; Gopher et al 1994). For example, some researchers are studying the viability of computer games for training complex tasks. Gopher et al (1994) tested the transfer of skills from a complex computer game to the flight performance of cadets in the Israeli Air Force flight school. They argued that the context relevance of the game to flight was based on a skill-oriented task analysis, which used information provided by contemporary models of the human processing system as the framework. Flight performance scores of two groups of cadets who received 10 hours of training in the computer game were compared with a matched group with no game experience. Results showed that the groups with game experience performed much better in subsequent test flights than did those with no game experience. Jentsch & Bowers (1998) and Goettl et al (1996) have reported similar findings.

Precisely why simulation and simulators work is not well known. A few studies have provided preliminary data (e.g. Bell & Waag 1998, Jentsch & Bowers 1998, Ortiz 1994), but there is a somewhat misleading conclusion that simulation (in and of itself) leads to learning. Unfortunately, most of the evaluations rely on trainee reaction data and not on performance or learning data (see Salas et al 1998). More systematic and rigorous evaluations of large-scale simulations and simulators are needed. Nonetheless, the use of simulation continues at a rapid pace in medicine, maintenance, law enforcement, and emergency management settings. However, some have noted (e.g. Salas et al 1998) that simulation and simulators are being used without much consideration of what has been learned about cognition, training design, or effectiveness. There is a growing need to incorporate the recent advances in training research into simulation design and practice. Along these lines, some have argued for an event-based approach to training with simulations

(Cannon-Bowers et al 1998, Oser et al 1999, Fowlkes et al 1998). According to this perspective, simulation-based training should be developed with training objectives in mind, and allow for the measurement of training process and outcomes, and provisions for feedback (both during the exercise and for debriefing purposes).

In related work, Ricci et al (1995) investigated the use of a computer-based game to train chemical, biological, and radiological defense procedures. In this case, the game was not a simulation (as discussed above), but a computer-based slot machine that presented trainees with questions about the material. Trainees earned points for correct answers, and received corrective feedback for incorrect ones. The authors argued that motivation to engage in this type of presentation (over text-based material) would result in higher learning. Results indicated that reactions and retention (but not immediate training performance) were higher for the game condition.

Behavior role modeling is another type of simulation-based training that has received attention over the years. Recently, Skarlicki & Latham (1997) found that a training approach that included role-playing, and other elements of behavior modeling, was successful in training organizational citizenship behavior in a labor union setting. Similarly, Smith-Jentsch et al (1996b) found that a behavior modeling approach emphasizing practice (i.e. role playing) and performance feedback was superior to a lecture only or lecture with demonstration format for training assertiveness skills. Also studying assertiveness, Baldwin (1992) found that behavioral reproduction (i.e. demonstrating assertiveness in a situation that was similar to the training environment) was best achieved by exposing trainees only to positive model displays. Conversely, the combination of both positive and negative model displays was most effective in achieving behavioral generalization (i.e. applying the skill outside of the training simulation) four weeks later.

Team training

As noted by Guzzo & Dickson (1996) and Tannenbaum & Yukl (1992), teams are heavily used in industry, government, and the military. Therefore, these organizations have invested some resources in developing teams (Tannenbaum 1997). A number of theoretically-driven team training strategies has emerged. These include cross-training (Blickensderfer et al 1998), team coordination training (Prince & Salas 1993), team leadership training (Tannenbaum et al 1998), team self-correction (Smith-Jentsch et al 1998), and distributed team training (Dwyer et al 1999). All of these have been tested and evaluated with positive results (see Cannon-Bowers & Salas 1998a).

The aviation community has arguably been the biggest advocate and user of team training (see Helmreich et al 1993). The airlines and the military have extensively applied a strategy labeled crew resource management (CRM) training. This strategy has a 20-year history in the aviation environment. It is used as a tool to improve teamwork in the cockpit but, more importantly, to reduce human error, accidents, and mishaps (Helmreich & Foushee 1993). CRM training has gone through several evolutions (Helmreich et al 1999) and is maturing. Systematic procedures for designing and developing CRM training have been developed (Salas et al 1999), and the evaluation data are encouraging (see Leedom & Simon 1995, Salas et al 1999, Stout et al 1997). CRM training seems to work by changing the crew's attitudes toward teamwork, and by imparting the relevant team competencies. Crew that have received CRM training exhibit more teamwork behaviors in the cockpit (Salas et al 1999, Stout et al 1997). However, more and better evaluations are needed. Most of the evaluations conducted have been in simulation environments. Only recently have evaluations begun to determine the transfer of this training to the actual cockpit.

Other research in team training has focused on developing strategies to train specific competencies (see also Cannon-Bowers & Salas 1998b). For example, Smith-Jentsch et al (1996b) examined determinants of team performance–related assertiveness in three studies. These studies concluded that, whereas both attitudinally focused and skill-based training improved attitudes toward team member assertiveness, practice and feedback were essential to producing behavioral effects. In addition, Volpe et al (1996) used shared mental model theory (Cannon-Bowers et al 1993) as a basis to examine the effects of cross-training and workload on performance. The results indicated that those who received cross-training were more effective in teamwork processes, communication, and overall team performance.

In sum, the literature has begun to provide evidence that team training works. It works when the training is theoretically driven, focused on required competencies, and designed to provide trainees with realistic opportunities to practice and receive feedback. Also, guidelines for practitioners have emerged (e.g. Swezey & Salas 1992, Salas & Cannon-Bowers 2000), tools for designing team training strategies have surfaced (e.g. Bowers et al 1993), and a number of strategies are now available for team training (e.g. Cannon-Bowers & Salas 1997). In the future, we need to know more about how to diagnose team cognitions during training. We also need better and more rigorous measurement protocols to assess shared knowledge. In addition, we need to understand better the mechanisms by which to conduct effective distributed team training.

Post-training conditions

Events that occur after training are as important as those that occur before and during training. Therefore, recent research has focused on improving the methods and procedures we use to evaluate training, and on examining the events that ensure transfer and application of newly acquired KSAs. In examining this body of work, we get a clear sense that it is in these two areas where we probably have made the most significant progress. There are theoretical, methodological, empirical, and practical advances. All the issues have not been solved, but meaningful advances have been made in the last decade. This is very encouraging. We first look at training evaluation and then at transfer of training.

Training evaluation

Kirkpatrick's typology and beyond

Kirkpatrick's typology (Kirkpatrick 1976) continues to be the most popular framework for guiding evaluations. However, recent work has either expanded it or pointed out weaknesses, such as the need to develop more diagnostic measures. For example, Kraiger et al (1993) proposed a multi-dimensional view of learning, implying that learning refers to changes in cognitive, affective, and/or skill-based outcomes. The proposed taxonomy can be used to assess and document learning outcomes. In a meta-analysis of studies employing Kirkpatrick's model, Alliger et al (1997) noted that utility-type reaction measures were more strongly related to learning and performance (transfer) than affective-type reaction measures. Surprisingly, they also found that utility-type reaction measures are more predictive of transfer than learning measures. Kraiger & Jung (1997) suggested several processes by which learning outcomes can be derived from instructional objectives of training. Goldsmith & Kraiger (1997) proposed a method for structural assessment of an individual learner's knowledge and skill in a specific domain. This model has been used with some success in several domains (e.g. Kraiger et al 1995, Stout et al 1997).

Clearly, Kirkpatrick's typology has served as a good foundation for training evaluation for many decades (Kirkpatrick 1976). It has been used, criticized, misused, expanded, refined, adapted, and extended. It has served the training research community well—but a richer, more sophisticated typology is needed. Research needs to continue finding better, more diagnostic and rigorous assessments of learning outcomes. The next frontier and greatest challenge in this area is in designing, developing, and testing on-line assessments of learning and performance. As we rely more on technology for training delivery, we need better and more protocols to access learning not only after but also during training (e.g. Ghodsian et al 1997).

Evaluation design issues

Training evaluation is one of those activities that are easier said than done. Training evaluation is labor intensive, costly, political, and many times is the bearer of bad news. We also know that it is very difficult to conduct credible and defensible evaluations in the field. Fortunately, training researchers have derived and tested thoughtful, innovative and practical approaches to aid the evaluation process. For example, Sackett & Mullen (1993) proposed other alternatives (e.g. posttesting-only, no control group) to formal experimental designs when answering evaluation questions. They suggested that those questions (e.g. How much change has occurred? What target performance has been reached?) should drive the evaluation mechanisms needed, and that each requires different designs. Haccoun & Hamtiaux (1994) proposed a simple procedure for estimating effectiveness of training in improving trainee knowledge—the internal referencing strategy.

This situation tests the implicit training evaluation notion that training-relevant content should show more change (pre-post) than training-irrelevant content. An empirical evaluation using internal referencing strategy versus a more traditional experimental evaluation indicated that the internal referencing strategy approach might permit inferences that mirror those obtained by the more complex designs.

The costs of training evaluation have also been addressed recently. Yang et al (1996) examined two ways to reduce costs. The first method is by assigning different numbers of subjects into training and control groups. An unequal group size design with a larger total sample size may achieve the same level of statistical power at lower cost. In a second method, the authors examined substituting a less expensive proxy criterion measure in place of the target criterion when evaluating the training effectiveness. Using a proxy increases the sample size needed to achieve a given level of statistical power. The authors described procedures for examining the tradeoff between the costs saved by using the less expensive proxy criterion and the costs incurred by the larger sample size. Similar suggestions have been made by Arvey et al (1992).

Evaluations

It is refreshing to see that more evaluations are being reported in the literature; we hope this trend continues. It is only by drawing lessons learned from past evaluations that the design and delivery of training will continue to progress. Several field training evaluations have been reported in team training settings (e.g. Leedom & Simon 1995, Salas et al 1999), sales training (e.g. Morrow et al 1997), stress training (e.g. Friedland & Keinan 1992), cross-cultural management training (e.g. Harrison 1992), transformational leadership training (e.g. Barling et al 1996), career self-management training (e.g. Kossek et al 1998), workforce diversity training (e.g. Hanover & Cellar 1998) and approaches to computer training (e.g. Simon & Werner 1996). All suggest that training works. However, an examination of evaluations where training did not work is also needed (and we suspect there are many). Some important lessons can be learned from these types of evaluations as well.

Transfer of training

Transfer of training is conceptualized as the extent to which KSAs acquired in a training program are applied, generalized, and maintained over some time in the job environment (Baldwin & Ford 1988). There has been a plethora of research and thinking in the transfer of training area (see Ford & Weissbein 1997). This emerging body of knowledge suggests a number of important propositions and conclusions. For example, (*a*) the organizational learning environment can be reliably measured and varies in meaningful ways across organizations (Tannenbaum 1997); (*b*) the context matters (Quinones 1997)—it sets motivations, expectations, and attitudes for transfer; (*c*) the transfer "climate" can have a powerful impact on the extent to which newly acquired KSAs are used back on the job (e.g. Tracey et al 1995, Thayer & Teachout 1995); (*d*) trainees need an opportunity to perform (Ford et al 1992, Quinones et al 1995); (*e*) delays between training and actual use on the job create significant skill decay (Arthur et al 1998); (*f*) situational cues and consequences predict the extent to which transfer occurs (Rouiller & Goldstein 1993); (*g*) social, peer, subordinate, and supervisor support all play a central role in transfer (e.g. Facteau et al 1995, Tracey et al 1995); (*h*) training can generalize from one context to another (e.g. Tesluk et al 1995); (*i*) intervention strategies can be designed to improve the probability of transfer (e.g. Brinkerhoff & Montesino 1995, Kraiger et al 1995); (*j*) team leaders can shape the degree of transfer through informal reinforcement (or punishment) of transfer activities (Smith-Jentsch et al 2000); (*k*) training transfer needs to be conceptualized as a multidimensional construct— it differs depending on the type of training and closeness of supervision on the job (Yelon & Ford 1999).

As noted by Ford & Weissbein (1997), much progress has been made in this area. There are more studies using complex tasks with diverse samples that actually measure transfer over time. However, much more is needed. Specifically, we need more studies that actually manipulate the transfer climate (e.g. Smith-Jentsch et al 2000). The measurement problems remain. Most studies still use surveys as the preferred method for measuring transfer. Other methods need to be developed and used. Finally, we need to assume that learning outcomes at the individual level will emerge to influence higher level outcomes. Vertical transfer of training is the next frontier. Vertical transfer may be a leverage point for strengthening the links between learning outcomes and organizational effectiveness (see Kozlowski et al 2000).

Taken together, these studies validate the importance of the organizational environment in training. In the future we need to continue to determine which factors affect transfer so that we can maximize it.

Final observations, conclusions, and the future

In closing, we draw on the extensive literature just reviewed to offer the following observations:

1 As Tannenbaum & Yukl (1992) predicted, the quality and quantity of research has increased. We truly have seen an explosion of theoretical, methodological, and empirical work in training research, and we do not see an end to this trend. This is very encouraging, and we believe this body of work will pay off as we learn more about how to design and deliver training systems. Therefore, we contend that training research is here to stay and prosper.
2 The progress in theoretical development, especially the attention given to cognitive and organizational concepts, is revolutionizing the field. These new developments promise to change how we conceptualize, design, implement, and institutionalize learning and training in organizations. In the future, we

will need a deeper understanding of these concepts, we must strive for more precision and clarity of constructs, and our methods must be more rigorous.

3. The body of literature generated over the past decade suggests that the field does not belong to any single discipline anymore. In the past, industrial/ organizational and educational psychologists primarily conducted training research. A closer look at the literature now suggests that cognitive, military, engineering, human factors, and instructional psychologists are involved in training research to an equal degree. In fact, computer scientists and industrial engineers are also researching learning, training technology, and training systems. As many others have observed, we need more cross-fertilization, collaboration, and dialogue among disciplines. To start, we need to read each other's work, and leverage each other's findings, ideas, and principles

4. Technology has influenced—and will continue to do so for the foreseeable future—the design and delivery of training systems. Whether we like it or not, technology has been embraced in industrial, educational, and military institutions as a way to educate and train their workforces. Technology may, or may not, have instructional features because it is often employed without the benefit of findings from the science of training. However, as we learn more about intelligent tutoring systems, modeling and simulation, multimedia systems, learning agents, Web-based training, distance learning, and virtual environments, this state of affairs may change. It is encouraging that basic and applied research is currently going on to uncover how these technologies enhance learning and human performance (e.g. Cannon-Bowers et al 1998). More research is needed, and the prospects of it happening are very promising. Specifically we need to know more about how to best present knowledge over the Internet, how and when to provide feedback, which instructional strategies are best for Web-based applications, what role instructors and trainees play in these modern systems, and how effectiveness can best be evaluated.

5. The distinction between training effectiveness and training evaluation is much clearer. Kraiger et al (1993) provided the seed for this important distinction. Training effectiveness is concerned with why training works and it is much more "macro" in nature. That is, training effectiveness research looks at the training intervention from a systems perspective—where the success of training depends not only on the method used but on how training (and learning) is positioned, supported, and reinforced by the organization; the motivation and focus of trainees; and what mechanisms are in place to ensure the transfer of the newly acquired KSAs to the job. Training evaluation on the other hand, examines what works and is much more "micro" (i.e. focused on measurement). It looks at what was learned at different levels and is the basis for determining the training effectiveness of a particular intervention. This distinction has made some significant contributions to practice possible and, more importantly, is helping avoid the simplistic view of training (i.e. that training is just a program or curriculum rather than the complex interaction of

many organizational factors). More research aimed at uncovering why training works is, of course, desirable.

6 Much more attention has been given to discussing training as a system embedded in an organizational context (e.g. Dipboye 1997, Kozlowski & Salas 1997, Kozlowski et al 2000, Tannenbaum & Yukl 1992). This is refreshing and welcome. For many decades, training researchers have ignored the fact that training cannot be isolated from the system it supports. In fact, the organizational context matters (e.g. Quinones 1997, Rouillier & Goldstein 1993) and matters in a significant way. Research aimed at studying how organizations implement training and why even the best-designed training systems can fail is encouraged.

7 Research has begun to impact practice in a more meaningful, and it is to be hoped, quantifiable way. We can offer principles and guidelines to organizations regarding how to analyze, design, develop, implement, and evaluate training functions. Much needs to be done, but it is only through mutual reciprocity—science and practice—that real progress will be made (see Salas et al 1997). As already stated, we have seen more evaluations conducted, there are more guidelines for designers and practitioners, and viable strategies that seem to impact organizational outcomes and the link between learning and performance are more tangible today (Bassi & Van Buren 1999).

A number of training issues need considerable attention in the next few years (in addition to the ones we have noted throughout this chapter). In particular, we need research that helps us get a better understanding of what, how, and when on-the-job training works. On-the-job training is a common practice in organizations, but few principles and guidelines exist on how to optimize this strategy. We need a deeper understanding of how to build expertise and adaptability through training. Although some work has started (e.g. Kozlowski 1998, Smith et al 1997), longitudinal studies in the field are desirable. How learning environments are created and maintained in organizations needs to be researched and better understood. A related issue is how, and under what circumstances, individuals and teams learn from informal organizational activities. In addition, as organizations become older and more diverse, more attention must be paid to the special training needs of nontraditional workers (especially given the anticipated reliance on high-tech systems). Moreover, as organizations allow more flexibility in how work is accomplished (e.g. telecommuting), training practices must keep pace. In fact, organizations will increasingly depend on workers who can develop, maintain, and manage their own skills, requiring attention to the challenge of how to develop and attract self-directed learners. Finally, as noted, training researchers need to embrace and investigate new technologies. We know that organizations will; we hope that new developments in training are driven by scientific findings rather than the band wagon.

In conclusion, we are happy to report that, contrary to charges made by our predecessors over the years, training research is no longer atheoretical, irrelevant, or dull. Exciting advances in all areas of the training enterprise have been realized. Training research has also been called faddish, a characteristic we hope is beginning to fade as well. However, we wonder whether there is compelling evidence to suggest that training practitioners in organizations are actually applying what has been learned from the research. This brings us back to a question we raised at the beginning of this chapter; namely, to what degree does the science of training affect organizational training practices? In other words, can we find evidence that organizations are implementing the lessons being learned from training research (especially the work reviewed here), or are practitioners still prone to latch on to the latest training craze? The answer is, quite simply, that we just do not know. This is due, at least in part, to the fact that detailed records documenting training practices (and more importantly, the rationale that went into developing them) are not typically available. However, one thing seems clear: The stage for the application of training research is set. We say this because, as noted, organizations are beginning to question the value-added of human resource activities (including training), and to pay more attention to human capital. Simply put, organizations want to know what the return is on their training investment.

Assuming this trend continues, it should force training professionals to turn to the science of training for empirically verified guidelines regarding how to optimize training outcomes (including transfer), and how to evaluate whether training has been effective in reaching organizational goals. As the pressure grows to show an impact on the bottom line, training practitioners will do well to employ sound principles, guidelines, specifications, and lessons learned from the literature, rather than relying on a trial-and-error approach. For this reason, we believe a new era of training has begun—one in which a truly reciprocal relationship between training research and practice will be realized.

Acknowledgments

We thank Clint Bowers, Ken Brown, Irv Goldstein, Steve Kozlowski, Kevin Ford, John Mathieu, Ray Noe, Paul Thayer, Scott Tannenbaum, and Will Wooten for their valuable comments and suggestions on earlier drafts of this chapter. We were aided in the literature review by two doctoral students in the Human Factors program from the University of Central Florida: Katherine Wilson and Shatha Samman.

Literature cited

Alliger GM, Tannenbaum SI, Bennett W, Traver H, Shotland A. 1997, A meta-analysis of the relations among training criteria. *Pers. Psychol.* 50:341–58

Anderson JR, Corbett AT, Koedinger KR, Pelletier R. 1995. Cognitive tutors: lessons learned. *J. Learn. Sci.* 4:167–207

Arthur W, Bennett W, Stanush PL, McNelly TL. 1998. Factors that influence skill decay and retention: a quantitative review and analysis. *Hum. Perform.* 11:79–86

Arthur W, Day EA, Bennett W, McNelly TL, Jordan JA. 1997. Dyadic versus individual training protocols: loss and reacquisition of a complex skill. *J. Appl. Psychol.* 82:783–91

Arthur W, Young B, Jordan JA, Shebilske WL. 1996. Effectiveness of individual and dyadic training protocols: the influence of trainee interaction anxiety. *Hum. Factors.* 38:79–86

Arvey RD, Salas E, Gialluca KA. 1992. Using task inventories to forecast skills and abilities. *Hum. Perform.* 5:171–90

Baker D, Prince C, Shrestha L, Oser R, Salas E. 1993. Aviation computer games for crew resource management training. *Int. J. Aviat. Psychol.* 3:143–56

Baker D, Salas E, Cannon-Bowers J. 1998. Team task analysis: lost but hopefully not forgotten. *Ind. Organ. Psychol.* 35:79–83

Baldwin TT. 1992. Effects of alternative modeling strategies on outcomes of interpersonal-skills training. *J. Appl. Psychol.* 77:147–54

Baldwin TT, Ford JK. 1988. Transfer of training: a review and directions for future research. *Personnel Psychol.* 41:63–105

Baldwin TT, Magjuka RJ. 1997. Training as an organizational episode: pretraining influences on trainee motivation. See Ford et al 1997, pp. 99–127

Barling J, Weber T, Kelloway EK. 1996. Effects of transformational leadership training on attitudinal and financial outcomes: a field experiment. *J. Appl. Psychol.* 81:827–32

Bassi LJ, Van Buren ME. 1999. *The 1999 ASTD State of the Industry Report.* Alexandria, VA: Am. Soc. Train. Dev.

Bell H, Waag W. 1998. Evaluating the effectiveness of flight simulators for training combat skills: a review. *Int. J. Aviat. Psychol.* 8:223–42

Blickensderfer E, Cannon-Bowers JA, Salas E. 1998. Cross training and team performance See Cannon-Bowers & Salas 1998b, pp. 299–311

Blickensderfer E, Cannon-Bowers JA, Salas E, Baker DP. 2000. Analyzing knowledge requirements in team tasks. In *Cognitive Task Analysis,* ed. JM Schraagen, SF Chipman, VJ Shalin. Mahwah, NJ: Erlbaum

Bowers CA, Morgan BB Jr, Salas E, Prince C. 1993. Assessment of coordination demand for aircrew coordination training. *Mil. Psychol.* 5:95–112

Brett JF, Vande Valle D. 1999. Goal orientaion and goal content as predictors of performance in a training program. *J. Appl. Psychol.* 84:863–73

Bretz RD Jr, Thompsett RE, 1992. Comparing traditional and integrative learning methods in organizational training programs. *J. Appl. Psychol.* 77:941–51

Brinkerhoff RO, Montesino MU. 1995. Partnership for training transfer: lessons from a corporate study. *Hum. Res. Dev. Q.* 6:263–74

Buttom SB, Mathieu JE, Zajac DM. 1996. Goal orientation in organizational research: a conceptual and empirical foundation. *Organ. Behav. Hum. Decis. Process.* 67:26–48

Campbell JP. 1971. Personnel training and development. *Annu. Rev. Psychol.* 22:565–602

Cannon-Bowers J, Burns J, Salas E, Pruitt J. 1998. Advanced technology in decision-making training. See Cannon-Bowers & Salas 1998b, pp. 365–74

Cannon-Bowers JA, Salas E. 1997. Teamwork competencies: the interaction of team member knowledge, skills, and attitudes. In *Workforce Readiness: Competencies and Assessment,* ed. HF O'Niel, pp. 151–74. Mahwah, NJ: Erlbaum

Cannon-Bowers JA, Salas E. 1998a. Individual and team decision making under stress: theoretical underpinnings. See Cannon-Bowers & Salas 1998b, pp. 17–38

Cannon-Bowers JA, Salas E, eds. 1998b. *Making Decisions Under Stress: Implications for Individual and Team Training.* Washington, DC: Am. Psychol. Assoc.

Cannon-Bowers J, Salas E, Converse S. 1993. Shared mental models in expert team decision making. In *Individual and Group Decision Making: Current Issues,* ed. NJ Castellan Jr, pp. 221–46. Hillsdale, NJ: Erlbaum

Cannon-Bowers JA, Salas E, Tannenbaum SI, Mathieu JE. 1995. Toward theoretically-based principles of trainee effectiveness: a model and initial empirical investigation. *Mil. Psychol.* 7:141–64

Christoph RT, Schoenfeld GA Jr, Tansky JW. 1998. Overcoming barriers to training utilizing technology: the influence of self-efficacy factors on multimedia-based training receptiveness. *Hum. Res. Dev. Q.* 9:25–38

Cole ND, Latham GP. 1997. Effects of training in procedural justice on perceptions of disciplinary fairness by unionized employees and disciplinary subject matter experts. *J. Appl. Psychol.* 82:699–705

Colquitt JA, LePine JA, Noe RA. 2000. Toward an integrative theory of training motivation: a meta-analytic path analysis of 20 years of research. *J. Appl. Psychol.* In press

Colquitt JA, Simmering MS. 1998. Consciousness, goal orientation, and motivation to learn during the learning process: a longitudinal study. *J. Appl. Psychol.* 83:654–65

Dipboye RL. 1997. Organizational barriers to implementing a rational model of training. See Quinones & Ehrenstein 1997, pp. 119–48

Driskell JE, Johnston JH. 1998. Stress exposure training. See Cannon-Bowers & Salas 1998b, pp. 191–217

Driskell JE, Willis RP, Copper C. 1992. Effect of overlearning on retention. *J. Appl. Psychol.* 77:615–22

Dubois DA, Shalin VL, Levi KR, Borman WC. 1997/1998. A cognitively-oriented approach to task analysis. *Train. Res. J.* 3:103–41

Dweck CS. 1986. Motivational processes affecting learning. *Am. Psychol.* 41:1040–48

Dweck CS, Leggett EL. 1988. A social-cognitive approach to motivation and personality. *Psychol. Rev.* 95:256–73

Dwyer DJ, Oser RL, Salas E, Fowlkes JE. 1999. Performance measurement in distributed environments: initial results and implications for training. *Mil. Psychol.* 11:189–215

Eden D, Aviram A. 1993. Self-efficacy training to speed reemployment: helping people to help themselves. *J. Appl. Psychol.* 78:352–60

Ehrenstein A, Walker B, Czerwinski M, Feldman E. 1997. Some fundamentals of training and transfer: Practice benefits are not automatic. See Quinones & Ehrenstein 1997, pp. 31–60

Elliot AJ, Church MA. 1997. A hierarchical model of approach and avoidance achievement motivation. *J. Pers. Soc. Psychol.* 72:218–32

Facteau JD, Dobbins GH, Russel JEA, Ladd RT, Kudisch JD. 1995. The influence of general perceptions for the training environment on pretraining motivation and perceived training transfer. *J. Manage.* 21:1–25

Fisher SL, Ford JR. 1998. Differential effects of learner efforts and goal orientation on two learning outcomes. *Pers. Psychol.* 51:397–420

Ford JK, Kozlowski S, Kraiger K, Salas E, Teachout M, eds. 1997. *Improving Training Effectiveness in Work Organizations.* Mahwah, NJ: Erlbaum. 393 pp.

Ford JK, Quinones MA, Sego DJ, Sorra JS. 1992. Factors affecting the opportunity to perform trained tasks on the job. *Pers. Psychol.* 45:511–27

Ford JK, Smith EM, Sego DJ, Quinones MA. 1993. Impact of task experience and individual factors on training-emphasis ratings. *J. Appl. Psychol.* 78:218–33

Ford JK, Smith EM, Weissbein DA, Gully SM, Salas E. 1998. Relationships of goal-orientation, metacognitive activity, and practice strategies with learning outcomes and transfer. *J. Appl. Psychol.* 83:218–33

Ford JK, Weissbein DA. 1997. Transfer of training: an updated review and analysis. *Perform. Improv. Q.* 10:22–41

Fowlkes J, Dwyer D, Oser R, Salas E. 1998. Event-based approach to training. *Int. J. Aviat. Psychol.* 8:209–22

Friedland N, Keinan G. 1992. Training effective performance in stressful situations: three approaches and implications for combat training. *Mil. Psychol.* 4:157–74

Ghodsian D, Bjork R, Benjamin A. 1997. Evaluating training during training: obstacles and opportunities. See Quinones & Ehrenstein 1997, pp. 63–88

Goettl BP, Yadrick RM, Connolly-Gomez C, Regian WJ, Shebilske WL. 1996. Alternating task modules in isochronal distributed training of complex tasks. *Hum. Factors.* 38:330–46

Goldsmith T, Kraiger K. 1997. Structural knowledge assessment and training evaluation. See Ford et al 1997, pp. 19–46

Goldstein IL. 1980. Training in work organizations. *Annu. Rev. Psychol.* 31:229–72

Goldstein IL. 1993. *Training in Organizations: Needs Assessment, Development and Evaluation.* Monterey, CA: Brooks/Cole. 3rd ed.

Gopher D, Weil M, Bareket T. 1994. Transfer of skill from a computer game trainer to flight. *Hum. Factors* 36:387–405

Guzzo RA, Dickson MW. 1996. Teams in organizations: recent research on performance and effectiveness. *Annu. Rev. Psychol.* 47:307–38

Guzzo RA, Yost PR, Campbell RJ, Shea GP. 1993. Potency in groups: articulating a construct. *Br. J. Soc. Psychol.* 32:87–106

Haccoun RR, Hamtiaux T. 1994. Optimizing knowledge tests for inferring learning acquisition levels in single group training evaluation designs: the internal referencing strategy. *Pers. Psychol.* 47:593–604

Hanover JMB, Cellar DF. 1998. Environmental factors and the effectiveness of workforce diversity training *Hum. Res. Dev. Q.* 9:105–24

Harrison JK. 1992. Individual and combined effects of behavior modeling and the cultural assimilator in cross-cultural management training. *J. Appl. Psychol.* 77:952–62

Helmreich RL, Foushee HS. 1993. Why crew resource management? Empirical and theoretical bases of human factors training in avaiation. See Wiener et al 1993, pp. 3–45

Helmreich RL, Merritt AC, Wilhelm JA. 1999. The evolution of crew resource management training in commercial aviation. *Int. J. Aviat. Psychol.* 9:19–32

Helmreich RL, Wiener EL, Kanki BG. 1993. The future of crew resource management in the cockpit and elsewhere. See Wiener & Kanki 1993, pp. 479–501

Howard A, ed. 1995. The *Changing Nature of Work.* San Francisco: Jossey-Bass

Hunter JE. 1986. Cognitive ability, cognitive aptitudes, job knowledge, and job performance. *J. Vocat. Behav.* 29:340–62

Huselid MA. 1995. The impact of human resource management practices on turnover, productivity, and corporate financial performance. *Acad. Manage. J.* 38:635–72

Jacobs JW, Dempsey JV. 1993. Simulation and gaming: fidelity, feedback, and motivation. In *Interactive Instruction and Feedback,* ed. JV Dempsey, GC Sales, pp. 197–229. Englewood Cliffs, NJ: Educ. Technol.

Jentsch F, Bowers C. 1998. Evidence for the validity of PC-based simulations in studying aircrew coordination. *Int. J. Aviat. Psychol.* 8:243–60

Johnston JH, Cannon-Bowers JA. 1996. Training for stress exposure. In *Stress and Human Performance,* ed. JE Driskell, E Salas, pp. 223–56. Mahweh, NJ: Erlbaum

Kaemar KM, Wright PM, McMahan GC. 1997. The effects of individual differences on technological training. *J. Manage. Issues.* 9:104–20

Kanfer R. 1991. Motivational theory and industrial and organizational psychology. In *Handbook of Industrial and Organizational Psychology,* ed. MD Dunnette, LM Hough, M Leaetta, 2:75–170. Palo Alto, CA: Consult. Psychol, 2nd ed.

Kirkpatrick DL. 1976. Evaluation of training. In *Training and Development Handbook,* ed. RL Craig, Ch. 18. New York: McGraw-Hill. 2nd ed.

Kirlik A, Fisk AD, Walker N, Rothrock L. 1998. Feedback augmentation and part-task practice in training dynamic decision-making skills. See Cannon-Bowers & Salas 1998b, pp. 247–70

Kossek EE, Roberts K, Fisher S, Demarr B. 1998. Career self-management: a quasi-experimental assessment of the effects of a training intervention. *Pers. Psychol.* 51:935–62

Kozlowski SW. 1998. Training and developing adaptive teams: theory, principles, and research. See Cannon-Bowers & Salas 1998b, pp. 247–70

Kozlowski SWJ, Brown K, Weissbein D, Cannon-Bowers J, Salas E. 2000. A multilevel approach to training effectiveness: enhancing horizontal and vertical transfer. In *Multi-level Theory, Research and Methods in Organization,* ed. K Klein, SWJ Kozlowski. San Francisco: Jossey-Bass

Kozlowski SWJ, Salas E. 1997. A multilevel organizational systems approach for the implementation and transfer of training. See Ford et al 1997, pp. 247–87

Kraiger K, Ford JK, Salas E. 1993. Application of cognitive, skill-based, and affective theories of learning outcomes to new methods of training evaluation. *J. Appl. Psychol.* 78:311–28

Kraiger K, Jung K. 1997. Linking training objectives to evaluation criteria. See Quinones & Ehrenstein 1997, pp. 151–76

Kraiger K, Salas E, Cannon-Bowers JA. 1995. Measuring knowledge organization as a method for assessing learning during training. *Hum. Perform.* 37:804–16

Latham GP. 1988. Human resource training and development. *Annu. Rev. Psychol.* 39:545–82

Leedom DK, Simon R. 1995. Improving team coordination: a case for behavior-based training. *Mil. Psychol.* 7:109–22

London M, Moore EM. 1999. Continuous learning. In *The Changing Nature of Performance,* ed. DR Ilgen, ED Pulakos, pp. 119–53. San Francisco: Jossey-Bass

Martocchio JJ. 1992. Microcomputer usage as an opportunity: the influence of context in employee training. *Pers. Psychol.* 45:529–51

Martocchio JJ. 1994. Effects of conceptions of ability on anxiety, self-efficacy and learning in training. *J. Appl. Psychol.* 79:819–25

Martocchio JJ, Baldwin TT. 1997. The evolution of strategic organizational training. In *Research in Personnel and Human Resource Management,* ed. RG Ferris, 15:1–46. Greenwich, CT: JAI

Martocchio JJ, Judge TA. 1997. Relationship between conscientiousness and learning in employee training: mediating influences of self-deception and self-efficacy. *J. Appl. Psychol.* 82:764–73

Martocchio JJ, Webster J. 1992. Effects of feedback and cognitive playfulness on performance in microcomputer software training. *Pers. Psychol.* 45:553–78

Mathieu JE, Martineau JW. 1997. Individual and situational influences in training motivation. See Ford et al 1997, pp. 193–222

Mathieu JE, Martineau JW, Tannenbaum SI. 1993. Individual and situational influences on the development of self-efficacy: implication for training effectiveness. *Pers. Psychol.* 46:125–47

Mathieu JE, Tannenbaum SI, Salas E. 1992. Influences of individual and situational characteristics on measures of training effectiveness. *Acad. Manage. J.* 35:828–47

McKenna JA. 1990. Take the "A" training: Facing world-class challenges, leading-edge companies use progressive training techniques to stay competitive. *Ind. Week* 239:22–26

Mitchell TR, Hopper H, Daniels D, George-Falvy J, James LR. 1994. Predicting self-efficacy and performance during skill acquisition. *J. Appl. Psychol.* 79:506–17

Morrow CC, Jarrett MQ, Rupinski MT. 1997. An investigation of the effect and economic utility of corporate-wide training. *Pers. Psychol.* 50:91–119

Neerincx MA, Griffoen E. 1996. Cognitive task analysis: harmonizing tasks to human capacities. *Ergonomics* 39:543–61

Noe RA, ed. 1999. *Employee Training and Development.* Boston: Irwin/ McGraw-Hill

Noe RA, Wilk SL. 1993. Investigation of the factors that influence employees' participation in development activities. *J. Appl. Psychol.* 78:291–302

Ortiz GA. 1994. Effectiveness of PC-based flight simulation. *Int. J. Aviat. Psychol.* 4:285–91

Oser RL, Cannon-Bowers JA, Salas E, Dwyer DJ. 1999. Enhancing human performance in technology-rich environments: guidelines for scenario-based training. In *Human/Technology Interaction in Complex Systems,* ed. E Salas, 9:175–202. Greenwich, CT: JAI

Phillips JM, Gully SM. 1997. Role of goal orientation, ability, need for achievement, and locus of control in the self-efficacy and goal-setting process. *J. Appl. Psychol.* 82:792–802

Prince C, Salas E. 1993. Training and research for teamwork in the military aircrew. See Wiener et al 1993, pp. 337–66

Quick JC, Joplin JR, Nelson DL, Mangelsdorff AD, Fiedler E. 1996. Self-reliance and military service training outcomes. *Mil. Psychol.* 8:279–93

Quinones MA. 1995. Pretraining context effects: training assignment as feedback. *J. Appl. Psychol.* 80:226–38

Quinones MA. 1997. Contextual influencing on training effectiveness. See Quinones & Ehrenstein 1997, pp. 177–200

Quinones MA, Ehrenstein A. 1997. *Training for a Rapidly Changing Workplace: Applications of Psychological Research.* Washington, DC: Am. Psychol. Assoc.

Quinones MA, Ford JK, Sego DJ, Smith EM. 1995. The effects of individual and transfer environment characteristics on the opportunity to perform trained tasks. *Train. Res. J.* 1:29–48

Randel JM, Main RE, Seymour GE, Morris BA. 1992. Relation of study factors to performance in Navy technical schools. *Mil. Psychol.* 4:75–86

Ree MJ, Carretta TR, Teachout MS. 1995. Role of ability and prior job knowledge in complex training performance. *J. Appl. Psychol.* 80:721–30

Ree MJ, Earles JA. 1991. Predicting training success: not much more than G. *Pers. Psychol.* 44:321–32

Ricci KE, Salas E, Cannon-Bowers JA. 1995. Do computer based games facilitate knowledge acquisition and retention? *Mil. Psychol.* 8:295–307

Rogers W, Maurer T, Salas E, Fisk A. 1997. Task analysis and cognitive theory: controlled and automatic processing task analytic methodology. See Ford et al 1997, pp. 19–46

Rouillier JZ, Goldstein IL. 1993.The relationship between organizational transfer climate and positive transfer of training. *Hum. Res. Dev. Q.* 4:377–90

Sackett PR, Mullen EJ. 1993. Beyond formal experimental design: towards an expanded view of the training evaluation process. *Pers. Psychol.* 46:613–27

Saks AM. 1995. Longitudinal field investigation of the moderating and mediating effects of self-efficacy on the relationship between training and newcomer adjustment. *J. Appl. Psychol.* 80:221–25

Salas E, Bowers CA, Blickensderfer E. 1997. Enhancing reciprocity between training theory and training practice: principles, guidelines, and specifications. See Ford et al 1997, pp. 19–46

Salas E, Bowers CA, Rhodenizer L. 1998. It is not how much you have but how you use it: toward a rational use of simulation to support aviation training. *Int. J. Aviat. Psychol.* 8:197–208

Salas E, Cannon-Bowers JA. 1997. Methods, tools, and strategies for team training. See Quinones & Ehrenstein 1997, pp. 249–80

Salas E, Cannon-Bowers JA. 2000. The anatomy of team training. In *Training and Retraining: A Handbook for Business, Industry, Government and the Military,* ed. S Tobias, D Fletcher. Farmington Hills, MI: Macmillan. In press

Salas E, Fowlkes J, Stout RJ, Milanovich DM, Prince C. 1999. Does CRM training improve teamwork skills in the cockpit?: two evaluation studies. *Hum. Factors.* 41:326–43

Salas E, Klein G, eds. 2000. *Linking Expertise and Naturalistic Decision Making.* Mahwah, NJ: Erlbaum. In press

Salas E, Rhodenizer L, Bowers CA. 2000. The design and delivery of CRM training: exploring the available resources. *Hum. Factors.* In press

Schmidt RA, Bjork RA. 1992. New conceptualizations of practice: Common principles in three paradigms suggest new concepts for training. *Psychol. Sci.* 3:207–17

Schraagen JM, Chipman SF, Shalin VL, eds. 2000. *Cognitive Task Analysis.* Mahwah, NJ: Erlbaum. 392 pp.

Schreiber D, Berge Z, eds. 1998. *Distance Training: How Innovative Organizations Are Using Technology to Maximize Learning and Meet Business Objectives.* San Francisco: Jossey-Bass

Shebilske WL, Jordan JA, Goettl BP, Paulus LE. 1998. Observation versus hands-on practice of complex skills in dyadic, triadic, and tetradic training-teams. *Hum. Factors.* 40:525–40

Shebilske WL, Regian JW, Arthur W Jr, Jordan JA. 1992. A dyadic protocol for training complex skills. *Hum. Factors.* 34:369–74

Shute VJ, Gawlick LA. 1995. Practice effects on skill acquisition, learning outcome, retention, and sensitivity to relearning. *Hum. Factors.* 37:781–803

Shute VJ, Gawlick LA, Gluck KA. 1998. Effects of practice and learner control on short- and long-term gain. *Hum. Factors.* 40:296–310

Simon SJ, Werner JM. 1996. Computer training through behavior modeling, self-paced, and instructional approaches: a field experiment. *J. Appl. Psychol.* 81:648–59

Skarlicki DP, Latham GP. 1997. Leadership training in organizational justice to increase citizenship behavior within a labor union: a replication. *Pers. Psychol.* 50:617–33

Smith E, Ford K, Kozlowski S. 1997. Building adaptive expertise: implications for training design strategies. See Quinones & Ehrenstein 1997, pp. 89–118

Smith-Jentsch KA, Jentsch FG, Payne SC, Salas E. 1996a. Can pretraining experiences explain individual differences in learning? *J. Appl. Psychol.* 81:909–36

Smith-Jentsch KA, Salas E, Baker DP. 1996b. Training team performance-related assertiveness. *Pers. Psychol.* 49:110–16

Smith-Jentsch KA, Salas E, Brannick M. 2000. To transfer or not to transfer? An investigation of the combined effects of trainee characteristics and team transfer environments. *J. Appl. Psychol.* In press

Smith-Jentsch KA, Zeisig RL, Acton B, McPherson JA. 1998. Team dimensional training: a strategy for guided team self-correction. See Cannon-Bowers & Salas 1998b, pp. 247–70

Stajkovic AD, Luthans F. 1998. Self efficacy and work-related performance. A meta-analysis. *Psychol. Bull.* 124:240–61

Steele-Johnson D, Hyde BG. 1997. Advanced technologies in training: intelligent tutoring systems and virtual reality. See Quinones & Ehrenstein 1997, pp. 225–48

Sternberg RJ. 1997. Managerial intelligence: Why IQ isn't enough. *J. Manage.* 23:475–93

Stevens CK, Gist ME. 1997. Effects of self-efficacy and goal-orientation training on negotiation skill maintenance: what are the mechanisms? *Personnel Psychol.* 50:955–78

Stout RJ, Salas E, Fowlkes J. 1997. Enhancing teamwork in complex environments through team training. *Group Dyn.: Theory Res. Pract.* 1:169–82

Swezey RW, Salas E, eds. 1992. *Teams: Their Training and Performance.* Norwood, NJ: Ablex

Tannenbaum SI. 1997. Enhancing continuous learning: diagnostic findings from multiple companies. *Hum. Res. Manage.* 36:437–52

Tannenbaum SI, Cannon-Bowers JA, Mathieu JE. 1993. *Factors That Influence Training Effectiveness: A Conceptual Model and Longitudinal Analysis.* Rep. 93-011, Naval Train. Syst. Cent., Orlando, FL

Tannenbaum SI, Dupuree-Bruno LM. 1994. The relationship between organizational and environmental factors and the use of innovative human resource practices. *Group Organ. Manage.* 19:171–202

Tannenbaum SI, Smith-Jentsch KA, Behson SJ. 1998. Training team leaders to facilitate team learning and performance. See Cannon-Bowers & Salas 1998b, pp. 247–70

Tannenbaum SI, Yukl G. 1992. Training and development in work organizations. *Annu. Rev. Psychol.* 43:399–441

Tesluk PE, Farr JL, Mathieu JE, Vance RJ. 1995. Generalization of employee involvement training to the job setting: individual and situational effects. *Pers. Psychol.* 48:607–32

Thayer PW. 1997. A rapidly changing world: some implications for training systems in the year 2001 and beyond. See Quinones & Ehrenstein 1997, pp. 15–30

Thayer PW, Teachout MS. 1995. *A Climate for Transfer Model.* Rep. AL/HR-TP-1995-0035, Air Force Mat. Command, Brooks Air Force Base, Tex.

Tracey JB, Tannenbaum SI, Kavanagh MJ. 1995. Applying trained skills on the job: the importance of the work environment. *J. Appl. Psychol.* 80:239–52

VandeValle D. 1997. Development and validation of a work domain goal orientation instrument. *Educ. Psychol. Meas.* 57:995–1015

Volpe CE, Cannon-Bowers JA, Salas E, Spector PE. 1996. The impact of cross-training on team functioning: an empirical investigation. *Hum. Factors.* 38:87–100

Warr P, Bunce D. 1995. Trainee characteristics and the outcomes of open learning. *Pers. Psychol.* 48:347–75

Wexley KN. 1984. Personnel training. *Annu. Rev. Psychol.* 35:519–51

Wexley KN, Latham GP. 2000. *Developing and Training Human Resources in Organizations,* Vol. 3. Englewood Cliffs, NJ: Prentice-Hall. In press

Wiener EL, Kanki BG, Helmreich RL, eds. 1993. *Cockpit Resource Management.* San Diego, CA: Academic

Wilson MA, Zalewski MA. 1994. An expert system for abilities-oriented job analysis. *Comp. Hum. Behav.* 10:199–207

Yang H, Sackett PR, Arvey RD. 1996. Statistical power and cost in training evaluation: some new considerations. *Pers. Psychol.* 49:651–68

Yelon SL, Ford JK. 1999. Pursuing a multi-dimensional model of transfer. *Perform. Improv. Q.* 12:58–78

Zsambok C, Klein G, eds. 1997. *Naturalistic Decision Making.* Mahweh, NJ: Erlbaum

32

KIRKPATRICK'S LEVELS OF TRAINING CRITERIA

Thirty years later

George M. Alliger and Elizabeth A. Janak

Source: *Personnel Psychology* 42 (1989): 331–342.

Abstract

Kirkpatrick's model (1959a, 1959b, 1960a, 1960b) of training evaluation criteria has had widespread and enduring popularity. This model proposed four "levels" of training evaluation criteria: reactions, learning, behavior, and results. Three problematic assumptions of the model may be identified: (1) The levels are arranged in ascending order of information provided. (2) The levels are causally linked. (3) The levels are positively intercorrelated. This article examines the validity of these assumptions, the frequency of each level in published evaluation studies, correlations from the literature in regard to Assumptions 2 and 3, and implications for the researcher and training manager.

About 30 years ago, Kirkpatrick published a series of articles in which he outlined four categories of measures of the effectiveness of training outcomes (Kirkpatrick, 1959a, 1959b, 1960a, 1960b). Each category was termed a "step." Step 1 was termed *reactions* and defined as trainees' "liking of" and "feelings for" a training program. Note that a reaction measure is conceived in attitudinal rather than behavioral terms. Step 2, *learning*, was defined as "principles, facts, and techniques understood and absorbed" by the trainees. Step 3 was *behavior*, defined as "using [learned principles and techniques] on the job." Step 4, *results*, was spoken of simply as the ends, goals, or "results desired ... reduction of costs; reduction of turnover and absenteeism; reduction of grievances; increase in quality and quantity of production; or improved morale."

This proposed model or taxonomy of training evaluation criteria clearly met a felt organizational need for it quickly became well known in training departments around the country. Moreover, the field of industrial/organizational psychology has largely accepted this framework (Cascio, 1987).

The power of Kirkpatrick's model is its simplicity and its ability to help people think about training evaluation criteria. In other words, it provides a vocabulary and rough taxonomy for criteria. At the same time, Kirkpatrick's model, through its easily adopted vocabulary and a number of (often implicit) assumptions, can tend to misunderstandings and over-generalizations. We discuss the model in the light of three assumptions that appear to be largely implicit in the minds of researchers and trainers, although to all appearances unintended by Kirkpatrick himself when the model was proposed. These three assumptions, however, have been endorsed or can be identified in the literature.

The first assumption is that the "steps" are arranged in ascending value of information provided (Newstrom, 1978). A measure of learning provides more information than does a measure of reaction, and so forth. It is, in fact, now common to see the term "levels" of criteria referred to instead of the more purely procedural term "steps" (Goldstein, 1986a; we use the term "levels" in the remainder of the article). The second assumption is that these levels of evaluation are causally linked. For example, Hamblin (1974) states, "training leads to reactions which lead to learning which leads to changes in job behavior which lead to changes in the organization." A third assumption is that the levels are positively intercorrelated. That is, a set of essentially positive interrelationships, or "positive manifold," is posited to exist among levels of training evaluation (cf. Newstrom, 1978). Each of these three assumptions about Kirkpatrick's steps appears to be codified in what has been termed the "hierarchical model" of training evaluation (Hamblin, 1974; Noe & Schmitt, 1986), where "favorable outcomes at the lowest criterion level are seen to be necessary for favorable outcomes to occur at the next higher level, and so on" (Clement, 1982).

Examining the assumptions

It is our belief that each of these assumptions about levels of training evaluation is problematic. We address each theoretically and then discuss a literature overview, including relevant correlations from the literature to further examine the third assumption.

Assumption 1: Each succeeding level is more informative than the last.
This assumption has the flavor of reasonableness, which may explain a nearly absolute lack of discussion about it in the literature. There are, however, some questions that can be raised in regard to it. First, it is not clear that all training in organizations is meant to effect change at all four levels. Some training may be largely rewarding, spirit-building, or perquisite in nature. For example, programs designed to instill company pride or rejuvenate employees may be realistically expected to have impacts at the reaction level only. Similarly, training that is limited to inculcation of company history or philosophy may, in some cases, be

best and most appropriately measured by growth in knowledge: the goal may be a knowledgeable manager, and attendant behavior change, for example, may not be of immediate interest to the evaluator.

A point worth making in this regard is that Assumption 1 can lead to a perception of Level 4, results, as invariably the "best" measure, since it is highest in the hierarchy. Advocacy of the "dollar criterion" (Brogden & Taylor, 1950), having been championed in research journals (e.g., Reilly & Smither, 1985; Weekly, Frank, O'Connor, & Peters, 1985), now appears in popular practitioner journals (e.g., Fitz-enz, 1985; Sheppeck & Cohen, 1985) and management textbooks (e.g., Hall & Goodale, 1986). Such sources promise that techniques for dollar estimation of intervention effectiveness will help HRM managers to "strengthen their power and influence" (Hall & Goodale, 1986). Estimating intervention value in dollars is thus enthusiastically presented as one way to emerge from the dark ages of the "personnel" function and move into the new era of the "human resources" department, which is (in theory) happily revenue producing instead of resource draining. Nonetheless, even when practically possible, there may be times when dollar estimation is inappropriate, as when the plant manager argued against quantitative evaluation because it was important to keep the idea of the intervention in the fore (Saporito, 1986). That there is a tendency for the purely quantitative, as dollars surely are, to obscure the field of possible approaches to issues such as evaluation is attested to by Goldstein (1986b, p. 22):

> It is startling to discover that most I/O psychologists still believe that quantitative models are good while qualitative research models do not contribute.
>
> ... [But] the continuum from good to bad does not have anchors with quantitative on the good side and qualitative on the bad side.

Assumption 2: Each level is caused by the previous level.
Causality is difficult to prove or disprove. Several questions can be raised about this assumption, however. The first question is one of temporality. While Level 3 and 4 measures occur at some time after training, Levels 1 and 2 usually are administered directly after training (as well as possibly before, in the case of Level 2). Indeed, a single instrument may measure both reactions and learning (Alliger & Horowitz, 1989). There would seem, then, to be no temporal distinction between reactions and learning as far as their assessment. Why then assume the former causes the latter? Probably the rationale is that those students reacting well to training are attending to the training as well. But Lewicki's (1986) studies, for example, indicate that attending can be deleterious to learning; other psychologists have argued that people are not good at reporting their experiences of learning (Hofstadter & Dennett, 1981; Thorndike, 1935). Moreover, perhaps it is only when trainees are challenged to the point of experiencing the training as somewhat unpleasant that they learn: In such a case learning and reactions might be *negatively* correlated. Such negative correlations between Level 1 and Level 2 measures have

in fact been found in educational classroom research (Remmers, Martin, & Elliott, 1949; Rodin & Rodin, 1972). Or consider that humorous lectures are liked better (Level 1) but do not cause more learning (Level 2) (Kaplan & Pascoe, 1977).

There is some reason to believe, then, that reactions may not be expected to cause learning. (This is of course more likely to the extent that reaction measures are attitudinally and not behaviorally based.) At the same time, among learning, behavior, and results, some causal links should exist. Learning often should relate to behavior since, in some cases, grasp of some principle, sequence, or facts can be important to behavior. Level 3, behaviors, should cause Level 4, results. In a reverse causality, Level 4, results, should be important to the maintenance of Level 3, behaviors, since people will tend to continue behaviors that are perceived to be effective. That is, feedback sustains the behavior-results link. Figure 1 illustrates both the traditional hierarchical causal model (Clement, 1982) and this alternative proposed causal linking among levels of criteria, where Level 1 is unrelated to the other levels, Level 2 to some degree is important in the causality of Levels 3 and 4, and Levels 3 and 4 are causally interdependent.

Assumption 3: Each succeeding level is correlated with the previous level; or, more generally, there exists a "positive manifold": all correlations among levels are positive.

This assumption is clearly linked to the previous one. If each level is causally linked to the previous level, then positive correlations among measures should exist. But, considering the points already made about causal linking among levels, to what extent, is it in fact logical to assume this set of positive relationships? For example, it has been argued that perhaps no positive relationship should be predicted between reactions and learning. On the other hand, our theoretical expectations are that Levels 2, 3, and 4 would be intercorrelated.

To some degree, evidence against the validity of Assumption 3 is seen in the literature. Many evaluation studies that have evaluated training on two or more of

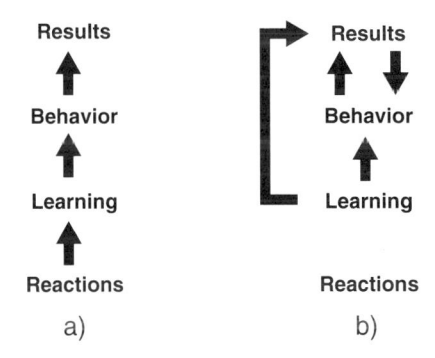

Figure 1 The a) causality in the hierarchical model and b) an alternative model of causality among Kirkpatrick's four levels of training criteria.

Kirkpatrick's levels have reported different effects of training for different levels (e.g., Campion & Campion, 1987; Decker, 1982; Meyer & Raich, 1983; Moffie, Calhoon, & O'Brien, 1964; Russell, Wexley, & Hunter, 1984). This provides indirect evidence against the likelihood of finding high positive intercorrelations among levels. An examination of correlations among levels, which provide a more direct examination of Assumption 3, follows.

An examination of the intercorrelation among levels

One way to examine empirically the accuracy of the above assumptions is to review the literature for reported correlations among criteria, categorized by Kirkpatrick's levels. Accordingly, a citation search was conducted on Kirkpatrick (1959a, 1959b, 1960a, 1960b, 1967, 1976, 1977, 1978, 1979, 1985) for the years 1969 to the present (the Social Science Citation Index began in 1969). Of the 55 articles so located, only 8 dealt with the actual evaluation of a training program; none reported correlations between levels. Consequently, a literature search was conducted for any article dealing with evaluation of a training program in several journals that might be expected to publish such articles. Journals were reviewed from 1959 to present, if possible. Specifically, we reviewed *Academy of Management Journal*, *Academy of Management Review* (first published in 1976), *Journal of Applied Behavioral Science*, *Journal of Applied Psychology*, *Personnel Psychology*, *Personnel*, and *Training and Development Journal* (*Journal of ASTD* until 1966). Table 1 shows the number of articles found by journal and category. Only one relevant article was found in *Academy of Management Review*; it did not report criteria, and so that journal is not included in Table 1.

Table 1 illustrates some interesting facts. First, most articles in the journals reviewed look at a single level of evaluation. Second, in contrast to the results of Catalanello & Kirkpatrick's (1968) and Kirkpatrick's (1978) industry surveys, most studies do not focus on reactions alone. In all probability this reflects the difference between practice and publishing: in practice, most training is evaluated on the reaction level only, while editors for the reviewed journals may look for evaluation results measuring learning, behavior, or results. Third, field studies are well represented (70% of total). It should also be noted that our search turned up numerous articles that addressed training evaluation but that did not report an evaluation study. For example, *Training and Development Journal* actually published in this time period 214 articles on training evaluation; only the 32 shown in Table 1 reported an evaluation study.

Unfortunately, of the articles in Table 1, only eight reported intercorrelations among two or more levels of evaluation. Consequently, we widened our search again by following leads from reference lists in these articles and appropriate other articles and books. In the end, we found 16 articles reporting 30 appropriate correlations. Four of these articles were academic samples relating teacher ratings and student evaluations; our interest was in industrial training. Consequently, our final data set consisted of only 12 articles reporting 26 correlations.

Table 1 Breakdown of literature review by journal and level of criteria

	Journal						
	AMJ	JABS	JAP	PP	P	TDJ	Total
Years reviewed	59–88	65–88	59–88	59–88	59–88	60–88	
No. articles reporting training evaluation results	18	41	79	21	10	32	203
Criteria levels used							
1	1	1	2	–	1	6	11
2	8	9	29	9	2	4	61
3	5	16	34	4	2	5	66
4	–	5	3	–	2	1	11
1, 2	1	1	6	3	–	2	13
1, 3	–	6	–	1	1	10	18
1, 4	–	–	–	1	–	1	2
2, 3	1	1	4	1	–	1	8
2, 4	–	–	–	–	–	–	0
3, 4	1	1	–	–	1	–	3
1, 2, 3	1	–	1	–	1	–	3
1, 2, 4	–	–	–	–	–	–	0
1, 3, 4	–	1	–	–	–	1	2
2, 3, 4	–	–	–	–	–	–	0
1, 2, 3, 4	–	–	–	2	–	1	3
Design							
Field	14	33	38	19	10	30	134
Laboratory	4	8	41	2	0	2	57

Note: AMJ = *Academy of Management Journal*, JABS = *Journal of Applied Behavioral Science*, JAP = *Journal of Applied Psychology*, PP = *Personnel Psychology*, P = *Personnel*, TDJ = *Training and Development Journal*.

Although disappointed in this small number of usable results, we felt our search was relatively successful, given the apparent sparsity of correlational data of this type: Clement (1982) reported being unable to locate in the literature *any* correlations between levels of Kirkpatrick's model. Actually, the fact that the vast majority of articles reviewed did not report inter-level correlations, even when it was highly likely the data would have allowed such correlations to be calculated, may signify that the hierarchical model is simply assumed to be correct. Table 2 provides a list of the 11 articles, and information about the samples studied. Table 3 provides the correlations between levels of evaluation, listed in descending magnitude. Sample size-weighted mean correlations for each pair of levels are found in parentheses.

Results and discussion

As can be seen, the number of available correlations between pairs of levels ranged from one to eight. This small number of correlations means, obviously, that generalizations should be made with care. An examination of the mean sample

Table 2 Articles reporting correlations between levels of evaluation

Author(s)	N	Type of sample	Description of measures (Level: Type)
Alliger	90	1st- to 5th-level managers	2: Posttest 3: Questionnaire
Alliger & Horowitz	1,259	1st-level managers	1: Questionnaire 2: Pre posttest
Bolman	118	Workers (type unspecified)	1: Questionnaire 2: Self-ratings
Clement	50	1st-level supervisors	1: Questionnaire 2: Pre posttest 3: Self-ratings 4: Subordinate ratings
Eden & Shani	105	Male soldiers	1: Questionnaire 2: Posttest
Miles	34	School Principals	2: Observer ratings 3: Peer ratings
Noe & Schmitt	60	School Administrators	1: Questionnaire 2: Observer ratings 3: Observer ratings 4: Supervisor ratings
Reeves & Jensen	173	Workers (type unspecified)	1: Questionnaire 3: Self-ratings
Severin	50[a]	——[a]	2: Training grades 3: Supervisor ratings 4: Production records
Smith	60	Branch office managers	2: Pre posttest 4: Customer satisfaction
Stroud	103	Supervisors	1: Questionnaire 3: Self-ratings Supervisor ratings
Wexley & Baldwin	256	Management students	1: Questionnaire 2: Posttest 3: Self ratings Observer ratings

[a] Severin's article was itself a compendium of many studies; the median N was 50, and the nature of the samples varied.

size-weighted correlations for each cell in Table 3 indicates that Level 1 may tend to correlate only slightly with the other levels: $r_{1,2} = .07$; $r_{1,3} = .05$; and $r_{1,4} = .48$ (but this last is based on a single correlation). On the other hand, the weighted mean correlations among Levels 2, 3, and 4 could be said to be slightly larger: $r_{2,3} = .13$; $r_{2,4} = .40$; and $r_{3,4} = .19$. Is it in fact possible that attitudinal reactions to training should be considered in a category independent from such constructs as learning or behavior, as these mean correlations might

Table 3 Correlations between levels of evaluation

	Level 2	Level 3	Level 4
Level 1	.79[e]	.12[k]	.48[g]
	.50[d]	.04[l]	
	.35[c]	.06[g]	
	.17[g]	.01[h]	
	.07[l]	(.04)	
	−.03[b]		
	(.03)		
Level 2		.74[j]	.53[g]
		.40[d]	.24[i]
		.16[a]	(.40)
		.06[f]	
		.06[l]	
		−.02[d]	
		−.05[d]	
		−.15[g]	
		(.18)	
Level 3			.48[i]
			.41[g]
			.20[d]
			.00[d]
			−.07[d]
			(.19)

Note: For Noe and Schmitt data, original study correlations determined by adding residual to reproduced correlations; for Reeves Jenkins, an average r is presented; for Severin, and Wexley Baldwin, median correlations are reported; for Stroud, correlation in table represents midpoint of range reported (.036 to .211). Mean sample size-weighted correlations for each cell are in parentheses.
[a] Alliger (1988); [b] Alliger & Horowitz (1989); [c] Bolman (1971); [d] Clement (1982); [e] Eden & Shani (1982); [f] Miles (1965); [g] Noe & Schmitt (1986); [h] Reeves & Jensen; [i] Severin (1952); [j] Smith (1976); [k] Stroud (1959); [l] Wexley & Baldwin (1986).

suggest and as is depicted in Figure 1? The data from our literature search certainly do not warrant a definite answer to this question. For example, it is certainly possible that some of these correlations are artifactually small, due to the reduced variance typical of reaction measures (cf. Alliger & Horowitz, 1989). The variance of the reaction measures was available for only five of the articles listed in Table 2; when we examined the variance relative to the means for those measures, reduced reaction measure variance could be concluded as probable in some cases but not in others. In any case, the proposed model of Figure 1 may perhaps stand as an alternative that, even if ultimately incorrect, may stimulate further research. Such research would seem useful, since practitioners and researchers in training are often faced with decisions regarding the nature of training evaluation data.

Clement (1982), has stated that correlations that do not support the hierarchical model fail to do so because of noise from intervening variables such as motivation, context of transfer, trainee attitudes, and so forth. No doubt these variables account for some of the variation among correlations in Table 3.

In this regard, one question that might be raised from Assumptions 2 and 3 is whether all correlations in Table 3 may be seen as arising from a single distribution, sampling error accounting for differences among correlations. That is, if all levels are intercorrelated to about the same degree, then sampling error might be the only source of variance among correlations within and among levels. However, predicted variance due to sampling error accounts for less than 15% of the variance of the distribution consisting of all correlations in Table 3.

An issue of interest not addressed in this article is the relationship among criteria *on the same level*. Should researchers be satisfied that a single criterion on a given level will completely capture that level, or that other criteria on that level would have told the same story about training effectiveness? We would like to suggest that caution is needed here: the measurement of different criteria on the same level could show different results. Consider, for example, that behavior learned in a training class might be differentially displayed to, and evaluated by, superiors, peers, or subordinates.

Kirkpatrick's model may never have been meant to be more than a first, global heuristic for training evaluation. As such it has done well. There are, in fact, several other models of training evaluation criteria, most of them very similar to Kirkpatrick's (e.g., Jackson & Kulp, 1978; Warr, Bird, & Rackham, 1970). However, we have proposed that each of three assumptions apparently implicit in the general understanding of Kirkpatrick's model, and in that of most other models as well, can be logically questioned. We have also shown that much of the literature available underscores the problematic nature of these assumptions.

Acknowledgments

The authors wish to thank Michael Britt for aiding in the literature search and Steven Cronshaw, Kevin Williams, Wilson Wong, and the editor Paul Sackett and an anonymous reviewer for their helpful comments on an earlier version of this article.

References

Alliger GM. (1988). [Evaluating training effectiveness for upper-level managers]. Unpublished raw data.

Alliger GM, Horowitz HM. (1989). IBM takes the guessing out of testing. *Training and Development Journal, 43*(4), 69–73.

Bolman L. (1971). Some effects of trainers on their t-groups. *Journal of Applied Behavioral Science, 7*, 309–326.

Brogden HE, Taylor EK. (1950). The dollar criterion—Applying the cost accounting concept to criterion construction. *Personnel Psychology, 3*, 133–154.

Campion MA, Campion JE. (1987). Evaluation of an interviewee skills training program in a natural field setting. *Personnel Psychology, 40*, 675–691.

Cascio WF. (1987). *Applied psychology in personnel management* (3rd ed.). Englewood Cliffs, NJ: Prentice-Hall.

Catalanello RF, Kirkpatrick DL. (1968). Evaluating training programs—The state of the art. *Training and Development Journal, 22*(5), 2–9.

Clement RW. (1982). Testing the hierarchy theory of training evaluation: An expanded role for trainee reactions. *Public Personnel Management Journal, 11*, 176–184.

Decker PJ. (1982). The enhancement of behavior modeling training of supervisory skills by the inclusion of a retention process. *Personnel Psychology, 35*, 323–332.

Eden D, Shani AB. (1982). Pygmalion goes to boot camp: Expectancy, leadership, and trainee performance. *Journal of Applied Psychology, 67*, 194–199.

Fitz-enz J. (1985). HR measurement: Formulas for success. *Personnel Journal, 64*(10), 53–60.

Goldstein IR. (1986a). *Training in organizations: Needs assessment, development, and evaluation.* Pacific Grove, CA: Brooks/Cole.

Goldstein IR. (1986b). *Presidential address to the Society of Industrial-Organizational Psychology.* Washington, DC.

Hall DT, Goodale JG. (1986). *Human resource management: Strategy, design, and implementation.* Glenview, IL: Scott, Foresman and Company.

Hamblin AC. (1974). *Evaluation and control of training.* New York: McGraw-Hill.

Hofstadter DR, Dennett DC. (1981). *The mind's I: Fantasies and reflections on self and soul.* New York: Bantam Books.

Jackson S, Kulp MJ. (1978). Designing guidelines for evaluating the outcomes of management training. In Peterson RO (Ed.), *Determining the payoffs of management training* (pp. 1–42). Madison, WI: ASTD.

Kaplan RM, Pascoe GC. (1977). Humorous lectures and humorous examples: Some effects upon comprehension and retention. *Journal of Educational Psychology, 69*, 61–65.

Kirkpatrick DL. (1959a). Techniques for evaluating training programs. *Journal of ASTD, 13*(11) 3–9.

Kirkpatrick DL. (1959b). Techniques for evaluating training programs: Part 2—Learning. *Journal of ASTD, 13*(12), 21–26.

Kirkpatrick DL. (1960a). Techniques for evaluating training programs: Part 3—Behavior. *Journal of ASTD, 14*(1), 13–18.

Kirkpatrick DL. (1960b). Techniques for evaluating training programs: Part 4—Results. *Journal of ASTD, 14*(2), 28–32.

Kirkpatrick DL. (1967). Evaluation of training. In Craig RL, Bittel LR (Eds.), *Training and development handbook* (pp. 87–112). New York: McGraw-Hill.

Kirkpatrick DL. (1976). Evaluation. In Craig RL (Ed.), *Training and development handbook* (pp. 301–319). New York: McGraw-Hill.

Kirkpatrick DL. (1977). Evaluating training programs, evidence vs. proof. *Training and Development Journal, 31*(11), 9–12.

Kirkpatrick DL. (1978). Evaluating in-house training programs. *Training and Development Journal, 32*(9), 6–9.

Kirkpatrick DL. (1979). Techniques for evaluating training programs. *Training and Development Journal, 33*(6), 78–92.

Kirkpatrick DL. (1985). Effective training and development, Part 2: In house approaches and techniques. *Personnel, 62*(1), 52–56.

Lewicki P. (1986). *Nonconscious social information processing.* New York: Academic Press.

Meyers HH, Raich MS. (1983). An objective evaluation of a behavior modeling training program. *Personnel Psychology, 36,* 755–761.

Miles MB. (1965). Changes during and following laboratory training: A clinical experimental study. *Journal of Applied Behavioral Science, 1,* 215–242.

Moffie DJ, Calhoon R, O'Brien JK. (1964). Evaluation of a management level program. *Personnel Psychology, 17,* 431–440.

Newstrom JW.(I978). Catch-22: The problems of incomplete evaluation of training. *Training and Development Journal, 32*(11), 22–24.

Noe RA, Schmitt NM. (1986). The influence of trainee attitudes on training effectiveness: Test of a model. *Personnel Psychology, 39,* 497–523.

Reeves ET, Jensen JM. (1972). Effectiveness of program evaluation. *Training and Development Journal, 26*(1), 36–41.

Reilly RR, Smither JW. (1985). An examination of two alternative techniques to estimate the standard deviation of job performance in dollars. *Journal of Applied Psychology, 70,* 651–661.

Remmers HH, Martin D, Elliot DN. (1949). *Student achievement and instructor evaluations in chemistry: Studies in higher education.* West Lafayette, IN: Purdue University.

Rodin M, Rodin B. (1972). Student evaluations of teachers. *Science, 177,* 1164–1166.

Russell JS, Wexley KN, Hunter JE. (1984). Questioning the effectiveness of behavior modeling training in an industrial setting. *Personnel Psychology, 37,* 465–481.

Saporito B. (1986). The revolt against working smarter. *Fortune, 114*(2), 58–67.

Sheppeck MA, Cohen SL. (1985). Put a dollar value on your training program. *Training and Development Journal, 39*(11), 59–62.

Severin D. (1952). The predictability of various kinds of criteria. *Personnel Psychology, 5,* 93–104.

Smith PE. (1976). Management modeling training to improve morale and customer satisfaction. *Personnel Psychology, 29,* 351–359.

Stroud P. (1959, November/December). Evaluating a human relations training program. *Personnel, 36,* pp. 52–60.

Thorndike EL. (1935). *The psychology of wants, interests, and attitudes.* New York: Appleton-Century.

Warr P, Bird M, Rackham N. (1970). *Evaluation of management training.* London: Gower Press.

Weekly JA, Frank B, O'Connor EJ, Peters LH. (1985). A comparison of three methods of estimating the standard deviation of performance in dollars. *Journal of Applied Psychology, 70,* 122–126.

Wexley KN, Baldwin TT. (1986). Post training strategy for facilitating positive transfer: An empirical exploration. *Academy of Management Journal, 29,* 503–520.

33

TRANSFER OF TRAINING

A review and directions for future research

Timothy T. Baldwin and J. Kevin Ford

Source: *Personnel Psychology* 41 (1988): 63–105.

Abstract

Transfer of training is of paramount concern for training researchers and practitioners. Despite research efforts, there is a growing concern over the "transfer problem." The purpose of this paper is to provide a critique of the existing transfer research and to suggest directions for future research investigations. The conditions of transfer include both the generalization of learned material to the job and the maintenance of trained skills over a period of time on the job. The existing research examining the effects of training design, trainee, and work-environment factors on conditions of transfer is reviewed and critiqued. Research gaps identified from the review include the need to (1) test various operationalizations of training design and work-environment factors that have been posited as having an impact on transfer and (2) develop a framework for conducting research on the effects of trainee characteristics on transfer. Needed advancements in the conceptualization and operationalization of the criterion of transfer are also discussed.

Positive transfer of training is defined as the degree to which trainees effectively apply the knowledge, skills, and attitudes gained in a training context to the job (Newstrom, 1984; Wexley & Latham, 1981). Transfer of training, therefore, is more than a function of original learning in a training program (Atkinson, 1972; Fleishman, 1953). For transfer to have occurred, learned behavior must be generalized to the job context and maintained over a period of time on the job.

There is growing recognition of a "transfer problem" in organizational training today (Michalak, 1981). It is estimated that while American industries annually spend up to $100 billion on training and development, not more than 10% of these expenditures actually result in transfer to the job (Georgenson, 1982). While researchers have similarly concluded that much of the training conducted in organizations fails to transfer to the work setting (e.g., I. Goldstein, 1986; Mosel, 1957; Wexley & Latham, 1981), a comprehensive review and critique of the empirical research on transfer has not appeared.

Several researchers have stated that the existing literature on transfer offers little of value to trainers concerned with maximizing positive transfer (Gagne, 1962; Wexley, 1984). On the other hand, Hinrichs (1976) has suggested that trainers often fail to apply the scientific knowledge that does exist. Rather than argue for one viewpoint or the other, it is our belief that it is more beneficial to investigate systematically what we do know about transfer of training and to consider how we can proceed to learn more. Rather than continue to bemoan what is a widely recognized concern, we must begin to specify the type of investigations needed to generate the knowledge base for improving our understanding of transfer issues.

The purpose of this paper is to provide a critique of the existing transfer research and to suggest directions for future research investigations. First, we will provide an organizing framework outlining the factors we believe affect transfer of training. Second, we will review the existing research on factors affecting transfer. Third, we will present a critique of the research and highlight critical research gaps. Finally, we will specify the types of research needed to improve our understanding of the transfer process.

A Framework for examining training transfer

Examination of transfer issues requires a clear understanding of what is meant by transfer as well as the identification of factors that affect transfer. Figure 1 presents a framework for understanding the transfer process. In Figure 1, the transfer process is described in terms of training-input factors, training outcomes, and conditions of transfer. The conditions of transfer include both the (1) generalization of material learned in training to the job context and (2) maintenance of the learned material over a period of time on the job. Training outcomes are defined as the amount of original learning that occurs during the training program and the retention of that material after the program is completed. Training-input factors include training design, trainee characteristics, and work-environment characteristics. The major training-design factors are the incorporation of learning principles (Bass & Vaughan, 1966), the sequencing of training material (Gagne, 1962; Tracy, 1984), and the job relevance of the training content (Campbell, 1971; Ford & Wroten, 1984). Trainee characteristics consist of ability or skill, motivation, and personality factors. Work-environment characteristics include climatic factors such as supervisory or peer support as well as constraints and opportunities to perform learned behaviors on the job.

As the model indicates, training outcomes and training-input factors are posited to have both direct and indirect effects on conditions of transfer. These effects are specified in terms of six linkages, which are critical for understanding the transfer process. Working backwards in the model, training outcomes of learning and retention are seen as having direct effects on conditions of transfer (Linkage 6).

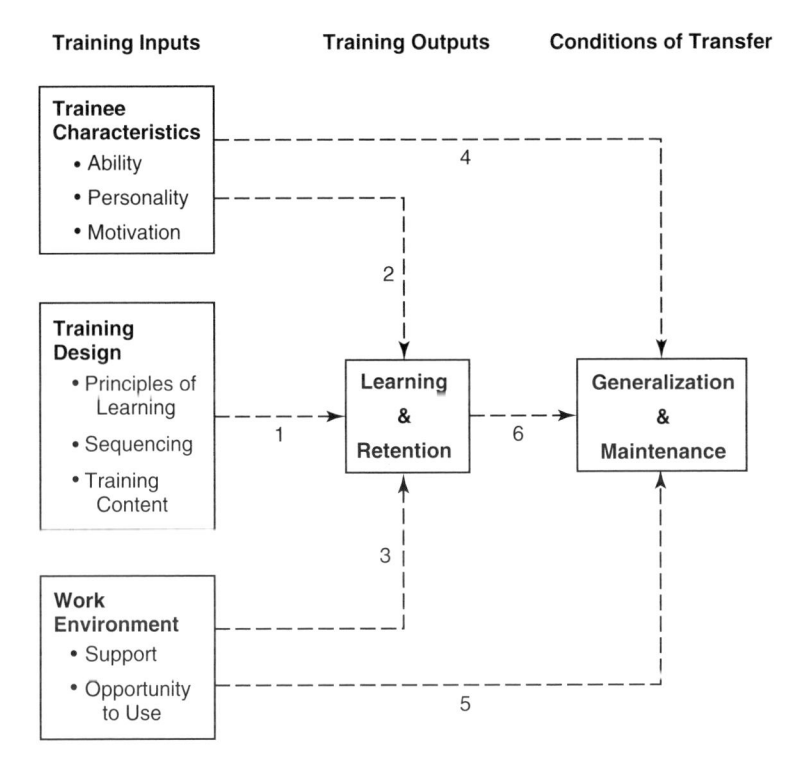

Figure 1 A model of the transfer process.

That is, for trained skills to transfer, training material must be learned and retained (Kirkpatrick, 1967). Trainee characteristics and work-environment characteristics are also hypothesized to have direct effects on transfer regardless of initial learning during the training program or retention of the training material (Linkages 4 and 5, respectively). For example, well-learned skills may not be maintained on the job due to lack of motivation or lack of supervisory support. Finally, training outcomes (learning and retention) are viewed as directly affected by the three training inputs of training design, trainee characteristics, and the work-environment characteristics (Linkages 1, 2, and 3 respectively). These three training inputs, therefore, have an indirect effect on transfer through their impact on training outcomes.

The model in Figure 1 provides a framework for describing the transfer process. The literature examining transfer issues will now be reviewed and then be critiqued in relation to the impact of training-input factors on training outcomes and conditions of transfer.

Literature review

For this review, empirical studies cited in the major works of the organizational-training literature (e.g., Bass & Vaughan, 1966; Campbell, 1971; Campbell,

Dunnette, Lawler & Weick, 1970; Decker & Nathan, 1985; Ellis, 1965; I. Goldstein, 1980, 1986; McGehee & Thayer, 1961; Wexley, 1984; Wexley & Latham, 1981) were examined. Other studies were identified through an extensive literature search and cross-referencing of cited studies. Therefore, this review provides an examination of the transfer-issue research that has been referenced in the organizational-training literature.

The review was based on the framework provided in Figure 1; that is, the research was reviewed in terms of the effects of training design, trainee characteristics, or work-environment factors on either learning and retention of trained material (training outcomes) or generalization and maintenance of training (conditions of transfer). A summary of the findings will be followed by a critique of the existing research.

Training design

A large proportion of the empirical research on transfer has concentrated on improving the design of training programs through the incorporation of learning principles. Research has centered on four basic principles: (1) identical elements, (2) teaching of general principles, (3) stimulus variability, and (4) various conditions of practice.

Identical elements

The notion of identical elements was originally proposed by Thorndike and Woodworth (1901). They hypothesized that transfer is maximized to the degree that there are identical stimulus and response elements in the training and transfer settings. Empirical research supports the use of identical elements as a means of increasing the retention of both motor (Crafts, 1935; Gagne, Baker, & Foster, 1950) and verbal behaviors (Duncan & Underwood, 1953; Underwood, 1951).

General principles

Teaching through general principles maintains that transfer is facilitated when trainees are taught, not just applicable skills, but also the general rules and theoretical principles that underlie the training content (McGehee & Thayer, 1961). For example, Judd (1908) and Hendrickson and Schroeder (1941) demonstrated the usefulness of teaching through general principles by using rules of light infraction to improve proficiency in underwater shooting. Crannell (1956), in a series of three studies, showed the value of teaching general principles for problem solving by improving subjects' ability to learn card-sorting tricks. Goldbeck, Bernstein, Hillix, and Marx (1957) found that individuals instructed in the principles of analyzing problems were better able to locate problems with malfunctioning electronic equipment.

Stimulus variability

Stimulus variability is the notion that positive transfer is maximized when a variety of relevant training stimuli are employed (Ellis, 1965). Proponents state that several examples of a concept to be learned strengthen the trainee's understanding so that he/she is more likely to see the applicability of a concept in a new situation (Duncan, 1958; Ellis, 1965). The principle of stimulus variability has received empirical support with respect to training outcomes. For example, Shore and Sechrest (1961) found that using a moderate number of different examples that were repeated a few times each was more effective in enhancing learning than using one example repeatedly.

Conditions of practice

Conditions of practice include a number of specific design issues, including massed or distributed training, whole or part training, feedback, and overlearning. Massed versus distributed training is the issue of whether or not to divide training into segments. Research evidence suggests that material learned under distributed practice is generally retained longer than material learned by massed practice (Briggs & Naylor, 1962; Naylor & Briggs, 1963). There is also evidence that difficult and complex tasks result in higher performance when massed practice sessions are given first, followed by briefer sessions with more frequent rest intervals (Holding, 1965).

Whole versus part training concerns the relative efficiency of practice with all the material as opposed to practice on one part at a time. Evidence suggests that the whole method is advantageous for enhancing training outcomes when (1) the intelligence of the learner is high, (2) practice is distributed rather than massed, and (3) the training material is high in task organization but low in task complexity (Naylor & Briggs, 1963).

Feedback, or knowledge of results, refers to information provided to trainees about their performance. Evidence shows that feedback is a critical element in achieving learning and that timing and specificity are critical variables in determining its effects (e.g., Wexley & Thornton, 1972). Some authors have suggested that the optimal specificity of feedback may be dependent on the trainee and the stage of learning (Blum & Naylor, 1968), although empirical evidence is lacking.

Overlearning refers to the process of providing trainees with continued practice far beyond the point when the task has been performed successfully (McGehee & Thayer, 1961). Research indicates that the greater the amount of overlearning, the greater the subsequent retention of the trained material (Atwater, 1953; Gagne & Foster, 1949; Mandler, 1954). More recently, Hagman and Rose (1983) reported the results of several studies sponsored by the Army Research Institute that provide empirical support for the value of overlearning on retention in military training contexts.

While researchers have also stressed the importance of design issues such as sequencing and the relevance of training content, (e.g., Gagne, 1962), empirical research is lacking. One exception is the work of Decker (1980, 1982), who has explored the effects of different types of learning points on the reproduction and generalization of skills taught in behavior-modeling programs.

Trainee characteristics

A wide variety of trainee characteristics thought to affect transfer have been suggested in the practitioner literature (e.g., Robinson, 1984; Trost, 1982); however, empirical investigations of ability, personality, and motivational effects on training and transfer outcomes are quite limited.

Existing research evidence shows that trainee success in early stages of training or on training samples predicts transfer on some training tasks (Downs, 1970; L. Gordon, 1955; M. Gordon & Cohen, 1973; McGehee, 1948). And investigations of a variety of ability and aptitude tests also show moderate success for such measures as predictors of trainability (e.g., M. Gordon & Kleiman, 1976; Neel & Dunn, 1960; Robertson & Downs, 1979; Ryman & Biersner, 1975; M. Smith & Downs, 1975; C. Taylor, 1952; E. Taylor & Tajen, 1948; Tubiana & Ben-Shakhar, 1982). But Ghiselli's (1966) review of the literature in the area characterized the typical predictive power of aptitude tests for the prediction of trainability as "far from impressive" (p. 125).

With respect to personality variables, Noe and Schmitt (1986) found limited support for the effects of locus of control on pretraining motivation and learning. Baumgartel, Reynolds, and Pathan (1984) found that managers high in need for achievement and having an internal locus of control were more likely to apply new knowledge gained in training to work settings. On the other hand, Miles (1965), in a study of a sensitivity program, concluded that personality factors had no direct effect on transfer.

Several studies have investigated the effects of motivational factors on transfer. Ryman and Biersner (1975) found a significant relation between trainee confidence in the successful completion of a Navy diving training program and subsequent class success and dropout rate. Tubiana and Ben-Shakhar (1982) found a significant relation between motivation to succeed in training and a composite criterion of training performance, a probability assessment of promotion potential, and a sociometric measure of the trainee's popularity with peers. Results from a study by Hicks and Klimoski (1987) show that a trainee's perception that he/she had a choice to attend (or not attend) a managerial-skills training program influenced motivation to learn and subsequent learning in the program. Noe and Schmitt (1986) found that trainees with high job involvement were more motivated to learn and transfer skills to the work setting. Baumgartel et al. (1984) showed that managers who believed in the value of training were more likely to apply skills learned in training. Finally, Eden and colleagues (Eden & Ravid, 1982; Eden &

Shani, 1982) found that higher self-expectancies led to higher training performance in two studies of military personnel.

Post-training interventions such as goal setting and feedback have been used to increase the motivation of the trainee to transfer skills learned in training. For example, Wexley and Nemeroff (1975) found that trainees assigned goals after a management development program were significantly better at applying their learning than were members of a control group. Reber and Wallin (1984) showed that both feedback and goal setting produced higher levels of skill transfer to the work setting than did either approach separately.

Work-environment characteristics

While the practitioner literature on training (e.g., Eddy, Glad, & Wilkins, 1967) stresses that positive transfer is highly contingent on factors in the trainee's work environment, empirical evidence is sparse. Baumgartel and his associates (Baumgartel & Jeanpierre, 1972; Baumgartel et al., 1984; Baumgartel, Sullivan, & Dunn, 1978) have conducted a line of research indicating that managers in favorable organizational climates (with freedom to set goals and a supportive environment) are more likely to apply new knowledge to work settings. And Hand, Richards, and Slocum (1973) concluded that positive changes in human-relations skills 18 months after training were due to organizational decisions such as salary and promotions that reinforced the attitudes learned in training. Huczynski and Lewis (1980) found that a management style that included pre-course discussion with one's boss and subsequent boss sponsorship contributed most to the transfer of skills.

Critique of the existing literature

Tables 1, 2, and 3 present outlines of the research on the effects of training design, trainee characteristics, and work-environment characteristics, respectively. The next section provides a critique of the research to identify what is known about transfer and to aid in the specification of the type of research needed to improve our understanding of the transfer process.

Training input factors

Table 1 presents the studies referenced by training researchers (e.g., I. Goldstein, 1986; Wexley & Latham, 1981) as the empirical basis for what is known with respect to training design and learning principles. An examination of the table reveals that the research on learning principles was typically completed before 1970. The sample used for most of the studies was composed of college students completing relatively straightforward memory and psychomotor-skills tasks. For example, to examine the impact of identical elements, Underwood (1951) used a sample of 54 college students, whose task was to pair adjectives. In a more recent

Table 1 Empirical studies of transfer of training—training input factors: design of training

Author(s)	Sample	Task or training content	Variables	Design[a]	Criteria
Adams (1955)	127 Military trainees	Distinguishing spatial arrangements of a stimulus pair	Stimulus variability	E	Immediate[b] proficiency on an arrangement task
Atwater (1953)	32 College students	Pairing words	Conditions of practice (overlearning)	E	Immediate proficiency in pairing words correctly
Baldwin (1987)	72 College students	Behavior modeling of assertive skills	Stimulus variability	E	Immediate measure of learning; immediate reproduction of skills; generalization of skills to a novel context four weeks later; unobstrusive measure of skill use four weeks later
Briggs & Naylor (1962)	144 College Students	Maintaining control of a compensatory tracking system	Conditions of practice (whole vs. part)	E	Immediate measure of tracking proficiency
Briggs & Waters (1958)	160 ROTC college students	Pilot training; simulator tracking task	Conditions of practice (whole vs. part)	E	Immediate measure of total number of errors in sorting cards to illustrate understanding
Callentine & Warren (1955)	120 College students	Concept attainment with geometric figures	Stimulus variability	E	Immediate measure of total number of errors in sorting cards to illustrate understanding
Cominsky (1982)	34 Graduate students	Teaching reflection of feeling	General principles and stimulus variability	Q-E	Taped role plays, immediately after program completion
Crafts (1935)	64 College students	Card sorting	Identical elements	E	Immediate ability on test card sorting task
Crannel (1956) reports results of three experiments	248 College students	Card trick problems	General principles	E	Immediate measure of number of problems completed in one hour (Experiments 1 & 2); 6-week measure of whether two problems could be completed in 10 minutes (Experiment 3)

Decker (1980)	90 College students	Behavioral modeling of assertive skills	Type of learning points	E	Immediate reproduction of skills; immediate generalization of skills
Decker (1982)	24 First-line supervisors	Coaching and handling employee complaints	Type of learning points	Q-E	Immediate reproduction of skills; immediate generalization of skills
Digman (1959)	41 College students	Hitting a target button with rotor	Conditions of practice (massed vs. spaced)	E	Immediate task proficiency
Duncan (1958)	600 College students	Movement of a lever into one of 13 slots	Stimulus variability	E	Two proficiency tests given: (1) 24 hours after training, (2) 48 hours after training
Duncan & Underwood (1953)	186 College students	Moving a lever into slots in response to color-light stimuli	Identical elements	E	Retention of learning 24 hours and 14 months after acquisition
Forgus & Schwartz (1957)	39 Female college students	Learning a new alphabet	General principles	E	Immediate recall, simple transposition, and a measure of problem solving proficiency
Fryer & Edgerton (1950)	334 Military trainees	Gunnery training	Conditions of practice (massed vs. spaced) (instruction methods)	E	Immediate test of learning and retention of learning after 2 months
Gagne & Foster (1949)	145 Enlisted navy men	Reaction to light by pressing control panel switch	Conditions of practice (overlearning)	E	Immediate measures of (1) amount of time to complete trials, (2) no. of errors
Goldbeck, Bernstein, Hillix, & Marx (1957)	40 Male college students	Troubleshooting problems with electronic equipment	General principles	E	Immediate test of troubleshooting proficiency
Hagman & Rose (1983) results of 13 experiments	Military personnel	Variety of military tasks	Conditions of practice	Q-E/E	Both immediate proficiency and retention over time
Haselrud & Meyers (1958)	76 College students	Deciphering word codes (taught coding rules)	General principles	E	Immediate number of correct codings

(Continued)

Table 1 Cont'd

Author(s)	Sample	Task or training content	Variables	Design[a]	Criteria
Hendrickson & Schroeder (1941)	90 Eighth grade boys	Shooting an air gun at submerged underwater targets (taught principle of light infraction)	General principles	E	Immediate measure of accuracy on hitting underwater targets
Hilgard, Irvine, & Whipple (1953)	60 High-school students	Card trick problems	General principles	E	(1) Overnight measure of retention; (2) proficiency on simple transposition task; (3) proficiency on three problem-solving tasks
Hilgard, Edren, & Irvine (1954)	150 High-school students	Card trick problems	General principles	E	Overnight retention, number and type of errors made
Judd (1908)	Unspecified number of fifth and sixth grade boys	Shooting darts at submerged underwater targets (taught principle of light infraction)	General principles	E	Immediate accuracy on hitting underwater target with depth charge
Macpherson, Dees, & Grindley (1948)	200 College students	Line drawing, pushing a lever, pressing a Morse key	Feedback	E	Immediate task proficiency
Mandler (1954)	60 College students	Operating hand switches in sequences on a switchboard having six switches arranged in a hexagon; stimuli were letters of the alphabet	Conditions of practice (overlearning)	E	Immediate errorless trials
Mandler & Heinemann (1956)	60 College students	Assembly of verbal units from nonsense syllables	Conditions of practice (overlearning)	E	Immediate number of correct trials

Morrisett & Hovland (1959)	63 High-school students	Discriminating pairs of geometric figures	Stimulus variability	E	Immediate ability to discriminate between pairs
Naylor & Briggs (1963)	112 Female college students	Markov prediction task	Conditions of practice (whole vs. part)	E	Immediate number of correct predictions
Reynolds & Bilodeau (1952)	612 Basic trainee airmen	(1) Rudder control, (2) complex coordination, (3) rotary pursuit	Conditions of practice (massed vs. spaced)	E	Immediate proficiency and retention after 10 weeks
Schendel & Hagman (1982)	38 Reserve soldiers	Disassembly/assembly of M60 machine gun	Conditions of practice (overlearning)	E	8-week Retention interval
Shore & Sechrest (1961)	64 College students	Concept attainment	Stimulus variability	E	Immediate number of correct tests of concept attainment
Thorndike (1927)	24 People varying in age from 20 to 42+	Estimating length of paper strips blindfolded	Feedback	E	Immediate accuracy of length estimates
Thorndike & Woodworth (1901)	5 College students	Observing words for certain characteristics	Identical elements	E	Immediate speed and accuracy in word recognition
Trowbridge & Cason (1932)	60 College students	Drawing lines blindfolded	Feedback	E	Immediate proficiency of line drawing
Underwood (1951)	54 College students	Pairing adjectives	Identical elements	E	Immediate number of correct responses
Wexley & Thornton (1972)	261 College students	Introductory psychology course	Feedback	E	Course exams
Woodrow (1927)	76 College students	Memorization tasks (taught memory rules)	General Principles	E	Immediate memory scores

[a] E=Experimental; Q–E = Quasi–experimental.
[b] In this context, the term immediate denotes a period directly after the training took place; that is, no significant time elapsed between training and measurement of trained skills.

Table 2 Empirical studies of transfer of training—training input factors: trainee characteristics

Authors(s)	Sample	Training content	Variables	Criteria Source & (timing)	Measures & Results
Baumgartel & Jeanpierre (1972)	240 Indian managers	Management development program	Demographic (educ., age, job-income level); motivation (value & relevance of training); personality (composite scale)	Self (immediate)[a]	*Effort to apply*—41% of respondents indicated some intended effort to apply. Significantly related to job income but no other significant relationship with trainee characteristics.
				Self (unknown)	*Perceived success in transferring*—Of those indicating effort to apply, 47% indicated high success, 38% medium, and 15% low or no success. No r's with trainee characteristics reported.
				Supervisor (unknown)	*Attempt to Use*—21 % of bosses indicated some subordinate attempt to use. No r's with trainee characteristics reported.
Baumgartel, Reynolds, & Pathan (1984) Study 1	260 American managers	Human relations	Demographic (rank-job level); Motivation (value of training); personality (locus of control)	Self (immediate)	*Effort to apply*—Significantly related to locus of control. Relation with other trainee characteristics measured was n.s.[b]
				Self (unknown)	*Perceived success in transferring*—Significantly related to belief in the value of training. Relation with other trainee characteristics measured was n.s.
Baumgartel, Reynolds, & Pathan (1984) Study 2	246 Indian managers	Management development program	Personality (locus of control, need to achieve)	Self (immediate)	*Effort to apply*—Significantly related to locus of control and need achievement. Others were n.s.

Downs (1970)	82 Sewing machinists	Sewing machine training	Ability (training sample)	Instructor (immediate)	*Final instructor rating*—Significantly related ($r = .50$) to score on training sample.
Eden & Ravid (1982)	60 Military personnel	Clerical skills	Motivation (self & instructor expectancy)	Instructor (immediate)	*Learning exams*—Significant main effect for self-expectancy. High expectancy conditions had greater exam score average than controls. 27–30% of variance explained by self-expectancy.
Eden & Shani (1982)	105 Military personnel	Military combat command course	Motivation (instructor expectancy)	Instructor (immediate)	*Learning exams*—Significant main effect for instructor expectancy. High expectancy conditions had greater exam score average than controls. Instructor expectancy explained 73% of variance in learning exam performance.
Fleishman (1953)	122 Manufacturing foremen	Leadership training	Demographic (age, educ., tenure, number of subordinates)	Self (before training & varied from 2–24 after training)	*Leader behaviors (LBDQ)*—All relationships with trainee characteristics were n.s.
Gordon (1955)	400 Military recruits	Radio code training	Ability (early training time required)	Instructor (immediate)	*Radio code test score*—Significantly related to early training time required for three separate groups varying in previous radio code exposure.
Gordon & Cohen (1973)	58 Welding program trainees	Plate welding	Ability (early training performance)	Instructor (immediate)	*Time required to complete training*—Significantly related to early training performance on each of the first four tasks in training.
Gordon & Kleiman (1976)	101 Police trainees	Fundamentals of police work	Ability (training sample, IQ)	Instructor (immediate)	*Sum of graded exercises*—Significantly related to both work sample tests and IQ tests but the work sample tests yielded significantly higher r's in most cases.

(Continued)

Table 2 Cont'd

Authors(s)	Sample	Training content	Variables	Criteria Source & (timing)	Measures & Results
Hicks & Klimoski (1987)	85 Managers	Two-day performance review training	Motivation (degree of choice to select training, realistic preview)	Self (immediate) Self (immediate) Self (immediate) Self (immediate) Instructor (immediate) Trained observers (immediate)	*Appropriateness of training*—Main effects for degree of choice and type of prior info. *Profit from training*—Main effects for degree of choice and type of prior info. *Satisfaction w/ training*—Main effects for degree of choice. *Learning*—Main effects for degree of choice. *Achievement test*—Main effects for degree of choice. *Role play*—No significant effects.
Huczynski & Lewis (1980)	48 Electronic managers	Three-day network analysis training program	Motivation (attend on own, value of training, prior course discussion)	Self (4 months after training)	*Attempt to transfer*—35% of respondents made some attempt to transfer. Those who attempted transfer were more likely to have (1) attended the course on their own initiative, (2) believed the course would be beneficial, and (3) had prior discussions of the course.
Komacki, Heinzemann, & Lawson (1980)	55 Vehicle maintenance personnel	One-hour safety training	Motivation (reinforcing feedback)	Trained observers (weekly up to 40 weeks)	*Safety behaviors exhibited*—Significant increases in safety performance occurred when training was combined with feedback (15% over training only and 26% over baseline).

McGehee (1948)	21 Rug-mill trainees	Preparation of rug-spools	Ability (initial effectiveness in OJT training)	Instructor (immediate)	*Time required to attain acceptable average production*—Significantly related to time required to complete early training periods. Most significant increase in prediction was from 1st to 2nd period.
Miles (1965)	34 Elementary school principals	Two-week human relations	Demographic (tenure, no. of subs); personality (ego strength, flexibility, need affiliation) motivation (desire for change, feedback received, involvement, unfreezing)	Self (immediate)	*Perceived change from training*—Significantly related to feedback received. Relation with all other personality and motivation variables was n.s.
				Peer (immediate)	*Perceived change from training*—Significantly related to unfreezing, involvement, and feedback received. Relation with desire for change and other variables was n.s.
				Self (8 months after training)	*On-the-job change*—Significantly related to unfreezing. Relation with other variables was n.s.
Neel & Dunn (1960)	32 Supervisory trainees	10-week supervisory skills training	Ability (IQ-Wonderlic); personality ("How Supervise", authoritarianism)	Instructor (immediate)	*Course examinations*—Significantly related to Wonderlic ($r = .25$), "How Supervise" scale ($r = .69$), and authoritarianism ($r = .39$).
Noe & Schmitt (1986)	60 School educators	Managerial skills	Motivation (expectancies, motive to learn, exploratory behavior, job involvement); personality (locus of control)	Trained Raters (immediate)	*Learning (in-basket exercises)*—Relation with all trainee characteristics n.s. Rresidual value for job involvement = (.41).
				Self (varied 1–3–4 mos. after training)	*Motivation to transfer*—Relation with all trainee characteristics n.s.
				Supervisor (3 mos. after training)	*Behavior*—Relation with all trainee characteristics n.s.
				Peers (3 mos. after training)	*Behavior (peer)* Relation with all trainee characteristics n.s.

(Continued)

Table 2 Cont'd

Authors(s)	Sample	Training content	Variables	Criteria Source & (timing)	Measures & Results
Reber & Wallin (1984)	105 Farm machinery workers	Safety procedures	Motivation (reinforcing feedback and goals)	Trained observers (weekly up to 40 weeks)	*Safety behaviors exhibited*—Main effects for each of three interventions: (1) safety rule training alone, (2) goal setting, (3) feedback and goal setting. Percentage of safety behaviors exhibited varied such that (control) 62.80%, (1) 70.85%, (2) 77.54%, (3) 95.39%.
Ryman & Biersner (1975)	548 Military personnel	Technical (diving & underwater) skills	Motivation (course expectations, confidence, leadership efficacy, concern); personality (conformity)	File data (immediate)	*Program graduation*—Across 3 programs, successful graduation had a significant positive relationship with training motivation, leadership, and conformity and was negatively related to training concerns.
Smith & Downs (1975)	236 Shipbuilding apprentices	Variety of shipbuilding skills	Ability (trainability assessment)	Instructor (3–12 months after trainability assessment)	*Performance test*—Trainability assessments were successful in predicting performance after a 3-month period in the skill for which they were designed. They were less successful after a 12-month period and no single assessment predicted performance for all skills.
Taylor (1952)	120 Automotive mechanic trainees	Mechanic skills	Ability (aptitude test battery)	Instructor (immediate)	*Performance test*—Aptitude test battery was effective in identifying trainees who had the necessary knowledge and skills to skip the first four weeks to training and still do approximately as well as those who took the whole course.
Taylor & Tajen (1948)	313 Clerical trainees	Clerical, record-keeping skills	Ability (numeric score on test battery)	Instructor (immediate)	*Performance test*—Individuals' performance test scores on IBM punch card equipment were predicted with a one-hour pretraining test battery such that 70% of the selected trainees did better than the average unselected trainee.

Tubiana & Shakhar (1982)	459 Israeli military	Basic military training	Demographic (education); ability (language test, 2 IQ tests); motivation (motive to serve in combat); personality (activeness, sociability, responsibility, independence, & promptness)	Superior officer (immediate)	*Performance potential*—Officer rating of potential had a significant positive relationship to education ($r = .21$), language test scores ($r = .24$), intelligence ($r = .32$) and composite of personality & motivation ($r = .33$).
Wexley & Baldwin (1986)	256 College students	Time management	Motivation (goal setting, relapse prevention)	Instructor (immediate) Self (8 weeks after training) Observer (8 weeks after training) *Behavior*—No significant effects observed.	*Learning*—Main effect for assigned goal setting. *Behavior*—Main effects for assigned & participative goal setting.
Wexley & Nemeroff (1975)	27 Health care managers	Two-day supervisory skills program	Motivation (goal setting)	Self (60 days after training) Subordinate (60 days after training)	*Behavior*—Goal setting treatments were significantly more effective than a control group in improving the leader behavior of managers. *Behavior*—Assigned goal-setting group was most effective in increasing subordinate work satisfaction.

[a] Immediate denotes that no significant time elapsed between training and measurement of trained skills.
[b] n.s. denotes statistically nonsignificant.

Table 3 Empirical studies of transfer of training—environmental factors

Authors(s)	Sample	Training content	Variables	Criteria Source & (timing)	Measures & Results
Baumgartel & Jeanpierre (1972)	240 Indian managers	Management development program	Perceptions of transfer climate	Self (immediate)[a]	*Effort to apply*—Favorable organization climate perceptions were significantly and positively related to effort to apply.
Baumgartel, Reynolds, & Pathan (1984) (Study 1)	260 American managers	Human relations	Perceptions of transfer climate	Self (immediate)	*Effort to apply*—Favorable organization climate perceptions were significantly and positively related to effort to apply; the most favorable organization climate was characterized by high appreciation for performance and innovation, encouragement of risk taking and freedom to set own performance goals.
Baumgartel, Reynolds, & Pathan (1984) (Study 2)	246 Indian managers	Management development program	Perceptions of transfer climate	Self (immediate)	*Effort to apply*—Favorable organization climate perceptions were significantly and positively related to effort to apply. The most favorable organization climate was characterized by high appreciation for performance and innovation, a climate of freedom, a rational reward system, and openness in relationships among managers.
Fleishman (1953)	122 Manufacturing foremen	Leadership training	Perceptions of leadership climate	Self (varied 2–24 mos. after training)	*Leader behavior(LBDQ)*—Leader behavior was significantly affected by the leadership climate in the trainee's work environment. Trainees who returned to supervisors high in consideration exhibited more consideration. No such change occurred for those returning to supervisors lower in consideration.

Hand, Richards, & Slocum (1973)	21 Middle managers	Human relations training	Perceptions of transfer climate	Self (3 & 18 mos. after training)	*3-Month evaluation*—No significant changes in attitudes or behaviors of trainees were observed. *18-Month evaluation*—Significant positive changes in attitudes were observed in the experimental group; negative changes existed in the control group. Three climate perceptions (whether the organization favors participation by subordinates, innovative behavior, and independence of thought), moderated the findings.
Huczynski & Lewis (1980)	48 Electronic managers	Three-day network analysis training program	Supervisor support & perceptions of transfer climate	Self (4 mos. after training)	*Attempt to transfer*—Transfer attempts were more likely when the trainees had pre-training discussions with boss and where the boss "sponsored" the new idea. The management style and attitudes of the trainee's boss were found to be the most important factor in attempt to transfer.
Miles (1965)	34 Elementary school principals	Two-week human relations program	Perceptions of transfer climate	Self (8 mos. after training)	*Perceived on-the-job change*—Organizational factors (security, autonomy, power, & problem-solving adequacy) mediated the perceived change associated with laboratory training.

---

[a] Immediate denotes that no significant time elapsed between training and measurement of trained skills.

study, Schendel and Hagman (1982) had 38 soldiers disassemble machine guns under various conditions of overlearning.

The criterion measure of interest for all the studies was oriented toward training outcome. Typically, measures of retention were taken immediately after completion of the training task. Mandler and Heinemann (1956), for example, used the number of correct trials immediately after training to examine the effects of overlearning on retention. The research indicates that learning principles have an effect on learning and immediate retention of training material. Nevertheless, attempts to examine retention over time or the effects of retention on the generalization and maintenance of skills have been rare.

To summarize, Table 1 shows that studies examining training-design factors have used college students working on simple memory and motor tasks, with immediate learning or retention as the criterion of interest (Linkage 1 of the transfer model in Figure 1). From an examination of these study characteristics, two basic limitations of the existing research become evident.

First, the tasks used limit generalizability of the results to short-term, simple motor tasks and memory-skills training. The use of such tasks is problematic, given that organizational training is often conducted to enhance individual competence on long-term, complex skills such as interpersonal communication and managerial problem solving. The effect of these learning principles on training outcomes for more complex and interrelated tasks is unknown. While it is relatively straightforward to operationalize principles such as overlearning in controlled experimental settings with motor or memory tasks, the appropriate operationalization of learning principles in more complex organizational-training programs is problematic. For example, there is no empirical data regarding how much and in what ways a trainer should incorporate learning principles such as stimulus variability into a behavior-modeling program to enhance the transfer of managerial skills. In addition, W. Schneider (1985) suggests that several training-design maxims (e.g., practice makes perfect) are fallacious when training for "high performance" skills.

Second, the criterion measures of interest in these studies have been learning and short-term retention. While these measures are certainly appropriate, given the goals of the original research, any claims by training researchers regarding the implications of these "robust" findings for enhancing transfer of training must be made with caution. Training outcomes of learning and retention constitute necessary but not sufficient conditions for generalization and maintenance of skills. Therefore, we need research that explicitly examines the direct effects of training-design factors on training outcomes (Linkage 1) and then examines the effects of training outcomes on conditions of transfer (Linkage 6).

Trainee characteristics

Table 2 presents the studies that have examined the relation of trainee characteristics to transfer of training. There are fewer such studies, but they are more recent than those focusing on training-design characteristics. Examination of the table reveals a variety of different samples, training tasks, and designs used. The sample includes managers, college students, and line personnel. The training tasks range from general interpersonal skills such as human-relations training to specific skills programs such as time management.

The criterion measure typically used in these studies was retention of the learned material (Linkage 2). Retention was commonly measured through written tests, which asked trainees to recall trained material immediately or shortly after completion of the training program (see, for example, Wexley & Baldwin, 1986). In some studies, information on generalization and maintenance of trained skills to the job (Linkage 5) was also gathered. The major source of information about behavioral change was the trainee him/herself, with such information being gathered soon after completion of the training program. For example, upon completion of a network-analysis training program, Huczynski and Lewis (1980) asked trainees about their intentions to transfer skills learned. Four months later they asked them for their perceptions of their success in transferring skills from the training program. Few studies used behavioral ratings (Noe & Schmitt, 1986) or observed and recorded actual behaviors (e.g., Komacki, Heinzemann, & Lawson, 1980; Reber & Wallin, 1984) to evaluate the extent of transfer.

The research on trainee characteristics has two critical problems, which reduce its usefulness for understanding the factors affecting the transfer process. The first problem is the lack of theoretical frameworks to guide research. A number of individual-difference factors have been examined, including job involvement (Noe & Schmitt, 1986), need for achievement (Baumgartel & Jeanpierre, 1972; Baumgartel et al., 1984), belief in the value of training (Baumgartel et al., 1984; Ryman & Biersner, 1975), and intelligence level (Tubiana & Ben-Shakhar, 1982). Some motivational strategies have also been examined for their impact on transfer; they include goal setting (Reber & Wallin, 1984; Wexley & Baldwin, 1986; Wexley & Nemeroff, 1975), feedback (Komaki et al., 1980; Reber & Wallin, 1984), choice in attending training (Hicks & Klimoski, 1987; Huczynski & Lewis, 1980), realistic information about the training program (Hicks & Klimoski, 1987), and relapse prevention (Wexley & Baldwin, 1986). Despite these efforts, the lack of a systematic approach to this area has resulted in minimal improvements in our understanding of the transfer process. Systematic research is needed in which models would be developed, tested, and revised on the basis of empirical research. Noe (1986) has provided an initial attempt to identify key personality and motivational factors that affect transfer and to hypothesize expected linkages and relationships among these factors and transfer. More efforts at model development are needed.

A second critical issue is the lack of adequate criterion measures of transfer in the studies examining the effects of trainee characteristics. Self-report measures of transfer are not adequate for developing a data base regarding the relation of trainee characteristics to transfer or for determining which interventions have the greatest effect on transfer. For example, Wexley and Baldwin's (1986) conclusion that a post-training goal-setting intervention was more effective than a relapse-prevention intervention must be tempered by the fact that the conclusion was based solely on self-reported generalization of skills and not on actual behavioral changes.

Environmental characteristics

Table 3 presents information about the seven studies that have examined the relation of environmental characteristics to transfer of training. We located no studies in which an intervention was made to change the work environment and the effects of those changes on the extent of transfer was examined. Instead, studies used large-scale surveys to examine the relationships of correlates such as work climate (Baumgartel et al., 1984), leadership climate (Fleishman, 1953) and supervisory support (Huczynski & Lewis, 1980) to transfer criteria.

Most of the training programs studied were interpersonal-skills (human-relations) programs. Given that behavioral changes in interpersonal relations are difficult to operationalize, it is not surprising that the transfer criterion measure frequently used was a self-reported measure of effort to transfer (e.g., Baumgartel & Jeanpierre, 1972, Baumgartel et al., 1984). Many of the measures were gathered immediately or soon after the training program was completed. A few studies, such as Hand et al., (1973), collected self- and supervisor reports of behavior change at more than one point in time after completion of the training program.

There are two major problems with the research examining work-environment characteristics and transfer. The first issue is the static nature of the research in relation to the dynamic nature of the transfer process. The "strong" support for the importance of environmental characteristics to transfer is based solely on correlational studies in which causality can not be inferred. What is needed is the identification of key work-environment variables and the operationalization of these variables. For example, while research suggests that supervisory support is an important component affecting transfer, there is little attempt to understand the supervisory behaviors that lead to perceptions of support by trainees. Only by clearly operationalizing work characteristics such as support can interventions be developed and their effects on generalization and maintenance of training be examined.

A second issue is the criterion problem. The studies on environmental characteristics have typically used self-reports of behavioral change as the major measure of transfer. In fact, Baumgartel and his associates have often used an "intention to transfer" measure, which is actually a "motivation to transfer" measure rather than a measure of the extent of generalization and maintenance of trained skills. Only one study, Hand et al. (1973), examined maintenance of trained behaviors across time as they measured self-reports and supervisory reports of behavior 3 months and 18 months after completion of the training program. The results indicated no change in behavior at 3 months but changes in behavior after 18 months. Given only two data points in time and the fact that process measures were not taken, it is impossible to determine why these results were found. Research is needed in which measures are taken at multiple intervals to examine the interactive effects of work characteristics and time on skill utilization and skill decrements after completion of a training program.

Overall critique of the research

While the limited number and the fragmented nature of the studies examining transfer are disturbing by themselves, a critical review of the existing research reveals that the samples, tasks, designs, and criteria used limit even further our ability to understand the transfer process. This review and critique of the research brings to mind a quote by Campbell (1971) that "we know a few things but not very much" (p. 593). Yet the review and critique has also led to the identification of specific problems with research conducted in this area. The next section provides a more specific and detailed discussion of needed future directions for research into the transfer process.

Future research directions

The critique of the transfer literature indicates that there are a number of research gaps that need to be addressed. The following section suggests needed future research directions regarding training design, trainee characteristics, work environment, and criterion issues relevant to transfer.

Training design

Of the transfer research completed, it is clear that the experimental work on improving the training process is the most developed and rigorously researched. The results of research on the effects of the learning principles of identical elements, general principles, conditions of practice, and stimulus variability on retention has been quite robust. Nevertheless, we are still confronted with the problem of generalizing from these results to actual organizational-training settings.

In this section, several salient operational questions associated with the learning principles will be identified and illustrated with the use of a common organizational-training example. For this purpose, the case of training a new sales representative to sell computer equipment will be used. The salient operational questions will lead to a discussion of needed research questions. For illustrative purposes, operational issues relevant to principles of identical elements and stimulus variability will be highlighted.

Identical elements

The principle of identical elements predicts that transfer will be maximized to the degree that there are identical stimulus and response elements in the training and transfer settings. The critical operational problem is: "What, specifically, in the training program must be made identical to the actual work environment to facilitate learning, retention, and transfer?" One aspect of similarity is the degree to which the actual conditions of the training program (surroundings, tasks, equipment) match the work environment (physical fidelity). A second aspect of similarity is the degree to which trainees attach similar meanings in the training and organizational context (psychological fidelity). While there is some evidence that physical fidelity is less important than psychological fidelity (Berkowitz & Donnerstein, 1982), the concepts and their relative importance for different training content and skills have been neglected in the industrial-training literature.

To use the example of the new sales representative, one training tactic might be to replicate the relevant physical characteristics of the sales context exactly, including products, types of clients, office surroundings, and common distractions. Or, the training could focus on creating accurate reproduction of behavioral and cognitive processes that are necessary for performing the sales job. One could create training stimuli that necessitate the same responses and decision-making processes that the trainee should use in real sales situations. Research is needed to explore the type and level of fidelity needed to maximize transfer, given time and resource constraints. Unfortunately, the industrial-training literature does not provide specifications for what constitutes optimal levels of physical and psychological fidelity in various types of industrial-training programs. It is necessary to understand the type of learning involved and the instructional events being considered before it is possible to choose the most effective learning procedures, or operationalization of principles.

Stimulus variability

Maximizing stimulus variability is based on the notion that transfer is maximized when a variety of relevant training stimuli are employed (e.g., Ellis, 1965). Kazdin (1975) has noted that transfer is enhanced by developing a variety of situations or by using differentially reinforced stimuli to avoid the problem of training becoming attached to a narrow range of stimuli and responses. In this way, variability can serve to strengthen understanding of the applicability of the training to new situations (Duncan, 1958) and to foster innovation and generalization of skills (Bandura, 1977).

Operationalization of stimulus variability in organizational-training programs is problematic. Consider the example of developing models for a behavior-modeling program on building interpersonal skills for a new sales representative. Modeling is intended to provide the majority of the cognitive aspects of the training, including attention to a modeling display, mental coding, and mental rehearsal (Decker & Nathan, 1985; A. Goldstein & Sorcher, 1974). Yet, in behavior-modeling training, models are typically very simple and often redundant, and trainees are conditioned to think that the specific behaviors modeled and reinforced are universally applicable in handling problem situations on the job (Parry & Reich, 1984).

Three options for increasing stimulus variability in the modeling component of behavior-modeling training are character, situational, and model-competence variability. With character variability, a variety of different model characteristics (age, sex, organizational level) can be displayed. A second direction is to vary the situations modeled. For example, if one modeling tape entitled "assertive communication" portrays a salesperson assertively requesting a customer to reconsider a product, a second model could be shown that portrays a salesperson assertively requesting that the order department fill his/her order as soon as possible. A third way to increase variability is to vary the competence of the models. Models might be varied in terms of the extent to which they correctly demonstrate the key behaviors (high to low competence). Current behavior-modeling programs typically use effective models that are repeatedly shown. Yet, concept formation and problem-solving research suggest that negative models, in addition to positive models, can improve the process of retention and generalizability of skills (e.g., Bourne, 1970; Bourne & Guy, 1968; Craik & Lockhart, 1972).

Consequently, in the sales example, variability can be increased via different models, situations, and/or levels of model effectiveness. Also, while the focus in this section has been on the model displays, it should be noted that behavior modeling is a multi-stage process that should also include instructor input, role playing, and feedback. Thus, stimulus variability might also be introduced by the instructor (e.g., by providing varied examples or experiences) or by participants themselves in the role-playing scenarios. Unfortunately, at the present time, decisions regarding the focus and extent of stimulus variability in organizational-training programs such as behavior modeling must be based on intuition and conjecture rather than empirical support.

Baldwin (1987) has begun applied work examining the impact of stimulus variability within a behavior-modeling program. Variability has been operationalized in terms of the inclusion of different situations and different levels of effectiveness (effective or ineffective modeling) for assertive behaviors displayed by a videotaped model. Results suggest that increases in the variability of model competence enhance trainee generalization of learned skills. Similarly, in a counseling setting, Cominsky (1982) used different therapists (character variability) for the same patient rather than continuous work with one therapist and found that the increased stimulus variability led to enhanced treatment gains.

It is evident that there is much to be learned about the operationalization of training-design principles. Extending beyond the domain of organizational-training literature, recent research in the areas of information processing and instructional theory holds promise for furthering our understanding of training-design issues.

Cormier (1984) contends that an information-processing perspective has implications for training design. He points out that the principle of identical elements can be reconceptualized by using what we know about encoding and retrieval processes. More specifically, a training stimulus is conceptualized as a collection of attributes or elements (E. Smith, Shoben, & Rips, 1974; Underwood, 1969) that vary in terms of redintegrative capacity (Flexser & Tulving, 1978). Redintegration refers to the capacity of one part of a stimulus complex to re-evoke or cue the entire complex (Cormier, 1984). The redintegrative value of the available retrieval information is the critical determinant of its effectiveness. Applying this notion to transfer of training suggests that transfer should be the highest when the stimulus attributes with the highest redintegrative capacity are present in the task. In this view, it is not fidelity (either physical or psychological) per se that contributes to high positive transfer, but rather, the presence of retrieval information that has a high redintegrative capacity. Even low-fidelity training stimuli can be effective in producing transfer by providing the trainee with the essential cuing relationships between the stimulus attributes of the task environment and the appropriate responses.

While the task of identifying which attributes in training environments have high or low redintegrative value remains, the value of this conceptualization and framework for training is relatively straightforward. The fidelity of a training stimulus to the actual stimuli can be based on those attributes with high redintegrative value for correct responses. Those attributes with lower redintegrative value can be modified or eliminated without substantial loss of transfer (Cormier, 1984). These suggestions have considerable practical implications since high fidelity is often very difficult and expensive to create.

Research on information processing also suggests new avenues for better understanding the design principle of stimulus variability. An information-processing perspective suggests that when individuals are exposed to a variety of related or similar material across different presentations, they can more easily integrate new material with that already in memory into a common representation. From this perspective, stimulus variability is thought to aid transfer by providing a means by which an individual distinguishes relevant from irrelevant attributes (abstraction) and by enhancing the probability that additional relevant attributes are encoded into the functional representation of the to-be-remembered item. Therefore, research on the extent to which variability induces the formation of higher-order concepts or facilitates the abstraction of critical dimensions of task performance and stimulus recognition is needed.

The work of instructional theorists such as Gagne and Briggs (1979) is also relevant for transfer researchers interested in training-design issues. Gagne and Briggs developed a set of learning categories that permits them to analyze tasks and code behavior into one of several learning outcomes (e.g. intellectual skills, motor skills, cognitive strategies). Further, they have begun to examine each of the outcomes and determine the conditions of learning and instructional events that best support that learning outcome. While Gagne and Briggs (1979) focus on learning outcomes, a logical extension of the model would be the inclusion of the transfer outcomes of generalization and maintenance discussed earlier.

To further illustrate this point, consider that much of the conduct being modeled in training programs designed to teach motor skills is exactly prescribed.

Therefore, it is desirable for trainees to adopt the modeled behaviors in essentially the same form as they are portrayed (Bandura, 1977). For example, there is little leeway permitted in the proper way to safely operate a power tool or perform a surgical operation. Consequently, the objective is to have trainees mimic behavior as closely as possible. In the case of interpersonal or supervisory skills, however, the objective is more to inculcate generalizable rules or concepts (specifying a class of behaviors to be used, given certain stimuli) and not simply to enable the trainee to reproduce only those behaviors specifically modeled. In fact, in the training of interpersonal and supervisory skills, the title "behavior" modeling is perhaps a misnomer. The training objective is to have observers extract the common attributes exemplified in modeled responses and formulate the rules for generating behavior with similar structural characteristics. Stated simply, the ultimate goal in complex skill-modeling training is to teach the trainee one or more principles (not strictly a list of behaviors) that will allow him/her to learn, generalize, and apply behaviors different from those modeled. It is clear that investigation directed at building a contingency model of transfer-oriented instructional design would provide information important for developing training environments more conducive to positive transfer.

Trainee characteristics

A limited amount of research has examined ability, motivational, and personality characteristics for their effects on transfer. We need research that more clearly identifies the important trainee characteristics and applies them in organizational settings. An interactive approach to research is also needed to begin testing for optimal matches between trainee characteristics and training-program design and content.

The research on ability and personality characteristics has failed to identify those factors that are most critical in a training context. In addition, the focus of this research has been on distinguishing between individuals who are successful and those who are unsuccessful in transferring skills rather than on placing individuals into programs that optimally match their characteristics.

Empirical evidence suggests that need for achievement (Baumgartel & Jeanpierre, 1972; Baumgartel et al., 1984), locus of control (Noe & Schmitt, 1986), and general intelligence (Neel & Dunn, 1960; Robertson & Downs, 1979) can be factors in learning and transferring skills. While further identification of key individual-difference variables is needed, there is a critical need for the development of a research perspective that attempts to understand the relationships of trainee characteristics and training-program design to transfer. The major application of the existing research on stable individual differences is that transfer can be facilitated by carefully selecting individuals who have certain personality and/or ability characteristics for the training program.

Given that in many organizations selection of trainees is not a viable option (everyone must be trained), researchers must begin a program of research on placement, rather than selection, of individuals into the type of program that is optimal (in terms of transfer), given certain trainee characteristics. The existing research does not speak to the issue of placement because the instructional methodology (e.g., lecture, case study, discussion) of specific types of training programs (e.g., assertiveness, human relations, time management) have been held constant in the studies completed. Studies are needed in which personality/ability factors are measured and individuals placed into training programs under different conditions of instructional methodology to determine which "types" of individuals best match which types of programs for effective transfer of skills to the job.

Cronbach and Snow (1977) have labelled this concern for providing each trainee with the appropriate model of instruction the "aptitude–treatment interaction." When an aptitude–treatment interaction is found, trainees should be assigned differentially to alternative training methods to maximize the probability of transfer. Similarly, we posit that a "personality–treatment interaction" would call for assigning trainees with external locus of control, for example, to a different method of instruction than trainees with an internal locus of control. As noted by I. Goldstein (1986), the examination of how individual differences moderate the effectiveness of different training methods requires refinement of individual-difference measures and the development of a typology of instructional methodology of the sort proposed by Gagne and Briggs (1979) discussed earlier.

Research examining motivational issues of transfer lacks a coherent framework for understanding factors affecting the transfer process. We propose that the expectancy model (Lawler, 1973; Vroom, 1964) provides just such a useful heuristic for integrating research on transfer motivation and for leading to new directions for transfer research.

The expectancy model provides a useful heuristic for understanding transfer because of its interactive perspective on motivation. Perceptions—and therefore motivation—are affected by both individual and work-environment factors, which must be interpreted by an individual and translated into choices among various behavioral options. This perspective has not been adequately acknowledged in the transfer literature: few studies have attempted to examine multiple influences on motivation to learn or motivation to transfer skills. From the expectancy framework (Lawler, 1973), it can be seen that there are numerous factors (locus of control, self esteem, past experience, communications from others) that need to be examined for their relevance to the transfer process. For example, social interaction regarding the usefulness of a training program may affect an individual's expectancies regarding the relationship between doing well in the program and attaining valued outcomes.

Second, the expectancy framework stresses the importance of a dynamic perspective on motivation. Individuals are seen as active information processors who adapt their attitudes, behaviors, and beliefs to their social context and to their own past experiences. Organizational procedures and reward systems, as well as information obtained from interactions with peers and superiors in the work environment, affect an individual's construction of the reality within the work setting, including perceptions of expectancies (Daft & Weick, 1984). This implies that new experiences, once integrated into a person's construction of reality, can result in changes in these expectancies. Unfortunately, most studies examining motivational factors and transfer have examined motivation from a static perspective, gathering information at one period of time. Similarly, all the research on motivational effects on transfer has focused on the effects within a single training program. Given that expectancies can change over time, important issues that have not been researched are the cumulative effects of past training experiences on an individual's expectancies and subsequent motivation to transfer currently trained skills to the job.

Environmental characteristics

Progress in the research on environmental characteristics requires the operationalization of key variables such as climate and supervisory support at a level of specificity that allows for the development of interventions for changing environmental characteristics and testing their effects on transfer of training. I. Goldstein (1985) has discussed environmental characteristics as either facilitating or inhibiting the transfer of training, and more research is needed to identify and operationalize variables that significantly facilitate or inhibit transfer. Also needed is research that examines the effects of environmental characteristics from a levels-of-analysis perspective. Such a perspective would lead to the examination of the effects of differences in climate or support across workgroups, and even across organizations.

Supervisory support

Supervisory support for training has been cited as a key work-environment variable affecting the transfer process (e.g., see Fleishman, 1953; House, 1968). Employees look towards their supervisor for important information regarding how to work successfully within the social environment of the organization. As Huczynski & Lewis (1980), state, employees who perceive that a training program is important to the supervisor will be more motivated to attend, learn, and transfer trained skills to the job. While support is critical, development of a concept of what is meant by support has lagged far behind anecdotal evidence of the importance of support. In addition, those trained skills and behaviors most affected by supervisory support have not been examined.

Supervisory support is clearly a multidimensional construct, which could include encouragement to attend, goal-setting activities, reinforcement activities, and modeling of behaviors (Baumgartel et al., 1984; Eddy, Glad, & Wilkins, 1967; Huczynski & Lewis, 1980; Maddox, 1987). A supervisor can demonstrate encouragement to attend through both verbal and nonverbal cues. For example, a supervisor may demonstrate a lack of knowledge about the content of the training program or show his/ her reluctance to allow subordinates to attend by rescheduling training when minor crises arise in the department. In relation to goal setting, supervisors can discuss the content and benefits of the program and set goals prior to (focus on improving these skills) and subsequent to (action plans for applying skills) attendance in the program (Wexley & Baldwin, 1986). Reinforcement refers to the provision of rewards for using behaviors developed in the training program. Supervisors can first insure that trainees have the opportunity to use the new skills in which they are trained. Then, the supervisor can provide praise, better assignments, and other extrinsic rewards for trainees who utilize their new skills. Reinforcement processes can also work in reverse; for example, a supervisor who ignores the use of a new skill or actively attacks the use of new skills can cause the trained behaviors to "extinguish." Finally, modeling has been shown to be a powerful force in affecting behavioral change (Sims & Manz, 1982). Employees tend to imitate supervisors who have power over them in order to gain rewards. Therefore, the extent to which the supervisor behaves in ways congruent with the training objectives will have a major impact on transfer of trained skills by subordinates.

Empirical work is needed so that the supervisory-support factors that have the greatest impact on transfer can be identified. With this information, interventions can be developed to change managerial behaviors to increase supervisory support prior to subordinate attendance in a specific training program.

Levels-of-analysis issues

The existing research on influences of the work environment on transfer has been correlational in nature. Perceptions of supervisory support by individual trainees are correlated with self- or other reports of transfer of trained skills to the job. Such measures, which are often collected soon after completion of the training program, are clearly inadequate for developing a base of knowledge about the transfer process. In addition to serious criterion problems, this type of study is problematic as it focuses solely on the individual level of analysis.

The literature describing research into climate (B. Schneider, 1983) indicates that there are often reliable differences in level of support and other climate factors across workgroups within an organization as well as across different organizations. Organizations and departments within organizations can be differentiated in terms of goal orientation, time orientation, formality of structure, and interpersonal orientation (Lawrence & Lorsch, 1969). For example, an organization's philosophy about its people (interpersonal orientation) can have important implications for the transferring of skills from a human-relations training program. This perspective calls for research at the organizational level of analysis in which the same training program is offered across multiple organizations. Similarly, from a group level of analysis, a research and development department with a long time perspective may be more supportive of interpersonal-skills training programs that do not have immediate, objective payoffs while production departments under time pressures would be less supportive of such programs.

Consequently, an organization-wide training program for improving interpersonal skills will most likely lead to different amounts of transfer across departments, depending on the support or congruence of the training program with the climate or philosophy of the various departments within the organization. An examination of the transfer literature reveals no existing attempts to empirically examine the effects of work environmental characteristics on transfer from a levels-of-analysis perspective.

Criterion issues

The conditions of transfer include generalization of skills or behaviors learned in the training program and the maintenance of those skills and behaviors over a specified period of time. The review of the transfer literature reveals that research has concentrated on the training-input factors that might affect transfer rather than focusing on the appropriate measurement of the conditions of transfer. This neglect of criterion issues is surprising, given the long-standing concern of applied psychologists over the "criterion problem" (Cascio, 1982; Wallace, 1965). The usefulness of the empirical research on transfer is severely limited by the use of criterion measures that are deficient and contaminated. Advancement in criterion measurement requires a greater appreciation of the issues relevant to measuring generalization and maintenance of skills and behaviors.

Generalization

To examine the successful generalization of trained skills or behaviors, a clear identification of the knowledge, skills, and behaviors expected to be transferred to the job is needed. Then a systematic collection of the appropriate information is needed to make effective training decisions related to the value of various training programs (I. Goldstein, 1986) and to systematically reassess training needs for possible redesign of the training program (Ford & Wroten, 1984).

To develop appropriate measures of generalization requires a linkage of needs-assessment information, the specification of training objectives, and the determination of criteria to use to determine how much of the knowledge, skills, and behaviors learned in training are transferred to the actual job. In addition, the relevance of the skills learned for effective job performance must be determined. While these suggested linkages are certainly not new, few attempts have been made in the transfer literature to list the criteria of success that one should expect on the basis of training objectives and training evaluation criteria. Such an approach is critical to the development of an empirical base regarding transfer.

Once the knowledge, skills, and behaviors that should be exhibited on the job are specified, the next step is to determine baselines that describe how often we can expect trainees to exhibit those knowledge, skills, and behaviors on the job.

A task analysis is needed to detail the importance and frequency of the tasks performed on the job. The tasks that are affected by the trained behaviors and skills can then be identified. Other analysis techniques, such as the collection of critical incidents, can help provide a taxonomy of situations that call for the use of the trained skills or behaviors. The combination of task importance and frequency and a taxonomy of situations can provide a baseline for determining how often one should expect trained behaviors to be exhibited on the job. This would force the explicit recognition that an important component in developing transfer measures of generalization is the identification of how often and in what situations a trainee could reasonably be expected to demonstrate the trained behaviors or skills.

Maintenance

While generalization refers to the extent to which trained skills and behaviors are exhibited in the transfer setting, maintenance concerns the length of time that trained skills and behaviors continue to be used on the job. Decreases in the use of trained skills on the job could be a result of skill decrements over time. Or, the decrease in use could be a result of decreased motivation to use the skills due to constraints in the work environment or a lack of rewards for using the skills. Regardless, this perspective requires a highly dynamic approach to the study of transfer that is lacking in the literature.

Such a dynamic perspective has been taken in research examining the amount of learning that occurs in training or educational settings over time. Researchers in the learning field have represented the dynamic process of learning in the form of "learning curves" (e.g., see Bass & Vaughan, 1966). Learning curves represent how well a certain skill is learned and the speed with which an individual acquires that skill. The kind of task being trained, the design of the training program, and the characteristics of the trainee have been found to have major impacts on how quickly an individual attains the level of performance that meets established standards (Blum & Naylor, 1968).

Similarly, we posit that a useful way to think about maintenance of trained knowledge, skills, and behaviors is through the use of "maintenance curves," which represent the changes that occur in the level of knowledge, skills, or behaviors exhibited in the transfer setting as a function of time elapsed from completion of the training program. The development of a maintenance curve requires the consideration of three issues. First, a baseline of the level of knowledge, skill, or behavior that a trainee exhibits prior to and at the end of the training program must be established. The amount of differentiation between pre- and post-training levels indicates the decrement that must occur to return to the pre-training baseline. Second, an adequate time interval that allows for the determination of overall trends or variations in skill or behavior levels must be established. Third, at multiple time intervals, measurements must be taken to examine changes in the shape and slope of the maintenance curve over time.

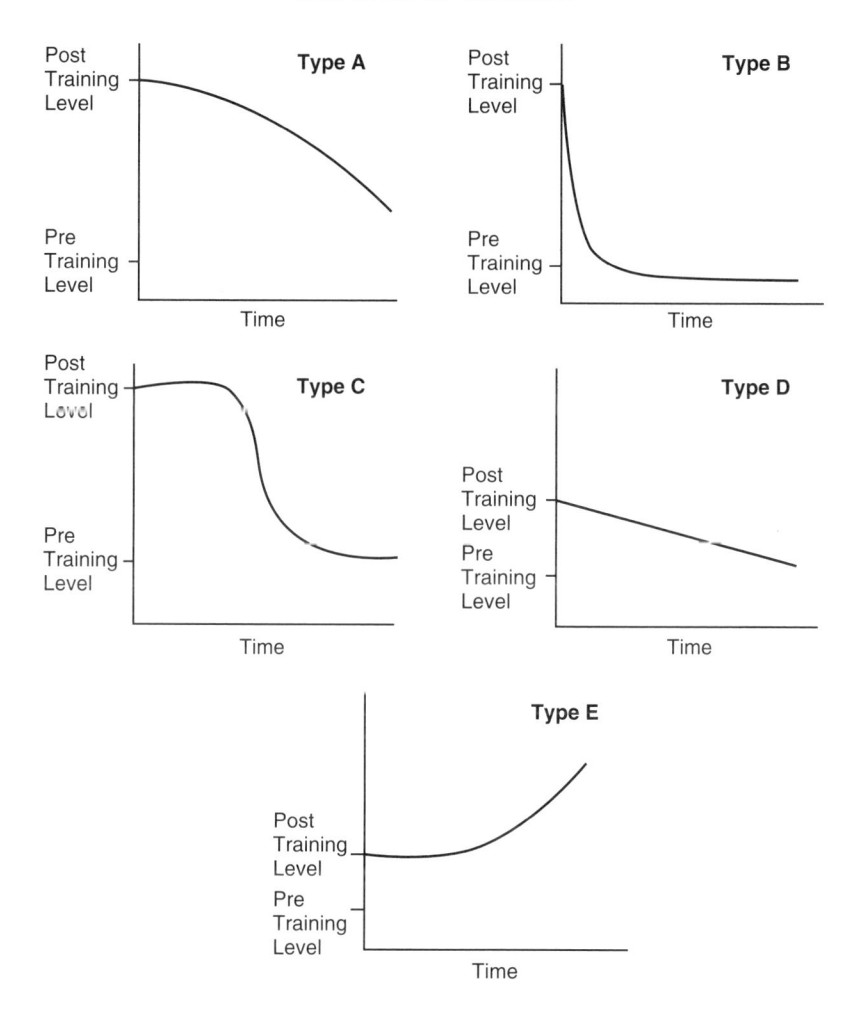

Figure 2 Types of transfer maintenance curves.

The five types of maintenance curve presented in Figure 2 illustrate the points made above. Type A demonstrates a curve in which there is a slow tapering off of a trained skill over time towards the pre-training baseline. This indicates the successful transfer of skills that is maintained over time but is in need of a "booster" session at some point to return to post-training baseline conditions. Type B indicates a failure in transfer as the post-training level drops immediately upon returning to the work site. In this case the person has demonstrated an ability to use the skill appropriately (based on performance in the training) but immediately reverts back to old ways of doing things on the job, for whatever reason. The third example, Type C, demonstrates an attempt by the trainee to use the skills trained on the job for a period of time, which is followed by a sharp decline in the use of a skill towards the pre-training baseline. This decline could occur due to the lack of success in using a trained skill on the job, perceived lack of support for using the skill, or some combination. Type D highlights the situation in which a trainee's learning and retention of trained material was minimal. In this case, there is little chance for the skills to generalize and be exhibited on the job. Finally, Type E demonstrates a situation in which the skill level actually increases over time once back on the job. For example, a supervisor may learn some behavioral modeling skills in giving performance feedback. Positive reactions by subordinates to the skills exhibited by the trainee once back on the job may result in more opportunities to exhibit those behaviors and an increase in the level of performance of those behaviors over time.

It is highly probable that the shape or "type" of maintenance curve found is affected by the type of skills trained (e.g., behavioral, psychomotor, cognitive), the proficiency level or amount of material retained by trainees at the completion of training, and supportiveness in the work environment for applying the new skill. For example, it might be predicted that psychomotor skills (other factors being constant) will be maintained over a longer period of time than will behavioral skills. In addition, maintenance curves can be examined at the individual level or the group level of analysis. For example, similarity of individual maintenance curves within a department would suggest a work-environment effect. Given reliable measures, a large variance in maintenance curves across individuals within a department would suggest individual-characteristics effects. Similarly, maintenance curves for different departments undergoing the same training program could be examined to identify differences in patterns. Then factors in the work environment that have systematic effects on the patterns found through the maintenance curves could be identified.

Conclusion

This paper has provided a review and critique of the transfer research reported in the organizational-training literature. Future research to increase our understanding of the factors affecting transfer has been outlined, and it has been stated that we must take into account a variety of factors and linkages that, to date, have not been adequately examined. One important step in doing this would be to take a more eclectic orientation toward transfer by focusing on a number of other literatures neglected by industrial-training researchers.

For example, with respect to the issue of conducive transfer environments, the literatures in the areas of counseling (Spevak, 1981), and psychotherapy (A. Goldstein & Kanfer, 1979) are potentially rich sources of ideas for testing and application to organizational settings. To illustrate, researchers in those areas have investigated the value of "buddy systems" for facilitating transfer (Barrett, 1978; Karol & Richards, 1978). A buddy system refers to two trainees being paired to reinforce each other in order to maintain learning, provide advice, and be alert for signs of relapse in themselves and the buddy. In a study of habitual smoking reduction, Karol and Richards (1978) found that the buddy system condition exhibited substantially less relapse to smoking than did a control condition.

Another strategy investigated in a counseling context has been that of "booster sessions" (Ashby & Wilson, 1977; Kingsley & Wilson, 1977). A booster session is an extension of training and usually involves periodic face-to-face contact of either a planned or unplanned nature between trainee and trainer. An obesity study by Kingsley and Wilson (1977) found that the inclusion of booster sessions at 2-, 3-, 4-, and 5-week intervals induced a significantly greater percentage of maintained weight loss than did the absence of boosters.

Marx (1982) has begun a program of research adapting a transfer strategy termed "relapse prevention," which was originally designed and successfully implemented in the treatment of addictive behaviors (Marlatt & J. Gordon, 1980; Perri, Shapiro, Ludwig, Twentyman, & McAdoo, 1984) to industrial settings. As Marx has noted, this approach seems particularly applicable as a post-training transfer strategy for industrial training. The relapse prevention model consists of both cognitive and behavioral components designed to facilitate the long-term maintenance of learned behaviors by teaching individuals to understand and cope with the problem of relapse.

In the area of educational psychology, Wlodkowski (1985) recently presented a comprehensive list of strategies for enhancing adult motivation to learn. While the author's focus was primarily on learning (not transfer) outcomes, and empirical evidence presented was quite limited, such work could serve as a departure point for empirical investigations aimed at investigating transfer in organizational contexts.

Aside from exploring other literatures, it is also readily apparent that we need to begin research that takes a more interactive perspective. Most of the existing research has focused exclusively on one input factor (design, trainee, work environment) rather than attempting to develop and test a framework that incorporates the more complex interactions among these training inputs. Consequently, we have a quite limited knowledge base about which input factors have the greatest impact on transfer under various conditions (such as type of organization and type of training program). A recent paper by I. Goldstein and Musicante (1985) is one of the first attempts to bring together several of the different factors usually examined independently (principles of learning, environment characteristics) and apply them together to an organizationally relevant (rater training) context.

In addition, training research cannot continue to ignore the job relevance of the training content as a critical factor affecting what is learned, retained, and transferred to the work setting. Transfer research has implicitly assumed the job relevance of the training content without attempting to specify what the desired skills or behaviors are or what the training content should be to insure skill acquisition. When training content is not valid, trainees may actually be successful in learning and transferring knowledge and skills that are inappropriate for effective job performance. Ford and Wroten (1984) and I. Goldstein (1986) have developed techniques for examining the content validity of training programs. Information from these analyses can then be used to refine training content and to increase the job relevance of the training program. In future studies on transfer, researchers should provide evidence of the job relevance of the training material before examining the effects of other input factors on generalization and maintenance of trained skills.

Perhaps most importantly for the present, there is a critical need to conduct research on transfer with more relevant criterion measures of generalization and maintenance. Conclusions from the existing research are problematic, given the relatively short-term, single-source, perceptual data base that has been created. It is hoped that the model presented, the review conducted, and the suggestions given in this paper will help spur further efforts at examining transfer from a broader and more dynamic perspective.

Acknowledgment

A previous draft of this manuscript was presented at the 47th annual meeting of the National Academy of Management. New Orleans, August, 1987.

Authors contributed equally and are listed alphabetically.

The authors wish to thank Ray Noe and two anonymous reviewers for their helpful comments.

References

Adams JA. (1955). Multiple vs. single problem training in human problem solving. *Journal of Experimental Psychology, 48*, 15–18.

Ashby WA, Wilson GT. (1977). Behavior therapy for obesity: Booster sessions and long-term maintenance of weight loss. *Behavior Research and Theory, 15*, 451–463.

Atkinson RC. (1972). Ingredients for a theory of instruction. *American Psychologist, 27*, 921–931.

Atwater SK. (1953). Proactive inhibition and associative facilitation as affected by degree of prior learning. *Journal of Experimental Psychology, 46*, 400–404.

Baldwin TT. (1987, August). *The effect of negative models on learning and transfer from behavior modeling: A test of stimulus variability.* Presented at the 47th annual meeting of the Academy of Management, New Orleans, LA.

Bandura A. (1977). *Social learning theory.* Englewood Cliffs, NJ: Prentice-Hall.

Barrett CJ. (1978). Effectiveness of widow's groups in facilitating change. *Journal of Consulting and Clinical Psychology, 46*, 20–31.

Bass BM, Vaughan JA. (1966). *Training in industry: The management of learning.* Belmont, CA: Wadsworth.

Baumgartel H, Jeanpierre F. (1972). Applying new knowledge in the back-home setting: A study of Indian managers' adoptive efforts. *Journal of Applied Behavioral Science, 8*(6), 674–694.

Baumgartel H, Reynolds M, Pathan R. (1984). How personality and organizational-climate variables moderate the effectiveness of management development programmes: A review and some recent research findings. *Management and Labour Studies, 9*, 1–16.

Baumgartel H, Sullivan GJ, Dunn LE. (1978). How organizational climate and personality affect the pay-off from advanced management training sessions. *Kansas Business Review, 5*, 1–10.

Berkowitz L, Donnerstein E. (1982). External validity is more than skin deep: Some answers to criticisms of laboratory experiments. *American Psychologist, 37*, 245–257.

Blum ML, Naylor JC. (1968). *Industrial psychology: Its theoretical and social foundations.* New York: Harper Row.

Bourne LE. (1970). Knowing and using concepts. *Psychological Review, 77*, 545–556.

Bourne LE, Guy DE. (1968). Learning conceptual rules: The role of positive and negative instances. *Journal of Experimental Psychology, 77*, 488–494.

Briggs GE, Naylor JC. (1962). The relative efficiency of several training methods as a function of transfer task complexity. *Journal of Experimental Psychology, 64*, 505–512.

Briggs GE, Waters LK. (1958). Training and transfer as a function of component interaction. *Journal of Experimental Psychology, 56*, 492–500.

Callentine MF, Warren JM. (1955). Learning sets in human concept formation. *Psychological Reports, 1*, 363–367.

Campbell JP. (1971). Personnel training and development. *Annual Review of Psychology, 22*, 565–602.

Campbell JP, Dunnette MD, Lawler EE, Weick KE. (1970). *Managerial behavior, performance and effectiveness.* New York: McGraw-Hill.

Cascio WF. (1982). *Costing human resources: The financial impact of behavior in organizations.* Boston: Kent Publishing.

Cominsky IJ. (1982). Transfer of training in counselor education programs: A study of the use of stimulus variability and the provision of general principles to enhance the transfer of the skill of reflection of feeling. *Dissertation Abstracts International, 43*(1–A), 76.

Cormier S. (1984). *Transfer of training: An interpretive review.* (Technical Report No. 608). Alexandria, VA: Army Research Institute for the Behavioral and Social Sciences.

Crafts LW. (1935). Transfer as related to number of common elements. *Journal of General Psychology, 13*, 147–158.

Craik FIM, Lockhart RS. (1972). Levels of processing: A framework for memory research. *Journal of Verbal Learning and Verbal Behavior, 11*, 671–684.

Crannell CW. (1956). Transfer in problem solution as related to the type of training. *The Journal of General Psychology, 54*, 3–14.

Cronbach LJ, Snow RE. (1977). *Aptitudes and instructional methods.* New York: Irvington.

Daft RL, Weick KE. (1984). Toward a model of organizations as interpretation systems. *Academy of Management Review, 9*, 284–295.

Decker PJ. (1980). Effects of symbolic coding and rehearsal in behavior modeling training. *Journal of Applied Psychology, 65*, 627–634.

Decker PJ. (1982). The enhancement of behavior modeling training of supervisory skills by the inclusion of retention processes. *Personnel Psychology, 32*, 323–332.

Decker PJ, Nathan BR. (1985). *Behavior modeling training.* New York: Praeger Publishers.

Digman JM. (1959). Growth of a motor skill as a function of distribution of practice. *Journal of Experimental Psychology, 57*, 310–316.

Downs S. (1970). Predicting training potential. *Personnel Management, 2*, 26–28.

Duncan CP. (1958). Transfer after training with single versus multiple tasks. *Journal of Experimental Psychology, 55*, 63–72.

Duncan CP, Underwood BJ. (1953). Transfer in motor learning as a function of degree of first task learning and inter-task similarity. *Journal of Experimental Psychology, 46*, 445–452.

Eddy WB, Glad DD, Wilkins DD. (1967). Organizational effects on training. *Training and Development Journal, 22*(2), 36–43.

Eden D, Ravid G. (1982). Pygmalion versus self-expectancy: Effects of instructor and self-expectancy on trainee performance. *Organizational Behavior and Human Performance, 30*, 351–364.

Eden D, Shani AB. (1982). Pygmalion goes to boot camp: Expectancy leadership and trainee performance. *Journal of Applied Psychology, 67*, 194–199.

Ellis HC. (1965). *The transfer of learning.* New York: Macmillan.

Fleishman E. (1953). Leadership climate, human relations training, and supervisory behavior. *Personnel Psychology, 6*, 205–222.

Flexser AJ, Tulving E. (1978). Retrieval independence in recognition and recall. *Psychological Review, 85*, 153–171.

Ford JK, Wroten SP. (1984). Introducing new methods for conducting training evaluation to program redesign. *Personnel Psychology, 37*, 651–666.

Forgus RH, Schwartz RJ. (1957). Efficient retention and transfer as affected by learning method. *Journal of Psychology, 43*, 135–139.

Fryer DH, Edgerton HA, (1950). Research concerning off-the-job training. *Personnel Psychology, 3*, 262–284.

Gagne RM. (1962). Miltary training and principles of learning. *American Psychologist, 17*, 83–91.

Gagne RM, Baker K, Foster H. (1950). On the relation between similarity and transfer of training in the learning of discriminative motor tasks. *Psychological Review, 57*, 67–79.

Gagne RM, Briggs LJ. (1979). Principles of instructional design. New York: Holt, Rinehart Winston.

Gagne RM, Foster H. (1949). Transfer to a motor skill from practice on a pictured representation. *Journal of Experimental Psychology, 39*, 342–354.

Ghiselli EE. (1966). *The validity of occupational aptitude tests.* New York: John Wiley & Sons.

Georgenson DL. (1982). The problem of transfer calls for partnership. *Training and Development Journal, 36*(10), 75–78.

Goldbeck RA, Bernstein BB, Hillix WA, Marx MH. (1957). Application of the half split technique to problem solving tasks. *Journal of Experimental Psychology, 53*, 330–338.

Goldstein AP, Kanfer FH. (1979). *Maximizing treatment gains: Transfer enhancement in psychotherapy.* New York: Academic Press.

Goldstein AP, Sorcher M. (1974). *Changing supervisory behavior.* New York: Pergamon Press.

Goldstein IL. (1980). Training in work organizations. *Annual Review of Psychology, 31*, 229–272.

Goldstein IL. (1985, August). *Organization analysis and evaluation models.* Presented at the 1985 meeting of the American Psychological Association, Los Angeles, CA.

Goldstein IL. (1986). *Training in Organizations: Needs assessment, development and evaluation.* Monterey, CA: Brooks/Cole.

Goldstein IL, Musicante GA. (1985). The applicability of a training transfer model to issues concerning rater training. In Locke E (Ed.), *Generalizing from laboratory to field settings* (pp. 83–98). Lexington, MA: Lexington Books.

Gordon LV. (1955). Time in training as a criterion of success in radio code. *Journal of Applied Psychology, 39*, 311–313.

Gordon ME, Cohen SL. (1973). Training behavior as a predictor of trainability. *Personnel Psychology, 26*, 261–272.

Gordon ME, Kleiman LS. (1976). The prediction of trainability using a work sample test and an aptitude test: A direct comparison. *Personnel Psychology, 29*, 243–253.

Hagman JD, Rose AM. (1983). Retention of military tasks: A review. *Human Factors, 25*(2), 199–213.

Hand HH, Richards MD, Slocum JM. (1973). Organization climate and the effectiveness of a human relations program. *Academy of Management Journal, 16*, 185–195.

Haselrud GM, Meyers S. (1958). The transfer value of given and individually derived principles. *Journal of Educational Psychology, 49*, 293–298.

Hendrickson G, Schroeder W. (1941). Transfer of training in learning to hit a submerged target. *Journal of Educational Psychology, 32*, 206–213.

Hicks WD, Klimoski RJ. (1987). Entry into training programs and its effects on training outcomes: A field experiment. *Academy of Management Journal, 30*, 542–552.

Hilgard ER, Edren RD, Irvine RP. (1954). Errors in transfer following learning with understanding: Further studies with Katona's card-trick experiments. *Journal of Experimental Psychology, 47*, 457–464.

Hilgard ER, Irvine RP, Whipple JE. (1953). Rote memorization, understanding and transfer: An extension of Katona's card-trick experiments. *Journal of Experimental Psychology, 46*, 288–292.

Hinrichs JR. (1976). Personnel Training. In, Dunnette MD (Ed.), *Handbook of Industrial and Organizational Psychology* (pp. 861–88). Chicago: Rand McNally.

Holding DH. (1965). *Principles of training.* London: Pergamon Press.

House RJ. (1968). Leadership training: Some dysfunctional consequences. *Administrative Science Quarterly, 12*, 556–571.

Huczynski AA, Lewis JW. (1980). An empirical study into the learning transfer process in management training. *Journal of Management Studies, 17*, 227–240.

Judd CH. (1908). The relation of special training and general intelligence. *Educational Review, 36*, 42–48.

Karol RL, Richards CS. (1978, November). *Making treatment effects last: An investigation of maintenance strategies for smoking reduction.* Presented at the meeting of the Association for Advancement of Behavior Therapy, Chicago, IL.

Kazdin AE. (1975). *Behavior modification in applied settings.* Homewood, IL: Dorsey Press.

Kingsley RG, Wilson GT. (1977). Behavior therapy for obesity: A comparative investigation of long-term efficacy. *Journal of Consulting and Clinical Psychology, 45*, 288–298.

Kirkpatrick DL. (1967). Evaluation of training. In Craig RL, Bittel LR (Eds.), *Training and development handbook* (pp. 87–112). New York: McGraw-Hill.

Komacki J, Heinzemann AT, Lawson L. (1980). Effects of training and feedback: Component analysis of a behavioral safety program. *Journal of Applied Psychology, 65*, 261–270.

Lawler EE III. (1973). *Motivation in work organizations.* Monterey, CA: Brooks/Cole.

Lawrence PR, Lorsch JW. (1969). *Organization and environment: Managing differentiation and integration.* Homewood, IL: Irwin.

MacPherson SJ, Dees V, Grindley GC. (1948). The effect of knowledge of results on performance: II. Some characteristics of very simple skills. *Quarterly Journal of Experimental Psychology, 1*, 68–78.

Maddox M. (1987). *Environmental and supervisory influences on the transfer of training.* Unpublished manuscript, Michigan State University, E. Lansing, MI.

Mandler G. (1954). Transfer of training as a function of response overlearning. *Journal of Experimental Psychology, 47*, 411–417.

Mandler G, Heinemann SH. (1956). Effects of overlearning of a verbal response on transfer of training. *Journal of Experimental Psychology, 52*, 39–46.

Marlatt GA, Gordon JR. (1980). Determinants of relapse: Implications for the maintenance of behavior change. In Davidson PO, Davidson SM (Eds.), *Behavioral medicine: Changing health lifestyles* (pp. 410–452). New York: Brunner/Mazel.

Marx RD. (1982). Relapse prevention for managerial training: A model for maintenance of behavioral change. *Academy of Management Review, 7*, 433–441.

McGehee W. (1948). Cutting training waste. *Personnel Psychology, 1*, 331–340.

McGehee W, Thayer PW. (1961). *Training in Business and Industry.* New York: Wiley.

Michalak DF. (1981). The neglected half of training. *Training and Development Journal, 35*(5), 22–28.

Miles MB. (1965). Changes during and following laboratory training: A clinical-experimental study. *Journal of Applied Behavioral Science, 1*, 215–242.

Morrisett L, Hovland CI. (1959). A comparison of three varieties of training in human problem solving. *Journal of Experimental Psychology, 58*, 52–55.

Mosel JN. (1957). Why training programs fail to carry over. *Personnel, 4*, 56–64.

Naylor JC, Briggs GE. (1963). The effect of task complexity and task organization on the relative efficiency of part and whole training methods. *Journal of Experimental Psychology, 65*, 217–224.

Neel RG, Dunn RE. (1960). Predicting success in supervisory training programs by the use of psychological tests. *Journal of Applied Psychology, 44*, 358–360.

Newstrom JW. (1984, August). *A role-taker time differentiated integration of transfer strategies.* Presented at the 1984 meeting of the American Psychological Association, Toronto, Ontario.

Noe R. (1986). Trainees' attributes and attitudes: Neglected influences on training effectiveness. *Academy of Management Review, 11*, 736–749.

Noe RA, Schmitt N. (1986). The influence of trainee attitudes on training effectiveness: Test of a model. *Personnel Psychology, 39*, 497–523.

Parry SB, Reich LR. (1984). An uneasy look at behavior modeling. *Training and Development Journal, 30*(3), 57–62.

Perri MG, Shapiro RM, Ludwig WW, Twentyman CT, McAdoo WG. (1984). Maintenance strategies for the treatment of obesity: An evaluation of relapse prevention training and post treatment contact by mail and telephone. *Journal of Consulting and Clinical Psychology, 52*, 404–413.

Reber RA, Wallin JA. (1984). The effects of training, goal setting, and knowledge of results on safe behavior: A component analysis. *Academy of Management Journal, 27*, 544–560.

Reynolds B, Bilodeau IM. (1952). Acquisition and retention of three psychomotor tests as a function of distribution of practice during acquisition. *Journal of Experimental Psychology, 44*, 19–26.

Robertson I, Downs S. (1979). Learning and the prediction of performance: Development of trainability testing in the United Kingdom. *Journal of Applied Psychology, 64*, 42–50.

Robinson JC. (1984). You should have sent my boss. *Training, 21*(2), 45–47.
Ryman DH, Biersner RJ. (1975). Attitudes predictive of diving training success. *Personnel Psychology, 28,* 181–188.
Schendel JD, Hagman JD. (1982). On sustaining procedural skills over a prolonged retention interval. *Journal of Applied Psychology, 67,* 605–610.
Schneider B. (1983). Interactional psychology and organizational behavior. In Cummings LL, Staw BM (Eds.), *Research in Organizational Behavior* (Vol. 5, pp. 1–31). Greenwich, CT. JAI Press.
Schneider W. (1985). Training high performance skills: Fallacies and guidelines. *Human Factors, 27*(3), 285–300.
Sims HP, Manz CC. (1982, January). Modeling influences on employee behavior. *Personnel Journal,* pp. 45–51.
Shore E, Sechrest L. (1961). Concept attainment as a function of positive instances presented. *Journal of Educational Psychology, 52,* 303–307.
Smith EE, Shoben EJ, Rips LJ. (1974). Structure and process in semantic memory: A feature model for semantic decisions. *Psychological Review, 81,* 214–241.
Smith MC, Downs S. (1975). Trainability assessments for apprentice selection in shipbuilding. *Journal of Occupational Psychology, 48,* 39–43.
Spevak PA. (1981). Maintenance of therapy gains: Strategies, problems and promise. *JSAS Catalog of Selected Documents in Psychology, 11,* 35. (MS. No. 2255).
Taylor CW. (1952). Pretesting saves training costs. *Personnel Psychology, 5,* 213–239.
Taylor EK, Tajen C. (1948). Selection for training: Tabulating equipment operators. *Personnel Psychology, 1,* 341–348.
Thorndike EL. (1927). The law of effect. *American Journal of Psychology, 39,* 212–222.
Thorndike EL, Woodworth RS. (1901). The influence of improvement in one mental function upon the efficiency of other functions. *Psychological Review, 8,* 247–261.
Tracy WR. (1984). *Designing training and development systems.* New York: Amacom.
Trost A. (1982). They may love it but will they use it? *Training and Development Journal. 36*(1), 78–81.
Trowbridge MH, Cason H. (1932). An experimental study of Thorndike's theory of learning. *Journal of General Psychology, 7,* 245–260.
Tubiana JH, Ben-Shakhar G. (1982). An objective group questionnaire as a substitute for a personal interview in the prediction of success in military training in Israel. *Personnel Psychology, 35,* 349–357.
Underwood BJ. (1951). Associative transfer in verbal learning as a function of response similarity and degree of first-line learning. *Journal of Experimental Psychology, 42,* 44–53.
Underwood BJ. (1969). Attributes of memory. *Psychological Review, 76,* 559–573.
Vroom VH. (1964). *Work and motivation.* New York: Wiley.
Wallace SR. (1965). Criteria for what? *American Psychologist, 20,* 411–417.
Wexley KN. (1984). Personnel training. *Annual Review of Psychology, 35,* 519–551.
Wexley KN, Baldwin TT. (1986). Post-training strategies for facilitating positive transfer: An empirical exploration. *Academy of Management Journal, 29,* 503–520.
Wexley KN, Latham GP. (1981). *Developing and Training Human Resources in Organizations.* Glenview, IL: Scott Foresman.
Wexley KN, Nemeroff W. (1975). Effectiveness of positive reinforcement and goal setting as methods of management development. *Journal of Applied Psychology, 64,* 239–246.

Wexley KN, Thornton CL. (1972). Effect of verbal feedback of test results upon learning. *Journal of Educational Research, 66*, 119–121.

Wlodkowski RJ. (1985). *Enhancing adult motivation to learn.* San Francisco: Jossey-Bass.

Woodrow H. (1927). The effect of type of training upon transference. *Journal of Educational Psychology, 18*, 159–172.

34
APPLICATION OF COGNITIVE, SKILL-BASED, AND AFFECTIVE THEORIES OF LEARNING OUTCOMES TO NEW METHODS OF TRAINING EVALUATION

Kurt Kraiger, J. Kevin Ford and Eduardo Salas

Source: *Journal of Applied Psychology* 78(2) (1993): 311–328.

Abstract

Although training evaluation is recognized as an important component of the instructional design model, there are no theoretically based models of training evaluation. This article attempts to move toward such a model by developing a classification scheme for evaluating learning outcomes. Learning constructs are derived from a variety of research domains, such as cognitive, social, and instructional psychology and human factors. Drawing from this research, we propose cognitive, skill-based, and affective learning outcomes (relevant to training) and recommend potential evaluation measures. The learning outcomes and associated evaluation measures are organized into a classification scheme. Requirements for providing construct-oriented evidence of validity for the scheme are also discussed.

Training evaluation is the systematic collection of data regarding the success of training programs (I. L. Goldstein, 1986). Constructive evaluation occurs when specified outcome measures are conceptually related to intended learning objectives. Evaluation is conducted to answer either of two questions: whether training objectives were achieved (learning issues), and whether accomplishment of those objectives results in enhanced performance on the job (transfer issues).

Although both questions are important, Campbell (1988) stressed that the most fundamental issue of evaluation is whether trainees have learned the material covered in training. Shuell (1986) also argued that evaluation should be conducted first to determine whether the intended outcomes of training have been achieved. Unfortunately, there are no conceptual models to guide researchers in decisions about how to evaluate learning. Therefore, this article focuses on issues related to specification and measurement of learning. Our objective is to derive a conceptually based scheme for evaluating learning outcomes; this classification scheme would then serve as a starting point for the development of a true training evaluation model.

The assumptions underlying our approach are that learning outcomes are multidimensional and that progress in the training field requires taking a construct-oriented approach to learning. By multidimensional, we mean that learning may be evident from changes in cognitive, affective, or skill capacities. This perspective contrasts approaches taken in other assessment models, which have either ignored learning outcomes or have treated learning as a unidimensional construct. The need for a construct-oriented approach to learning is consistent with the views of various reviewers of the training literature who have continually bemoaned the absence of theory in training research (Campbell, 1971; I. L. Goldstein, 1980; Latham, 1988; Wexley, 1984). Whereas theoretical progress has been made in other training subsystems (Cannon-Bowers, Tannenbaum, Salas, & Converse, 1991; Tannenbaum & Yukl, 1992), less progress has been made in the area of evaluation.

The absence of a conceptual basis for evaluating learning is characteristic of prior models. Historically, the most popular evaluation model, proposed by Kirkpatrick (1976, 1987), identifies four levels of evaluation: trainee reactions, learning, behavior, and organizational results. Within this model, learning is measured by examining the extent to which trainees have acquired relevant principles, facts, or skills and could be assessed using traditional multiple-choice tests. Learning was conceptualized both as a causal result of positive reactions to training and as a causal determinant of changes in trainee behavior (Alliger & Janak, 1989).

Although there are a number of conceptual flaws in the model (Alliger & Janak, 1989; Clement, 1982; Snyder, Raben, & Farr, 1980), in the present context, its greatest shortcomings are a lack of clarity regarding what specific changes may be expected as a function of trainee learning and the difficulty in identifying what assessment techniques are appropriate given those expectations. For example, it is not clear whether Kirkpatrick (1976, 1987) thought of learning skills and learning facts as synonymous and whether the same assessment tools are appropriate for each. As Kirkpatrick's recommendations continue to represent state-of-the-art training evaluation, there has been insufficient research as to what constitutes learning and how learning outcomes should be assessed.

More recently, other researchers have embedded learning indices into conceptual models of training effectiveness. The phrases *training evaluation* and *training effectiveness* have often been used interchangeably (e.g., Ostroff, 1991), yet each addresses very different research questions. Training evaluation refers to a system for measuring whether trainees have achieved learning outcomes. It is concerned with issues of measurement and design, the accomplishment of learning objectives, and the attainment of requisite knowledge and skills. In contrast, training effectiveness models seek to explicate why training did or did not achieve its intended outcomes. This objective is accomplished by identifying and measuring the effects of individual, organizational, and training-related factors on training outcomes such as learning and transfer of training (Tannenbaum, Mathieu, Salas, & Cannon-Bowers, 1991). Issues of transfer of training and training effectiveness are necessarily broader than issues of training evaluation. However, it is critical to recognize that these models require substantive criterion variables provided by good evaluation theories. It is equally important to note that conceptually sound measures of learning have been absent from these models.

An examination of training effectiveness models illustrates the central role of learning. For example, Baldwin and Ford (1988) discussed trainee, training design, and organizational characteristics that may affect the transfer of training. They included learning and retention as mediating variables between these characteristics and the generalization and maintenance of trained behaviors on the job. I. L. Goldstein (1991; Rouillier & Goldstein, 1991) derived a transfer climate model that identified and tested specific situational cues and consequences in the organizational environment that affect training transfer. The amount of learning obtained by a trainee was recognized as an important precursor to transfer. Whereas the work of these authors highlights the importance of learning and transfer issues, we believe additional benefits can be derived from multidimensional perspectives on learning and learning outcomes.

Finally, Noe (1986) and Tannenbaum et al. (1991) derived broader models of training effectiveness that identified situational and individual factors that affected both learning and posttraining outcomes; learning during training was again proposed as a mediating variable between situational factors and desired organizational outcomes. However, even in these models, learning is treated as a unidimensional construct and different learning outcomes are not defined.

Thus, despite the critical role of trainee learning in the training process, previous models of training evaluation (e g., Kirkpatrick, 1976, 1987)and transfer of training or training effectiveness (e.g., I. L. Goldstein, 1991; Tannenbaum et al., 1991) have defined it in a simplistic and unidimensional way. To date, there has been little attention given to conceptualizing and measuring these learning outcomes.

Toward a classification scheme of learning outcomes

Generally, the training field has envisioned learning outcomes solely as changes in verbal knowledge or behavioral capacities. These learning outcomes are unnecessarily restrictive and out of step with modern learning theories. In other disciplines, more complex and extensive taxonomies of learning outcomes highlight the true multifaceted nature of learning (Bloom, 1956; Gagne, 1984; Krathwohl, Bloom, & Masia, 1964). Decades ago, Bloom (1956) proposed that cognitive outcomes beyond recall or recognition of verbal knowledge are legitimate learning outcomes and proposed a taxonomy of cognitively based learning outcomes. Krathwohl et al. (1964) expanded this taxonomy further to include affect-oriented objectives such

[Figure: A diagram with "LEARNING" at top branching into three boxes:
- Cognitive Outcomes: Verbal knowledge, Knowledge organization, Cognitive strategies
- Skill-Based Outcomes: Compilation (Proceduralization, Composition), Automaticity
- Affective Outcomes: Attitudinal, Motivational (Motivational disposition, Self-efficacy, Goal setting)]

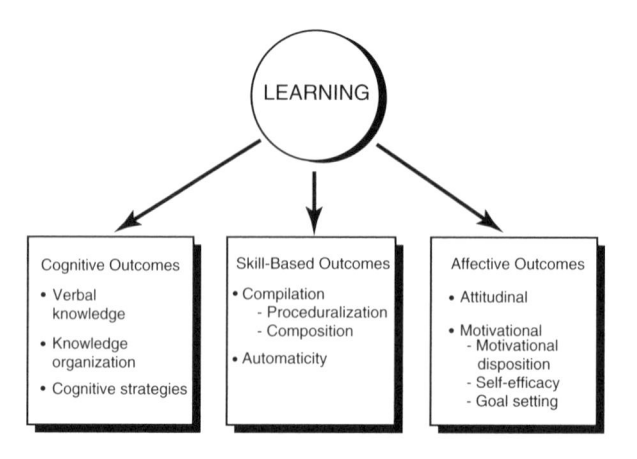

Figure 1 A preliminary classification scheme of learning outcomes.

as awareness and appreciation. Gagne (1984) was also critical of limiting instructional objectives to the behavioral domain and reinforced the need to examine various cognitive, skill-oriented, and attitudinal learning outcomes.

To advance the science and practice of training evaluation, it is necessary to move toward a conceptually based classification scheme of learning based on such a multidimensional perspective. Drawing from Bloom's (1956) and Gagne's (1984) taxonomies, we propose three categories of learning outcomes: cognitive, skill-based, and affective.

Figure 1 presents an overview of the three learning outcomes and the constructs that are the focus of this article. In line with Gagne (1984), the learning constructs most relevant for the cognitive category include verbal knowledge, knowledge organization, and cognitive strategies. Skill-based outcomes include skill compilation and automaticity. Finally, attitudinal outcomes (attitude object and strength) and motivational outcomes such as disposition, self-efficacy, and goal setting are proposed as key affective learning outcomes.

For each of the three categories, we will review relevant theory or research from a wide variety of psychological domains and identify constructs that are indicators of each learning outcome. Measurement issues relevant for each learning construct are provided and methods for training evaluation proposed. A summary classification scheme is provided in the discussion section, following the presentation of all outcomes.

Cognitive learning outcomes

Cognition refers to a class of variables related to the quantity and type of knowledge and the relationships among knowledge elements. An important goal of cognitive science is to generate theoretical systems or models that specify how people function (Lord & Maher, 1991). With respect to evaluation, a cognitive perspective focuses not only on static states of trainee knowledge, but on the dynamic processes of knowledge acquisition, organization, and application.

Traditionally, knowledge acquisition in the training domain has been assessed by achievement tests administered at the end of training. Trainees may be presented with a series of questions in either multiple-choice or true-false format and are required to indicate whether each stimulus exists in memory For example, matching the term *active listening* to the clause "use of body language, empathy, and paraphrasing to discern content and meaning" would reflect knowledge of a concept covered in a supervisory skills training course. Such formats are best suited for testing the retention of verbal or declarative knowledge (Gagne, 1977).

In contrast, research in other psychological domains has highlighted the complex and dynamic nature of the knowledge acquisition process. Although the acquisition of verbal knowledge serves as a foundation for cognitive skill development (Anderson, 1982), measures of verbal knowledge may be unable to discriminate among learners at higher levels of cognitive development. Thus, we have adapted Gagne's (1984) three categories of cognitive learning objectives to suggest three general categories of cognitively based evaluation measures: verbal knowledge, knowledge organization, and cognitive strategies. Whereas all three outcomes may be useful for evaluating trainees at any level of development, generally, the three are ordered chronologically with respect to anticipated changes in trainees. That is, measures of verbal knowledge would be the most sensitive for trainees during the initial stages of skill acquisition, and strategy-based measures would be more useful for advanced trainees.

In the following sections, we will discuss measurement issues relevant to each cognitively based measure. We have purposely presented less information on verbal knowledge measures, given that these are fairly common in the training field. Instead, we have focused our presentation on theory and applications related to the other two categories.

Verbal knowledge

Encoded knowledge exists in different forms, including declarative knowledge (information about what), procedural knowledge (information about how; Anderson, 1982), and strategic (Greeno, 1980) or tacit knowledge (information about which, when, and why; Wagner, 1987). Most theories of cognitive skill development agree that the acquisition of declarative knowledge must precede higher order development (Ackerman, 1987; Anderson, 1982; Fitts & Posner, 1967). Accordingly, specifying and measuring trainees' retention of declarative knowledge is most appropriate in the initial stages of training.

However, it should be noted that developing a foundation of verbally based, task-relevant knowledge is a necessary but not sufficient condition for higher order skill development. Ackerman (1986, 1987) argued convincingly that the latent abilities influencing task performance differ according to the developmental stage. Specifically, general intelligence factors seem to be the most critical for determining performance on novel tasks; trainees competent at inferring relations or memorizing information will be more successful early in training. However, with continued practice, task behaviors become internalized, and performance levels are influenced as much by psychomotor differences (e.g., speed of encoding or responding) as they are by general intellectual capabilities (Ackerman, 1987). Clearly, the danger is that whereas typical paper-and-pencil tests may be the most appropriate measure for assessing trainees' initial learning, the conceptual relationship between learning and achievement may be confounded by trainees' general intelligence. That is, if a traditional multiple-choice exam is given early in training, then it may be erroneous to conclude that the highest scorers on the exam are the ones most likely to continue to succeed in training, given that those who are the most intelligent will have an (early) edge in acquiring declarative knowledge and in displaying it on a more traditional measure.

Measurement implications

At one level, the implications for evaluating declarative knowledge vary little from the suggestions of Kirkpatrick (1976, 1987) or from how organizations typically measure learning. The acquisition of declarative knowledge can be assessed through multiple-choice, true-false, or free-recall exams. At another level, it should be recognized that there are two different approaches for assessing the amount of declarative knowledge held by trainees. Speed tests assess the number of items answered in a given time or the reaction time to any single item. Power tests assess the number of items answered correctly, given unlimited time. Ackerman and Humphreys (1990) noted that given similar content, speed and power tests actually measure different constructs—an argument supported by empirical studies (e.g., Lohman, 1979; Lord, 1956). Ackerman and Humphreys suggested that format choice should depend on the construct to be measured. Power tests measure the accuracy of stored information; such tests should be used when recall accuracy is valued or the consequences of errors are high. Speed tests measure the rate at which individuals can access knowledge; they are more appropriate when recall speed is the focal learning outcome.

In practice, many evaluations confound the two constructs, such as when the number of correct answers are counted on a timed test. Ackerman and Humphreys (1990) offered their own criticisms of such tests, and the interested reader is referred to their chapter for more details. For present purposes, the immediate implications are that when selecting tests to evaluate initial knowledge acquisition, thought should be given to the precise nature of the construct in question and that the choice of testing format should reflect that construct.

The second measurement implication is more direct. To maximize the value of traditional measures of declarative knowledge, these tests should be given closer to the beginning of training than to the end. There are two reasons for this. First, as a feedback mechanism, such tests should be given early enough to identify knowledge gaps that may hinder the rate of subsequent (higher-order) learning. Second, from a psychometric perspective, variance among trainees in declarative knowledge should be greater earlier in training than near the end. Consequently, earlier evaluation scores would have the greatest use for predicting other learning outcomes.

Knowledge organization

As skill learning advances beyond initial acquisition phases, several interrelated changes in processing occur as a function of continued practice (Anderson, 1982; Fitts & Posner, 1967). First, learners begin to focus less on declarative knowledge and more on procedural knowledge. Concurrent with an increase in procedural knowledge is the development of meaningful structures for organizing knowledge. In recent years, many researchers have stressed that of equal or greater importance than the amount or type of knowledge stored in memory is the organization of that knowledge (Johnson-Laird, 1983; Rouse & Morris, 1986).

The term *mental model* has been used to describe how people organize their knowledge. Mental models serve as mechanisms trainees use to describe functions and forms of tasks, explain and observe integration of tasks, and anticipate future task requirements (Rouse & Morris, 1986). Synonyms for mental models include knowledge structures, cognitive maps, or task schemata. Incumbents are believed to possess separate models for multiple functions on the job. For example, a military pilot may possess distinct mental models for preflight briefings, takeoffs, landings, tactical engagements, and aircrew coordination. Mental models provide a context for the interpretation of objects and events; they not only organize existing information, but influence the acquisition of new knowledge (Messick, 1984).

One important characteristic of mental models is the type or complexity of the stored elements. Studies of expert/novice differences suggest that whereas novices create different mental models for problem definition and solution strategies, experts form more complex knowledge structures that contain both problem definition nodes and solution nodes (Glaser & Chi, 1989). The advantage of this model is that having identified the problem, experts are able to quickly access a solution strategy because that strategy is closely linked (in memory) to the problem node. In contrast, solution times are slower and less fluid as the novices must engage in one search to identify the problem and another to solve it (Glaser, 1986).

A second important characteristic of mental models is the organization or interrelationships among model elements. Research on expert/novice differences reveals that experts' knowledge bases are characterized by hierarchical storage and strong paths between critical elements (Glaser & Chi, 1989). *Hierarchical storage* refers to the way in which new information is integrated and the way in which existing knowledge is organized. Additionally, through experience, paths between diagnostic nodes and solution nodes are solidified, increasing solution speed.

Measurement implications

One direct implication of the previous discussion is that trainees' understanding of course material may be best assessed by measuring their supportive cognitive structures. There are numerous strategies for directly measuring these structures (Flanagan, 1990). The modal technique requires judgments of similarity or closeness among a previously defined set of core elements. Elements are then mapped either by having the learners physically arrange the elements using a free-sort task within a problem space (e.g., Champagne, Klopfer, Desena, & Squires, 1981) or by submitting the judgments to a clustering or scaling algorithm (e.g., Cooke & McDonald, 1987; Naveh-Benjamin, McKeachie, Lin, & Tucker, 1986; Shavelson, 1974). This latter strategy is referred to as *structural assessment* (Goldsmith & Johnson, 1990).

The resulting map can be "scored" by assessing its similarity to a prototype or to the instructor's map (Goldsmith & Davenport, 1990) or by determining its level of complexity (Champagne et al., 1981). For example, the greater the number of levels or the greater the differentiation among elements within a level, the more complex the map. Other scorable elements of a mapped structure include counting the number of levels (as an indicator of hierarchical organization), determining the distance or number of links between key nodes (e.g., between diagnoses and solutions), or assessing overlap to a prototype after weighting links by their importance to job success or future development.

A good example of the use of mental models to evaluate training programs is found in the research of Goldsmith and Johnson (1990; Goldsmith, Johnson, & Acton, 1991). Goldsmith and Johnson assessed changes in the knowledge domain over a 16-week undergraduate course on psychological research methods. Working with the department faculty, they defined a list of 30 core concepts to be covered during the course (e.g., confound, design, error, interaction). The rating task presented students with all possible pairs of concepts and required them to judge the relatedness of the concepts using a 7-point scale. Forty subjects completed the ratings during the 1st, 8th, and 15th weeks of the semester. The rating task assumes that the less related students perceive two items, the further apart the concepts exist in their knowledge structures. The ratings were analyzed using a procedure called Pathfinder (Schvaneveldt, Durso, & Dearholt, 1985). Pathfinder creates a link-weighted network, a configuration in which concepts are depicted as nodes and relationships are depicted as links between nodes. A similarity index was computed between each student's representation and the instructor's for each measurement occasion. The index is approximately equal to the number of common links between two networks divided by the total number of links in both (Goldsmith & Davenport, 1990).

Goldsmith and Johnson (1990) did not attempt to assess learning over the course of the semester, so there were no data comparing students' structures from the beginning of the semester to the end. Of interest though are analyses of the validity of end-of-semester cognitive maps for predicting total semester points. The correlation between the similarity index and final course points was .74. Thus, the more a student's mental representation of psychological research matched the instructor's, the better the student did in the course.

More recently, the same technique has been applied in true training settings. Kraiger and Salas (1992) administered both the Pathfinder technique and a more traditional (multiple-choice) exam at the end of two training programs—one on aircrew coordination training for Navy pilots and the other on $SPSS_x$ programming to graduate students in psychology. Kraiger and Salas found that the similarity between trainees' cognitive maps and those of training experts (those who designed the training, delivered the training, or both) were correlated with the traditional knowledge-based measure for Navy pilots and with traditional measures and task-specific self-efficacy and later transfer of training to classroom performance for the graduate students.

Cognitive strategies

A final category of cognitive measures, drawn from Gagne's (1984) learning objectives, centers on the development and application of cognitive strategies. Individual differences exist in the extent to which knowledge can be accessed or applied more rapidly or more fluidly (Anderson, 1982; Kanfer & Ackerman, 1989). Anderson's (1982) theory proposed that skill development is a continuous process, and as knowledge and procedures continue to be compiled, more elegant task strategies emerge. Kanfer and Ackerman's (1989) theory proposed that through continued practice, complex behaviors are internalized; the greater the internalization, the more cognitive resources are available for executive functions or strategy development. Given that these executive skills or strategies are evident primarily at the highest levels of skill acquisition, measures of such would serve as capstones for training evaluation.

The term *metacognition* has been used to refer to both the knowledge of one's own cognition and the regulation of such (Brown, 1975; Leoncsio & Nelson, 1990). Metacognitive skills include planning, monitoring, and revising goal-appropriate behavior (Brown, Bransford, Ferrara, & Campione, 1983; Schoenfeld, 1985) or understanding the relationship between task demands and one's capabilities (Pressley, Snyder, Levin, Murray, & Ghatala, 1987). They also include skills in regulating or evoking appropriate strategies (Bereiter & Scardamalia, 1985). *Strategies* refer to a broad range of mental activities that facilitate knowledge acquisition and application (Prawat, 1989).

Research in cognitive psychology has shown that the metacognitive skills of experts are superior to those of novices. In contrast to novices, experts are more likely to discontinue a problem-solving strategy that would ultimately prove to be unsuccessful (Larkin, 1983), are more accurate about judging the difficulty of new problems (Chi, Glaser, & Rees, 1982), and are better able to estimate the number of trials they will need to accomplish a task (Chi, 1987). Similarly, good readers are more aware than are poor readers whether they are comprehending text as they read it (Pressley et al., 1987). In sports psychology, evidence of tennis strategy and effective decision making has been found to be a precursor to motor skill development and enhanced performance (McPherson & French, 1991; McPherson & Thomas, 1989).

These findings are relevant in two ways. First, they indicate that metacognitive skills of awareness are correlates of cognitive skill development and, hence, suitable indices of learning. For example, one study by Peterson, Swing, Stark, and Waas (1984) found that measures of students' cognitive processes were better predictors of achievement test scores than were observers' ratings. Measures of awareness, self-evaluated learning, needed development, and so forth would all seem to hold a place in the training evaluation domain as evidence of learning.

Second, because metacognitive skills of self-regulation are important to successful task performance, they also warrant measurement. For example, safety trainers in a nuclear power plant would certainly be interested in knowing which trainees could detect their own errors and which could not. Here, the emphasis is on the regulatory functions (Nelson & Narens, 1990). Knowing trainee skill levels of self-regulation or self-control of cognitive processing may provide valuable information when making job assignments, reassignments to training, and so forth. Furthermore, there is some evidence that the lack of these skills can lead to "production deficiencies" in subsequent learning and problem solving (Hertel & Hardin, 1990). A production deficiency occurs when the incumbent has the necessary abilities and knowledge to perform the task but lacks the metacognitive skills that facilitate the access to and use of these resources (Slife & Weaver, 1992).

Measurement implications

There are numerous ways in which the measurement of metacognitive skills can support inferences of learning during training. One commonality of these approaches is that each attempts to test for higher levels of understanding than that shown by mere recall or recognition. Measures of understanding should be designed to assess trainees' awareness of steps undertaken or progress toward a goal.

Gott and her associates (e.g., Glaser, Lesgold, & Gott, 1986; Means & Gott, 1988) developed a method called *probed protocol analysis to* assess trainees' understanding of their task behavior relative to a superordinate goal. Working with a subject matter expert, they first defined, in detail, the steps necessary to solve a problem (e.g., an electronic troubleshooting task). Trainees were asked to describe what they would do at each step. Metacognitive awareness was assessed by asking trainees pre-specified probe questions at each step. Examples of such questions are: "Why would you run this test, and what would it mean if it fails?",

"How does this test help you solve the problem?", and "Are there any alternatives to the test you just ran?" Responses to these probes indicate whether trainees were generating and testing hypotheses, operating under goals, or understood when or whether they were making progress toward a solution. If probes are written to reflect breakdowns in routines, or goal blockages, the protocol analysis technique can be extended to assess self-regulatory skills, that is, the trainees' skill at initiating corrective responses.

Gill, Gordon, Moore, and Barbera (1988) used a protocol analysis to investigate the effectiveness of an instructional videotape. Gill et al. compared the diagnostic sensitivity of a set of question probes to free recall. The researchers found that the probe strategy resulted in a better representation of students' knowledge structures than did the free-recall task and that the knowledge structures built using these probes were highly correlated ($r = .73$) with problem-solving strategies. Kraiger and Salas (1992) developed a paper-and-pencil version of Means and Gott's (1988) probed protocol analysis technique. Responses were collected from graduate students after a 3-hour $SPSS_x$ training course delivered during the third week of a multivariate statistics course. Responses were scored for thoroughness and understanding by three subject matter experts. Post-training scores correlated .68 and .74 with two final exam $SPSS_x$ problems administered 12 weeks later.

Research on meta-cognition reinforces the value of measuring trainees' self-assessments of learning outcomes. A strategy suggested by Bloom and his colleagues is to use self-reports of awareness or understanding (Krathwohl et al., 1964). Self-report measures should reflect trainees' awareness of knowledge gained. Questions about trainees' awareness of level of the proceduralization, degree of additional learning needed, or awareness of mistakes are appropriate. The extent to which trainees' answers coincided with empirical verification would indicate the extent to which they were developing expert like representations of the job. For example, studies in instructional psychology have found students' reports of attention and cognitive processing to be valid predictors of academic achievement (Peterson, Swing, Braverman, & Buss, 1982; Peterson et al., 1984). Similarly, Slife and Weaver (1992) reported that subjects' estimates of the precision of their problem-solving efforts are reasonable correlates of actual performance.

A good example of this type of approach can be found in a training study conducted by Fisk and Gallini (1989). Fisk and Gallini attempted to compare a traditional training program (for learning base-5 arithmetic) to one based on conceptually based information processing principles. Among their evaluation measures was a test of Perceived Readiness for Examination Performance (PREP; Pressley et al., 1987). PREP requires examinees to predict how many items they expect to answer correctly on a test. It assesses the ability to judge whether material is adequately learned and understood for future applications. Fisk and Gallini found that subjects receiving the hypothetically superior form of training scored higher on the PREP and scored higher on more traditional measures of learning as well.

The success of the self-assessment measures discussed above suggests that learners may yield accurate portrayals of current knowledge states, provided that the information has been properly elicited. This conclusion is supported by several reviews documenting the validity of self-assessments for psychological assessment (Shrauger & Osberg, 1981) and academic ability (Mabe & West, 1982).

One clever example of the use of self-ratings as indices of awareness can be found in a training study by Schendel and Hagman (1982). These researchers sought to determine if individuals could estimate in advance how much refresher training they would require to regain a certain level of proficiency. Soldiers were put through a training program on how to disassemble and reassemble an M60 machine gun. Training was completed to a point of overlearning. After a period in which the skill was not practiced or rehearsed, the soldiers were asked to estimate the number of trials required to return to their original levels of proficiency after the original training. The results comparing the actual number of trials with the self-assessments indicated that the soldiers were fairly accurate in their predictions.

Skill-based learning outcomes

The second category of learning outcomes concerns the development of technical or motor skills. Characteristics of skill development include a goal orientation and a linking of behaviors in a sequentially and hierarchically organized manner (Weiss, 1990).

Traditionally, skill development has been evaluated by observing trainee performance in role plays (simulations at the end of training) or in actual job behaviors. Behavioral observation may be an appropriate evaluation tool, provided the assessment strategy is developed in concert with a theoretical conceptualization of skill development.

Theories of skill development generally posit three definable stages: (a) initial skill acquisition, (b) skill compilation, and (c) skill automaticity (Anderson, 1982; Fitts & Posner, 1967). Initial skill acquisition involves the transition from knowledge that is declarative to knowledge that is procedural (Neves & Anderson, 1981). Procedural knowledge enables the reproduction of trained behaviors. Compilation skills occur with continued practice beyond initial successes at reproducing trained behavior. Performance at this stage is characterized by faster, less error-prone performance and by the integration of discrete steps into a single act. With subsequent automaticity, individuals not only perform tasks quickly but are able to maintain parallel rather than successive processing of activities (e.g., Shiffrin & Dumais, 1981). Individuals at this stage are more likely to detect the appropriate situations for using a skill (Gagne, 1986) and to individualize skilled acts.

Although initial acquisition must precede higher order skill development, it is during the latter steps that successful initial learning is translated into adaptive skills. Therefore, in this section, we focus on the learning outcomes evident at the compilation and automaticity stage as they represent the higher levels of skill development that are often the desired outcomes of skill-oriented training programs.

Compilation

If advanced skills are defined by smooth, fast performance (Gagne, 1984), then trainee behavior at the initial skill acquisition stage of development may be characterized as rudimentary in nature. Trainees may reproduce trained behavior but only through a heavy reliance on working memory and mental rehearsal of previously learned routines (Weiss, 1990). Accordingly, performance is slow and the trainees' ability to attend to task-irrelevant information or to react to novel task-relevant stimuli is low.

In contrast, trainee performance at the compilation stage is decidedly faster and more fluid. Errors are reduced, verbal rehearsal is eliminated, and behavior is more task-focused. According to Anderson (1982), compilation is the result of two interrelated processes: proceduralization and composition. During proceduralization, the trainee builds smaller, discrete behaviors into a domain-specific production or routine. For example, a computer programmer builds and learns to apply different debugging strategies for different types of problems. Composition begins simultaneously with proceduralization but may continue after it. During composition, the trainee mentally groups steps by linking successive (previously learned) procedures into a more complex production. For example, whereas a less advanced tennis player may have proceduralized separate skills related to following through on shots and approaching the net, after composition, the player executes both acts as a single, fluid behavior.

With compilation, individuals are in a better position to determine the situations in which trained skills are useful or not useful. Individuals also learn to apply newly learned behaviors to unique settings (generalization) and to modify existing skills depending on the situation (discrimination) (Anderson, 1982).

Measurement implications

In many domains, it would be useful to track trainees' skill development to assess progress and to design or modify other training interventions. For example, knowing that trainees have reached the compilation stage may lead to the provision of greater opportunities for practice under constant mapping conditions to enable movement toward automaticity (Shiffrin & Schneider, 1977).

To adequately sample and track changes in compilation as a function of training requires the measurement of highly specific criteria (Smith, 1976) that reflect maximal performance (Cronbach, 1960). High specificity involves the observation and description of discrete behaviors of an individual. Maximal performance measures focus on what an individual *can* do rather than on typical performance.

One way to measure the development of compilation skills is through targeted behavioral observations (Komaki, Heinzman, & Lawson, 1980). This methodology requires timed observations randomly spaced and for a long enough period to draw valid inferences. Observation categories should reflect specific, anticipated changes related to learning objectives. For example, trainees can be asked to demonstrate their skills on learned tasks, while observers track criteria such as the frequency of desired or undesired behaviors, time to completion, steps necessary to complete a task, the sequencing of steps, or the number of task-related errors. Compilation can be inferred from evidence such as plateaus in the rate of increase of desired behaviors, a sustained decrease in the frequency of undesired behaviors or number of errors, a rapid increase in the completion of steps, the reordering or elimination of more trivial steps, or the appearance of synthesis across previously discrete steps.

Hands-on performance measurement is a second technique for assessing compilation. Both the Army (Campbell & Associates, 1990) and the Air Force (Hedge & Teachout, 1991) have developed hands-on tests. In these, a series of steps are identified as important for successfully completing a number of tasks. Individuals are then observed performing the tasks by trained observers who either record whether each step was taken (go/ no-go) or provide an evaluation of the quality of step completion (pass/fail) (Borman & Hallam, 1991).

Two disadvantages of hands-on testing are the long time required to administer such tests and, for technical jobs, the necessity of assembling and disassembling costly equipment. An appealing alternative is a structured situational interview (Latham, Saari, Pursell, & Campion, 1980). This process permits detailed and targeted evaluation by asking trainees to state how they would perform or complete a task. For example, in the Air Force, airmen are shown a piece of equipment and asked to describe the steps necessary to complete a particular task. Results indicate that the situational interview is a reliable method for collecting information (Kraiger, 1991) and that performance on a situational interview correlates highly with performance on actual hands-on performance tests (Hedge & Teachout, 1991; Kraiger, 1991).

With either the hands-on or interview methodology, compilation can be assessed using many of the same criteria described under the behavioral observation methodology (measuring the frequency of undesired behavior, timing step completion, or watching for the elimination of steps). A more novel approach is to instruct the trainee to perform the hands-on task(s) twice—once under instructions to perform a task the way they would normally and a second time with instructions to perform the task as they were trained to do. Smoother, quicker, better performance with the use of fewer steps under "normal" conditions would permit inferences of compilation. If the trainee is proficient at the task but unable to simulate the more mechanical, trained method, evidence exists that the trainee has passed through the compilation stage (Kraiger, 1988).

Compilation is also characterized by the capacity to modify learned behaviors to new task settings. This characteristic can be assessed by examining trainees' ability to generalize skills beyond the situations trained and to discriminate when skills need to be adapted to fit a changing situation. For example, in behavioral modeling, trainees could be asked to attend to a situation by closely following the learning points from the training program across a variety of situations. In another scenario, trainees could be asked to adapt their trained behaviors to deal effectively with a unique situation that could be encountered on the job. Compilation skills would be evident when individuals are able to generalize skills to situations not specifically trained and when they are able to quickly and successfully adapt skills to unique situations with little effort or thought.

This approach was used in a study of salesperson effectiveness in customer relations (Leong, Busch, & John, 1989). In one scenario, salespeople had to recognize the similarities across various situations and respond by using trained skills. In a subsequent scenario, salespeople were presented with an atypical sales situation (customer characteristics did not match a trained profile). In this setting, the degree of compilation can be assessed from the extent to which the salespeople varied their selling approaches and tailored them to the individual needs of the customer. Those salespeople high in compilation skills should be able to incorporate more distinctive actions and be more adaptive in atypical situations.

Automaticity

Through continual practice, trainees may reach the automaticity stage. Although compilation and automaticity are most appropriately thought of as points on a continuum rather than discrete stages, there are certain characteristics of automatized behavior that are not evident during the compilation stage. The development of automaticity implies a shift in operational modes, from controlled to automatic processing (Schneider & Shiffrin, 1977; Shiffrin & Schneider, 1977). With automaticity, performance is fluid, accomplished, and individualized.

Because the learner can no longer verbalize intended behaviors or processes, automatization enables task accomplishment without conscious monitoring and enables concurrent performance on additional tasks (Shiffrin & Dumais, 1981). Furthermore, because attentional requirements decrease when behaviors are automatized (Ackerman, 1987), task behaviors are not affected by other demands for cognitive resources (e.g., distracting thoughts, situational pressures, secondary tasks, etc.). With automaticity, individuals have greater cognitive resources available to cope with extraneous demands. Finally during the automaticity stage, skill capabilities may be expected to undergo additional "tuning" (Rummelhart & Norman, 1978). Tuning involves changes such as improved accuracy, generalized applicability specialized applicability, and determination of a prototype or typical case (Gagne, 1984). For example, most drivers have automated important skills related to operating a car. This capacity allows them to converse with passengers while monitoring the road, changing speeds, or reacting to environmental changes.

Measurement implications

Collecting measures that assess automaticity also provides valuable information on the degree of trainee learning. Strategies effective for tracking compilation are not as applicable at this stage, given that automaticity is marked by significantly different cognitive and attentional processes.

Instead, automaticity would have to be assessed through measures specifically designed for that purpose. Cognitive psychologists typically have measured automaticity by examining artificial tasks (e.g., learning nonsense syllables) under rigorous experimental conditions that would not be found in applied contexts. This has led some writers to express doubt as to whether automaticity can be measured in organizational settings (Glaser et al., 1986). At least three strategies, however, hold some promise.

The first strategy directly parallels work by cognitive psychologists and requires trainees to perform the trained tasks while simultaneously performing a secondary task. Ideally, multiple measures on both tasks would be collected during training. Because automaticity minimizes cognitive effort or attention necessary to complete the primary task, as the trainee shifts from controlled to automatic processing, performance on the secondary task should increase. When performance on both tasks stabilizes (and reaches proficiency on the secondary task), automaticity may be inferred. For example, Tyler, Hertel, McCallum, and Ellis (1979) required subjects to unscramble anagrams such as "drootc" (which produces "doctor"). After each item was presented, a tone was delivered at one of four intervals through headphones worn by the subjects. Their secondary task was to monitor and respond as quickly as possible to the tone while solving the anagrams. One training analog for this task would be in the assessment of skill development in a plant operator. If trainees were instructed to gradually monitor more and more stimuli (e.g., meters, screens, etc.), stable performance on the primary task coupled with enhanced performance on the secondary task would suggest automaticity.

A second strategy is to use a single task but to have subjects solve both normal and interference problems. An interference problem resembles a normal one but with key information altered. For example, in math, an interference equation would be "$4 + 5 = 20$." This equation is false as presented but could be true if the addition sign were changed to a multiplication sign (Zbrodoff & Logan, 1986). If automaticity has not occurred, interference problems (in this case, evaluating an equation as true or false) should not take longer, or be more difficult, than normal problems. As automaticity develops, the learner processes larger chunks of information and may not attend to discrete, though critical, pieces of information. Thus, performance decrements on interference tasks permit inferences of automaticity. Again, multiple measures during training will provide a baseline and lead to more confident judgments of the onset of automatization. Soloway, Adelson, and Ehrlich (1988) used such a task in a study of expert/novice differences in computer programming. Subjects were asked to provide a missing line in either a normal or "distractor" program. The distractor program ran successfully but contained elements that violated rules of programming discourse (e.g., a function that returned the minimum of a set of values was assigned to a variable named MAX). As expected, performance differences between proficient and nonproficient subjects were more pronounced on the distractor programs.

A third strategy is not to measure automaticity directly but to embed a concern for it in all measures collected during or after training (Glaser et al., 1986). Evaluation is focused on other dimensions of knowledge or behavior. However, variations in the context or methods of assessment may enable inferences of automatization. For example, suppose that pilot training is to be assessed using two behaviorally based simulated flights at the end of training. By constructing one scenario to be context-rich, with multiple interference tasks, and a second to be context-simple, automaticity is implied by the absence of performance differences between tasks. Another indication of automated processing would occur when trainees appear to stop monitoring their own behavior (or report less awareness of their actions). This observation may be confirmed by investigating whether trainees' performance subsequently declines when they are explicitly asked to attend to their behavior. Other embedded measures suggested by Glaser et al. (1986) include determining whether goal structures exist independent of technical guidelines (e.g., Can a mechanic correct a malfunction without a repair manual?) or giving trainees a randomized list of steps to a task and asking them to select and order the important tasks. Here, the omission of initial steps (e.g., consult manual) could suggest automaticity.

Affectively based learning outcomes

Gagne (1984) included attitudes as a learning outcome, reasoning that attitudes can determine behavior or performance, that there are a variety of mediums devoted to affecting attitudes (e.g., advertising), and that there is evidence that attitudes can be changed. Gagne defined an *attitude* as an internal state that influences the choice of personal action. Accepting this definition, we broadened this category of learning outcomes to include motivational and affective outcomes. We believe this treatment is consistent with Gagne's classification because motivation is also an internal state that affects behavior.

An emphasis on behavioral or cognitive measurement at the expense of attitudinal and motivational measurement provides an incomplete profile of learning and the learning process (Gagne, 1984; Messick, 1984). Unfortunately, Kirkpatrick (1976, 1987) and others in the training field have ignored affectively based measures as indicators of learning. Instead, training researchers have collected what are termed *reaction measures*—indicants of how well trainees liked the training, perceptions of how well organized the training program was, and whether trainees found the training useful. These measures provide feedback on the quality of training delivery but are not direct measures of individual learning. Our intent in this section is to propose a broader range of affectively or attitudinally based outcomes that may be measured and used to infer learning during training.

Taking this broader perspective, we refer to affectively based measures of training evaluation as a class of variables encompassing issues such as attitudes, motivation, and goals that are relevant to the objectives of the training program. In addition, like Bloom and his associates (Bloom, 1956; Krathwohl et al., 1964) and Gagne (1977), we conceptualize this class of variables as indicators of learning, rather than simply precursors to learning. If a trainee's values have undergone some change as a function of training, then learning has occurred.

For purposes of classification, we have placed in this final category all those learning outcomes that are neither cognitively based nor skill based. These remaining outcomes are generally of two types: those that target attitudes or preferences as the focus of change and those in which motivational tendencies are an indirect target of change.

Attitudinal outcomes

The field is replete with examples of training programs that establish affective change as a focus of training. The incorporation of affective outcomes into the training curriculum is most clearly seen in the development of training programs (e.g., police recruits) that not only impart knowledge and skills but are also powerful socialization agents (Feldman, 1989). Among the affective outcomes in organizations that may be acquired by training are creative individualism (defined as the acceptance of pivotal norms and values and the rejection of all others; Schein, 1968), organizational commitment (Louis, Posner, & Powell, 1983), recognition of what is important to learn (Becker, Geer, Hughes, & Strauss, 1961), group norms (Feldman, 1984), and tolerance for diversity (Geber, 1990).

Training objectives may also include desired outcomes such as inner growth, self-awareness, and changing values. For example, safety training programs often seek to influence the valences trainees attach to safe behaviors (e.g., Gregorich, Helmreich, & Wilhelm, 1990; McIntire, 1973). A less obvious example involves one of the major training methods in the field, behavioral modeling. What researchers and practitioners often overlook is that this technique sets changing attitudes and value systems as its ultimate goal. An examination of the theory behind the behavioral modeling method reveals that skills must first be developed through observation, practice, and reinforcement. Once the new behavioral patterns are found to be effective in solving real problems in organizations, the individuals should come to recognize the value of those new and effective behaviors and then internalize attitudes and values congruent with the new behavioral patterns (A. P. Goldstein & Sorcher, 1974; Kraut, 1976).

Measurement implications

The achievement of outcomes such as tolerance for diversity or concerns for safety can best be measured by following principles for attitude measurement. Measures of attitudes must take into account both the direction of feelings toward the attitude object and the strength of the reaction to the object. In the case of training evaluation, the attitude object is defined by the specific learning objective(s). The first focus of measurement should be whether the direction of attraction toward the attitude object is consistent with the learning objective(s). The direction of attitudes is assessed in several ways. Most commonly, the attitude objects are listed with a scale that allows the respondent to indicate a preference or rejection of the object (e.g., an agree/disagree scale).

The second focus of measurement concerns attitude strength, that is, how deeply an individual holds the attitude (Chaiken & Stangor, 1987). There are a number of different conceptualizations of attitude strength including attitude accessibility (Fazio, 1988), attitude centrality (Kronsnick, 1986), and internalization or conviction (Abelson, 1988). *Accessibility* refers to the number of cognitive associations between an object and its evaluation. These associations are formed through the individual actively processing information about an object. *Attitude centrality* focuses on the degree of interconnectedness between the individual and the attitude object. *Internalization* or *conviction* focuses on the acceptance by the individual of the attitudes, codes, principles, or sanctions that become a part of an individual and that affect value judgments and determine conduct (Krathwohl et al., 1964).

Abelson (1988) suggested a number of ways of using self-report measures to operationalize attitude strength. These include how strongly individuals hold to their views; how important their views are to their self-perceptions; how concerned they are about the issue in question; how often they think about the issue; and how often they express views on the issue to friends, co-workers, and family members. Other potential indicators of attitude strength include steadfastness (how likely they are to change their minds on an issue), affect (to what extent do they feel angry or good when thinking about an issue), certainty (how correct do they think their views are), and centrality (how many other issues come up when discussing the issue in question) (Abelson, 1988).

Once the learning objective is specified as the attitude object, measures of attitude strength can be useful for inferring learning during training. Specifically, pre- and posttraining measures of attitude strength that indicate a change from conformity and passivity to active participation and identification with training goals would signal that learning has occurred. Additionally, attitude strength may be expected to affect future processing of information relevant to an existing attitude (Chaiken & Stangor, 1987). With training, those who become more committed to an attitude or value are more likely to pay attention or process new information relevant to that value than those who are simply passive or noncommittal to training goals.

Gregorich et al. (1990) provided one example of assessing attitude change (although not specifically addressing attitude strength) to evaluate a training program. The program consisted of a seminar on cockpit resource management that was delivered to captains, first officers, and flight engineers. The researchers developed a Cockpit Management Attitudes Questionnaire that consists of 25 items chosen to measure attitudes related to cockpit resource management. More than 500 flight captains, first officers, and flight engineers completed the questionnaire before and after training. The results indicated that there were significant changes in stated attitudes in the desired direction especially in relation to attitudes toward communication and coordination, command responsibility, and the recognition of stressor effects.

Motivational outcomes

The second type of affective outcomes in training concern motivational tendencies. In some circumstances, changes in trainee motivation may be an intended outcome of training. A popular example of enhanced motivation as an intended outcome is a "free" real estate or money management seminar intended to increase attendees' desire to attend (and pay for) additional training. More commonly, however, motivational change is a secondary training outcome. That is, although the primary objective may be to build skill sets, motivational changes are anticipated as well. In subsequent sections, we discuss three motivational outcomes that may be secondary objectives of training: motivational dispositions, self-efficacy, and goal setting. Each has been the focus of considerable research in other psychological disciplines, and each shows promise as a measure of secondary learning in training.

Motivational disposition

Research on cognitive development in children has led to the recognition of two distinct motivational dispositions within the classroom: mastery or performance orientations (Dweck, 1986; Dweck & Elliott, 1983). A *mastery orientation* is characterized by a concern for increasing one's competence regarding the task at hand. A *performance orientation* is marked by an intention to do well and to gain a positive evaluation by others. A young baseball pitcher who tries to use his fastball to strike out all batters displays a performance orientation, whereas another who risks a bad outing to work on developing other pitches displays a mastery orientation.

People with a performance orientation perceive their capacities as fixed or immutable to change, whereas people adopting a mastery orientation perceive their skills and abilities as malleable and therefore establish learning goals to develop those qualities (Dweck & Leggett, 1988). A mastery orientation implies a tendency to make internal attributions for success and failure; to see learning as personally determined; and to view goals as flexible and individual, rather than normative and immediate (Prawat, 1989).

Although the performance and mastery orientation was originally conceived of as an individual difference variable (Dweck & Elliott, 1983), more recent research has characterized it as a general motivational tendency that is adaptable to situations or interventions. For example, researchers have shown that the best disposition depends on the material to be learned or the level of instruction (Ames & Archer, 1987; Biggs & Rihn, 1984) and that superior learners are able to adopt the orientation most appropriate to the context (Biggs & Rihn, 1984).

In a posttraining context, the best disposition may be a function of the nature of the task and the incumbents' level of sophistication. Mentoring is one developmental activity that typically seeks to instill a mastery orientation in learners. For example, diagnosing illnesses from X-rays is a very difficult task to learn, requiring as many as 200,000 trials to achieve expertise (Lesgold et al., 1989). As in many other domains, the developmental pattern for radiological diagnosis begins with high levels of declarative knowledge, ingraining of repeatable patterns, and initial attempts at hypothesis formation and testing (Lesgold et al., 1989). Presumably, doctors faced with the task of training residents would attempt to instill a mastery orientation during the initial stages of skill development. Residents should be willing to make and learn from their mistakes. However, near the end of their residency, when the trainees assume greater responsibility for patient outcomes, a performance orientation (getting it right) should predominate. Periodic measurement of these orientations (e.g., Ames & Archer, 1987) would indicate the extent to which the training staff was affecting the proper motivation.

Self-efficacy

Self-efficacy refers to one's perceived performance capabilities for a specific activity (Bandura, 1977a). Self-efficacious perceptions are generally believed to be task-specific and are hypothesized to influence one's choice of activities, effort expended, persistence, and task performance (Bandura, 1977a). Numerous studies have reported positive relationships between self-efficacy beliefs and task performance (e.g., Barling & Beattie, 1983; Stumpf, Brief, & Hartman, 1987; Weinberg, Gould, & Jackson, 1979). According to Bandura (1977a), psychological procedures such as training change behavior in part by creating and strengthening self-efficacy.

Accordingly changes in trainees' self-efficacy may be a useful indicator of learning or skill development during training. In some instances, enhanced self-efficacy will be a formal objective of the training. For example, sports psychologists believe performance expectancies and self-efficacy to be important determinants of athletic success (Feltz & Doyle, 1981; Feltz & Weiss, 1982). Consequently, numerous authors have advocated various coaching and training strategies to directly enhance athletes' self-efficacy, including ensuring performance accomplishments (Weinberg et al., 1979) or providing various forms of modeling (Gould & Weiss, 1981; McAuley, 1985).

Alternatively, enhanced self-efficacy may be an unintended outcome of other, well-designed training programs. When difficult tasks are broken down into component parts (Blum & Naylor, 1968) and trainees are able to develop competency on simpler tasks before proceeding to more complex tasks (Briggs, 1968), the trainees are likely to develop stronger perceptions of self-efficacy concurrent with greater skill capacities. In a similar vein, Schunk (1985) postulated that as students work on a learning task, their perceived capabilities are influenced by such factors as their ability to cognitively process directions and instructions, early successes and failures, and other contextual factors such as rewards or social comparisons. Regardless of whether changes in self-efficacy are formal or unintentional training outcomes, it is clear that such changes occur and that they may be related to other training criteria of interest.

There are several reasons why perceptions of self-efficacy should be included as posttraining measures of learning. As stated before, enhanced self-efficacy may be a formal training objective. Additionally, such beliefs may moderate the relationship between knowledge acquisition and subsequent performance. It is a well-accepted fact that there is a difference between possessing relevant skills and applying them in diverse, appropriate situations. Perceptions of self-efficacy may be one factor that determines whether or not trainees apply the skills they have acquired (cf. Bandura, 1983). Finally, posttraining self-efficacy beliefs may be useful predictors of long-term transfer or skill maintenance (Marx, 1982). For example, Kraiger and Salas (1992) reported that self-efficacy judgments collected at the end of training predicted scores on performance tests administered 3 months later better than a traditional test of learning did.

Goal setting

Considerable research has implicated the role of goals and goal setting in motivational processes (e.g., Locke & Latham, 1990; Naylor, Pritchard, & Ilgen, 1980). The mechanisms presumed to operate through goal setting are also those that characterize motivated behavior: direction, arousal, and persistence of effort (Locke & Latham, 1990). Research indicates that individuals who set specific, difficult goals and who are committed to those goals are more likely to exert effort and perform at a high level (Locke, Latham, & Erez, 1988; Mento, Steele, & Karren, 1987; Tubbs, 1986).

The importance of goal setting to training evaluation rests on three assertions. First, individuals differ in the extent to which they are active in self-management processes, including setting and working toward goals (Manz, 1986). Thus, it is reasonable to assume that, irrespective of an intervention or evaluation, there will be variability among trainees regarding the difficulty, complexity or specificity of their goals for the application and development of recently acquired skills.

Second, individual differences in the type and structure of goals have been identified as an important difference between task experts and novices. This is important because training has been likened to a process of turning novices into experts (Howell & Cooke, 1989; Kraiger, 1988). Accordingly, it can be argued that difference in goal quality is a useful indicator of trainees' development. Glaser (1986) noted that experts and novices differ in their goal clarity and specificity. In contrast to novices, experts are characterized by well-differentiated, hierarchical goal structures. Thus, trainees who have learned the most will exhibit better quality goals and can be expected to exert more effort in desirable directions, be able to work toward concurrent subgoals, and have contingency plans in the event of goal blockage.

There are other predictable differences between the goal structures of experts and novices (Glaser et al., 1986). For example, one common weakness of novice goal structures is that subgoals are nonindependent; for example, a new assistant professor may set conflicting first-year subgoals of winning a teaching award and establishing a broad-based research agenda. Additionally, novices also set goals based on known methods rather than on methods best suited for the problem at hand. Thus, the new faculty member may set out to win the teaching award by using lecturing as the predominant instructional method, regardless of whether it is the most appropriate format for the specific learning objectives of each class.

Finally, it is asserted that individual differences in the presence and quality of goals may hold additional implications for the extent to which knowledge and skills acquired in training are applied to the job. Goal setting is viewed as an important factor influencing transfer of learned behaviors to the job (Baldwin & Ford, 1988; Wexley & Baldwin, 1986). To illustrate, a study by Farrell and Dweck (1985; cited in Dweck & Leggett, 1988) differentiated students who held learning goals (of acquiring new skills or extending their mastery) from students with performance goals (of establishing the adequacy of their ability or avoiding giving evidence of inadequacy or both). Students who held learning goals were more likely to actively attempt transfer tasks and scored significantly higher on such tasks. Not surprisingly, a strong goal-setting component is also included in relapse prevention strategies (Marx, 1982). Numerous studies have supported the hypothesis that awareness of goal setting increases the likelihood that knowledge and skills acquired in training are applied on the job (Frayne & Latham, 1987; Gist, Bavetta, & Stevens, 1990; Latham & Frayne, 1989; Wexley & Baldwin, 1986; Wexley & Nemeroff, 1975).

Measurement implications

A direct implication of the preceding discussion is that changes in trainees' motivational states (motivational disposition, self-efficacy, and goals) may be inferred as evidence of their development during training. Various techniques exist for measuring these motivational states. The standard procedure for assessing the magnitude and strength of self-efficacy perceptions is straightforward (Bandura, 1977b). Trainees are given a set of specific performance outcomes of increasing difficulty and asked to indicate whether they are capable of accomplishing the objective and, if so, their confidence in doing so (see Gist, 1989, for an example).

Several direct measures of mastery and performance orientations exist as well (Ames & Archer, 1987; Nimmer, 1991). Nimmer's measure assesses both goal and affective dimensions of the mastery orientation, has been validated on a college-age sample, and includes items such as "When I approach a new task, I am usually confident in my ability to master the task" and "My enjoyment with working on tasks tends to be overshadowed by my concern over others' evaluations."

Trainees' goals may be measured by direct assessment of their goal commitment (e.g., Earley & Kanfer, 1985; Latham & Steele, 1983). Goal commitment is perceived as a reasonable surrogate of goal acceptance (Locke et al., 1988). A more sensitive measure of training success may be to assess trainees' goal structures. For a variety of tasks, but particularly those involving problem solving or decision making, trainees can be asked to demonstrate their goal structures using methods such as free recall, focused interviews, and think aloud verbal protocols. The similarity between trainees' structures and those of job experts can be assessed and used to infer training success. Dimensions on which similarity can be assessed include goal complexity, goal specificity, goal difficulty, and contingency planning. Alternatively, goal structures can be measured and compared using methods similar to those used to assess cognitive structures (Naveh-Benjamin et al., 1986; Schvaneveldt et al., 1985; Shavelson, 1974).

Generally, main effects for training on motivational out comes may be expected whenever the training was intended to affect those states. That is, in many instances, there should be an a priori learning objective targeting the motivational outcome to guide the measurement process. In such instances, pre-and postevaluations are critical given that variables such as mastery and performance orientation and self-efficacy are often conceptualized as individual difference variables. When trainees' motivational states change as intended, learning during training may be inferred, and subsequent posttraining evaluation may not be necessary to draw conclusions regarding the success of the intervention.

For example, Gist (1989) used changes in self-efficacy perceptions to compare two methods for training managers in idea generation. The two training formats were compared on a measure of self-efficacy and on the quantity and quality of trainees' performance on two idea-generation tasks. Consistent with hypotheses, the cognitive-modeling strategy (Meichenbaum, 1975) resulted in both greater self-efficacy and task performance. Moreover, within training groups, self-efficacy was significantly correlated to task performance.

In other contexts, changes in motivational states may be an unintended consequence of training programs. Schunk (1985) argued that reinforcement associated with the routine, administrative aspects of classrooms may trigger increases in students' self-efficacy that generalize to trained tasks. In addition, some trainees' may spontaneously set difficult, challenging goals whereas others may not. Measures of unintentional motivational change may be useful not only as immediate measures of training success but as potential moderators of transfer of training or skill maintenance. Thus, one trainee with a low level of knowledge acquisition during training but a strong mastery orientation or feelings of self-efficacy may show strong distal transfer, whereas another trainee who scores high on a measure of declarative knowledge but lacks well-articulated transfer and application goals may not demonstrate long-term skill maintenance.

Discussion

Both the theory and practice of training evaluation have been hampered by the absence of a thorough, conceptually based model of training evaluation. We have suggested that this is in large part due to a reliance on incomplete theories of what learning is and how it should be evaluated. Accordingly, we discussed learning as a function of changes in cognitive, skill-based, and affective states. For each state, we reviewed relevant research from other psychological domains, proposed potential changes as a function of training, and recommended alternative methods for evaluating learning in training.

A classification scheme

As a result of these efforts, we are in a position to derive a preliminary, conceptually based classification scheme of learning outcomes for training evaluation. This scheme, presented in Table 1, is organized by the cognitive, skill-based, and affective learning outcomes. For each learning outcome, the table describes relevant learning constructs, appropriate foci for measurement, and potential evaluation measures. The classification scheme in Table 1 summarizes the constructs and measures we have proposed throughout this article. The scheme advances the training evaluation by providing a broadened definition of learning, a construct-oriented approach to learning outcomes, and the rudiments of a nomological network necessary to build models of training evaluation and training effectiveness. These contributions are clarified below.

Definition of learning

Traditionally, industrial/organizational (I/O) psychologists have used definitions of learning such as "a relatively permanent change in behavior that occurs as a result of practice" (Wexley & Latham, 1991, p. 73) while ignoring more multi-faceted definitions (Gagne, 1984; Messick, 1984). In contrast, and as indicated in Table 1, training and training evaluation can target a number of learning constructs, including declarative knowledge relevant to valued skill; development of complex and useful mental models for storing, organizing, and applying knowledge; development of strategies and executive functions for monitoring and regulating skilled performance; development of compilation skills such as proceduralization and composition; development of fluidity or automaticity in retaining and accessing knowledge; development and internalization of appropriate attitudes toward the focus of instruction; and changes in motivational tendencies.

It should be noted that these learning outcomes are not discrete but are often interrelated; that is, changes in one learning outcome may imply changes in another. For example, as trainees build accurate mental models, they must understand the task, equipment, co-workers, and the interrelationships among these elements (Cannon-Bowers, Salas, & Converse, in press; Rouse, Cannon-Bowers, & Salas, in press). In turn, these models lead to expectations about the elements and their interrelationships (Rouse et al., in press). These expectations fall closer to the affective domain than to the cognitive realm because they allow the learner to "sense" the correctness of current situations or "anticipate" nontrained phenomena.

Table 1 A classification scheme for learning outcomes for training evaluation

Category	Learning construct(s)	Focus of measurement	Potential training evaluation methods
Verbal knowledge	Declarative knowledge	Cognitive outcomes Amount of knowledge Accuracy of recall Speed, accessibility of knowledge	Recognition and recall tests Power tests Speed tests
Knowledge organization	Mental models	Similarity to ideal Interrelationships of elements Hierarchical ordering	Free sorts Structural assessment (e.g., Pathfinder)
Cognitive strategies	Self-insight Metacognitive skills	Self-awareness Self-regulation	Probed protocol analysis Self-report Readiness for testing
Compilation	Composition Proceduralization	Skill-based outcomes Speed of performance Fluidity of performance Error rates Chunking Generalization Discrimination Strengthening	Targeted behavioral observation Hands-on testing Structured situational interviews

Automaticity	Automatic processing Tuning	Attentional requirements Available cognitive resources	Secondary task performance Interference problems Embedded measurement
Attitudinal	Targeted object (e.g., safety awareness) Attitude strength	Affective outcomes Attitude direction Attitude strength Accessibility Centrality Conviction	Self-report measures
Motivation	Motivational disposition	Mastery versus performance orientations Appropriateness of orientation	Self-report measures
	Self-efficacy	Perceived performance capability	Self-report measures
	Goal setting	Level of goals Complexity of goal structures Goal commitment	Self-report measures Free recall measures Free sorts

It is evident from Table 1 that the adoption of a broader, multidimensional definition of learning leads to the consideration of a broader range of conceptually based evaluation measures. We have attempted to lay the foundation for a more comprehensive training evaluation model by adapting measures of various psychological constructs from other disciplines. The evaluation measures that we have suggested include power or speed tests of recognition or recall of declarative knowledge; knowledge elicitation techniques for measuring mental models such as verbal protocol analyses or cognitive mapping methods such as Pathfinder; probed protocol analysis and self-reports of awareness and readiness to perform as measures of metacognitive strategies; alternative behavioral sampling methodologies for measuring compilation such as hands-on testing, structured interview testing, and behavioral observations; embedded tests for automaticity such as the use of distractor tasks; and perceptually based measures such as the assessment of attitude strength or goal complexity and pre- and postcomparisons of self-efficacy or motivational dispositions. In some instances, our recommended measures have yet to be used in an actual training environment. However, the success of these procedures for other purposes in other domains yields optimism that they would be similarly successful as mechanisms for training evaluation.

Construct-oriented approach

Throughout this article, we have advocated a construct-oriented approach to the conceptualization of learning states and to the development of training evaluation measures. We have used the term learning construct to connote both a final state (e.g., proficiency, declarative knowledge) and a process for achieving that state (e.g., knowledge organization).

A construct-oriented approach to training evaluation has two clear benefits. First, it forces researchers to be explicit in identifying not only the instructional objectives (e.g., specific knowledge, skills, and abilities) but also the most appropriate mechanisms for facilitating trainee development toward those objectives. Although in this article we have focused on the evaluation of training, implicit in this discussion is the need to be more explicit about the intended changes of training. Depending on the anticipated learning outcome, evidence of the success of the training program may be derived from mean differences (between pre- and posttests or trained and untrained groups), measures of convergence to a prototype, or measures of variability across trainees. For example, the compilation and automaticity constructs make different predictions about the degree of consistency across trainees during skill development. Thus, over repeated measures of skill-based testing, evidence of reduced variability over response patterns would support inferences of compilation, whereas subsequent evidence of increased variability would support inferences of automaticity (as trainees' individualize performance).

A second benefit of a construct-oriented approach concerns the potential for validating the actual training measures used. Researchers typically have shown less interest in the construct validation of criterion measures than of predictors (Binning & Barrett, 1989; Schmitt, 1989). This orientation toward predictor constructs has been attributed both to a lack of clarity regarding the requirements of construct validation of performance measures (Austin, Villanova, Kane, & Bernardin, 1991) and to a lack of agreement regarding the nature or scope of performance constructs (cf. Borman, 1991; Campbell, Campbell, & Associates, 1988; Fleishman & Quaintance, 1984). Although the identification and estimation of both relevant and irrelevant sources of variance remains a vexing problem in performance appraisal (Waldman & Spangler, 1989), these same issues are potentially solvable in the context of training evaluation. Given that the performance domain is more narrowly defined through learning outcomes, measured variables can be more readily linked to latent variables (intended learning outcomes), and extraneous sources of variance can be controlled or measured through the experimental or quasi-experimental designs commonly used in training evaluation.

Development of a nomological network

Other researchers have likened construct validation to theory development (cf. Clark, 1983). This comparison is relevant to the present case because we aspire to a theory or model of training evaluation. As a first step, we have developed a conceptual scheme to organize relevant learning outcomes, have identified appropriate learning constructs within this conceptual framework, and have specified multiple measurement techniques that can be applied to specific learning outcomes.

The next step is to identify a nomological network of multiple concepts, measures, and their interrelationships (Cronbach & Meehl, 1955). A nomological network requires the development and testing of hypotheses about the interrelationships among the learning constructs identified in Table 1, the relations of the learning constructs with other training outcomes such as behavioral changes on the job, and the predictive impact of factors such as trainee characteristics and training design on learning outcomes. Each step in building a nomological network for learning outcomes is described below.

An implicit assumption of the conceptual scheme presented in Table 1 is that there is a complex set of relationships among the measures of the various learning constructs. Several principles can guide the development of hypotheses for testing the interrelationships among these measures. First, stronger relationships should be expected among measures of the same learning construct than among measures of different constructs. That is, there should be evidence of convergent validity among multiple measures of the same learning construct, but there should be evidence of discriminant validity between measures of different learning constructs. More generally, operational measures of sequential learning constructs should be more highly correlated than measures of distal constructs. For example, measures of verbal knowledge should be more highly correlated with measures of either knowledge organization or compilation than with measures of metacognitive skills or automaticity. Furthermore, because metacognitive skills and automaticity are both indicative of higher order skill development, measures of these constructs should be highly intercorrelated.

A second step is to examine the relationship between changes in learning outcomes and other important training outcomes. As noted by Alliger and Janak (1989), Kirkpatrick's (1976, 1987) four steps of reaction, learning, behavior, and results have been codified in the training literature as a hierarchical approach to evaluation. For example, it is now accepted that learning is a necessary but not sufficient condition for behavioral changes on the job (e.g., see Clement, 1982; Noe & Schmitt, 1986). Alliger and Janak questioned this hierarchical approach and presented an alternative causal, plausible ordering. In their thinking, reactions to training are unrelated to learning, and learning can have a direct influence on results criteria as opposed to the indirect results it has on behavioral change.

The problem is not which causal ordering is preferable. Rather, from a construct validation perspective, the problem is that linkages have been identified without articulating reasons why or how such measures are logically related. Furthermore, a more substantive issue has rarely been addressed—under what conditions should different learning constructs be related to different behavioral change measures such as skill generalizability and maintenance. For example, it is likely that trainees who develop compilation skills will generalize training to more appropriate job situations than will those at the initial skill acquisition stage. Similarly, trainees who develop skills at the automaticity stage should maintain those skills over a longer period on the job than will those who leave training at the compilation stage. Relating learning criteria to intended learning outcomes enables the identification of such conditions.

A third step in building a nomological network is to specify and test relationships between the learning measures and predictor variables such as trainee characteristics and training design characteristics. Recent research on training characteristics and learning outcomes provides directions for such research (e.g., Tannenbaum et al., 1991). For example, Ackerman (see Ackerman & Humphreys, 1990) has shown that general intelligence is a good predictor of individual differences at the initial skill acquisition stage but is less of a predictor for trainees at the automaticity stage. Kanfer and Ackerman (1989) conducted three studies that indicated the complex interactions of type of training (e.g., declarative or procedural). These studies focused on ability differences, goal setting, and self-regulatory activities. For example, one study showed that goal-setting manipulations during initial training led to more self-regulatory activities and higher levels of performance.

Generally, learning measures would be expected to show the greatest effects when there is congruence between the learning objectives, instructional designs, and the method of assessment. For example, Glaser (1986) discussed several training techniques for improving learners' mental models. It should be expected that operationalizations of learning constructs relevant to mental models (e.g., similarity to an ideal) should show greater pre- to posttest changes when improving or building mental models are instructional objectives and when these mental modeling training techniques are used as opposed to the more traditional lecture and discussion methods of instruction. Similarly, measures of affective or motivational change should show the strongest effects in programs that make these outcomes an explicit training objective.

Conclusion

In this article, we have integrated theory and research from a number of diverse disciplines and have provided a multidimensional perspective to learning outcomes. We have advanced the theory of training evaluation by providing a conceptually based scheme of learning constructs, measurement foci, and measurement techniques. The value of our construct-oriented approach is that it provides a systematic framework for conducting training evaluation research. The ultimate criterion for such work is whether it spurs additional research in training that advances our understanding of training evaluation and training effectiveness.

Acknowledgments

The views expressed herein are those of the authors and do not reflect the official position of the organizations with which they are affiliated.

We thank three anonymous reviewers for comments on earlier versions of this article.

References

Abelson, R. P. (1988). Conviction. *American Psychologist, 43,* 267–275.

Ackerman, P. L. (1986). Individual differences in information processing: An investigation of intellectual abilities and task performance during practice. *Intelligence, 10,* 109–139.

Ackerman, P. L. (1987). Individual differences in skill learning: An integration of psychometric and information processing perspectives. *Psychological Bulletin, 102,* 3–27.

Ackerman, P. L., & Humphreys, L. G. (1990). Individual differences theory in industrial and organizational psychology. In M. D. Dunnette & L. M. Hough (Eds.), *Handbook of industrial and organizational psychology* (2nd ed., Vol. 1, pp. 223–282). Palo Alto, CA: Consulting Psychologists Press.

Alliger, G. M., & Janak, E. A. (1989). Kirkpatrick's levels of training criteria: Thirty years later. *Personnel Psychology, 42,* 331–342.

Ames, C., & Archer, J. (1987, April). *Achievement goals in the classroom: Student learning strategies and motivation processes.* Paper presented at the annual meeting of the American Educational Research Association, Washington, DC.

Anderson, J. R. (1982). Acquisition of a cognitive skill. *Psychological Review, 89,* 369–406.

Austin, J. T., Villanova, P., Kane, J. S., & Bernardin, H. J. (1991). Construct validation of performance measures: Definitional issues, development, and evaluation of indicators. *Research in Personnel and Human Resources Management, 9,* 159–233.

Baldwin, T. T., & Ford, J. K. (1988). Transfer of training: A review and directions for future research. *Personnel Psychology, 41,* 63–105.

Bandura, A. (1977a). Self-efficacy: Toward a unifying theory of behavioral change. *Psychological Review, 84*, 191–215.

Bandura, A. (1977b). *Social learning theory*. Englewood Cliffs, NJ: Prentice-Hall.

Bandura, A. (1983). Self-efficacy determinants of anticipated fears and calamities. *Journal of Personality and Social Psychology, 45*, 464–469.

Barling, J., & Beattie, R. (1983). Self-efficacy beliefs and sales performance. *Journal of Organizational Behavior Management, 5*, 41–51.

Becker, H. S., Geer, B., Hughes, E. C., & Strauss, A. L. (1961). *Boys in white*. New Brunswick, NJ: Transaction Books.

Bereiter, C., & Scardamalia, M. (1985). Cognitive coping strategies and the problem of "inert" knowledge In S. Chipman, J. W. Segal & R. Glaser (Eds.), *Thinking and learning skills: Vol. 2. Research and open questions* (pp. 65–80). Hillsdale, NJ: Erlbaum.

Biggs, J. B., & Rihn, B. (1984). The effects of interventions on deep and surface approaches to learning. In J. R. Kirby (Ed.), *Cognitive strategies and educational performance* (pp. 279–293). San Diego, CA: Academic Press.

Binning, J.F., & Barrett, G. V. (1989). Validity of personnel decisions: A conceptual analysis of the inferential and evidential bases. *Journal of Applied Psychology, 74*, 478–494.

Bloom, B. (1956). *Taxonomy of educational objectives: The cognitive domain*. New York: Donald McKay.

Blum, M. L., & Naylor, J. C. (1968). *Industrial psychology: Its theoretical and social foundations*. New York: Harper & Row.

Borman, W. C. (1991). Job behavior, performance, and effectiveness. In M. D. Dunnette & L. M. Hough (Eds.), *Handbook of industrial and organizational psychology* (2nd ed., Vol. 2, pp. 271–326). Palo Alto, CA: Consulting Psychologists Press.

Borman, W. C., & Hallam, G. L. (1991). Observation accuracy for assessors of work-sample performance: Consistency across task and individual-differences correlates. *Journal of Applied Psychology, 76*, 11–18.

Briggs, L. J. (1968). *Sequencing of instruction in relation to hierarchies of competence*. Palo Alto, CA: American Institutes of Research.

Brown, A. L. (1975). The development of memory: Knowing, knowing about knowing, and knowing how to know. In H. W. Reese (Ed.), *Advances in child development and behavior* (Vol. 10, pp. 103–152). San Diego, CA: Academic Press.

Brown, A. L., Bransford, J. D., Ferrara, R. A., & Campione, J. C. (1983). Learning, remembering, and understanding. In J. H. Flavell & E. M. Markman (Eds.), *Handbook of child psychology* (4th ed., Vol. 3, pp. 77–166). New York: Wiley.

Campbell, J. P. (1971). Personnel training and development. *Annual Review of Psychology, 22*, 565–602.

Campbell, J. P. (1988). Training design for productivity improvement. In J. P. Campbell & R. J. Campbell (Eds.), *Productivity in organizations* (pp. 177–215). San Francisco: Jossey-Bass.

Campbell, J. P., & Associates. (1990). The Army selection and classification project. *Personnel Psychology, 43*, 231–378.

Campbell, J. P., Campbell, R. J., & Associates. (1988). *Productivity in organizations*. San Francisco: Jossey-Bass.

Cannon-Bowers, J. A., Salas, E., & Converse, S. A. (in press). Shared mental models in expert decision making teams. In N. J. Castellan, Jr. (Ed.), *Current issues in individual and group decision making*. Hillsdale, NJ: Erlbaum.

Cannon-Bowers, J. A., Tannenbaum, S. I., Salas, E., & Converse, S. A. (1991). Toward an integration of training theory and technique. *Human Factors, 33*, 281–292.

Chaiken, S., & Stangor, C. (1987). Attitudes and attitude change. *Annual Review of Psychology, 38*, 575–630.

Champagne, A. B., Klopfer, L. E., Desena, A. T., & Squires, D. A. (1981). Structural representations of students' knowledge before and after science instruction. *Journal of Research in Science Technology, 18*, 97–111.

Chi, M. T. H. (1987). Representing knowledge and metaknowledge: Implications for interpreting metamemory research. In F. E. Weinert & R. H. Kluwe (Eds.), *Metacognition, motivation and understanding* (pp. 239–266). Hillsdale, NJ: Erlbaum.

Chi, M. T. H., Glaser, R., & Rees, E. (1982). Expertise in problem-solving. In R. Sternberg (Ed.), *Advances in the psychology of human intelligence* (Vol. 1, pp. 7–75). Hillsdale, NJ: Erlbaum.

Clark, A. (1983). Hypothetical constructs, circular reasoning, and criteria. *Journal of Mind and Behavior, 4*, 1–12.

Clement, R.W. (1982). Testing the hierarchy theory of training evaluation: An expanded role for trainee reactions. *Public Personnel Management, 11*, 176–184.

Cooke, N. M., & McDonald, J. E. (1987). The application of psychological scaling techniques to knowledge elicitation for knowledge-based systems. *International Journal of Man-Machine Studies, 28*, 533–550.

Cronbach, L. J. (1960). *Essentials of psychological testing* (2nd ed.). New York: Harper & Row.

Cronbach, L. J., & Meehl, P. (1955). Construct validity in psychological tests. *Psychological Bulletin, 52*, 281–302.

Dweck, C. S. (1986). Mental processes affecting learning. *American Psychologist, 41*, 1040–1048.

Dweck, C. S., & Elliott, E. S. (1983). Achievement motivation. In E. M. Hetherington (Ed.), *Handbook of child psychology* (Vol. 4, pp. 643–691). New York: Wiley.

Dweck, C. S., & Leggett, E. L. (1988). A social-cognitive approach to motivation and personality. *Psychological Review, 95*, 256–273.

Earley, P. C., & Kanfer, R. (1985). The influence of component participation and role models on goal acceptance, goal satisfaction and performance. *Organizational Behavior and Human Decision Processes, 36*, 378–390.

Fazio, R. (1988). On the power and functionality of attitudes: The role of attitude accessibility. In A. R. Pratkanis, S. J. Breckler, & A. G. Greenwald (Eds.), *Attitude structure and function* (pp. 153–179). Hillsdale, NJ: Erlbaum.

Feldman, D. C. (1984). The development and enforcement of group norms. *Academy of Management Review, 9*, 47–53.

Feldman, D. C. (1989). Socialization, resocialization, and training: Re-framing the research agenda. In I. L. Goldstein & Associates (Eds.), *Training and development in organizations* (pp. 376–414). San Francisco: Jossey-Bass.

Feltz, D. L., & Doyle, L. A. (1981), Improving self-confidence in athletic performance. *Motor Skills: Theory into Practice, 5*(2), 112–122.

Feltz, D. L., & Weiss, M. (1982). Developing self-efficacy through sport. *Journal of Physical Education, Recreation, and Dance, 53*(2), 24–26, 36.

Fisk, A. D., & Gallini, J. K. (1989). Training consistent components of tasks: Developing an instructional system based on automatic/controlled processing principles. *Human factors, 31*, 453–463.

Fitts, P. M., & Posner, M. (1967). *Human performance*. Monterey, CA: Brooks/Cole.

Flanagan, D. L. (1990). *Techniques for eliciting and representing knowledge structures and mental models*. Unpublished manuscript, Naval Training Systems Center, Orlando, FL.

Fleishman, E. A., & Quaintance, M. (1984). *Taxonomies of human performance*. San Diego, CA: Academic Press.

Frayne, C., & Latham, G. P. (1987). Application of social learning theory to employee self-management of attendance. *Journal of Applied Psychology*, *72*, 387–392.

Gagne, R. M. (1977). *The conditions of learning*. New York: Holt, Rinehart & Winston.

Gagne, R. M. (1984). Learning outcomes and their effects: Useful categories of human performance. *American Psychologist*, *39*, 377–385.

Gagne, R. M. (1986). Research on learning and retaining skills. In I. L. Goldstein, R. M. Gagne, R. Glaser, J. M. Royer, T. J. Shuell, & D. L. Payne (Eds.), *Learning research laboratory: Proposed research issues* (AFHRL-TP-85-54, pp. 5–19). Brooks Air Force Base, TX: Manpower and Personnel Division, Air Force Human Resources Laboratory

Geber, B. (1990). Coverstory: Managing diversity. *Training*, *27*(7), 23–30.

Gill, R., Gordon, S., Moore, J., & Barbera, C. (1988). The role of conceptual structures in problem-solving. In *Proceedings of the Annual Meeting of the American Society of Engineering Education* (pp. 583–590). Washington, DC: American Society of Engineering Education.

Gist, M. E. (1989). The influence of training method on self-efficacy and idea generation among managers. *Personnel Psychology*, *42*, 787–805.

Gist, M. E., Bavetta, A. G., & Stevens, C. K. (1990). Transfer training method: Its influence on skill generalization, skill repetition, and performance level. *Personnel Psychology*, *43*, 501–523.

Glaser, R. (1986). Training expert apprentices. In I. L. Goldstein, R. M. Gagne, R. Glaser, J. M. Royer, T. J. Shuell, & D. L. Payne (Eds.), *Learning research laboratory: Proposed research issues* (AFHRL-TP-85-54, pp. 20–28). Brooks Air Force Base, TX: Manpower and Personnel Division, Air Force Human Resources Laboratory.

Glaser, R., & Chi, M. T. (1989). Overview. In M. T. Chi, R. Glaser, & M.J. Farr (Eds.), *The nature of expertise* (pp. xv–xxviii). Hillsdale, NJ: Erlbaum.

Glaser, R., Lesgold, A., & Gott, S. (1986, July). *Implications of cognitive psychology for measuring job performance*. Paper prepared for the Committee on the Performance of Military Personnel, National Academy of Sciences, Washington, DC.

Goldsmith, T. E., & Davenport, D. M. (1990). Assessing structural similarity of graphs. In R. W. Schvaneveldt (Ed.), *Pathfinder associative networks: Studies in knowledge organization* (pp. 75–87). Norwood, NJ: Ablex.

Goldsmith, T. E., & Johnson, P. J. (1990). A structural assessment of classroom learning. In R. W. Schvaneveldt (Ed.), *Pathfinder associative networks: Studies in knowledge organization* (pp. 241–254). Norwood, NJ: Ablex.

Goldsmith, T. E., Johnson, P. J., & Acton, W. H. (1991). Assessing structural knowledge. *Journal of Educational Psychology*, *83*, 88–96.

Goldstein, A. P., & Sorcher, M. (1974). *Changing supervisor behavior*. New York: Pergamon Press.

Goldstein, I. L. (1980). Training in work organizations. *Annual Review of Psychology*, *31*, 229–272.

Goldstein, I. L. (1986). *Training in organizations: Needs assessment, design, and evaluation*. Monterey, CA: Brooks/Cole.

Goldstein, I. L. (1991). Training in work organizations. In M. D. Dunnette & L. M. Hough (Eds.), *Handbook of industrial and organizational psychology* (2nd ed., Vol. 2, pp. 507–620). Palo Alto, CA: Consulting Psychologists Press.

Gould, D., & Weiss, M. (1981). The effects of model similarity and model talk of self-efficacy and muscular endurance. *Journal of Sport Psychology, 3,* 17–29.

Greeno, J. G. (1980). Some examples of cognitive task analysis with instructional implications. In R. E. Snow, P. A. Federico, & W. E. Montague (Eds.), *Aptitude, learning, and instruction* (Vol. 2, pp. 1–21). Hillsdale, NJ: Erlbaum.

Gregorich, S. E., Helmreich, R. L., & Wilhelm, J. A. (1990). The structure of cockpit management attitudes. *Journal of Applied Psychology, 75,* 682–690.

Hedge, J. W., & Teachout, M. S. (1991, April). *The conceptual development and implementation of a job performance measurement system.* Paper presented at the Sixth Annual Meeting of the Society for Industrial and Organizational Psychology, St. Louis, MO.

Hertel, P. T., & Hardin, T. S. (1990). Remembering with and without awareness in a depressed mood: Evidence of deficits in initiative. *Journal of Experimental Psychology: General, 119,* 45–59.

Howell, W. C., & Cooke, N. J. (1989). Training the human information processor. In I. L. Goldstein (Ed.), *Training and development in organizations* (pp. 121–182). San Francisco: Jossey-Bass.

Johnson-Laird, P. (1983). *Mental models.* Cambridge, MA: Harvard University Press.

Kanfer, R., & Ackerman, P. L. (1989). Motivation and cognitive abilities: An integrative/aptitude-treatment interaction approach to skill acquisition [Monograph]. *Journal of Applied Psychology, 74,* 657–690.

Kirkpatrick, D. L. (1976). Evaluation of training. In R. L. Craig (Ed.), *Training and development handbook: A guide to human resource development* (2nd ed., pp. 18-1–18-27). New York: McGraw-Hill.

Kirkpatrick, D. L. (1987). Evaluation of training. In R. L. Craig (Ed.), *Training and development handbook: A guide to human resource development* (3rd ed., pp. 301–319). New York: McGraw-Hill.

Komaki, J., Heinzman, A. T., & Lawson, L. (1980). Effect of training and feedback: Component analysis of a behavioral safety program. *Journal of Applied Psychology, 65,* 261–270.

Kraiger, K. (1988, April). *Implications of expert/novice differences for training assessment and design.* Paper presented at the third annual meeting of the Society for Industrial and Organizational Psychology, Dallas.

Kraiger, K. (1991, April). *Generalizability theory as evidence of the reliability and validity of work sample tests and proficiency ratings.* Paper presented at the sixth annual meeting of the Society for Industrial and Organizational Psychology, St. Louis, MO.

Kraiger, K., & Salas, E. (1992). *Development of cognitively based measures of learning during training.* Manuscript submitted for publication.

Krathwohl, D. R., Bloom, B. S., & Masia, B. B. (1964). *Taxonomy of educational objectives: The classification of educational goals.* White Plains, NY: Longman.

Kraut, A. I. (1976). Developing managerial skills via modeling techniques: Some positive research findings—A symposium. *Personnel Psychology, 29,* 325–328.

Kronsnick, J. A. (1986). *Policy voting in American presidential elections: An application of psychological theory to American politics.* Unpublished doctoral dissertation, University of Michigan, Ann Arbor.

Larkin, J. H. (1983). The role of problem representation in physics. In D. Gentner & A. L. Stevens (Eds.), *Mental models* (pp. 75–98). Hillsdale, NJ: Erlbaum.

Latham, G. P. (1988). Human resource training and development. *Annual Review of Psychology, 39,* 545–582.

Latham, G. P., & Frayne, C. A. (1989). Self-management training for increased job attendance: A follow-up and a replication. *Journal of Applied Psychology, 74,* 411–416.

Latham, G. P., Saari, L. M., Pursell, E. D., & Campion, M. A. (1980). The situational interview. *Journal of Applied Psychology, 65,* 422–427.

Latham, G. P., & Steele, T. R. (1983). The motivational effects of participation versus goal setting on performance. *Academy of Management Journal, 26,* 406–417.

Leonesio, R. J., & Nelson, T. O. (1990). Do different metamemory judgments tap the same underlying aspects of memory? *Journal of Experimental Psychology: Learning, Memory, and Cognition, 16,* 464–470.

Leong, S. M., Busch, P. S., & John, D. R. (1989). Knowledge bases and salesperson effectiveness: A script-theoretic analysis. *Journal of Marketing Research, 26,* 164–178.

Lesgold, A., Rubinson, H., Feltovich, P., Glaser, R., Klopfer, D., & Wang, Y. (1989). Expertise in a complex skill: Diagnosing X-ray pictures. In M. T. Chi, R. Glaser, & M. J. Farr (Eds.), *The nature of expertise* (pp. 311–342). Hillsdale, NJ: Erlbaum.

Locke, E., & Latham, G. R. (1990). *A theory of goal setting and task performance.* Englewood Cliffs, NJ: Prentice-Hall.

Locke, E., Latham, G. P., & Erez, M. (1988). The determinants of goal commitment. *Academy of Management Review, 13,* 23–39.

Lohman, D. (1979). *Spatial ability: A review and reanalysis of the correlational literature* (Tech. Rep. No. 8). Stanford, CA: Stanford University, School of Education.

Lord, F. M. (1956). A study of speed factors in tests and academic grades. *Psychometrika, 21,* 31–50.

Lord, R. G., & Maher, K. J. (1991). Cognitive theory in industrial/organizational psychology. In M. Dunnette & L. M. Hough (Eds.), *Handbook of industrial and organizational psychology* (2nd ed., Vol. 2, pp. 1–62). Palo Alto, CA: Consulting Psychologists Press.

Louis, M. R., Posner, B. Z., & Powell, G. N.(1983). The availability and helpfulness of socialization practices. *Personnel Psychology, 36,* 857–866.

Mabe, P. A., & West, S. G. (1982). validity of self-evaluation of ability: A review and meta-analysis. *Journal of Applied Psychology, 67,* 280–296.

Manz, C. C. (1986). Self-leadership: Toward an expanded theory of self-influence processes in organizations. *Academy of Management Review, 11,* 585–600.

Marx, R. D. (1982). Relapse prevention for managerial training: A model for maintenance of behavioral change. *Academy of Management Review, 7,* 27–40.

McAuley, E. (1985). Modeling and self-efficacy: A test of Bandura's model. *Journal of Sport Psychology, 7,* 283–295.

McIntire, R. W. (1973). Behavior modification guidelines. In T. C. Tuttle, C. B. Grether, & W. T. Liggett (Eds.), *Psychological behavior strategy for accident control: Development of behavioral safety guidelines* (Final Report for the National Institute for Occupational Safety and Health, Contract No. HSM-99-72-27). Columbia, MD: Westinghouse Behavioral Safety Center.

McPherson, S. L., & French, K. E.(1991). Changes in cognitive strategies and motor skill in tennis. *Journal of Sport & Exercise Psychology, 13,* 26–41.

McPherson, S. L., & Thomas, J. R. (1989). Relation of knowledge and performance in boys' tennis: Age and expertise. *Journal of Experimental Child Psychology, 48,* 190–211.

Means, B., & Gott, S. P. (1988). Cognitive task analysis as a basis for tutor development: Articulating abstract knowledge representations. In J. Psotka, L. D. Massey, & S. A. Mutter (Eds.), *Intelligent tutoring systems: Lessons learned* (pp. 35–57). Hillsdale, NJ: Erlbaum.

Meichenbaum, D. (1975). Enhancing creativity by modifying what subjects say to themselves. *American Educational Review, 12*, 129–145.

Mento, A. J., Steele, R. R., & Karren, R. J. (1987). A meta-analytic study of the effects of goal setting on task performance: 1966–1984. *Organizational Behavior and Human Decision Processes, 39*, 52–83.

Messick, S. (1984). Abilities and knowledge in educational achievement testing: The assessment of dynamic cognitive structures. In B. S. Plake (Ed.), *Social and technical issues in testing: Implications for test construction and usage* (pp. 156–172). Hillsdale, NJ: Erlbaum.

Naveh-Benjamin, M., McKeachie, W. J., Lin, Y., & Tucker, D. G. (1986). Inferring students' cognitive structures and their development using the "ordered tree technique." *Journal of Educational Psychology, 78*, 130–140.

Naylor, J. C., Pritchard, R. D., & Ilgen, D. R. (1980). *A theory of behavior in organizations.* San Diego, CA: Academic Press.

Nelson, T. O., & Narens, L. (1990). Metamemory: A theoretical framework and some new findings. In G. Bower (Ed.), *The psychology of learning and memory* (pp. 125–173). San Diego, CA: Academic Press.

Neves, D. M., & Anderson, J. R. (1981). Knowledge compilation: Mechanisms for the automatization of cognitive skills. In J. R. Anderson (Ed.), *Cognitive skills and their acquisition* (pp. 335–359). Hillsdale, NJ: Erlbaum.

Nimmer, J. G. (1991). *Development and validation of the Mastery Orientation Measure.* Unpublished manuscript, University of Colorado at Denver.

Noe, R. A. (1986). Trainees' attributes and attitudes: Neglected influences on training effectiveness. *Academy of Management Review, 11*, 736–749.

Noe, R. A., & Schmitt, N. (1986). The influence of trainee attitudes on training effectiveness: Test of a model. *Personnel Psychology, 39*, 497–523.

Ostroff, C. (1991). Training effectiveness measures and scoring schemes: A comparison. *Personnel Psychology, 44*, 353–374.

Peterson, P. L., Swing, S. R., Braverman, M. T., & Buss, R. (1982). Students' aptitudes and their reports of cognitive processes during direct instruction. *Journal of Educational Psychology, 74*, 535–547.

Peterson, P. L., Swing, S. R., Stark, K. D., & Waas, G. S. (1984). Students' cognitions and time on task during mathematics instruction. *American Educational Research Journal, 21*, 487–516.

Prawat, R. S. (1989). Promoting access to knowledge, strategy, and disposition in students: A research synthesis. *Review of Educational Research, 59*, 1–41.

Pressley, M., Snyder, B. S., Levin, J. R., Murray, H. G., & Ghatala, E. S. (1987). Perceived Readiness for Examination Performance (PREP): Produced by initial reading of text and text containing adjunct questions. *Reading Research Quarterly, 22*, 219–236.

Rouillier, J. Z., & Goldstein, I. L. (1991, April). *The determinants of positive transfer of training climate through organizational analysis.* Paper presented at the Sixth Annual Meeting of the Society for Industrial and Organizational Psychology, St. Louis, MO.

Rouse, W. B., Cannon-Bowers, J. A., & Salas, E. (in press). Mental models and training for complex decision-making tasks. *IEE—Systems, Man, and Cybernetics.*

Rouse, W. B., & Morris, N. M. (1986). On looking into the black box: Prospects and limits in the search for mental models. *Psychological Bulletin, 100,* 349–363.

Rummelhart, D. E., & Norman, D. A. (1978). Accretion, tuning and restructuring: Three models of learning. In J. W. Cotton & R. Klatsky (Eds.), *Semantic factors in cognition* (pp. 37–53). Hillsdale, NJ: Erlbaum.

Schein, E. H. (1968). Organizational socialization and the profession of management. *Industrial Management Review, 9,* 1–16.

Schendel, J. D., & Hagman, J. D. (1982). On sustaining procedural skills over a prolonged retention interval. *Journal of Applied Psychology, 67,* 605–610.

Schmitt, N. (1989). Construct validity in personnel selection. In B. J. Fallon, H. Pfister, & J. Brebner (Eds.), *Advances in industrial and organizational psychology* (pp. 331–341). Amsterdam: Elsevier.

Schneider, W., & Shiffrin, R. M. (1977). Controlled and automatic human information processing: I. Detection, search, and attention. *Psychological Review, 84,* 1–66.

Schoenfeld, A. H. (1985). *Mathematical problem solving.* San Diego, CA: Academic Press.

Schunk, D. H. (1985). Self-efficacy and classroom learning. *Psychology in the Schools, 22,* 208–223.

Schvaneveldt, R. W., Durso, F. T., & Dearholt, D. W. (1985). *Pathfinder: Scaling with network structures* (Memorandum in Computer and Cognitive Sciences, MCCS-85-9). Las Cruces: New Mexico State University, Computing Research Laboratory.

Shavelson, R. J. (1974). Methods for examining representations of subject-matter structure in a student's memory. *Journal of Research for Science Teaching, 11,* 231–249.

Shiffrin, R. M., & Dumais, S. T. (1981). The development of automatism. In J. R. Anderson (Ed.), *Cognitive skills and their acquisition* (pp. 111–140). Hillsdale, NJ: Erlbaum.

Shiffrin, R. M., & Schneider, W. (1977). Controlled and automatic human information processing: II. Perceptual learning, automatic attending, and a general theory. *Psychological Review, 84,* 127–190.

Shrauger, J. S., & Osberg, T.M. (1981). The relative accuracy of self-predictions and judgments by others in psychological assessments. *Psychological Bulletin, 90,* 322–351.

Shuell, T. J. (1986). Contributions of cognitive psychology to learning from instruction in Air Force training. In I. L. Goldstein, R. M. Gagne, R. Glaser, J. M. Royer, T. J. Shuell, & D. L. Payne (Eds.), *Learning research laboratory: Proposed research issues* (AFHRL-TP-85-54, pp. 29–44). Brooks Air Force Base, TX: Manpower and Personnel Division, Air Force Human Resources Laboratory.

Slife, B.D., & Weaver, C. A., III. (1992). Depression, cognitive skill, and metacognitive skills in problem solving. *Cognition and Emotion, 6,* 1–22.

Smith, P. C. (1976). Behavior, results, and organizational effectiveness: The problem of criteria. In M. D. Dunnette (Ed.), *Handbook of industrial and organizational psychology* (pp. 745–775). Chicago: Rand McNally.

Snyder, R. A., Raben, C. S., & Farr, J. L. (1980). A model for the systematic evaluation of human resource development programs. *Academy of Management Review, 5,* 431–444.

Soloway, E., Adelson, B., & Ehrlich, K. (1988). Knowledge and processes in the comprehension of computer programs. In M. T. Chi, R. Glaser, & M. J. Farr (Eds.), *The nature of expertise* (pp. 129–152). Hillsdale, NJ: Erlbaum.

Stumpf, S. A., Brief, A. P., & Hartman, K. (1987). Self-efficacy expectations and coping with career-related events. *Journal of Vocational Behavior, 31,* 91–108.

Tannenbaum, S. I., Mathieu, J. E., Salas, E., & Cannon-Bowers, J. B. (1991). Meeting trainees' expectations: The influence of training fulfillment on the development of commitment, self-efficacy, and motivation. *Journal of Applied Psychology*, *76*, 759–769.

Tannenbaum, S. I., & Yukl, G. (1992). Training and development in work organizations. *Annual Review of Psychology*, *43*, 399–441.

Tubbs, M. E. (1986). Goal setting: A meta-analytic examination of the empirical evidence. *Journal of Applied Psychology*, *71*, 474–483.

Tyler, S. W., Hertel, P. T., McCallum, M. C., & Ellis, H. C. (1979). Cognitive effort and memory. *Journal of Experimental Psychology: Human Learning and Memory*, *5*, 607–617.

Wagner, R. K. (1987). Tacit knowledge in everyday intelligent behavior. *Journal of Personality and Social Psychology*, *52*, 1236–1241.

Waldman, D. A., & Spangler, W. D. (1989). Putting together the pieces: A closer look at the determinants of job performance. *Human Performance*, *2*, 29–59.

Weinberg, R. S., Gould, D., & Jackson, A. (1979). Expectations and performance: An empirical test of Bandura's self-efficacy theory. *Journal of Sport Psychology*, *1*, 320–331.

Weiss, H. M. (1990). Learning theory and industrial and organizational psychology. In M. D. Dunnette & L. M. Hough (Eds.), *Handbook of industrial and organizational psychology* (2nd ed., Vol. 1, pp. 171–221). Palo Alto, CA: Consulting Psychologists Press.

Wexley, K. N. (1984). Personnel training. *Annual Review of Psychology*, *35*, 519–551.

Wexley, K. N., & Baldwin, T. T. (1986). Post training strategy for facilitating positive transfer: An empirical exploration. *Academy of Management Journal*, *29*, 503–520.

Wexley, K. N., & Latham, G. P. (1991). *Developing and training human resources in organizations*. New York: HarperCollins.

Wexley, K. N., & Nemeroff, W. (1975). Effectiveness of positive reinforcement and goal setting as methods of management development. *Journal of Applied Psychology*, *60*, 446–450.

Zbrodoff, N. J., & Logan, G. D. (1986). On the automaticity of mental processes: A case study of arithmetic. *Journal of Experimental Psychology: General*, *115*, 118–130.

35

BUILDING A LEARNING ORGANIZATION

David A. Garvin

Source: *Harvard Business Review 71* (July–Aug. 1993): 78–91.

Continuous improvement programs are sprouting up all over as organizations strive to better themselves and gain an edge. The topic list is long and varied, and sometimes it seems as though a program a month is needed just to keep up. Unfortunately, failed programs far outnumber successes, and improvement rates remain distressingly low. Why? Because most companies have failed to grasp a basic truth. Continuous improvement requires a commitment to learning.

How, after all, can an organization improve without first learning something new? Solving a problem, introducing a product, and reengineering a process all require seeing the world in a new light and acting accordingly. In the absence of learning, companies – and individuals – simply repeat old practices. Change remains cosmetic, and improvements are either fortuitous or short-lived.

A few farsighted executives – Ray Stata of Analog Devices, Gordon Forward of Chaparral Steel, Paul Allaire of Xerox – have recognized the link between learning and continuous improvement and have begun to refocus their companies around it. Scholars too have jumped on the bandwagon, beating the drum for "learning organizations" and "knowledge-creating companies." In rapidly changing businesses like semiconductors and consumer electronics, these ideas are fast taking hold. Yet despite the encouraging signs, the topic in large part remains murky, confused, and difficult to penetrate.

Meaning, management, and measurement

Scholars are partly to blame. Their discussions of learning organizations have often been reverential and utopian, filled with near mystical terminology. Paradise, they would have you believe, is just around the corner. Peter Senge, who popularized learning organizations in his book *The Fifth Discipline,* described them as places "where people continually expand their capacity to create the results they truly desire, where new and expansive patterns of thinking are nurtured, where collective aspiration is set free, and where people are continually learning how to learn together."[1] To achieve these ends, Senge suggested the use of five "component technologies": systems thinking, personal mastery, mental models, shared vision, and team learning. In a similar spirit, Ikujiro Nonaka characterized knowledge-creating companies as places where "inventing new knowledge is not a specialized activity...it is a way of behaving, indeed, a way of being, in which everyone is a knowledge worker."[2] Nonaka suggested that companies use metaphors and organizational redundancy to focus thinking, encourage dialogue, and make tacit, instinctively understood ideas explicit.

Sound idyllic? Absolutely. Desirable? Without question. But does it provide a framework for action? Hardly. The recommendations are far too abstract, and too many questions remain unanswered. How, for example, will managers know when their companies have become learning organizations? What concrete changes in behavior are required? What policies and programs must be in place? How do you get from here to there?

Most discussions of learning organizations finesse these issues. Their focus is high philosophy and grand themes, sweeping metaphors rather than the gritty details of practice. Three critical issues are left unresolved; yet each is essential for effective implementation. First is the question of *meaning*. We need a plausible, well-grounded definition of learning organizations; it must be actionable and easy to apply. Second is the question of *management*. We need clearer guidelines for practice, filled with operational advice rather than high aspirations. And third is the question of *measurement*. We need better tools for assessing an organization's rate and level of learning to ensure that gains have in fact been made.

Once these "three Ms" are addressed, managers will have a firmer foundation for launching learning organizations. Without this groundwork, progress is unlikely, and for the simplest of reasons. For learning to become a meaningful corporate goal, it must first be understood.

What is a learning organization?

Surprisingly, a clear definition of learning has proved to be elusive over the years. Organizational theorists have studied learning for a long time; the accompanying quotations suggest that there is still considerable disagreement (see the insert "Definitions of Organizational Learning"). Most scholars view organizational learning as a process that unfolds over time and link it with knowledge acquisition and improved performance. But they differ on other important matters.

Some, for example, believe that behavioral change is required for learning; others insist that new ways of thinking are enough. Some cite information processing as the mechanism through which learning takes place; others propose shared insights, organizational routines, even memory. And some think that organizational learning is common, while others believe that flawed, self-serving interpretations are the norm.

> **Definitions of Organizational Learning**
>
> **Scholars have proposed a variety of definitions of organizational learning. Here is a small sample:**
>
> Organizational learning means the process of improving actions through better knowledge and understanding.
> **C. Marlene Fiol and Marjorie A. Lyles, "Organizational Learning,"** *Academy of Management Review, October 1985.*
>
> An entity learns if, through its processing of information, the range of its potential behaviors is changed.
> **George P. Huber, "Organizational Learning: The Contributing Processes and the Literaturers,"** *Organization Science***, February 1991.**
>
> Organizations are seen as learning by encoding inferences from history into routines that guide behavior.
> **Barbara Levitt and James G. March, "Organizational Learning,"** *American Review of Sociology***, Vol. 14, 1988.**
>
> Organizational learning is a process of detecting and correcting error.
> **Chris Argyris, "Double Loop Learning in Organizations,"** *Harvard Business Review***, September-October 1977.**
>
> Organizational learning occurs through shared insights, knowledge, and mental models and builds on past knowledge and experience-that is, on memory.
> **Ray Stats, "Organizational Learning - The Key to Management Innovation,"** *Sloan Management Review***, Spring 1989.**

How can we discern among this cacophony of voices yet build on earlier insights? As a first step, consider the following definition:

> A learning organization is an organization skilled at creating, acquiring, and transferring knowledge, and at modifying its behavior to reflect new knowledge and insights.

This definition begins with a simple truth: new ideas are essential if learning is to take place. Sometimes they are created de novo, through flashes of insight or creativity; at other times they arrive from outside the organization or are communicated by knowledgeable insiders. Whatever their source, these ideas are the trigger for organizational improvement. But they cannot by themselves create a learning organization. *Without accompanying changes in the way that work gets done, only the potential for improvement exists.*

This is a surprisingly stringent test for it rules out a number of obvious candidates for learning organizations. Many universities fail to qualify, as do many consulting firms. Even General Motors, despite its recent efforts to improve performance, is found wanting. All of these organizations have been effective at creating or acquiring new knowledge but notably less successful in applying that knowledge to their own activities. Total quality management, for example, is now taught at many business schools, yet the number using it to guide their own decision making is very small. Organizational consultants advise clients on social dynamics and small-group behavior but are notorious for their own infighting and factionalism. And GM, with a few exceptions (like Saturn and NUMMI), has had little success in revamping its manufacturing practices, even though its managers are experts on lean manufacturing, JIT production, and the requirements for improved quality of work life.

Organizations that do pass the definitional test – Honda, Corning, and General Electric come quickly to mind – have, by contrast, become adept at translating new knowledge into new ways of behaving. These companies actively manage the learning process to ensure that it occurs by design rather than by chance. Distinctive policies and practices are responsible for their success; they form the building blocks of learning organizations.

Building blocks

Learning organizations are skilled at five main activities: systematic problem solving, experimentation with new approaches, learning from their own experience and past history, learning from the experiences and best practices of others, and transferring knowledge quickly and efficiently throughout the organization. Each is accompanied by a distinctive mind-set, tool kit, and pattern of behavior. Many companies practice these activities to some degree. But few are consistently successful because they rely largely on happenstance and isolated examples. By creating systems and processes that support these activities and integrate them into the fabric of daily operations, companies can manage their learning more effectively.

1. Systematic problem solving

This first activity rests heavily on the philosophy and methods of the quality movement. Its underlying ideas, now widely accepted, include:

- Relying on the scientific method, rather than guesswork, for diagnosing problems (what Deming calls the "Plan, Do, Check, Act" cycle, and others refer to as "hypothesis-generating, hypothesis-testing" techniques).
- Insisting on data, rather than assumptions, as background for decision making (what quality practitioners call "fact-based management").
- Using simple statistical tools (histograms, Pareto charts, correlations, cause-and-effect diagrams) to organize data and draw inferences.

Most training programs focus primarily on problem-solving techniques, using exercises and practical examples. These tools are relatively straightforward and easily communicated; the necessary mind-set, however, is more difficult to establish. Accuracy and precision are essential for learning. Employees must therefore become more disciplined in their thinking and more attentive to details. They must continually ask, "How do we know that's true?", recognizing that close enough is not good enough if real learning is to take place. They must push beyond obvious symptoms to assess underlying causes, often collecting evidence when conventional wisdom says it is unnecessary. Otherwise, the organization will remain a prisoner of "gut facts" and sloppy reasoning, and learning will be stifled.

Xerox has mastered this approach on a company-wide scale. In 1983, senior managers launched the company's Leadership Through Quality initiative; since then, all employees have been trained in small-group activities and problem-solving techniques. Today a six-step process is used for virtually all decisions (see the insert "Xerox's Problem-Solving Process"). Employees are provided with tools in four areas: generating ideas and collecting information (brainstorming, interviewing, surveying); reaching consensus (list reduction, rating forms, weighted voting); analyzing and displaying data (cause-and-effect diagrams, force-field analysis); and planning actions (flow charts, Gantt charts). They then practice these tools during training sessions that last several days. Training is presented in "family groups," members of the same department or business-unit team, and the tools are applied to real problems facing the group. The result of this process has been a common vocabulary and a consistent, companywide approach to problem solving. Once employees have been trained, they are expected to use the techniques at all meetings, and no topic is off-limits. When a high-level group was formed to review Xerox's organizational structure and suggest alternatives, it employed the very same process and tools.[3]

2. Experimentation

This activity involves the systematic searching for and testing of new knowledge. Using the scientific method is essential, and there are obvious parallels to systematic problem solving. But unlike problem solving, experimentation is usually motivated by opportunity and expanding horizons, not by current difficulties. It takes two main forms: ongoing programs and one-of-a-kind demonstration projects.

Ongoing programs normally involve a continuing series of small experiments, designed to produce incremental gains in knowledge. They are the mainstay of most continuous improvement programs and are especially common on the shop floor. Corning, for example, experiments continually with diverse raw materials and new formulations to increase yields and provide better grades of glass. Allegheny Ludlum, a specialty steelmaker, regularly examines new rolling methods and improved technologies to raise productivity and reduce costs.

Xerox's Problem-Solving Process

Step	Question to Be Answered	Expansion/ Divergence	Contraction/ Convergence	What's Needed to Go to the Next Step
1. Identify and select problem	What do we want to change?	Lots of problems for consideration	One problem statement, one "desired state" agreed upon	Identification the gap "Desired state" described in available terms
2. Analyze problem	What's preventing us from reaching the "desired state"?	Lots of potential causes identified	Key cause(s) identified and verified	Key cause(s) documented and ranked
3. Generate potential solutions	How could we make the change?	Lots of ideas on how solve the problem	Potential solutions clarified	Solution list
4. Select and plan the solution	What's the best way to do it?	Lots of criteria for evaluating potential solutions	Criteria to use for evaluating solution agreed upon	Plan for making and monitoring the change
		Lots of ideas on how to implement and evaluate the selected solution	Implementation and evaluation plans agreed upon	Measurement criteria to evaluate solution effectiveness
5. Implement the solution	Are we following plan?		Implementation of agreed on contingency place [if necessary]	Solution in place
6. Evaluate the solution	How well did it work?		Effectiveness of solution agreed upon Continuing problems (if any) identified	Verification that the problem is solved, or Agreement to address continuing problems

Successful ongoing programs share several characteristics. First, they work hard to ensure a steady flow of new ideas, even if they must be imported from outside the organization. Chaparral Steel sends its first-line supervisors on sabbaticals around the globe, where they visit academic and industry leaders, develop an understanding of new work practices and technologies, then bring what they've learned back to the company and apply it to daily operations. In large part as a result of these initiatives, Chaparral is one of the five lowest cost steel plants in the world. GE's Impact Program originally sent manufacturing managers to Japan to study factory innovations, such as quality circles and kanban cards, and then apply them in their own organizations; today Europe is the destination, and productivity improvement practices the target. The program is one reason GE has recorded productivity gains averaging nearly 5% over the last four years.

Successful ongoing programs also require an incentive system that favors risk taking. Employees must feel that the benefits of experimentation exceed the costs; otherwise, they will not participate. This creates a difficult challenge for managers, who are trapped between two perilous extremes. They must maintain accountability and control over experiments without stifling creativity by unduly penalizing employees for failures. Allegheny Ludlum has perfected this juggling act: it keeps expensive, high-impact experiments off the scorecard used to evaluate managers but requires prior approvals from four senior vice presidents. The result has been a history of productivity improvements annually averaging 7% to 8%.

Finally, ongoing programs need managers and employees who are trained in the skills required to perform and evaluate experiments. These skills are seldom intuitive and must usually be learned. They cover a broad sweep: statistical methods, like design of experiments, that efficiently compare a large number of alternatives; graphical techniques, like process analysis, that are essential for redesigning work flows; and creativity techniques, like storyboarding and role playing, that keep novel ideas flowing. The most effective training programs are tightly focused and feature a small set of techniques tailored to employees' needs. Training in design of experiments, for example, is useful for manufacturing engineers, while creativity techniques are well suited to development groups.

Demonstration projects are usually larger and more complex than ongoing experiments. They involve holistic, systemwide changes, introduced at a single site, and are often undertaken with the goal of developing new organizational capabilities. Because these projects represent a sharp break from the past, they are usually designed from scratch, using a "clean slate" approach. General Foods's Topeka plant, one of the first high-commitment work systems in this country, was a pioneering demonstration project initiated to introduce the idea of self-managing teams and high levels of worker autonomy; a more recent example, designed to rethink small-car development, manufacturing, and sales, is GM's Saturn Division.

Demonstration projects share a number of distinctive characteristics:

- They are usually the first projects to embody principles and approaches that the organization hopes to adopt later on a larger scale. For this reason, they are

more transitional efforts than end-points and involve considerable "learning by doing." Mid-course corrections are common.
- They implicitly establish policy guidelines and decision rules for later projects. Managers must therefore be sensitive to the precedents they are setting and must send strong signals if they expect to establish new norms.
- They often encounter severe tests of commitment from employees who wish to see whether the rules have, in fact, changed.
- They are normally developed by strong multifunctional teams reporting directly to senior management. (For projects targeting employee involvement or quality of work life, teams should be multilevel as well.)
- They tend to have only limited impact on the rest of the organization if they are not accompanied by explicit strategies for transferring learning.

All of these characteristics appeared in a demonstration project launched by Copeland Corporation, a highly successful compressor manufacturer, in the mid-1970s. Matt Diggs, then the new CEO, wanted to transform the company's approach to manufacturing. Previously, Copeland had machined and assembled all products in a single facility. Costs were high, and quality was marginal. The problem, Diggs felt, was too much complexity.

At the outset, Diggs assigned a small, multifunctional team the task of designing a "focused factory" dedicated to a narrow, newly developed product line. The team reported directly to Diggs and took three years to complete its work. Initially, the project budget was $10 million to $12 million; that figure was repeatedly revised as the team found, through experience and with Diggs's prodding, that it could achieve dramatic improvements. The final investment, a total of $30 million, yielded unanticipated breakthroughs in reliability testing, automatic tool adjustment, and programmable control. All were achieved through learning by doing.

The team set additional precedents during the plant's start-up and early operations. To dramatize the importance of quality, for example, the quality manager was appointed second-in-command, a significant move upward. The same reporting relationship was used at all subsequent plants. In addition, Diggs urged the plant manager to ramp up slowly to full production and resist all efforts to proliferate products. These instructions were unusual at Copeland, where the marketing department normally ruled. Both directives were quickly tested; management held firm, and the implications were felt throughout the organization. Manufacturing's stature improved, and the company as a whole recognized its competitive contribution. One observer commented, "Marketing had always run the company, so they couldn't believe it. The change was visible at the highest levels, and it went down hard."

Once the first focused factory was running smoothly – it seized 25% of the market in two years and held its edge in reliability for over a decade – Copeland built four more factories in quick succession. Diggs assigned members of the initial project to each factory's design team to ensure that early learnings were not lost; these people later rotated into operating assignments. Today focused factories remain the cornerstone of Copeland's manufacturing strategy and a continuing source of its cost and quality advantages.

Whether they are demonstration projects like Copeland's or ongoing programs like Allegheny Ludlum's, all forms of experimentation seek the same end: moving from superficial knowledge to deep understanding. At its simplest, the distinction is between knowing how things are done and knowing why they occur. Knowing how is partial knowledge; it is rooted in norms of behavior, standards of practice, and settings of equipment. Knowing why is more fundamental: it captures underlying cause-and-effect relationships and accommodates exceptions, adaptations, and unforeseen events. The ability to control temperatures and pressures to align grains of silicon and form silicon steel is an example of knowing how; understanding the chemical and physical process that produces the alignment is knowing why.

Further distinctions are possible, as the insert "Stages of Knowledge" suggests. Operating knowledge can be arrayed in a hierarchy, moving from limited understanding and the ability to make few distinctions to more complete understanding in which all contingencies are anticipated and controlled. In this context, experimentation and problem solving foster learning by pushing organizations up the hierarchy, from lower to higher stages of knowledge.

3. Learning from past experience

Companies must review their successes and failures, assess them systematically, and record the lessons in a form that employees find open and accessible. One expert has called this process the "Santayana Review," citing the famous philosopher George Santayana, who coined the phrase "Those who cannot remember the past are condemned to repeat it." Unfortunately, too many managers today are indifferent, even hostile, to the past, and by failing to reflect on it, they let valuable knowledge escape.

A study of more than 150 new products concluded that "the knowledge gained from failures [is] often instrumental in achieving subsequent successes. ... In the simplest terms, failure is the ultimate teacher."[4] IBM's 360 computer series, for example, one of the most popular and profitable ever built, was based on the technology of the failed Stretch computer that preceded it. In this case, as in many others, learning occurred by chance rather than by careful planning. A few companies, however, have established processes that require their managers to periodically think about the past and learn from their mistakes.

Boeing did so immediately after its difficulties with the 737 and 747 plane programs. Both planes were introduced with much fanfare and also with serious problems. To ensure that the problems were not repeated, senior managers commissioned a high-level employee group, called Project Homework, to compare the development processes of the 737 and 747 with those of the 707 and 727, two of the company's most profitable planes. The group was asked to develop a set of "lessons learned" that could be used on future projects. After working for

> **Stages of Knowledge**
>
> Scholars have suggested that production and operating knowledge can be classified systematically by level or stage of understanding. At the lowest levels of manufacturing knowledge, little is known other than the characteristics of a good product. Production remains an art, and there are few clearly articulated standards or rules. An example would be Stradivarius violins. Experts agree that they produce vastly superior sound, but no one can specify precisely how they were manufactured because skilled artisans were responsible. By contrast, at the highest levels of manufacturing knowledge, all aspects of production are known and understood. All materials and processing variations are articulated and accounted for, with rules and procedures for every contingency. Here an example would be a "lights out," fully automated factory that operates for many hours without any human intervention.
>
> In total, this framework specifies eight stages of knowledge. From lowest to highest, they are:
>
> 1. Recognizing prototypes (what is a good product).
> 2. Recognizing attributes within prototypes (ability to define some conditions under which process gives good output).
> 3. Discriminating among attributes (which attributes are important? Experts may differ about relevance of patterns, new operators are often trained through apprenticeships).
> 4. Measuring attributes (some key attributes are measured, measures may be qualitative and relative).
> 5. Locally controlling attributes (repeatable performance; process designed by expert, but technicians can perform it).
> 6. Recognizing and discriminating between contingencies (production process can be mechanized and monitored manually).
> 7. Controlling contingencies (process can be automated).
> 8. Understanding procedures and controlling contingencies (process is completely understood).
>
> *Adapted from work by Ramachandran Jaikumar and Roger Bohn*

three years, they produced hundreds of recommendations and an inch-thick booklet. Several members of the team were then transferred to the 757 and 767 start-ups, and guided by experience, they produced the most successful, error-free launches in Boeing's history.

Other companies have used a similar retrospective approach. Like Boeing, Xerox studied its product development process, examining three troubled products in an effort to understand why the company's new business initiatives failed so often. Arthur D. Little, the consulting company, focused on its past successes. Senior management invited ADL consultants from around the world to a two-day "jamboree," featuring booths and presentations documenting a wide range of the company's most successful practices, publications, and techniques. British Petroleum went even further and established the post-project appraisal unit to review major investment projects, write up case studies, and derive lessons for planners that were then incorporated into revisions of the company's planning guidelines. A five-person unit reported to the board of directors and reviewed six projects annually. The bulk of the time was spent in the field interviewing managers.[5] This type of review is now conducted regularly at the project level.

At the heart of this approach, one expert has observed, "is a mind-set that... enables companies to recognize the value of productive failure as contrasted with unproductive success. A productive failure is one that leads to insight, understanding, and thus an addition to the commonly held wisdom of the organization. An unproductive success occurs when something goes well, but nobody knows how or why."[6] IBM's legendary founder, Thomas Watson, Sr., apparently understood the distinction well. Company lore has it that a young manager, after losing $10 million in a risky venture, was called into Watson's office. The young man, thoroughly intimidated, began by saying, "I guess you want my resignation." Watson replied, "You can't be serious. We just spent $10 million educating you."

Fortunately, the learning process need not be so expensive. Case studies and post-project reviews like those of Xerox and British Petroleum can be performed with little cost other than managers' time. Companies can also enlist the help of faculty and students at local colleges or universities; they bring fresh perspectives and view internships and case studies as opportunities to gain experience and increase their own learning. A few companies have established computerized data banks to speed up the learning process. At Paul Revere Life Insurance, management requires all problem-solving teams to complete short registration forms describing their proposed projects if they hope to qualify for the company's award program. The company then enters the forms into its computer system and can immediately retrieve a listing of other groups of people who have worked or are working on the topic, along with a contact person. Relevant experience is then just a telephone call away.

4. Learning from others

Of course, not all learning comes from reflection and self-analysis. Sometimes the most powerful insights come from looking outside one's immediate environment to gain a new perspective. Enlightened managers know that even companies in completely different businesses can be fertile sources of ideas and catalysts for creative thinking. At these organizations, enthusiastic borrowing is replacing the "not invented here" syndrome. Milliken calls the process SIS, for "Steal Ideas Shamelessly"; the broader term for it is benchmarking.

According to one expert, "benchmarking is an ongoing investigation and learning experience that ensures that best industry practices are uncovered, analyzed, adopted, and implemented."[7] The greatest benefits come from studying *practices,* the way that work gets done, rather than results, and from involving line managers in the process. Almost anything can be benchmarked. Xerox, the concept's creator, has applied it to billing, warehousing, and automated manufacturing. Milliken has been even more creative: in an inspired moment, it benchmarked Xerox's approach to benchmarking.

Unfortunately, there is still considerable confusion about the requirements for successful benchmarking. Benchmarking is not "industrial tourism," a series of ad hoc visits to companies that have received favorable publicity or won quality awards. Rather, it is a disciplined process that begins with a thorough search to identify best-practice organizations, continues with careful study of one's own practices and performance, progresses through systematic site visits and interviews, and concludes with an analysis of results, development of recommendations, and implementation. While time-consuming, the process need not be terribly expensive. AT&T's Benchmarking Group estimates that a moderate-sized project takes four to six months and incurs out-of-pocket costs of $20,000 (when personnel costs are included, the figure is three to four times higher).

Benchmarking is one way of gaining an outside perspective; another, equally fertile source of ideas is customers. Conversations with customers invariably stimulate learning; they are, after all, experts in what they do. Customers can provide up-to-date product information, competitive comparisons, insights into changing preferences, and immediate feedback about service and patterns of use. And companies need these insights at all levels, from the executive suite to the shop floor. At Motorola, members of the Operating and Policy Committee, including the CEO, meet personally and on a regular basis with customers. At Worthington Steel, all machine operators make periodic, unescorted trips to customers' factories to discuss their needs.

Sometimes customers can't articulate their needs or remember even the most recent problems they have had with a product or service. If that's the case, managers must observe them in action. Xerox employs a number of anthropologists at its Palo Alto Research Center to observe users of new document products in their offices. Digital Equipment has developed an interactive process called "contextual inquiry" that is used by software engineers to observe users of new technologies as they go about their work. Milliken has created "first-delivery teams" that accompany the first shipment of all products; team members follow the product through the customer's production process to see how it is used and then develop ideas for further improvement.

Whatever the source of outside ideas, learning will only occur in a receptive environment. Managers can't be defensive and must be open to criticism or bad news. This is a difficult challenge, but it is essential for success. Companies that approach customers assuming that "we must be right, they have to be wrong" or visit other organizations certain that "they can't teach us anything" seldom learn very much. Learning organizations, by contrast, cultivate the art of open, attentive listening.

5. Transferring knowledge

For learning to be more than a local affair, knowledge must spread quickly and efficiently throughout the organization. Ideas carry maximum impact when they are shared broadly rather than held in a few hands. A variety of mechanisms spur this process, including written, oral, and visual reports, site visits and tours, personnel rotation programs, education and training programs, and standardization programs. Each has distinctive strengths and weaknesses.

Reports and tours are by far the most popular mediums. Reports serve many purposes: they summarize findings, provide checklists of dos and don'ts, and describe important processes and events. They cover a multitude of topics, from benchmarking studies to accounting conventions to newly discovered marketing techniques. Today written reports are often supplemented by videotapes, which offer greater immediacy and fidelity.

Tours are an equally popular means of transferring knowledge, especially for large, multidivisional organizations with multiple sites. The most effective tours are tailored to different audiences and needs. To introduce its managers to the distinctive manufacturing practices of New United Motor Manufacturing Inc. (NUMMI), its joint venture with Toyota, General Motors developed a series of specialized tours. Some were geared to upper and middle managers, while others were aimed at lower ranks. Each tour described the policies, practices, and systems that were most relevant to that level of management.

Despite their popularity, reports and tours are relatively cumbersome ways of transferring knowledge. The gritty details that lie behind complex management concepts are difficult to communicate secondhand. Absorbing facts by reading them or seeing them demonstrated is one thing; experiencing them personally is quite another. As a leading cognitive scientist has observed, "It is very difficult to become knowledgeable in a passive way. Actively experiencing something is considerably more valuable than having it described."[8] For this reason, personnel rotation programs are one of the most powerful methods of transferring knowledge.

In many organizations, expertise is held locally: in a particularly skilled computer technician, perhaps, a savvy global brand manager, or a division head with a track record of successful joint ventures. Those in daily contact with these experts benefit enormously from their skills, but their field of influence is relatively narrow. Transferring them to different parts of the organization helps share the wealth. Transfers may be from division to division, department to department, or facility to facility; they may involve senior, middle, or first-level managers. A supervisor experienced in just-in-time production, for example, might move to another factory to apply the methods there, or a successful division manager might transfer to a lagging division to invigorate it with already proven ideas. The CEO of Time Life used the latter approach when he shifted the president of the company's music division, who had orchestrated several years of rapid growth and high profits through innovative marketing, to the presidency of the book division, where profits were flat because of continued reliance on traditional marketing concepts.

Line to staff transfers are another option. These are most effective when they allow experienced managers to distill what they have learned and diffuse it across the company in the form of new standards, policies, or training programs. Consider how PPG used just such a transfer to advance its human resource practices around the concept of high-commitment work systems. In 1986, PPG constructed a new float-glass plant in Chehalis, Washington; it employed a radically new technology as well as innovations in human resource management that were developed by the plant manager and his staff. All workers were organized into small, self-managing teams with responsibility for work assignments, scheduling, problem solving and improvement, and peer review. After several years running the factory, the plant manager was promoted to director of human resources for the entire glass group. Drawing on his experiences at Chehalis, he developed a training program geared toward first-level supervisors that taught the behaviors needed to manage employees in a participative, self-managing environment.

As the PPG example suggests, education and training programs are powerful tools for transferring knowledge. But for maximum effectiveness, they must be linked explicitly to implementation. All too often, trainers assume that new knowledge will be applied without taking concrete steps to ensure that trainees actually follow through. Seldom do trainers provide opportunities for practice, and few programs consciously promote the application of their teachings after employees have returned to their jobs.

Xerox and GTE are exceptions. As noted earlier, when Xerox introduced problem-solving techniques to its employees in the 1980s, everyone, from the top to the bottom of the organization, was taught in small departmental or divisional groups led by their immediate superior. After an introduction to concepts and techniques, each group applied what they learned to a real-life work problem. In a similar spirit, GTE's Quality: The Competitive Edge program was offered to teams of business-unit presidents and the managers reporting to them. At the beginning of the 3-day course, each team received a request from a company officer to prepare a complete quality plan for their unit, based on the course concepts, within 60 days. Discussion periods of two to three hours were set aside during the program so that teams could begin working on their plans. After the teams submitted their reports, the company officers studied them, and then the teams implemented them. This GTE program produced dramatic improvements in quality, including a recent semifinalist spot in the Baldrige Awards.

The GTE example suggests another important guideline: knowledge is more likely to be transferred effectively when the right incentives are in place. If employees know that their plans will be evaluated and implemented – in other words, that their learning will be applied – progress is far more likely. At most companies, the status quo is well entrenched; only if managers and employees see new ideas as being in their own best interest will they accept them gracefully.

AT&T has developed a creative approach that combines strong incentives with information sharing. Called the Chairman's Quality Award (CQA), it is an internal quality competition modeled on the Baldrige prize but with an important twist: awards are given not only for absolute performance (using the same 1,000-point scoring system as Baldrige) but also for improvements in scoring from the previous year. Gold, silver, and bronze Improvement Awards are given to units that have improved their scores 200, 150, and 100 points, respectively. These awards provide the incentive for change. An accompanying Pockets of Excellence program simplifies knowledge transfer. Every year, it identifies every unit within the company that has scored at least 60% of the possible points in each award category and then publicizes the names of these units using written reports and electronic mail.

Measuring learning

Managers have long known that "if you can't measure it, you can't manage it." This maxim is as true of learning as it is of any other corporate objective. Traditionally, the solution has been "learning curves" and "manufacturing progress functions." Both concepts date back to the discovery, during the 1920s and 1930s, that the costs of airframe manufacturing fell predictably with increases in cumulative volume. These increases were viewed as proxies for greater manufacturing knowledge, and most early studies examined their impact on the costs of direct labor. Later studies expanded the focus, looking at total manufacturing costs and the impact of experience in other industries, including shipbuilding, oil refining, and consumer electronics. Typically, learning rates were in the 80% to 85% range (meaning that with a doubling of cumulative production, costs fell to 80% to 85% of their previous level), although there was wide variation.

Firms like the Boston Consulting Group raised these ideas to a higher level in the 1970s. Drawing on the logic of learning curves, they argued that industries as a whole faced "experience curves," costs and prices that fell by predictable amounts as industries grew and their total production increased. With this observation, consultants suggested, came an iron law of competition. To enjoy the benefits of experience, companies would have to rapidly increase their production ahead of competitors to lower prices and gain market share.

Both learning and experience curves are still widely used, especially in the aerospace, defense, and electronics industries. Boeing, for instance, has established learning curves for every work station in its assembly plant; they assist in monitoring productivity, determining work flows and staffing levels, and setting prices and profit margins on new airplanes. Experience curves are common in semiconductors and consumer electronics, where they are used to forecast industry costs and prices.

For companies hoping to become learning organizations, however, these measures are incomplete. They focus on only a single measure of output (cost or price) and ignore learning that affects other competitive variables, like quality, delivery,

> **The Half-Life Curve**
>
> Analog Devices has used half-life curves to compare the performance of its divisions. Here monthly data on customer service are graphed for seven divisions. Division C is the clear winner even though it started with a high proportion of late deliveries, its rapid learning rate led eventually to the best absolute performance. Divisions D, E, and G have been far less successful, with little or no improvement in on-time service over the period.
>
> On-Time Customer Service Performance – Monthly Data (August 1987-July 1988)
>
> [Chart: Percentage of lines rate (log scale, 1 to 100) vs Half-life in Months [time required to reduce late shipments by one-half] for Divisions A (0), B (1.5), C (4), D (No improvement), E (60+), F (12), G (60+), Total (13)]
>
> Source: Ray Stata: "Organizational Learning – The Key to Management Innovation," *Sloan Management Review*, Spring 1989, p. 72.

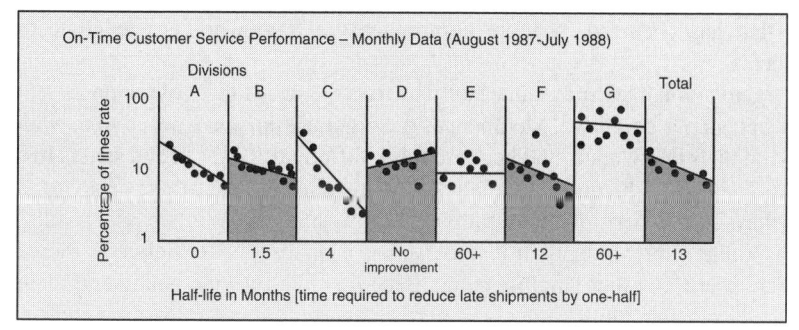

or new product introductions. They suggest only one possible learning driver (total production volumes) and ignore both the possibility of learning in mature industries, where output is flat, and the possibility that learning might be driven by other sources, such as new technology or the challenge posed by competing products. Perhaps most important, they tell us little about the sources of learning or the levers of change.

Another measure has emerged in response to these concerns. Called the "half-life" curve, it was originally developed by Analog Devices, a leading semiconductor manufacturer, as a way of comparing internal improvement rates. A half-life curve measures the time it takes to achieve a 50% improvement in a specified performance measure. When represented graphically, the performance measure (defect rates, on-time delivery, time to market) is plotted on the vertical axis, using a logarithmic scale, and the time scale (days, months, years) is plotted horizontally. Steeper slopes then represent faster learning (see the insert "The Half-Life Curve" for an illustration).

The logic is straightforward. Companies, divisions, or departments that take less time to improve must be learning faster than their peers. In the long run, their short learning cycles will translate into superior performance. The 50% target is a measure of convenience; it was derived empirically from studies of successful improvement processes at a wide range of companies. Half-life curves are also flexible. Unlike learning and experience curves, they work on any output measure, and they are not confined to costs or prices. In addition, they are easy to operationalize, they provide a simple measuring stick, and they allow for ready comparison among groups.

Yet even half-life curves have an important weakness: they focus solely on results. Some types of knowledge take years to digest, with few visible changes in performance for long periods. Creating a total quality culture, for instance, or developing new approaches to product development are difficult systemic changes. Because of their long gestation periods, half-life curves or any other measures focused solely on results are unlikely to capture any short-run learning that has occurred. A more comprehensive framework is needed to track progress.

Organizational learning can usually be traced through three overlapping stages. The first step is cognitive. Members of the organization are exposed to new ideas, expand their knowledge, and begin to think differently. The second step is behavioral. Employees begin to internalize new insights and alter their behavior. And the third step is performance improvement, with changes in behavior leading to measurable improvements in results: superior quality, better delivery, increased market share, or other tangible gains. Because cognitive and behavioral changes typically precede improvements in performance, a complete learning audit must include all three.

Surveys, questionnaires, and interviews are useful for this purpose. At the cognitive level, they would focus on attitudes and depth of understanding. Have employees truly understood the meaning of self-direction and teamwork, or are the terms still unclear? At PPG, a team of human resource experts periodically audits every manufacturing plant, including extensive interviews with shop-floor employees, to ensure that the concepts are well understood. Have new approaches to customer service been fully accepted? At its 1989 Worldwide Marketing Managers' Meeting, Ford presented participants with a series of hypothetical situations in which customer complaints were in conflict with short-term dealer or company profit goals and asked how they would respond. Surveys like these are the first step toward identifying changed attitudes and new ways of thinking.

To assess behavioral changes, surveys and questionnaires must be supplemented by direct observation. Here the proof is in the doing, and there is no substitute for seeing employees in action. Domino's Pizza uses "mystery shoppers" to assess managers' commitment to customer service at its individual stores; L.L. Bean places telephone orders with its own operators to assess service levels. Other companies invite outside consultants to visit, attend meetings, observe employees in action, and then report what they have learned. In many ways, this approach mirrors that of examiners for the Baldrige Award, who make several-day site visits to semifinalists to see whether the companies' deeds match the words on their applications.

Finally, a comprehensive learning audit also measures performance. Half-life curves or other performance measures are essential for ensuring that cognitive and behavioral changes have actually produced results. Without them, companies would lack a rationale for investing in learning and the assurance that learning was serving the organization's ends.

First steps

Learning organizations are not built overnight. Most successful examples are the products of carefully cultivated attitudes, commitments, and management processes that have accrued slowly and steadily over time. Still, some changes can be made immediately. Any company that wishes to become a learning organization can begin by taking a few simple steps.

The first step is to foster an environment that is conducive to learning. There must be time for reflection and analysis, to think about strategic plans, dissect customer needs, assess current work systems, and invent new products. Learning is difficult when employees are harried or rushed; it tends to be driven out by the pressures of the moment. Only if top management explicitly frees up employees' time for the purpose does learning occur with any frequency. That time will be doubly productive if employees possess the skills to use it wisely. Training in brainstorming, problem solving, evaluating experiments, and other core learning skills is therefore essential.

Another powerful lever is to open up boundaries and stimulate the exchange of ideas. Boundaries inhibit the flow of information; they keep individuals and groups isolated and reinforce preconceptions. Opening up boundaries, with conferences, meetings, and project teams, which either cross organizational levels or link the company and its customers and suppliers, ensures a fresh flow of ideas and the chance to consider competing perspectives. General Electric CEO Jack Welch considers this to be such a powerful stimulant of change that he has made "boundarylessness" a cornerstone of the company's strategy for the 1990s.

Once managers have established a more supportive, open environment, they can create learning forums. These are programs or events designed with explicit learning goals in mind, and they can take a variety of forms: strategic reviews, which examine the changing competitive environment and the company's product portfolio, technology, and market positioning; systems audits, which review the health of large, cross-functional processes and delivery systems; internal benchmarking reports, which identify and compare best-in-class activities within the organization; study missions, which are dispatched to leading organizations around the world to better understand their performance and distinctive skills; and jamborees or symposiums, which bring together customers, suppliers, outside experts, or internal groups to share ideas and learn from one another. Each of these activities fosters learning by requiring employees to wrestle with new knowledge and consider its implications. Each can also be tailored to business needs. A consumer goods company, for example, might sponsor a study mission to Europe to learn more about distribution methods within the newly unified Common Market, while a high-technology company might launch a systems audit to review its new product development process.

Together these efforts help to eliminate barriers that impede learning and begin to move learning higher on the organizational agenda. They also suggest a subtle shift in focus, away from continuous improvement and toward a commitment to learning. Coupled with a better understanding of the "three Ms," the meaning, management, and measurement of learning, this shift provides a solid foundation for building learning organizations.

References

1. Peter M. Senge, *The Fifth Discipline* (New York: Doubleday, 1990), p. 1.
2. Ikujiro Nonaka, "The Knowledge-Creating Company," *Harvard Business Review*, November–December 1991, p. 97.
3. Robert Howard, "The CEO as Organizational Architect: An Interview with Xerox's Paul Allaire," *Harvard Business Review,* September–October 1992, p. 106.
4. Modesto A. Maidique and Billie Jo Zirger, "The New Product Learning Cycle," *Research Policy,* Vol. 14, No. 6 (1985), pp. 299, 309.
5. Frank R. Gulliver, "Post-Project Appraisals Pay," *Harvard Business Review,* March–April 1987, p. 128.
6. David Nadler, "Even Failures Can Be Productive," *New York Times,* April 23, 1989, Sec. 3, p. 3.
7. Robert C. Camp, *Benchmarking: The Search for Industry Best Practices that Lead to Superior Performance* (Milwaukee: ASQC Quality Press, 1989), p. 12.
8. Roger Schank, with Peter Childers, *The Creative Attitude* (New York: Macmillan, 1988], p. 9.
9. Ramchandran Jaikumar and Roger Bohn, "The Development of Intelligent Systems for Industrial Use: A Conceptual Framework," *Research on Technological Innovation, Management and Policy,* Vol. 3 (1986), pp. 182–188.